CAMBRIDGE LIBRARY COLLECTION

Books of enduring scholarly value

Philosophy

This series contains both philosophical texts and critical essays about philosophy, concentrating especially on works originally published in the eighteenth and nineteenth centuries. It covers a broad range of topics including ethics, logic, metaphysics, aesthetics, utilitarianism, positivism, scientific method and political thought. It also includes biographies and accounts of the history of philosophy, as well as collections of papers by leading figures. In addition to this series, primary texts by ancient philosophers, and works with particular relevance to philosophy of science, politics or theology, may be found elsewhere in the Cambridge Library Collection.

The Principles of Political Economy

Henry Sidgwick, (1838–1900), philosopher, classicist, lecturer and fellow of Trinity College, Cambridge, and supporter of women's university education, is well known for his *Method of Ethics* (1874), a significant and influential book on moral theory. First published in 1883, this work considers the role the state plays (and ought to play) in economic life, and whether economics should be considered an Art or a Science. Sidgwick applies his utilitarian views to economics, defending John Stuart Mill's 1848 treatise of the same name. The book calls for a return to traditional political economy by eliminating 'needless polemics'. Sidgwick also outlines the need to bridge the gap between his analytical or deductive method and the inductive method employed by Mill's critics, the new generation of economic philosophers including John Elliot Cairnes and William Stanley Jevons. The second edition, reissued here, was published in 1887.

Cambridge University Press has long been a pioneer in the reissuing of out-of-print titles from its own backlist, producing digital reprints of books that are still sought after by scholars and students but could not be reprinted economically using traditional technology. The Cambridge Library Collection extends this activity to a wider range of books which are still of importance to researchers and professionals, either for the source material they contain, or as landmarks in the history of their academic discipline.

Drawing from the world-renowned collections in the Cambridge University Library, and guided by the advice of experts in each subject area, Cambridge University Press is using state-of-the-art scanning machines in its own Printing House to capture the content of each book selected for inclusion. The files are processed to give a consistently clear, crisp image, and the books finished to the high quality standard for which the Press is recognised around the world. The latest print-on-demand technology ensures that the books will remain available indefinitely, and that orders for single or multiple copies can quickly be supplied.

The Cambridge Library Collection will bring back to life books of enduring scholarly value (including out-of-copyright works originally issued by other publishers) across a wide range of disciplines in the humanities and social sciences and in science and technology.

The Principles of Political Economy

Henry Sidgwick

CAMBRIDGE
UNIVERSITY PRESS

CAMBRIDGE UNIVERSITY PRESS

Cambridge, New York, Melbourne, Madrid, Cape Town,
Singapore, São Paolo, Delhi, Tokyo, Mexico City

Published in the United States of America by Cambridge University Press, New York

www.cambridge.org
Information on this title: www.cambridge.org/9781108037013

© in this compilation Cambridge University Press 2011

This edition first published 1887
This digitally printed version 2011

ISBN 978-1-108-03701-3 Paperback

This book reproduces the text of the original edition. The content and language reflect the beliefs, practices and terminology of their time, and have not been updated.

Cambridge University Press wishes to make clear that the book, unless originally published by Cambridge, is not being republished by, in association or collaboration with, or with the endorsement or approval of, the original publisher or its successors in title.

THE PRINCIPLES

OF

POLITICAL ECONOMY

THE PRINCIPLES

OF

POLITICAL ECONOMY

BY

HENRY SIDGWICK,

AUTHOR OF "THE METHODS OF ETHICS."

> 'Tis the day of the chattel,
> Web to weave and corn to grind:
> Things are in the saddle,
> And ride mankind.
> — EMERSON.

SECOND EDITION

London:
MACMILLAN AND CO.
AND NEW YORK.
1887

[*The Right of Translation is reserved.*]

Cambridge:
PRINTED BY C. J. CLAY, M.A. AND SONS,
AT THE UNIVERSITY PRESS.

PREFACE.

THE character and scope of this treatise I have endeavoured to explain fully in the introductory chapter; it remains for me here to acknowledge my debts to the works that have chiefly aided me in composing it. After J. S. Mill's book, from which I first learned political economy, and on which the present work must be understood to be primarily founded, I believe that I owe most to Jevons' *Theory of Political Economy*, the leading ideas of which have been continually in my thoughts. I am also considerably indebted both to Cairnes' *Leading Principles of Political Economy* and to the *Economics of Industry*, by Mr and Mrs Alfred Marshall, together with some papers by Mr Marshall on the theory of Value diagrammatically treated, which have been privately printed[1]. I have also derived valuable suggestions from Mr Hearn's *Plutology*, and from Mr F. A. Walker's *Wages;* also from Mr Macleod, as regards the theory of Money, and

[1] Mr Marshall also lent me for perusal, several years ago, some MSS on Foreign Trade which have not—so far as I know—been printed.

to some extent in treating of Wealth and Capital—though I do not agree with most of Mr Macleod's views. I must also express my obligations to the writer of an article on 'Industrial Monopolies' in the *Quarterly Review* of October 1871.

Among foreign writers, I have derived most assistance from the works of Professor A. Wagner and the late Professor A. Held; especially from the former's elaborate systematic treatise on the subject. I am also indebted to Cournot's *Principes Mathématiques de la Théorie des Richesses*, and to Schäffle's *Quintessenz des Socialismus* and *Bau und Leben des Socialen Körpers*.

Finally, I must acknowledge gratefully the aid that many friends have kindly given me, by supplying information or suggesting corrections required for various portions of the work while it was in progress; among whom I must particularly mention Mr F. W. Maitland, of Lincoln's Inn, and Mr J. N. Keynes, of Pembroke College, Cambridge. To the latter I am especially indebted for his kindness in reading and criticising the proof-sheets of the greater part of the book: which has enabled me to improve it in many respects.

In revising the book for a second edition I have carefully considered all the published criticisms of it that I have seen, and also the criticisms that have been kindly sent me in private by several persons—among whom I ought especially to thank Mr F. Y. Edgeworth, Mr Carveth Read, and Mr P. H. Wicksteed. I have usually modified, and sometimes rewritten, the passages criticised: but I have not altered my views on any point of fundamental importance. I have also endeavoured to shorten and simplify several parts of my exposition which appeared to me needlessly prolix or complicated: and have thus been able to make room for a certain amount of new matter without materially adding to the size of the book. Further, I have been aided in my revision by some of the books on Political Economy which have appeared since my first Edition; to some of these I have had occasion to refer by name in notes: of those to which I have not so referred the most important is the *Handbuch der politischen Oekonomie*, edited by G. Schönberg. I must also thank Mr Keynes and Professor Foxwell for useful suggestions which they have made, at my request, on certain sections of the book while it was passing through the press.

CONTENTS.

INTRODUCTION.

CHAPTER I.

THE PRESENT STATE OF ECONOMIC CONTROVERSY IN ENGLAND AND THE SPECIAL AIM OF THE PRESENT WORK.

		PAGES
1.	During the last thirty years Political Economy in England has risen from the state of controversy on fundamental principles and method into that of an apparently established science, and again relapsed into the state of controversy.	1—7
2.	My special aim is to eliminate needless polemics by a guarded restatement of traditional doctrines, with due recognition of the advances made in economic theory by recent writers.	7—11

CHAPTER II.

THE SCOPE OF POLITICAL ECONOMY.

1.	Is Political Economy a Science, concerned with what is, or an Art, concerned with what ought to be done?	12—14
2.	Originally it was conceived as an Art, and is formally so defined by Adam Smith; but the substance of the latter's doctrine inevitably rendered his exposition mainly that of a science;	14—18
3.	but not entirely, since the doctrine of *laisser faire*, characteristic of Adam Smith and his school, belongs to Art;	18—24
4.	and, in the department of Production, the line between Science and Art is difficult to draw.	24—25
5.	In this treatise, all questions as to proper governmental interference in economic matters are treated separately (in Book III.) as questions belonging to the 'Art of Political Economy.'	25—27

CHAPTER III.

THE METHOD OF ECONOMIC SCIENCE.

1. The ordinary treatment of the Theory of Production is mainly inductive and analytical—e.g. Mill's treatment is so. . . . . 28—32
2. The traditional method of determining the Laws of Distribution and Exchange is primarily deductive and hypothetical, but obviously requires for application to concrete cases the aid of induction. . . . . 32—35
3. Both the general legitimacy of this method and its necessary limitations may be briefly shown by considering its chief hypotheses. . . . . 35—41
4. In using the method, quantitative precision should be attained as far as possible; but the limits of attainable precision should also be carefully noted. . . . 41—42

BOOK I.

PRODUCTION.

CHAPTER I.

THE THEORY OF PRODUCTION.

1. In this book industry is viewed primarily as a function of the human community, without regard to the terms on which its members co-operate. . . . . 45—47
2. But in order to use the notion of wealth with quantitative precision, we need a clear view of the measure of wealth, and therefore of value. . . . . . 47—48

CHAPTER II.

THE DEFINITION AND MEASURE OF VALUE.

1. Search for a definition is often the best way of examining what has to be defined. The definition often cannot be both useful for scientific purposes and in strict conformity with usage. . . . . 49—53

CONTENTS. xi

PAGES

2. In making the notion of Exchange Value precise, the main difficulty is to find a measure of variations of value : since Labour is not the measure we require,—at any rate in measuring amounts of wealth. . . . . 53—59
3. The best attainable measure is liable to inevitable inexactness, owing to the changes in relative quantity and in quality of the commodities that make up the aggregate of wealth. . . . . 59—64
4. The distinction between "objective" and "subjective" value in use, and between "real value" in exchange and the estimated value which determines actual price, are instructive ; but this notion of "real value" is difficult to employ with precision. . . . . . . 64—67

CHAPTER III.

WEALTH.

1. The difficulties of measuring Value apply also to the measurement of Wealth ; and other difficulties arise from the varying relations of purchased and unpurchased utilities : . . . . 68—71
2. however we cannot take Utility as a measure, discarding value ; . . . . 71—74
3. especially considering the variations in Needs. . 74—76
4. We must distinguish Producers' wealth from Consumers' wealth, being primarily concerned with the latter, in estimating the wealth of a community : and 'wealth' cannot include services (though 'Produce' may), . . 76—79
5. nor Culture or Skill,—though skill may be a form of investment of capital. . . . . 79—81
6. In discussing the questions whether Debts, Patents, Copyrights, Goodwill, &c., are wealth, we should distinguish (1) Producers' wealth from Consumers' wealth and (2) wealth of individuals from social wealth. . . 81—86

CHAPTER IV.

CAUSES OF VARIATIONS IN PRODUCTION.

1. Taking Produce to include all commodities derived from the application of man's labour to his material environment, ... 87—90

		PAGES
2.	variations in amount of produce may be referred to several different causes :	90—92
3.	partly, to differences in men's physical circumstances,	93—96
4.	partly, to differences in the quantity and quality of their labour.	96—98
5.	These latter, again, are largely due to variously caused differences in the strength of motives to labour.	98—104
6.	Efficiency of labour is greatly increased by Cooperation, especially by Division of Employments :	104—107
7.	also depends much on the terms of Cooperation : (e.g.) is increased by 'piece-work' where applicable, and in some cases by 'profit-sharing.'	107—114
8.	Also by Invention—the development of which has at once aided, and been aided by, that of Cooperation—: also by Capital—largely required in consequence of Invention.	114—117

CHAPTER V

CAPITAL.

		PAGES
1.	'Capital' has to be differently defined from the point of view of the individual and that of the community; 'individual's capital' is wealth employed for profit;	118—121
2.	and therefore includes (a) finished products in possession of producers and traders, and (b) land; but from the social point of view we must distinguish capital and land,	121—123
3.	restricting capital to results of human labour, but not excluding immaterial results, such as business connexion,	123—125
4.	and skill; but not physical strength, so far as this results from consumption that is not merely a means to future production.	125—127
5.	The accumulated stock of capital consists mainly of instruments, not food of labourers;	127—129
6.	which, in the labourers' possession, is not 'capital' in the ordinary sense, though in a wider sense it may be called (consumers') capital; as may all unconsumed wealth, so far as it is the intermediate result of labour employed for future utility, and more productive of utility through postponement of consumption.	129—132
7.	(Producers') Capital—the need of which has grown steadily with the progress of industry—is now largely owned by persons other than those who manage it.	132—134

CHAPTER VI.

LAWS OF PRODUCTION.

1. By 'Laws' I mean quantitative statements as to the operation of different causes of greater or less production. . . . . 135—136
2. They cannot generally be laid down with any exactness. 136—140
3. Malthus' 'Law of Population,' and the Law of Diminishing Returns from Land are valid, when duly qualified, as abstract statements of tendencies; also the concrete statement that in old countries population is limited by the difficulty of procuring subsistence; but the limit is not rigid, and the 'standard of comfort' that partly determines it is variable. . . . . . . 140—150
4. The Law of increase of individuals' capital is not definitely ascertainable; . . . . 150—156
5. still less the Law of increase of social capital. . . 156—159

BOOK II.

DISTRIBUTION AND EXCHANGE.

CHAPTER I.

INTRODUCTION.

1. The fundamental question of Distribution is 'how does produce tend to be competitively shared among the different classes who cooperate—through exchange—in production.' . . . . 163—167
2. The theory of Distribution, thus conceived, has therefore close affinity to the Theory of Exchange value of material products; and it is convenient to take the latter first. . 167—170

CHAPTER II.

THEORY OF EXCHANGE VALUE OF MATERIAL COMMODITIES.

1. The deductive theory of value depends on certain assumptions, which require to be carefully stated :—mainly on the assumptions of 'commercial' and 'industrial' competition. . . . . 171—174

		PAGES
2.	Mill's exposition of the theory is in the main sound, but some of the cardinal terms—especially 'increase of demand'—involve ambiguities that need to be removed.	174—180
3.	'Equation of supply and demand' is formally inadequate to determine price, if both supply and demand vary with price.	180—182
4.	This is exemplified by the indefinite number of values possible in the case of a monopolized article;	182—183
5.	compared with that of a 'simply scarce' article.	183—185
6.	In explaining Market Value of commodities produced under ordinary conditions, we have to show how Supply tends to be determined by prospects of loss and gain in holding back;	185—187
7.	and to note the diverse effects of speculation.	187—189
8.	But cost of production—estimated, as it must be, in terms of *remuneration*, not *sacrifice*—cannot be assumed to be independent of demand.	189—195
9.	Hence the Ricardian doctrine of value needs important qualification.	195—198
10.	The determination of values of products industrially connected is more complex :	198—200
11.	also that of durable products, partly sent back into the market by consumers.	200—201

CHAPTER III.

THEORY OF INTERNATIONAL VALUES.

1.	There are various causes of economic gain through trade between distant places.	202—205
2.	The peculiarity of the theoretical determination of the values of the products of such trade depends primarily not on the imperfect mobility of labour, but on the cost of carriage.	205—209
3.	The combined laws of demand of different wares exchanged tend to determine how much of the double cost of carriage is to be added to the 'real price' of each when sold :	210—213
4.	The fluctuations of Foreign exchanges may be used to illustrate this theory, but need careful handling.	213—215
5.	The term 'International' may be objected to in this connexion, but is defensible.	215—216

CHAPTER IV.

DEFINITION OF MONEY.

		PAGES
1.	The denotation of the term money is obscure and fluctuating; but, as commonly used in discussions about the money-market, it certainly includes Bankers' Liabilities:	217—222
2.	though this fact has not received adequate recognition.	222—225
3.	This denotation seems on the whole most convenient.	225—231

CHAPTER V.

VALUE OF MONEY.

1. The value of metallic money, freely coined, may be regarded as depending on the value of the metal. . . 232—236
2. The value of gold is slowly and irregularly affected by industrial competition: if we suppose the quantity given, variations in the value of a gold standard will be determined by variations in the monetary work of gold coin, together with the demand for gold in the arts. . 236—240
3. They will therefore be partly due to changes, difficult to measure, in commodities in general. . . . . 240—243
4. Bankers' obligations have the same actual value as the coin they represent; though, of course, a less value than coin would have if they were not used; and a more variable value. This must be distinguished from the value of money—i.e. of the use of money—in the money-market; this latter again is not to be identified with the rate of interest on capital generally. . . . . . 243—247
5. There are, however, certain connexions between the purchasing power of money and the rate of discount in the money-market which explain the common confusion. . 247—250
6. A double standard with a fixed ratio will be stable against minor variations of supply, the fixed ratio causing an adjustment of demand to supply. . . . . . 250—252
7. The value of inconvertible currency is determined by the relation of supply to demand. . . . . 252—254

CHAPTER VI.

INTEREST.

1. By 'Interest', in the theory of Distribution, is meant the share of produce obtained by the owner of capital as such. 255—259

		PAGES
2.	By 'rate of interest' is meant the commonly expected average yield of newly invested capital; which with certain qualifications, may be taken as approximately uniform in a modern community at any given time.	259—264
3.	It depends on conditions of demand and supply combined: —so far as demand goes, in a modern industrial society, it depends mainly on industrial demand.	264—267
4.	It tends to correspond to average additional produce expected to be obtained by employment of last increment of floating capital, *minus* 'employer's fee'; therefore varies with variations in recognised opportunities of profitably using capital to aid labour.	268—272
5.	The reaction of changes in the rate of interest on the saving that supplies capital has an important, but not definitely measurable, tendency to keep the rate stable.	273—275
6.	The yield of most—but not all—old investments tends to decrease.	276—277

CHAPTER VII.

RENT.

1.	Ricardo's view of agricultural rent, as price paid for 'original powers' of soil, and his account of the origin and history of rent, are unacceptable:	278—283
2.	and his formula for competitive determination of rent is only acceptable with certain important qualifications.	283—288
3.	Difficulties arise in framing rent-contracts from possibilities of improving or deteriorating land; similarly, in the case of mines, from deterioration.	288—291
4.	Ricardo's conception is really most applicable to building land in towns. There are various other extra profits more or less analogous to rent.	291—293

CHAPTER VIII.

THE REMUNERATION OF LABOUR.

1.	Competition does not tend to give the labourer the real wages required to make his labour most efficient.	295—298
2.	Nor can I accept the 'Wages-Fund Theory', which professes to determine general wages by 'ratio of capital to population'.	298—302
3.	Wages should not be regarded as paid out of capital.	302—305

CONTENTS. xvii

PAGES

4. The remuneration of labour—including the labour of employers—may be regarded as the share of produce that remains after paying for the use of capital and land; and thus, supposing the quantity and quality of labour to be given independently of its remuneration, the latter would depend partly on the efficiency of labour, partly on the price paid for the use of 'producers' wealth'. . . . . 305—310
5. However, the reaction of the remuneration of labour on the supply of labourers has a certain tendency to counteract changes in this remuneration :—but to a very varying extent as circumstances vary. . . . 310—315

CHAPTER IX.

PARTICULAR WAGES AND PROFITS.

1. The proposition that industrial competition tends to equalise the remunerations of average labourers requires important limitations. . . . . . . 316—320
2. The inequalities in the wages of different classes are partly compensation for differences of sacrifice entailed by their work, or by the training required for it, partly due to scarcities of persons able or willing to afford the outlay required for superior qualities of labour, partly to scarcities of natural gifts. . . . . . . 320—327
3. The inequalities of average earnings of employers of different amounts of capital are to be referred chiefly to these two kinds of scarcity combined. . . . . . 328—334

CHAPTER X.

MONOPOLY AND COMBINATION.

1. Monopoly resulting from combination is a normal element of the industrial society with which our theory deals. . . . . 335—337
2. We have to distinguish various modes and degrees of monopoly—extending the term to include 'buyers'' monopoly; . . . . 337—342
3. and to note special characteristics of monopoly resulting from combination—open or tacit—and different methods of attaining the end in view. . . . . . . 342—347
4. Under certain conditions, bodies of hired labourers may

xviii   CONTENTS.

PAGES

       increase their earnings by combination, without counterbalancing loss to themselves or to other hired labourers.   347—351
5. A normal rate of exchange between opposing combinations of buyers and sellers cannot be ascertained, by the methods of economic science. . . . . . 351—353

CHAPTER XI.

TRANSIENT AND LOCAL VARIATIONS IN DISTRIBUTION.

1. After a summary of the five preceding chapters, in which we have discussed the determination of Normal rates of remuneration for industrial services, ... 354—358
2. we notice that these normal rates are exposed to continual fluctuations—especially the profits of business— . . 358—361
3. and proceed to analyse the causes of these, as due to moral and intellectual shortcomings, to accidents, to inventions and other improvements ; . . . . . . 361—366
4. to miscalculations of demand causing (so-called) 'over-production'; . . . . 366—368
5. to changes in rate of interest, consequent on 'over-production' or otherwise caused, and changes in purchasing power of money. . . . . 368—371
6. This leads us to notice local variations in the prices of products, due to physical and historical causes combined . . . . 371—374
7. and consequent inequalities in returns to labour and capital, kept up by obstacles to migration and frequent industrial changes. . . . . 374—377
8. Any forecast of future economic changes must necessarily be vague and conjectural, except so far as it is avowedly hypothetical. . . . . 377—384

CHAPTER XII.

CUSTOM.

1. Distinguishing from Custom = the tendency to do as others do, Habit = the tendency to do as one has done before, we observe that the economic effects of Habit are various . . . . 385—388
2. as also of Custom . . . . 388—390
3. and that only a part of these effects is excluded by the assumptions of the competitive system—viz. (1) the mere blind tendency to follow use and wont, and (2) Custom as morally obligatory. . . . . . 390—392

BOOK III.

THE ART OF POLITICAL ECONOMY.

CHAPTER I.

	PAGES
The Art of Political Economy, as here treated, consists mainly of the theory of what ought to be done by government to improve Production or Distribution, and to provide for governmental expenditure.	395—398

CHAPTER II.

THE SYSTEM OF NATURAL LIBERTY CONSIDERED IN RELATION TO PRODUCTION.

1. The general argument in favour of leaving industry alone has much force, but needs important qualifications and exceptions, ... 399—402
2. even in the most abstract theoretical treatment, owing to divergence between utility to the individual and utility to society; illustrated generally in reference to Bequest and Contract; . . . . 402—406
3. exemplified further by special cases, in which the utility of socially useful services cannot be adequately appropriated by the persons who might render them : . 406—408
4. also where the gain of a change is largely counterbalanced by loss; and in the case of monopoly, especially monopoly resulting from combination. 408—410
5. Sometimes, however, governmental intervention is needed to secure such combined action or abstinence as is socially advantageous: 410
6. Note also the imperfectly employed labour that competition normally involves, and the labour spent in attracting business : . . . . 410—412
7. also the case of utilities distant in time. . . 412—413
8. Hence complete *laisser faire* is not to be taken as a political ideal : the problem for the statesman is to balance its disadvantages against the disadvantages of extending the sphere of government. . . . . . . 413—416
9. Our reasoning so far has left unassailed the assumption that the individual is a better judge than government of his economic interests: but this assumption is not completely true, nor even tending to become so. 416—418

CHAPTER III.

THE RELATIONS OF GOVERNMENT TO INDUSTRY.

PAGES

1. The strictly economic interferences of government are to be distinguished from its interferences with industry in the exercise of its necessary functions. . . . . 419—421
2. Such interferences are of various kinds and degrees of intensity, ... 421—422
3. may take place for national defence, ... 422—423
4. for protection of life, health, reputation of individual citizens, adults or children, ... 423—427
5. or for protection from theft or fraud. Observe, too, that governments have importantly restricted their enforcement of contracts—e.g. by bankruptcy laws—and, under the guise of judicial interpretation, have practically determined the conditions of ordinary engagements. . 427—432
6. Again many important questions as to the limits of the right of property have to be determined by government; e.g. in the case of land, patents, copyrights, inheritance. . . . . 432—436

CHAPTER IV

IMPORTANT CASES OF GOVERNMENTAL INTERFERENCE TO PROMOTE PRODUCTION.

1. Governments (central or local) have interfered specially in businesses concerned with transfer; partly from their tendency to become monopolies, partly from the importance of their indirect utilities: . . . 437—439
2. as in the case of ordinary roads, . . 439—440
3. of railways and canals . . . . 441—445
4. and the post-office. On somewhat similar grounds they have intervened in the provision for gas and water. . 445—446
5. Coining is obviously adapted for governmental management, on various grounds; but there seems no reason why it should not pay its expenses. . . . . 446—448
6. A bimetallic currency may be maintained under certain conditions and has certain advantages. . . . 448—454
7. The establishment of a Tabular Standard would much reduce fluctuations in the value of deferred payments: but it would be a matter of difficulty. . . . 454—456
8. The issue of convertible notes should be at least regulated, and there are important advantages in its being undertaken by government; . . . . . 457—460

CONTENTS.

		PAGES
9.	which render it desirable that government should form a special connexion with a bank; but not that it should undertake ordinary banking business—though certain kinds of lending seem suited to government.	460—464
10.	There are certain other departments in which governments have intervened partly with a view to production: thus in providing for education and culture they have partly aimed at making labour more efficient.	464—467
11.	They have partly on similar grounds assisted emigration:	467—470
12.	and arranged the sale of unoccupied lands on other than strictly commercial principles.	470—475
13.	Even in fully occupied countries, there are reasons for keeping certain portions of land under governmental management, as forests; for restricting private property in mines;	475—478
14.	and perhaps—though this is more doubtful—for interference with the tenure of agricultural land, in order to promote production.	478—484

CHAPTER V.

PROTECTION.

1. Temporary Protection, though not practically to be recommended, is under certain circumstances defensible in abstract economic theory; . . . . . . 486—489
2. even from a cosmopolitan point of view: especially to foster a new industry: . . . . 489—493
3. still more from a purely national point of view, in spite of important drawbacks. . . . . 493—496
4. And Free Trade may tend, in certain cases, to be accompanied by a displacement of population between the trading communities. . . . . . . 496—498

CHAPTER VI.

THE PRINCIPLES OF DISTRIBUTIVE JUSTICE.

1. The present individualistic organization of society cannot be maintained to be theoretically just, on account of its long duration, or unjust on account of its origin. . . 499—502
2. The institution of private property, as extended to land, cannot be defended as strictly 'realizing freedom', or 'securing the fruits of labour'; though the gain to labour

		PAGES
	in the aggregate from the accumulation of capital that the institution has caused vastly outweighs its loss through exclusion from appropriated land.	502—503
3.	It does not however appear that private property and free contract together tend to give each labourer the wages he deserves. But exact remuneration of desert seems an unattainable ideal.	503—506
4.	It has been believed that *laisser faire* gives, or will give, the greatest possible equality of opportunities to labour: but it certainly leaves room for serious inequality from monopoly and combination, from fluctuations of industry,	506—510
5.	from the unearned increment in the value of land,	510—513
6.	from the large earnings of owners of capital, and from the payment of interest, which would not be required if capital were accumulated by the community. The grounds for not removing these inequalities by governmental interference are *productional*, not *distributional*.	513—517

CHAPTER VII.

ECONOMIC DISTRIBUTION.

1.	A more equal distribution of wealth tends *primâ facie* to increase happiness:	518—520
2.	but we have to allow for loss through increased idleness, decreased saving, lessened efficiency of capital, pressure of population, checked growth of culture.	521—525
3.	It seems impossible to dispense, as Communism seeks to do, with the individualistic stimulus to labour and care, and check to population.	526—528
4.	But the ideal of Socialism is not open to the same objections; and a certain advance in the direction of this ideal, by a judicious and gradual extension of governmental functions, is not opposed to sound economic theory.	528—533
5.	The chief communistic institution, actually established in England, is the provision for poor-relief; this, however might perhaps be made in other ways.	533—538
6.	Other distributional interferences have been usually—and rightly—designed also to benefit production. In determining the proper limits of such interference, one important consideration is the efficiency of voluntary provision for social needs.	538—541

CONTENTS. xxiii

7. In determining a 'fair' division of produce between opposing combinations, an arbitrary point of departure is necessary: political economy can only assist in showing how 'fairness' arbitrarily defined is to be maintained under changing conditions. . . . 541—544

CHAPTER VIII.

PUBLIC FINANCE.

1. We have to treat generally of the provision for public expenditure (the amount of which must partly depend on the possibilities of conveniently providing for it). . . . . 545—547
2. The commodities required for the use of government are generally obtained by free purchase; though under certain circumstances it is more economical to obtain services—especially of soldiers—by direct compulsion. 547—549
3. The funds for such purchases may come from (1) Rents, or (2) Loans—which are under certain circumstances legitimate, whether for productive employment, or as a means of lightening an occasional burden by spreading it over a longer period, ... 549—554
4. or (3) from payments for commodities supplied by government—the price of which, when they are monopolised, may be determined on various principles. . . . . 554—560
5. Taxes, commonly so called, can be only to a very limited extent treated as payments for services rendered by government. . . . . 560—564
6. Distinguishing 'taxes proper' from such payments, we may note the complexity of considerations, political and economical, productional and distributional, which ought to have weight in the selection of taxes. . . . 564—566
7. We should aim at proportioning taxation mainly to that part of the income which is not spent in necessaries, nor in ways socially useful, nor saved: the adjustment can at best be rough, especially if taxes be largely laid on commodities—a method however which is on several grounds to be recommended. . . . . . 566—571
8. The incidence of taxes is hard to determine, from the varying degrees of completeness and rapidity with which their burden tends to be transferred: illustrated by taxes on Incomes, taxes on Land, . . . 571—576

		PAGES
9.	and taxes on Production—which as 'indirect' taxes are sometimes thought to be transferred completely to the consumers; but the rapidity and even the extent of the transference varies much according to circumstances.	576—578
10.	Such taxes are liable to cause an extra loss to consumers, over and above the gain to the treasury.	578—581
11.	Taxes on inheritance require special and separate treatment.	581—582

CHAPTER IX.

POLITICAL ECONOMY AND PRIVATE MORALITY.

1.	Political economy tends to influence the common notion of fair dealing especially in respect of taking advantage of (a) ignorance,	583—587
2.	and (b) need. Properly understood, it does not generally justify a man in exacting more than the normal competitive price for his service; but it shows the danger of condemning any one for taking full advantage of competition, except in case of extreme need, when humanity requires some gain to be foregone.	587—590
3.	Economic teaching has had a doubtful effect on the current dislike of 'rings' and other combinations—and the severer censure commonly passed on 'making work,' 'scamping work,' &c.	590—592
4.	The egoistic influences of the individualistic organisation of industry need to be counteracted: hence the moral value of Cooperation.	592—593
5.	Political economy has exploded the fallacy that the luxurious expenditure of the rich benefits the poor; but it has also drawn attention to the dangers of almsgiving.	593—595

INTRODUCTION.

CHAPTER I.

THE PRESENT STATE OF ECONOMIC CONTROVERSY IN ENGLAND AND THE SPECIAL AIM OF THE PRESENT WORK.

§ 1. SOME twenty years ago, both the Theory of Political Economy in its main outlines, and the most important practical applications of it, were considered as finally settled by the great majority of educated persons in England. Two causes appear to have chiefly cooperated in producing this result. The prosperity that had followed on the abolition of the corn-laws had given practical men a most impressive and satisfying proof of the soundness of the abstract reasoning by which the expediency of Free Trade had been inferred; and a masterly expositor of thought (J. S. Mill) had published in a convenient treatise a skilful statement of the chief results of the controversies of the preceding generation; in which the doctrines of Ricardo were presented with many of the requisite explanations and qualifications, and much of what was sound in the objections and supplementary suggestions of other writers was duly taken into account. It seemed that the science had at length emerged from the state of polemical discussion on fundamental notions and principles, and that whatever further remained to be done would be building on a foundation already laid. J. S. Mill's language had a considerable share in producing this belief. No English thinker, since Locke, who has exercised so wide and intense an influence on his contemporaries, has been generally so little open to the charge of overrating the finality—as regards either substance or form—of the theories he has expounded: and no one since Bacon has been more concerned to point the way to the illimitable worlds of knowledge that remain to be conquered. Hence it is all the more remarkable that he should have commenced his account of value with the unhesitating assertion that "there is nothing in the laws of value which remains "for the present or any future writer to clear up: the theory "of the subject is complete." It is not surprising that the younger generation, to whom his treatise soon became the chief—and often the sole—source of economic knowledge, should be equally confident; and that it should become the fashion to point to Political Economy as unique among moral sciences for the clearness and certainty of its method and the admitted trustworthiness of its conclusions.

Probably many of the generation taught by J. S. Mill are not aware how recent is the date of this confident tone. In fact, however, during the second quarter of the present century almost every English writer on Political Economy took note in some form or other of the rudimentary and unsettled condition of his study. For example, Senior, in an Introductory Lecture delivered before the University of Oxford in 1826, spoke of the science as "in that state of imperfect "development, which...throws the greatest difficulty in the way "of a beginner and consequently of a teacher, and offers the "fairest scope to the objections of an idle or interested adver-"sary." Malthus[1] in the following year remarked that "the "differences of opinion among political economists" have "of "late been a frequent subject of complaint." The Edinburgh Reviewer of McCulloch's first edition (1831) characterized Political Economy as "a moral science of which the "doctrines are not recognised": and McCulloch himself through his successive editions, was obliged to note that "the differences

---

[1] *Definitions in Political Economy* (preface).

"which have subsisted among the most eminent of its professors "have proved exceedingly unfavourable to its progress, and "have generated a disposition to distrust its best established "conclusions." Even in 1852 when Senior again addressed the University of Oxford, he announced that his subject was still "in a state of imperfect development," and devoted his first lecture to an explanation of "the causes that have retarded its "progress."

No doubt many of these writers express a confident hope that this 'retardation' will soon cease. McCulloch has no doubt that "the errors with which the science was formerly infected "are fast disappearing," and Colonel Torrens ventures to prophesy more definitely that "twenty years hence there will scarcely "exist a doubt respecting any of its more fundamental principles." And by the time that Mill's work had gone through several editions an impression began to prevail widely that this better time had actually arrived. The generation whose study of Political Economy commenced about 1860 were for the most part but dimly conscious of the element of stormy controversy from which the subject had so recently emerged[1]. It is

[1] The following extract from the *Edinburgh Review*, Vol. 114, seems to me to represent accurately the view of the subject which was current about the time (1861) that it was written: and it is all the better evidence of the general state of opinion, because it occurs incidentally in an article on 'English Jurisprudence.' "That some departments of human conduct are capable of being classified "with sufficient exactness to supply the materials of a true science is conclu-"sively proved by the existence of Political Economy."......" Political Economy "is the only moral science in which definitions of fundamental terms suffi-"ciently accurate to obtain general currency amongst all persons conversant "with the subject have yet been produced. The consequence has been that "the conclusions of those who understand the science are accepted and acted "on with a degree of confidence which is felt in regard to no other speculations "that deal with human affairs. Political Economists can appeal to the only test "which really measures the truth of a science—success—with as much con-"fidence as astronomers. The source of their success has been that they have "succeeded in affixing a precise meaning to words which had for ages been "used by millions who attached to them vivid but not definite notions, such as "wages, profits, capital, value, rent, and many others of the same kind."

The preface to Fawcett's Manual—first published in 1863—exhibits the same undoubting confidence in the established scientific character of Political Economy. It begins with the following sentences:

"I have often remarked that Political Economy is more frequently talked "about than any other science, and that its principles are more frequently

true that there were still loud voices heard on the opposite side; but comparatively little notice was taken of them. For instance, the condemnation of Political Economy by Auguste Comte was generally disregarded—in spite of the great and growing interest that was then taken in the Positive Philosophy—as being plainly irrelevant to Mill's exposition of the subject; in fact, it seemed to be based on a misunderstanding nearly as palpable as that involved in the vulgar dislike of the political economist as a preacher of the gospel of Mammon and selfishness. I hardly think that even the eloquent diatribes of Mr Frederic Harrison[1] induced any considerable number of readers—outside the working classes—even to doubt the established position of economic science. Nor did the elaborate attacks made by Mr Macleod[2] on the received doctrines succeed in attracting public attention: his books were bought and read, but were valued almost exclusively for their information on the special subject of Banking. Mr F. D. Longe's refutation of the Wages-Fund Theory (1867) fell quite dead: even the *Quarterly Review*, which in 1871 attacked Thornton for ignoring his obligations to Mr Longe, and sneered at Mill for admitting when urged by a friend a hostile argument to the force of which he had previously remained deaf, had up to that date never found occasion to mention Mr Longe's name.

In 1871, however, these halcyon days of Political Economy had passed away. Their termination was of course not abrupt; but so far as any date can be fixed for it, I should place it at the appearance of Mill's notice of Thornton's book *On Labour* in the *Fortnightly Review* of March, 1869. I do not think that the work itself, apart from the review, would have produced so much effect; since Thornton's criticism of the Theory of Value showed so serious a misapprehension of the general relation which economic theory necessarily bears to economic facts, that a disciple of Mill might be pardoned for

"appealed to in the discussions of ordinary life. No science, however, is "perhaps more imperfectly understood. I believe that profound mathema-"ticians, or accomplished geologists and botanists, are far more numerous than "real masters of the principles of Political Economy."

[1] Cf. *Fortnightly Review*, 1865.

[2] In his *Theory of Banking*, 1855-6, and his *Dictionary of Economical Philosophy*, 1863.

underrating the real use and importance of this and other parts of Thornton's book. But the manner in which Mill replied to this criticism appeared to most of his disciples highly unsatisfactory, and the facility with which he resigned a doctrine (the old 'Wages-Fund Theory') which he had taught for years caused them an unexpected shock; thus they were naturally led to give a more respectful attention not only to Thornton's assaults, but also to other utterances of dissent from economic orthodoxy to which they had hitherto turned a deaf ear. A second shock was given in 1871 by the publication of Jevons' *Theory of Political Economy;* which took up in reference to the received mode of treating the subject an attitude almost similar to that which each new metaphysical system has hitherto adopted towards its predecessors. Again, in 1874, Cairnes' *Leading Principles of Political Economy,* though written by a disciple of Mill and in fundamental agreement with his doctrines, still contributed to impair the unique prestige which Mill's exposition had enjoyed for nearly half a generation. As a controversialist Cairnes, though scrupulously fair in intention, was deficient in intellectual sympathy; he could hardly avoid representing any doctrine that he did not hold in such a way as to make it almost inconceivable to his readers that it could possibly have been maintained by a man of sense; and when this treatment was applied to some of his master's most important statements, the expressions of personal regard for Mill by which it was accompanied only made the result seem more damaging to a reader who was convinced by Cairnes' reasoning. Meanwhile the strife between Labour and Capital had come to occupy more and more of the attention of cultivated society; and the conviction had gradually gained ground that Political Economy had failed to ascertain the "law "that determines the stable equilibrium of work and wages[1]": and even that "the attempt to solve great industrial questions "on the hypothesis which Mr Mill states to be the fundamental "one of Political Economy"—i.e. that men are governed by self-interest only—"is to confuse rather than to elucidate the "problems which it behoves us to investigate."

[1] Cf. *Edinburgh Review*, vol. 138, 1873.

In short, when the concluding quarter of this century began, it was evident that Political Economy had returned to the condition in which it was in the second quarter; and that McCulloch's melancholy admission that "the differences which "have subsisted among the most eminent of its professors have "proved exceedingly unfavourable to its progress, and have "generated a disposition to distrust its best established con- "clusions" was again only too applicable. This unfortunate result would, I think, have been brought about merely by the disputes and divergences of opinion among economists who adhered to the mode of treating the subject which has prevailed in England since Ricardo. But a powerful contribution to it was supplied by a thoughtful and independent writer, Cliffe Leslie; who in 1870, in an article on the Political Economy of Adam Smith, began that attack on the 'Ricardian' or 'à priori' method which he continued in several subsequent articles, afterwards reprinted in his *Essays Moral and Political.* One part of Cliffe Leslie's work consisted in drawing the attention of English economists to the movement in opposition to their method which had for some time been carried on in Germany, and which, during the last twenty years, has continually gained strength. The leaders of this movement, however widely they also differ among themselves, are generally agreed in repudiating as "Manchesterthum"—or even "Smithianis- "mus"—the view of Political Economy mainly adopted in England; and their influence constitutes an additional force under which the disputes as to particular doctrines among the English Economists tend to broaden into more fundamental controversy as to the general method of dealing with economic questions.

At the same time the opposition of influential artisans to the traditional Political Economy has not diminished, if I may judge from Mr Howell's *Conflict of Labour and Capital;* it has only changed somewhat from sullen distrust to confident contempt. While, finally, the great practical success of Free Trade—which, as I said at the outset, contributed largely to the prestige enjoyed by Political Economy during its halcyon days in the third quarter of this century—has recently been called in question by an apparently growing party of practical men; and is certainly rendered dubious through the signal disappointment of Cobden's confident expectations that the example of England would be speedily followed by the whole civilised world.

§ 2. This brief sketch of the recent history and present condition of Political Economy in England has seemed to me necessary in order to explain the exact object of the present work; which on the one hand does not aim at originality, while on the other hand it is not precisely an elementary treatise. It is written in the belief that the reaction above described against the treatment of Political Economy as an established science was inevitable and even salutary; but that it has been carried too far, so that the waves of disputation are in danger of submerging the really sound and valuable results of previous thought. My primary aim, then, has been to eliminate unnecessary controversy, by stating these results in a more guarded manner, and with due attention to the criticisms and suggestions of recent writers. Several valuable contributions to abstract economic theory have been made by Cairnes, Jevons, and others who have written since Mill; but in my opinion they generally admit of being stated in a form less hostile to the older doctrines than their authors suppose. In the same way I think that the opposition between the Inductive and Deductive Methods has been urged by writers on both sides in needlessly sharp and uncompromising terms. I shall endeavour to show[1] that there is an important part of the subject to which economists are generally agreed in applying a mainly inductive or "realistic" treatment. On the other hand, few, I think, would deny the utility and even indispensability of deductive reasoning in the Theory of Distribution and Exchange; provided only the assumptions on which such reasoning proceeds are duly stated, and their partially hypothetical character continually borne in mind. I fully admit the importance of this latter proviso; accordingly in those parts of this work in which I have used chiefly deductive reasoning, I have made it my special aim to state explicitly and keep clearly in view the limited and conditional applicability of the conclusions attained by it.

[1] Cf. *post*, Chap. III.

With this view I have been generally careful to avoid any dogmatic statements on practical points. It is very rarely, if ever, that the practical economic questions which are presented to the statesman can be unhesitatingly decided by abstract reasoning from elementary principles. For the right solution of them full and exact knowledge of the facts of the particular case is commonly required; and the difficulty of ascertaining these facts is often such as to prevent the attainment of positive conclusions by any strictly scientific procedure.

At the same time the function of economic theory in relation to such problems is none the less important and indispensable; since the practical conclusions of the most untheoretical expert are always reached implicitly or explicitly by some kind of reasoning from some economic principles; and if the principles or reasoning be unsound the conclusions can only be right by accident. For instance, if a practical man affirms that it will promote the economic welfare of England to tax certain of the products of foreign industry, a mere theorist should hesitate to contradict him without a careful study of the facts of the case. But if the practical person gives as his reason that "one-sided "free trade is not free trade at all," the theorist is then in a position to point out that the general arguments in favour of the admission of foreign products are mostly independent of the question whether such admission is or is not reciprocated. So again, if it is argued that, in the present agricultural depression, a restriction of freedom of contract and freedom of bequest is imperatively required, it would be presumptuous to affirm dogmatically that such restrictions are undesirable. But if the advocate of these restrictions explains that they are required in order that more farming capital may be applied to the land, it then becomes opportune to show him that *so far as* land in England is cultivated, on the average, with an amount of capital larger than that which would give the greatest proportional produce, and *so far as* the fall in farmers' profits is due to increased facilities of foreign importation, the mere application of more capital to the land would tend to aggravate the fall. And similarly in dealing with other questions of the day, abstract economic arguments almost always come in, and are almost never by themselves decisive.

In thus making prominent the hypothetical character of the deductive reasonings of Political Economy, I am merely following the lines laid down by J. S. Mill in his general account of economic method—as expounded most fully in his *Essays on Unsettled Questions in Political Economy* (1843). This view of the subject rendered his whole treatment of it more profoundly different from that of Ricardo and James Mill, than is at first apparent to hasty readers; though, as was only natural, the modifications which its consistent application required in the old doctrine were not always carried out with perfect precision and completeness. Still, the work that was actually done by Mill in supplying corrections and limitations to the dogmatism of the earlier Ricardian school, seems to me to have an importance which some recent critics have overlooked; and to which, in my present attempt to carry this work a stage further, I am especially called upon to do justice.

Note on Ricardo and J. S. Mill.

In the preface to the second edition of Jevons' *Theory of Political Economy*—the most important contribution to economic theory that has been made in England for a generation—the lamented author announces as a conclusion to which he is "ever more clearly coming, "that the only hope of attaining a true system of Economics is to "fling aside, once and for ever, the mazy and preposterous assump- "tions of the Ricardian School[1]." He subsequently speaks of the doctrines of this school as "Ricardo-Mill Economics," explaining how "that able but wrong-headed man, David Ricardo, shunted the "car of economic science on a wrong line, a line, however, on which "it was further urged towards confusion by his equally able and "wrong-headed admirer, John Stuart Mill[2]."

The expression of opinion in these passages appears to me exaggerated and violent, even so far as Ricardo is concerned; while so far as it applies to Mill I cannot but regard it as entirely false and misleading. I certainly should agree with Jevons in deprecating as excessive and overstrained the eulogistic language in which many competent judges have described the work of Ricardo. Though

---

[1] *Theory of Political Economy*, preface, p. xlix.
[2] *L. c.* p. lvii.

undoubtedly an original and important thinker, I cannot perceive that Ricardo was a thoroughly clear and consistent reasoner; and it has always seemed to me highly unfair to the deductive method of economics to treat Ricardo's writings as a peculiarly faultless specimen of its application. At the same time I hold that many of the characteristic doctrines of Ricardo, stated with proper qualifications and reserves, ought to find a place in any complete exposition of economic theory; and I have been careful to give them, in the present treatise, the place which appears to me to belong to them: though I equally hold that the statement of them by Ricardo himself has frequently serious, and sometimes glaring, deficiencies. In some cases, as in the determination of Wages and Profits, while recognising an element of truth in Ricardo's view, I think that the defects of his doctrine are beyond patching, and that an entirely new treatment of the subject has to be adopted. On the other hand, as regards the relation of Value to Cost of Production, Ricardo's doctrine is of fundamental importance (though requiring to be qualified and supplemented); and any teaching which ignores or obscures it appears to me fatally defective. But, whatever judgment may be passed on the work of Ricardo, it is certainly misleading to say that Mill "urged the car of economic science further towards "confusion" on the "wrong line" on which Ricardo had shunted it. Indeed I am unable to conjecture how Jevons would have supported a statement which appears to me so perverse. He cannot, I think, refer to the general theory of Value, where Mill corrects and supplements Ricardo's view, by giving due place to the operation of Supply and Demand in the determination of market-price; and where he quietly gets rid of Ricardo's serious confusion between Measure of Value and Cause or Determinant of Value. Nor can he have been thinking of the theory of Rent; for here Mill's exposition of the Ricardian doctrine is improved and guarded in several important respects; especially by the account taken of Carey's indisputable limitation of the law of diminishing returns, and by the stress laid on the influence of general industrial progress in counteracting this law. Nor, again, can he have in view the theory of Wages and Profits; in which, among other improvements, Mill reduces to harmlessness Ricardo's dangerous paradox that "wages cannot rise with-"out profits falling." Nor, finally, can his statement relate to the theory of International Values; since he expressly says that this is probably the most valuable part of Mill's work. But if Jevons' charge cannot be justified in relation to any of the four topics that

I have mentioned, it is difficult to conceive how so strong a statement can possibly be justified at all. It must be admitted that on more than one important point Mill has not made clear to the reader the interval that separates his doctrine from Ricardo's: which, with Cliffe Leslie, I partly attribute to that "piety of a disciple" which Mill always manifests towards Ricardo's teaching. This disposition has had some unfortunate consequences, and must be regarded as a weakness; still, in a subject where most writers have shown so marked a tendency to emphasize the novelty of their ideas, and exaggerate their divergence from their predecessors, it appears to me a weakness that "leans to virtue's side."

CHAPTER II.

SCOPE OF POLITICAL ECONOMY.

§ 1. POLITICAL Economy, in England at least, is now almost universally understood to be a study or inquiry concerned with the Production, Distribution, and Exchange of Wealth. I shall afterwards[1] propose, in certain parts of the enquiry, to substitute for 'wealth' a term which will include the transient utilities resulting from labour—which we call 'services'—as well as the utilities "embodied in material objects" to which the term 'wealth' is commonly restricted. But since the relations of men to Wealth, strictly taken, will in any case constitute the chief object of our study, we may acquiesce provisionally in the definition above given: understanding that by 'Production of 'wealth' is meant the production of new value or utility in preexisting materials; and that, under the head of 'Distribution 'and Exchange' we examine, not the material processes by which goods are conveyed from place to place[2], or the legal processes by which they are transferred from owner to owner, but the different proportions in which the produce of industry is shared among the different economic classes that have co-operated in producing it, the ratios in which different kinds of wealth are exchanged for each other, and the causes determining these proportions and ratios.

A more fundamental divergence of opinion relates to the point of view from which Political Economy contemplates these

[1] Cf. B. I. Chap. III.
[2] It may be observed that "distribution" in this material sense is, in the view of the political economist, a kind of production, since it adds to the utility and value of the goods conveyed.

CHAP. II.]   SCOPE OF POLITICAL ECONOMY.   13

relations. Is its primary aim to establish certain general propositions, either positively or hypothetically true, respecting the coexistence and sequence of facts, or to give practical rules for the attainment of certain ends? Is it, in short—to use an old distinction recently revived in this connexion—a Science or an Art? The former view is that which has been adopted, I believe, by all writers on economic theory in England for the last thirty years. No doubt an important part of the subject as treated by Mill and other systematic writers belongs admittedly to Art rather than to Science; viz. the discussion of the principles on which Taxation should be managed and of the general nature and limits of Governmental interference, so far as it affects the amount or the distribution of the national wealth. But these matters are generally handled by the writers in question under the head not of Political Economy strictly speaking, but of its application to Politics or the Art of Government. They hold that the precepts or rules of this department of practice are properly based, in a great measure, on the generalisations or deductions of Economic Science; but they do not mean these rules of Art when they speak of the 'laws of Political Economy'; and they have frequently censured as a vulgar error the habit of thinking and speaking of economic 'laws' as liable to 'violation,' and as needing to be realised by voluntary conformity or even enforced by public opinion. Still this habit has been found very difficult to eradicate[1]; and indeed, the sharp distinction which English economists are at present disposed to draw between Economic Theory and its application to practice is almost confined to themselves and their more docile disciples: it has not worked itself into the common thought of even cultivated persons here, and it has not been generally accepted by Continental writers. When, in discussing the same matters, one set of disputants blend the consideration of 'what exists' or 'tends to exist' with the consideration 'what ought to be done,' while another set emphatically distinguish the two questions, the gravest misunderstanding is likely to result: hence it

[1] I think it may be said that, at least in nine cases out of ten, when reference is made by public speakers or journalists to the laws of Political Economy, it is implied that Political Economy *prescribes* "freedom of contract," and does not merely assume it as a condition of the applicability of its conclusions.

seems very important to examine carefully the causes and the justification, if there be any, of this widespread confusion —or at least fusion—of distinct inquiries.

§ 2. The causes are partly historical or linguistic; partly, again, they lie deep in the nature of the subject and the normal conditions of the application of the human intellect to practice. To begin with the former, we may observe that the generic term Economy has always denoted an Art or method of attaining a practical end rather than a Science, and that it has naturally been found difficult to alter its meaning altogether in prefixing to it the epithet Political; especially since, the compound 'politico-economical' having been found unendurable, the simple 'economical' has been used to do adjectival duty both for 'economy' and 'political economy.' Recent writers, it is true, have generally used 'economic' as the adjective corresponding to political economy': but though they have thereby obviated an ambiguity of language, they have not done away with the general impression that Political Economy is one branch of a larger subject which includes, e.g., Domestic Economy as another branch. This, of course, was the relation of the two studies as originally conceived: otherwise the term Political Economy would never have come into use. It was because a monarch or statesman was conceived to have the function of arranging the industry of the country somewhat as the father of a family arranges the industry of his household, that the Art which offered him guidance in the performance of this function was called Political Economy. If we turn, for example, to Sir James Steuart, the first of our systematic writers, we find that his *Inquiry into the Principles of Political Economy* (published 1767) commences with the following account of the subject:

"Economy in general is the art of providing for all the "wants of a family with prudence and frugality......The whole "economy must be directed by the head, who is both lord and "steward;......as lord he establishes the laws of his economy, as "steward he puts them into execution......

"What economy is in a family, Political Economy is in a "state,......but the statesman is not master to establish what "form of economy he pleases;...the great art therefore of Politi-

"cal Economy is first to adapt the different operations of it to
"the spirit, manners,. habits and customs of the people, and
"afterwards to model these circumstances so as to be able to
"introduce a set of new and more useful institutions.

"The principal object of this science is to secure a certain
"fund of subsistence for all the inhabitants, to obviate every
"circumstance which may render it precarious; to provide
"everything necessary for supplying the wants of the society,
"and to employ the inhabitants (supposing them to be freemen)
"in such a manner as naturally to create reciprocal relations
"and dependencies between them, so as to make their several
"interests lead them to supply one another with their reciprocal
"wants......Political Economy in each country must necessarily
"be different;......it is the business of a statesman to judge
"of the expediency of different schemes of economy, and by
"degrees to model the minds of his subjects so as to induce
"them, from the allurement of private interest, to concur in the
"execution of his plan."

Nine years after Steuart's book was published appeared the epoch-making *Wealth of Nations*, enforcing an essentially different view of a statesman's duties. But notwithstanding the gulf that separates Adam Smith's economic doctrine from Steuart's, he is equally decided in regarding Political Economy as a study with an immediate practical end[1]. "Political "Economy," he says, in the introduction to the fourth book, "proposes two distinct objects: first, to provide a plentiful "revenue or subsistence for the people, or, more properly, to "enable them to provide such a revenue or subsistence for "themselves; and secondly, to supply the state or common "weal with a revenue sufficient for the public service. It "proposes to enrich both the people and the sovereign." Accordingly by the "systems of Political Economy" of which he treats in this book he seems at the outset to mean not systems in the scientific sense, i.e. connected sets of general statements

[1] No importance is to be attached to the fact that Steuart, Adam Smith, and others *call* Political Economy a Science while defining it as (what we should now call) an Art. The present general recognition of the distinction between the two terms, in its application to economic matters, is due, I think, to the combined influence of Senior and J. S. Mill, and cannot be traced further back. McCulloch, for instance, altogether ignores it.

of fact; but modes of organized governmental interference with a view to "enriching the people and the sovereign." But each of these systems was of course based upon certain quasi-scientific principles, a certain view of economic facts; for instance, the "mercantile" system of restraints on importation, encouragements of exportation, &c., rested on the supposition that the balance of gold and silver procured by any branch of national industry and commerce was a trustworthy criterion of its advantage to the country. Hence in his discussion of the mercantile system Adam Smith naturally expounds and refutes this quasi-scientific doctrine (and the confusions and errors on which it was founded) along with the practical deductions drawn from it; though he is chiefly occupied in describing these latter and tracing their consequences. So far there is no particular disadvantage in the ambiguity of the term 'system'; as it might legitimately denote either a body of scientific doctrines or a set of practical precepts, there is no serious confusion caused by using it for a combination of the two.

But when Adam Smith passes in Ch. IX. to treat of the "Agricultural Systems," the ambiguous term becomes a manifestly awkward instrument for the conveyance of his meaning, and is certainly liable to cause a confusion in the reader's mind. For we naturally expect to find in an agricultural 'system' the same kind of organized governmental interference in the interest of agricultural producers that we found in the mercantile system in the interest of manufacturers and merchants; and in fact Adam Smith's own language expressly suggests this antithesis. He introduces his account of the views of Quesnay and the other French Physiocrats, which occupies two-thirds of this chapter, by a reference to Colbert's protective policy; remarking that "as in the plan of "Mr Colbert the industry of the towns was certainly overvalued "in comparison with that of the country, so in their system it "seems to be as certainly undervalued." He passes on from his discussion of the Physiocrats to speak of the policy of China, Indostan and ancient Egypt, which, as he says, "favours "agriculture more than all other employments"; he also refers to the ancient republics of Greece and of Rome, whose policy "honoured agriculture more than manufactures (though it

"seems rather to have discouraged the latter employments than
"to have given any direct or intentional encouragement to the
"former)." And he concludes by arguing that "those agricul-
"tural systems...which preferring agriculture to all other em-
"ployments, in order to promote it, impose restraints upon
"manufactures and foreign trade...really and in the end dis-
"courage their own favourite species of industry...and are
"therefore more inconsistent than the mercantile system";
and that, therefore, "all systems of preference and restraint
"should be completely taken away." Hence the careless reader
might excusably carry away the impression that Quesnay's
doctrine, which was certainly a "system of preference" for
agriculture, was like the "plan of Mr Colbert," a system of legal
regulation and restraint: and even the careful reader, if not
previously informed on the subject, must be startled when he
suddenly learns that in Quesnay's view "perfect liberty" was
"the only effectual expedient" for encouraging agriculture;
and that the only positive governmental interference proposed
by the Physiocrats, as a deduction from their speculative
preference for agriculturists, was the raising of all revenue by
an "impôt unique" on rent.

The truth is that Adam Smith has really not seen the
extent to which, in the hands of the Physiocrats as well as
his own, the method of Political Economy has changed its
fundamental character and become the method of a science
rather than an art: since the change is due not to any
difference in the question primarily asked by the economic
inquirer, but to the entirely different answer now given to it.
The question is still the same, "How to make the nation as rich
"as possible": but as the answer now is "By letting each
"member of it make himself as rich as he can in his own way,"
that portion of the old art of Political Economy which professed
to teach a statesman how to "provide a plentiful revenue or
"subsistence for the people" becomes almost evanescent: since
the only service of this kind which the sovereign can render—
besides protecting his subjects from the violence of foreigners
and from mutual oppression and injustice—is to "erect and
"maintain certain public works and certain public institutions,
"which it can never be for the interest of any individual, or any

"small number of individuals, to erect and maintain." What remains for Political Economy to teach the statesman is merely how to provide himself with a "revenue sufficient for the public "services" in the best possible way: and accordingly such teaching, since Adam Smith's time, has constituted the sole or chief part of Political Economy considered as an art. As regards the "plentiful revenue or subsistence of the people," Adam Smith, instead of showing the statesman how to provide it, has to show him how Nature herself would make ample provision if only the statesman would abstain from interfering with her processes: instead of recommending laws (in the jurist's sense) by which the national production and distribution of wealth *ought to be* governed, he has to trace the laws (in the naturalist's sense) by which these processes actually *are* governed. In short, the substance of his economic doctrine naturally leads him to expound it in the form of the science to which later writers have applied the name of Political Economy; before entering (in Book V.) on the discussion of the principles of the Art of Political Economy, of which the legitimate sphere is, in his view, reduced to the principles of governmental expenditure and taxation.

§ 3. But however great the change that was thus made, through the teaching of the Physiocrats and Adam Smith combined, in the current conception of Political Economy; it is important to observe that the transition thus effected from Art to Science was, in the nature of the case, incomplete. Political Economy became primarily a study of 'what is' rather than of 'what ought to be done': but this was because the two notions were, at least to a considerable extent, identified in the political economist's contemplation of the existing processes of the production and distribution of wealth. He described and analysed these processes, not only to show what they were, but also to show that they were not likely to be improved by human restraints and regulations. This is true not only of Adam Smith, but of almost all his disciples and successors for more than half a century. It should be noted, however, that they have maintained this identity of the actual with the ideal in very different degrees and on very different grounds; and that a considerable amount of mutual misunderstanding and mistaken inference has resulted from not observing these differences. Such misunderstanding has been a good deal aided by the ambiguity of the term 'natural,' applied by Adam Smith, Ricardo, and others, to the shares of different producers as determined by the economic laws which these writers expound. For by the term 'natural' as commonly used, the notion of 'what generally is,' or 'what would be apart from human interference,' is suggested in vague combination with that of 'what ought to be' or what is intended by a benevolent Providence': and it is not always easy to say in what proportions the two meanings are mixed by any particular writer. Indeed it is somewhat difficult to determine this even in the case of Adam Smith himself. There is no doubt that—as Mr Cliffe Leslie[1] has pointed out—Adam Smith's advocacy of the "obvious and simple sys-"tem of natural liberty" is connected with his strongly marked theistic and optimistic view of the order of the physical and social world. He is convinced that "all the inhabitants of the "universe are under the immediate care and protection of that "great, benevolent, and all-wise Being, who directs all the "movements of nature, and who is determined, by his own "unalterable perfections, to maintain in it, at all times, the "greatest possible quantity of happiness[2]": and this conviction gives him a peculiar satisfaction in tracing the various ways in which the public interest is "naturally" promoted by the spontaneous cooperation of individuals seeking each the greatest pecuniary gain to himself. At the same time he is too cool an observer of social facts to carry this optimism to an extravagant pitch. He takes care to point out, for instance, that the "inte-"rest of the employers of stock" has "not the same connexion "with the general interest of society" as that of landlords and labourers: and even that "the interest of the dealers in any "particular branch of trade or manufactures is always in some "respect different from and even opposite to that of the "public[3]." So again when he speaks of "hands *naturally* "multiplying beyond their employment" in the stationary state

---

[1] In an essay on the Political Economy of Adam Smith, recently reprinted in *Essays in Political and Moral Philosophy*.
[2] *Theory of Moral Sentiments*, Pt. VI. § II. ch. iii.
[3] *Wealth of Nations*, Bk. I. ch. xi.

of a country's wealth, and describes the "starving condition of "the labouring poor as a *natural* symptom of the declining "state," we can hardly suppose that the term "natural" is intended directly to imply the design of a benevolent Providence. The Natural is here what actually exists or what tends to exist according to general laws, apart from casual disturbances and deliberate human interference. In consideration of these and similar passages we should, I think, refrain from attributing to Adam Smith a speculative belief in the excellence of the existing arrangements for producing and distributing wealth, to any further extent than is required to support his practical conclusion that they were not likely to be bettered by the interference of government. Still less should we attribute to him any intention of demonstrating that these arrangements realise distributive justice, in the sense that each man's remuneration is an exact measure of the service that he renders to society. On the contrary, he expressly affirms the opposite of this in the case of the landlord, whose rent "costs him neither "labour nor care" and is "not at all proportional to what the "landlord may have laid out upon the improvement of the land, "or to what he can afford to take; but to what the farmer can "afford to give." If at the same time, as a Moralist and Natural Theologian, he holds that there is nothing unjust in the established order of distribution, and that each individual is duly provided for by a beneficent Providence; it is not because he considers that each enjoys wealth in proportion to his deserts, but rather because he sincerely believes in the delusiveness—so far as the individual is concerned—of the common struggle to get rich, and holds that happiness is equally distributed among the different ranks of society in spite of their vast inequalities in wealth[1].

There is therefore a great interval between the position of Adam Smith and that, for instance, of Bastiat. In Bastiat's conception of the fundamental problem of Political Economy the questions of Science and Art are completely fused; his aim being, as his biographer says, "to prove that that which is"—or rather *would* be, if Government would only keep its hands off—

[1] Cf. *Theory of Moral Sentiments*, Pt. IV. ch. i.

"is conformable to that which ought to be": and that every one tends to get exactly his deserts in the economic order of unmodified competition. None of the English followers of Adam Smith has ever gone so far in this direction as Bastiat; and the most eminent of them, Ricardo, represents, we may say, the opposite pole in the development of Adam Smith's doctrine. When Ricardo, using Adam Smith's term to denote a somewhat different fact, speaks of the "natural" price of labour, his phrase carries with it no optimistic or theistic suggestions whatsoever; he means simply the price which certain supposed permanent causes are continually tending to produce. Indeed he explains that "in an improving society" the market-price of labour may remain an indefinite time above the "natural" price; and he contemplates with anything but satisfaction the result of the "natural advance of society," which in his view tends to the benefit of landlords alone. He remains true, no doubt, to Adam Smith's "system of natural liberty" as regards the distribution of produce no less than the direction of industry; but he is further even than Adam Smith from any attempt to demonstrate a necessary harmony of interests among the producers whom he would leave to settle their shares by free contract. In fact, two of his most characteristic doctrines are diametrically opposed to any such harmony: his demonstrations, namely, that marked improvements in agriculture have a tendency to diminish rent, and that the substitution of machinery for human labour is often very injurious to the interests of the class of labourers. And though he is averse to any direct legislative interference with the natural determination of wages, he is disposed to encourage "some effort on the part of the legislature" to secure the comforts and well-being of the poor by regulating the increase of their numbers. This last suggestion indicates a main source of the difference between Ricardo's teaching and that of his great predecessor. It is the Malthusian view of Population which has rendered the optimism of the eighteenth century impossible to English economists of the nineteenth. If the tendency of Nature left alone was to produce, as the ultimate outcome of social progress, a multitude of labourers on the verge of starvation, it was difficult to contemplate her processes with anything like enthusiasm. A less "jaundiced" mind than that of the hero of *Locksley Hall* might well feel depressed at the prospect,

"Slowly comes a hungry people, as a lion creeping nigher
"Glares at one that nods and winks beside a slowly dying fire."

Hence, though English economists have, speaking broadly, adhered to Adam Smith's limitations of the sphere of government, the more thoughtful among them have enforced these limitations sadly rather than triumphantly; not as admirers of the social order at present resulting from "natural liberty," but as convinced that it was at least preferable to any artificial order that government might be able to substitute for it.

Still it remains true that English Political Economy, in whatever tone it has been expounded, has generally included an advocacy of *Laisser Faire;* and that not only in treating of the attempts to regulate Production, with which Adam Smith was practically most concerned, but also in dealing with the questions of Distribution, which the movement of nineteenth century thought has brought into continually greater prominence. Our economists have not commonly confined themselves to tracing the laws that determine the remuneration of services, so far as it depends on free contract among persons aiming each at obtaining the greatest pecuniary gain for a given amount of effort, abstinence, or other sacrifice; but they have also, for the most part, opposed all attempts to introduce, either by law or public opinion, any different division of wealth. If they have not gone the length of maintaining that distribution by free competition is perfectly *just*, as proportioning reward to service; they have still generally maintained it to be practically the best mode of dividing the produce of the organized labour of human beings; they have held that through the stimulus it gives to exertion, the self-reliance and forethought that it fosters, the free play of intellect that it allows, it must produce more happiness on the whole than any other system, in spite of the waste of the material means of happiness caused by the luxurious expenditure of the rich. Or if they have not even gone so far as this, they have at any rate taught that it is inevitable, and that any attempt to deviate from it will be merely throwing effort away. Thus, by one road or another, they have been led to the same practical conclusion in favour of non-interference;

and it is hardly surprising that practical persons have connected this conclusion with the economic doctrines with which it was found in company, and have regarded it as an established "law of political economy" that all contracts should be free and that every one should be paid exactly the market-price of his services.

It must be obvious, however, as soon as it is pointed out, that the investigation of the laws that determine actual prices, wages and profits, so far as these depend on the free competition of individuals, is essentially distinct from the inquiry how far it is desirable that the action of free competition should be restrained or modified—whether by the steadying force of custom, the remedial intervention of philanthropy, the legislative or administrative control of government, or the voluntary combinations of masters or workmen. So far as the purely scientific economist studies primarily the results that tend to be produced by perfectly free competition, it is not because he has any predilection for this order of things—for science knows nothing of such preferences—but merely because its greater simplicity renders it easier to grasp. He holds that a knowledge of these simpler relations precedes, in the order of study, the investigation of the more complex economic problems that result from competition modified by disturbing causes[1]. But the adoption of perfectly free competition as a *scientific* ideal—a means of simplifying the economic facts which actual society presents, for the convenience of general reasoning—does not imply its adoption as a *practical* ideal, which the statesman or philanthropist ought to aim at realising as completely as possible. We may perhaps be led to hold with Bastiat that unrestricted competition would give every man his deserts and otherwise bring about the best of all possible economic worlds: but in order to reach this conclusion

---

[1] The statement in the text represents, I think, the general view of economists, which I am here trying to give; but it does not exactly represent my own view as regards one of these disturbing causes, viz. voluntary Combination. For Combination among the sellers of any commodity places the persons combining in a position economically similar to that of a monopolist; and though the laws that govern prices under the condition of monopoly are different from those that result from free competition, I do not perceive that they are necessarily more complex. Cf. *post*, Bk. II. ch. ii. and ch. x.

we must adopt some principle for determining what a man's deserts are, some criterion of social wellbeing which carries us beyond the merely scientific determination of wages, profits and prices. In short, as regards the whole department of distribution and exchange, the Art of Political Economy—if we admit the notion of Art at all—is easily and completely distinguishable from the scientific study of economic facts and laws.

§ 4. The case is different with Production: and it is to be observed that in the original treatment of Political Economy as a directly practical inquiry it was the improvement of Production rather than Distribution that was taken as its practical end. Thus Adam Smith's opening paragraphs represent as his main object the investigation of the conditions which determine a nation's annual supply of the necessaries and conveniences of life to be abundant or scanty. His first book begins with a discussion of "the causes of the improvement in the productive powers of "labour"; in his second book he is occupied in considering the fundamental importance of "stock" to production, and "the different quantities of labour which it puts in motion, "according to the different ways in which it is employed." In the third he describes the diverse plans that nations have followed in the general direction of labour, with the aim of making its produce as great as possible; and, as we have seen, the "systems of political economy" discussed in his fourth book were systems framed with a view to the same end. On the other hand he hardly considers Distribution as a practical problem; and so far as he does raise the question, how a more "liberal "reward of labour" may be attained, his answer seems to be that it can only be attained by "increasing the national "wealth," or in other words by solving the practical problem of Production. So again, in the brief but pregnant treatise on the Elements of Political Economy written a generation later by James Mill, it is noticeable that in describing the scope of his chapter on Production he puts prominently forward its directly practical aim: its object is, he says, to "ascertain by what "means the objects of desire may be produced with the greatest "ease and in greatest abundance, and upon these discoveries, "when made, to form a system of rules skilfully adapted to the "end." Whereas, when he comes to speak of the laws of Distribution, it never occurs to him even to hint that the process investigated admits of being improved, and that the student ought to keep this improvement in view. And in the account of the objects of Political Economy given ten years later by McCulloch, this difference in the treatment of the different enquiries is equally marked.

Nor is it difficult to understand how this difference comes to be maintained. In dealing with questions of Production, the obvious and uncontroverted aim of all rational effort—public or private—is, other things being equal, to produce as much as possible in proportion to the cost. The extent to which this aim is realised is the most interesting point to observe in examining the actual process of production in different ages and countries; and this is also the criterion which we adopt naturally and without reflection, when we judge different methods of production to be better or worse. Hence the transition from the point of view of Science to that of Art is, in this part of the subject, easy and almost imperceptible; the conclusions of the former are almost immediately convertible into the precepts of the latter. Accordingly we find that even the most careful of the writers who, like J. S. Mill, have taken special pains to present Political Economy as primarily a science, give a prominent place in this part of their work to the discussion of the good and bad results of different modes of production. They analyse the gain derived from the Division of Labour, and note the counterbalancing drawbacks; they compare the advantages and disadvantages of the "grande" and "petite culture." in farming; they consider what kinds of business are adapted to management by joint-stock companies—all topics which clearly belong to the discussion of Production regarded as an Art. I am myself disposed to think that these practical questions should not be discussed at any length in a general exposition of Economic Science; but I have not attempted to draw any sharp line: I regard it as the chief business of a Scientific Theory of Production to investigate the causes by which the labour of any society is rendered more or less productive of wealth: and such an investigation necessarily goes far to supply an answer to the question "how the produce "of labour may be made as great as possible."

§ 5. At the same time, though in discussing the conditions more or less favourable to Production we inevitably approach the margin which divides Art from Science, I have thought it expedient to reserve as much as possible for a separate inquiry the discussion of the principles of governmental interference with industry:—whether with a view to a better organized Production or a more satisfactory Distribution of wealth: since I conform so far to the older and more popular view of my subject as to consider the discussion of these principles an integral part of the theory of Political Economy. This discussion, then, will occupy the main part of a separate and final book on "Political "Economy considered as an Art[1]." The Science of Political Economy, as it is ordinarily conceived in England, forms the subject of the first two books, on (1) Production and (2) Distribution and Exchange, respectively. The precise manner in which I distinguish and connect these three topics, and the grounds on which I have combined the theory of Exchange with that of Distribution, will be better explained somewhat later.

Besides the subjects above mentioned, economists since Say have often introduced, as a separate department, a discussion of the laws of Consumption; and the indispensability of such a discussion has been strongly urged by Jevons; who goes the length of saying that "the whole theory of Economy depends "upon a correct theory of Consumption." I quite agree with Jevons as to the fundamental importance of certain propositions

---

[1] I have already explained, in the preceding section, why I do not hold with one of my reviewers that "the art of political economy considered as a study of "what ought to be is contained in the science." It is of course true that the examination of the effects of any kind of governmental interference, either on Production or on Distribution and Exchange, may be treated as a problem of Economic Science: but in the case of Distribution and Exchange, as I have before said, it is clearly not enough for practical purposes to determine what kind of effects on incomes and prices will be produced by any measure: we have further to consider whether these effects are desirable or the reverse. On this latter point very different views are explicitly or implicitly maintained by thinkers, statesmen, reformers, philanthropists of different schools: a careful, thorough and impartial examination of these different views appeared to me, when I wrote my book, to be a great *desideratum:* and it is this desideratum which I have mainly endeavoured to supply in that part of my third book which deals with Distribution.

relating to Consumption; and I also think that their importance has not been adequately apprehended by many recent writers. Still, it has appeared to me most convenient, in such a treatise as the present, to introduce these propositions in discussing the questions relating to Production, Distribution and Exchange which they help to elucidate: I have therefore not thought it necessary to bring them together under a separate head.

Before concluding I may observe that the current use of the adjective "economic" affords a good illustration of what has been said above of the essential difference between Production and Distribution when considered from the point of view of Art or Practice. For when the word "economic" is used either along with such terms as "gain," "loss," "advantage," "drawback," or as a term of approval implying gain or advantage, it always refers to the relation of cost or expenditure to the quantity of some result attained by it. An arrangement "economically" preferable to some other is one that produces either a given result at a less cost or a greater amount of a certain kind of result at no greater cost: there is an "economic gain" when either *cost* is saved or *produce* increased, and an "economic loss" when the reverse of either process occurs. There is no similar use of the term to imply an ideal system of distributing wealth; we should not, for instance, speak of laws relating to property as *economically* advantageous or desirable, meaning that they led to a right division of property. We might no doubt speak of an "economic" distribution of wealth, no less than of labour; but this is really a confirmation of the view just stated; since in so speaking we should be understood to be assuming that the end of the distribution was to *produce* the greatest possible amount of happiness or satisfaction, and affirming that the arrangement spoken of as "economic" was well adapted to this end.

This peculiar use of the adjective "economic" should be carefully noticed; as it is almost indispensable, while at the same time it is a little liable to confuse the reader.

CHAPTER III.

METHOD OF ECONOMIC SCIENCE.

§ 1. THE result arrived at in the last chapter may be summed up thus. The Science—as distinct from the Art—of Political Economy, of which the general principles will be expounded in the first two books of this treatise, deals mainly with the laws or general facts of the Production, Distribution, and Exchange of wealth; and also with the general facts of the Consumption of wealth, so far as these are connected with the former. This definition of the subject coincides broadly with that adopted by most English writers; but there exist considerable differences of opinion as to the method by which the subject should be investigated: differences which—as was before observed—have been brought into special prominence in recent controversies. These controversies have turned mainly on two fundamental questions, which it will be convenient to consider together, since they are closely connected. It is disputed, first, whether the science of Political Economy can be advantageously treated separately from the general Science of Society: and secondly, whether its method is properly deductive and *à priori*, or inductive and historical.

It does not appear to me that any instructive result can be attained by discussing either of these points, unless we carefully distinguish between different inquiries which, as we have seen, have been included under the name of Political Economy; and examine each separately in relation to the questions above raised. If we attend to this distinction I think it will appear that, though the divergences of view above noticed are likely always to exist to a certain extent, the controversy arising from them may at any rate be reduced to a much smaller space than it at present tends to occupy.

Let us begin, then, by considering the two questions of method above mentioned in relation to the Theory of Production. If we ask whether the investigation of the causes, by which the labour of any society is rendered more or less productive of wealth, can be properly separated from other parts of the general science of society, it is, I think, clearly wrong to answer such a question in an absolute way, either negatively or affirmatively. On the one hand, every economist ought to admit with Mill[1] "the universal consensus of social phenomena, whereby "nothing which takes place in any part of the operations of society "is without its share of influence on every other part;" on the other hand, this is no reason why the study of the industrial or wealth-producing organization of society should not be pursued as a "separate though independent branch of sociological "speculation," just as in the natural body we study separately the physiology and pathology of each of the principal organs and tissues, though every one is acted on by the state of all the others.

And it is to be observed that the relations of industry[2] to other factors of social life vary indefinitely in closeness and importance; so that the question how far it is needful to investigate them is one which has to be answered very differently in relation to different economic enquiries. Thus, in considering generally the causes of the improvement in the productive powers of labour, the importance of a healthy condition of social morality must not be overlooked; but it is not therefore the economist's duty to study in detail the doctrine or discipline of the different Christian churches: if, however, we are studying historically the causes that have affected the interest of capital, the views of Christian theologians with regard to usury will require careful attention. So, again, the conditions and development of the Fine Arts will not generally demand more than a very brief and summary treatment from the economist: if,

---

[1] *Logic*, Bk. VI. ch. ix. § 3.
[2] I use the term "industry" in a wide sense, to include all kinds of trade, as well as agriculture, mining, and manufactures.

however, we are investigating the share taken by a particular community in the international organization of industry, the special artistic faculties and sensibilities of its members may become a consideration of much importance. Similarly the influence exercised on industry by government has often been an economic factor of the first magnitude: still it is obvious that, in modern European communities, at the existing stage of social development, changes in the industrial organization of the civilised part of mankind are largely independent of changes in their political organization. For instance, in the present century, we have seen France pass from Absolute Monarchy to Limited Monarchy, from Limited Monarchy to Republic, from Republic to Empire, and from Empire to Republic again; and yet none of these changes—except the third during a transient crisis—have appreciably affected its industrial system; whereas this latter has been materially modified during the same period by causes unconnected with politics, such as the invention of railways and of electric telegraphs. At the same time I should quite admit that most English economists a generation ago hardly foresaw the extent to which political conditions would continue to affect industry up to the present date: and, similarly, the relations between the development of industry and other factors of social life, such as the progress and diffusion of knowledge, and the changes in national character or in the habits and sentiments of special classes, have hardly met with due consideration. Still the modifications which appear to me necessary on this score are of a subordinate kind; they do not amount to a fundamental difference of treatment.

If now we ask whether the method of such an investigation as we have been considering should be 'inductive' and 'historical' or 'deductive' and 'à priori,' it again seems to me clear that there is not really room for much controversy. At any rate, I know of no economist who has attempted to ascertain the "causes of "the improvement in the productive powers of labour" by a method purely—or even mainly—*à priori* and unhistorical. A certain amount of deductive reasoning, no doubt, has commonly been introduced into this investigation; but this seems inevitable. In particular, we require for the comprehension of economic facts some interpretation of the motives of human agents; and this has necessarily to be supplied, to a large extent, from our general knowledge[1] of human nature—modified, of course, by any special knowledge that we may be able to gain as to the peculiar mental characteristics of the class of persons whom we are considering. But in the general analysis of the conditions favourable to effective production, which Mill and other writers who have followed him have given in the first part of their exposition, the deductive element has always been quite subordinate; and so far as the method adopted is different from what would ordinarily be called 'inductive,' it is not because it is in any sense an *à priori* method; but because it chiefly consists in getting a clearer and more systematic view, through reflective analysis, of general facts which common experience has already made familiar.

Thus, when Mill in his first six chapters states the requisites of production, labour, capital and natural agents; when he defines the notion of labour, considers its relation to the natural agents on which it operates, and classifies the different kinds of labour and the different species of utility produced by it; when he makes clear the notion of capital, as wealth diverted from the purpose of directly satisfying its owner's needs, and employed, whether in the form of instruments or labourers' necessaries, in producing other wealth: when he points out how capital is continually consumed and reproduced, but with various degrees of rapidity, according as it is fixed or circulating;—it is obvious that all these results, however interesting, are obtained by merely analysing and systematizing our common empirical knowledge of the facts of industry. So, again, when he goes on to consider the conditions on which the degree of productiveness of different productive agents depends; his method is again merely that of comparing and generalising from observed facts. Thus he studies quite *à posteriori* the differences in the natural advantages of different countries; the differences among human

---

[1] How far this general knowledge is itself acquired by induction of some sort is not, of course, the question. As Mill explains, in the passage referred to in the next note, the economic "method *à priori*" is not a "mode of philosophizing "which does not profess to be founded on experience at all"; but is merely distinguished from the "method *à posteriori*" by not requiring, as the basis of its conclusions, *specific* experience of economic facts.

beings in habits of energetic work, in capacity of exertion for distant objects, in keenness of desire for wealth, and in other intellectual and moral qualities; and the differences in the security afforded "by government, and against government" at different times and places. So further, in the discussion of the advantages of division of labour, and in the comparison of production on a small scale with production on a large scale, his argument though partly deductive still relies greatly on specific experience. Then again, when he states the law of the increase of labour, the causes that actually counteract the capacity of increasing population inherent in human beings, and the extent of their operation, are investigated inductively (Ch. X.); and so are the actual variations in the "effective "desire of accumulation," which causes the increase of capital (Ch. XI.). In both these cases we could, no doubt, without conscious induction, lay down certain incontrovertible abstract propositions; but in the former case we should hardly get beyond the truths of elementary arithmetic, and in the latter case we should hardly get beyond such trivial maxims as that "wealth "is increased by industry and thrift," &c.

I have gone into these details, not because I wish to lay stress on Mill's authority, but because none of the "orthodox" critics of his widely-read book has ever attacked his general method of treating the Theory of Production. What therefore we have to remark is not merely that Mill's treatment of this part of his subject is mainly inductive and analytical; but that it never seems to have occurred to any "à priori" economist that it ought to have been different.

§ 2. Why then, it may be pertinently asked, does Mill say— as he certainly does say[1]—that Political Economy is essentially an abstract science, that its method is essentially "the method *à* "*priori*," and that it "has been so understood and taught by all "its most distinguished teachers"? The only answer I can give is that in this and similar passages Mill is thinking, not of the Theory of Production as he himself conceives and expounds it,

---

[1] See in particular the Essay "On the Definition and Method of Political "Economy," in his *Essays on some unsettled Questions in Political Economy*. The doctrine here laid down is also maintained in his *Logic*, B. VI. c. IX. § 3; where a long quotation from this essay is introduced.

but of the Theory of Distribution and Exchange: and primarily of that portion of this latter subject which he distinguishes as "statical" and not "dynamical[1]"—i.e. that which treats of the determination of the reward of services and the value of products in the existing condition of industry. This is the part of the subject to which, since Ricardo, the attention of economic theorists has been chiefly directed (though they have often not distinguished it clearly from other parts): and it is easy to show how a method largely different from that adopted in treating the question of Production naturally suggests itself here. The broad and striking fact which originally led and still leads reflective minds to discuss the question "how a nation is made wealthy" is the vast difference between the amounts of wealth possessed by different nations and by the same nation at different periods of its history; especially the great increase in the most recent times, in consequence of what we speak of vaguely as "advance of civilisation," "progress of arts and sciences," "development of trade and commerce," &c. Hence in our method of dealing with this question induction from historical facts is naturally prominent; though a certain amount of deduction inevitably comes in when we analyse the combined play of the forces of economic change whose effects history presents to us. And we may, of course, examine the phenomena of Distribution from the same point of view of Comparative Plutology; we may ask why the share of wealth annually obtained by an English miner is larger than that obtained by a German miner, or why English landowners now obtain higher rents than they did 100 years ago: and if in our answers we "include directly or remotely, the operation of all the causes" that have combined in causing the differences investigated, it seems evident that our method of investigation must be—just as in the case of Production—a primarily inductive and historical one. We shall have to note and explain differences and changes in national character generally, in the habitual energy, enterprise, and thrift of special classes, in law and administration and other political circumstances, in the state of knowledge,

[1] I ought perhaps to say that I do not regard as satisfactory either the line that Mill draws by means of this pair of terms, or his manner of treating the questions that he distinguishes as "dynamical."

the state of general and special education, and other social facts; and in this explanation the "method à priori" can evidently occupy but a very subordinate place.

But such questions are not, I think, those which most obviously suggest themselves in connexion with the phenomena of distribution. Here the broad and striking fact, that at once troubles the sympathy and stirs the curiosity of reflective persons, is the great difference between the shares of different members of the same society at the same time. Thus what economists have been primarily concerned to explain is how the complicated division of the produce of industry among the different classes of persons who have co-operated to produce it is actually determined here and now; and what is likely to be the effect of any particular change that may occur in the determining conditions, while the general state of things remains substantially the same. Similarly as regards the phenomena of exchange, the most natural and obvious question is why each of the vast number of articles that make up what in the aggregate we call wealth is exchanged and estimated at its present price; and how far any particular event, other things remaining the same, would tend to raise or lower its price.

It is in answering these questions that the general theory of Political Economy, as commonly treated, uses mainly an abstract, deductive, and hypothetical method. That is, it considers the general laws governing the determination of remunerations and prices, in a state of things taken as the type to which modern civilised society generally approximates, in which freedom of exchange and freedom in choice of calling and domicile are supposed to be—broadly speaking—complete within a certain range, and in which the natures and relations of the human beings composing the industrial organization are supposed to be simpler and more uniform than is actually the case in any known community. By means of this simplification we obtain exact answers to our general economic questions through reasonings that sometimes reach a considerable degree of complexity. It is obvious that answers so obtained do not by themselves enable us accurately to interpret or predict concrete economic phenomena; but I hold that when modified by a rough conjectural allowance for the difference between our hypothetical premises and the actual facts in any case, they do materially assist us in attaining approximate correctness in our interpretations and predictions.

It is, however, evident that the applicability and utility of such hypothetical reasonings will depend largely on two conditions: first on the degree of success attained in forming our original suppositions, so that they may correspond as closely as possible to the facts, without becoming unmanageably complex; and secondly on the extent to which we recognise and attend to the divergence from facts which is—in most cases—inevitable in such abstract reasonings, and the insight and skill which we show in conjecturing roughly the effect of modifying causes whose operation we cannot precisely trace. To secure success in either of these respects we require an accurate knowledge of the general characteristics of the matter with which we are dealing; and I do not see how we are to obtain this knowledge without an inductive study of economic facts. It is not perhaps necessary that the deductive and inductive investigation of any class of economic phenomena should be always carried on simultaneously, or even by the same persons; but the latter is certainly an indispensable supplement to the former.

§ 3. To illustrate the necessary place of Induction even in connexion with the ordinary reasonings of the deductive Political Economy, it may be convenient to examine briefly the fundamental assumptions of the latter. The first and most fundamental is, that all persons engaged in industry will, in selling or lending goods or contracting to render services, endeavour *ceteris paribus* to get as much wealth as they can in return for the commodity they offer. This is often more briefly expressed by saying that Political Economy assumes the universality and unlimitedness of the desire for wealth. Against this assumption it has been urged that men do not, for the most part, desire wealth in general, but this or that particular kind of wealth: in fact, that "the desire of wealth is an abstraction, "confounding a great variety of different and heterogeneous "motives which have been mistaken for a single homogeneous "force[1]." It does not, however, appear that there is necessarily

---

[1] Cliffe Leslie, *Essays in Political and Moral Philosophy*, p. 238.

any such mistake as Mr Cliffe Leslie here supposes. For so far as the objects of these different and heterogeneous desires are all exchangeable and commensurable in value, they all admit of being regarded as definite quantities of one thing—wealth; and it is just because the "desire of wealth" may, for this reason, be used to include "all the needs, appetites, passions, tastes, "aims, and ideas which the various things comprehended under "the word wealth satisfy," that we are able to assume, to the extent required in deductive political economy, its practical universality and unlimitedness. There is no particular species of wealth of which it would be approximately true to say that every one desires as much of it as he can get. But there is no class of persons engaged in industry of whom it cannot be said with approximate truth that they would always like more of some kind of wealth if they could get it without the least sacrifice. Even the richest capitalists and landowners, who are merely connected with industry as lenders of wealth, are found to have a desire of wealth sufficiently strong to prevent them from letting indifferent persons have the use of their property at less than the market rate.

At the same time it is equally true that there are other things obtainable by labour, besides wealth, which mankind generally, if not universally, desire; such as power, and reputation: and it is further undeniable that men are largely induced to render services of various kinds by family affection, friendship, compassion, national and local patriotism and other kinds of *esprit de corps*, and by other motives. The amount of unpaid work that is done from such motives, in modern civilised society, forms a substantial part of the whole: and political economists are perhaps fairly chargeable with an omission in making no express reference to such work—with the exception of the mutual services rendered by husbands and wives, and by parents and children. It is however to be said that services altogether unremunerated by money occupy no important place in the organization of industry; they belong chiefly to the exercise of governmental or literary functions, or the management of property (trust-funds), or to some part of that complex system of eleemosynary labour and expenditure, which actually supplements the deficiencies of the industrial distribution. And so far as paid services are concerned, all economists, from Adam Smith downwards, have recognised the operation of other motives—as for instance the love of reputation—as a cause of the difference of remuneration in different employments. All therefore that they have explicitly assumed is that, *other things being equal*, a man will prefer a larger price or remuneration to a smaller. This qualification includes, of course, disagreeable things that have to be borne, as well as desirable things that may be acquired; indeed Adam Smith draws express attention to the differences in the agreeableness and disagreeableness of different employments as a cause of diversity in wages.

Among the disagreeable things that have to be borne Labour itself generally occupies a prominent place, in the view of the deductive economists. Mill, for instance, speaks of "aversion to "labour" as a "perpetually antagonizing principle" to the desire of wealth: and it has been customary to attribute to it an equal degree of universality; it being affirmed not merely that "every "one desires to obtain as much wealth as possible," but that he also desires to obtain it by "the least possible amount of "labour." This proposition, however, is open to the obvious objection that many persons get more happiness out of their work than they do out of a good deal of their expenditure. And in fact it does not appear to me necessary, in ordinary economic reasonings on problems of distribution, to assume that mankind are "averse to labour" generally. The assumption usually required is merely that every man will require payment for his work if he can get it; but this immediately follows from the desire of wealth, if he has no special inducement for performing gratuitously the particular work in question; since the fact that a man likes his work is not a reason why he should consent to do it for nothing, if he can get something that he desires by his labour[1].

---

[1] It may perhaps be urged that an aversion to labour must at any rate be supposed to operate at the point at which the labourer leaves off; since otherwise he would not leave off, provided he could obtain any object of desire by continuing to work. And, no doubt, it would be usually safe to infer that at the close of any worker's daily task of paid labour he likes such labour decidedly less than some other unremunerated employment of his time. Still the argument is not conclusive: for a man may cease to labour merely because it would be bad economy of his powers to continue, since additional work to-day would cause a

At the same time it is no doubt important in justifying, as against communism, the existing individualistic organization of industry, to show that men in general are not likely to work—to the extent required for the satisfaction of the wants of society—without the powerful motive supplied by their desire of wealth for themselves and their families. And certainly we seem able to infer, from observation of the manner in which even the respectable rich employ their time, that no important part of the labour required for the production of wealth is likely to be carried on to an adequate extent, with adequate perseverance throughout the day and from day to day, by such beings as men now are, except under the influence of some motive more powerful than an average man's liking for work. Whether any communistic scheme can be expected to supply such motives adequately is a question which we may afterwards take occasion to discuss. Meanwhile, for ordinary economic reasonings, we may accept the proposition "that every "one desires as much wealth as possible at the least possible "sacrifice," without necessarily adding that he always regards as a sacrifice the labour by which he is able to produce or earn wealth.

From this fundamental assumption we may immediately infer, that so far as freedom of contract exists, similar exchanges will be made on approximately similar terms, at least within the limits of the same market; meaning by a market[1] a body of persons in such commercial relations that each can easily acquaint himself with the rates at which certain kinds of exchanges of goods or services are from time to time made by the others. For it is obvious that, if A prefers a greater gain to a smaller, he will not sell his goods or his services to B at a rate lower than what he thinks he could obtain from C or D; allowance being made for any trouble, expense, or other sacrifice that he would incur in getting the more favourable terms. This inference is often broadly expressed by the statement that "where there is open competition, there cannot be two prices

---

more than proportionate decrease in efficiency for work hereafter. I suppose that this explanation would be frequently true, as regards the higher kinds of intellectual work.

[1] Cf. Jevons, *Theory of Political Economy*, c. iv. "Definition of a market."

"in one market for the same commodity." Such a statement, as ordinarily understood, implies that the market-price is determined by the unconcerted action of individual exchangers. We have, however, no ground for assuming *à priori* that the uncontrolled action of enlightened persons seeking each his own greatest pecuniary gain may not under certain circumstances result in a deliberate combination of sellers or buyers to dictate terms of exchange. And I shall afterwards show that the question what price enlightened self-interest will prompt such a combined body to demand is not outside the range of the deductive method; it is only a special case of the determination of the value of a monopolized article, which may be made the subject of abstract reasoning as suitably as any other determination of value. But it is convenient and customary to use the term 'competition' to imply the absence of such combination; and I shall so use it.

The operation of competition above described, by which the terms of *similar* exchanges are kept approximately similar, should be carefully distinguished from that other action of competition, by which certain inequalities in the remuneration of *dissimilar* services tend to be continually removed, though more slowly and indirectly. In this latter case we have to consider the influence exercised by the desire of wealth, and the knowledge of current rates of remuneration, not on the terms of particular bargains, but on men's choice of—or adhesion to—their respective trades or professions. The existence of this influence may be inferred from the assumptions already made as immediately and cogently as the influence of competition on similar exchanges. That is, we may infer that persons considering what trade or profession to select among those open to them will, other things being equal, select those that they (or their advisers) believe to be best remunerated; and further that persons will leave a badly remunerated trade when they think that they can obtain elsewhere a remuneration sufficiently higher to compensate for the trouble and annoyance —and in most cases extra risk—involved in the change.

To complete our list of the assumptions ordinarily made by English political economists we should have to include other propositions relating to several different social facts, such as

Population, Agriculture and Government. But the principles of competition above given are certainly the chief and cardinal axioms of deductive economics: and perhaps they will serve for our present purpose. As I have stated them, they seem to me incontrovertibly legitimate as corresponding broadly to the facts of modern industrial societies. But I see no adequate ground for assuming these principles *à priori, except* with the qualifications above given; and as so qualified, they do not enable us confidently to explain or predict the economic phenomena of any actual society without additional data, which can only be obtained by induction. We may affirm *à priori* that men will prefer a greater gain to a less, *other things being equal;* but we can draw no positive inferences from this without ascertaining how far other things are equal: and we can only learn by a careful study of facts the force of the other motives, of which all economists admit the existence and importance; especially of the powerful but unobtrusive impulses which lead a man to do what other people do, and what he himself has done before. Similarly we may affirm that in a perfectly organized market, in which the terms of all bargains may be ascertained without more trouble than average exchangers are able and willing to take, the price of similar commodities will be approximately the same, allowance being made for the trouble and expense of conveying the commodity; but we can only learn by a study of facts how far in any given society at any given time the conditions of sale of any particular commodity approximate to those of a perfectly organized market. With what degree of precision the required knowledge can be obtained, what exertions, intellectual or physical, are needed to obtain it, what the probability is of these exertions being made by average sellers or buyers of the commodity in question, are all points that can only be determined empirically. So again, it may be granted that competition tends to equalise the remunerations, so far as they are known, of dissimilar services, involving equal sacrifices and rendered by persons with equal natural qualifications and opportunities. But before we can apply this principle in any concrete case, we have obviously to ascertain how the different persons or classes of persons concerned estimate particular sacrifices, and what their qualifications and opportunities are; that is, to what extent, and by what expenditure of time and means, they are really able to fit themselves for each of the different careers that they are legally free to enter.

§ 4. These limitations to the use of the deductive method in Political Economy appear to me obvious and incontrovertible: and I have endeavoured always to keep them in view throughout the discussion of the laws of Distribution in Book II. I must admit, however, that they have not always been duly recognised by deductive economists; who have in consequence been led to make somewhat too sweeping assumptions as to concrete facts. I think that writers of the opposite school have done good service in criticizing these assertions, and the confident and dogmatic tone in which they have been enunciated. But I cannot accept the conclusion which some of them have proceeded to draw, that the traditional method of English Political Economy is essentially faulty and misleading. I quite admit that the direct utility of the deductive method, as a means of interpreting and explaining concrete facts—though not its validity, so long as it is regarded as merely abstract and hypothetical—depends on its being used with as full knowledge as possible of the results of observation and induction. But its indirect utility, as a means of training the intellect in the *kind* of reasoning required for dealing with concrete economic problems, depends to a far less degree on such empirical knowledge; and I cannot see that this indirect utility is materially affected by any divergences that have been shown to exist between the premises of current deductions and the actual facts of industry. On the other hand, I think that both the validity and the utility of the current deductions have been somewhat impaired by a want of thorough explicitness as to the assumptions on which these reasonings depend, and by a want of clearness in the cardinal notions employed in them. In order to guard against this latter defect, I have been led to perform with rather unusual elaborateness the task of defining the cardinal terms of Political Economy. The precise advantages that I have hoped to gain by this are explained in the second chapter of the following book, in which the task is commenced: I trust that I shall convince the reader that the process, however tedious, is absolutely indispensable to that exact treatment of economic questions, to which alone the epithet 'scientific' ought to be applied.

Here I may notice the discussion that has recently been raised[1] on an issue still wider than that debated between the advocates of the "à priori" economics, and the Inductive or "realistic" school; viz. on the pretensions of Political Economy to be a science at all. I certainly think the language sometimes used by economic writers, suggesting as it does that the doctrines they expound are entitled in respect of scientific perfection to rank with those of Physics, is liable to be seriously misleading. But I am not disposed to infer from this that we ought deliberately to acquiesce in treating Political Economy unscientifically. My inference would rather be, not that we ought not to aim at being as scientific as we can, but that we ought to take care not to deceive ourselves as to the extent to which we have actually attained our aim: that, for instance, so far as we are treating Political Economy positively, we should avoid mistaking a generalisation from limited experience for a universal law; and so far as we are treating it hypothetically, we should take care not to use words in different meanings without being aware of the difference, nor suppose our notions to be quantitatively precise when they are really indefinite. The endeavour to be scientific in this sense will not lead to hasty and mistaken dogmatism; on the contrary, it will, I hope, deliver us from the hasty and mistaken dogmatism, caused by loose and confused thinking, to which 'common sense' or 'natural intelligence' is always liable.

[1] See especially Professor Price's *Practical Political Economy*.

BOOK I.

CHAPTER I.

THE THEORY OF PRODUCTION.

§ 1. THE fundamental question with which we shall be concerned in the present Book may be simply stated thus: Under what conditions, or by the operation of what laws, does a nation become more or less wealthy? The need of a more precise definition of this question, and the proper mode of meeting this need, will be explained as we go on; at the outset this more obvious and popular statement seems sufficient.

In considering this question the first point which presents itself is the difficulty of separating the study of Production from the study of Distribution and Exchange. It is easily seen that the kinds of wealth produced in any society depend largely on the manner in which wealth is distributed among the members of the society. In a community where there is a large middle class, there will probably be an abundance of cheap luxuries; while where there are only a few rich persons among a multitude of poor, we shall expect to find a production mainly of necessaries, with a small amount of costly and elaborate commodities. Similarly, distribution cannot fail to influence the *amounts* of wealth produced; since both the nature and the intensity of the motives, that normally prompt men either to labour or to save, vary considerably according to their position in the scale of wealth and poverty. The precise importance of the influence thus exercised on production is no doubt hard to estimate. Indeed if we were able to estimate it exactly,—if (e.g.) we could tell how far the improvement in industrial instruments and processes would go on as at present, if the inventors and managers of industry had not the present keen spur of private gain—the controversy between Socialists and advocates of *laisser faire* would be much nearer settlement than it is. But however we may answer such questions as this, we are bound to take note of the effects of the existing distribution of wealth, as supplying to the different classes engaged in production the stimulus that actually prompts the energetic and sustained labour and the extensive outlay of wealth for remote results, which we find them undertaking.

None the less does it seem to me desirable that we should practise ourselves in contemplating the process of production from the point of view of society as a whole, abstracting as far as possible from the 'adjustment of the terms of co-opera-'tion[1]' among producers; so that the total gain or loss in wealth resulting from any given change to the aggregate of human beings concerned may be habitually distinguished from those gains and losses of individuals which, regarded from the point of view of society, are mere transfers. Normally, no doubt, what is productive of wealth to an individual tends to increase the wealth of the community of which he is a part : but this is not always the case,—e. g. a man may make money by promoting a joint-stock company that fails—and even when the two effects are combined, they may be combined in indefinitely varying proportions. And to confound the effect of any cause on the wealth of a part with its effect on the whole wealth is one of the commonest forms of error in popular economic discussion ; the operation of a new law, a tax, a war, or other important social event, in increasing or diminishing the wealth of some particular class of persons, being specially striking and impressive, attracts the attention of ordinary observers to the exclusion of all other effects. Further, many of the cardinal notions of Political Economy, such as Capital, Profit, Cost of Production—even the more elementary notion of Wealth—are naturally conceived somewhat differently from the point of view of the individual and from that of society ; and it

---

[1] The phrase is quoted from Hearn's *Plutology*. I take the opportunity of acknowledging the assistance that I have derived from this well-written and instructive work, in composing the present portion of my treatise.

CHAP. I.] THE THEORY OF PRODUCTION. 47

is important to recognise clearly this doubleness of meaning, so as to guard against the confusions that are liable to arise out of it.

Accordingly I propose in the present Book, to keep as consistently as possible to the social view of industry. We shall consider the members of the human family as combining, on certain terms, the determination of which we do not at present investigate, in the work of adapting their material environment to their joint needs and uses; we shall examine the circumstances that have been favourable or adverse to this combined operation, and try to forecast, so far as may be, the prospect of greater or less success in it hereafter. We must take notice of variations in the amounts of the products of industry, falling to the lot respectively of the different classes of persons who have combined, personally or by lending their property, to produce them; indeed we shall have to consider these varying shares from two distinct points of view, both as motives to labour and saving, and as means to the efficient performance of functions: but we shall not yet inquire how the proportional amount of each share comes to be neither more nor less than it is.

§ 2. But though I thus agree with Mill in separating the Theory of Production from that of Distribution and Exchange, I cannot agree with him in separating the discussion of the fundamental notions employed in the former from the discussion of Value. It is clearly impossible to form any precise idea of amounts of wealth, of increase or decrease of wealth, greater or less efficiency of production, before we have settled how wealth is to be measured; and since wealth is currently measured by its value—for when we say that a man's wealth is increased, we do not usually mean that he owns more matter, but that what he owns is more valuable—it seems desirable, in order to attain a scientific method of measuring it, to begin by examining the notion of Value: and then to attempt to determine the notion of Wealth so far as is needful for the purpose of the present enquiry. The examination of these two fundamental conceptions occupies the two following chapters. In the third chapter I proceed to what I may call a 'qualitative analysis' of the conditions of Production; in the course of which the relation of Capital to other factors of industrial progress comes naturally to be indicated. But to make this relation quite clear, it is necessary to take up again the task of definition and affix a precise meaning to the term Capital. Then in a concluding chapter I examine how far we can determine the general laws of operation of the causes on which the increase or decrease of wealth in any society has been found to depend.

CHAPTER II.

THE DEFINITION AND MEASURE OF VALUE.

§ 1. BEFORE attempting to make the common notion of value clear and quantitatively precise, it may be useful to explain my general view of the work of definition, which will occupy so large a space in this part of my treatise. For, in spite of all that has been written, by authors of deserved repute, on the place of Definition in Economic Science, it still seems to me that this introductory part of the study is rarely treated from such a point of view as would enable us to derive the maximum of instruction from it. The economists who have given most attention to the matter seem to me commonly to fall into two opposite errors at the same time. They underrate the importance of *seeking* for the best definition of each cardinal term, and they overrate the importance of *finding* it. The truth is,—as most readers of Plato know, only it is a truth difficult to retain and apply,—that what we gain by discussing a definition is often but slightly represented in the superior fitness of the formula that we ultimately adopt; it consists chiefly in the greater clearness and fulness in which the characteristics of the matter to which the formula refers have been brought before the mind in the process of seeking for it. While we are apparently aiming at definitions of terms, our attention should be really fixed on distinctions and relations of fact. These latter are what we are concerned to know, contemplate, and as far as possible arrange and systematize; and in subjects where we cannot present them to the mind in orderly fulness by the exercise of the organs of sense, there is no way of surveying them so convenient as that of reflecting on our use of common terms. And this reflective contemplation is naturally stimulated by the effort to define; but when the process has been fully performed, when the distinctions and relations of fact have been clearly apprehended, the final question as to the mode in which they should be represented in a definition is really—what the whole discussion appears to superficial readers—a question about words alone. Hence in comparing different definitions our aim should be far less to decide which we ought to adopt, than to apprehend and duly consider the grounds on which each has commended itself to reflective minds. We shall generally find that each writer has noted some relation, some resemblance or difference, which others have overlooked; and we shall gain in completeness, and often in precision, of view by following him in his observations, whether or not we follow him in his conclusions. I may observe that there is a natural tendency to estimate the results of intellectual, as of other, labour in proportion to their cost; hence the more difficulty we have found in drawing a line of definition, the more inclined we are to emphasize its importance when once drawn, and to overlook or underrate the points of resemblance which objects excluded by it have to those included. Whereas the very difficulty of drawing the line is most likely due to the importance of these points of resemblance; and instead of forgetting them when the work of definition has been performed to our satisfaction, we ought to take special pains to keep them before our minds. Often, indeed, we have to admit that—even when a distinction is of fundamental importance—no sharp line of definition can be drawn, owing to the gradual manner in which the cases near the line shade off into each other.

I have said that in the work of definition, the final question—the point which we directly raise and settle—must be merely a question as to the use of words. In saying this I do not at all mean to depreciate its importance, or to justify a careless treatment of it. No doubt if our view of the subject is tolerably complete, and our notions clear and precise, it is of secondary importance what verbal tools we use in reasoning, so long as we use them consistently; but this secondary importance is sufficiently great to claim our most careful consideration. There seem to be two conditions which it is on different grounds desirable that a definition should satisfy as far as possible; but we should bear in mind that we frequently cannot completely satisfy either—still less both together. In the first place, we should keep as closely as we can to the common use of language: otherwise we are not only exposed to the danger of being misunderstood by others, through the force of habitual usage overcoming the impression produced by express definition; but we further run serious risk of being inconsistent with ourselves, on account of the similar effect of habit on our own minds. Secondly, our definitions should be precisely adapted to the doctrine that we have to expound; so that we may avoid as far as possible the continual use of qualifying epithets and phrases. In aiming at the first of these results, we should not forget that common usage may be inconsistent; on the other hand, we should not hastily assume that this is the case. Economists have sometimes missed the useful lessons which common thought has to teach, by deciding prematurely that a word is used in two or more distinct senses, and thus omitting to notice the common link of meaning that connects them. Still, it will of course often happen that we cannot fit a word for scientific use without cutting off some part of its ordinary signification: hence it is very important that we should keep carefully distinct the two very different questions (1) What *do* we commonly mean by the terms, Value, Wealth, Capital, Money, &c.? and (2) What *ought* we to mean by them—what meaning is it, for scientific purposes, convenient to attach to them? I think that a good deal of unnecessary controversy has been due to a want of clear separation between these two very different inquiries, and the different methods of discussion respectively appropriate to them. It seems to be forgotten that the former question is not strictly an economic question at all, but a linguistic one; we may even add that it is a linguistic question which those who are most acquainted with economic facts find themselves least able to solve succinctly and satisfactorily: since in attempting to give to common terms the precision which their own view of the facts requires, they inevitably raise questions which are not raised in ordinary thought, and to which therefore it is illusory to suppose that common usage gives even an implicit answer. Again, in trying to adapt our terms to scientific purposes, we must remember that, dealing as we are with facts whose relations of resemblance and difference are highly complex, we may often require to classify them somewhat differently for the purposes of different inquiries; and that hence a definition which would be most suitable for one investigation will require some modification to render it convenient for another. Economists have frequently found this; and have been content to meet the difficulty by using the same word with slight differences of meaning. This seems to me often the best course to adopt, provided the change is clearly stated and kept before the reader's mind. I find, however, that even careful writers have been too much inclined to slur over the differences of meaning, and keep them in the background, especially when they are not considerable in amount: a procedure which dangerously tends to encourage looseness of thought.

I have spoken once or twice of the importance of making our thought precise. I do not mean that we should necessarily aim at quantitative exactness in all our statements of economic laws. I quite agree with the writers (such as Cairnes) who have warned us against the futility of such an aim. But the more inevitable it is that our conclusions should be merely rough and approximate, the more important it becomes that we should be thoroughly aware when and how far they are wanting in exactness; and in order that we may be aware of this, we should make our *conceptions* as precise as possible, even when we cannot make our *statements* so. Only in this way can we keep before our minds the inadequacy of our knowledge of particulars to supply answers to the questions which our general notions lead us to ask. And if, as is sometimes the case, even our general conceptions cannot be reduced to perfect exactness; it is still desirable that we should know why this is the case, and what obstacles the fact presents to our efforts to think precisely about it. This last precaution seems to me to have been specially neglected by economists. Most of the objects about which they reason are conceived as possessing definite quantity. Yet (e.g.) some of the most eminent of them[1] have

[1] Cf. post, B. II. c. II.

CHAP. II.] *DEFINITION AND MEASURE OF VALUE.* 53

not always seen that it is impossible to think definitely of the quantity of any aggregate of diverse elements, except so far as these elements admit of being reduced to a common quantitative standard; and that unless this is done, when we speak of such an aggregate as having increased or decreased in amount, or of something else as "varying in proportion to" it, we are using words to which there are necessarily no definite thoughts corresponding.

Bearing in mind then these general considerations, let us attempt to deal with the much controverted notion of Value upon the principles above laid down.

§ 2. Economists have usually followed the Physiocrats in attributing to the term value two different meanings, utility and power of purchasing. The distinction thus drawn between "Value in use" and "Value in exchange" is certainly important; but the account usually given of the two notions overlooks the connexion between them; which lies in the comparison of equivalents which the term value in either sense essentially implies. For let us consider what we mean when we speak of a man setting value on, or attaching value to, things to which the idea of exchange is inapplicable—whether this inapplicability be due to circumstances isolating the man, as, for instance, if we think of Robinson Crusoe on his island; or to the fact that no one else would buy the things, as in the case of old letters and other memorials, knowledge of various kinds, &c. We do not, I think, mean exactly that the things are useful to him; though no doubt they *are* in a certain sense useful, that is, they satisfy or prevent some want or desire which is or would be felt in the absence of them[1]. But we mean that the man would, if

[1] This seems to be the accepted meaning of the terms "useful," "utility," &c., in the present discussion. It is not, I think, quite convenient to say with Professor Jevons that 'useful' is that which gives pleasure; and to measure 'utility,' in the Benthamite way, by the balance of pleasurable over painful consequences. For *primâ facie* there are many valued things—alcohol, opium, &c.—which not only have an actual tendency to produce a balance of painful consequences to their consumers, but are even known to have this tendency by the persons who nevertheless value and consume them. And in dealing with the determination of value we are not concerned—except in a very indirect way—with these painful consequences: what we are concerned with, is the intensity of the desire or demand for the articles in question, as measured by the amount of other things, or of labour, that their consumers are prepared to give for them.

necessary, *give something* to gain them or prevent their destruction. This something may be some useful material thing, or it may be labour of some kind; the general notion of value leaves this quite indefinite, provided only the giving of the matter or labour would not occur unless there were something to be got or preserved by it. All that it distinctly involves is the notion of something else, presented as a possible alternative for the thing valued.

If this, then, be the fundamental conception of Value when exchange is out of the question, it does not seem to be essentially altered in the more ordinary case when, in speaking of the value of a thing, we no doubt have in view its Exchange Value. Only in this latter case we mean that *other people* would give something for the article in question: that if offered for sale it would fetch a price in the market. If we only wanted a *qualitative* definition of the common notion of value, we need not press our inquiries beyond this; we need not go on to ask *what* it is that other people would give in exchange. But if we use the notion *quantitatively*, as we commonly do, and as we require to do for the purposes of economic science; if we think of a thing A as having *more* or *less* value than a thing B, we must mean that some purchasers will give for A more or less of a certain kind of thing than any purchaser would give for B. That is, we require a Standard of Value. And further, if we make our quantitative comparison precise, and think of one thing as being (e.g.) *twice* as valuable as another, we necessarily imply what economists call a "perfect "market," in which there cannot be two prices for the same thing at the same time. So long as this market is thought of at a particular place and time, the conception of a standard of value presents no difficulty. Obviously, any thing we choose will serve for a standard; for if cloth (e.g.) will sell in a perfect market for more of any one thing than linen will, it will sell for more of any other thing.

But a perplexity arises when we compare the values of the same thing at different times, and speak of things increasing or decreasing in value. For here we can no longer take anything we like as a standard of value; since we do not think a thing more valuable because it will sell for more of something that has grown cheaper. When therefore we say that a thing has risen in value, what do we exactly mean? To this question one of two answers is commonly given; either (1) that the thing would sell for more of things in general, or (2) that it would sell for more of something which itself had not varied in value. Neither of these answers is altogether satisfactory. The first is at once abstract and vague; we cannot actually exchange an article for 'things in general;' and it is not easy to see how we can state its value in terms of such an aggregate, if the elements composing the aggregate have in the mean time varied in value relatively to each other, as may easily be the case. The second answer appears to avoid this difficulty; but this appearance is soon dispelled. For reflection shows us that the notion of '*not* varying in value' must be exactly as hard to define as the opposite notion of 'varying in value.' The second answer, therefore, still leaves us asking 'What 'does variation in value mean and how is it to be measured?'

There is, however, a mode of meeting this difficulty, which is given in perhaps the clearest form by Cairnes[1]. He has no doubt that when in discussing an advance in the price of butcher's meat, we ask whether meat has risen or money fallen in value, "obviously there is a tacit reference to the "causes on which value depends: and the question really raised "is not strictly as to the change in the exchange value of meat "and money, but as to the cause or causes which have produced "the change. If we believe that the change is traceable to a "cause primarily affecting meat, we say that meat has risen in "value," &c. I cannot agree that this interpretation of the ordinary notion of change in value is "obviously" correct; as I think that many persons would speak of a thing as having fallen in value, when they found that it had fallen relatively to all other things, even though they might know the change to be due to causes affecting primarily these other things[2]. And

---

[1] *Some Leading Principles*, Part I. c. I. § 1. Cf. also Mill, *Pol. Econ.* B. III. c. I. § 3.

[2] The current discussion of the appreciation of gold shews that there is a disagreement on this point as to the meaning of words: for some disputants, admitting that the general purchasing power of gold has increased, affirm that gold has not 'really risen in value' because this change is due to the improve-

I think that most persons would find it difficult to distinguish clearly the causes of change in value that 'primarily affect' a particular article from those that primarily affect other things. Take the common case of a rise in price due to an intensification in the demand for an article. This intensified demand may itself be merely caused by an increase in the supply of other things; as when society growing richer wants more old silver and is prepared to pay more for it. We can hardly call such a phenomenon a "cause primarily affecting" the old silver; yet I think we should commonly say that old silver had risen in value under such circumstances. Suppose, again, that the intensified demand were due merely to an alteration in social habits, without any increase of general wealth; still, even in this case, being the expression of an increased preference for old silver as compared with certain other luxuries, it is the effect of a cause simultaneously affecting these other articles.

On the whole, I think, that strictly speaking, the "causes "primarily affecting" a thing that varies in exchange value must be understood to be causes affecting its supply—if Cairnes' interpretation of "change in value" is to have any definite significance. Of such causes the most important, in the case of most articles, is a change in the amount of labour required for producing either the article itself or the instruments and materials employed in its production. In this way we are led to Ricardo's view that a "commodity which at all "times required the same sacrifice of toil and labour to produce "it" would be "invariable in value[1];" which implies, what he elsewhere expressly says, that "labour is a measure by which "the *real* as well as the *relative* value" of things "may be "estimated." But on this view the "real value" of things must be different from their "exchangeable value"—even relatively to labour; since the proportion that labourers obtain of what they produce admittedly varies. I am not aware that Ricardo anywhere expressly draws attention to this distinction

---

ments which have enabled other things to be produced at less cost: while others mean by appreciation' or rise in value the admitted increase in general purchasing power, and consider that the only question is as to the *causes* of the appreciation.

[1] Ricardo, *Political Economy*, c. xx.

between the "cost or real value" of things and their "ex-"changeable value[1];" but it is definitely stated by his disciple McCulloch; who affirms that "real value or cost is to be esti-"mated by the quantity of labour directly or indirectly expended "on its acquisition[2];" while admitting that it is only under special circumstances that the "exchangeable value," even of a "freely produced commodity," exactly corresponds to its real value.

It is remarkable that Ricardo and McCulloch could deliberately adhere to the statements above quoted, while they at the same time drew attention to the differences in the value of different products due to the different degrees of durability of the capital employed in producing them:—or, which (as Ricardo says) is the same thing, the different lengths of time required to elapse in each case between the application of productive labour and the transfer of its product to the consumer. At any rate all economists—except those Socialists who have perverted Ricardo's inconsistency into an argument against the remuneration of capitalists—would now agree that in McCulloch's estimate of cost "labour and delay" (or some corresponding term) must be substituted for "labour" simply.

With this qualification, the Ricardian interpretation of the common notion of "real value" appears to me tenable; especially when we consider value from the social point of view. It does not seem forced or strained to say that things in general have grown "really cheaper," meaning that society would not have to give so much labour and time in order to obtain them. As was before said, in the 'comparison of equivalents' which I hold to be essentially implied in the common notion of value, the exact nature of the equivalents compared is not determined; and when we consider in the aggregate the valuable products of the labour of any community it is natural to compare this aggregate of products with the labour (and delay) that it would cost to reproduce them—so far at least, as we should desire to reproduce them. Hence I regard the question 'whether 'a thing costs more to produce' as an admissible interpretation

---

[1] As I have already said, I am of opinion that Ricardo does not quite clearly distinguish between a theory of the causes of a change in value and a view of what constitutes such a change.

[2] McCulloch, *Political Economy*, Part II., c. I.

of the question 'whether its value has really risen[1].' I do not,

[1] The doctrine of Ricardo's that we have been discussing should be carefully distinguished—as it is by its author—from the view taken by Adam Smith in adopting labour as the "real measure of exchangeable value," for Adam Smith means not the labour expended in producing anything, but the labour that it would buy. The reason that he gives for his view is that "labour never "varies in its own value." In saying this he does not of course mean that labour does not vary in its *exchange value:* he is perfectly aware that "it may "sometimes purchase a greater and sometimes a smaller quantity of goods." What he means is that labour is always the same sacrifice to the labourer: has always, we may say, the same negative "value in use" for him. But even this statement if unqualified, is in palpable contradiction to common experience. An amount of work which would cause no sensible inconvenience to a man in health would be a grievous burden to an invalid; and almost all men like tasks, which they are conscious of being able to accomplish well, better than if they could only perform them indifferently. In fact, when we consider the higher kinds of skilled labour, it must be evident that the labourer often gets more enjoyment out of his work than he does out of anything else in life. So much, indeed, Adam Smith seems by implication to allow. He is thinking only of common labour; and even as regards this he only maintains that "equal "quantities of labour, at all times and places, may be said to be of equal value "to the labourer," in the sense that "in his ordinary state of health, strength "and spirits, in the ordinary degree of his skill and dexterity, he must always "lay down the same portion of his ease, his liberty, and his happiness." *Wealth of Nations*, B. I. c. v. The qualifications thus introduced are considerable; but even when so qualified, the statement appears to me inadmissible. For by "equal quantities of labour" Adam Smith must, I suppose, be understood to mean labour of equal intensity for equal times: but then as Jevons says, "intensity of labour may have more than one meaning: it may mean the "quantity of work done, or the painfulness of the effort of doing it." It is the latter of these characteristics which Jevons chooses for measuring labour: but if we take this view of quantity, Adam Smith's proposition is reduced to the tautology that equally painful labour is always equally painful to the labourer; if, on the other hand, we measure intensity of labour by quantity of work done, Adam Smith's proposition comes into glaring conflict with facts; as will be evident if we imagine ourselves proposing to an average Bengalee in his ordinary condition to raise through a given space in a given time the amount of weight which would be cheerfully lifted by an average English navvy in his ordinary condition. If, however, we measure "quantity of labour" by time only, the statement is even more clearly opposed to common experience.

There seems therefore to be no sense in which Adam Smith's proposition can be accepted. But even if it were granted that labour has always the same negative 'value in use' for the labourer, I cannot see that this would be a sufficient ground for taking it as the standard of exchange value. For since at the same time and place the labour of one class of men certainly differs in exchange value from that of another class, we shall still have to choose which kind of labour is to be taken for the standard; and any such choice must necessarily be arbitrary, as the reason given applies equally to all kinds.

however, think that Ricardo or any of his followers has fully faced the difficulty of making this notion of cost quantitatively precise. For to do this we require a common measure for labour and delay and for different kinds of labour: and if we take—as the customary measure—the market price of these different sacrifices, we get a result which may continually vary while the sacrifices remain unchanged. Also though the higher wages paid for higher qualities of labour partly represent the extra labour that has been employed in training the superior labourer, it is evident that they partly correspond to natural superiorities—in physical strength or other useful qualities— which have no necessary relation to sacrifice of any kind[1]. We might ask also if by "cost" is meant cost according to the most economical method of production which is known and used, or according to that ordinarily employed, or average actual cost, or what is or might be the cost of the costliest portion required to meet the demand: for all these might be different. But to pursue these difficulties further would involve an anticipation of the Theory of Distribution and Exchange, to be set forth in the following Book: and this is not needful for our present purpose, since at any rate Value in the sense in which it is equivalent to Cost cannot serve as a measure of "amounts of wealth[2]": for the very point of an improvement in industry is that it enables us to produce more wealth in proportion to the cost.

§ 3. Shall we then fall back on the answer first suggested, and try to give as exact a meaning as we can to the notion of 'change 'in value relatively to things in general'? The difficulties of this attempt are so serious that many writers decline them altogether: they refuse to answer the question whether a thing has risen or fallen in value relatively to things in general; and only consider whether it has risen or fallen relatively to some specified commodity. In the chapter in which Mill discusses

---

[1] Ricardo's statement (*Pol. Econ.* c. i. § 2), that "the estimation in which "different qualities of labour are held comes soon to be adjusted in the market "with sufficient precision for all practical purposes" seems to me palpably, inadequate to meet the difficulty; since these "adjustments of the market" are continually varying, and the error involved in treating them as stable is not of the kind that economic theory can legitimately neglect.

[2] This Ricardo, of course, clearly sees; cp. next chapter p. 71.

the 'Measure of Value' he seems to adopt this view. "A "measure of exchange value" [of the same thing at different times and places], he says, "is impossible[1]." We find, however, that Mill has no hesitation in pronouncing on the extent of the rise in the value of gold, during the last five years of our long struggle with Napoleon; when the notes of the Bank of England were, to judge merely from the market-price of gold, depreciated thirty per cent. He tells us that "the state of Europe at that "time was such...that the value of the standard itself was "considerably raised; and the best authorities, among whom it "is sufficient to name Mr Tooke, have, after an elaborate inves-"tigation, satisfied themselves that the difference between "paper and bullion was not greater than the enhancement "in the value of gold itself...the evidences of the fact are con-"clusively stated in Mr Tooke's *History of Prices*[2]." But if so definite a variation in the value of gold, between two different points of time, can be established on conclusive evidences, it seems clear that it must be possible to "measure the value "of the same thing at different times," relatively to things in general, with sufficient exactness for practical purposes. And, indeed, the default of such a measure would seriously affect our ordinary comparisons between amounts of wealth possessed by individuals or nations at different times. For we commonly perform such comparisons by taking the money value of each of the quantities composed, and making what we consider due allowance for a rise or fall in the purchasing power of money during the intervening period. If then we are unable to measure changes in the value of the money standard, relatively to things in general, it must be impossible to compute the increase or decrease of wealth between two different times; unless some other measure than exchange value is taken, which will involve a serious deviation from the ordinary view of amounts of wealth.'

It therefore seems to me important to ascertain precisely how far we can give a definite meaning to the question, 'whether 'the value of a thing relatively to things in general,' or its 'general purchasing power,' has risen or fallen: and, for the

[1] Book III. c. xv.   [2] c. xiii. § 6.

reason just given, we may conveniently take as an example the particular commodity by which we commonly measure other values. Suppose, then, that we are investigating the change in the value or purchasing power of gold between two points of time. If we found that the prices in gold of all commodities had risen [or fallen] in the same ratio, we should obviously take that ratio to represent the fall [or rise] in the value of gold. But this could only occur by the rarest of accidents : the question therefore is if we find the changes in price unequal, and especially if we find that some prices have risen and others fallen, on what principle are we to combine these different changes into one result? As Jevons has noticed, different alternatives present themselves at this point of the inquiry, and " the exact mode in which preponderance of rising or falling " prices ought to be determined is involved in doubt. Ought " we to take all articles on an equal footing in the determination? " Ought we to give most weight to those which are least " intrinsically variable in value ? Ought we to give additional " weight to articles according to their importance, and the total " quantities bought and sold ?"

" The question," he adds, " seems to be one that no writer " has attempted to decide—nor can I attempt to decide it[1]."

I think that if we are guided by the practical interest which men in general have in asking the question, we must consider different articles of consumption[2] as important in proportion to the value of the total quantities consumed; notwithstanding an element of inexactness which, as will presently appear, this view inevitably involves. To make this clear, let us begin by considering the matter from the point of view of an individual. When a man asks how much gold will have changed in value twenty years hence, what he is practically concerned to know is how far at the end of this

[1] The quotation is from a pamphlet on "A Serious Fall in the Value of " Gold."

[2] The distinction thus introduced between "articles of consumption" and commodities that are only useful for the production of other wealth is further explained and justified in the following chapter (§ 4). In a later chapter (Book II. c. v.) it will be shown that a somewhat different interpretation of the notion of "general purchasing power" is required in investigating the effects of a change in the value of money on trade.

time his money will go in purchasing the articles which he habitually consumes. And if we assume that his consumption will remain unchanged, the question can be simply answered when the time arrives—supposing the requisite statistics attainable—by summing up the amounts of money paid for the things consumed, at the old and the new prices respectively, and taking the ratio of the difference to the whole amount expended. No doubt the result obtained by this method is likely to be different for different individuals, even at the same place: suppose for instance that at the end of the time corn has risen in price and the finer kinds of manufactures generally have fallen; we shall probably find that a rich man has got to pay less for his habitual consumption, and a poor man more. But this does not seem to be in itself any reason against applying the method to ascertain the change in the purchasing power of gold for a whole community[1]; since we have simply to treat the aggregate consumption of the individuals comprising the community as if it were the consumption of a single individual. The real difficulty does not lie here, but in the fact that the habitual consumption, whether of individuals or of societies, does not really remain unchanged between any two points of time. Even if we leave out of account all changes in habitual and conventional needs and desires, the mere fact that men generally buy somewhat more of things in proportion to their cheapness will cause alterations in the amounts of the different elements of their consumption. Under these circumstances the proposed method presents us with two alternatives; we may either take the total amounts of things purchased at the later period and consider how much they would have cost twenty years before, or we may exactly reverse the process. It is manifest, however, that these alternative procedures might lead to different and even opposite answers to the question, 'What change has occurred in the general purchasing power of money?' since it may be that men would have both had to pay more twenty years ago for what they buy now, and also more

---

[1] In what follows—to the end of the next paragraph—I assume, for simplicity's sake, that the community may be considered to be in the same place, and to have only a single market.

now for what they bought twenty years ago. So far as this is the case, we must say that the question whether gold has risen or fallen in value does not properly admit of a single exact answer by the method of comparing prices: there must always be a margin of inexactness in our determination of the amount of change, corresponding to the difference between the results of the two procedures. So far as this margin is concerned, we have to abandon the *primâ facie* exact method of comparing prices, and to substitute the inevitably more indefinite procedure of comparing the amounts of ability or satisfaction obtainable respectively from the different aggregates of hypothetical purchases[1].

And we have to deal similarly with a further source of inexactness introduced into this calculation by the progress of the industrial arts. The products of industry keep changing in quality; and before we can say whether any kind of thing—e.g. cloth—has really grown cheaper or dearer we must compare the quality—that is, the degree of utility—of the article produced at the beginning of the period with that of the more recent ware. This source of difficulty reaches its maximum in the case where entirely new kinds of things have been produced or brought into the country by trade. To leave them out altogether might clearly vitiate the result: for a nation might be unable to buy for a given sum of money an equal amount of the articles that it used to consume, and yet might be able to procure a completer satisfaction of its wants by spending the money on newly introduced wares: while, further, the raised price of the former commodities might be indirectly due to the production or importation of the latter.

So far we have been considering the difficulty of carrying a standard of value from one *time* to another. But precisely similar obstacles stand in the way of our obtaining definite results, when we compare the different values of gold (or any other ware) in different places at the same time: and they can

[1] In such cases we may often obtain a sufficient approximation to accuracy by the simpler method of confining our attention to the articles of common consumption at both periods. But if we wish to get the *closest possible* approximation to the answer that we are really seeking, we have to fall back on a rough comparison of amounts of utility.

only be partially overcome, by methods similar to that just explained[1].

One point more remains to be considered. In speaking of the aggregate of "articles" with which any particular commodity has to be compared, in order to ascertain the amount of change in its general purchasing power, I have tacitly assumed that only *material* commodities are included in the aggregate. And this, I think, would be the case, if we were considering the particular commodity as a measure of *wealth*, strictly taken. But if our ultimate aim is—as has been supposed in the preceding section—to compare the different amounts of purchased utility corresponding to the same money incomes at different times and places, we have to take note of the fact that a certain portion of a man's income is usually employed in purchasing not material things but services of various kinds. He buys from Government the service of sending his letters and telegrams; he buys from railway companies the service of conveying himself and his luggage from place to place; if he is comparatively rich, he probably spends a considerable sum in buying domestic services. We cannot omit these services from the aggregate of commodities with which the standard of value is compared, when our aim is to infer—as exactly as possible—from the nominal income of any body of persons their real command over the necessaries and conveniences of life[2].

§ 4. In a previous section I have discussed the conception of "real value"—as distinguished from exchange value—held by Ricardo and McCulloch: according to which the "real" value of a thing is measured by the labour and delay that would be required to produce it, or to produce something

---

[1] I may observe that the language of some economists would suggest that, for measuring value during an interval of time, the problem was to find a *concrete* identical standard, some actual *thing* that did not vary in value. But the difficulty lies much deeper. For our present purposes it would not matter how much gold, or any other concrete standard, varied in value, if we had the power of accurately measuring its variations; since this power would give us an *ideal* invariable standard, which is all that we require for the exact measurement of wealth. But as it is we are unable to make even this ideal standard exact beyond a certain point.

[2] Some further discussion of the relation of services to material wealth will be found in the next chapter (§ 4).

equally useful[1]. But it is not uncommon to use the term "real" "value" without any reference to cost, and merely as implying the ordinary antithesis between "fact" and "opinion"; as when the estimate of the value of a thing formed by a certain individual, or generally current in the market, is said to be above or below its "real" value or worth. A somewhat similar distinction is sometimes taken, especially by German writers, between "subjective" and "objective" value. It is desirable to examine briefly the significance of these antitheses.

We may begin by considering their application to "value in use." It may be thought that this kind of value must be "subjective," as being obviously relative to the individual who uses: and no doubt when we speak—as I before spoke—of the "value attached" by an individual to any article, we generally mean an estimate of its comparative capacity of satisfying needs and desires of which he alone has immediate knowledge. Still, even so, his present estimate may be shown by subsequent experiences to have been mistaken: he may find that the article really affords him less satisfaction than he might have derived from something else to which he preferred it. And if the utility of the article consists in its capacity of satisfying some common physical or some industrial need—and most of the articles that make up the aggregate which we call wealth are useful in one or other of these ways—it can obviously be estimated without any reference to the subjective feelings of the individual using it. In this way (e.g.) we may estimate the "objective" or "real" value in use of different kinds of fuel, or stone for building, or food for nutrition: and, similarly we might speak of the really higher value in "productive use" or "business-use" of certain instruments of production as compared with others, measuring their superiority by the extra *quantum* of produce obtainable by using them. Generally speaking, this "value in business-use" does not determine the value in exchange of such instruments[2]:

[1] This qualification is introduced to meet such cases as that of instruments which we should not reproduce at all, if they were destroyed, but should replace by something less costly though equally useful. In a progressive state of the arts of industry, such cases are frequent.

[2] It will be afterwards explained that the market-value of any kind of commodity does not tend to correspond to its *total* utility—as compared with any other commodity—but to what Jevons has called its *final* utility; i.e. the

but in dealing with land cases occur in which recourse must be had to this value in business-use, in order to arrange a fair exchange. Thus when a railway company takes a portion of land from a farm, it may not be possible to determine the compensation that it ought to pay by the exchange value of the land taken, since it may easily happen that, if sold separately, its price would fall much below its value to the farmer: the only fair way of determining compensation is by estimating the value of the land, for purposes of agricultural production, to the person who possesses or uses the remainder[1]. And since in any such estimate the future as well as the present conditions of agriculture would have to be taken into account, it is easy to see that the estimates of different persons might be very different, and even that the "real" value in use of the land in question may turn out to be very divergent from any of the prospective estimates.

In this way we see how the exchange value of a permanent instrument of production, such as land, may be different from what we may fairly call its "real" value in exchange: for— owing, let us say, to a "scare" as to the prospects of agriculture—the future exchange value of its produce may be underestimated, and the present exchange value of the land may be proportionally depressed. In this case what we mean by "real" value, is the hypothetical exchange value which would result from the substitution of truth for error in the minds of actual and possible purchasers. This use of the term "real "value" is convenient in ordinary discourse. I think, however, that it should be avoided in a treatise that aims at scientific precision, except in cases where there can be no doubt or dispute as to the particular kind of error or ignorance which we suppose to be replaced by truth. For in many cases, we should find various kinds and degrees of error in the minds of the persons whose judgments determine the price of a commodity;

utility of the last portion which it is found advantageous to purchase. Cp. next Chap. § 2 and Book II. ch. II.

[1] It should be observed that in the case supposed in the text, a certain extra compensation, over and above the equivalent for agricultural value, would be claimed for "value in use" of a more subjective kind: e.g. for the loss of a portion of an estate to which the owner may be attached from old association.

and it would generally be quite arbitrary to select one of these and regard its elimination as the one thing needful to make the current opinion of value correspond to the reality. And if, in order to determine the real value of any thing, we were to suppose knowledge of all facts materially affecting its value, in the estimate of intelligent persons, to be substituted for ignorance and error in the minds of all the persons concerned, we should generally get a hypothesis so remote from reality that it would be at once impossible to calculate the hypothetical value, and absurd, if we could calculate it, to call it "real." For the limitations of knowledge actually existing in the minds of producers, dealers, and consumers are among the most important of the facts on which any particular intelligent dealer bases his estimate of value: the removal of such limitations would be a fundamental alteration of the facts. To take a very simple case: suppose that a private bank of issue with a large and steady business was at a given time, owing to heavy losses, not in a condition to meet its liabilities if a run had been made on it compelling it to stop payment: but that as the secret was kept, it passed safely through the crisis, and is now in a condition of complete solvency. What shall we say was the "real value"—according to the current usage of the term—of the bank's promise to pay, at the time of crisis? If its condition had been generally known, they would have been worth less than their nominal value; but as it was not known they have actually been as valuable as the coin they represented. The question, therefore, is surely too indeterminate to admit of a decided answer. And much greater perplexities would arise in other more complex cases: therefore, if this notion of "real value" as divergent from actual price is introduced at all, it ought at least to be accompanied by a statement of the particular substitution of knowledge for ignorance or error which is implicitly supposed.

CHAPTER III.

WEALTH.

§ 1. IN the preceding chapter I have tried to make clear the kind and degree of inexactness which necessarily enters into all comparisons between amounts of wealth possessed by persons or communities living respectively at different times or in distant places, so long as we adhere to the commonly accepted method of measuring wealth by its exchange value. The difficulties of such measurement hardly appear so long as we are merely considering and comparing the wealth of individuals (or even of classes) at any particular time and place[1]. The wealth of any individual is usually considered to include all useful things—whether material things, as food, clothes, houses, &c., or immaterial things, as debts, patents, copyrights &c.—which being at once valuable and transferable admit of being sold at a certain price. And this aggregate is suitably measured by its exchange value; the common standard of value, money, being taken for convenience' sake. Our object in such estimates is to compare the potential control of any one individual here and now, over all purchaseable commodities, with that of any other individual; and, so far as such control is transferable, the ordinary mode of measurement enables us to make this comparison with as much accuracy as the imperfection of markets allows.

But when we try to compare the amounts of wealth possessed by persons or communities living at different times or in remote

---

[1] By "place" must be understood a region sufficiently limited in size not to admit of any material variation in the purchasing power of money within it.

places, we are met by the difficulties that we have been examining in the preceding chapter. So long, indeed, as we are only contemplating some one element of wealth, some particular kind of valuable article (of which the quality is supposed to be the same at the different times and places considered), we naturally estimate its amount as wealth by the ordinary measure of quantity. But when we have to compare aggregates of wealth made up of heterogeneous elements, it becomes necessary to reduce the units of quantity of these different elements to some common standard of measurement; and if we adhere to our original standard of exchange value, we have to deal with the problem of keeping this measure identical, in spite of the variations in relative value among the elements measured. But, as we have seen, this problem does not admit of a complete solution. Such a measure—except under purely hypothetical circumstances—is liable to a certain amount of inexactness, the limits of which we can define, but which we are unable to remove; and in the effort to make it as exact as possible, we are reduced in many cases to an inevitably vague comparison between the utilities of diverse commodities.

But again, such comparisons are liable to be further vitiated by the varying relations of purchased to unpurchased utilities, at different times and places. We have already observed that in ordinary thought wealth is measured by its money value: thus it is natural that economists, while pointing out the defectiveness of this measure, should still have retained the characteristic of "possessing exchange value" as an essential part of the definition of wealth; and that in so doing they should have conceived themselves to be in harmony with the common sense of mankind. Accordingly they have excluded from the notion of wealth such unpurchased though useful things as the sun's light and heat, air, the rain that waters the ground, water in rivers and seas, &c. They do not, however, seem to have observed the difficulties that this view involves, so soon as we try to compare the amounts of wealth possessed by human societies, inhabiting different regions of the earth's surface. For we find not merely that such useful unbought things are indispensable, as instruments or auxiliary materials, to the production of things that have exchange-value; but also—which is the important point—that they are instruments and materials of very various degrees of efficiency in different regions. Now since a large part of what is valued and exchanged as wealth consists in instruments and materials only useful as means of producing other wealth, it is paradoxical to draw a sharp line between purchased and unpurchased instruments and materials, so as to call a community "richer" because it possesses more of the former, though it may actually have less means on the whole of producing things directly useful. The difficulty becomes greater when the purchased and unpurchased instruments have a close resemblance to each other; as in the case where the water-ways of a country consist partly of canals and partly of rivers and creeks. The difficulty extends in range when we observe how, as civilisation progresses, so important an instrument as land tends to pass over from the class of unpurchased to that of purchased utilities. It seems contrary to common sense to say that a nation's wealth has increased because an instrument that it previously possessed has become valuable by becoming scarce. Thornton[1] has shown effectively the kind of error that may thus be introduced, in comparing the average wealth possessed by members of the same social class at different periods of a country's history. He points out that though an English peasant in the seventeenth century may have only had 5s. weekly wages, he often enjoyed also a rent-free site for his cottage, taken from the neighbouring waste, and unpurchased grazing on the neighbouring common for cows, sheep, pigs, and poultry. These things ought certainly to be taken into account, no less than changes in the value of money, in comparing such a peasant's share of wealth with that of an agricultural labourer now.

Again, exchange value is an obviously inappropriate measure of wealth, in the case of durable products of labour which, from their special adaptation to certain unique public uses, are not properly transferable, and have no market-price; such as roads, cathedrals, the houses of parliament. Such things are clearly part of the wealth of the community; but we cannot measure the *quantum* of wealth contained in them by the price at which

[1] *On Labour*, Introduction.

CHAP. III.] WEALTH. 71

they would sell if they had to be sold; nor, again, by the price at which they could be produced, for it may easily be that if they were destroyed it would not be worth while to reproduce them. In such cases, then, the standards of the market fail us; we have to fall back upon 'value in use.'

The same considerations apply, in a minor degree, to any kind of property that is more useful to the owner than it is to any one else. A man's command over the necessaries and conveniences of life is not affected by any fall in the market value of his property, except so far as he wishes—or may wish—to sell it: in proportion as he neither has nor is likely to have such a wish, exchange value becomes a manifestly irrelevant consideration in the estimate of his wealth.

§ 2. If, then, the common measurement of wealth by exchange value requires to be thus variously corrected and supplemented by estimates of utility, would it not be simpler, and really more consistent with ordinary thought, to take utility as the sole standard?

This is the view of Ricardo: who, regarding the value of a thing as directly proportioned to "the quantity of labour "employed in producing it,"—was necessarily led to separate the measure of wealth altogether from the measure of value; since, otherwise, he would have incurred the absurdity of denying that a country's wealth is increased by an enlarged supply of products due to increased facility of production. How then are we to measure utility? Ricardo[1] treats this as a very simple matter. "A man is rich or poor according to the amount of "necessaries and luxuries that he can command;" and therefore, if he gets two sacks of corn where he could only get one before, he gets "double the quantity of riches, double the quantity of "utility, double the quantity of what Adam Smith calls value "in use." But surely any man who got two sacks of corn where he had only counted on one would willingly exchange a great part of the second for things which he would not take in exchange for an equal part of the first: if such an exchange is out of the question, though he may find a use for the second sack it will certainly not be as useful as the first. And this is no less true of a community. Suppose a harvest of double the

[1] *Principles of Political Economy and Taxation*, ch. xx.

ordinary abundance in a fertile isolated country: the additional quantum of corn will obviously not have a corresponding quantum of social utility; it may even be of no use except to burn, as is said to have been sometimes the case in the Western States of North America. In fact, as Jevons has admirably explained[1], the variations in the relative market values of different articles express and correspond to variations in the comparative estimates formed by people in general, not of the *total* utilities of the amounts purchased of such articles, but of their *final* utilities; the utilities, that is, of the last portions purchased. From the fact that when things become dearer people generally buy somewhat less of them, we may infer that they estimate the portion which they refrain from buying as only just worth the money that they previously gave for it, while considering what they still buy to be worth the higher price[2]. If the price rose further, a further reduction of purchases would similarly indicate that another portion of the article was generally judged to be less useful than the amount still bought; and so on, for each rise in price. Hence when the supply of any article has been increased and its price consequently fallen, it is not really correct to reckon the total utility of the article as having increased in proportion to the increase in quantity; any more than it is correct to regard it as having decreased in proportion to the decrease in value. We ought to regard the additional quantum—so far, at least, as it is supplied to the previous consumers—as composed of parts of continually decreasing utility; the rate of decrease being measured by the fall in price, supposing the purchasing power of money relatively to all other articles to remain unchanged. If we assume the rate of decrease to be approximately uniform, we may regard the decrease in the average utility of the increment of supply as corresponding roughly to about half the fall in price. In this way we not only avoid the difficulties that arise in the measure-

---

[1] *Theory of Political Economy*, c. 4.

[2] It should be observed that there is one case—not without importance when we are dealing with luxuries—to which this principle does not apply. This is the case of things desired and valued on account of their rarity. Of such things the total, and not merely the final, utility *pro tanto* is decreased by an increase of supply. A similar exception must be made in the case of money, as is noticed later. (Cp. Book II. ch. v., note at the end of the chapter.)

ment of wealth by exchange value; we also obtain a satisfactory explanation of these difficulties.

On the other hand it must be admitted that this measurement by utility brings us into an awkward conflict with usage, when we consider it as applied to variations in amount of things of any one kind; or even to variations in an aggregate of things that do not vary in relative value. Suppose that owing to improvements in production the English nation became possessed of twice the amount of each kind of commodity that it now consumes; it would be paradoxical to say that its wealth had not doubled, as we should be obliged to do according to the view just explained. Further, the demonstration above given that "final "utility" decreases as supply increases involved the assumption that the additional supply of the cheapened article is purchased and consumed by the consumers of the previous supply; it is therefore inapplicable so far as the article is bought by different purchasers in different pecuniary circumstances. If tea, becoming cheaper, is bought by a poorer class, what reason have we for saying that what they purchase is not as useful as the dearer tea previously purchased by the rich? Indeed, is it not reasonable to suppose that a given commodity is more useful when bought by the poor, because the poor have fewer luxuries and therefore get more enjoyment out of what they have? In fact we are merely extending to wealth generally the principle established by Jevons in respect of particular kinds of wealth if we assume that, on the average, each additional increment to the amount possessed by any one individual has a decreased utility. But in this case, if we measure wealth simply by its utility, 'amount of wealth' will partly be determined by the manner in which the wealth is distributed; and we cannot say how much wealth there was in a country, till we know how it was shared among its inhabitants. Nay, we shall even have to ascertain how it is managed in each separate household; since a given supply of material products is less useful in proportion as it is uneconomically consumed.

These considerations are important when we are endeavouring to estimate the amount of utility or satisfaction derived by a community from the aggregate of things which make up its wealth. At the same time they show that to measure wealth simply by utility would cause an inconvenient divergence from common thought and common language; and therefore, though in Book III. we shall have to deal with the difficulties of measuring social utility, I do not propose to adopt this standard for determining 'amounts of wealth' in ordinary economic enquiries. It seems best to acquiesce in the ordinary method of measuring amounts of wealth of the *same* kind by quantity, and comparing amounts of wealth of *different* kinds by their exchange value; being content to get over the difficulties of carrying this measure from one time or place to another, in the imperfect manner above explained; and including even commodities gratuitously enjoyed in one term of the comparison[1], if things similar in kind are included (as having market value) in the other term. Only we must bear in mind that "amount of "wealth," thus estimated, corresponds but imperfectly to "amount of utility" derived by the community from the things that constitute its wealth.

§ 3. There is another difficulty lurking in the conception of Utility as a measure of wealth, which it will be instructive to discuss. By the Utility of material things, as before explained, we mean their capacity to satisfy men's needs and desires. And so long as we regard these latter as constant, it seems easy and straightforward to say that men are richer in proportion as they are able to satisfy their needs and desires. But it is not quite so easy to deal with the case in which their needs and the means of satisfying them have increased *pari passu;* especially if the additional need is a need of protection against some pain or danger which did not previously threaten. Suppose (e.g.) that a country is visited by a new peril of inundation; and that, by the extra exertions of its inhabitants, an embankment is constructed. Are we to say that it has thereby become a richer country than before? Or again, suppose that climate renders the inhabitants of one country liable to diseases that do not occur in another. Are we to say that the former country is the richer of the two, if its excess of wealth consists merely in remedies, palliatives, and prophylactics of diseases specially

---

[1] Such is the produce of waste land before mentioned. The values of such gratuitously obtained commodities would of course have to be supplied from the corresponding articles included in the other term of the comparison.

incident to its climate? A similar question may be raised as regards means of protection against noxious animals; or, again, as regards material securities against mutual injury on the part of the citizens. Shall we say that one country is richer than another, so far as the former has castles with battlements and towers, which civil peace and security render unnecessary in the latter? If, on the other hand, we allow ourselves to be led by this kind of consideration to limit the common denotation of the term wealth, where are we to stop? For the greater part of the material products of any country are useful as means of protection against the organic pains due to cold, inanition, &c.; and in different regions very different amounts of the produce of labour are required to make such protection effective: hence it may be said that inhabitants of cold climates are not really richer because they require more elaborate houses, more clothing, more food, and far more fuel than the dwellers in warmer regions. I think it must be allowed that the significance of comparisons between the amounts of wealth possessed by different groups of persons is liable to be seriously impaired by any important variations in their needs and desires: and that anything more than a vague and general comparison between (e.g.) the annual produce of England and that of a tropical island would be obviously idle. But there is not the same objection to a quantitative comparison between the wealth of England and that of Germany or France; as the physical needs of the populations of these countries may be assumed to be approximately the same: and a similar assumption is, on the whole, legitimate in comparing England now with England a century or half a century ago. For the primary needs of an Englishman, the food, clothing, shelter, &c., that his race and climate render necessary for his health, can hardly have changed materially; and though secondary needs of tea, tobacco, newspapers, &c., may have developed themselves in him we may fairly regard the satisfaction of these needs as a gain in the aggregate of utility derived from material objects.

So far as we compare the wealth of societies differing very widely in elementary needs, the important question is not whether either has not more wealth on the whole than the other, but whether it has more wealth to spare; more wealth that could be safely taken from its inhabitants, without interfering either with their health or with their productive efficiency[1].

§ 4. If, however, our main object in comparing "amounts "of wealth" is to obtain useful data for estimating the comparative amounts of satisfaction derived from material sources by different communities, or the same community at different times, a further distinction should be taken between the two portions of a country's material wealth which we may distinguish as Consumers' wealth and Producers' wealth respectively. By Consumers' wealth I mean such material things as are directly available for satisfying human needs and desires; Producers' wealth being only useful indirectly as a means of obtaining the former. What is commonly prominent in the thought of men when they speak of the increase or decrease of a country's wealth is certainly its stock of consumers' wealth; indeed we sometimes find in such discussions that the general term wealth is used in this more restricted signification. The distinction does not naturally suggest itself when we are contemplating wealth from the point of view of an individual: since an individual may at any moment exchange his land or his factory for any portion of consumers' wealth that he may desire; so that they are to him at least *potentially* consumers' wealth to the extent of their market value. But this consideration is in the main inapplicable to the whole community, which cannot similarly sell its land, factories, &c.: hence when we are discussing social

---

[1] It should be observed that what the members of a given society at a given time could spare—in the sense above defined—depends in an uncertain and varying degree upon previous habits, and upon mental and social conditions that are themselves variously modifiable, and, further, that there is no sharp line to be drawn between the expenditure which increases efficiency and that which does not; in most cases, before we come to quite superfluous expenditure, we shall find a certain portion which increases the consumers' efficiency in a continually diminishing ratio to the amount consumed: thus a labourer may do a better day's work by eating meat rather than bread, while yet the difference between the value of the meat and that of the bread may be greater than the value of the additional produce of his labour. Still, in spite of this indeterminate margin, we may with advantage mark off—as clearly as may be—the spare or superfluous portion of the wealth of a community from that which is required to keep its members in proper working condition.

wealth our attention is fixed in the first instance on things directly useful. Such things, in short, seem to be social wealth in a primary and special sense; while other things, only used and valued as a means to the production or conservation of these, are only to be called wealth in a secondary and wider signification of the term. It must be admitted that the boundary line between the two classes cannot be sharply drawn; there is an indeterminate margin of things which might plausibly be placed in either or both of these classes. Still this margin does not appear to be of great importance as compared with the aggregate of either class; and here as in other cases the impossibility of drawing a sharp line ought not to lead us to abandon a broadly important distinction, provided that we bear in mind the imperfect precision with which our classes are defined.

When this distinction is once taken, it is easy to see how misleading it may be to add the amount of Consumers' wealth in a country at any time to that of Producers' wealth, and present the sum of the two as the "total wealth" of the country. For since there is no constant proportion between the two parts of the total thus heterogeneously composed, a country might thus fallaciously be represented as having grown richer in proportion to the number of its inhabitants, owing to an increase in the number and elaborateness of its instruments, when in fact its produce per head, prospective as well as actual, might have really decreased. It is to be observed, too, that the exchange value of durable instruments (including land) may easily increase without any addition to their productive efficiency: since what people are willing to give for instruments of production does not depend entirely on the amount that they expect to produce with them, but partly also on the current rate of interest. If the rate of interest falls, owing to the decreasing productiveness of the latest additions to the capital of the country, previously existing instruments of permanent utility— among which land is the most important—will rise in value without necessarily becoming more productive: and therefore if we simply measured the amount of wealth contained in such instruments by its exchange value, the country would seem to have received a large increment of wealth, merely through a fall in the rate of interest. It seems therefore best, in an enquiry into the "wealth of nations," to take—as Adam Smith does—for our primary object of investigation what I have called 'Consumers' wealth,' the "necessaries and con-"veniences of life which a nation annually consumes."

But when we thus fix our attention on the "real income" of the community as distinguished from its resources, another consideration comes into view, which was noticed in the preceding chapter. A man's money is not entirely, though it is mainly, spent in consumable things—food, clothing, fuel &c.: it is partly spent in what may be called 'consumable services'; i.e. utilities furnished by the labour of others, which are not "fixed and embodied in matter": such as the services of domestics, physicians, actors, carriers. Ought we then to extend the conception of "wealth" to include such services? There is something to be said for this. The two kinds of utility are to some extent alternatives; and there would seem to be a certain absurdity in saying that people are poorer because they cure their diseases by medical advice instead of drugs, improve their minds by hearing lectures instead of reading books, guard their property by policemen instead of man-traps and spring-guns, or amuse themselves by hearing songs instead of looking at pictures[1]. It may be observed too that, in ordinary estimates of the aggregate income of the inhabitants of a country, directly useful—or, as we might say, "consumable"—services are commonly included: for as such services are reckoned as paid out of income, if we add the nominal incomes, estimated in money, of those who render such services as well as those who receive them, the result will only represent the aggregate

[1] It is worth noticing that, as Senior pointed out, *Political Economy*, p. 51 (2nd edition), the line drawn by common language between utilities "embodied" in material products, and utilities that are merely services, depends "on "differences existing not in the things themselves...but in the modes in which "they attract our attention." When our attention is principally called to the *result* of labour, in altering the qualities of matter, we call this result a new material product; when it is principally called to the act of altering, we consider this act as a *service* applied to a product previously existing. Thus the mending of shoes is commonly treated as a service because we pay for it separately; but we consider that the cook at a restaurant 'produces' a dish, because our payment for his operations is lumped together with our payment for the material on which they were exercised.

CHAP. III.]   WEALTH.   79

real income[1] of the country, if this latter notion is extended so as to include services. Hence when we pass to consider, in the following book, how this aggregate real income is distributed among the members of the community, it would be inconvenient and misleading not to enlarge our conception of the aggregate distributed so as to include services as well as material products. If, as I think, the term wealth is by usage restricted to stores or sources of utility comparatively permanent, some other term must be found to include, along with the wealth annually consumed, what I have called directly consumable services: and I propose accordingly, in the following book, to employ the terms "commodities" and "produce of labour" in this extended way. When, however, we are analysing the causes which render a community more or less liberally supplied with the necessaries and conveniences of life, it seems best to limit the object of investigation in a manner somewhat different from that which is appropriate in treating of Distribution; and to confine ourselves to such utilities as result from the application of labour to man's material environment. For the variations that we find in considering the command of different societies over this class of utilities differ greatly in their nature and causes from the variations in the quality and abundance of professional and domestic services; and it would serve no useful purpose to include the latter in the same investigation with the former.

§ 5. But the view above taken of material wealth as composed of permanent sources of utility raises a new question. Suppose we grant that services are not wealth on account of their transiency; still, there are other immaterial things which are permanent sources of utility, and why should not these be included in the notion of wealth? For instance, we consider that a chief result of a truly liberal education is to impart culture; that is to develope in human beings the capacities for realising certain elevated and delightful modes of mental existence, consisting in attainment of knowledge, exercise of

---

[1] It should be observed that the aggregate nominal income represents more than the aggregate consumption of material wealth and services; since it includes also that portion of income which is really saved, that is, which takes the form of additional instruments, materials, &c.

sympathy, or æsthetic emotion of some kind. Such modes of existence commonly require some of the material products ordinarily thought of as wealth, such as books, microscopes, pictures, &c.; but the capacities themselves are by far the most difficult and expensive conditions of making actual the possible utilities "embodied" in these luxuries. A man can buy the plays of Shakespeare for 3s. 6d. or less; but he cannot buy the capacity for enjoying Shakespeare without a vastly greater expenditure of his own and others' labour than 3s. 6d. would remunerate. Are we not then, it may be asked, to regard this culture, when acquired, as wealth, as much as the less important source of utility which we possess in the three-and-sixpenny volume? Certainly the facts just indicated should not be overlooked by the economist; it should be borne in mind that the expenditure of wealth and labour in imparting culture is an indispensable condition of realising the most important part of the utilities which we commonly but imperfectly conceive as attached to the material things that we call luxuries. Not only, however, is usage clearly opposed to our calling culture wealth; but—what is more important—the investigation of the causes of improvement in quality and increased diffusion of culture has for the most part but little natural connexion with an investigation of the causes of improvement in our supply of material commodities.

This latter argument, however, does not apply to the case of technical knowledge and trained skill. It is clear that a community may increase its means of producing commodities as much by improving the mechanical knowledge and skill of its inhabitants as by adding to its stock of inanimate instruments[1]; and that it depends on circumstances which of these two courses is at any time the more profitable employment of national wealth and labour. Hence—though, as skill is not directly

---

[1] It may be worth while to observe that the non-transferability of skill has a certain effect in diminishing the reasonable expectation of national advantage from producing it; since it somewhat increases the danger that the utility aimed at may not ultimately be realised. We may assume, generally speaking, that a machine will be used so long as it is worth using; since if its present owner is too lazy to use it he can sell it; but as skill cannot so be transferred, it may remain unused, merely because its possessor can obtain as much wealth as he wants in some other way.

exchangeable, it is contrary to usage to call it wealth—still, as I shall hereafter argue, we can hardly deny that so far as it results from labour it may be a form of investment of capital[1].

§ 6. There are, however, other immaterial things, such as debts, copyrights, &c., which being (unlike culture and skill) exchangeable, are—as we saw—commonly included in our estimate of the wealth of individuals. The question then arises how far we should include these in our conception of the aggregate wealth of the community? We will take first the case of Debts. A debt may be regarded either as the creditor's Right to receive a certain sum of money or a debtor's Obligation to pay it; the two notions merely representing two opposite views of the same fact. Such a right or obligation, being transferable, is a thing that possesses a definite exchange value; and the least reflection will show how very large is the amount of these valuable immaterial articles owned by Englishmen; indeed most of the wealth of those who are not landowners or personally engaged in business consists of the debts owed them by governments, companies, bankers, or private persons. It is clear, however, that such debts would not be properly included in an inventory of the aggregate wealth of Englishmen, except so far as they are debts of foreigners; since whatever be the positive value of a creditor's right to receive money, his debtor's obligation to pay it must have a corresponding negative value; though as there is no market for the obligations of debtors, as distinct from the rights of their creditors, this negative value does not usually force itself on our observation. At the same time, it ought to be recognised that this estimate overlooks the increase in utility on the whole, which generally speaking results from the transfers of material wealth effected by means of debts. A well-organized system of credit increases the productive resources of a country, just as a well-organized system of railway communication does; and this effect is especially striking in the case of certain kinds of debts, viz. those of bankers and merchants, which are used over and over again in transfers of wealth; and thus come to be a medium of exchange, which to a large extent takes the place of gold coin. Now so far as such debts (or the printed or written

[1] See ch. v.

acknowledgments of them) serve as substitutes for the precious metals in the machinery of exchange, it would be misleading to include the latter in our account of a country's resources—or 'producers' wealth,' as I have called it—and reject the former: for if a country substitutes an adequate currency of banknotes for a portion of its gold currency, and buys goods from abroad with the coin saved, it is evident that its power of obtaining 'consumers' wealth' has been increased by the change. And what is true of bankers' obligations will be admitted to be true of other debts, so far as they perform the same useful function of enabling material wealth to be transferred to the persons to whom it is most useful.

At the same time it is important to observe that, in estimating for purposes of comparison the wealth of a community, the ordinary standards of Quantity and Exchange Value are altogether inapplicable to the portion of wealth used as a medium of exchange. Quantity is almost an irrelevant consideration, since the social utility of a medium of exchange has no tendency to vary directly with its amount. Within very wide limits the function of money, so far as its employment within a country is concerned, will be no better performed by a larger quantity than by a smaller; provided that our habits and customs of distribution and exchange are duly adapted to the smaller amount. And exchange value is clearly misleading when the medium of exchange consists partly of metallic money and partly of bankers' debts. For while the actual functions of the two portions are the same, so long as the coin is used within the country, the coin has the special utilities of being both available for foreign payments and capable of being melted down and turned to other uses without any considerable loss. For these reasons—while it would be absurd to deny money to be wealth—it seems to me most convenient to omit the medium of exchange altogether in our comparisons of the wealth of different societies (or of the same society at different times); and to treat it as something *sui generis*. But whether we do this or not is not a question of great importance, for the purpose of our present enquiry: provided that we give due weight to the distinction before drawn between 'consumers' commodities,' whether material or immaterial, and 'producers' wealth' that is socially useful only as a means of producing consumers' commodities; since the medium of exchange is at any rate to be considered as producers', not consumers', wealth, and is therefore to be estimated, from a social point of view, by its productive efficiency.

And we should treat similarly the other valuable immaterial things which—as was before said—are commonly and rightly included in our estimate of the wealth of individuals. Take, for example, the rights to prohibit imitation of one's inventions and literary compositions by others, known as Patents and Copyrights. It is obvious that the exchange value of such things is no guide at all to their social utility. The primary effect of patents and copyrights is generally to decrease the amount of consumers' wealth produced in the country. The utility of the invention on which the patent is based may be very great; but it would be *primâ facie* greater if there were no patent at all, so that every producer might use it freely. Still, we believe that the ultimate effect of the establishment of patent rights is to increase the stock of directly useful commodities, through the stimulus given to inventive activity. But what a country gains in this way cannot be estimated with quantitative exactness, any more than what it gains by other important differences between a good and bad system of legislation; and it would be manifestly illusory to measure this advantage by reckoning the average exchange value of patents.

In the next chapter I shall take note of the importance to a country of its political organization[1] (including its system of law) as a source of increased production: but this, being common to all members of the community, is not represented

---

[1] There is a certain element of truth in the fallacious reasoning by which it has been argued that our national debt should be included in the inventory of England's wealth, as much as capital sunk in land or railways; as the interest paid on it is paid for the use of money which has been thoroughly well invested in rearing the historic polity of which we enjoy the benefits.

"Tantæ molis erat Romanam condere gentem,"

and the "civis Romanus" has naturally to pay, like the shareholder in a railway, for the borrowed capital used in this great construction. The analogy is undeniable; only we must not infer that England—any more than a railway—is worth more because it has cost us so much; still less that it is worth more because we had to borrow the money.

in any ordinary commercial estimate of the wealth of individuals. The case is otherwise with certain elements of that more indefinite and spontaneous social organization which, viewed as a whole, is a hardly less indispensable factor in the actual production of the aggregate of utilities enjoyed by the community. The established relations of individual traders and professional men with other members of the community, who habitually deal with them, are sources of gain to these individuals, admitting of more or less definite valuation. This is the case to some extent even with relations that are only partially transferable; as the Credit[1] of a banker or merchant, which may be handed on through the continuity of a firm, but cannot be exactly sold to a successor. In a certain sense it is legitimate to reckon this credit as a part of the wealth of such a firm since it is certainly a part of its productive resources, of which the value is measurable by the additional profit that it enables the firm to obtain. And the character of (individual's) wealth belongs still more clearly to what is variously known as Practice, Goodwill or Connexion;—terms by which we denote the fact that a considerable though indeterminate number of persons habitually use the services of a particular trader or professional man, and from the force of habit will mostly continue to use the services of any one who obviously steps into his place. Such settled habits of other persons, which in many industries give to old-established houses a qualified monopoly of business, are of course a considerable source of profit to the person whose services are employed. So far, then, as such 'Goodwill' is capable of being transferred at a definite exchange value, we ought no doubt to include it in any estimate of the wealth of the person enjoying it. And I admit that this immaterial wealth of individuals may to a certain extent be rightly considered as a part of the productive resources of the community: for, as was before said, the establishment of certain definite channels of business, certain fixed

---

[1] I may observe that in discussing the case of bankers' and merchants' obligations, employed as a medium of exchange, I have avoided the term "credit," as signifying ambiguously both the confidence which a creditor feels in his debtor, and the legal obligation to pay money which the latter incurs in return for the wealth lent him: it is in the former of these meanings that the term is here used.

habits of dealing with particular persons and companies, is a normal element of social organization; and we cannot conceive it annihilated without serious inconvenience to society. But it is clear that the social utility of the Goodwill or Connexion of individual traders cannot in the least be inferred from its exchange value, any more than the social utility of their credit or reputation.

It may be noticed that in the case of 'Goodwill' or 'Business Connexion' what is actually bought and sold is commonly the legal right of using the name (as well as the actual buildings &c.) of the dealer from whom the Goodwill is purchased. In the case of a physician's Practice, however, no similar external symbols of continuous succession are exchanged; what the physician undertakes to give in return for the money paid him is merely his absence and his recommendation; and it is a remarkable illustration of the force of mere habit, even in so important a matter as the choice of medical advice, that this recommendation—even when currently known to have been purchased—should have so high an exchange value as it appears actually to possess. But in neither case is the habit of dealing, on which the profit of the purchase depends, really secured by any legal right. I draw attention to this point, because even in the case of patents, copyrights, &c., considered as portions of an individual's wealth, it does not appear to me exactly correct to say with Mr Macleod that the wealth consists in the legal right; but rather that it consists in the special productive advantage or utility, the means of making extra profit, which is *derived* from the fact of non-imitation, though *secured* by the legal right. For if the legal right were annihilated, the owner of the patent would obviously remain just as rich as before, if only a general habit of non-imitation could be maintained— by public opinion or otherwise—among rival producers[1]. Similarly in the case of any portion of material wealth, that which constitutes a thing wealth is the possibility of enjoying the utilities or satisfactions to which it is a means, secured to its owner by his legal right to non-interference on the part of others; and not this right itself. Hence in con-

[1] I do not mean to suggest that this supposition is within the limits of probability.

sidering material wealth, though legal ownership is presumed, it is hardly necessary to draw attention to it.

We have now examined the chief questions that have been raised with regard to the definition of wealth. The results that we have obtained, so far as they are important at the present stage of our investigation[1], will perhaps be most conveniently summed up at the outset of the following chapter.

[1] Some further discussion of Producers' Wealth—under the more familiar name of Capital—will be found in chap. v.

CHAPTER IV.

CAUSES OF VARIATIONS IN PRODUCTION.

§ 1. THE lengthy discussion in the preceding chapter will not, I trust, have been thrown away, if it has assisted us in forming a clearer conception of the object that we have in view, in investigating the laws or conditions of Production. The term Wealth, as we have seen, is variously used in ordinary discourse, and may with perfect scientific propriety be diversely defined for the purpose of different inquiries. But in studying the Wealth of Nations what we are concerned to know is, Under what conditions different communities of men, or the same communities at different times, come to be "better or "worse supplied with all the necessaries and conveniences for "which they have occasion[1]." Hence our attention should be concentrated upon those directly useful commodities which I have called Consumers' Wealth to distinguish them from the instruments and materials which are only useful and valuable as means of producing other wealth. Again in comparing— with any aim at precision—the supply of such commodities enjoyed by different communities, or the same community at different times, we must limit ourselves to cases in which the primary needs of the persons concerned are not materially different. I may here observe that, if we are considering the same community at two different periods of its history, we ought not to overlook the durability of a portion of Consumers' wealth which has often been left rather out of sight by economists. When Adam Smith, for instance, speaks of the

[1] Adam Smith, Introduction.

"annual produce of labour," the term calls to mind the food that is eaten from day to day or the clothes that are worn out in a few years, rather than the houses, gardens, parks, pictures, jewels, &c., that are handed down from generation to generation. At the same time these latter must not be omitted in estimating the community's command over the "conveniences" —and even the "necessaries"—of life. A man's house does not the less shelter him from the elements because it was built in the reign of Elizabeth; and if we ask why England now is richer than England 300 years ago, a part of the answer must be that each generation has added somewhat to the stock of such durable wealth as is not, except accidentally, destroyed in the using.

At the same time, this is no doubt a very small part of the answer required; especially since this stock of wealth not only requires continual expenditure of labour in care and repairs, and continual additions to take the place of what is slowly consumed, but also continual adaptation to the changing tastes— and sometimes the changing needs—of successive consumers. And it seems most convenient for the present to neglect this small element of inherited consumable commodities and consider society as continually supplying what it continually consumes, in respect of the comparatively durable part of its consumers' wealth no less than of that which is rapidly destroyed and reproduced[1]. But we must not forget the amount of error involved in this limitation of view; and we must also bear in mind that carelessness in preserving what has been produced, and the instability of taste and fashion which impairs the satisfaction derived from it, tend practically to reduce the available supply of commodities.

Further; I argued that, in a complete view of the conveniences of life, we ought to consider along with consumers' wealth what I have called, for analogy's sake, "consumable "services": and I accordingly propose to extend the terms "produce" and "commodities," so as to include such services as

[1] As will be seen, a different view of this durable consumers' wealth is attained in the following chapter, in which its analogy to Producers' capital is brought out; but the difference is not very important for the present investigation.

well as material products. I also pointed out that, since a portion of wealth consists of books, pictures, microscopes, and other material means of literary, artistic, and scientific culture, and since the utilities embodied in these objects cannot be realised except by persons who have been more or less elaborately trained, it would be a mistake for us to leave out of sight the culture that results from this training, and the skill that is acquired and used as a source of immediate enjoyment, as a private person's skill in painting or piano-playing. Though we do not call permanent skill and culture, any more than transient services, by the name of wealth; still, since they resemble wealth in the two important characteristics of being results of labour and sources of satisfaction, the economist no less than the statesman or the philanthropist must keep them in view, in contemplating the growth of the resources of refinement and elevation of life which the progress of civilisation tends to furnish in continually increasing abundance.

At the same time, I pointed out a decisive practical reason for not including any reference to culture, or to the labour by which in each generation it is developed and transmitted, in our present examination of the causes why different societies are better or worse supplied with commodities generally: viz. that the most important changes that we have to note and explain in society's command over material wealth, are very different in their nature and causes from the most important changes that have taken place as regards the possession and enjoyment of culture. Under the latter head, for instance, the varying quality and abundance of the services of painters, poets, educators, even priests would be a prominent object of investigation; and would obviously take us into regions very remote from that of Political Economy as ordinarily understood. The same may be said of most other professional services. On the other hand, it would be equally misleading to confine our view of produce to the material things—food, fuel, clothing &c.— that producers are continually handing over to consumers: since there are other commodities, not transferred in a material form, but equally derived from the application of labour to matter, of which the increased supply that a modern civilised community continually enjoys is due to causes similar to those that have increased its command over material commodities; and of which therefore the production is naturally and suitably considered along with the production of the latter. Such, for example, are the commodities of Conveyance and Correspondence;—so far as they are what I have called consumers' commodities: i.e. so far as railways and telegraphs convey tourists and the messages of friends, no less than goods, commercial travellers, and messages of business[1].

The 'produce,' therefore, of which we are to examine the variations in amount must be conceived as something of which material wealth is the chief but not the sole constituent. For brevity's sake it will be convenient sometimes to refer to it as wealth: but we must be understood to have in view all the commodities derived from the application of the labour of a society of human beings to their material environment.

According to the ordinary view of "production" of material products, the process so named is conceived to terminate when the portion of matter to which it is applied has received its final quality and shape; the conveyance and sale of such finished products being regarded as separate and subsequent processes. Here, however, in consistency with the extended meaning which I give to the term 'produce,' we must regard as 'productive' all the labour employed about a thing until its consumption commences: that is, we must include the labour of carriers and traders, no less than that of farmers and manufacturers.

§ 2. The fundamental questions, then, which the Theory of Production attempts to answer, may now be precisely stated as follows: (1) What are the causes that make the average annual produce per head[2] of a given community at a given

[1] The quantity of such commodities may be measured by (1) the number of persons and messages conveyed within a given period, and (2) the space through which they are conveyed: increased speed of conveyance is an improvement in quality which can only be roughly estimated.

[2] We investigate the average supply per head, and not the total supply; because it is to the former that all assertions as to the greater or less wealth of a society commonly relate—we do not think that a nation has grown richer merely because, having grown larger, it consumes more food, clothing, &c. And we take the supply as annual, because the principal products of agriculture are actually produced at intervals of about a year; otherwise, of course, any other period would do equally well.

time greater than that of another whose primary wants are not materially different, or greater than its own produce at a previous stage of its history? and (2) What are the laws of their operation? The answer of the former of these questions is somewhat complicated, but in no way doubtful or obscure: it merely requires a little care in reflective analysis to distinguish the different elements that enter into the productiveness of industry; though their mutual connexion is so close and intricate that it is a matter of some little difficulty to expound them in a clear order. But when we attempt to measure accurately the operation of any of these causes in the past, and still more when we try to forecast the extent to which they may be expected to operate in the future, we touch on points which controversy has found—or rendered —difficult and perplexing. It has therefore seemed to me desirable to treat these two questions separately; and to confine myself in the present chapter to a merely qualitative analysis of the conditions of Production, reserving for a future chapter the discussion of the more precise quantitative statements, which for distinctness' sake I propose to call the 'Laws' of Production.

The whole process of Production—the application of the labour of a community to adapt external matter, organic or inorganic, to the satisfaction of its wants—has various degrees of complexity according to the nature of the utility produced. Ordinarily, we can distinguish three chief *stages* involving a somewhat larger number of leading *species* of industry. First comes the labour required to get possession of some material thing in its natural state, or with no further modification than is needed to render it moveable: i.e. either mainly the labour of pursuit or enticement and capture—e.g. of game or fish—, or mainly the labour of initiating or fostering the natural growth of tame animals and vegetables, or the labour of detachment or extraction, as in the case of forest trees and minerals. Then follows the labour of manufacture in which this raw material undergoes mechanical or chemical changes more or less extensive to adapt it to human uses: then, finally, comes the labour of the carriers who convey the finished goods from place to place, and of the traders who enable them to be obtained promptly and easily by the members of the community who may from time to time require them. It is evident that, for a given population, this whole process—or any part of it—will tend to yield more or less of the utilities at which it aims, according as the labour is (i) applied under more or less favourable circumstances, or (ii) is greater in quantity, or (iii) more efficient in quality. I include under the term labour all kinds of voluntary exertion, intellectual as well as muscular, which contributes directly or indirectly to the increase of produce as above defined: and I mean by "quantity of labour" merely *extensive* quantity, measured in two ways, by length of time and number of labourers. On this view we may distinguish four different ways in which the labour of one community may be less than the labour of another, in proportion to the whole number of the population; for either the workers may bear a smaller ratio to the non-workers, or the number of years during which they work may bear a smaller ratio to the whole period of life, or they may work for fewer days in the year, or for fewer hours in the day. It may however be urged that we ought to regard labour as having *intensive* as well as extensive quantity; and no doubt we commonly speak of men as doing more or less work in the same time, meaning not merely that they produce more or less result, but that they make more or less effort. But since I cannot find any satisfactory measure of the amount of such effort, applicable to all kinds of labour alike, it seems best to include this source of variation under the third head of 'efficiency' of labour. The question is not of great practical importance; because the variations in quantity and quality of labour respectively are on any view largely due to the same causes[1].

[1] Jevons, in his *Theory of Political Economy* (c. v.), considers labour as possessing intensive quantity: but his view of this characteristic does not appear to me very clear or consistent. In one passage (p. 185, 2nd ed.) he says that "intensity of labour may have more than one meaning; it may mean the "quantity of work done, or the painfulness of the effort of doing it." But surely "quantity of work done"—or, as he afterwards says, "amount of "produce"—varying as it must with the material to which the labour is applied, the skill with which it is directed, the instruments that aid it, &c., &c., cannot possibly measure the mere quantity (in any sense) of the labour. And though the "painfulness" of labour is a characteristic of fundamental economic importance, it cannot possibly supply a universal measure of labour; since, as

§ 3. Let us begin, then, by analysing briefly the differences in the productiveness of labour that are due to external conditions. In the first place the "spontaneous bounties of nature" (as they are called) are very unequally distributed: in some regions things directly consumable, or the materials required for making them—game or fish, wood or coal for fuel, or useful metals—are much more abundant than elsewhere, or more easily obtained, preserved, or applied to their appropriate uses These variations are obvious and familiar; and almost equally obvious are the differences in the degrees in which land and water, the great permanent instruments of production (including conveyance), are naturally adapted for this purpose or capable of being made so. It should be observed, however, that these material advantages do not remain the same in all stages of industrial development: but vary with the varying amounts of labour applied and the varying efficiency of instruments and processes. Thus in newly settled countries the lands first cultivated are commonly not those that ultimately prove most fertile: so again the river-system of a country is fundamentally important for communication till railways are invented, but not afterwards: and similarly the ocean was long a barrier to navigators of inland seas.

Secondly, as we pass from one part of the earth's surface to another, we find similar variations in the conditions unfavourable to production or to the preservation of what has been produced: either periodic conditions of inorganic nature such as extreme dampness[1] or extreme heat; or occasional disturbances

I have already argued, the assumption that labour is universally painful is in conflict with facts.

In another passage (p. 221) Jevons says that "we may approximately "measure the intensity of labour by the amount of physical force undergone "in a given time." This view appears to me quite different from the one just discussed; since by "amount of physical force undergone" must be meant some effect on the labourer's organism, not on the material modified by his labour. But what the precise nature of this organic effect is, or by what standard, applicable to all kinds of labour alike, Jevons proposes to measure it, I cannot discover from his examples.

[1] "During the rainy season, in the region of the upper Ganges, mushrooms "shoot up in every corner of the houses; books on shelves swell to such an "extent that three occupy the place previously occupied by four; those left on "the table get covered over with a coat of moss one-eighth of an inch in thick- "ness." Roscher, *Political Economy* (Lalor's translation) § CLIX.

as floods, storms, earthquakes, &c.; or plants or insects noxious in various ways. Here also we may notice (1) the direct physical effect of climate on the labourer's energy, as well as (2) its effects in varying the period during which labour can be usefully employed in agriculture[1].

In short, the external world upon which man operates requires in its original state very different degrees of adaptation to extract from it the same *quantum* of utility for human needs. We have now to observe that, in the regions of the earth which have been for some time in the possession of civilised man, each succeeding generation receives its portion of the earth's surface in a somewhat different condition from the preceding generation. For the most part it finds its inheritance in a state more favourable to labour; the benefits of its predecessor's work being inextricably mingled with the "spontaneous bounties" of nature. These benefits may have been to some extent intentional, as when men plant trees that their children may reap the fruits; but for the most part each generation carries on primarily for its own ends the process which, from a human point of view, we may call the 'improvement' of the external world; only a considerable part of this improvement, being permanent in its nature, profits posterity as much as the improvers themselves. The later-born generation finds, along with fields originally fertile, others that have become so through labour spent in clearing and draining, embankments to ward off floods, tanks or canals for irrigation, &c. It finds that the beasts of prey that used to inhabit its land are either extinct, or reduced in numbers and scared from the haunts of men. It finds rivers made navigable and freed from "snags "and rafts, rapids and shallows," harbours made more commodious, roads and railroad levels constructed. To maintain some of these improvements will require, no doubt, some labour of its own; but indefinitely less labour than was required for their original construction. So again, it finds species of plants and animals which have not only been tamed, but also

---

[1] "In the countries on the Danube," says Professor Hearn (*Plutology*, pp. 74, 5), "the cultivation of the ground and the reaping of the crop are "spread over seven months; in the countries on the north of the Volga they "must be concluded in four months."

by gradual breeding have been rendered more fit than they originally were for the satisfaction of human wants. This improvement, also, is not strictly speaking permanent: it might conceivably be lost: but it is not likely to be lost without a social catastrophe, and, generally speaking, it does not entail any additional labour on the generation that succeeds to it.

On the other hand, we have to notice certain respects in which the earlier generations are liable to render the land they live in worse adapted for the requirements of their successors. They tend to exhaust the useful minerals that are most conveniently situated for extraction—and also certain useful organic products accumulated in previous ages, such as Peruvian guano. They may exhaust the fertility of certain soils by frequent crops, so that these soils will afterwards require more labour to render them as fertile as they were originally. They tend to diminish the number of useful wild animals and drive them into places where they are more difficult to catch; and to carry the clearing of forests beyond the point at which the tree is less useful than the ground on which it stands. But these and other similar deteriorations, so far as we have yet had experience of them, cannot be said to weigh heavily in the balance against the improvements before mentioned.

There is however one specially important way in which a generation may find itself with a material environment less adapted to its needs, through the action of its predecessors. It may find that, through the increase in its numbers, the country it inhabits has become too small for the most effective application of the aggregate of its labour: that is, the increase in the advantages of Division of employments (to be presently noticed) may be more than neutralised by the diminution in the proportional amount of agricultural produce that can be annually extracted from the land, in return for the extra labour applied to it[1].

---

[1] To what extent and under what conditions this tends to occur are fundamentally important questions which we shall have to consider carefully when we come to discuss the Law of Diminishing Returns in chap. vi. of this Book.

Then, further, we have to observe that the gifts of nature are only useful so far as they are known; and that our knowledge of them has continually increased. As civilisation progresses, men discover, or enter into effective communication with, regions unknown to their ancestors,—regions containing new useful plants and animals whose products they may appropriate by exchange; they discover new possibilities of acclimatizing foreign plants and animals already known; they find new minerals in their own land. New combinations of matter, again, are accidentally produced in the development of industries, which are afterwards ascertained to possess unexpected utilities. To a still larger extent useful properties previously unknown or almost unknown are discovered in things already known, or new modes of combining properties already known so as to increase their utility. In all these ways the available bounties of nature come to be continually increased, by the progress of knowledge, for each successive generation. Here again the improvement is not absolutely permanent; it may be lost through the intellectual inertness of the later-born inhabitants; indeed, like some of the material improvements before-mentioned, it requires a continual expenditure of labour to maintain it. But this expenditure is trifling in comparison with the utility of its results; and is not likely to be pretermitted by any civilised society in its normal condition.

§ 4. In dealing with the first class of conditions of variable productiveness, I have been led to include one that might equally be placed in the third class. For the increase of our knowledge of matter and its properties, taking effect in what we call Inventions of new industrial processes, is properly regarded as one of the most important causes of improvement in the efficiency of human labour. In another respect, again, the distinction above drawn between improvements in Man and in Nature, though on the whole convenient, is somewhat forced. For Man is a part of Nature; the productive qualities of man no less than those of plants and animals, exhibit differences that are, relatively speaking, original—that is, of which the origin is lost in prehistoric obscurity; and at the same time they are similarly susceptible of improvements that may be transmitted through physical heredity. This is true not only of such qualities as strength, energy, fineness of sense, &c., but also of higher intellectual aptitudes.

Again, as we have already seen, both the quantity and the quality of labour are directly affected by climatic influences, which render the labourer himself languid and inert, or render important kinds of work impossible for him at certain periods.

Passing from these conditions, which are in the main unalterable, we may notice variations in the quantity and personal efficiency of labourers which depend on such physical and social circumstances of the labourers' lives as admit of being at any time modified by the action either of individuals or of the society to which they belong. In the first place, it is obvious that the proportion of effective workers to the rest of the community will be less, other things being equal, where the population is increasing rapidly, owing to the larger number of children that have to be supported; it will be less, again,—for any given rate of increase of adult population—the greater the number of children that die in infancy, owing to want of care or want of proper food, clothing, &c. Again, unsanitary conditions of life tend in another way to reduce the quantity of labour performed by a given population; by diminishing, through premature death or early and prolonged decrepitude, the average proportion which the working period of life bears to the whole; and again, by diminishing the number of working days in the year, through increased frequency of incapacitating disease.

Similarly, bad air and water, uncleanliness, over-indulgence in alcohol, and other unhealthy habits may lower the physical tone of the labourer and thus impair the quality of his work without causing positive illness; on the other hand the strength and energy of the labourer may be largely increased by an ampler supply of the necessaries of life[1].

Even more important than the differences in the physical strength and vigour of labourers are the variations that we find

[1] Hence—as we shall afterwards notice—differences in cost of labour to employers are often much slighter than, and sometimes even in opposite direction to, differences in the labourers' remuneration.

in their skill and intelligence, their foresight, quickness, vigilance, and resource in availing themselves of advantages that further production and avoiding or removing all that impairs it. Superiorities in these respects are partly, as I have said, congenital and transmitted through physical heredity: but to a great extent they are handed down from generation to generation by conscious training and learning; primarily by technical training and learning of special arts and processes, though the effect of general education in developing industrial intelligence must not be overlooked. We must also bear in mind the extent to which industrial efficiency is transmitted by association and unconscious imitation. "The child," says Mr F. A. Walker, "becomes a better workman simply by reason "of being accustomed, through the years of his own inability to "labor, to see tools used with address, and through watching "the alert movement, the prompt cooperation, the precise "manipulation, of bodies of workmen. The better part of "industrial as of every other kind of education is unconsciously "obtained. And when the boy is himself apprenticed to a "trade, or sets himself at work, he finds all about him a "thorough and minute organization of labor which conduces "to the highest production; he has examples on every side to "imitate; if he encounters special obstacles, he has only to "stop, or hardly even to stop, to see some older hand deal with "the same[1]." This unconscious imitation operates powerfully in keeping up the habitual energy of individuals in a society when a high average standard of energetic work is maintained.

§ 5. Still, in explaining differences in the degree of energy of individual labourers or groups of labourers, as well as differences in the (extensive) quantity of the labour performed by a given population, a chief place must be given to differences in the strength of the motives for work presented to their minds.

Among these varying motives the most powerful is undoubtedly that "desire for wealth" which economists have often treated as the sole possible spring of industrial activity. In a previous chapter[2] I have argued that the very fact that this desire is derived from, or is a generalised form of, an

[1] *The Wages Question*, c. 3. [2] Introduction, c. iii.

indefinite number of more particular impulses, renders it practically legitimate to assume its universal presence; since there is at least no important class of persons who do not desire, either for their own present satisfaction, or as provision for the future, or for donation or bequest to others, a larger supply of *some* kind of purchaseable commodity. None the less is it important to observe the different degrees of intensity in which the desire of wealth actually operates, in consequence of variations in the strength of the more particular impulses from which it is derived or generalised. Of these the most universal and imperious are the primary wants of food, clothing, shelter, and other necessaries. These primary needs, as we have already observed, are considerably modified by differences of climate and of the physical constitution of different races; and also somewhat by the traditional habits of different communities and classes. But even assuming them to be approximately uniform, the amount of labour required for their satisfaction must obviously be affected by changes in the productiveness of labour; and the stimulus to labour supplied by them will vary accordingly. Hence improvements in production, of which the benefit accrues to the labourers, have some tendency to cause a diminution in the quantity of labour instead of an increase in the quantity of produce: since if a man's earnings are already sufficient to satisfy all his keenly felt needs, the power of earning more by the same amount of labour must partly operate as an inducement to work less.

It is, no doubt, a general law of human nature, that when these primary needs are satisfied, other desires requiring more or less wealth for their gratification tend to be developed, and to fill up the vacuum of impulse thus created. But the strength of these secondary impulses, as compared with the aversion to additional labour which acts as a counterforce, is a far more variable element than the urgency of the primary needs. The sensibility to "comforts", or the means of warding off slighter physical annoyances; the taste for sensuous "luxuries", that is, for the means of increasing the positive pleasures that normally attend the satisfaction of physical wants, by variety and elaborateness in food, drink, furniture, &c.; the taste for ornament, elevated gradually into artistic sensibility; the demand for the emotional and intellectual gratifications furnished by literature, science, &c.;—all these springs of action are operative in very various degrees in different communities and classes at different periods of their history. The progress of civilisation tends generally to increase their force—in fact such increase is implied in our common notion of the complex change that we call 'progress of civilisation'—but the tendency is not uniform in kind or degree. Foreign Trade has historically been a most powerful and important agent in the diffusion of these secondary desires:—it is, indeed, noteworthy that the advantage of foreign trade which was most prominent in the view of pre-Smithian economists of the last century, was not that it tends to supply more amply and economically needs and desires already existing; but rather that it "rouses men from "their indolence, and presenting the gayer and more opulent "part of the nation with objects of luxury which they never "heard of before, raises in them a desire of a more splendid 'way of life than their ancestors enjoyed[1]." The influence of these desires as developed in individuals is further modified by the varying extent and manner in which custom and social sentiment intervene; either as prescribing certain comforts or luxuries as "decencies" of life in certain classes, or as stimulating efforts to rise above the standard socially prescribed in any class, in order to gain the higher social rank or reputation attached to the possession or exhibition of wealth; or, on the other hand, as reprobating luxury generally or particular species of luxurious expenditure. We have further to take into account the varying operation of the Affections, which multiply the attractive force of all objects of desire by extending the range of the persons for whom they are desired; and the play of the moral sentiments which variously combine with natural affections in prompting to such extension—thus (e.g.) the provision of wealth for children is an end sought with very different degrees of eagerness by average persons at different times and places. Nor must we neglect the influence of the political organization of the community, in rendering political power more or less dependent on the possession of wealth. Again, it is to be observed that several of the

[1] Hume, *Essay on Commerce.*

desires above enumerated require leisure as well as wealth for their full satisfaction; also that very varying amounts of wealth are required for any given gratification—as in the case of the primary needs. Finally the resultant force of this complex play of motives is of course affected by any variations in the average dislike of labour; in considering which we may especially notice the powerful effect of social sentiments and opinions; labour generally, or certain kinds of labour, having frequently been regarded as more or less degrading.

But the stimulus given to labour by the desire for wealth does not vary simply according to the strength of this resultant impulse; it is modified at least equally by the extent to which the labourer is impressed with the belief (1) that additional wealth may be obtained and kept by additional labour, and (2) that there is no other more easy and agreeable way of obtaining it. Here it is to be observed, in the first place, that the range of opportunities of obtaining wealth has been largely extended and restricted by the varying action of governments. What political conditions are most effective in securing the proportionment of reward to labour is a much controverted question, which will demand our consideration later[1]. But there is no question that this security has often been impaired by the fact that adequate protection of earnings from spoliation has not been provided—as Mill epigrammatically says—"by "the government and against the government." Lack of protection by the government obviously involves the double detriment of discouraging honest labour, and encouraging the socially unproductive industry of plundering others;—effects which are aggravated when the plunderers are armed with, or sheltered by, the authority of government; but "protection "against the government" must be understood to include security not merely against the arbitrary seizure of property, but also against such oppressive taxation as discourages the accumulation of wealth.

On the other hand there is equally little question that the well intentioned tutelage of government has often gone too far; that (e.g.) in civilised Europe in the 18th century the opportunities of obtaining wealth were seriously diminished by the

[1] See Book III. cc. iii. and iv.

restraints which governments have imposed on free choice of domicile and calling, and on the processes of industry and trade; or again that the sustenance gratuitously provided for non-workers, by the English Poor-law from 1782 to 1823, dangerously impaired the motives to industry. This latter effect may of course be also produced by indiscriminate private almsgiving without the intervention of government. And similarly even when the government leaves individuals perfect freedom in the choice of calling and domicile, the want of "mobility" in the labour of the community may seriously interfere with its productiveness; ignorance, or routine, or social sentiment, or strong local attachment may prevent workers from choosing the business in which their exertions would be most productive and best remunerated.

Supposing the species of industry determined, the strength of the labourer's motive to exertion and care depends, of course, partly on the amount of his earnings; but partly also on the connexion between his earnings and his efforts; and this, again, varies greatly with the mode in which industry is organized. The connexion is most simply effective when a labourer works independently and owns the whole produce of his labour. So far as this simple arrangement is precluded by its incompatibility with the full advantages of co-operation, the labourer's interest in production has to be secured by some artificially contrived correspondence between his remuneration and his work. Different arrangements for attaining this result will be presently considered; here we need only observe that the deficiency of stimulus in the case of a hireling who works for a fixed wage may be partially supplied by careful supervision, if his wages can be easily raised or lowered at his employer's will, and if the competition for work among labourers is keen. Hence, distinguishing the work of employed labourers generally from that of their manager (whether the employer or his agent), we may draw attention to the special importance of adequate motives for exertion and care in the case of the latter: not merely because skilful management implies vigilant oversight and prompt command, but also because men catch skill, promptitude, and energy by unconscious imitation from their chief, and further feel a certain stimulus from the satisfaction of taking part in effectively organized performance. For though, under present circumstances, the strongest stimulus to the energy of average men—whether employed or employers—is undoubtedly supplied by the desire of gaining wealth for themselves or their families; still we ought to recognise, as actual forces, both the desire of turning out good work, and the *esprit de corps*, which the mere fact of cooperating habitually for a given end tends to produce in average human beings, if the tendency is not overpowered by adverse influences, such as the consciousness of conflicting interests.

The foregoing analysis has led us more than once to consider differences in the moral qualities of labourers, as causes of variations in production. The economic importance of these may be briefly summed up thus; so far as it is made each labourer's interest to work his utmost, the more prudence and self-control he has, the more he will increase the wealth of the community: while again, the more he is actuated by sense of duty and wide public spirit, the more productive his labour will be under circumstances in which the coincidence between his own interest and that of society is wanting or obscure. The dishonest workman who scamps piece-work and is slothful if paid by the day, the dishonest manufacturer who employs labour and capital in producing the illusory semblance of utility, the tradesman who spoils his wares by adulterating them, all diminish produce. But besides self-interest on the one hand, and the influence exercised by common morality and regard for the general good on the other, we have to take special note of the narrower *esprit de corps* fostered by combinations of persons with similar interests; especially among the labourers in particular industries by such organizations as Trades-unions. So far as the rules of such associations, and the general opinion and sentiment which they produce or intensify, are directed towards the maintenance of a high standard of workmanship, their effect on production is likely to be beneficial. In some cases, however, the rules and practices of Trades-unions have acted in an opposite direction, by resisting measures designed to economize labour; it being considered to be the interest of labourers in any particular industry that the field of employment should be as large as possible. How far this view is sound we do not now consider; here we have merely to observe that the prevalence of this belief causes this narrower *esprit de corps* to diminish the productive efficiency of the aggregate labour of the community[1].

§ 6. In examining variations in the personal efficiency of individual labourers, we have been led to treat of the indirect effects of cooperation and association of workers, in developing skill and energy and *esprit de corps*. Let us now pass to consider the more obvious and important gains in productiveness of labour, due directly to the same association and cooperation.

We may notice first the more elementary advantages obtained by cooperation in its simplest form. There are many things which one man alone cannot do, but which are readily accomplished by the simultaneous action of several men. The raising of a given weight, for example, requires a certain force, which may be obtained when the power of two men is simultaneously applied, where it could not be obtained by any amount of successive effort on the part of either working singly. But further, it is soon found that frequently little or no more labour is required to render a given service to several persons than is required to render it to one. "The fire and the water "and the care requisite to prepare the food of one person will "equally prepare the food of three or four. Consequently "when two men have to do two different things, if in place "of each performing his two several acts, they can with the "same or nearly the same effort perform for their joint benefit "each one act sufficient for the two, there is a clear saving of "half their labour[2]." Thus as simple cooperation increases power, Division of Employments, or as it has been called by economists since Adam Smith, "Division of Labour," economizes its use; and in this way division of employments would in many cases cause a most important gain, independently of any consequent increase of aptitude in the labourers whose functions are thus specialized. Postal communication affords a striking example of this. There is not much room for increase

---

[1] The loss to production caused by conflicts between labourers and employers as to wages will be noticed later in this chapter.

[2] Cp. Hearn, *Plutology*, pp. 124, 208.

of dexterity in the simple process of delivering a letter; the economic advantage of making letter-carrying a separate employment depends almost entirely on the great diminution of labour that each separate delivery requires, when one man delivers all the letters in the same street. In many cases, again, there is a great advantage in saving the time lost in passing from one set of actions to another; especially when the subdivision of employments is carried—as it is in many modern manufactures—so far that each worker has only to perform one very short series of actions, repeated as often as possible. Still by far the most striking advantage of the division of employments is the increased dexterity of the workmen; the vastly greater ease, rapidity, and accuracy which constant repetition gives to the performance of any act or set of acts. Probably no paragraph in Adam Smith's works is so widely known as that in which he contrasts the number of pins that a man could make by himself with the number that he can make when in combination with others he confines himself to a single part of the process; and certainly the degree of additional efficiency that a worker can acquire, in work of a tolerably simple and uniform kind, under a highly developed system of divided employment, is greater than anyone without specific experience would have imagined. There is a further economic advantage in the fact that the training required to bring each labourer up to full efficiency tends to become shorter and less expensive, as the work he has to do becomes limited and simplified[1]. A more important gain than this last consists in the economy of aptitudes that becomes possible, through the continually increasing variety of employments; there is thus greater opportunity of setting different individuals to do what they can do best; especially all new gifts and talents become indefinitely more profitable to society when their possessor can be set free from all work except that for which he is specially

[1] To some extent this advantage is purchased by a corresponding risk of the labourer's being reduced to inefficiency, in case of his employment failing; but it may be observed that separation of employments in any particular industry does not always involve a corresponding specialisation of labour: as the particular tasks allotted to a given class of labourers in one branch of industry may have counterparts more or less closely correspondent in other branches.

gifted[1]. We may notice as an instance of this that the chief part of the knowledge, foresight, and power of complicated calculation, that are indispensable to the successful conduct of many industries, need only be possessed by the comparatively small number of persons required for the function of management. Finally, the division of employments enables mankind to utilise to the utmost not only the special qualities of human beings, but similarly the superior natural provision of the materials or instruments of production in different countries and districts. Through this division each article consumed by any one may be produced in the place where the labour of producing it is most effective, due allowance being made for the labour and time lost in carrying it to the consumer; and also for certain other disadvantages and risks which I shall presently notice.

The division of employments has different economic effects according as the co-operating workers are organized under one management, or under several different managements. So far as the simultaneous, or nearly simultaneous, combination of a number of different acts is required for the accomplishment of a single result, it is necessary that the labourers should be in one place, and generally expedient that their work should be under the direction of one mind. And even when the operations to be performed on the same material, before it becomes a finished product, are merely successive, there is still a considerable economic advantage in uniting the labourers under one management, and, so far as is possible, either in one building or buildings nearly adjacent. For in the first place the most difficult and valuable kind of labour, that of management, is thus both economized and made more efficient in important respects; e.g. it is easier to adapt the product to the changing needs and tastes of society when all the required changes in production can be carried out under one direction; again, a more exact adjustment is possible of the supply of each kind of labour required, so that every class of producers can be kept in full work; and further, there is less loss of

[1] Economists, however, have rightly drawn attention to the danger that threatens the mental development of the labourer through an excessive sameness in his work.

labour and time in carrying the product in different stages from one set of producers to another, and taking care of it till it is wanted.

For similar reasons, an economy of labour, especially the labour of management, as well as of the utility of buildings and other instruments, tends to be realised, generally speaking, by any considerable (if well adjusted) increase in the scale on which a business is organized. A large business, too, can afford various kinds of expenditure on the whole profitable, which are too costly or too uncertain for smaller concerns: such as the employment of elaborate machinery, or highly skilled and specialised labour, outlay for experiments, for obtaining information[1], &c. The extent of these advantages, however, varies greatly with the nature of the industry; and in estimating it with a view to practical conclusions, we have to compare it with the drawbacks that attend industry on a large scale, especially if the terms of cooperation are adjusted in the manner that is at present most common.

§ 7. We have already noticed that the conditions on which labourers working under one management agree to cooperate may differ materially. In England at the present time the greater part of the labour purchased by employers is sold for a price simply proportioned to its time; so that the labourer has not nearly so strong a motive for exerting energy, skill and care as he would have if he were working on his own account. The consequent diminution in the productiveness of his labour can be but partially prevented by watchful supervision; and of course, where overseers have to be hired, supervision is similarly liable to be less efficient. When payment is made by the "job" or "piece" this detriment is obviated, so far as mere quantity of work is concerned: and it tends to be at least much reduced if, besides a fixed minimum payment for time, the worker receives an addition proportioned to his efficiency or economy, as tested by certain definite results;—as when a shopman is partly remunerated by a payment proportioned to the amount of his sales, or as when a railway company en-

[1] I do not mention the advantage that a large business has in gaining connexion and custom; as it is more a private gain in Distribution than a social gain in Production.

courages thrift in fuel and grease by adding to the wages of its employees a certain proportion of the expenditure saved by them. But in many kinds of work it is difficult to devise a satisfactory test for ascertaining the amount gained by the extra energy and thrift of the workers: and, in particular, "piece-wages[1]" are often found impracticable or inconvenient from the difficulty of dividing the work to be done into sufficiently independent parts. Moreover this mode of payment, though an adequate stimulus to *quantity* of work, is liable to render its *quality* inferior through careless haste—or even deliberate "scamping"—unless the worker's task can be quite definitely marked out and its quality easily tested and estimated[2]. Hence in the industries whose produce tends to be largely, yet somewhat indefinitely, increased or preserved by minute and vigilant attention to details, together with occasional intensity of effort to meet emergencies, the keen interest which one who works on his own account feels in the result is a peculiarly important spring of effective labour; and an organization of industry which tends to multiply this force is proportionally advantageous. In such industries, therefore, it may be economically best—even at a partial sacrifice of the advantages of division of labour—to maintain separate businesses on a scale so small as to enable the employer's supervision to be everywhere effective, or even to render oversight almost unnecessary, the chief labour being that of the employer himself and his family; especially if the industry be one in which expensive machinery either is not profitable or is only occasionally needed and may be conveniently hired. This latter seems to be at present the case in certain kinds of agriculture; and it is with regard to these that the advantage of Production on a small scale has been chiefly urged[3]. The probability of

[1] I have adopted from Mr Lalor, the translator of Roscher's *Political Economy*, this translation of the German "Stücklohn," as a convenient abbreviation of "wages paid for piece-work."

[2] It is also to be observed that the method of piece-work has no tendency to prevent unthrifty use of the employer's instruments and auxiliary materials, so far as these have to be entrusted to the labourers.

[3] Cf. Mill, Book I. c. ix, where the kinds of culture mentioned include "not only the vine and the olive, where a considerable amount of care and "labour must be bestowed on each individual plant, but also roots, leguminous "plants, and those which furnish the materials of manufacture."

superior management on the part of the small employer is of course diminished in proportion as he has to share with any one else the increment of produce obtainable thereby. This diminution is most simply and completely prevented when the cultivator is also the *owner* of the land he cultivates; where this is not the case, a nearly equivalent result might be attained by suitable contracts between the owner and the cultivator[1]; but such contracts have frequently been wanting.

Where organisation on a large scale is clearly most economical, it would seem to be generally the interest both of the employer and of the community to find some plan of remunerating labour which may supply stronger motives to energy and thrift than mere time-wages can furnish. This may be done either by piece-work given out to individuals—which is extensively used in many industries[2]; or by contracting for piece-work in larger lots with groups or "gangs" of labourers—a method sometimes available where ordinary piece-work is impracticable; or, again, by some plan of adding to time-wages a premium or bonus allotted to labourers who have shown efficiency or economy above a certain standard. But, as was before said, none of these methods is universally applicable; nor can they be relied on to prevent a further risk of detriment to the aggregate production of the community, which the customary mode of dividing the earnings of industry between labourers and employers involves;—the danger, namely, of obstinate disagreement as to the price to be given for the labourers' services, resulting in more or less extensive and prolonged stoppages of work. Such stoppages naturally tend to be more frequent and

---

[1] Some writers, who have followed Mill in advocating Peasant Proprietorship, seem to regard it as something more than a means of securing to the cultivator all the fruits of his labour; they speak as if the mere sense of ownership of the land on which a man labours supplied a peculiar stimulus to energetic labour. Without denying the existence of this sentiment, I may point out that it can hardly be included in the "desire of wealth," which Mill and other economists treat as summing up all the springs of labour attributed to men in economic reasonings; and the motive is of too refined a kind to justify us, without more evidence than has yet been given, in assigning to it an important place among the springs of action of average men.

[2] Thus "in the tailoring trades, in shoemaking, and in most of the other "industries engaged in the manufacture of articles for personal wear, payment "by the piece is nearly universal." Howell, *Capital and Labour*, ch. vi.

more prolonged in the present stage of our industrial development, in which combinations of labourers tend to be vigorous and active; and, whether immediately due to 'strikes' of labourers, or to retaliatory 'lock-outs' of masters, inevitably cause much loss of wealth to the community.

With a view of avoiding the evils of these obstinate disagreements—and also of securing adequate stimulus to exertion and thrift—the plan of giving the labourer a share in the profits of the business in which he is employed, has been, in recent times, strongly recommended both by theorists and by practical men; and many experiments have been, and are being, made in this direction, some of which have had a striking amount of success. So far, however, as this method of Participation of Profits appeals to the ordinary economic motive of private interest, it can hardly be as directly effective as the method of piece-work, or even as adequate and properly graded premiums for extra exertion and thrift; since the labourer who is paid by the piece, or by an adequate premium or bonus, depends entirely on his own energy and care for the addition to his wages, whereas when the workmen share profits each individual's gain is mainly determined by the efficiency and economy of others. And this objection becomes stronger, the more the profit of the business depends on the energy and skill of the management; since, so far as this is the case, what the workmen who participate in profits divide may really have been in the main produced by the manager's labour[1]. On the other hand, in industries in which overseeing by the employer or his agent is difficult and liable to be ineffective, the mutual supervision of the workmen, stimulated by the interest that all have in the results of each other's labour, is a valuable advantage: especially if piece-work is inapplicable. And further, it is to be noted that the chief advocates of Profit-sharing do not merely regard it as appealing to the workman's private interest: rather, in their view, one of its chief advantages lies in the habit of working for the common interest—with a sense that private interest is therewith bound up—which the system tends to develope. It is largely

[1] It may be observed, however, that in such cases there is a strong reason for making the manager—and any leading subordinates who share his important work—participate in profits.

through this moral effect that it is held to be preventive of obstinate disagreement about wages. It seems probable, however, that the realization of this last advantage depends largely on the employer's possession of personal qualities that win the confidence of those whom he employs: for a new danger of conflict is introduced by the necessity of agreeing upon a scale of participation. Even where such confidence is established, the participation of all employees in profits must tend to divulge the financial condition of a business; and this loss of secrecy may be a material disadvantage in competition with other businesses, either by inviting rivalry when times are good or by impairing the employer's credit in times of pressure. Hence the plan seems more suitable for adoption in the case of management by joint-stock companies—where the advantages of secrecy have already been given up—than by private employers, unless as philanthropists. Again, the method seems not easily applicable to work of which the profit is remote;—e.g. to large building works that may last some years—since the motive supplied by the prospect of a share is in such cases too weak to give the required stimulus to the minds of average workmen; nor where it is difficult to estimate precisely; nor perhaps where it is very fluctuating, and liable to alternate with heavy loss[1], which the workmen cannot be expected to share.

Still, with all deductions and limitations, the amount of success attained by the system of profit-sharing in certain cases remains a striking and noteworthy fact, and—though it is perhaps doubtful how far we can argue from success in a few cases, in which the stimulus of unfamiliar gain is likely to have been exceptionally effective,—there is certainly ground for hopeful further experiments, especially in businesses whose conditions are peculiarly adapted for it. Such—as we have seen—are businesses which are making an easily estimated and comparatively steady *quantum* of profit, where management is comparatively easy and straightforward, where much may be gained by the industry and thrift which an average man can be induced to exercise by the prospect of a moderate addition to his income,

---

[1] This difficulty may perhaps be satisfactorily met by the establishment of a reserve fund; and by making workmen's shares take partly the form of savings, of which they will reap the benefit in times of adversity.

and where the mutual watchfulness of workmen is likely to be decidedly more effective than supervision from above.

So far I have been chiefly considering the principle of profit-sharing as applied in what is called "Industrial Partnership"; that is, I have here supposed that the capital employed in the business is mainly or entirely owned by a few persons, who retain the whole management of the concern in their hands, and are in fact merely capitalist employers who have agreed to give their employees a share of their profits. Another application of the same principle, differing importantly from that which we have been discussing, is exhibited by what is often called in a special sense Cooperative Production[1]; in which the capital employed in the business is owned (or borrowed) by the labourers employed in it, who accordingly form a joint-stock company with a salaried manager; and divide among themselves whatever profit they make, after paying wages at the market-rate and what is regarded as fair interest on capital. Here the stimulus exercised on the cooperators by the prospect of profits is at its maximum; but this advantage seems inevitably compensated, by a corresponding diminution in the manager's motive to activity,—so far as he is actuated by self-interest,—in comparison with the motives that act on an ordinary capitalist employer. There are the further dangers, (1) that a body of shareholders receiving little more than the ordinary wages of manual labourers may be inclined to the mistaken economy of paying their manager inadequately, and so buying inferior management at a price dear though low; and (2) that labourers having the ultimate control of the business in which they labour may not leave their manager sufficient freedom of deciding large matters that cannot wait, nor render him sufficiently prompt obedience in the ordinary course of the work.

It is to be observed further that neither of these forms of Profit-sharing—not even the last-mentioned—affords complete security against conflicts among the cooperating workers.

[1] It should be observed that the term is sometimes used to include businesses carried on in connexion with the artisans' Cooperative Stores, and accordingly managed by associations of consumers who do not share profits with their employees as such. This system may be economically advantageous, as an extension of the business of Cooperative Stores: but its principle is altogether different from that discussed in the text.

Wages, as I said, are to be paid at the market-rate; but it is precisely *against* the market-rate that strikes take place; and the labourers of any particular class within the concern may feel their community of interests with members of the same class outside, more strongly than they feel their community of interests with the differently paid labourers—including the manager—of their own business[1]; especially when the cooperative business is not sufficiently flourishing to allow them a substantial bonus out of profits. They will no doubt avoid one source of conflict between labour and capital, as their knowledge of their own business will prevent them from having exaggerated views of the profits that capitalist employers are at any time obtaining; and it has been justly urged that in this way the "Cooperators" (in this narrow sense) may render an important service to other labourers and employers. It does not appear, however, that the plan has yet been applied so extensively and successfully as to enable this service to be largely realized: and indeed the whole principle of Participation of Profits is as yet more important on account of what is hoped from it in the future by thoughtful and instructed persons, than in virtue of the results that have been achieved by it up to the present time[2].

I now pass to consider the other mode of arranging the division of employments; according to which labourers or groups of labourers work independently and merely cooperate by exchanging their products. This form of cooperation occurs as an alternative, in certain industries, to the combination under one management of the different parts of a complex process

---

[1] Lord Brassey (*Lectures on the Labour Question*, VI. p. 131) mentions the occurrence of a strike in the Ouseburn Engine Works, which he calls "the most important experiment in cooperative production hitherto attempted in this country."

[2] I defer for the present the discussion of other expedients for settling or preventing disagreements as to wages:—such as Boards of Conciliation, arbitration, and automatic "sliding scales" by which the wages in certain industries are made to vary with the prices of the products of the industries according to a fixed ratio. Such expedients do not aim at improving production except negatively by the prevention of conflict; what they primarily seek to attain is a satisfactory division of the proceeds of industry between employers and employees: it therefore seems more appropriate to discuss them under the head of Distribution. See Book II. ch. x. § 5, and Book III. ch. vii. § 7.

performed on the same material: but it will be evident at a glance that it has a far wider scope. Indeed we may say that cooperation, in this sense, is nothing less than the fundamental principle on which the whole industrial organization of society is based. It is manifest that the aggregation of particular sets of workers in single large establishments, of which we have been speaking, is only rendered possible through the tacit and unconscious consent of the rest of society to employ the services of these workers by purchasing their products. Without exchange, division of employment could not be conveniently carried very far, so long as the present system of private ownership was maintained unaltered: through exchange it might easily embrace the whole inhabited globe in one vast scheme of cooperation: and in fact its development only tends to stop at the point at which its advantages are outweighed by the drawbacks incident to production for distant consumers. The most obvious of these drawbacks lies in the additional labour and time spent in conveyance and communication between producer and consumer; but we have also to take into account the increased difficulty of adjusting supply to demand, owing to the difficulty that the producer has in obtaining full information as to the consumers' needs; which entails normally an increased expenditure of time and labour in keeping finished products in warehouses and shops. In some few cases an absolute waste of such products has resulted from a great oversupply of a particular ware; the demand for which has been miscalculated. More frequently this kind of miscalculation has caused wares to be left in the hands of producers or traders for an inordinate length of time; has rendered expensive machinery and acquired skill temporarily or even permanently useless; and has inflicted on the industries thus disorganized, and others to whom the effect spreads from them, the more indefinite evils of general depression of energy and enterprise. These drawbacks and dangers, however, are in some cases at least not found sufficient to neutralize the advantages of producing even at the distance of a great semicircle of the earth's surface from the consumer.

§ 8. The wonderful development and spontaneous organization of industries, which we have just been contemplating,

CHAP. IV.] IN PRODUCTION. 115

would not have taken place without a corresponding and simultaneous development in two other fundamentally important aids to the efficiency of labour, which we must now expressly notice. We may take first the one of which we have already had occasion to speak; the growth of man's knowledge of the external world, and also of his ingenuity in applying that knowledge, which, when combined, constitute what we call the "Progress of Invention." So long as invention was comparatively undeveloped, the extent of profitable cooperation, within the range of each particular industry, was closely limited: since so long as the processes of production are simple and rude, the economic advantages of breaking them up into parts are comparatively soon exhausted: it is not till Invention has rendered these processes elaborate and complicated that the brilliant triumphs of "Division of Labour" can be won. On the other hand, as cooperation through exchange is developed, and the general demand for the product of any particular industry extended, the field of the economic application of inventions is correspondingly increased: it may not be possible to use costly machinery, however ingeniously adapted to its work, unless the demand for its products is sufficient to keep it in constant employment. Division of Labour, again, supplies more favourable conditions for Invention, since when the labourer's attention is concentrated on a few acts, he is more likely to discover improvements in the mode of performing them[1]; while at the same time his increased skill renders him more qualified to profit by delicate and elaborate inventions.

In considering Invention as a source of increased production, we must extend the meaning of the term to include all expedients for saving labour or augmenting its utility; whether introduced in particular departments of industries, or in the great social organization of industries through exchange; and whether introduced with full deliberation by single individuals, or through the half spontaneous and unconscious concurrence

---

[1] It should be observed that the most striking and (so to say) *revolutionary* improvements in industry have often been made by persons of inventive genius not employed in the industry. But a number of smaller improvements, individually less noticeable but important in the aggregate, are continually suggested by workmen.

8—2

of many. In this sense the transition, in an early stage of social development, from barter to money may be spoken of as an invention of the greatest importance; and similarly any later improvements in the machinery of exchange, such as the substitution of a good paper currency for gold and the development of a good system of banking, or even the adoption of the decimal system of measurement. So again, we might regard the system of Profit-sharing—if it ever should realize the hopes of its most sanguine promoters—as an invention of first-class social utility; and we may even now so regard the remarkable economy of labour in the retail trade effected by the artisans' Cooperative Stores in Great Britain; which, chiefly by an effective combination of the advantages of ready money payments with the advantages—gradually gained—of organization of business on a large scale, have within 25 years accumulated some £10,000,000 of capital owned by over 750,000 members. It should be observed, too, that many of the most useful improvements at a particular time and place in production are obtained by the application of inventions already known, but hitherto neglected from ignorance, inertness or some other cause. The economic history of all countries affords abundant instances of this; in recent times the introduction or development of systems of canals and railways in different countries are particularly impressive examples.

There are important economic differences between different kinds of Invention. In the first place what is invented may be either a new instrument or merely a new process. In some cases a great saving of labour may be effected by a new application of natural forces to produce a desired result, without the intervention of any new tools. The application of the sun and air in bleaching, and of fire in clearing land for cultivation, exemplify this first kind of Invention. But it mostly happens that the new process discovered requires also new instruments or auxiliary materials which are themselves products of labour. In this latter case it is important to notice that the use of a more efficient instrument would not always involve a gain in the efficiency of labour on the whole: since the better instrument may require more labour to make and keep in repair, and it is possible that this extra labour might be more productive if applied in some other way. Thus an invention *technically* successful may fail *economically*.

But further, even when Invention has shown the way to a manifest saving of labour by the adoption of a new process, either with or without new instruments, it may still be impossible or inexpedient for the labourers to adopt it. For the new process may involve an increased delay in producing the desired result; and the labourers—or those who purchase their labour—may be unable or unwilling to afford this delay. Or again, the new instruments may require other instruments or materials to make them at all, or to make them economically; and they may not be able to procure these. In either case we should ordinarily describe the obstacle by saying that the Invention was not carried into effect for want of Capital. We are thus led to what economists have commonly held to be the most important source of increase in the efficiency of labour; viz., the accumulation of Capital. Unfortunately, this cardinal term is used variously and often ambiguously by different writers; and, as we shall see, it has to be used differently for the purposes of different economic enquiries. Hence it seems desirable, before we proceed further, to obtain a clear view of the different conceptions which the term represents, and of their mutual relations.

CHAPTER V.

CAPITAL.

§ 1. THE terms Value and Wealth, which we have in previous chapters attempted to define, are in the fullest sense *common* terms: that is, they enter habitually into the ordinary thought and speech of all civilised men. "Capital" on the other hand is, when the scientific economist first begins to deal with it, already a semi-technical term; being habitually used not by men generally in their ordinary thought, but by men of business and others when discussing industrial matters. The meaning, however, that it has thus acquired is not that which is most convenient for the purposes of the present investigation. For the man of business means by "Capital" wealth employed so as to bring its possessor a surplus, which we may call in a wide sense "profit[1]". But it is obvious that wealth may yield a surplus to the individual owning it, even when, from the point of view of the community, it is wasted without return—as (e.g.) the money that a usurer lends to a spendthrift. Such money is properly regarded as a portion of the aggregate capital of individual members of the community, when—in the Theory of Distribution—we consider the return to capital as determined by supply and demand[2]; but it is clearly not a part of the wealth that aids in increasing the annual produce of labour; it is not therefore "capital" in the sense appropriate to the Theory of Production. Capital in the *productional* sense must, I conceive, be wealth employed to bring a surplus or profit not

---

[1] It is convenient here to use the term "profit" in a wide sense, so as to include the "interest" of money lent, as one species of profit. See next chap. page 154.

[2] Cf. ch. VI. § 3 of the following Book.

to the individual owner only, but to the industrial community of which he is a member: and this—which we may distinguish as 'social' capital—is what Political Economists generally, from Adam Smith downward, have been chiefly concerned to define and discuss. But the distinction between social capital and individuals' capital does not appear to me to have been worked out with sufficient thoroughness, or applied consistently to all the questions that emerge when we try to form an exact notion of Capital.

To attain this result, let us begin by asking what is exactly meant from the point of view of the individual capitalist, by "wealth employed to bring a profit." It does not mean that the wealth is necessarily in the form of instruments or materials for making new wealth, or in the form of food, clothing, &c., for the labourers who are using the instruments: for, as we have seen, it does not matter to the individual whether his wealth is used productively or unproductively, so long as he gets his profit. It merely means that the individual is using his wealth—either personally, or by lending it to others—in such a way that he continually finds himself possessed of the equivalent of what was originally devoted to such use, together with some additional wealth; this additional wealth being what is called profit. Or, more precisely, we should say that the *hope* of finding himself possessed of this profit is his motive for thus using his wealth; since we should agree that capital does not lose its essential characteristics by becoming actually profitless. We have, therefore, first to ascertain what portion of a man's wealth is being employed with the aim of making its owner continually richer; and then to distinguish the capital from the profit. In the case of wealth that has been lent to some one else, there is of course no difficulty; as the sum which the debtor pays for the use of the wealth is clearly profit, and the sum which he is bound to replace clearly capital. And the line drawn in this case can be ideally extended to include the case where the wealth has been spent in purchasing a perpetual annuity; for though here there is no one under legal obligation to pay at any fixed time an equivalent for the principal, still actually the annuity can be at any time sold at its market value, so that we may regard this possible price as the capital. In this case, however, the price at any time may be less or more than the sum originally spent; and therefore in calculating profit we have to subtract from or add to the sums annually received a sum sufficient to compensate for the difference. A rather more difficult question arises when we consider the wealth of a man employed in business. A good deal of it is, of course, clearly capital. "A manufacturer, for "example, has one part of his capital in the form of buildings, "fitted and destined for carrying on his branch of manufacture. "Another part he has in the form of machinery. A third "consists, if he be a spinner, of raw cotton, flax or wool; if a "weaver, of flaxen, woollen, silk or cotton thread, and the like; "according to the nature of the manufacture[1]." But it is not quite so clear how we are to regard the money that he keeps uninvested, or the finished goods that he has in his warehouses; for though he will partly employ the former, and the proceeds of the latter, in paying his workpeople, replenishing his stock of materials, repairing or replacing his buildings or machinery, he may also employ part in supplying luxuries to himself and his family. Mill's view is that this question must be answered by considering what the manufacturer *intends* to do with his money, and with the proceeds of his goods when he has sold them. "The distinction between capital and not capital lies in "the mind of the capitalist—in his will to employ them for one "purpose rather than another." I agree that we should take the intention of the owner of wealth, rather than the consequences of his acts, to determine whether that wealth is or is not capital; but it is, I think, more according to analogy to regard the wealth as becoming capital, not when the owner's intention is formed, but when it is executed; that is, not when the wealth is "destined" for profitable employment, but when it is actually used for this purpose. On this principle whatever part of the money that the capitalist keeps uninvested is held to be required for current use in his business, should be regarded as capital. It may not be always possible to determine with certainty how much this is; the capitalist may not know exactly what money he keeps for business purposes and what for private consump-

---

[1] J. S. Mill, *Political Economy*, I. ch. IV. § 1.

tion; and if he does not know, it is not easy for any one else to decide. But for purposes of general reasoning we may ignore this slight margin of uncertainty and suppose the line between the two portions clearly drawn—as it would be by a careful man of business—and regard the money that is kept for current use in business as a part of the owner's capital. His stock of finished goods, again, so long as it remains unsold, is capital; but capital, if I may so say, pregnant with profit; the greater part of its value is of course merely an equivalent for the value of the materials spent in producing the goods, the wear and tear of the instruments used, the wages of the labourers employed, and other incidental expenses of production; but, so long as the industry is prospering, there is always a surplus which should be viewed as *potential* profit, to become actual when the goods are sold.

§ 2. It follows of course that, from the individual's point of view, we must reject as too restricted the definition of capital adopted by Ricardo, James Mill, and others, which states it to consist of "the food and other articles consumed by the "labourers, the raw material on which they operate, and the "instruments of all sorts which are employed in aiding their "labours[1]"; thus excluding the finished products of the manufacturers of gold-lace, champagne, velvet, &c. For, obviously, such finished goods are a form in which some part of the wealth employed for a profit by manufacturers, and an important part of the wealth so employed by traders, must always exist.

Further, from the same point of view the definition of capital would seem clearly to include *land* as being, to a great extent, wealth employed so as to obtain profit for the individual owner or tenant; hence it is rather surprising that English economists generally agree in making an unqualified separation between land and capital[2]. Partly, perhaps, they may have been unconsciously influenced by the older "mercantilist" view of capital (still lingering in common thought and discourse), which conceived it by preference as money: since land is the one kind of

---

[1] James Mill, *Elements of Political Economy*, ch. i.; cp. Ricardo, ch. v.

[2] In ch. vii. of the following Book I shall examine the grounds for this distinction between Capital and Land in the Theory of Distribution. Here I will only point out that in considering the various industries in which land is

wealth which—even when the Mercantile System was in fullest sway—was always broadly distinguished from Money. The mode, however, in which, for the most part, they have formally tried to distinguish capital from land, is by introducing a new characteristic into the definition of capital; that namely of being the "saved produce of past labour." But the distinction can hardly be thus justified from the individual's point of view, when it has once been admitted that the definitions of 'in-'dividual's' and 'social' capital do not coincide; for there is much other capital that has not been created by the labour or the saving of its possessor, and it cannot matter to him whether or not others have laboured or saved to produce it.

Even when we turn to regard capital from the point of view of the community, if we define it merely as wealth employed productively—i.e. in adding utility to matter—we must of course include land as the great primary instrument and source of materials for human industry. But this definition is not the one most suitable for the purposes of the present discussion. If we are to consider capital as an aid in the application of man's labour to his material environment; we clearly cannot define the term so as to include this environment itself, in its unlaboured condition; and therefore must restrict it to such utilities—whether attached to land or otherwise—as result from the modification of the environment by human labour[1]. Among these utilities we must certainly include in capital from the social no less than from the individual's point of view those embodied in the finished products of which I before spoke. For we have seen reason to extend the term Production

employed, it would often be equally unusual and inconvenient not to be able to speak of the producers as having a certain portion of their capital in the form of land. Take, for instance, the case of a railway company; it is manifest that an important part of the real wealth represented by the nominal capital of the company consists of the land on which the lines run.

[1] Accordingly the continual adaptation of the earth to human uses, which in the preceding chapter has been stated as one of the conditions of increasing production, is to be regarded as an accumulation of capital.

In accepting the proposition that capital is the result of labour, I must guard myself from being supposed to accept implicitly the doctrine that the value of capital or of other wealth is *due* solely to labour. As we shall hereafter see, there are cases when the labour employed is insignificant compared to the value of its product.

to the whole process of conveying wealth into the hands of the consumer; and it is evident that if champagne and velvet are to form part of the produce that is annually consumed, the whole aggregate of wealth employed in the process of 'pro- 'ducing' it must always include a certain amount of champagne and velvet ready for sale, in the hands of wine-growers, manufacturers, merchants and retail traders.

§ 3. In the last paragraph I applied the term 'capital' to the utilities resulting from labour embodied in what are commonly called "products" rather than to these "products" themselves. And this seems to me the most proper use of the term, though custom and convenience render it undesirable to adhere to it strictly; since if we define capital so as to exclude land, in its unlaboured condition, consistency requires us equally to exclude the *matter* of all movable wealth—as distinct from the new relations of that matter due to human volition. We must now observe that the results of past labour—such as the labour of a consulting chemist whose advice is taken on the processes of a manufacture,—may be as permanently productive as the labour of manual workers; though we could hardly say that the results of the chemist's work were "embodied" in the plant of the manufacture[1]. Still less should we say this of the labour of the lawyer who defends a railway project before a Parliamentary Committee, or of the 'promoters' who float the shares of a new company; yet if the employment of this labour is either absolutely indispensable, or is the most economical mode of starting the new business, the mere immateriality of its results seems an irrelevant reason for establishing a distinction between it and the labour spent in the physical construction of the instruments used in the business. When we ask what the shareholders have got for the money paid up, the complete answer is not given by enumerating the buildings and instruments; we must add that—through the labours of lawyers, promoters &c.—they have got a working concern; and if the concern is a profitable one, we have just as much ground

[1] It is not easy to draw a clear line between the results of labour that are, and those that are not, "embodied" in matter; and I have not thought it worth while to complicate the discussion by trying to draw it exactly, since the drift of my argument is that it is manifestly unimportant.

for including the immaterial part of its construction in the capital of the community, as we have in the case of the material part.

This leads me to consider a source of profit, noticed in a preceding chapter, which exhibits the immaterial results of labour and expenditure as still more clearly separate from any material capital than in the cases just discussed. I mean the saleable article, called "goodwill" or "business connexion." Let us take for example, the business of publishing a newspaper. The sale of a newspaper when it first starts is ordinarily so limited that its proceeds do not repay the current expenses of production; so that the business has to be carried on for some time at a loss. Hence, in order that the undertaking should be on the whole a profitable one, it is necessary that the proceeds of the sale should ultimately be sufficient to pay profit, not only on the material capital actually employed in production, but upon all the wealth and labour that has been spent without return in the earlier years of the undertaking. The business may be regarded as having capital sunk in it, which would be recovered in its price, if it came to be sold; though it is actually represented merely by a certain habit of purchasing the newspaper that exists in the community at large. This potential price is properly reckoned as part of the wealth and capital of the individual owning the business; and so far as the establishment of such habits of purchasing are useful to the community,—but only so far—we may also regard them as a part of 'social capital.'

A striking example of the definite value of this source of profit is furnished by the business of banking. A banker's profit is largely derived from the tacit consent of the community to use his obligations to pay money on demand as a medium of exchange, equivalent to actual coin. In ordinary times, until a run on the bank occurs, these obligations are transferred from one customer to another, without payment being exacted. Hence, though in estimating the banker's wealth these obligations would be reckoned on the negative side, still, so long as he is not required to meet them, he is able to take as profit the whole or part[1] of the interest which he

---

[1] Part only, if he has to pay interest on the money that he owes.

receives on the wealth, elsewhere invested, by which he would meet his obligations if required. Thus he may be only just solvent, and yet be, so long as his credit lasts, a wealthy man. This fact, I conceive, is what is meant by saying that the credit of such a bank is a part of its capital; and the expression seems to me legitimate, provided we are careful to point out that such capital is of fragile nature, liable to sudden destruction in case of a panic. And, as we saw, there are strong reasons for regarding bankers' credit generally as an addition to the resources of the country; since the country gains by means of it a medium of exchange, which it costs very little to produce and maintain, and which at the same time is for some purposes even more useful than coin[1].

§ 4. We thus see that the results of labour may persist in various forms—material and immaterial—which we may call "investments" of capital: and in following the normal process of any manufacture, we can observe how at each stage of the process a considerable portion of the capital employed changes its form, passing from raw material to half-finished products, then becoming goods finished and ready for sale, then through sale turning into money and so into raw material again. The question is thus suggested whether the productive skill that results from wealth laid out in education, and is an indispensable factor in the production of new wealth, is to be classed among the forms in which capital may exist. I have already pointed out that such skill, not being transferable, lacks one of the characteristics that common usage regards as essential to wealth. Still, it is evident that the wealth spent in producing such skill may be as profitably employed, both for the individual and for the community, as if it were invested in inanimate instruments; and if this outlay has been incurred with a view to gain, I think we should regard it as a form of investment of capital; though it will be well to denote its results by some

[1] It may be urged that the credit that is the immaterial source of this useful commodity is not the result of labour: but a man cannot get his obligations currently accepted as a medium of exchange, unless he goes into banking as a business; and a banking business cannot be created at one stroke, or unless the place and time for starting it be skilfully selected, nor can it be maintained without careful management—not to speak of the labour of subordinates.

such term as 'personal capital,' to express their peculiar characteristic of non-transferability.

Similarly we might extend the term Capital to include all the wealth consumed from infancy upwards, by productive workers, so far as it has been serviceable in developing or maintaining productive qualities—physical strength as well as skill: and we might regard the productive vigour that results from this consumption as a form in which social capital is actually existing. And if we define capital, from a social point of view, merely as wealth employed so as continually to reproduce itself with a (social) profit, we ought in consistency to take this view. I think however that for the purposes of the Theory of Production we usually require a more restricted conception of capital: we have to consider it as a joint factor with labour in social production, by the aid of which the labourers of the community are enabled to produce more than they would otherwise do; and in order to keep this view of it clear, we have to maintain the distinction between capital and labourers, just as we have to maintain the distinction between capital and land—or man's material environment—in its unlaboured condition. For this purpose therefore, we must regard as social Capital not *all* the results of labour that are employed so as to produce a social profit; but only such results as would not exist in their present form, or would not be used in their present manner, except as a means to this end. On this view it is only so far as the labourer's consumption is distinctly designed to increase his efficiency, that it can properly be regarded as an investment of capital. No doubt, if an individual adopts a more expensive diet in order that he may be enabled to work harder without injury to health, the increase in his expenditure thus caused is for all economic purposes similar to outlay on fuel or other auxiliary materials in a manufacture. Similarly if statesmen or philanthropists are considering the desirability of measures tending to increase the labourers' share of food, clothing, house-room, &c., they may fairly recommend this outlay as having the essential characteristics of an investment of capital for the community, so far as it may be reasonably expected to lead to more vigorous and effective labour. But, generally speaking, we must, I think, regard the consumption of produce, for the preservation or enjoyment of life, as the final end of the series of changes that make up the process of production; and accordingly must distinguish it broadly from consumption that would not be incurred, except as a means to further production; treating as a gift of nature any undesigned gain in productive efficiency that may result from it[1].

It is not of course denied that the products consumed by the labourers will, generally speaking, have previously formed part of the capital of individual capitalists. But, obviously, they can no longer form part of the employer's capital after he has exchanged them for the results of the labourer's work, whatever that may be; for these results—in the form of extracted products, half-finished or finished goods, &c.—have become the new form of that part of his capital which, before the exchange, was in the form of money or commodities destined for wages[2]. Even if the labourers are fed at the capitalist's own table the case is not substantially altered; only the moment at which the food ceases to be employer's capital is deferred until the time at which it is actually eaten.

§ 5. Here I may observe that there is something misleading in the manner in which economists have spoken of capital as being "accumulated," and at the same time have put forward, as the prominent and typical form of capital, the food, clothing, and other commodities which the labourer consumes. For though, as we have seen, there must always be a certain stock of such commodities, finished but undistributed, which forms a part of the capital of manufacturers and traders; still the accumulation of capital, that industrial progress brings with it, does not, to any important extent, consist in an increase of this stock. Indeed, one of the economic advantages which the improvement of the machinery for conveyance brings with it,

[1] It must be admitted that social capital as above defined is something that we cannot measure exactly. But it is in any case impossible to estimate otherwise than very roughly the amount of aid that the community derives from the results of previous labour.

[2] Some writers seem to me to fall into the serious confusion of regarding *both* the real wages of the labourer *and* the results of his labour for which these wages are exchanged, as being *at the same time* parts of the capital of his employer.

lies in the diminution of the amount of these stocks which it becomes necessary to keep. What is really accumulated is mainly the results of labour in the form of what we may call generally instruments to make labour more efficient—including under the notion of instruments all buildings used in production, and all improvements of land.

It may assist to make this clearer if we conceive the community to be organized on a socialistic basis, its industry and the actual distribution of its commodities remaining in other respects unaltered: that is, if we suppose the instruments and materials of production to be owned by a government, which from time to time distributes the finished goods among the citizens, giving to the rich the luxuries that they now enjoy, on account of their superior deserts. Such a community, if governed with wisdom, and with due regard for the interest of posterity, would continue the accumulation of capital that is at present going on; that is, it would allot a certain portion of its produce to labourers employed in improving land, constructing railways, and other work yielding no *immediate* return of consumers' wealth. But it would be obviously forced and inappropriate to say that the produce so allotted was "saved" or "accumulated" and to call it therefore capital. What would really be accumulated, would be the railways, the machines, the additional productiveness of the land, &c.; or, to put it generally, the intermediate results of labour employed for remote ends, so that a possible increase in the immediate produce of consumable commodities is sacrificed for a greater increase in the ultimate produce. That the increase must ultimately be greater, unless the capital is wasted, is of course implied in the conception of capital as auxiliary to labour.

No doubt, in our actual individualistic society, this accumulation of instruments is brought about chiefly by the action of individual capitalists; who abstain from consuming the whole of their profits, in order to get more profit hereafter for themselves and their heirs. Hence it is a legitimate fiction to regard them as taking a part of their share in the food, clothing, &c., that constitute the real wages of their labourers; and to consider this accordingly as the primary form in which capital always has existed although the form in which most of it ultimately exists is, as we have seen, that of instruments. But we must take care not to imply that all or even a large part of capital could exist simultaneously in this form; or that it would be no loss to the community if the capital in the form of instruments were destroyed, provided it were supplied—say from abroad—with an equal amount of capital in the form of the current means of sustenance[1].

And we must bear in mind that the applicability of this conception of the primary form of capital depends not on the necessary conditions of the Production of wealth, but upon the actual conditions of its Distribution. The essential point in the formation of capital is the employment of labour for remote ends, not the saving of sustenance in order that it may be employed as the real wages of hired labourers; and a good deal of the actual capital of any civilized community, while it is the result of labour diverted from the supply of immediate needs, has not been produced by labour hired with a view to profit. At the same time it should be clearly recognized that in the existing economic condition of society the employment of labour in making instruments is principally due to the voluntary action of persons who, having the alternatives of "saving" and 'spending[2]" presented to them, prefer the former; and a fundamentally important part of the process initiated by their "saving" consists in the transfer of food, clothing, &c., from the stocks of traders to labourers, in return for the transfer to their employers of the results of their labour.

§ 6. So far, in speaking of Capital I have only had in view what in a previous chapter I have called 'producers' 'wealth': that is I have implicitly followed Adam Smith[3] in distinguishing from capital that portion of the "general stock "of any society" which is "reserved for immediate consumption,

---

[1] No doubt the instruments could all be made over again in time, provided the labourers could be supported while making them; but obviously their labour would be of greatly inferior efficiency during the period that would elapse until the instruments were made: hence we must regard the form "instruments"— in the extended sense before mentioned—as that in which the greatest part of capital must necessarily exist, if capital is duly to fulfil the function of increasing the efficiency of labour.

[2] That is, spending in luxuries for themselves or their families.

[3] *Wealth of Nations*, Bk. II. ch. i.

"but not yet entirely consumed", on the ground that it "does not afford a revenue or profit." The distinction is obvious, and should be continually kept in view; but, reflection will, I think, show that it is less fundamental than is commonly supposed.

This will be most easily seen if we begin by considering the class of products which we have already distinguished as "durable "consumers' wealth"—houses, furniture. Such things, says Adam Smith, may yield a revenue to their owner, if they are let or hired out, and so " serve the function of a capital to him " but they cannot yield any revenue to the community; they are gradually consumed without replacement, whereas the capital employed in production, if prudently invested, is continually replacing itself with a profit. But it will appear I think, on closer examination, that the notion of 'wealth replacing itself 'with a profit' is ambiguous, and that so far as it is applicable to (at least[1]) a large part of the capital employed in industry, it is no less applicable to the durable consumers' wealth that I am now considering. For at least a large part of the wealth employed in Production—viz. all instruments and auxiliary materials employed in the production of luxuries, and even products consumed by labourers if engaged in producing luxuries—can only be said to "replace itself with a profit" in the sense that the consumable utilities which it is the means of producing have a higher social value than the wealth destroyed in producing them—so that a portion of the price of the produce is sufficient to compensate for the consumption of materials and the deterioration and depreciation of instruments. And in this sense the wealth invested in a house may with equal truth be said to replace itself with a profit; for if we value the annual use of a house at its market-price, we shall find—if the house has been economically purchased—that after subtracting ordinary interest on its original price a sufficient quantum of value will remain to compensate for its deterioration.

---

[1] The statement applies to capital generally, according to the view that I have taken of it in the preceding section: but even if the necessaries consumed by labourers, and the productive qualities of the labourers thereby sustained, are included as part of the capital of the community, the statement in the text remains true.

In short the essential characteristic of the aid that capital in the form of instruments gives to labour is that by interposing an interval of time between the application of labour (i.e. of the labour spent in making the instrument) and the enjoyment of its result, the utility produced is ultimately greater than it would have been if the labour had been spent in some manner yielding more rapid returns: and this characteristic is no less present in the case where a certain kind of utility,—as that of shelter, &c.,—can only be obtained by making a durable article that will be useful for many years[1]. And the same may be said of all durable products from which we expect to derive continued or repeated utilities in the future; the thing itself in relation to its future utilities has the essential characteristics of Capital. The difference between the case of wealth that is employed and valued as a means of obtaining other *wealth*, and wealth from which we only expect future *utility*, and wealth that is only valued in view of produce to be hereafter enjoyed, is, as I have said, of great importance: we may perhaps represent it by designating the former as "producers' capital" and the latter as "consumers' capital." But in taking this distinction we must bear in mind that many most important instruments that are "producers' capital" from the individual's point of view are at least partly "consumers' capital" from the point of view of the community;—such as railways and steamships so far as they carry tourists, and merely furnish the immaterial commodity of a desired change of place.

But further; even the consumers' stocks of food, fuel and other things consumed in a single use, have in a certain sense,

[1] So far as the alternatives of making a more or less durable house are presented, the question whether it will be economically advantageous to spend the extra labour required for the more durable building is clearly similar to the question that arises (as we have already observed) in considering whether an instrument that is undeniably useful is also profitable; we have to consider in either case whether the additional utility is worth purchasing at the price of the additional labour, taking into account the time that must elapse between the application of the labour and the consumption of the utility. No doubt up to a certain point these alternatives are not presented; there is an irreducible minimum of durability which a house must possess, in order that the utilities derived from it may be obtained at all: but a similar irreducible minimum is found in the case of producers' wealth—we cannot have corn at all without some kind of plough.

so far as their amount is economically regulated, the essential characteristics of capital. Such commodities do not, indeed, usually increase in utility by being kept, but are rather liable to deterioration : still, so far as they are prudently kept they save the labour of multiplied purchases and journeys which would otherwise be necessary. The keeping of such stocks therefore is as essentially a labour-saving expedient for the individual as the use of an instrument in production. The stocks in the hands of manufacturers and traders fulfil a similar function for the community; the social advantage of having more or less of such stocks is to be measured by the extent to which their existence either saves the labour of sale and conveyance, or increases the utility of the commodity by equalizing its consumption, or renders the labour of manufacture more productive by enabling it to be more continuous and uniform, and organised on a larger scale, than would otherwise be the case[1]. And as we saw, it is only so far as they are thus useful that the community gains from the "accumulation" of such products.

It would seem then that the term 'capital,' in its scientific application, is most appropriately used, to express an aspect which all accumulated wealth presents—so far as it is produced and used with due regard to economy[2]—up to the very moment of consumption: as being, namely, the intermediate results of labour employed for future utilities, which in some way or other are greater in proportion to the labour required for enjoying them, through the prolongation of the interval between the labour and the enjoyment.

§ 7   Hence, when it is said that, in a given society at a given time, an invention tending admittedly to render labour more productive cannot be carried into effect for want of capital, the essential fact implied, from a social point of view, is that the community cannot or will not spare the required labour

[1] Here too there is an irreducible minimum. Corn and other agricultural products must be kept between one harvest and another, in order that they may be continuously consumed: and in other cases we should often have to go without things altogether, if there were no stocks.

[2] It should be admitted that this aspect is actually presented, for the most part, in a less degree by Consumers' capital than it is by Producers' capital; inasmuch as the former is commonly managed with a less strict regard to economy. This difference, however, is by no means universally to be found.

from work more immediately—though less ultimately—productive. In our existing societies, however, the future gain of labour thus spared for the making of new capital does not usually accrue to the labourers personally; but to others who purchase the results of his labour with money which might have been employed in purchasing an equivalent amount of directly consumable commodities; and are therefore said to "save" whatever addition is thus made to the real capital of the community.

Though, as we saw in the preceding chapter, the progress of Invention—including the developments of the great system of cooperation through exchange—does not *necessarily* increase the need of capital, it has, on the whole tended continuously and decidedly in this direction: the increase in the amount of consumable commodities obtainable by a given amount of civilized labour has been attended by a continual increase in the amount of real capital required to furnish these commodities to the consumer. And since, further, one feature of this progress has consisted in the organization of businesses—on the whole, though with important exceptions—on a continually increasing scale, the capital has been required in continually larger masses under single management. This aggregation of capital has been partly brought about by the successful industry of capitalist employers, who have extended their businesses by means of their own increasing wealth: but to a large extent the new capital has resulted from the savings of persons who either have not been employers of capital to any extent or have been unable to employ it profitably in their own businesses. In this case the capital has been chiefly collected either (1) by borrowing—largely through the medium of banks —or (2) by the union of several small portions of capital in joint-ownership, mainly on the basis of limited liability. In both these ways vast masses of capital have been placed in the hands of persons better able than their owners to employ them productively, and industrial enterprise has been greatly promoted; but with the serious drawback that the employers of other people's capital have less motive for using it skilfully and carefully than they would have if they owned it. This drawback is specially important in the case of joint-stock companies; as persons who form these are, for the most part, industrial experts obtaining capital from non-experts; whereas producers who have obtained loans or discounts from banks—while substantially they may be regarded as employing capital belonging to the depositors and note-holders who are the creditors of the banks—yet do this through the intervention of persons professionally concerned to refuse reckless or untrustworthy borrowers. Accordingly, the loss of capital through reckless or unskilful management on the part of joint-stock companies tends to be considerable;—not to speak of the opportunities that they have afforded for the deliberately fraudulent acquisition of wealth under the pretext of productive enterprise. Still, however the balance of disadvantages and advantages may lie as regards businesses of smaller dimensions, at any rate the capital required for the great enterprises of modern industry—such as canals and railways, water-works and gas-works, and the modern developments of banking—could hardly have been brought together except by some form of joint-ownership, and consequently delegated management; whether the joint-ownership be that of a voluntary association of individuals, or of the compulsory association which we call the state.

CHAPTER VI.

THE LAWS OF PRODUCTION.

§ 1. IN Chapter IV. we were occupied in surveying the causes of variation in the productiveness of labour in different ages and countries. We first distinguished and briefly analysed the conditions of man's material environment that are favourable or adverse to production; and noted the differences—whether original or superinduced by human labour—in the adaptation to human uses of the portions of land inhabited by different communities, and their bordering or intersecting rivers and seas. We then passed to consider the causes of variation in the quantity and quality of labour performed, in proportion to the number of the population supported by it. We observed the important modifications in both quantity and quality due (1) to the varying physical conditions of the labourer's existence, and (2) to the varying strength of his motives for work. We analysed the complexity of the elementary impulses that constitute the 'desire of wealth' for self and family which is undoubtedly the mainspring of industry in our actual societies; and noted the manifold and complicated ways in which the strength of this resultant impulse tends to be modified by the degree of civilisation, the political structure, the moral state, the customs and prevalent opinions of any community considered as a whole, or again by the moral and social influences predominant in special classes; and especially by the varying extent and manner in which the industrial organisation maintains the correspondence of reward to exertion. We then examined this industrial organisation in another aspect, analysing the advantage obtained by the combination of labour,—that is, mainly by the Division of Employments,—and noting the attendant drawbacks. We further observed the striking variations in the efficiency of labour that are due to intellectual conditions; partly to differences in the average technical skill of the individuals actually working; still more to differences in the development of the industrial arts—through Invention—in the community as a whole. Finally we have dwelt on the importance of Capital; considered either in the concrete as (mainly) an already accumulated stock of instruments auxiliary to labour, or more abstractly as the power of directing labour to the attainment of greater but remoter utilities, through the control over the produce of labour possessed by the owners of accumulated wealth.

We have now to consider how far we can establish important general propositions as to the extent to which these different causes operate. It is to such propositions that I have desired to restrict the term "Laws of Production." In a wider sense the mere statement of a cause of the greater or less productiveness of labour might be called the statement of a Law of Production; but the description would sound somewhat ambitious, and economists who have propounded such 'laws' have certainly been understood to imply by the term some definite knowledge as to the *quantity* of effect to be attributed to one or more of the different causes determining production. It should be observed, however, that the propositions thus denoted belong to two very different classes; they may be (1) abstract and hypothetical, or (2) concrete and positive. That is, they may either state (1) the amount of effect that any cause, supposed to be given in quantity as well as quality, would produce under certain supposed conditions, or *tends* to produce under actual conditions so far as it is not counteracted or modified by the operation of other causes; or they may state (2) to what extent any particular cause has been found, or may be expected, to operate either in human communities generally or in the modern civilised societies with which we are primarily concerned. The importance of maintaining the essential difference between these two species of laws will appear in the course of this chapter.

§ 2. Before, however, we proceed to examine in detail the chief laws (of either kind) that have been propounded by economists, it is necessary to recall those limitations to the possibility of exactly measuring the productiveness of labour, which our previous discussions on the measure of value and wealth have led us to notice. We saw that so far as the commodities which are consumed in different communities—or in the same community at different times—were different in kind, a comparison between the different amounts of produce in the two cases respectively must necessarily reduce itself to a rough balancing of utilities; and that even if the commodities were similar in kind, but were produced under such different conditions (of demand, supply, &c.) in the two terms of the comparison as to vary materially in relative value, this variation introduced an irremediable element of inexactness into any quantitative comparison of the two aggregates of wealth thus variously composed.

These inexactnesses are not generally of material importance when we are considering changes in the amount produced by any community at short intervals of time, or comparing neighbouring countries similar in industrial and climatic conditions; but they may easily become very considerable when we are trying to deal with secular variations, or to include remote countries in some wide generalisation.

We saw further that, even if our result were free from this source of inexactness, it would still have no real significance, as an answer to the question which prompts us to make the comparison, if there were any marked difference in the primary needs of the different sets of human beings whose wealth we are comparing. And when we consider the needs of labourers as such we see that these needs vary with the labour required of them: and hence that we may measure their productive efficiency either by the total value of the commodities produced or by the excess of this over the value of what they consume so far as this consumption contributes to efficiency[1].

---

[1] As we have already had occasion to observe, no sharp line can be drawn between necessary and superfluous consumption. There is a broad margin of expenditure which increases the productive efficiency of the persons who benefit by it, though not sufficiently to make the resulting increment of produce balance the expenditure.

The exact limits of this margin seem to me very difficult to ascertain. Who shall say precisely to what extent the stimulating food and drink, commodious dwellings, expensive amusements enjoyed by the best paid class of

The latter measurement is suggested by the analogy of the instruments—especially the living instruments—employed by the labourers; since in measuring the productiveness of useful animals we should always consider not their *gross* produce but their *net* produce, after subtracting the value of the food, &c., consumed by them. The analogy is too obvious and irresistible to be ignored; and we must admit this measurement of the productive efficiency of labourers as valid for some purposes; for instance, any employer who undertook to feed his labourers would rightly use this measurement in reckonings of his private business[1]. But, for the reason given incidently in the preceding chapter, it is not, I conceive, the measurement normally applicable in our present consideration of the matter from the point of view of the community; so far, that is, as the additional consumption which causes the additional efficiency is held to be desirable, in itself or in its results of bodily or mental vigour, as an amelioration of the labourer's life, and therefore an element of the ultimate end to which the whole process of production is a means. I shall therefore in the present chapter mean, by the 'produce' of which we are to examine the laws, the *gross* produce of consumable commodities; including along with this whatever new capital may be brought into existence within the period under consideration. This latter must obviously be taken into account; as it would be absurd to regard the productiveness of labour, at any given time and place, as affected by the question whether the utilities resulting from it are immediate or remote[2].

Let us then, taking in order the conditions of greater or less production which have been above enumerated, consider how far we can lay down laws as to the extent to which these conditions either (1) are actually found or may be expected to

skilled workers (barristers, physicians, men of business, &c.) contribute to the more effective performance of their functions?

[1] It should be observed that in the calculations of private employers a different measurement again has commonly to be applied; the value of what the labourer produces has to be compared not with the value of the materials of his necessary consumption, but with the wages that he is willing to take.

[2] A certain amount of error, as was before noticed, may be introduced by including new 'producers' wealth,' reduced to a common measure with directly consumable commodities by the standard of exchange value; but this element of possible error is not important for our present purposes.

operate in increasing or diminishing produce, or (2) would operate in the absence of counteracting causes.

The first class of conditions examined in Chapter IV have not—with one important exception [1]—been thought to afford material for the statement of any general economic laws. In the economic history, even in the social and political history of the human race, it is doubtless indispensable to note the different advantages and opportunities for production (including trade) presented by different countries. Thus the historian will point out how the special fertility of plains watered by large rivers, and the facilities of conveyance afforded by these rivers, furnished the decisively favourable conditions for the early establishment of large societies in China, Bengal, Mesopotamia, and Egypt; how, again, to the opportunities of communication provided in peculiar abundance by an inland sea studded with islands and invaded by peninsulas, may be attributed that development of trade in the Ægean and the Mediterranean generally which led to the Græco-Roman civilisation as one of its consequences. These and similar *apercus* are of great interest and importance. But the differences in the advantages and drawbacks thus presented to human industry by man's material environment are so various and complicated, and change so continually as the power of mankind to utilise advantages or overcome obstacles grows with the development of knowledge and of social organization; that we cannot usefully attempt to frame any general and definite quantitative statements as to the various and changeful effect of these conditions on production.

Again, the gradual changes that have taken place in the economic relation of man to his environment, through its adaptation by human labour, constitute, for the most part, merely a special case of the aid given to labour by the accumulation of capital; and will be most appropriately examined later from this point of view.

I pass therefore to consider, as causes of variation in amount of produce, the differences that are found in the quantity and

---

[1] I refer to the effect of limited space of land in diminishing the productiveness of the labour of the community inhabiting it—as expressed in the Law of Diminishing Returns, discussed later on in this chapter.

quality of labour applied, in proportion to the number of the population consuming the produce. Let us take first the differences in quantity. Here I do not find that any economist has thought it possible to lay down concrete laws as to the differences or probable changes either in the proportion of workers to non-workers in civilized societies, or in the average time for which they work. A small part of the very complex influences that we noted as determining these quantities does perhaps admit of being prognosticated; we may predict, for example, that civilized society will become more definitely industrial than it has yet become in European countries, and thus the slight social discredit still attaching to labour will entirely die away; but the rate of this change and the amount of effect it is likely to produce appear to be beyond calculation.

Again, as regards the abstract laws of the relation of "amount "of produce" to "quantity of labour," we have to observe that the obvious arithmetical law "the more work the more wealth" has undoubtedly to be qualified by the empirical generalization that, after a certain point, any increase in the quantity of labour performed by man within a given time tends to be accompanied by some deterioration in its quality. But in the present state of our knowledge it is not possible, I conceive, to establish even an approximate numerical law connecting the deterioration in quality with the increase in quantity.

§ 3. Here, however, it should be observed that it is not the proportion of labour to the population supported by it that recent economists have usually considered, in investigating what they call the "Law of the increase of Labour;" but rather the increase in the total number of human beings in any country. "The increase of labour," says Mill, "is the increase of man-"kind; of population." Still it seems clear that the determination of the rate of increase in the numbers of a nation does not come *primâ facie* within the general problem of Production as I, after Adam Smith, have stated it; for, as was said, we do not consider that a nation is richer or "better supplied with "the necessaries and conveniences of life," because having more members to feed and clothe it produces proportionately more food and clothing. It is therefore not primarily because the increase of a nation's numbers involves an increase in the

CHAP. VI.]   *THE LAWS OF PRODUCTION.*   141

quantity of its labour, that we are here called upon to deal with the large controversy raised by Malthus' famous Essay on Population; but because of the relation which the Malthusian doctrine maintained between increase of numbers in a given country and decrease in the proportional productiveness of the correspondingly increased labour. Or to use the phrases that have now become familiar, the 'Law of Population' chiefly interests us because it involves the 'Law of Diminishing 'Returns.'

But the connexion of these two questions is so intimate that it seems desirable here to sum up briefly the results of the long discussion started by Malthus' essay; especially as it is not, I think, difficult at the present stage of the discussion to state these results, so far as they are important for our present purposes, in a form not open to attack.

It is now generally admitted by competent judges that the human race—normally if not always and everywhere—has been to a great extent kept down to its actual numbers by the difficulty of supplying the physical wants of the population that, but for this difficulty, would have existed. This check to population has operated in the different ways, which Malthus distinguished as "preventive" and "positive": that is, either (1) by the fear of an insufficient supply of the material means of existence, causing abstinence from marriage, with or without vice, or artificial limitation of families, generally more or less vicious[1]; or (2) by the actual effect of the insufficient supply in causing the destruction of life; whether (a) through simple starvation, or voluntary exposure of children, or wars due to economic causes and constituting a mode of the struggle for sustenance among different parts of the human race; or (b) through diseases caused or aggravated by want of nourishment, or neglect of children or unhealthy manners of life caused by the necessity of earning a livelihood,—which are the positive checks chiefly operative in modern civilised societies[2].

[1] The practice of abortion may be classed with "preventive" or "positive" checks according to the view taken of the point at which human life begins.

[2] Malthus (Princ. of Pop. I. ch. ii.) includes in his account of both "preventive" and "positive" checks "vice and misery" not due to want of food: and this is doubtless legitimate when the question of population is considered in reference to the possibilities of social improvement imagined by

Accordingly, in a certain very important sense, it may be affirmed that "population has a constant tendency to increase "beyond the means of subsistence"; provided that we understand by the word "tendency" that the proposition relates to what would happen, if the checks in question were removed, not to what may be expected to happen in the actual future of our own or any other community. The proposition, though abstract and hypothetical, is not, of course, demonstrable *a priori*; it rests on inductive evidence: but such evidence has been adequately provided, so far at least as concerns large portions of the human race; and it has been provided with special definiteness in respect of the English race, while living in countries of the temperate zone under existing social conditions.

As regards this portion of the human race—to which I shall for the present confine my attention—we may state what is substantially the Malthusian doctrine with somewhat more quantitative precision. Suppose that all Englishmen married at the time of life at which, apart from prudential restraint, they were inclined to do so and observed the rules of chastity and monogamy to the extent that experience would justify us in expecting; that they did not artificially limit the number of their families; could obtain without seriously unhealthy toil the amount of food, clothing, fuel and house-room required for health; had the amount of protection from death and bodily injury which is actually afforded by the Governments of civilised Europe in time of peace; and took such measures to ward off preventable diseases, from themselves and their children, as ordinarily careful persons would take in the present state of medical knowledge. We may, I think, safely affirm that—apart from exceptional calamities—the population would double itself within a period less than 30 years[1].

optimistic writers such as Godwin. But in analysing the forces which keep population to its actual numbers it seems important to distinguish the vice and misery which are ultimately due to the difficulty of satisfying physical wants, from such vice and misery as mere economic improvement would have no tendency to remove.

[1] There are serious difficulties in the way of determining exactly this hypothetical period of duplication. The most important evidence is that supplied by the growth of the population in the United States,—where the increase, between 1790 and 1840, was from 3·9 to 17·1 millions, in a period

CHAP. VI.] *THE LAWS OF PRODUCTION.* 143

Secondly, it may be affirmed that if the process of doubling and re-doubling of the population were continued, upon any given portion of the earth's surface, the means of subsistence obtainable from the region in question would within a certain time become barely sufficient to support the population; so that the supposed increase could no longer continue,—the time at which this stoppage would be reached varying, of course with the density of the population[1].

Thirdly, we may affirm that our past experience of the growth of the industrial arts affords no justification for the assumption that the future development of agriculture will enable us to increase food in a ratio at all corresponding to the supposed increase of population.

It is in examining the nature of the ultimate barrier to increase of population, affirmed in the second of the propositions above given, that we come upon what has been called the Law of Diminishing Returns. Before discussing this, it should be observed that the greater rapidity in the increase of population which we have supposed would involve necessarily a smaller proportion of workers to non-workers. Assuming, however, that the arts of industry were sufficiently developed to enable this smaller proportion, duly aided by instruments, to provide adequate nourishment, clothing, &c., for the whole population, and that no greater proportion of the produce of labour took the form of luxuries; it is evident that if the productiveness of labour did not diminish, the increase of population might go on until it was checked by non-preventable diseases due to over-crowding. The "Law of Diminishing Returns", then, affirms that the productiveness of labour does tend to diminish, as the proportion of labourers to land increases, after a certain

in which the immigration was proportionally small. But even in this case it is difficult to estimate exactly the effect of emigration, on the one hand, and, on the other hand, we can only guess roughly the extent to which "misery" or "vice" or prudence actually diminished the population even of this exceptionally prosperous community. Accordingly in the numerical estimate given in the text I have allowed a large margin beyond the 25 years which Malthus gave as the time required for population to double itself, when unchecked.

[1] For simplicity's sake I have supposed foreign trade to be excluded—a legitimate supposition, as we may take the district of any size and any density of population.

degree of density of population—much below what would be on other grounds insanitary—has been reached. The degree of density, it should be observed, varies with the development of the industrial arts, and the accumulation of capital: it tends to be continually advanced by the progress of Invention, provided that, through the accumulation of capital, the improvement of processes which Invention renders possible is actually realized. The necessity—to which Carey drew attention[1],—of thus limiting the scope of the law of diminishing returns to communities of a certain density, is now generally recognised. In fact, in a thinly-peopled country we have to note a tendency to increasing returns; every additional labourer tends to make labour on the average more productive, since he enables the whole body of labourers to realize more fully the advantages of cooperation. And this tendency to increasing returns continues to operate, in all branches of industry except agriculture and mining, without any known limit from density of population, except such as arises from sanitary considerations. The closer human beings live to one another, the greater tends to be the *quantum* of utility derived from a given *quantum* of labour in conveyance and communication; the greater, therefore, tends to be the development of cooperation by exchange; and as the scale on which each particular branch of manufacture may be profitably organized becomes thus proportionally larger, the production itself tends correspondingly to become more economical, as has been already explained[2].

Hence the Law of Diminishing Returns may be understood both in a narrower and in a wider signification; and there is some danger of confounding the two. It may either mean (1) that the productiveness of agricultural and extractive labour tends, *ceteris paribus*, to diminish with every increase of population, even though capital increases proportionally; or (2) that, notwithstanding increased returns from the labour employed in manufactures and internal trade, the productiveness of labour generally tends so to diminish :—the degree of density at which the former tendency would begin to operate being of course lower than that which would introduce the latter.

[1] *Princ. of Social Science*, Vol. i. ch. iv.
[2] Cf. *ante* ch. iv. § 6.

CHAP. VI.]   *THE LAWS OF PRODUCTION.*   145

Still, even in its wider application to the productiveness of labour generally[1], the tendency to diminishing returns may be legitimately inferred to be operative in England at present; from the decidedly greater productiveness of labour and capital when applied in the countries to which Englishmen have migrated; as manifested in the larger remuneration of similar labour, and the higher interest on capital, in these countries as compared with Great Britain[2]. We may therefore assume that the growth of our population has passed the point at which the average efficiency of labour tends to be decreased by any addition to its quantity, other things remaining the same, even though capital has been accumulated to a proportional extent[3].

[1] The operation of the 'Law of Diminishing Returns' in agriculture will be specially examined in a later chapter (Book II. ch. vii). For the purposes of the present argument, it may, I think, be assumed.

[2] These differences of course vary from place to place and are continually fluctuating; but as to their general nature there is not, I conceive, any dispute. I find, for example, that the result of a comparative investigation of weekly wages in Massachusetts and Great Britain, as stated in the sixteenth Annual Report of the Massachusetts Bureau of the Statistics of Labour, is "that the "general average weekly wage of the employés in 24 industries in Massachusetts "is 62+ per cent. higher than the general average weekly wage of the employés "in the same industries in Great Britain": while the allowance to be made on the other side for the higher prices of the necessaries of life in Massachusetts, did not amount to 6 per cent. An equally definite result is more difficult to state in the case of interest, because capital is so easily transferred from England to the United States, that the extra interest obtainable from American investments must be taken to represent extra risk in such investments for Englishmen, as estimated by English investors generally. But in certain investments it is evident that this extra risk arises largely from the additional difficulty that a foreigner has in ascertaining and guarding against the dangers that may from time to time threaten them: so that in such investments—e.g. in mortgage on real estate—there can be no doubt that interest in the United States is much higher *to residents* than interest in England to Englishmen; after making all allowance for risk.

There is to be set on the other side the greater proportion of produce allotted as rent in England: but from this, again, we must subtract what is really, from a social point of view, interest on capital, being paid for the use of the results of past labour: and what remains—though it cannot be exactly estimated—can only be a very small percentage of the aggregate earnings of Englishmen.

[3] It is not of course meant that there is no possible application of labour and capital in England, according to the methods of industry at present understood, which would be more productive than some applications at present

S. P. E.

But then as other things do not remain the same, as on the contrary the improvement in the arts of industry—including improvement in the system of Cooperation through Exchange with less densely peopled countries,—is continually going on, a tendency of growing population to decrease proportional produce in England is continually counteracted by the tendency of industrial progress to increase it; and our evidence does not enable us to lay down any concrete law, formulating the actual influence which the two forces combined may be expected to exercise in determining the average produce per head for a given density of population. If indeed we excluded Foreign Trade, we might confidently affirm that no degree of improvement in industry known to us by experience could counteract the effect in decreasing the average productiveness of labour which the actual rate of increase of population in England would cause; so that the decrease in average supply must soon check the rate of increase. But then this exclusion of Foreign Trade makes such an affirmation purely abstract and hypothetical. Supposing Foreign Trade to go on, we have to decide whether the region whose production we are examining is to include all the mutually trading countries or only one. But on neither view can we frame any definite concrete 'law of 'diminishing returns,' applicable to a country like England; on the former view because the population of the whole region with which England trades cannot be said to have reached the point at which returns diminish; on the latter view because the possibilities of England's obtaining additional subsistence by trade have only a remote and indefinite limit. If the dream of Free-Traders were realized, if all the world were willing to allow free ingress to our manufactures, it seems to be quite

made. Such a statement would be absurd; as there is a good deal of capital actually employed which is yielding no return at all. What is meant is that, *ceteris paribus*, any considerable increment of capital-aided labour, *applied with average skill*, would be less productive than the average of such labour actually applied. It should be observed that agricultural labour is sometimes liable to become more unproductive, in consequence not merely of the increase of population, but of a disproportionate employment of the additional labour in agriculture: e.g. through an excessive subdivision of farms. But in this case the loss in productive efficiency is not entirely due to the law of diminishing returns; but partly to the defect of an industrial organization too inert to respond adequately to a change in its circumstances.

possible that the whole of England might become almost as thickly populated as Middlesex, without any decrease in the average productiveness of her labour.

So far, therefore, as we go beyond the abstract proposition that the proportional returns to capital and labour in England tends *ceteris paribus* to be decreased by any increase of population, we can only infer from the evidence before mentioned that actually the proportional returns to capital and labour in England are less than they would be if England were less densely populated. Let us now return to the more strictly 'Malthusian' law which affirms that the population of countries like England would increase at a decidedly more rapid rate than the present, were it not for the operation of either the prudential or the positive checks. This statement, as I have said, is hardly now disputed, by competent persons; but there is an ambiguity in the phrase "prudential restraint" which it is important to point out. Prudence, in this application, means the foresight and consequent avoidance of danger; but Malthus' disciples have not always made it clear whether the danger to which they referred was the danger of being in want of the necessaries of life (for oneself or one's children), or the danger of being in want of comforts, decencies, or luxuries[1]. It is obvious that the motive which actually restrains all classes in the community above the lowest is fear of the latter, not the former danger. It is necessary to premise this before considering the concrete law which some writers have preferred to give as the main Malthusian doctrine: the proposition, namely, that "population presses closely on the "limits of subsistence." In a certain very important sense this proposition is generally true and generally admitted in respect of civilized and fully-peopled countries; in the sense, namely, that population increases when the means of subsistence increase in such a way as will enable the mass of the community to obtain an ampler supply of necessaries. From this, however, it cannot be absolutely inferred, that even the lowest class in the community is on the verge of starvation; it may be merely

---

[1] Malthus himself expressly distinguishes these different applications of prudence at the outset of his *Essay*; but I am not sure that he has always kept the distinction sufficiently before his mind.

that they are in a position in which the supply of necessaries is an important element in the consideration whether or not it is prudent to marry. Still, it may be stated as a concrete law that holds good in England and other European countries, that there is a compression exercised on population by the difficulty of procuring the necessaries of life. The compression is not rigid: in England for example population might easily increase with greater rapidity than at present, if all classes restricted their consumption of luxuries—especially harmful luxuries: but a strong elastic pressure undoubtedly exists. If any statesman or philanthropist cherished the somewhat old-fashioned aim of increasing the population of his country, the best course he could adopt would be to promote the increase of its means of subsistence[1], especially of the mass of the population; since, though this is not the only means by which population can be increased, it is a means that may be relied on as effectual; and it is the only means that can be adopted without bringing the population nearer to the danger of the varied sufferings entailed by insufficiency of food.

But it is one thing to affirm that if subsistence increased, population would increase also; it is quite a different thing to maintain that the latter increase will in all cases be sufficient to

[1] The term "increase of the means of subsistence" is not free from ambiguity: for instance, the question may be raised whether a nation really increases its means of subsistence if a portion of it adopts a cheaper instead of a more expensive food, supposing that the former is abundant in proportion to its cheapness. I conceive that if the cheaper food be equally adapted to support life,—or even if it be merely more adapted in proportion to its cost—, the nation must be regarded as having more command over the means of subsistence: and that the change constitutes a distinct gain in utility. And I think that economists who have taken the opposite view have too hastily assumed the proposition combated in the next section; namely, that the classes consuming the cheaper food would necessarily "people down" to the thus lowered limit of subsistence. Even if this consequence followed it would not necessarily involve any suffering, though it would undoubtedly increase the danger of suffering from any accidental diminution of income; because if they had continued to consume the dearer food they would under certain circumstances have had the resource—which they have now lost—of descending to the cheaper article. But, as I urge in the next section, there is no necessity to suppose that the consumers of the cheaper food cannot raise their standard of living; and if they do this they will not only have more present command over the conveniences of life, but also—on the whole—more security as regards the future, than they would otherwise have had.

absorb the former. That this effect would be produced in the state of society of which he had actual experience Malthus certainly held: and a similar assumption is the foundation of the doctrine of a 'natural rate of wages' which occupies a cardinal position in Ricardo's theory of distribution; and to which attention has recently been attracted by Lassalle and other German Socialists, under the ominous name of the "iron law of "wages[1]." Ricardo does not indeed fall into the error of supposing—as Lassalle and others appear to have understood—that the "natural rate" of wages is that which gives the labourer only the bare necessaries of life; though he sometimes incautiously uses language that suggests this meaning, as when he says that "the natural price of labour is that price which "is necessary to enable the labourers, one with another, to "subsist and perpetuate their race[2]." Elsewhere he repeatedly recognises that the natural price of labour "essentially de- "pends upon the customs of the people," or "the quantity " of food necessaries and conveniences become essential to them "from habit;" adding that "many of the conveniences now "enjoyed in an English cottage would have been thought "luxuries at an earlier period of our history." This last sentence shews further that he did not regard the natural price of labour, estimated in commodities, as a constant quantity. On the contrary he is careful to state that "it varies at different "times in the same country;" and he speaks of the effort to raise it, by "stimulating the taste of the labouring classes for "comforts and enjoyments," as one of the worthiest aims of philanthropy. But he did, I think, assume that a mere increase of subsistence had in itself no tendency to produce this effect; that, even though the "market rate of wages" were to "remain "for an indefinite period above the natural rate,"—which he expressly states to be possible—the latter would still during this period have no tendency to rise towards the former. At any rate this assumption seems to be involved in the main part of his reasonings on wages: it is however opposed to what our general knowledge of human nature would lead us to infer:

[1] "Ehernes (brazen) Lohngesetz."
[2] This passage and those afterwards quoted are all taken from the same Chapter (v.) of Ricardo's *Principles of Political Economy*.

and, so far as I know, a duly comprehensive study of economic facts does not tend to support it[1]. I conceive, indeed, that in the actual restriction of the numbers of English manual labourers "positive" checks have, for the most part, operated more strongly than "preventive[2]". But so far as any class of labourers is restrained preventively, by a "standard of "comfort," from increasing its numbers, I see no reason to doubt that such a standard will tend to be somewhat raised, if any increase in the productiveness of the labour in question should cause a material and long sustained increase in its remuneration.

§ 4. We thus arrive at the question which remains to be discussed, in order to complete the enquiry proposed for the present chapter; viz. whether we can determine the laws of variation in the productive efficiency of labour. So far as the *personal* efficiency of the labourers is concerned, no economist (I believe) has ever claimed to possess the knowledge required for this task. Indeed it seems evident that any one who attempted to explain the differences in the physical, intellectual and moral qualities of labourers, and in the motives presented to them by their social and industrial circumstances, sufficiently to enable us to predict even roughly the future operation of these conditions, must in fact claim a prescience of the whole development of civilized society, beyond the pretensions of the most confident of living sociologists. While, again, the ultimate causes of

[1] It was the opinion of Malthus (*Princ. of Pol. Econ.* ch. iv. § 2) that a "decided elevation in the standard of the comforts and conveniences of the "English working classes" had been caused by the unusual succession of fine harvests in the fifty years from 1715 to 1765.

[2] That prudential motives, however, do operate to an important extent, even in this part of our population, may be legitimately inferred from the fluctuations in the marriage-rate, which Dr Farr has called the "barometer of national "prosperity": and which in England varied between 17·9 per 1000 persons in 1853, when industry was feeling the full stimulus of the Australian gold-discoveries, to 14·4 in 1879, a year in which a prolonged commercial depression reached its lowest point. See *Vital Statistics*, (from the writings of) William Farr, Part II. pp. 74, 5.

By "positive" checks I mean, chiefly, not actual starvation but (1) increased mortality of adults from diseases caused or aggravated by insufficient supply of necessaries, (2) mortality of children from this cause or from parental neglect due to the necessities of breadwinning, and (3) premature deaths from unhealthy or dangerous occupations.

THE LAWS OF PRODUCTION.

these differences are so complicated and their effects so intermingled, that it seems rash even to attempt any precise statement as to the effect that any particular change would produce if isolated. Whether we consider (e.g) changes in the labourer's habit of diet, or changes in the educational machinery applied to them, or in their social customs and opinions, or the terms on which they usually cooperate,—though we can often pronounce with confidence on the kind of effect on production to be expected from a given cause—we can hardly ever predict, even hypothetically, the quantity of effect.

It remains to consider how far the case is different with that element in the productiveness of labour which depends on the aid afforded it by capital; whether we can determine the "law of the increase of capital." I must first remark that Mill and others who have dealt with this question appear to me to present a somewhat one-sided view of the process of accumulation of what I have called concrete capital;' i.e. instruments and other intermediate results of labour employed for remote ends. It is right to dwell on the fact that—at least in civilized communities as organized—this accumulation actually depends, in the main, on the saving of individuals: but it should also be pointed out that this saving can only take effect in aiding production so far as instruments or processes have been discovered by which labour may be made more productive, through delay, in its final result of consumable commodities. Or, to use a current phrase, there must be a 'field for the 'employment of capital' if profit is to be gained; and the existence and continual enlargement of this field depends on Invention—in the extended sense in which I have before used the term to include all improvements in the general organization of industry, as well as in special industrial processes.

Now I conceive that no important quantitative generalizations can be established as to the variations in this second factor of the growth of social capital. We have no means of predicting the rate at which either our knowledge of the laws of nature or the application of this knowledge to industry is likely to progress in the future; it may be very much more rapid and extensive than it has been even during the last hundred years; on the other hand it may be very much slower, or may even come almost to a standstill—putting out of sight the possibility of any such social disturbances as might lead to an actual retrogression in civilization. And it is further to be observed that even if we could predict roughly the amount of improvement which the industry of the future may be expected to receive from invention, it would still be uncertain how far this improvement will involve the enlargement of the field of employment for capital. Hitherto, inventions have generally had the effect of complicating and prolonging the processes of industry, while at the same time increasing the ultimate productiveness of labour. But this has not always been the case; and so far as I know, there is no definite reason why the inventions of the future should not be chiefly in the direction of simplifying and abbreviating industrial processes; so that at each step of improvement the demand for capital will be restricted instead of being enlarged.

Bearing this in mind, let us consider whether we can ascertain the abstract law of the other factor in the growth of concrete capital; whether, supposing the field of employment for capital determined, we can say how far the capital will be furnished. Now the applications of labour, in the making of instruments or otherwise, by which its ultimate net production is increased, are of varying degrees of profitableness; the increment of produce obtained by delay is in some cases greater, in others less. We have therefore to inquire (1) how far the community can afford labour for remote results, and (2) how far it is likely so to apply its labour; and, as regards this second point, we have to ask, in particular, how far the individuals whose saving mainly determines this direction of labour will be willing to prefer remote results to immediately consumable utilities.

The fund from which saving might be made is what, in § 1 I proposed to call the net produce of labour of the community; i.e. what can be produced by any society in any given period, over and above what is required to supply the necessaries of life to all engaged in production,—and to children and others necessarily dependent on them—, and to compensate for the deterioration of the previously existing capital. This, so far as it can be determined, gives the maximum of

CHAP. VI.] *THE LAWS OF PRODUCTION.* 153

possible saving within the period. But as we have seen, the line between "necessary" and "superfluous" consumption cannot be sharply drawn; and it is the less necessary to attempt to draw it with precision, since the maximum above indicated has never been approached in any community of human beings; the motives which prompt men to save having always proved weaker than the motives which prompt them to spend, long before this maximum was reached. Still, so far as we limit our investigation to cases where we may assume that the primary needs of the human beings considered are an approximately constant quantity[1], we may clearly lay down that the possible maximum of saving increases as the gross produce of labour (per head) increases, but in a greater ratio. Hence, if the resultant force of the impulses that prompt men to save when balanced against those that prompt them to spend could also be assumed to be constant, the accumulation of capital—when it once had fairly commenced—would tend to increase at a continually accelerated rate.

But this latter assumption manifestly diverges widely from facts. The tendency to save, like the tendency to spend, is the complex result of a number of different impulses, some self-regarding, some sympathetic; and continually varies, partly in proportion to the strength of these, partly from variations in the intellectual condition of human beings, and partly from external causes. Even if we suppose the desires of the personal enjoyments derivable from wealth to remain unaltered; any important change either (1) in the prospects of security afforded by the physical or political circumstances of the community, or (2) in the average individual's power of foresight and capacity of being moved to action by the representation of remote consequences, or (3) in the range or intensity of his sympathetic interests, especially those due to family affection or patriotism local and general, must affect materially the general disposition to save. Now no economist, so far as I know, has attempted to determine

[1] This assumption is often manifestly untrue when we are comparing the productive efficiency of different races. E.g. the reason why the competition of "Chinese cheap labour" is so menacing to the English race in America and Australia seems to lie in the smaller necessary consumption of the average Chinaman, as compared with that of an average Englishman; which renders the net produce of the former's labour greater, though the gross produce is less.

the laws of variation of these conditions. In fact, the only general "law of the increase of capital"—beyond a mere statement of the above-mentioned conditions of variation—that Mill[1] (e.g.) appears to lay down, is the abstract proposition that, other things being equal, the "effective desire of accumulation" will vary directly with the "pecuniary inducement" to accumulate; that is, with the rate of interest[2]. Thus, other things being the same, if the rate of interest falls, the supply of new capital on which the interest will have to be paid will tend to be less: if it rises more. This abstract proposition is probably true on the whole; but even this seems to me less simple and certain than Mill represents it, since the total effect of a fall in interest is the result of a number of tendencies which to an important extent act in contrary directions. So far, indeed, as a man is induced to save not by the desire to attain any particular definite end, but by a general estimate of future resources as compared with present enjoyments for himself, his family, or others whom he may wish to benefit, it is obvious that any diminution in the yield of his savings must *pro tanto* decrease this inducement. But it would seem that in most cases the motives for accumulation are not of this general character. In the first place men in business and the professions save, to a great extent, with a view of obtaining a certain income from their

[1] *Political Economy* Book I. ch. xi.

[2] In this passage, as in another quoted soon after, Mill appears to use the terms 'interest' and 'profit' as practically convertible, though he elsewhere carefully distinguishes them. This does not seem to me contrary to usage; as 'profit' is I think often used in a wide sense for all 'returns to capital,' so as to include as one species 'interest,' which always denotes the additional wealth continually obtained by the mere ownership of capital, or the price paid for the temporary use of it by the employer of capital who does not own it. Still, it seems to me more convenient, when we are endeavouring to ascertain as precisely as possible the law of the increase of capital, to distinguish the terms; and to denote by 'profit' the yield of capital to the employer who is also the owner. If this distinction is taken, it will evidently be 'interest' rather than 'profit' which supplies the motive to accumulation, in the case of all persons except those who employ their own capital; and it will be so even as regards these latter, so far as they are able to borrow what they can profitably employ in their business at the ordinary rate of interest, allowance being made for risk. Hence it seems to me best to use 'interest' exclusively in the present discussion; though it ought to be borne in mind that so far as an employer believes that he could advantageously use capital that he is not able to borrow at the ordinary rate, he will have an additional stimulus to save.

savings; the amount of which they conceive beforehand with more or less definiteness, whether their aim is to retire from business themselves or to provide for their children. It is obvious that a lowering of the rate of interest, as it would render a larger amount of saving necessary to obtain a given income, would have a certain tendency to *increase*—instead of decreasing—the amount annually saved by such persons. Again a large amount is annually saved, especially by poorer persons, not so much for the sake of the interest as in order to have the principal "against a rainy day:" all such saving will be scarcely at all affected by any change in the rate of interest. Further, we have to take into account the great influence of habit and social custom in determining the apportionment of income between expenditure and accumulation. Many persons have a nearly fixed standard of living, and so long as their income is more than sufficient to provide for this, they merely save the surplus whatever it may happen to be. In proportion as this is the case, their saving will only be diminished by a fall in interest so far as their income is diminished by it: and it is in no way necessary that a fall in interest should be accompanied by a decrease in the average income of individual members of the community. In fact, as Mill points out, "a fall in "the rate of interest is frequently itself the result of a great "accumulation of capital; and the income derived from a large "amount of capital at a low rate of interest generally gives a "greater total power of saving than the income derived from a "small amount of capital at a high rate of interest."

It appears, therefore, that a fall in the yield of capital is likely partly to diminish the inducements to save, partly to increase them, partly to influence saving in a manner which we cannot precisely determine till we know the special causes of the fall. I think it probable that the first of these effects will generally preponderate over the others; but I do not think that we can say that this will certainly be always the case, still less to what extent it will be so.

On similar grounds I should regard as rather too dogmatic Mill's subsequent statement[1] that "there is at every time and

[1] Book IV. c. iv. Here again Mill must evidently be understood to use the term 'profit' as convertible with 'interest;' since in another paragraph he

"place some particular rate of profit which is the lowest that "will induce the people of that country and time to accumulate "savings and to employ those savings productively." I do not doubt that this is true of England at the present time,—though I see no means of determining precisely what the minimum rate in question is, here and now. But I know no conclusive general reason for regarding the prospect of interest as the only possible spring of accumulation and productive investment; and I think it quite conceivable that, at some future period of the world's history, accumulation may go on much as at present with average net interest at or barely above zero[1].

§ 5. But even if the laws of the saving of individual

speaks of a "profit or interest of 3 or 4 per cent" as being "a sufficient motive "to the increase of capital in England at the present day."

[1] Such a fall would doubtless somewhat increase the accumulation of Consumers' Capital at the expense of productive investment; but it must be remembered that the keeping of consumers' capital must always involve some degree of risk, and some trouble or outlay. In connexion however with this conjectural forecast the following point should be noticed. The new savings of individuals are partly absorbed by sales of capital already invested by persons who wish to spend some of their capital: the saving of one set of people being thus balanced by the spending of others. Now in what has been said we have supposed that the community is adding to its real capital, and therefore that some part of the savings of individuals have to take the form of new instruments of industry. If, however, the rate of interest falls through this accumulation of instruments, such previously existing instruments—especially land—as have not had their utility impaired by the competition of the new capital, will (as we have already observed) have their selling value increased: and therefore the sales of such instruments by persons intending to consume the proceeds will absorb a continually increasing amount of savings. This consideration becomes important when we forecast the consequences of a continual fall in the rate of interest. Its effects will be most easily shewn by making an extreme supposition. Let us suppose that, owing to the steady increase of savings, more rapidly than the enlargement of the field of employment of capital through invention, &c., interest by 2000 A.D. has fallen to a third of its present rate in England; and that rents on the average have been doubled through the increasing scarcity of land. It is obvious that land will sell at six times its present price; and therefore the sale of any given portion will be capable of absorbing six times the amount of saving that it would absorb at present. And if we carry the supposition of a fall in interest still further, it will be evident—still assuming rents at least not to fall in value—that before saving could increase to such an extent as to make the interest on capital merely cover risk, so that investment was no better than hoarding, the value of land must have become infinite. And the same may be said of the value of any irredeemable perpetual annuities that may have been sold by governments or private corporations.

members of any community, within any given period, could be determined more precisely than appears to me to be the case, there are several reasons why the result would give us no exact guidance as to the increase of 'social capital'—i.e. of the productive resources of the community derived from past labour—within the period.

In the first place—if we mean by a "community" a single nation, and not the whole aggregate of human beings more or less united through exchange into one industrial organization,—it should be observed that communities may, and in modern times largely do, lend their capital to other communities instead of employing it themselves; so that the supply of new capital for home employment may be reduced, without any fall in the rate of interest, merely because more attractive openings for investment have presented themselves abroad. Of course this foreign investment of capital increases the share obtained by the community of the produce of the world's labour; but it does not increase the productiveness of the labour of the community, except in an indirect and uncertain way, so far as it extends the opportunities and increases the advantages of foreign trade. And secondly, even in the case of home investments, we must note that a large amount of the ordinary savings of the community may be absorbed in meeting physical or social emergencies, which impose large occasional outlays on the community as a whole, but do not make the labour of the community more productive. In modern times this is most conspicuously exemplified by the large loans of governments for purposes of war; the issue of any such loan tends to increase the aggregate capital of individuals without any real increase in social capital[1].

But even in the case of any productive home investment of savings the profit to the individual investing is a very uncertain indication of the advantage to the community. For the investment may destroy or reduce the utility of previously invested capital; as when a railway is constructed which takes away traffic from an already existing railway, or a shop with expensive front, fittings, &c., is successfully designed

[1] The occasional needs of a portion of the community may similarly absorb the savings of the rest to a very varying extent.

to attract custom from another shop. The progress of invention, which continually modifies the field of employment for capital, continually affords opportunities for fresh investments—as in newly invented machinery, &c.—inevitably tending to reduce the value of portions of capital already in existence, to an extent which varies indefinitely[1] and can hardly ever be exactly ascertained. In such cases, then, the gain to the community from the new investment may be much less than the interest earned by the investing individual; when we take into account the destruction of the utility of the previously existing capital. On the other hand, it is equally possible that it may be much more. For the social profit of an improvement in the instruments of production will obviously accrue in part to the consumers of the commodities produced, so far as producers using the improved instruments are forced by competition to reduce the price of their products below what was required to remunerate the less efficient production which they have superseded.

Further, while the progress of industrial civilization causes the depreciation of some previously existing capital, it adds value to other durable results of previous labour productively applied, which are protected by circumstances from competition, such as buildings in towns well situated for business. The resulting addition to the value of existing capital is, of course, not due to saving; while yet,—if caused by an actual increase in the utility of the durable wealth in question—it may be a real addition to social capital.

We must also note the large amount of results of labour for remote ends, more or less profitable to the community, which are not included in the "saving" of individuals as ordinarily estimated; and which come but vaguely and slightly (if at all) within the operation of the law of such saving, as above formulated. Under this head will come a large amount of the improvements of agricultural land under a system of small farming (especially if the cultivator be also the owner); and

---

[1] Improvements may easily be imagined which would annihilate vast portions of the productively invested wealth of individuals; such (e.g.) as a mechanical invention that superseded railways in England, or a development of trade that rendered English wheatgrowing unprofitable: and economic changes of this kind, though smaller in degree, are continually occurring.

similarly, a large part of the labour for remote results, that is spent in utilising the opportunities continually presented for the successful establishment of new lucrative businesses in trade. Such labour can be but slightly affected by changes in the rate of interest. Still less is such a consideration ordinarily operative in determining the accumulation of the durable wealth that we have called "consumers' capital;" so far at least as such wealth is commonly owned by the persons using it.

Finally, we must not leave out of our calculation the increase of social resources due to labour from time to time expended in founding and developing institutions of public utility—educational, sanitary, and the like—by which no profit is earned for individuals. Above all we must take account of the economic advantages of the greatest of human institutions, the State; in building up which so much toil and other sacrifices have been incurred for distant results, from motives of patriotism or love of glory, without any reckoning of pecuniary returns to the individuals who have laboured. A statement of the Laws of Production is undeniably incomplete without an attempt to estimate systematically the economic benefits and drawbacks that spring from different political institutions and different principles and methods of administration. It seems however most convenient to defer all consideration of the tendencies of different modes of Governmental interference, until in the concluding book we come to discuss these tendencies from the point of view of Art of Practice; and ask 'How far (if at all) 'and in what way *ought* Government to intervene with a view 'to making the produce of industry a maximum.' The answer to this question will indirectly supply an answer to the corresponding question that we should naturally here raise from the point of view of science; so far, that is, as it seems to be within the province of the theoretical economist to deal with this latter enquiry.

BOOK II.

DISTRIBUTION.

CHAPTER I.

INTRODUCTION.

§ 1. WE have now to consider what, in accordance with usage, I have given as the second part of the subject of economic science: The Theory of Distribution and Exchange. The notion of 'Exchange' may be taken as sufficiently clear: but 'Distribution' requires some further explanation[1]. In the first place it should be observed that it is not strictly the Distribution of Wealth, but the Distribution of Produce with which we are primarily concerned. We suppose a society in which the main part of the land and other instruments for producing wealth are already distributed among the members as their private property: and this pre-existing distribution of producers' wealth we do not profess to explain. Nor is it absolutely necessary, up to a certain point of our investigation, to make any general assumption with regard to it: but in working out the details of our theory, we shall have to take note of the inequality that is characteristic of this pre-existing distribution in all existing civilised societies. We shall have to suppose that some persons own land and some capital in varying and sometimes considerable amounts, and that others have little or none of either; and that in neither case are the owners and the users altogether coincident. And it is convenient to assume this inequality throughout.

[1] To prevent misunderstanding, I never employ the word 'Distribution'—as it is sometimes used—to denote or include the processes of conveyance and retail trade that intervene between the completed manufacture of a consumable article and the commencement of its consumption. According to the view taken in the present treatise, these processes are conceived as a part of the whole process of Production. See p. 12.

We may state, then, the main question which a Theory of Distribution attempts to answer as follows: 'According to what 'laws is the new increment of commodities, continually pro-'duced by the combination of the labour and unequally dis-'tributed capital (including land) of different members of the 'community, shared among the different classes of persons who 'have co-operated in producing it, either by their personal 'exertion—bodily or mental—or by allowing others to use their 'wealth, knowledge or other resources?' The main part of this produce consists of the food, clothing, and other kinds of consumable wealth that are continually being made by producers and transferred to consumers: but this is not the whole of it. For, firstly, it seems best to include under the term 'produce' all purchaseable commodities, whether "embodied in "material objects" or not; on the grounds urged in the preceding book[1] (where, however, this extension of the meaning of 'produce' was not fully adopted). Our object is to study the causes of the different extents of command over "neces-"saries and conveniences," obtained respectively by different members of the community, through the complicated system of co-operation by means of exchange on which the life of modern society depends; and since some portion of each one's money income is spent in purchasing not material wealth but education, professional advice, &c., we must regard these utilities, no less than the material products of industry, as practically 'distributed' through the medium of the money payments that determine the nominal incomes of individuals: and the laws that govern the exchange values of these immaterial commodities concern us as much as those regulating the values of material products.

Again, we have to bear in mind that the new wealth produced in a society that is growing richer will partly consist of new 'producers' wealth '—new railways, factories, warehouses and an increased supply of new raw materials to be hereafter transformed into consumers' wealth, and new auxiliary materials such as coal for steam-engines &c. Such additions,—so far as they are more than sufficient to compensate for the continual destruction, deterioration, and depreciation of capital—must be

---

[1] See ch. iii. § 4, p. 79.

regarded as part of the produce distributed: it is, in fact, mainly this part which is continually "saved" and added to the already existing accumulation of capital[1].

'Produce,' so understood, is nearly equivalent to the 'real income' of the community during the period; provided that we include in the notion of 'real income' the unpurchased utilities that a man derives from his own labour or the unpaid labour of members of his family—which are largely unrepresented in ordinary estimates of his money income. Such utilities, indeed, are not in any ordinary sense 'distributed'; still, we cannot leave them out of account in our investigation of the laws of distribution, at least if they have a market value or if the labour employed on them is of a kind that might—and under other circumstances would—be employed in producing saleable commodities. Of this kind, for instance, is the labour of cooking food, making or repairing or cleansing clothes and furniture, teaching children, carrying purchases from shops, and walking to and from places of work: when we contemplate the resulting utilities from the point of view of the community, we find that a portion of them, varying at different times and places, is commonly purchased, and another portion of them commonly unpurchased; hence it would be manifestly misleading to confine our attention to the former, and to leave the latter entirely out of sight.

A varying portion of this unpaid labour is employed in appropriating and utilising those "spontaneous gifts of nature" which at certain times and places are unpurchased (except by the labour of appropriation &c.) while elsewhere and at other times they command an extra price through scarcity. We have already seen[2] that in comparing the wealth of different societies at different times and places we must include these unpurchased utilities in one term of the comparison, if utilities of the same kind, having exchange value, are included in the other term; and the same principle will obviously apply to the comparisons

[1] There is some difficulty in determining precisely, yet so as to avoid paradox, the notion of *amount* of produce within a given period, when we include in 'produce' the additions to capital: but this difficulty—which is of no real importance in relation to the discussion which follows—will be more conveniently dealt with later on. See ch. vi. § 1.

[2] B. i. ch. iii. § 1.

that have to be made, in considering changes and differences in distribution.

Further, we have to note that an important part of the consumable utilities enjoyed by the members of a civilised community within any given period,—though properly included in the notion of "real income"—are not in any sense the result of the labour exerted within the period. I refer to the utilities derived from portions of consumers' wealth—such as land and buildings, pictures, statues, jewels, some kinds of books and furniture &c.—which are comparatively durable; and consequently, in civilised countries are often handed down from father to son for many generations. Such utilities are not commonly included by economists in the aggregate of which they investigate the distribution: but, obviously, they cannot be left out of account in estimating the command—either of individuals or of the community generally—over the necessaries and conveniences of life within any given period[1].

Still, these utilities derived from domestic labour or inherited consumers' wealth only concern us in a secondary and indirect way: our primary object of investigation is the distribution of the produce of the great system of co-operation through exchange, which forms the framework of modern industrial society. We are to examine the causes that determine the shares in which the aggregate of utilities continually produced by this system is divided among the independent individuals who have co-operated in producing it. We shall assume generally that this division is brought about, as it mainly is in a modern industrial community, by free bargaining among persons seeking each his private interest,—extending the term "private" to include "domestic" interest, in the case of husbands and parents. We shall, accordingly, only take note in a secondary way of the domestic redistribution of shares industrially earned, among members of a household who themselves earn little or nothing; and also of the almsgiving and donations of wealth for public objects by which the inequalities of the primary industrial

---

[1] Of course to some extent such utilities are strictly 'produced' within the period; so far, namely, as they are due to the labour required from time to time for repairing and keeping in good condition houses and other kinds of durable consumers' wealth.

CHAP. I.] *INTRODUCTION.* 167

distribution of produce are mitigated and its deficiencies supplemented;—i.e. only so far as these supplementary redistributions influence the primary industrial division[1]. And so far as industrial shares are to any considerable extent determined by law, custom or current opinion as to what is just or equitable, excluding or overriding free contract, our reasonings will only be applicable to them in a partial and qualified manner[2].

We shall also exclude from our present consideration the important share of the produce appropriated by Government, so far at least as concerns the transfer of this share from the possession of individuals to that of the state, by means of taxation: though when we consider the influence exercised on the determination of wages by the physical needs or "standard "of comfort" of the labourer or his family, we must of course take account of what he is required to pay for the services of government. Moreover, the redistribution of the collected taxes among the members and employees of Government, and in the way of governmental expenditure, so far as it proceeds by free contract, is to a great extent similar in its determination and effects to the distribution through free contract of the rest of the produce.

§ 2. The shares of this industrial distribution are classified in ordinary economic discussion as (1) Wages of labour—a term which may conveniently be extended to include what are more commonly called the Earnings or Salaries of the higher kinds of labourers; (2) Profits of persons employing labour together with capital and sometimes land; (3) Payments made to owners of land or other capital when employed by non-owners, further distinguished as (*a*) Rent paid for land or buildings and (*b*) Interest paid for the use of 'money' as is commonly said, or of 'capital' as economists generally say.

Without at present attempting a more exact demarcation of these different shares, it is easily seen that each share represents the price paid by society for a certain service or utility

[1] For instance, in investigating the minimum below which wages cannot permanently fall, the effects of almsgiving, and of public provision for paupers have to be taken into account.

[2] In the last chapter of this book I have endeavoured to reduce within its proper limits the currently recognised opposition between Competition and Custom.

contributed by the recipient of the share. In the case of Wages, Interest, and Rent, this fact is obvious; since Wages are paid directly for Labour, Rent for the use of land, and Interest for the use of money or other capital. A little more reflection is required to see the exact nature of the utility remunerated by Profits. The profit obtained in any year by a man of business is only ascertainable indirectly, by taking the value of his capital (including land) at the end of the year, adding what he has taken out of his business from time to time for consumption, and subtracting the value of his original capital. In many businesses the result of this calculation will vary very greatly in different years; sometimes, doubtless, falling considerably below zero. Still we may assume that, on the average, the profit obtained by a business in which a given amount of capital is employed must be materially greater than the interest that could be got by lending the same amount; and that the labour and thought required for the management of capital is not—like (e.g.) the labour of writing second-rate poems—supplied gratuitously by men of business as a class. This excess, then, of average profit over possible interest (and sometimes rent) is to be regarded as the price which society pays for the employer's labour; and we may call it, after Mill, the employer's Wages of Management[1].

It appears, then, that in all cases the different shares of the produce are obtained by what is, substantially if not formally, an exchange of certain services for the price that they will fetch in the market. The distribution, in fact, that we have to investigate is essentially Distribution through Exchange; involving usually a double exchange, of services for money and of money for consumable commodities. It is from this intimate connexion of the two notions that I am unable to follow Mill in separating the theory of distribution from the theory of the exchange value of material commodities. Mill's procedure was due, I think, partly to an erroneous view of the laws governing Wages and Profits; partly to a wish to lay stress on the extent to which the shares of

---

[1] Mill's own term is "Wages of Superintendence"; but "Superintendence" seems to me less adapted than "Management" to denote the whole of the complex function of the *entrepreneur* of a business.

produce have actually been determined not by free bargaining, but by custom. And it is, no doubt, a noteworthy fact in economic history that Wages, Interest, and Rent have continued to be more or less determined by Law or Custom long after the prices of products had come to be generally settled by the free "higgling of the market." But this divergence belongs to a stage in economic development which the most industrially advanced portions of civilised mankind have now, in the main, left behind: in the modern industrial community Wages Interest and Rent directly, and Profits indirectly, are, in the main, as much determined by free contract as the prices of material commodities.

It remains to decide whether we shall examine first the remunerations of producers or the prices of products. I have adopted the latter course, chiefly because in examining the prices of products, we shall be dealing approximately with concrete facts, phenomena of industry admitting of statistical investigation; whereas the remunerations of different classes of productive services, as defined by economists, are, to a greater extent, elements arrived at by abstract economic analysis. Accordingly, as one of my chief aims is to eliminate controversies due to an unguarded use of abstract conceptions, it seemed on the whole most convenient to begin as close as possible to concrete facts, and proceed gradually from them to such abstract notions as (e.g.) that of Ricardian Rent. I shall therefore occupy the two following chapters with an examination of the laws according to which the Exchange Value of material products tends to be competitively[1] determined. The value of Money will require a separate discussion, as the definition of the term Money has first to be carefully considered. Accordingly, the fourth and fifth chapters will be occupied respectively with the Definition of Money, and the theory of the Value of Money; from which latter subject we shall pass by an easy transition to the determination of Interest, with which, in the sixth chapter, the exposition of the Theory of Distribution will commence.

---

[1] I have adopted this phrase as a convenient abbreviation for "determined "under the influence of free competition."

NOTE. Mr Walker, in his instructive book on *The Wages Question* (chap. i.), states that "vast amounts of wealth are ex-"changed which are not distributed;" giving as an example the case of a small American farmer, proprietor of a farm in one of the Southern sea-board states, for which he and his family supply all the labour required. He says that all the cotton produced on such a farm is "not distributed," though it is "exchanged, being sold "to purchase breadstuffs, clothing, West-India goods, &c." This seems to me to imply a misleadingly narrow view of Distribution. The cotton, no doubt, is not distributed *by* the farmer; but I conceive that the breadstuffs, clothing, &c. are properly regarded as distributed *to* him. They constitute his share of the aggregate produce of the industrial society of which he is a member; a share which increases or diminishes, according as the value of the service rendered by him to society in producing cotton rises or falls—that is, as compared with the services rendered by the producers of breadstuffs, &c. And similarly, of course, the cotton sold by him will be distributed through exchange among other producers.

CHAPTER II.

THEORY OF EXCHANGE VALUE OF MATERIAL PRODUCTS.

§ 1. THE main assumptions on which English Economists since Ricardo have generally proceeded, in their investigations of the laws of value, have been briefly discussed in an earlier chapter[1]. But before examining the theory in detail, it will be desirable to state these assumptions again somewhat more fully; because, although the actual facts of industry correspond to them approximately, the degree of approximation varies very much in different cases.

1. We assume that every person concerned in the exchange of the article in question aims with ordinary intelligence at selling his goods for the highest price which he can get for them; neither Law nor Custom intervening so as seriously to affect the success of his endeavour. When this assumption is stated in its most general form, we must understand 'price' to mean 'balance of total advantages obtained by the trans-'action over any drawbacks that may be incident to it.' But, generally speaking, in the sale of material products, the only drawback is the expense of forwarding the article to the buyer (so far as this is undertaken by the seller) which may be simply subtracted from the price; while the advantages, with one important exception, are wholly comprised in the money-price of the article. The exception is that a dealer frequently has an interest in dealing with one class of purchasers rather than another, with a view to the establishment of a business. But within large limits it is in most cases true that any differences

[1] Introduction, c. iii.

among purchasers are indifferent to the seller of goods, except so far as one offers a higher money-price than another; and, for simplicity, I shall assume this to be the case in the following discussion.

Generally speaking, there are many independent buyers and sellers making similar exchanges at approximately the same time: and if they act without concert,—though the effort of each party to obtain the most favourable terms for himself will continually tend to produce an approximate uniformity in the rates of exchange for similar commodities—there will continually be slight variations, due to the varying needs, circumstances, and judgments of different sellers and purchasers; and the changes in price of which we are about to examine the causes will take place through an unconcerted coincidence in direction of these individual variations. This is the condition of things, denoted by the phrase "open competition," which is commonly assumed in economic reasonings. Under certain circumstances, however, it is the interest of dealers in a commodity to enter into a deliberate combination to dictate terms of exchange; and here and there an individual—say an eminent artist or the proprietor of a vineyard of special quality—controls the whole supply of some uniquely valuable commodity and can singly fix its price. More often, again, Monopoly and Competition are combined: an individual or combination controls so large a part of the supply of a certain article as to be able to raise or lower its price at will within certain limits, but not beyond them. Such cases of Monopoly, total or partial, do not ordinarily lie beyond the range of economic science: we can generally[1] determine the rate of exchange which enlightened self-interest will prompt the monopolist to offer by reasoning similar to that by which we determine the results to which open competition would lead: and it is important practically, as well as for theoretical completeness, to do this. In the present chapter, however, I shall only treat of monopoly briefly and by way of introduction to the theory of competitive prices; reserving a fuller discussion of monopoly and combination to a later chapter (Ch. x.).

[1] The chief exceptional case, in which such determination may be excluded, is where monopolist is bargaining with monopolist. See ch. x. § 5.

2. Here, therefore, except where it is otherwise stated, I assume that the competition of dealers in a market[1] is perfectly free and open; that the prices at which transactions actually take place are readily ascertainable by all dealers; and that, in consequence, at the same time and place wares of the same quality are sold for approximately the same money-price. Strictly speaking, we have no ground for assuming this identity of price, except where the quantities sold are approximately the same; since the trouble of the seller, the remuneration of which is included in the price, does not vary materially with the amount; so that we should expect a reduction of price for large transactions. And in fact such a reduction is actually made in certain dealings both wholesale and retail. E. g. it is partly on this account, partly from the importance of business connexion, that large dealers commonly sell to the retailers of their commodities at a price lower than that charged to purchasers for consumption. But in wholesale transactions among dealers it is generally convenient to have a fixed price (per unit) for all amounts in which it is worth while to deal at all; and for simplicity we will suppose this to be the case in the transactions which we examine. I shall assume, therefore, that 'the market price' of which we speak is at any given time and place the same *per unit* for all quantities sold. The market need not necessarily be at one place; only if it extend over a considerable space, the price cannot be assumed to be strictly the same, but the same allowing for expenses of transport.

3. I further assume that the products whose price we are investigating are made solely to be sold; and not partly for the consumption of the producer. In the existing organisation of industry, the extent to which any producer supplies his own consumption is trifling in most industries; and so far as the case is otherwise, we may conveniently avoid complication by the fiction of supposing the producer to sell to himself at the market-rate whatever share of his own products he and his family consume. Only wherever this share is a considerable proportion of the whole, as is sometimes the case with small agricultural producers, it must be borne in mind that the same individuals have to be regarded in two aspects at once, as pro-

[1] For the meaning of market, see p. 38.

ducers and consumers; and that their gains in the latter character will partially counterbalance any losses through cheapness that may befall them in the former character.

4. A minor deviation from facts which it is convenient to make is the assumption that variations in price are continuous. In reality, of course, the difference between the different prices of the smallest quantity customarily sold can hardly be less than the smallest current coin; and in retail sales of low-priced articles this necessity practically modifies to an important extent the effect on actual prices of changes in the forces determining value.

5. Besides "commercial competition"—to use Cairnes' phrases,—I also assume effective "industrial competition," within the region contemplated. That is, I assume that producers as well as traders aim at selling their services for the highest price attainable, and therefore tend to be attracted, by a higher rate of remuneration, both from district to district, and from industry to industry. Hence I infer (1) that approximately the same wages will tend to be paid for the same quality of labour in any one industry; and (2) that when the remuneration of labourers or capitalists in any industry is known to be higher than that of labourers or capitalists in some other industry not entailing materially greater sacrifice or outlay or requiring scarcer qualifications, the difference will tend to be gradually reduced by the attractions which this higher remuneration exercises on actual or prospective labourers or employers. The extent, however, to which this tendency may be assumed to operate, without deviating too widely from actual facts, will require careful discussion.

The theory of market values or prices, as determined by Supply and Demand, depends on the assumption of Commercial Competition (so far as combination is excluded): while the theory of "natural" or "normal" values or prices, so far as they are determined by Cost of Production, depends on the assumption of Industrial Competition.

§ 2. J. S. Mill, in the third book of his Political Economy, Ch. I—VI., has given an explanation, lucid and in the main sound, of the manner in which the operation of these two quite different kinds of competition is combined. Considering the

CHAP. II.] OF MATERIAL PRODUCTS. 175

wide popularity of Mill's treatise, it seems to me convenient to begin by giving a summary[1] of his exposition, slightly corrected, and afterwards to discuss more fully the points in which it seems to me to need qualification and further development.

"The temporary, or Market Value of a thing, depends on "the demand and supply; rising as the demand rises, and "falling as the supply rises. The demand, however, varies "with the value, being generally greater when the thing is "cheap than when it is dear; and the value always adjusts "itself in such a manner, that the demand is equal to the "supply.

"Besides their temporary value, things have also a per-"manent, or, as it may be called, a Natural Value, to which "the market value, after every variation, always tends to "return."

In considering the determination of this natural value, we will, in the first instance, assume that each commodity may be treated as the single result of an independent process of production[2]. Making this assumption, we have to distinguish three different classes of commodities. First, there is a small class of things which—either through natural scarcity or through monopoly—are so limited in quantity, that "their value is "entirely determined by demand and supply; save that their "cost of production (if they have any) constitutes a minimum "below which they cannot permanently fall." Secondly, there is an important class of things—chiefly manufactured articles in which the main element of cost is labour of some ordinary kind—of which the quantity produced may be increased to a practically indefinite extent, without any consequent material change in their cost of production. Any such article may, accordingly, be regarded as having at any given time a uniform average cost of production, independent of the amount produced: and this being so, such articles tend to "exchange for "one another in the ratio of their cost of production, or at what "may be termed their cost value:" that is, a value "sufficient to

---

[1] This summary is partly taken from Mill's own summary in his Book III. c. vi., partly from passages in the preceding chapters of the same book.

[2] The more complex case of commodities that have a joint cost of production is considered later (§ 10 of this chapter).

"repay the cost of production, and to afford besides the ordinary
"expectation of profit (regard being had to the degree of
"eligibility of the employment in other respects)." Hence the
value of such things "does not depend (except accidentally, and
"during the time necessary for production to adjust itself) upon
"demand and supply; on the contrary, demand and supply
"depend upon it....There is a demand for a certain quantity of
"each commodity at their cost value, and to that the supply in
"the long run endeavours to conform;" through the desire of
capitalists to make the highest possible profits, which causes
capital to be continually withdrawn from less profitable and
invested in more profitable industries. It must not be supposed
that this 'cost value' is something permanently fixed: it is
liable to change continually—and tends generally to fall somewhat—as industry progresses; and when such changes occur,
the market value may for a time deviate markedly from the
cost value. Still, it is not necessary, in order to make the value
of a thing conform approximately to its cost of production,
"that its supply should actually be either increased or di-
"minished....The mere possibility often suffices; the dealers
"are aware of what would happen, and their mutual com-
"petition makes them anticipate the result by lowering the
"price."

Finally there is a third class of commodities—exemplified
by most products of agriculture and mining—"which have not
"one but several costs of production; which can always be
"increased in quantity by labour and capital," but only at a
continually increasing cost. The natural value of such things
is "determined by the cost of that portion of the supply which
"is produced and brought to market at the greatest expense"—
so far as the expense is not due to unskill or exceptional ill-
fortune on the producer's part: the relation of natural to
market value being similar to that existing in the case just
discussed.

Further analysis shews that "Cost of Production consists
"of several elements, some of which are constant and uni-
"versal, others occasional. The universal elements of cost
"of production are, the wages of the labour, and the pro-
"fits of the capital. The occasional elements are, taxes, and

"any extra cost occasioned by a scarcity value of some of the "requisites.

"Omitting the occasional elements"; so far as things admit of indefinite increase at a uniform cost, they "naturally and "permanently exchange for each other according to the com- "parative amount of wages which must be paid for producing "them, and the comparative amount of profits which must be "obtained by the capitalists who pay those wages.

"If one of two things command, on the average, a "greater value than the other, the cause must be that it re- "quires for its production either a greater quantity of labour, "or a kind of labour permanently paid at a higher rate; or "that the capital, or part of the capital," employed in buying that labour, must be invested "for a longer period; or, lastly, "that the production is attended with some circumstance which "requires to be compensated by a permanently higher rate "of profit."

The further explanation and qualification of the theory above summarized, which I propose to give in the present chapter, may be conveniently commenced by removing some ambiguities in the cardinal terms used in stating it. In the first place, I ought to explain that I shall generally substitute the term 'price'—which, when used without qualification will always denote 'exchange value in money'—for the more abstract term 'value' which Mill prefers; believing that the greater familiarity and definiteness of the notion of 'price' will render it easier for the reader to follow the reasonings of this chapter. This use of Price for Value requires us to suppose that the purchasing power of money relative to commodities in general—exclusive of the one whose value is investigated— remains unchanged: but no material error is introduced by this supposition at the present stage of our discussion.

Secondly, the reader should bear in mind that in the notion of Cost of Production we include the cost of bringing to market the product in question. In investigating the prices of the products of International Trade we shall also take note of the further expenses that may have to be borne by the seller or the purchaser of the product, in conveying the equivalent of the commodity sold back from the market to the place where the seller wishes to use it. But this consideration may be omitted, without important error, in dealing with commodities produced and sold *within* such a country as England;—to which in the present chapter we may conveniently confine our attention.

Further, there is an ambiguity in the terms describing changes in Demand, which requires to be carefully removed. It seems to me, as to Mill, most convenient to mean by "increase of demand" increase of the quantity demanded of an article[1]: but if so, when we say (1) that a fall of value causes an "increased demand" and (2) again that "if the demand increases the value rises" there is an apparent inconsistency which needs to be explained. The explanation is that in affirming the first proposition we are supposing a change in the value of a commodity to take place in consequence of causes affecting its supply, while the purchasers' estimate of its comparative utility remains unchanged. We assume that for any given price there is a certain amount which purchasers are willing to take at that price; and that supposing other things unchanged this amount will be greater when the price is lower and less when it is higher. What the exact extent of any such variation in demand will be, for any given change in price, we have no means of knowing *a priori*[2], and we make no general assumption with regard to it. All that we assume is that for every rise [or fall] in the price of a commodity, other things remaining the same, there will be a decrease [or increase] in the amount of it which can be sold at the price[3]. On the other

---

[1] Cairnes prefers to measure demand not by 'quantity of commodity demanded' but by 'quantity of purchasing power offered for it'; and there are certainly some advantages in adopting this view: but, on the whole, I prefer Mill's. See note to p. 233.

[2] We may observe that these variations, in the case of most articles, are included within certain limits. That is, if the price rose beyond a certain point people could not afford to purchase the commodity at all; and if it fell to zero, the demand would still remain finite. But as the changes that actually occur fall considerably within these limits, we are not called upon to take account of them.

[3] This assumption, as Thornton has pointed out, is not found to hold in all sales that actually occur; it may easily happen that at a particular time and place a moderate change in the price of a given article would not alter the number of persons willing to purchase it. None the less is the assumption, I think, perfectly legitimate as a scientific hypothesis for the purposes of general

hand, when we speak of 'price rising as demand rises' we are contemplating the effect of some change in the causes of demand, other than variation of price. We are supposing that owing to some alteration in social needs or desires, or in the supply of some other commodity, or perhaps in the general wealth of society, the amount of the commodity in question demanded at the old price has increased. This effect, supposing the supply of the commodity to remain unchanged, is commonly expressed by saying that "the Demand is in excess of the Supply." But this being so, according to our general assumption of a continuous variation in demand corresponding, but in an opposite direction, to any variation in price, there will be some higher price at which the demand will be equal to the supply; it is obviously the interest of the sellers to raise their price till it reaches this point, and the competition of the buyers will enable them to raise it. It thus appears that the phrase "increase of demand" is currently used to denote two different facts: (1) the increase in quantity demanded which would result from any fall in price, supposing other conditions of demand to remain unchanged, and (2) an increase in the quantity demanded at a *given* price, due to changes in conditions of demand other than variation in price. It is, I think, convenient to have two unambiguous terms to distinguish these two different kinds of change in demand; and I think it will be in accordance with usage to speak of the former as an *extension* of demand, and of the latter as a *rise* or *intensification* of demand. I shall therefore always use these terms so; and similarly I shall use "reduction" and "fall" as the opposites of "extension" and "rise" respectively.

It ought to be borne in mind that not only may the demand for any one commodity vary quite differently from the demand for any other, but also that the demand for the same commodity may vary differently at different times. In fact, if we could construct a scale of the variations in demand for any

deductive reasoning; since it represents in a simple form, with approximate accuracy, the most important facts with which the theory is concerned;—viz., those of wholesale trade almost universally, and to a great extent those of retail trade and other exchanges, so far as regards commodities largely dealt in by purchasers of various degrees of wealth.

given commodity that would result *ceteris paribus* from any given series of variations in its price, we should doubtless find such a scale continually varying, as the amount of wealth in any community, the manner of its distribution, and social customs and fashions change. I have before[1] explained,—after Jevons— how the price of any ware tends to correspond to the "final utility" of the total quantity purchased; i.e. the utility of the last additional portion that, according to the resultant estimate of the aggregate of purchasers, it is just worth while to purchase at the price. But, in applying this conception, it must be borne in mind that, owing to the unequal distribution of wealth, the same price represents very different degrees of utility in relation to different purchasers. E g. if the price of a newspaper were reduced from $2d.$ to $1d.$, two men, one rich and one poor, might be thereby induced to take it in; but the $1d.$ would represent a much higher estimate of its value in use on the part of the poor man. Thus the quantity of a commodity demanded at any given price is the result of a number of very diverse estimates of its final utility made under indefinitely varying conditions: and each variation in demand, corresponding to a change in price, is generally a compound effect of a number of different readjustments of these estimates, rendered necessary by the change in price; hence any cause that affects materially any of these estimates will tend to alter the scale of variation. But for our present purpose it will be convenient to assume, where the contrary is not expressly stated, that the scale of demand for each of our commodities remains unaltered, during the period that enters into our consideration.

§ 3. Assuming then that the price of, and demand for, any commodity vary together continuously but in opposite directions according to a certain scale, it is evident that for any given quantity of the article "supplied" or offered for sale, there must be some price at which (to use Mill's phrase) "the "equation of demand and supply" would be realised,—that is, at which the quantity demanded by purchasers in general would be just equal to the given quantity. Hence, if the quantity of

---

[1] See pp. 72, 73.

the article supplied is fixed independently of its price, and has to be sold for any price that can be got for it, this Equation of Demand and Supply will determine the market-price of the article; and in the case of an article whose price is kept above cost value by the limitation of its quantity, the natural or normal value will be similarly determined. But, in most cases we cannot assume Supply to be independent of price: as Mill himself points out, demand and supply are frequently equalised, not by an extended demand resulting from cheapness, but by "withdrawing a part of the supply." So far as this is the case, the determination of value is necessarily more complicated than Mill's exposition recognizes, and requires a fuller investigation of the influence of Price on Supply.

In making this investigation, I shall suppose, in the first instance[1] that the commodities in question are obtained by dealers from producers, and that any second-hand supply, sent back into the market by persons who have purchased for consumption, may be neglected:—a supposition which is actually true of almost all commodities consumed in a single use, and approximately true of many others. It will be convenient to consider first commodities belonging to Mill's first class, of which the Natural no less than the Market Value is stated to be determined by Supply and Demand. These are commodities of which the supply is insufficient to satisfy the whole of the demand that would exist for them at their cost value. Mill[2] says that such things are at a "scarcity" or "monopoly" value. He thus uses as convertible two terms which I find it necessary to distinguish; since it makes an important difference in the determination of the value of a scarce article, whether its supply is (1) controlled by a single seller, or several sellers who combining act as one, or is (2) in the hands of several sellers, competing freely with one another. It will be convenient to use the term "monopoly" to imply the former state of things, and to call the latter case that of simple "scarcity." It should be observed that a monopolized article will not necessarily be scarce: since a man may control the sole supply of any ware

[1] The case of second-hand supply is discussed in the concluding section of this chapter.
[2] Following Adam Smith.

and yet be unable to sell it at a price exceeding the cost value: indeed it may easily happen that he has to sell it (if at all) for a lower price still, as is the case (e. g.) with the authors of unreadable books. But we need not here concern ourselves with a monopoly of this unprofitable kind.

§ 4. Let us then begin by considering how supply will be determined in the case of a profitable monopoly. Here it soon appears that the effects of monopoly on value are very different under different conditions. There are some monopolized commodities for which the demand is keen, while the whole amount that it is possible to produce is very limited, and the additional expense of production involved in producing a larger amount instead of a smaller is comparatively small. In the case of such commodities, the decrease in price required to extend the demand sufficiently to meet any possible extension of supply will never be so great as to make the total profit on a larger quantity less than the total profit on a smaller. E. g. if the average produce of the Johannisberg vineyard were increased by one-half, without any decline in quality, it would be necessary to lower the price a little to get all the vintage sold off; but it would not be necessary to decrease it by nearly so much as one-third, so that (allowing for the additional expense of production), the net revenue of the proprietor of the vineyard would be considerably increased. In all such cases, then, the determination of supply is very simple: since self-interest will lead the proprietor of the commodity to produce and offer for sale as large an amount as he can. In other cases the monopolist has to limit the supply artificially, in order to secure the highest possible net profit: thus—to take Mill's illustration—the Dutch East India Company used, in good seasons, to destroy a portion of the produce of the Spice Islands; judging that if they tried to force a market for the whole produce, the price would fall so much that their net profit would be materially reduced. In cases of this latter kind it is obviously possible that the sale of a larger quantity at a lower price may bring in the same profit as the sale of a smaller quantity at a higher price: so that there may be no economic reason why the monopolist should choose one of the two quantities rather than the other: the "equation of supply and "demand" may thus be established indifferently at either of the two different values[1].

So far the articles considered have been luxuries; for which the maximum price obtainable is closely limited and could not exceed an amount small in proportion to the whole resources of the purchasers. But it is quite conceivable that an article absolutely necessary to subsistence might be thus monopolized; in which case the possible pecuniary gain of the monopolist, on the assumption of perfect commercial freedom, would theoretically amount to the whole spare wealth of the region affected by the monopoly. In practice, no doubt, the fear of popular indignation or legal interference would generally keep the monopolist's charges far below this theoretical maximum.

§ 5. Let us now consider the case of what I have called "simple scarcity value;" i.e. where a commodity, kept through scarcity above cost price, is sold by a number of persons who do not combine. Here, generally speaking, the amount of supply will be practically settled by the dealers selling all that they can bring to market. But it may happen here—just as in the case of strict monopoly,—that if each individual seller aimed intelligently at obtaining the greatest possible profit, and were able to rely on an equal exercise of enlightened self-regard on the part of all the rest, each would artificially limit his supply: though the limitations thus introduced would generally be different from those of a strictly monopolized commodity. For a point at which it would be the combined interest of the sellers to stop the supply, if only each could rely on all the others doing the same, would generally be a point at which it would be any individual seller's immediate interest to add to his supply; since the fall in the price of his commodity caused by this addition would generally be more than compensated by the profit on the extra amount that he would sell; and thus self-interest without concert would prompt each and all to enlarge the supply until it reached the point at which each would immediately lose by going further. But the determination of

---

[1] For simplicity's sake I have omitted the consideration of the varying *time* required for disposing of the stock of a commodity, according to the price: for this see § 6.

this point has, I conceive, hardly any practical interest[1]; since in practice such sellers—if combination were for some reason impracticable—would be almost certain to go beyond this point, and to sell as much as they could. For though each would immediately lose somewhat by so doing, his own loss would be much less than the loss he would inflict on the rest; since the price would fall for all alike, while he alone would be partly compensated by his profit on the extra amount he sold. On the other hand, if one seller were mistakenly to limit his supply, he would injure himself alone, while slightly benefiting his rivals. Under these conditions the coolest self-interest would prefer to err in the direction of extending supply; so that each would find it better on the whole to guard against

[1] Merely for the sake of illustration, I have worked out the following example of what might occur if the supply of a commodity were controlled by a small number of persons who did not combine, supposing that the conditions of demand were precisely known and that each could thoroughly rely on the enlightened self-interest of the others. Let us suppose that there are two springs of mineral water of the same quality, possessed and worked by two different persons. Let us suppose that the necessary expense of working each spring is £50 a month (including ordinary profit on the capital laid out in the original purchase) and that the expense of bringing to market each additional dozen bottles of the water may be estimated at 1s. Let us suppose the demand to be of such a kind that 500 dozen bottles a month can be sold for 9s. 6d. a dozen, but that the price must be lowered to 5s. to take off 1000 dozen a month; while if the supply were increased further the price per dozen would have to be reduced so much that the gain on the additional amount sold would not compensate for the loss on the rest. Under these circumstances it would obviously be more profitable for the two, if they could act in concert, to produce only 500 dozen a month: as in this case they would divide an extra profit of £112. 10s. (500 × 8s. 6d. - £100), while if they sold 1000 dozen they would only divide £100 (1000 × 4s. - £100). But if there is no concert between them, it will not be the interest of each to limit his production to 250 dozen: for if either were to do this it would obviously be the interest of the other to increase his own production to 750 dozen; since by that means he would gain an extra profit of £100 (750 × 4s. - £50), while it would be a matter of indifference—or even satisfaction—to him that his rival's extra profit was simultaneously reduced to zero. Each therefore would extend his production to 500 dozen; but not further if he could rely entirely on the enlightened self-interest of the other.

As I have said in the text, the realization of the conditions supposed is practically out of the question: but the case has a certain theoretical interest, as a conceivable transitional link between Monopoly and Competition. My conception of it is derived from Cournot (*Principes Mathématiques de la Théorie des Richesses*).

the danger of such error on the part of others, by extending his own supply: so long, that is, as it remained at a scarcity value. Hence in the case of a scarce article sold under open competition, the equation of supply and demand is practically almost certain to be realized by the simple process of selling the whole supply for what it will fetch.

§ 6. Let us pass to consider how the market-price will be determined in the case of a commodity of which the supply can be indefinitely increased. We have seen that industrial competition continually tends to make such market-price gravitate towards what Mill calls the "natural" or "cost" price of the commodity, though, through transient variations in Supply or Demand, it is continually liable to deviate—up or down—from this natural price. The question then is, how the exact point which it at any time reaches in its oscillations will be competitively determined; since it is clear, as was said, that the quantity offered will depend on the price as well as the quantity demanded: dealers are continually decided to sell or hold their stocks by the price prevailing in the market. Let us assume in the first instance (1) that production and consumption continue at a uniform rate through the year, and (2) that the commodity is not one that will deteriorate through being kept. Then, if we take any single dealer who has a stock of the commodity, we see that he will gain by selling it, unless he has reason to expect that the price at some definite distance of time will be higher than the present price by an amount more than sufficient to compensate him for his loss of interest or profit[1] on the capital locked up in the unsold stock, together with the expense and trouble of taking care of the goods. Hence, if we suppose that all the dealers have full information and perfect foresight, and that none of them would have to pay more than ordinary interest on borrowed money, we may infer that competition will keep the price at the point at which there is equal expectation of advantage in selling or holding back:

[1] Whether the dealer will require to be compensated for loss of interest merely, or for loss of profit, depends upon the condition of his business. If he does not see his way to using money profitably in his own line of business, he will only consider that he has to be compensated for loss of interest: but if business is flourishing, he will consider that he could be earning traders' profit on the money locked up.

i. e., at which any expected rise in prices is estimated as just sufficient to compensate for expense and loss on the stock kept back. Thus, so long as the price at any time is raised above cost price, these hypothetical dealers will sell all their stocks, unless they foresee in the proximate future a rise in demand more than sufficient to counterbalance the increase of supply[1] which the high price will tend to cause. If, on the other hand, the market-price should fall below cost price, owing to a temporary over-production, the action of the dealers in keeping back supply will check the fall at the point at which the difference between cost price and market-price is estimated as about equal to the probable loss on the stock kept back, during the time expected to elapse before the price rises again to cost point. Such would be the result under the simplified conditions that we have supposed; and such will tend to be the result, in proportion as these conditions are approximately realised in practice. But actually, of course, the supply that is kept back in any market partly depends on differences of opinion on the part of different dealers as to the future prospects of supply (or demand). It also depends, to a perhaps greater extent, on differences in another condition in which the theory as above given assumed uniformity. We have spoken of "loss of interest" as if there were a uniform rate of interest for all dealers; but it commonly happens that any trading body includes dealers in very different pecuniary circumstances, and some who would have to borrow at a higher rate than others. Hence these dealers may gain by selling off their goods at a price at which others will gain by keeping them back.

It may be observed that, under our hypothetical conditions, a rise in the general rate of interest will tend to increase the oscillations of market-price, by rendering it more inexpedient for dealers to keep back supply. A similar effect will be produced by any liability to deterioration in an unsold commodity. In an extreme case the deterioration might be so inevitable and rapid that it would never be the dealer's interest to keep any part of the supply longer than a single day; in which case the

[1] This increase may be caused either by stimulating production within the area from which the market in question has previously been supplied; or by extending this area, and attracting supplies from more distant producers.

price would tend to be fixed so that the day's demand should take off the day's supply.

Finally, the same general principle—that supply will on the average tend to be held back to an extent just sufficient to repay the loss of interest involved in holding back—will enable us to solve the slightly more complicated problems presented by commodities of which the supply and demand are not approximately uniform and continuous. Suppose (e.g.) that an article is produced only in one part of the year, while the intensity of the demand for it is uniform throughout the whole year, as is the case with the chief agricultural products. Here the competition of producers and dealers will tend to adjust the supply actually brought to market so as to keep the price throughout the year at a level that gradually rises, as the time of completion of the last harvest recedes into the past; in order to compensate for the interest lost by keeping produce unsold—apart from any further rise or fall that may be caused by good or bad expectations of the coming harvest. But here again we have in practice to take account of differences in the knowledge, foresight, and pecuniary circumstances of different dealers; and also, of course, of the complex variations in supply, and in facilities for conveyance, which a world-wide trade involves.

§ 7. So far I have not expressly adverted to the effects of speculative sales and purchases. But in fact, in discussing the problem of market-value in an abstract and simplified form, it was tacitly assumed that the legitimate work of speculation, in reducing the fluctuations of price that would otherwise result from fluctuations of supply and demand, would be completely performed without any special class of speculators; through the enlightened self-regard of ordinary dealers, prompting them to hold stocks when the price fell and sell when it rose. And of course, even under the conditions of actual business this assumption is largely realised; and, so far as this result of speculation is concerned, the only consequence of the development of a special class of speculators is that—as in other cases of division of labour—the work is likely to be more expertly performed. But the question still remains, how far speculation tends normally to produce only this moderative effect. According to Mill, this is necessarily the case so far as the speculators themselves profit by their operations. He admits, of course, that these have sometimes the opposite effect of causing or aggravating fluctuations: but he holds that, whenever this happens, the speculators themselves are the greatest losers. Thus he concludes that "the interest of the "speculators as a body coincides with the interest of the "public;" and "they can only fail to serve the public interest "in proportion as they miss their own[1]."

If we exclude the supposition of monopoly effected by combination among the speculators, this conclusion seems to me in the main sound, at least so far as markets for material products[2] are concerned; since those who purchase these products for use generally consider themselves as good judges of their quality as the speculators can be, and are not likely to be deluded into buying bad or useless wares through any operations of the latter. But even with these limitations Mill's doctrine is not altogether true; since so far as the changes in value which the speculator foresees and profits by are not alternations but comparatively permanent steps in one direction or the other, his gains are often made at the expense of the public; inasmuch as his operations do not render prices more stable, but merely antedate the rise or postpone the fall in price that would have occurred without them.

If, however, the possibility of combination be admitted, Mill's reasoning obviously fails as regards all commodities for which the demand diminishes but slightly as the price rises, so that (within the limits that we have practically to consider) the total price of the amount that can be sold at each rate continually increases as the amount itself diminishes. In the

[1] *Pol. Econ.* Book IV. c. ii. § 5.

[2] If the reasoning is intended to apply to actual markets for *securities*, it involves the important error of neglecting the influence exercised by the example of the speculators on a public conscious of its ignorance of the articles purchased. In such markets it often happens that artificial fluctuations in the values of sound securities, and even artificial elevations of the prices of worthless ones, when once started by speculative sales and purchases, are carried considerably further by the blind imitation of *bonâ fide* investors; and so become a source of profit to the speculators who are able to sell at the inflated, or buy at the lowered, rates which they have thus indirectly caused.

case of all such commodities it is quite possible for a combination of dealers, by buying up the whole or a great part of the stock in the market, to gain, through the high price obtained for a portion of what they have engrossed, more than enough to compensate them for any loss on the remainder. Food and other necessaries of life, as Mill himself explains, are commodities of this class. There is no doubt (e.g.) that a combination to raise the price of corn might be a source of great profit at the public expense, if only the combining dealers could secure a sufficient hold of the stock in the market, and if an outburst of public indignation against such "forestalling and regrating" did not interfere with the operation[1].

§ 8. Let us now examine more closely the determination of "natural" or "cost" price. Mill and other economists of the Ricardian school usually speak as if this was determined independently of the demand for the commodity: but it is clear that this cannot be the case with commodities of Mill's third class, which can only be increased at a continually increasing cost. Mill says that the natural value in such cases is determined "by the cost of production of the portion of the supply which is produced and brought to market at the greatest expense": but, obviously, this cost is only determined when the whole amount that it is the producers' interest to produce is determined; and this, by Mill's own account, must depend on the demand. It is evident, therefore, that the cost price of commodities of this class depends on the conditions of production and demand taken together: it is the price which would just remunerate the producers of the most (necessarily[2]) costly portion of the whole amount demanded at that price. Competition will obviously tend to cause an extension of the supply until the price is brought down to this point: and, obviously, it cannot tend—except through transient error—to cause any

[1] The famous "gold ring" in New York in 1869 is a striking instance of a successful combination of this kind: for, as all wholesale trade was carried on upon a gold basis, the metal was indispensable to solvency though not to life; while as the ordinary currency consisted of inconvertible paper, the amount of gold easily obtainable was small enough to admit of being monopolized.

[2] I mean by "necessarily" that the extra cost is not due to want of average skill and good fortune on the producers' part.

further extension. For, after this point has been reached, any further increase of average supply would involve an increased cost of production of the most costly portion of the supply; while the extension of demand necessary to take off the increased supply would involve a decreased price; so that the producers would lose doubly.

It remains to ask whether there is, as Mill holds, a "large" class of commodities which may be properly regarded as having a cost of production independent of the quantity from time to time demanded and supplied. I think it probable that there is a large class in reference to which such an assumption would not involve any very material error: but it can only be through an accidental balance of diverse effects that changes in the demand for a commodity tend to leave its cost of production altogether unaltered. This will appear when we look more closely at the elements of this cost. The "universal elements," as Mill says, are wages and profits: the occasional elements, taxes and any extra cost occasioned by the scarcity value of some of the requisites. Omitting taxes, it is clear that when any instrument or material required, directly or indirectly, for the production of an article is so limited in supply as to have a scarcity value, an intensified demand for the product will tend to cause a rise in the price of the requisite and consequently a rise—of course proportionally smaller—in the price of the product. And this result must also tend to follow when the requisite belongs to Mill's third class of commodities which we have just been considering: for (as we have just seen) a rise of demand tends to cause an increase in what we may call —after Jevons—their "final" cost of production[1] and therefore is their "natural" price. And as this third class includes "generally all the rude produce of the earth," it would seem that this action of demand on price must affect everything made out of this rude produce,—that is, almost all the products of industry.

There are, no doubt, many manufactured articles in whose cost of production the raw produce required directly or indirectly constitutes so small an item that the tendency of a rise in the

---

[1] That is, the cost of production of the costliest portion.

demand for the manufactured product to increase this item may be neglected without material error. In the case of such products, then, we need only consider whether changes in demand tend to affect the "universal elements" of cost of production; which, according to Mill's analysis, are "wages and profits",—including the profits of the capitalist who finally brings the ware to market, as well as those of other capitalists whom he reimburses in his payments for machinery[1] &c. To this Cairnes[2] has forcibly objected that "cost of production" ought to mean the "sacrifices undergone by producers," and that Mill's use of the term "confounds things" so "profoundly op-"posed to each other as cost and the reward of cost;" and it is certainly important to draw attention to the difference between the amount of efforts and sacrifices involved in production, and the amount of remuneration which these efforts and sacrifices obtain. But in order to give meaning to Cairnes' own statement that, if competition be perfect, "commodities will exchange *in* "*proportion to* their costs of production," we require a common measure of these efforts and sacrifices[3]; and I conceive that this common measure can only be found in their price. For suppose (e.g.) that, other things remaining the same, there is a general fall in the price paid for the use of capital: industrial competition must certainly tend to reduce proportionally the price of commodities whose production requires much capital: and similarly if the price of any particular kind of labour falls relatively to any other.

If, however, we hold with Mill that cost of production has to be estimated in terms of *remuneration* and not of *sacrifice*, the statement that commodities tend to "exchange for one "another in the ratio of their cost of production" must be admitted to give only an incomplete account of the manner in

[1] Mill *suggests* (III. ch. iv. § 5) this extension of the notion of 'cost of 'production' though he does not exactly *adopt* it. It may seem paradoxical to include in cost of production profits that are not yet realized: but the paradox disappears when we consider that it is not the actual profit, but the *expectation* of profit, which—*ceteris paribus*—determines the flow of capital to one industry rather than another; and which is thus the efficient cause of the variations in supply which raise or lower the market price.

[2] *Some Leading Principles*, Part I. c. iii.

[3] We clearly cannot definitely think of anything being "in proportion to" an aggregate of incommensurables.

which their "natural" value is determined. It analyses the total value of any product into the partial values of which it is compounded,—chiefly the values of the services of different labourers and capitalists—; but it does not explain the determination of these partial values. Indeed without further explanation the proposition might be interpreted as an insignificant truism; since, in a certain sense, as Cairnes pointedly observes, wares must always exchange in the exact ratio of their cost of production: as what remains over of the price of any ware, after reimbursing outlay, is the actual profit of the capitalist who finally brings the ware to market. This, of course, is not Mill's meaning; by the rates of wages and profits that enter into the determination of natural value, he means the *normal* rates to which, under the influence of industrial competition, the wages and profits of any industry tend to approximate. How these normal rates are determined is a question which I shall examine more fully hereafter[1]: here I am chiefly concerned to point out that they cannot be assumed to be altogether independent of the demand for the product. Let us take first the case of wages. It is no doubt natural to suppose, that under a system of perfectly free competition no known differences in the reward of labour could be permanently maintained except such as are required to remunerate differences in the efforts and sacrifices made by the labourers; and many of the disciples of Adam Smith have followed their master in making this general assumption[2]. But Mill has pointed out, in a noteworthy passage[3], the conclusions of which Cairnes has adopted and developed, that there are important differences in normal wages, which are due to relative scarcities of various kinds: chiefly to scarcities arising from the unequal distribution of wealth, which limits the power of performing certain kinds of services to the minority of persons whose parents have been able to afford the expense of prolonged training and sustenance for their children. The freest competition has not in itself any tendency to remove these scarcities, unless the present in-

---

[1] See ch. ix. of this book.
[2] Cp. *Wealth of Nations*, ch. x. first paragraph.
[3] *Pol. Econ.* B. II. c. xiv. § 2.

equalities in the distribution of wealth are first removed: and it seems clear that so far as the labour of any social grade above the lowest is thus purchased at a price more than sufficient to compensate, with interest, for the above-mentioned outlay on prolonged training and sustenance, it must be classed among the requisites of production that have scarcity values; which as we have seen, tend to vary with the demand for the product[1].

Let us now examine how the matter stands with the other element of cost of production, profit. In Cairnes' view, normal profits—unlike normal wages—may be rightly assumed to be independent of demand. "The competition of capital," he says, "being effective over the entire industry of each commer-"cial country, it follows that so much of the value of com-"modities as goes to remunerate the capitalists' sacrifice will "throughout the range of domestic industry" be proportioned to that sacrifice. This statement, however, seems to me to need restriction in more than one respect. In the first place, it must be borne in mind, in all discussions of industrial competition, that the profits of private manufacturers and traders are not published in statistical tables open to the inspection of all persons desirous of employing capital. The most observant man of business can usually attain only a rough approximation to the truth, in calculating the profits made in other industries and districts; and hence the equalizing force of competition can only be assumed to act strongly and cer-

---

[1] The case of the lowest grade of labour is more doubtful: see ch. VIII. § 6 of this book. It should be observed that this division of society into grades, *within* which industrial competition is supposed to be perfect, and *between* which it is supposed non-existent, does not correspond precisely to the facts of modern industrial communities ; but it corresponds to these facts more closely than the older hypothesis of generally effective competition. Ricardo (*Principles*, ch. i. § 2) avoids the conclusions above given by assuming that the differences in the remuneration of different kinds of labour are fixed and stable; in which case they would of course be independent of changes in demand. "The "estimation," he says, "in which different qualities of labour are held, comes "soon to be adjusted in the market with sufficient precision for all practical "purposes...the scale when once formed is liable to little variation." In any practical application of the theory of value the extent to which such fixity is actually maintained by custom should be carefully noted; but to assume fixity as normal is obviously inconsistent with the hypothesis of perfect competition.

tainly upon industries in which profits are either considerably above or considerably below the average. Within a somewhat broad margin on either side of the average its operation cannot but be vague and feeble; and hence the normal cost of production that regulates supply must be conceived as having a similar indefiniteness.

But Cairnes' statement involves a more fundamental theoretical difficulty. He appears to assume—with Mill and others—that the rate not only of interest but of that other element of profit which I have called "wages of management" must tend to be the same not only for capitals of the same amount, but even for capitals of different amount. But this assumption is hardly reconcileable with the proposition before quoted, that the remuneration of the (employing) capitalist tends to be proportioned to his sacrifice; since there seems no general ground for assuming that the trouble or other sacrifice involved in the employment of capital tends to be exactly proportioned to the amount of capital employed. I think[1] it probable, indeed, that the average rate of employers' profit tends, for the most part, to be not cognizably less on large than it is on small capitals; chiefly because large capitalists willing to manage their own capital have important advantages in industrial competition. But I know no ground for supposing this to be uniformly the case in all industries: and so far as increased demand for products increases the scale of production in any industry—as is ordinarily the case in manufactures—it is at least not improbable that the employers who thus increase their capital may be ultimately forced by industrial competition to submit to a lowered proportional rate of profit *per cent.* of capital.

And there is another and more obvious way in which the increase of production caused by a rise in demand will tend to modify the cost of production: viz. through the "tendency of "every extension of the market to improve the processes of pro-"duction" which Mill notices later, in speaking of International Trade. He remarks very justly[2] that "a country which produces "for a larger market than its own, can introduce a more extended

---

[1] The grounds for this opinion will be more fully discussed in ch. ix. § 3 of this book.

[2] Book III. ch. xvii. § 5.

"division of labour, can make greater use of machinery, and is "more likely to make inventions and improvements in the "processes of production": and of course the statement applies equally where the market for any commodity *within* a country receives a material extension. The consequent diminution in cost of production will of course be very different in different cases: but we must recognize that any important rise in demand has a general tendency to cause such diminution[1].

§ 9. To sum up; the Ricardian theory of the determination of Value by Cost of Production appears to me incontrovertible, at least as applied to modern civilised communities, if it is understood in a broad and vague sense; i.e. if it is understood merely to affirm that industrial competition is a force constantly acting in the direction of equalizing the remunerations of producers of the same class in different departments of industry, by increasing the supply—and so lowering the price—of commodities of which the producers are known to be receiving remunerations above the average of their respective classes, and similarly diminishing the supply and raising the price of the products of less profitable industries. But in the more exact and definite form in which the theory is stated even by Mill, it appears to me open to grave objections. It is the least of these objections that the suppositions made are too simple and uniform to correspond closely to the facts; defects of this kind beset all hypotheses framed for deductive reasoning on social phenomena, and all that we can do to remedy them is to note carefully the errors that thus come in and make a rough allowance for them. Of this nature is the error before pointed out in the supposition that industrial competition tends to establish a definite normal rate of profit in each industry, even when the statement is limited to capitals of about the same amount. As I have said, it is true that industrial competition *tends* to produce this result; but in admitting this we ought to note how much the mutual knowledge of profits actually obtainable by producers falls short of the mutual knowledge of

[1] It does not follow from this that a fall in demand will have a similar tendency to increase the cost of production: in most cases the effect of such a fall would, I conceive, rather be to diminish the number of separate establishments in which the branch of production in question was carried on.

prices actually obtainable by dealers in a tolerably well-organized market of material products; and how in consequence the tendency to a normal rate of profits begins to act feebly and vaguely, at a considerable interval from the attainment of the supposed definite result. In the case of wages this particular source of error is of less importance, since the actual rate of wages in any industry is easier to ascertain than the actual rate of profits; but here on the other hand the proportion between remuneration and sacrifice that industrial competition tends to establish is actually subject to more serious retardation and interference from various causes; especially from the difficulty of attracting labour from district to district and from industry to industry, and the different degrees in which custom and combination together operate in keeping wages up (or down) in different employments. So far, however, as the operation of these causes is independent of the demand for the product of the labour remunerated, they are more important in the theory of distribution than in the general theory of exchange; since they do not necessarily prevent the establishment, at any given time and place, of a normal cost of production towards which the market price tends to return after any variation temporarily caused by changes in demand or accidental excesses or deficiencies in supply. But so far as differences of wages are admittedly due to causes of which the operation is necessarily affected by variations in the demand for different kinds of labour—and we have seen that this is the case according to Mill's own view of industrial grades—it is manifestly illegitimate to regard cost of production as independent of demand. And this is equally the case, so far as increased aggregate production of a commodity tends to economy in the amount of labour required for a given amount of product; and so far, on the other hand, as it tends to raise the price of the "raw produce" that it employs, directly or indirectly, as material. Hence it appears to me unscientific to say broadly that "the value of things which can be increased in quantity at "pleasure does not depend (except accidentally, and during the "time necessary for production to adapt itself) upon demand." Even where the cost of production can be assumed to be approximately the same for all producers, we should represent

CHAP. II.] *OF MATERIAL PRODUCTS.* 197

the facts more exactly by supposing that in any given social and industrial conditions this cost of production will vary with the amount produced, just as we suppose that the amount demanded will vary with the price; though the former variation will no doubt be generally much slighter than the latter. The proposition, therefore, that the natural price of any product of this kind is equal to its cost of production, is certainly a true statement—on the assumption and with the qualifications already explained—but it is in almost all cases theoretically insufficient. Our formula must rather be, that it is a price at which the amount demanded is equal to the amount that would permanently be produced at a cost equal to the price, supposing social and industrial conditions unchanged[1].

And in the case of products of Mill's third class, of which the cost of production must be taken to be different for different portions of the aggregate amount produced, and to increase steadily as the aggregate increases, the formula becomes somewhat more complicated; the natural price must be stated to be that at which adequate remuneration could just be afforded to the producers of the costliest portion that it would be permanently worth while to produce, if social and industrial conditions remained unaltered.

We are thus enabled to show the close relation, which Mill's phraseology certainly tends to obscure, between the competitive determination of Natural Price, and that of Market Price. Market Price—supposing it definite and single as it would be in a perfect market—was explained to be the price at which the demand for the product in question would be sufficiently extensive to take off the actual supply (allowing for the possible withdrawal of a part of this supply in view of a prospective rise in demand or diminution of supply); while Natural Price (as we have seen) is similarly determined as the price at which the demand would be sufficiently extensive to take off the supply which, assuming social and industrial conditions unchanged, might permanently[2] be expected to be

[1] It is quite conceivable that, as in the case discussed in § 4, there may be several such prices.

[2] "Permanently"—because from the risk of starting a new business, especially in industries where production is on a large scale, from the difficulty of

produced at that price. There is, in fact, no sharp line to be drawn between the determinants in the two cases; prospective changes in cost of production, if their effect may be expected to be rapid and considerable, will enter into the calculations of dealers that influence market-prices through supply, as much as any other conditions of prospective supply or demand.

§ 10. The dependence of Value on Cost of Production and Demand together is further exemplified by the numerous cases in which two or more products are jointly produced by the same industrial process. "For example, coke and coal gas are both "produced from the same material, and by the same operation. "In a more partial sense, mutton and wool are an example; "beef, hides and tallow," &c. The values of the articles thus industrially connected are, as Mill himself explains[1], determined by Cost of Production and Demand conjointly in a complicated manner, which varies with the nature and extent of the connexion. All that can be stated generally is that the prices and amounts of any such set of products, under the action of industrial competition, will tend to conform to two conditions. Firstly the prices will tend to be such that the sum of them will repay their joint cost of production, including normal profit[2] on the capital employed: secondly the amounts will tend to be such that the demand for each article at the price will just about take off the supply[3]. It should be observed that in the examples above given the products are so connected that their amounts must increase or decrease together: but often they are wholly or to some extent alternatives, so that an increase in the production of one will, in the first instance at least, be attended by a diminution in the production of another. For instance, chickens and eggs are connected in

---

removing capital durably invested in forms specially adapted to particular industries, and other similar causes, market prices, however perfect competition became, would often be liable to remain long above or below their corresponding natural prices.

[1] B. III. c. xvi.

[2] By "normal profit" I mean "profit not much above or below the average "profit to be obtained on equal amounts of capital in other industries that do "not impose more sacrifices or require scarcer qualifications."

[3] Here again it is possible that these conditions may be equally satisfied by several different adjustments of prices and amounts.

this latter way. In the former case any rise in the demand for one only of the connected products, since by raising the joint price it will increase the supply of both, must obviously tend to lower the price of the other; as the sale of this latter will have to be extended without any rise in the demand for it. In the second case, on the other hand, any sudden rise in the demand for either product is likely to raise the price of the other temporarily—and perhaps permanently—by causing restriction of its supply. A more indirect connexion of this second class is that which subsists between commodities of which the production requires the same kind of raw or auxiliary material. In all such cases a rise in the demand for one of the connected commodities will in the first instance tend to increase the cost of production of the other; but whether this increase will tend to be sustained will depend on whether the production of the material in question becomes more costly, in whole or in part, by being increased in amount.

Another case that may be classed under the head of joint production is that in which different commodities are produced by the same labourers, but by industrial processes altogether separate: as when cultivators of the soil supplement their agricultural earnings by domestic manufactures in winter. The primary tendency of industrial competition is to keep the *total* remuneration of any class of labourers approximately equal to that of any other class whose labour does not entail materially more sacrifices, or require scarcer qualifications or more costly preparation. It therefore, in the case we are considering, affects primarily the *aggregate* price of the labourers' different products —just as if they were produced by the same industrial process—: it only acts directly on the price of each separate kind of product, so far as the producers have competing opportunities of employing profitably the particular portion of work-time which this product absorbs. But when a man has two occupations, of which one is the main source of his income, while the other is merely taken up to fill the fragments of time left by the former, his opportunities of employing these fragments profitably are likely to be somewhat restricted: so that, if the supply of what is produced in these leavings of work-time is sufficient to meet the demand at a price below what industrial competition under ordinary conditions would require, the price of the product is likely to be determined mainly by the relations of Quantity and Demand,—so long as it is enough to induce the labourer to prefer work to leisure.

Finally, it should be noticed that the values of two commodities may be connected through Demand, as well as through Supply; so far as one of the two is, either in ordinary consumption or in any kind of production, a substitute for the other. Thus (e.g.) an extension in the demand for mutton, due to a fall in its value, would have the effect of restricting the demand for beef, and would tend thereby to affect its cost of production and value. Indeed this kind of connexion may be said to subsist, in an attenuated form, among commodities generally; since such an extension in the demand for any one commodity as makes the aggregate price paid for it a larger share of the income of the community, tends *pro tanto* to reduce the demand for all other articles of consumption. The actual extent to which any one commodity may thus become an alternative for any other is of course extremely different in different cases; and a careful examination of these varying connexions is a fundamentally important element in any investigation of the specific laws of demand of different commodities.

§ 11. The point last noticed is important in considering a case in the determination of value, which—to avoid needless complexity—I have left out of account in the preceding discussion: i.e. the case of durable products, of which the supply in the market at any time is to a material extent not obtained from producers, but consists of second-hand articles sent back into the market by consumers. Sometimes such second-hand commodities—as (e.g.) old books, furniture and works of art generally—rise more or less out of competition with any first-hand products, to a scarcity price which has no relation to cost of production. Even here, however, we cannot generally regard the supply as given independently of the price: since the quantity supplied will tend to be somewhat increased by any rise in price, just as the quantity demanded tends to be diminished: so that a rise in price caused by an intensification of demand tends to be partly counteracted by the increased inducement to consumers to send back the articles into the market. Sometimes, again, the second-hand commodity is practically only an alternative for a first-hand commodity of a different quality;—as in the case of second-hand clothes. Where the two kinds of supply compete effectively with each other,—as in the important case of houses—the second-hand supply of course tends to affect the price of the first-hand articles by lowering the demand for them, as above explained; while the cost of production of the first-hand commodity tends to affect the price of the second-hand one in a peculiar indirect way; the natural price of the latter tends to correspond to the cost of producing not the same article, but an article equally useful. The value thus determined may—through deterioration and change of fashion—be indefinitely less, not only than the cost of producing the original article, but even than the cost of reproducing it in its present condition. So long as the demand at the price thus determined cannot be satisfied by the second-hand supply, the market-price of the latter will be effectively maintained by the cost of producing an equally useful article: but if at any time the second-hand supply is more than sufficient to meet the demand at this 'natural' price, the market-price of the commodity may of course be for a time simply determined by the relation of Quantity to Demand. This (e.g.) is liable to be the case with certain portions of the supply of immovable articles, such as buildings.

CHAPTER III.

THEORY OF INTERNATIONAL VALUES.

§ 1. IN the preceding chapter the cost of carriage of commodities to the markets in which their price is actually determined, has been cursorily noticed as a normal element in the cost of production. It is almost superfluous to observe that it is an element to which the development of industry has hitherto tended to give continually increasing importance. Though the progress of invention has steadily operated to reduce the average cost of conveying a given weight of goods over a given space; still the amount of goods carried and the distances over which they are conveyed have continually increased in a greater ratio; so that, in the most civilised part of the world, the proportion of the labour and capital of mankind at present employed in the business of moving goods is larger than it was at any earlier period in the history of civilisation. This is so strikingly the case that the growth of a nation's foreign trade is sometimes vaguely spoken of as though it constituted absolute and unquestionable evidence of advance in industrial prosperity. It may therefore be useful to point out—what might otherwise seem too obvious to be worth stating—that it is *ceteris paribus* an economic disadvantage that any commodity should be produced at a distance from the market in which it is normally sold; and that if in any case this disadvantage can be got rid of —without incurring any equally serious drawback—through the production at home of some commodity hitherto imported from abroad, the resulting diminution of trade would obviously be a mark of industrial improvement, and not of retrogression. And *a priori* we have every reason to suppose that, in the

CHAP. III.] *THEORY OF INTERNATIONAL VALUES.* 203

continually changing conditions of industry, opportunities for this kind of improvement will continually present themselves; and that the *vis inertiæ* of custom is no less liable to maintain the importation from abroad of goods which might be advantageously produced in the proximity of their market, than it is to keep any other part of the process of production in an economically backward condition. And therefore while the progress of industry, under the stimulus of alert and enlightened self-interest, may be doubtless expected to extend and enlarge trade continually in some directions, it is at the same time probable that it will reduce and diminish it in others.

As in the present chapter I propose to consider the special conditions affecting the value of commodities produced at a considerable distance from their consumers, it seems expedient to obtain a clear view of the cases in which such production is likely to be remunerative, and may accordingly be assumed as a normal element of a competitively organized industrial society. The following are the chief cases which it is important to distinguish.

I. Some commodities for which there is a general demand cannot be produced at all except in certain localities, situated at a considerable distance from important sections of their consumers. This is the case, generally speaking, with metals and other products of extractive industry; and also with certain agricultural products, such as wines of special quality.

II. There are other staples of international trade which could generally be produced at a moderate distance from their consumers, at least over a large part of the region inhabited by civilised man; but which can be most economically produced, even in distant markets, if a portion at least of the required supply of them is transported thither from certain places which offer special natural advantages for their production. This is the case, to a varying extent, with corn and other important products of agriculture.

III. In other cases, again, commodities can be most economically produced for distant markets not on account of any special advantages afforded by the place in which they are made, but because the cost of carriage is outweighed by the economic gain through co-operation and division of labour, obtained by the concentration of a manufacture—or of several connected manufactures—in one locality. To some extent this gain consists merely in the substitution of a more important saving of carriage for a less important; the cost of conveying raw and auxiliary materials required in the manufacture, or of conveying the product itself from one set of workers to another, being reduced by the local concentration of connected industries to an extent that more than compensates for the additional cost of conveying the finished product to the consumer. But besides this, various other advantages, previously noticed[1], of production on a large scale are obviously only obtainable if a correspondingly large normal demand can be secured for the product; and in the case of commodities of which the amount consumed by any one individual is small, an extensive demand must necessarily be the demand of consumers scattered over a wide area.

IV. The gain thus derivable from co-operation rendering it economically advantageous for men to aggregate themselves in the large closely packed masses which we find in continually increasing size in modern industrial towns, it becomes correspondingly necessary to obtain the supply of food, fuel, and certain other commodities required in large amounts for the ordinary consumption of any such mass by bringing a large part of it from a considerable distance.

V. Finally, we have to notice the important case in which a commodity is most economically obtained from a distance, even though it could be produced in the neighbourhood of its market with no greater—or even less—expenditure of labour and capital; because the returns obtainable by equal labour and capital in some other employment are so much greater, that the loss involved in employing them to produce the commodity in question would more than counterbalance the saving in cost of carriage. A striking instance of this was furnished by the gold discoveries of Australia; one consequence of which was that Australia began to import cheese and butter largely from abroad, although the pastures of New South Wales and Victoria offer unusual facilities for dairy-farming. The

[1] Cf. Book I. c. iv. § 6.

CHAP. III.] *THEORY OF INTERNATIONAL VALUES.* 205

high average remuneration obtainable by labour in gold-mining had raised the wages of Australian labour generally—and therefore in dairy-farming—so much, that the consequent additional cost of making butter in Australia was greater than the cost of conveying it from Ireland[1].

§ 2. It is evident that this last cause of foreign trade can only operate, so far as physical or social obstacles render the mobility of labour temporarily or permanently imperfect. Had it been as easy to draw over Irish labourers to Australia as it is to bring them to England, their influx would soon have brought down wages to a point at which it would have been less expensive to produce the butter required by Australia in Australian dairies. Now, according to Mill, it is only on account of this imperfect mobility that a special formula is required for determining the values of commodities brought from distant places; because, owing to the differences which this imperfect mobility allows to subsist between the remuneration of labourers or capitalists or both in different countries, cost of production is prevented from determining the normal value of such imported commodities. To take Mill's illustration: suppose England imports wine from Spain, giving cloth in exchange: then "if the cloth and the wine were both made in Spain, they "would exchange at their cost of production in Spain; if they "were made in England, they would exchange at the cost of "production in England. But"—we are told—"all the cloth "being made in England and all the wine in Spain, they are "in circumstances to which the law of cost of production is not "applicable. We must accordingly fall back" upon what "may "be appropriately named the Equation of International Demand;" the principle, namely, that "the produce of a country exchanges "for the produce of other countries at such values as are "required in order that the whole of her exports may exactly "pay for the whole of her imports[2]."

This Equation of Reciprocal Demand—if the phrase be not too dignified for a formula that contains so little information— will doubtless tend to be realised in international as well as in domestic trade: but I cannot agree with Mill that Cost of

---
[1] Cf. Cairnes, *Essays in Political Economy*, I. p. 38.
[2] Mill, *Pol. Econ.* B. III. c. xviii. § 1.

Production is to be left out of account altogether in the former, any more than in the latter case. His error appears to me most simply manifested in the earlier part of his argument, in which, to exhibit the "elementary principle of International "Values," he supposes, for the sake of argument, that the carriage of commodities from one country to the other could be effected without labour and without cost. It is easy to show that, under the circumstances thus supposed, cost of production must determine the value of exported commodities just as much as the value of commodities consumed at home; unless we further suppose that, after the trade is established, there is no product *common* to the trading countries—a supposition manifestly extravagant in the case of England and Spain (which Mill takes as examples) and most other countries inhabited by modern nations[1]. For let us suppose that there is at least one other commodity—say corn—which is produced both in England and in Spain. According to Mill's general theory of value, discussed in the preceding chapter, the relative values of cloth and corn in England must be determined by their comparative costs of production; and, again, the relative values of wine and corn in Spain must be determined in the same way. But if we suppose cost of carriage to be eliminated, there is no reason why the value either of wine or cloth should be altered by exportation; hence, the values of

[1] A critic of this chapter—Mr Bastable, *Theory of International Trade*, Appendix C—says that I have "forgotten that Mill expressly regards" this further hypothesis "as a necessary consequence of the non-existence of cost of "carriage. 'But for it,' he says 'every commodity would be regularly imported "'or regularly exported. A country would make nothing for itself which it did "'not also make for other countries'" (*Principles*, iii. 18, § 2). This, however, does not amount to saying that there would be no product common to any two trading countries, if cost of carriage were non-existent: since, granting Mill's inference, two countries might still make the same thing for export to a third as well as for home consumption. But though Mill's statement is not quite so extravagant as that which Mr Bastable regards as its equivalent, it is certainly quite incorrect;—as, indeed, Mr Bastable points out. For it is obvious that in the case of any of the chief products of agriculture and mining, a country might be able to produce a portion of the quantity required for its own demand as economically as it could be produced elsewhere, and yet unable to produce more except at a cost rapidly increasing with the amount: in this case, if we suppose the cost of international carriage annihilated, it would still produce something for itself which it did not produce for other countries.

both wine and cloth relatively to corn, and therefore relatively to each other, must be as much determined by cost of production as the values of home commodities are[1]. The "Equation of "International Demand" will still be maintained, but it will have no effect in determining the value of wine or cloth; since, if we leave cost of carriage out of account, there can be no reason why the wine should be entirely paid for in cloth, or *vice versâ*; there can be no reason why any debt remaining on either side, after balancing the wine against the cloth, should not be liquidated in corn or some other commodity. As we have seen in the preceding chapter, the costs of production of all the commodities concerned will, generally speaking, tend to be somewhat modified by changes in the demand for them: but this consideration is not in itself a reason for special treatment of international values; since, under the circumstances supposed, the demands of the two different countries for each commodity might be treated as one aggregate demand.

It would seem then, that if cost of carriage were left out of account there would be no need of a special principle for determining International Values. And in fact it appears to me that this need essentially depends on a condition to which Mill has not adverted: viz. that in explaining the determination of international values—or rather of the values of wares interchanged between distant places—we have to take into account not merely the expense of conveying wares into the foreign country, but also the expense of bringing home their value in some form or other. If we take this double cost of carriage into account, we shall find that "Cost of Production including "carriage" has an important relation to the determination of the price of the products of foreign trade: as giving the limits between which the competitive price tends to vary according to the varying conditions of demand for foreign products in each country.

This will become clearer if we consider an exceptional case in which cost of production, thus understood, would determine

---

[1] It does not of course follow that the wine and cloth will exchange for each other in proportion to their respective costs; since, if (as Mill supposes) labour and capital are imperfectly mobile, the cost of producing corn may be different in the two countries.

the value of the products of foreign trade, on the assumption of free competition, as definitely as it can determine the value of commodities produced at home.

Suppose there are two countries A and B, precisely similar in their conditions of production as regards all commodities except silk, which is produced in A and is incapable of being produced in B, though it would be eagerly consumed there; and suppose that a trade previously prevented is now opened for the first time between A and B. Silk will undoubtedly be carried from A to B, but as the trader could take back nothing which would have a higher value in A than it had in B, he must to recoup himself sell the silk permanently at a value which will pay not only the whole expense (including normal profit[1]) of carrying it from A to B, but also the whole expense of carrying back something else—whatever can be most conveniently carried—from B to A. He must charge this, in order to get the ordinary profit; and competition would prevent him from charging more. In this case the normal value of silk in B will evidently exceed its value in A by exactly the double cost of carriage between the two countries; and will therefore be determined by the cost of production just as much as the value of silk in A was before the trade was opened.

The case supposed is no doubt highly improbable;—and even if it existed at the outset, it would most likely be modified in consequence of the trade itself. It is almost certain that there would be some commodity in the production of which the second country B had a certain advantage—which if produced in A had to be produced at a higher relative cost of production. Let us suppose that there is one such commodity; which we will take to be hardware. Then, even though the advantage be comparatively slight, and less than would be required to pay the cost of carrying the hardware from B to A, it is evident that the trader who exports the silk to B will gain something extra by bringing back the proceeds of its sale to A in hardware rather than any other article. And this extra gain—like any other diminution in the expenses of

[1] For the purpose of this hypothetical reasoning it is legitimate to suppose 'normal profit' to be more definitely and simply determined than we have seen to be actually the case.

CHAP. III.] *THEORY OF INTERNATIONAL VALUES.* 209

bringing an article to market—industrial competition will tend to transfer to the consumers. But the question still remains, To which set of consumers will it be transferred? to those of A or to those of B? If the amount imported from B is not sufficient to supply the whole demand for hardware in A, at the price at which it can be remuneratively produced in that country, the normal price of hardware in A may be kept up by its home cost of production; so that the consumers of silk in B will reap the whole extra gain. But if we suppose that, when the trade is fully established, neither of the wares exchanged is produced in the importing country; the principle that price 'must correspond to cost of production' does not determine in which of two different ways the traders' profits will tend to be brought down to the ordinary level;—whether by selling A's wares a little cheaper in B or B's wares a little cheaper in A. The combination of these two results that the competition of traders will tend to bring about will be determined *ceteris paribus*, as I shall presently explain, by the relation of the demand for A's wares in B to the demand for B's wares in A. But at any rate it must be a combination that will realise Mill's "Equation of International Demand": the trade will not be in equilibrium unless the quantity of A's wares sold in B equal in value the quantity of B's wares sold in A[1]: and the tendency to this result will operate equally, however many wares are exchanged on either side. The action of industrial competition must always be conceived as tending to bring about this equilibrium; though actually, as the laws of demand no less than the conditions of supply are continually varying, the point of equilibrium must be conceived to undergo corresponding variations; and, at any given time, the tendencies towards equilibrium may easily be less strong than tendencies in the opposite direction, due to unforeseen changes in trade or industry[2].

[1] I assume for the present that there are no payments to be made between the two countries on-account of other transactions than those of trade.

[2] Mill is right in pointing out that there may possibly be several points of equilibrium: the conditions of demand for the commodities exchanged may be such that the equation of reciprocal demand may be equally well established at any one of a number of different sets of prices. But this possibility is not peculiar to the theory of International Values.

§ 3. We may now observe that in the above reasoning it has not been explicitly assumed, that labour and capital do not move freely between the trading countries; but we have made this assumption implicitly so far as we have ignored effects on labourers and capitalists, regarded as purchasers, of any changes in the value of the wares exchanged in the trade. To this extent, the assumption of the imperfect mobility of capital is no doubt required to give scope for the operation of the law of international values above stated. For if we suppose a perfect mobility of labour and capital within any region, every change in the price of articles brought from a distance to any place in it must be conceived to have an effect proportional to its magnitude in attracting or repelling inhabitants from that place; and in this case the values of wares interchanged between two places within such a region will be determined ultimately not by the equation of reciprocal demand but by the tendency to equalize the aggregate of utilities obtainable by similar sacrifices in different localities. But if labourers duly supplied with capital will not transport themselves from A to B, merely in order to get B's exports cheaper at the cost of getting A's exports dearer; then, so far as trade between distant places exists, the normal values of the products of such trade will be determined by the Equation of International Demand.

No doubt the varying degrees of mobility of labour and capital will have important effects on the course of international trade; since—as we have seen—if wages and interest are considerably higher in one country than in another it may be profitable for the former to import commodities which it could produce with less labour and capital at home. But in any case an essential part of the reason why a special theoretical treatment has to be applied to the products of international trade, is that a double cost of carriage has here to be taken into account. In fact, we have here a special case of the kind discussed at the close of the preceding chapter, in which the values of two commodities are causally connected through their being the joint products of one process of production; the one process here being the process of double carriage, each half of which is commercially inseparable from the other.

I must now explain a proviso which I should have placed

CHAP. III.] *THEORY OF INTERNATIONAL VALUES.* 211

earlier in this chapter, only that it is more easily understood at the point of the discussion which we have now reached. We cannot, in treating of international trade, conceive 'price' as we conceived it in treating of the general theory of value: i.e. as money-price, the value of money being supposed to remain unchanged. For in treating of international trade, we cannot legitimately assume that the value of gold and silver bullion—the metallic money of commerce—remains unchanged as we pass from one country to another; since bullion, being itself an article of trade, will tend to have in a country which obtains it by trade a value higher than that which it has where it is produced, by some portion of the cost of its own carriage and of that of the equivalent brought home in exchange for it. In the present discussion, therefore, we must conceive price as estimated not in the actual money of any of the trading countries, but by a standard of value common to the countries, obtained by estimating and allowing for the differences in the value of actual money: and, for consistency, we must apply the same standard in estimating cost of production[1]. It will be convenient to distinguish the price so estimated as 'real price.' The manner in which this common standard of value is to be obtained, has been explained in an earlier chapter[2]; in which also the degree of inexactness to which it is liable has been pointed out.

With this proviso, we may say that, in the manner explained in the preceding section, each of two mutually trading countries can normally obtain the wares of the other at a price somewhat less than cost of production *plus* double carriage, owing to the comparative advantage that it will usually have over the other in the production of some commodity. It may happen, of course, that each product is sold at such a price that it exactly pays its own cost of carriage; but there is no general tendency to this result. We can only say generally that the home cost of production together with double cost of carriage

---
[1] It will be observed that I do not follow Mill in substituting "labour" for "wages" as the main element of cost, when treating of International Values. I think that the reason before given, for estimating cost of production in terms of remuneration and not of sacrifice, applies to the wares of international trade as much as to any other products.
[2] Book I. ch. ii.

gives us a *maximum* value, and home cost of production without cost of carriage a *minimum* value; between which the normal value of wares in a foreign country may vary indefinitely with the varying conditions of trade; but no wares can rise, unless very temporarily, above the former point, and only under very exceptional circumstances can any fall below the latter. In actual trade it never happens that either extreme is reached, at least by the aggregate of a country's exports; there are always some products to be found in producing which a country has at least a relative advantage as compared with some of the countries with which it trades; accordingly most (if not all) of the wares of international trade are normally sold in the countries importing them at prices which will pay at least some part of their cost of carriage, as well as their home cost of production. In speaking of the home cost of production of the wares exchanged, we must bear in mind that the cost of producing such wares—estimated separately from the cost of the trade itself—will often be materially altered by the extension of their sale which the trade brings about; and their prices as imports will of course be altered in the same direction (though not necessarily in precisely the same ratio). On the one hand, in the case of manufactured articles, the extension of sale is sometimes the cause of a material cheapening in their cost of production, by enabling the manufacture to be carried on upon a larger scale; while, on the other hand, in the case of agricultural produce, we can often observe that the initial rise of price which the foreign demand causes is sustained by a permanent increase in the cost of producing the costliest portion of the article. Apart from these reactions of demand on cost of production, the division of double cost of carriage between the two countries will depend upon the degree in which the demand in either country for the foreign wares of the other is more easily extensible than the corresponding demand on the other side—i.e. is of such a kind that a comparatively small fall in the prices of the foreign wares causes, *ceteris paribus*, a comparatively large extension in the purchases of them. The more this is the case, the larger will be the share of the double cost of carriage that will tend to be added to the imports of the country in question. For, through the oscillations of supply

CHAP. III.] *THEORY OF INTERNATIONAL VALUES.* 213

that practically determine, at any given time, the division of the double cost of carriage, this extensibility of demand will keep up the prices on the one side as compared with the other; so that the equilibrium of trade will tend to be attained at a rate of interchange favourable to the country where the demand for foreign wares is less extensible.

§ 4. The view above given of the determination of international values may—with due precautions—be illustrated by the familiar phenomenon of the fluctuations in exchange of money between two countries. For it is by means of these fluctuations that the transactions of Importation and Exportation are economically connected; since the payments due to foreigners in consequence of importation are normally liquidated by transferring the money-debts due from foreigners in consequence of exportation. When the exchange between two countries is at par, any such debt—assuming for simplicity that its payment is certain and immediate and that both countries have standard coin of the same metal—is purchasable on either side for an amount of coined metal equivalent to that which the debt renders payable on the other side ; the instrument of transfer being usually a bill of exchange,—i.e. a written order by the exporting merchant directing his correspondent in the country to which he has exported to pay the money due. In this way, when the exchange is at par between two countries, as the means of paying money due in either may be purchased in the other by an equivalent amount of domestic coin, the money-price of the wares of either in the other will tend to correspond to the money-cost of production at home together with the money-cost of carriage. But if the trade has produced an excess of debts on either side, it may not be possible to liquidate it without the payment of actual coin: and then competition may increase the price of bills payable in the country to which coin has to be sent by a premium equivalent to the total cost of sending bullion or foreign coin to the country in question, and transforming it into the current coin of that country. When the price of bills has risen to this point, it is evident that the cost of importing wares from the country in question, to be paid for by these high-priced bills, must substantially include the cost of conveying the money back as well as the cost of carriage of the wares themselves. On the other hand, when the opposite extreme of the fluctuation is reached, the cost of carriage of the wares themselves is at least partly paid by premiums on bills[1].

These fluctuations accordingly exemplify and in a sense *represent* the fluctuations in the real cost of obtaining foreign wares of which our theory gave an account. But, for the reason explained in the preceding section, the former do not exactly correspond to the latter: for if money have a greater purchasing power in (say) the United States than in England, the addition to the real price of English goods in the United States, over their real price in England, will be correspondingly greater than it appears; and *vice versâ*.

In the preceding discussion I have supposed for simplicity's sake that only two countries are engaged in trade, and that their mutual indebtedness arises only from the exchange of their respective produce. In applying the theory to concrete facts it must be borne in mind, first, that the mutual indebtedness of nations results "from the relative totals of all the "amounts expended by each upon the other, whether in "payment of produce and manufactures, or for the purchase "of shares and public securities, or for the settlement of profits, "commissions, or tributes of any kind, or for the discharge "of the expenses incurred in foreign residence or travel: in "fact, from the entire payments (or promises to pay) which "pass between the respective countries. The liability incurred "is identical in its effect, whatever its origin may be[2];" every such liability has to be liquidated by the transmission either of money or of an order to receive money payable in the foreign country. Still the greater part of the transactions by which debts are incurred between countries, and the means of paying such debts obtained, consists of the importations and exportations of produce.

And secondly, it must be borne in mind that the condition of the Foreign Exchanges of any country, and consequently the share that it pays of the cost of its foreign trade, depends on its relations of debit and credit not with each country sepa-

---

[1] I say 'at least partly,' because in most cases the expense of conveying goods is greater than the expense of conveying money.

[2] Goschen, *Foreign Exchanges*, c. 2.

rately, but with all countries taken together; since, through the process technically called arbitration of exchange, a payment due from country A to country B may be made by assigning to B a debt due from a third country C to A. "There is some little additional expense, partly commission "and partly loss of interest, in settling debts in this circuitous "manner, and to the extent of that small difference the ex- "change with one country may vary apart from that with "others; but in the main, the exchanges with all foreign "countries vary together, according as the country has a "balance to receive or to pay on the general result of its "foreign transactions[1]."

§ 5. The theory above expounded applies, of course, to trade within a country no less than to foreign trade;—unless, as·I said before, the necessity of considering the equation of reciprocal demand is superseded by the assumption of a perfect mobility of capital and labour. It is therefore strictly to be called a 'Theory of the values of wares exchanged between 'distant places,' rather than a Theory of International Values. It is true that in a country where the same paper currency was used throughout, the facts that we have been examining would generally escape notice; because as the cost of transmitting money would be trifling, there could be no manifest fluctuations of inland exchange. Still, none the less would money be more abundant and prices at a higher level in towns or districts for whose products there was a keen demand in other parts of the country: so that the former would really bear less than an equal share of the cost of the trade that they carried on with the latter. Accordingly, there is no sharp distinction to be drawn—apart from the effects of governmental interference—between the laws actually governing the values of products sold within the country in which they are produced, and the laws governing the values of imported wares. All that can be said is that in dealing with a modern civilised country, duly furnished with means of communication and conveyance and substitutes for coin, the error involved in our assumption that the market values of domestic products tend to be everywhere the same, allowing for the cost of their carriage

[1] Mill, Book III. c. xx. § 3.

to market, will generally speaking be comparatively slight; whereas in considering the values of the wares of international trade, a similar error would not unfrequently be material[1].

At the same time, it is only in the case of Foreign Trade that the investigation of the conditions of favourable interchange excite practical interest; because it is only in this case that there has ever been a serious question of governmental interference with a view of making the interchange more favourable. Whether such interference can ever be on the whole expedient I do not now propose to discuss: but it may be observed that the theoretical determination of the division of the expenses of Foreign Trade does not enable us to determine the total amount of the gain resulting from such trade to either nation. To know this, we must know what each nation would have produced with the labour and capital now employed in producing for foreign trade: which generally we can but vaguely guess.

Nor, again, does it in any way follow that the nation that pays the greatest share of the double cost of carriage is the one that gains least. Indeed the very opposite may very likely be the fact; as will appear if we look again at the hypothetical case considered in § 2, where we supposed an entirely unreciprocated demand in one country B for the products of another country A. Under these circumstances, as we saw, the trade tends to be carried on under the most unfavourable conditions possible for B, as far as the division of expenses is concerned; since the consumers in B have to pay the whole of the double cost of carriage. On the other hand it is not improbable that the consumers in B will have the greater gain in utility; since they obtain access by the trade to an entirely new commodity, whereas the inhabitants of A only obtain at best a somewhat more economical way of acquiring commodities producible at home.

[1] Hence, in the discussion of the preceding chapter, we neglected, for simplicity's sake, the differences in the purchasing power of money in different localities within the same country. These differences, as we have before seen, it is theoretically impossible to estimate with perfect exactness; but it should be observed that so far as they actually exist, a further theoretical imperfection is introduced into the determination of value by cost of production.

CHAPTER IV.

DEFINITION OF MONEY.

§ 1. In the course of the preceding chapter we have been led to see the importance, in the theory of "international" values, of a clear view of the nature and causes of variations in the values of money. But the very denotation of the term money is so fluctuating and uncertain, that before we discuss the laws by which its value is determined, it seems desirable to make a thorough and systematic attempt to define the term itself[1].

Here, as in previous attempts to obtain definition, it seems best to begin by a careful and unbiassed consideration

[1] Jevons, in his excellent little book on "Money," tells us that the ingenious attempts that have been made to define money "involve the logical "blunder of supposing that we may, by settling the meaning of a single word, "avoid all the complex differences and various conditions of many things, re-"quiring each its own definition." Without denying that this blunder has been sometimes committed, I think it misleading to suggest, as Jevons does, that the attempt to define a class-name necessarily implies a neglect of the specific differences of the things contained in the class. Indeed, when he goes on to say that the many things which are or may be called money—"bullion, standard "coin, token coin, convertible and inconvertible notes, legal tender and not legal "tender, cheques of various kinds, mercantile bills, exchequer bills, stock cer-"tificates, &c."—"require each its own definition," he apparently maintains the rather paradoxical position that it is logically correct to give definitions of a number of species, but logically erroneous to try to define their common genus. It is easy to show that several at least of these more special notions present just the same sort of difficulties when we attempt to determine them precisely as the wider notion "money" does. For instance, the distinction between bullion and coin seems at first sight plain enough; but when we ask under which head we are to classify gold pieces circulating at their market value in a country that has a single silver standard, we see that it is not after all so easy to define coin. The characteristic of being materially coined—that is, cut and stamped by authority—though it has always been combined in our own experience with the

of the actual usage of the term. And here we are met at the outset by a rather remarkable phenomenon. There seems to be a tolerable accord among persons who write about money in England at the present time, as to the denotation that ought to be given to the term when they directly attempt to define it; at any rate, the margin of difference is inconsiderable in comparison with the amount of their agreement. Unfortunately the denotation so given disagrees very widely with their customary use of the term when they are not trying to define it; and this discrepancy is not of a minor kind, but as fundamental as can well be conceived. When the question is expressly raised they have no doubt that by money they mean what they also call currency, that is, coin and bank-notes. They see the need of distinguishing the latter as paper money or paper currency; and they recognize the existence of a narrower definition which restricts the term money to coined metal, on the view that bank-notes are mere promises to pay money, which ought not to be confounded with

characteristic of being legal tender, is capable of being separated from it; so that we have to choose between the two in our definition. Similarly, we may inquire whether by calling notes convertible it is merely meant that their issuer has promised to convert them into coin on demand, or whether a belief is affirmed that he would so convert them if required? If the latter alternative be chosen, it must be evident that the legitimacy of such a belief must depend upon the nature and extent of the provisions made by the issuer for meeting demands of coin; so that in order to define convertibility precisely we shall have to determine what provisions are adequate, and whether all possible demands should be provided for or only such as may reasonably be expected. Then further, how shall we treat the case—which used to be common in the United States—of notes for which coin will almost certainly be paid if demanded, but not without a serious loss of good-will to the demander? In short, we cannot escape the proverbial difficulties of drawing a line, if we attempt to use any economic terms with precision; and instead of seeing in these difficulties—as Jevons seems to do—a ground for not making the attempt, I venture to take an exactly opposite view of them. I think that there is no method so convenient for bringing before the mind the "complex differences and various "conditions" of the matters that it is occupied in studying, as just this effort to define general terms. The gain derived from this process (as I have urged in a previous chapter) is quite independent of its success. We may find that the reasons for drawing any proposed line between money and things rather like money are balanced and indecisive. But since such reasons must consist in statements of the important resemblances and differences of the things that we are trying to classify, the knowledge of them must be useful in economic reasoning, whatever definition we may ultimately adopt.

money, however currently they may be taken for it. But they are generally disposed to reject this view as a heresy; and though the narrower sense is that adopted by several economists of repute, I imagine that it would be regarded as at least old-fashioned by practical men; except so far as the word is quite technically employed in relation to the details of banking business. Again, though in the 'Resumption' controversy in the United States it was maintained that inconvertible notes ought not to be regarded as money, I do not think a definition excluding such notes—but including convertible notes—has ever found favour in England; although English financial authorities are of course agreed that inconvertible paper is a bad kind of money. Further, our authorities allow that there is a certain resemblance between bank-notes and bills of exchange, letters of credit, promissory notes issued by private persons, &c.; but though they may regard these latter as constituting an "auxiliary currency," they do not consider them to be currency in the strictest sense, and therefore do not call them money. The only important point on which their utterances are doubtful or conflicting is the question whether notes issued by private banks and not made legal tender should be considered as money; the importance of this question, however, so far as England is concerned, is continually diminishing. But when bankers and merchants, or those who write for them, are talking of "money" in the sense in which, generally speaking, they are most practically concerned with it—of money which is said to be sometimes "scarce" and at other times "plentiful" in what is called the "money market",—they speak of something which must be defined quite differently. For though coin and bank-notes form a specially important part of money-market money, still, in such a country as England where deposit-banking is fully developed and payment by cheque customary, the greater part of such money must consist of bankers' promises to pay coin[1] on demand, not "embodied" or represented otherwise than by rows of figures in their books.

---

[1] It may be said that English bankers are not strictly liable to pay their debts in *coin*, as they may tender Bank of England notes instead. But as these notes are only legal tender so long as the Issue Department of the Bank of England gives coin for them on demand, the phrase in the text is substantially accurate.

What has just been said will appear to some of my readers a truism. But there are probably others to whom it will appear a paradox; and for the sake of these latter it will be well to pause and illustrate pretty fully this use of the term Money. I shall take my illustrations from Bagehot's *Lombard Street* as being a widely read book written by a distinguished economist for practical men. Now it is true that Bagehot never *says* that in speaking of the money of Lombard Street, the possession of which makes England "the greatest moneyed country in the world," he means a commodity of which the greater part exists only in the form of bankers' obligations to pay money on demand, not even embodied in bank-notes. But there are many passages in which it is clear that he can mean nothing else[1]. Take, for example, the following:—

"Every one is aware that England...has much more imme-
"diately disposable and ready cash than any other country.
"But very few persons are aware how much greater the ready
"balance—the floating loan-fund, which can be lent to any one
"for any purpose—is in England than it is anywhere else in the
"world. A very few figures will shew how large the London
"loan-fund is, and how much greater it is than any other. The
"known deposits—the deposits of banks which publish their
"accounts—are, in

"London (31st December, 1872) . .	£120,000,000
"Paris (27th February, 1873) . .	13,000,000
"New York (February, 1873) . .	40,000,000
"German Empire (31st January, 1873) .	8,000,000

"And the unknown deposits—the deposits in banks which do
"not publish their accounts—are in London much greater than
"those in any other of these cities. The bankers' deposits of
"London are many times greater than those of any other city—
"those of Great Britain many times greater than those of any
"other country[2]."

Here Bagehot clearly regards these bankers' deposits as "im-
"mediately disposable and ready cash." But if we ask ourselves

---

[1] There are, no doubt, other passages in *Lombard Street*—as will be presently noticed—where 'money' is used in the narrower sense of 'metallic money'.

[2] *Lombard Street*, c. I. p. 4.

CHAP. IV.]   DEFINITION OF MONEY.   221

where and in what form this "cash." exists, it must be evident that, at any given time, most of it exists only in the form of liabilities or obligations, acknowledged by rows of figures in the bankers' books; and that it is transferred from owner to owner, and thus fulfils all the functions of a medium of exchange, without ever assuming a more material shape. Most persons, no doubt, who have not specially considered the matter, have a vague impression that these figures in bankers' books "repre-"sent" sovereigns or bank-notes; which, though they are not actually in the banker's possession, have yet passed through his hands, and exist somewhere in the commercial world. But if this view does not vanish on a few moments' reflection, it must at any rate be effectually dispelled by a perusal of *Lombard Street;* since the main drift of that book is to bring prominently forward the fact that, in consequence of the "one-reserve sys-"tem" upon which English banking is constructed, but little of this immense "loan-fund which can be lent to any one" could possibly be presented in the shape of coin or bank-notes. Of course some portion of the money lent by London bankers is continually taken from them in this shape. But a little reflection on the mode in which it is borrowed and used will show how comparatively small this portion is. Such loans are chiefly made to traders, either directly by the bankers or through the agency of the bill-brokers; and when a trader borrows from his bank, he almost always does so by having the loan placed to his credit in his banker's books, and drawing against it by cheques; and the effect of such cheques, for the most part, is not to cause the money to be produced in the form of coin or notes, but merely to transfer the claim on the banker to some other customer of the same or some other bank. The bank-notes and gold are merely the small change of such loans; and it is only when money is lent to manufacturers and farmers, who have large sums to pay in wages, that the amount of this change bears even a considerable proportion to the whole loan. It may seem that when cheques on one bank are paid into another, material money must pass between bank and bank. But by the system of the Clearing House the mutual claims of the different banks are set off against each other; so that, even when the balance daily due from each bank to any other was paid in notes, the amount of these required was very small in proportion to the amount of liabilities transferred; and now no notes are commonly needed at all, as such balances are paid by drafts on the Bank of England, where the other banks keep the main part of their reserves.

But we may reach the same result more briefly by means of a few statistics, which I take from Mr Palgrave's *Notes on Banking*, published in 1873. Mr Palgrave estimates the whole amount of deposits held in English, Scotch, and Irish banks (exclusive of the discount-houses) on the 12th of March, 1873, at about 486 millions, the liabilities of the London banks alone being about 179 millions: while he estimates the metallic circulation of the whole kingdom in 1872 at about 105 millions, and the note circulation at 43 millions. If we consider that more than 10 millions of notes and coin, on the average, were kept as reserve by the Bank of England, and that the provincial banks require a considerably larger proportion of coin for their daily business than the London banks, we shall require no elaborate proof to convince us that the greater part of the "unequalled loan-fund" of Lombard Street can never emerge from the immaterial condition of bankers' liabilities[1].

The difficulty, indeed, is not to prove this, but rather to explain why this obvious truth is overlooked, or even implicitly denied; not merely, as has already been said, in all formal definitions of money, but in most of what is said and written about the functions of bankers. Mill, for instance, implies over and over again that the medium of exchange, which it is the business of bankers to collect from private individuals and lend to traders, consists altogether of coined metal—or at least of coin and paper substitutes for coin made legal tender by Government[2]: and a similar implication is contained in much of Bagehot's language[3].

---

[1] In a paper published by the Statistical Society in March 1876, Mr John Dun estimated the deposits of the banks of the United Kingdom to amount to over 590 millions of pounds.

[2] Compare, among other passages, B. III. c. xi. § 2, and c. xii. § 2.

[3] Cf. (e.g.) *Lombard Street*, c. VI. p. 143. The only English writers on currency known to me who adequately avoid this erroneous conception are Professor Bonamy Price and Mr Macleod: and I may take this occasion to acknowledge my obligations in the present chapter to Mr Macleod's *Theory of Banking*. In

§ 2. The explanation of this serious and wide-spread inaccuracy of thought and language is, I think, two-fold. In many cases it is due to an inadvertent inference from a part to the whole, of the kind that has caused so many economic fallacies. A practical man is aware that (in ordinary times) he can convert any portion of his banker's liabilities into gold or notes at will, and that he only leaves it in its immaterial condition for his own convenience,—being less afraid of the failure of his bank than he is of having his gold or notes stolen. Hence he naturally comes to think and speak of all the "money at his bank" as "ready cash"; and thus, with Bagehot, conceives England as having "more ready cash" than any other country. When, however, he comes to consider possible crises and collapses of credit, the difference between bankers' liabilities and their means of meeting them becomes only too palpable; the same thing that he has just called "cash" appears to him in its opposite character of "credit"; and—again with Bagehot—he views England's "cash in hand" as being "so exceedingly small that a bystander almost trembles at its minuteness compared with the immensity of the credit that rests upon it." These two views of "cash" or "money" exist side by side in his mind, without being brought into any clear or consistent relation to each other; and thus we get the paradoxical result which I noticed at starting, that when such a practical man is called upon to give an express definition of money, he formally ignores the greater part of the actual medium of exchange, of which in the ordinary course of his business he is continually thinking and speaking as "money."

So far, however, as this inadequate representation of the facts is common also to theoretical economists, it is rather because the existence of this immaterial money is obscured to their view, not by the material money into which the banker is bound to convert it, but by the goods other than money which the bankers' customers purchase by means of it.

For instance, Mill begins his chapter on the Value of Money by "clearing from our path a formidable ambiguity of language,"

saying this, I must guard myself against being understood to approve Mr Macleod's general treatment of Economics.

by which, as he explains, money is commonly confounded with capital.

"When one person lends to another," he says, "what he "really lends is so much capital; the money is the mere instru-"ment of the transfer. But the capital usually passes from the "lender to the receiver through the means either of money, or "of an order to receive money, and at any rate it is in money "that the capital is computed and estimated. Hence, bor-"rowing capital is universally called borrowing money; the "loan market is called the money market .... and the equiva-"lent given for the use of capital, or, in other words, interest, is "not only called the interest of money, but, by a grosser per-"version of terms, the value of money."

Now, I do not deny that there is a confusing ambiguity in the phrase, "value of money"; but the language that Mill uses in exposing it seems to me open to a similar objection. It is true that when the value of money is mentioned in Lombard Street, it is not the purchasing power of money, measured in commodities, that is intended; it is, however, strictly and precisely the value of the temporary use, not of capital generally, but of money (including bankers' obligations) in particular[1]; estimated, as other values are commonly esti- mated, in terms of money. Of course, a man ordinarily borrows money in order to buy something else, or to pay for something already bought; but what he actually borrows—and is legally bound to repay—is the medium of exchange, and it is materially inexact to represent him as borrowing anything else. In borrowing and lending, just as in ordinary buying and selling, the function of the medium of exchange is to facilitate—while also complicating—the transfer of other commodities: but that is no justification for suppressing the fact of its intervention, or misrepresenting its nature[2]. This intervention of course, is not

[1] The causes which tend to make the rate of interest or discount paid for the use of money diverge somewhat from the rate of interest on capital generally will be discussed in the next chapter.

[2] When Mill speaks contemptuously of an "extension of credit being talked "of....as if credit actually were capital," whereas it is only "permission to use "the capital of another person," it is to be observed that, in a certain sense it may be said of gold coin that its only function is to "permit" or enable its owner to obtain and use other wealth: and that it is only in this sense that

strictly indispensable; commodities might be exchanged directly for each other, or borrowed without the intervention of a medium, as houses and land, for the most part, actually are borrowed. And it may be useful sometimes, in giving a general view of economic facts, to omit the medium of exchange altogether from our consideration; and to represent the persons who purchase goods with 'money' borrowed from banks as *substantially* borrowing the goods from the bankers' customers. But in so doing we should bear in mind how much this simplified view of the facts diverges from the reality; and not mix it up with any statements that aim at representing the facts of exchange as they really are. It is undeniable that, in England now, wealth is chiefly transferred by the intervention of a medium of exchange complex in composition; consisting partly of gold and silver coin, partly of bank-notes, but to a greater extent of bankers' obligations to pay coin on demand, not represented by notes; and it is chiefly this medium that is actually lent and borrowed in commercial and industrial loan-transactions. And it is no less undeniable that the immaterial part of this instrument has functions precisely similar to those of the material portion; that it is as effective in purchasing goods; that borrowers pay the same interest or discount for the use of it; and that it, no less than metallic or paper money is, in ordinary times, currently accepted in final settlement of all debts—except, of course, the debts of bankers.

§ 3. For the reasons above given, I think it convenient for many purposes to keep close—as Bagehot implicitly does—to the use of the term money current in the money-market, and to denote by it the whole of the ordinary medium of exchange. The essential and fundamental function of money is to be used in exchanges, and other transfers of wealth where the object is to transfer not some particular commodity but command over commodities generally: it is as a medium of wealth-trans-

---

Mill's statement is true of the credit or liabilities which a banker lends to his customers, whether in the form of notes, or under the rather misleading name of "deposits." This credit, no doubt, is a comparatively fragile and perishable instrument for transferring wealth; but that is no reason for ignoring the fact that, in a modern industrial community, it is the instrument mainly used for this important purpose.

fer[1] that money is qualified for performing its other important function of measuring values[2]. If, then, we take this function as essential; if we understand by money "that which passes "freely from" owner to owner "throughout the community, in "final discharge of debts and full payment for commodities[3];"

[1] This would be a more strictly appropriate term than 'medium of exchange' in a general account of the functions of money: since there are many transfers of wealth which are not in any sense exchanges,—as payment of fines and damages, distribution of property or income among members of a family &c.—: but I have thought it best generally to use the more familiar term.

[2] Jevons (*Money*, ch. iii.) distinguishes "four functions which money fulfils in modern "societies." It is (1) a medium of exchange, (2) a measure of value, (3) a standard of value [i.e. as Mr Walker says a "standard for deferred "payments"], (4) a store of value. It is obvious that the second and third uses follow naturally—though not, as Jevons points out, necessarily from the first.

As regards the fourth function, I agree with Mr Walker in declining to attribute it to money in the present economic condition of the most civilised societies. No doubt, in an earlier stage of economic development, the precious metals are largely used for hoarding as well as for currency: and in a certain sense, any medium of exchange must always be also a store of value; that is, each man must keep somewhere, so as to be obtainable without material delay, a sufficient quantity of it for his ordinary purchases. But Jevons seems to mean by a "store of value" something that a person "may hoard away for a "time;" i.e. something which he does not intend to use for current purchases, but keeps for a remote occasion. In this sense—undoubtedly most appropriate to the term "store"—I must deny that metallic money is adapted to be a "store of value," or is ordinarily used for this purpose in modern societies. Debts payable before the remote occasion arrives (or portions of capital believed to be readily saleable) are the commodities chiefly used in this way by modern men of business. I may observe, moreover, that most of the language in which Jevons explains what he denotes by a "store of value" appears to me merely to describe a medium of international exchange. "It is worthy of "inquiry," he says, "whether money does not also serve a fourth distinct "purpose—that of embodying value in a convenient form for conveyance to "distant places...at times a person needs to condense his property into the "smallest compass, so that he may carry it with him on a long journey, or "transmit it to a friend in a distant country." But so long as the journey or transmission is within the range of "modern societies" what a man carries or sends is commonly some document transferring to a foreign banker a portion of his home banker's obligations to pay him money on demand; the foreign banker being ultimately repaid by having transferred to him some foreign merchants' debt that has been purchased by the home banker. The whole transaction is obviously one of international exchange.

[3] In the above quotation from Mr Walker (*Money, Trade, and Industry*, p. 4), I have substituted the phrase "from owner to owner" in the place of "from "hand to hand." It appears to be the difference between the two phrases which renders Mr Walker unwilling to recognise deposits in banks as money; since

then, in all ordinary conditions of modern commercial societies, bankers' debts payable on demand, however acknowledged and transferred, are as rightly called money as they are commonly so designated; and in all consideration of the quantity of money available for commercial or other purposes, this fact ought to be distinctly recognised.

It may be urged, perhaps, that bankers' debts are not accepted in final discharge of other debts, because they have to be discharged by the bankers themselves in coin or legal-tender notes. But though each banker is under a general obligation of liquidating any portion of his liabilities in this way, practically any such liquidation of liabilities in one case is balanced by an opposite transaction with some other customer by which the banker receives gold or notes in exchange for his own liabilities: so that, if we consider his transactions in the aggregate, it remains broadly true that, in ordinary times, bankers' liabilities are accepted in final discharge of ordinary debts. Still the fact that any banker may be at any time called upon to fulfil his legal obligation, of paying coin or legal-tender notes to the extent of his liabilities, constitutes an important distinctive characteristic of that part of the medium of exchange which consists of such liabilities: there is certainly a sense in which the discharge of

they cannot "pass from hand to hand," as notes do. But surely when payment is made by means of notes (not being legal tender), the important fact is not the mere physical transmission of pieces of paper, but the transfer of claims on the banker: which is equally effected when payment is made by cheques. No doubt the receiver of the cheque *might* demand payment in notes: but similarly the receiver of notes might pay them in and have the sum added to his account. The former, again, might ask for payment in gold; but so equally might the latter. From neither point of view does there appear to be any essential distinction between the two. In saying this, I do not mean to ignore the important practical difference that exists between payment by notes and payment by cheques. Cheques do not circulate as notes do: the receiver of a cheque commonly pays it in without delay and thus selects the banker whose liabilities he consents to take as money, whereas the receiver of a note usually exercises no such choice; so that the transfer of bankers' liabilities is more complicated in the former case than in the latter; since, as was before observed, there is a change of bankers as well as a change of bankers' customers. But none the less is the essence of the transaction a transfer of bankers' obligations "in final discharge of debts and full payment for commodities." Accordingly a definition of money which includes bank notes generally and excludes the rest of bankers' liabilities is, I think, quite unacceptable.

debts by gold or legal-tender notes is more final: and it is a tenable view that the term "money" should be strictly confined to what possesses this higher degree of finality. I think, however, that legal currency hardly gives a sufficiently important distinction in the case of notes convertible into coin on demand; since the equivalence of such notes to the coin they nominally represent is sustained not by their legal currency (which is of course no protection against depreciation by over-issue), but by the belief that they can be exchanged for coin at will. And though in some countries this belief may be firmer and better grounded where the credit of government is pledged to conversion than in the case of notes issued by private bankers, we cannot affirm this as a universal law: and at any rate the difference of security is only a difference of degree[1]. On the other hand, the characteristic of "finality" belongs in the highest degree to the inconvertible notes for which a modern government can usually secure practically complete currency, as an internal medium of exchange; by (1) undertaking to receive such notes at their nominal value and payment of taxes and other debts due to the public treasury, and (2) making them legal tender for the payment of all debts of money not contracted under the express condition that they are to be paid otherwise.

[1] It is sometimes forgotten that the notes of the Bank of England, though in a certain sense "legal money," are not so in the sense most important to the political economist; since their legal currency would cease, if the Issue Department ceased to give gold for them, and therefore could hardly be effective in sustaining their value, if this ever came to be seriously doubted. No doubt the quality of these notes is unique; in the severest crisis they would be taken as readily as gold. But this is not due to the fact that they are legal tender, but to the special provision made for maintaining their convertibility; and perhaps even more to the general belief that the credit of the English Government is practically pledged to maintain it. And here again it must be observed that the unique position of the Bank of England has now practically an almost equal effect in sustaining the currency of the liabilities of its banking department; in the worst of panics every one has considered "money deposited" with the Bank of England as safe as its bank-notes in his own strong chest.

Hence it seems to me that, in relation to English finance, the definition of money that includes bank-notes generally, and excludes the rest of bankers' liabilities, is specially indefensible; since it ignores the profound distinction that separates the credit of the Bank of England from the credit of all other banks, while it unduly emphasizes the more superficial distinction between the liabilities of provincial banks that are transferred by notes and the liabilities of the London joint-stock banks that are transferred by cheques.

But as the finality of such notes is only attained at the cost of rendering them liable to depreciation from over-issue, their inferiority to convertible notes is so palpable and so universally recognised that it would be practically very awkward to dignify the former by the title of money while refusing it to the latter.

Metallic money or coin is no doubt distinguished from the other constituents of our actual medium of exchange by the important attribute of being composed of a material that has a high value for other purposes; and also because, except in the case of an inconvertible paper currency, the value of all the rest of the medium of exchange depends on the belief that any given portion of it could be exchanged for coin at will. This fact is sometimes expressed by the statement that metallic money alone has "intrinsic value." But the phrase seems to me misleading; since it is not the difference in the source of the value of coin, confusedly expressed by the word "in-"trinsic," which is practically important, but the difference in its range and permanence. It is not because coin is made of a more expensive material that it is a better money than notes; but because it could be used as a medium of exchange over a wider area, and because its value is not liable to sudden destruction through the insolvency of the issuer, nor to sudden diminution in consequence of excessive issues. And it should be borne in mind that these distinctions are not of absolute and unvarying importance; there is no reason why we may not, some time or other, have an international circulation of bank-notes; and the progress of science and industry might so enlarge the supply of gold as to make it possible for a wise and stable government to devise a paper currency of more durable value than gold coin would then be, if still issued as at present.

Still, under existing circumstances, the distinction between metallic money and bankers' obligations—especially in a community that abstains from inconvertible paper—remains fundamentally important; and I should have no objection to restrict the term money to the former, if any short word, sanctioned by usage, could be found for the whole medium of exchange. Since however this is not the case, it seems ·best to use "money" in the wider signification which it has in the money-market, and refer to metallic money as "coin."

And it must be borne in mind that even this definition is not wide enough for certain purposes; as it does not cover the actual medium of exchange used in foreign—and to some extent internal—trade. The metallic money of commerce is properly bullion, not coin; the latter is used for the payment of foreign debts only so far as it is the most convenient form of bullion. And the non-metallic medium of commercial exchange still consists to a great extent of merchants', not bankers', obligations; that is of bills of exchange, so far as they still circulate among traders, and are not at once discounted. Again, there are certain widely accepted securities—the bonds of some governments, of some railways, &c.—which are so much more convenient for transmission than bullion that they are frequently used as substitutes for bullion in the payment of international debts. When such securities have come to be bought and sold with a view to the fulfilment of this function, to deny that they possess *pro tanto* the most essential characteristic of money, would be to make ourselves the slaves of language. Since, however, neither merchants' debts nor the debts of governments form a medium of exchange currently accepted throughout a community in final settlement of debts; it seems to me most convenient to call them not money, but 'substitutes for money.'

This leads me to notice an objection that is likely to be brought against the view above expounded. It may be said that what I have called Money is merely a part of what other economists have called Credit, and that it is more convenient to keep this term as indicating its real quality. And I should quite admit that for some purposes it is important to insist on the fact that bankers' debts are after all debts, no less than those of private individuals. But in a general consideration of the manner in which the functions of money are performed, it seems to me more important to point out that there is as much difference between one kind of credit and another, in respect of its currency, as there is between gold and "goods." If a private individual (A) obtains any valuable article from another (B) by promising to pay for it hereafter, and *does* pay for it, the credit he receives obviously does not operate as a substitute for money at all, in the long run—though it tends *pro tanto* to raise prices temporarily. Only if B uses A's debt to him as a means of purchasing another commodity from C does this credit begin to be a substitute for money: if C uses it similarly in a similar transaction with D, its efficiency as a substitute is doubled. But it is not until such a debt has come to be taken without any idea of using it otherwise than as a means of payment that it has completely acquired the characteristics of money. That this is, in ordinary times, the case with bankers' obligations taken in the aggregate, is undeniable; though (as I have said) the fact is obscured by the continual liquidation in gold of small portions of such obligations.

CHAPTER V.

VALUE OF MONEY.

§ 1. WE have seen in the preceding chapter that the medium of exchange, in a society like our own, with a fully developed banking system but without inconvertible paper, should be conceived as consisting partly of metallic money, but to a much larger extent of bankers' promises to pay metallic money on demand; such promises being partly represented by bank-notes which pass from hand to hand; in England, however, the greater part of these obligations are merely acknowledged in the bankers' books, and transferred by means of cheques. When a financial crisis occurs and mutual suspicion suddenly invades the commercial part of the community, the available amount of this immaterial medium of exchange is liable to shrink suddenly, through the widespread distrust of certain portions of it; so that the superiority in stability of other portions becomes of great practical importance. This superiority may be due to a special connexion between the Government of the society and a certain bank: for instance, we have already noticed that through the special relations existing between the Government and the Bank of England, the promises of the latter occupy a unique position among the promises of English bankers[1]. But however important may be the differences between different species of bankers' debts, they are all equally accepted—so far as they are used as a medium of exchange—as of equal value with the coin

[1] As has already been noticed, this is true not merely of the notes issued by the Issue Department, but also of the obligations of the Banking Department; though the confidence in the latter does not rest on the same grounds as the confidence in the former, and cannot exactly be placed on a par with it.

CHAP. V.]   *VALUE OF MONEY.*   233

into which they are nominally convertible on demand. Of course the use of these substitutes renders the demand[1] for metallic money—and therefore its value—less than it would have been, supposing metallic money alone available and the amount of exchanges to be mediated the same: but this supposition is an idle one, since the use of bankers' debts as money is an essential factor in the development of modern commerce, though the extent of its effects cannot be exactly estimated[2]. At any rate, so long as every portion of the aggregate of bankers'

---

[1] I may here note an inconsistency, pointed out by Cairnes (*Some Leading Principles*, c. ii. § 2, 3), in Mill's explanation of the term Demand. After laying down generally (III. c. ii. § 3) that "by demand we mean the quantity de-"manded," he states, in the special case of money, that "the demand for "money consists of all the goods offered for sale." If this inconsistency is to be avoided, it is on the whole best, in my opinion, to measure demand for money as well as for other things by quantity demanded. I admit that it is rather a strain on language to speak of a fall in prices as resulting from an "increased" (or, as I should say, "raised") "demand for money;" when the fact that the phrase denotes is not that the sellers want more money for their commodities at the old rate of exchange, but that there are more commodities to be sold for whatever money they will fetch. But it seems better to submit to this strain on ordinary language and thought in the one case of money, rather than adopt Cairnes' alternative, and measure demand for commodities generally by "quan-"tity of purchasing power offered for them." For this involves an equally marked, and a more extensive and inconvenient divergence from ordinary usage. What men commonly understand by an increase or rise in the "demand "for a commodity" is that an increased amount of it is demanded at the price at which it was selling before the increase. No one voluntarily offers to give more for anything than he is asked for it; if he thinks it cheap, he asks for more of it:—though the result of such asking, on the part of himself and others, may be that the price is raised instead of the supply being increased.

[2] There would seem to have been some confusion in the minds of those writers on currency a generation ago, who insisted on the importance of regulating the bank-note currency so as to make it "conform exactly to a "metallic standard" (see Mill, B. III. ch. xxiv. § 3). For if they meant that the value of bank-notes must conform to the *actual* value of the coin they nominally represented, the result would seem to be sufficiently secured so long as the convertibility of the notes is maintained; while if they desired to make the value of notes and coin conform to what *would have been* the value of coin if no notes had been used, their attempt was manifestly chimerical. It is impossible to estimate the extent to which the value of gold would have been greater than it now is, supposing that bankers' (and merchants') obligations had never been used as substitutes for coin; because it is impossible to say precisely how far the actual development of exchange, which would have occasioned this rise in value, would have taken place if the more convenient medium of exchange, afforded by these obligations, had never come into use.

debts is believed by the bankers' creditors to be convertible into coin at will, its exchange value at any given time cannot diverge from the value of the coin. Let us proceed, then, to consider the causes determining the value of metallic money.

I have already noticed that the term "value of money" is used in two ways: in economic treatises it usually means the purchasing power of money, or its exchange value measured in commodities other than money; in practical discussions about the "money-market" it denotes the rate of interest paid for the temporary use of money. I shall presently discuss both the confusion sometimes made between these different facts and their actual connexion: in the mean time I shall avoid the ambiguity as far as possible.

Let us ask, then, on what conditions the purchasing power of coin depends. In the first place, it should be observed that when the privilege of coining is, as it commonly is, monopolised by Government, it would be possible for the latter to raise the value of coin above what would be sufficient to defray the expenses of production, by limiting the amount coined. In fact this course is adopted by most modern Governments, in the case of coins used for very small payments only; to these a value is assigned, as representing a certain fraction of some higher coin, considerably above the value of the metal used in making them. Such coins are accordingly called 'tokens.' But no civilized government now adopts this plan in the use of coins current for larger payments: since on the one hand any money of which the value depends upon the limitation of its amount is always liable to be suddenly depreciated by large issues, and the resulting danger of violent derangement in the pecuniary relations of all debtors and creditors has an injurious effect on commerce and industry; while on the other hand if governments, through necessity or cupidity, are driven to disregard this consideration, they now prefer the far more profitable and hardly more dangerous course of issuing inconvertible paper-money[1].

[1] Many economists appear to me, in condemning this practice of "lowering "the standard," to use language calculated to mislead. For instance, Mill speaks of Governments "robbing their creditors by the shallow and impudent artifice... "which consists in calling a shilling a pound, that a debt of a hundred pounds "may be cancelled by the payment of a hundred shillings." These phrases certainly suggest the popular error that a debased coinage necessarily falls in

The question, indeed, that is now practically discussed in reference to coins is of the opposite kind; viz. whether it is not on the whole most advantageous for the community to coin not only *freely* but *gratuitously* for all individuals who desire it, defraying the expenses by taxation. This, however, together with the further question, how the inevitable loss through wear of the coins in use is to be made good, belongs rather to the Art of Political Economy[1]. Here we will merely assume that standard coins are coined freely for any person who brings gold to the government mint at a charge that at any rate does not exceed the cost of the process; while any serious depreciation of the old coinage, in consequence of loss of weight through wear or ill-treatment, is prevented by prohibiting the use of coins materially lighter than those issued by the Mint.

Under these circumstances we may, without material error, neglect the cost of coinage in considering how variations in the value of coin will be determined; and regard these as depending entirely on variations in the value of the metal used for standard coins. We will assume in the first instance that only one metal, gold, is so used; and, for simplicity, we will suppose that over the whole region which we are considering gold tends to have the same value allowing for cost of carriage from the mines. This supposition is not far from true of the economically most advanced parts of the civilised world, united by active commercial intercourse. Though, strictly speaking, as we have seen in the last chapter but one, we have to consider not a single but a double cost of carriage,

value in proportion to its debasement, even though the supply of the coinage is altogether under the control of the Government. Whereas such fall, as I have said, depends upon its being issued in excess—but it is to be observed that an amount may be excessive after debasement which was not so before; as a certain dislike of the coin is produced by the knowledge of its debasement, and this, together with the impossibility of using it for foreign payments, tends to diminish the demand for it.

It should be added that the value of token coins is not liable in the same way to depreciation through excessive issue; since the value of a token is intended to be determined entirely by that of the more valuable coin, to a certain fraction of which it is declared equivalent. If however such coins were issued in great excess, they might perhaps be used to some extent in payments of a larger amount than that for which they are legally current; and as so used, they would have a depreciated value.

[1] Cf. *post*, Book III. ch. iv. § 5.

which, in this as in other cases, may be divided unequally between the trading countries; and we have also to take account of the fact that a country does not merely receive gold as an export from countries where gold-mining is carried on; it may also receive it in payment of debt from any other country with which it is in commercial relations. Under these complex conditions, all that we can say generally is (1) that the value of gold in a country where there are no gold-mines will tend to be in excess of its value in a country from which it is profitable to import it, by some portion of the double cost of carrying gold one way and some kind of goods the other way; and (2) that in proportion as the products of a country are keenly demanded abroad, this excess will tend to be reduced. Hence any change in the conditions of trade may modify somewhat the value of gold in a particular district, without equally affecting its value elsewhere. But in the present discussion it is best to ignore these minor changes in local values; and to suppose the value of gold to change uniformly over the region contemplated, as would be approximately the case in an isolated country supplied from its own mines.

§ 2. In the first place, gold like other products of extractive industry, is a commodity produced simultaneously at very different costs; the cost of the least remunerative portion of its production tending to increase—so long as other things remain the same—as the total amount produced increases. As we have seen, so far as industrial competition operates, the value of such commodities will be affected—not only transiently but to some extent permanently—by any change either in the conditions of supply or in those of demand; a rise in the demand, other things remaining the same, tends to raise the value because the supply cannot be correspondingly increased without having recourse to more expensive production; and any increase in cost of the least remunerative part of the production, demand remaining unchanged, will tend to have ultimately a similar effect. Hitherto, however, the action of industrial competition has been particularly irregular in the case of gold; owing to the various and uncertain nature of the returns of the industry, and to the fact that the working of alluvial deposits—from which by far the largest part of the gold in the world has been derived—can generally be carried on with very little capital. Further, in consequence of the great durability of gold, and the fact that the gold used as money is practically always in the market, any change in the cost of production of the metal is likely to take a long time to produce its full effect on exchange value. "Hence the "effects of all changes in the conditions of production of the "precious metals are at first, and continue to be for many "years, questions of quantity only, with little reference to cost "of production[1]."

Let us then consider how the value of a given quantity of gold will be affected by the conditions of demand. The total demand for gold is composed, in an advanced industrial community, mainly of two elements, which have to be kept distinct in considering the causes of its variations; (1) the monetary demand—including the demand for bullion as the metallic money of international trade—and (2) the demand for ornamental or technical use. Any rise (or fall) in either demand must affect the value of the whole; but it will obviously affect it to a less extent than if there were only one kind of demand, as its effect will be partly counteracted by the reduction (or extension) in the other demand, consequent on the change in value. We may assume of course that both demands alike exhibit the general relation of demand to value, extending as the latter falls and shrinking as it rises; but so far as the demand for ornamental or technical uses is concerned we have no reason to assume any particular quantitative relation between a given change in value and the consequent change in extent of demand.

The case is different with the monetary demand. But before analysing this more minutely, I must notice a third kind of demand, comparatively unimportant in an advanced stage of industrial development, but very important at lower stages;— I mean the demand for hoarding. It is somewhat difficult to distinguish it sharply from either of the other two kinds of demand: for (1) in the stage of economic development in which

---

[1] Mill, III. c. ix. § 2.

hoarding takes place to a considerable extent, ornaments of gold and silver are often partly valued as a form of hoarding; and (2) on the other hand it is difficult to draw a sharp line between hoarding coin and keeping it for current use; since what is hoarded is intended to be used sometime as a means of obtaining other wealth. This latter difficulty may be illustrated by the fact that some economists class bank-reserves of gold with hoards; and, no doubt, such reserves are kept for security against needs that may never arise—and which, certainly, the bankers hope to avoid altogether. Nevertheless this classification seems to me misleading; since the employments of gold thus placed together are as unlike as possible in their real relations to the ordinary monetary work of gold: for gold hoarded is—for the time at least—withdrawn from this work, whereas gold kept in bank-reserves, by sustaining the convertibility of bankers' debts, indirectly performs monetary work in a higher degree than coin.

In short the monetary utility of gold, as an internal medium of exchange, has to be viewed in relation to two distinct uses; (*a*) the use of coin for mediating directly in certain transfers of wealth, generally of small amounts, and (*b*) the use of coin or bullion as the basis of a medium of exchange currently accepted as equivalent to coin but larger in quantity than the gold which sustains its convertibility;—larger in varying degrees, according to the nature of the system for supplying substitutes for gold. Now it is clear that a mere change in the value of gold, consequent on a change in its quantity, has no general tendency —supposing other things unchanged—to affect the relative proportions in which coin and its substitutes are respectively used; since the value of such substitutes, supposing their convertibility complete, must rise and fall *pari passu* with that of coin. Nor, again, supposing the exchanges of commodities requiring the mediation of money to remain constant, has a change in the quantity of gold any tendency to affect the monetary efficiency of coin or its substitutes in the way of altering their 'rapidity of circulation,'—i.e. altering the number of exchanges in which the same coin or debt is used over again within a given time. Hence, so far as the quantities and relative values of the commodities exchanged remain the same, the quantity of gold demanded for the work of mediating exchanges may be taken to vary simply in inverse ratio to its purchasing power:—for the obvious reason that, as the price of anything rises, a proportionally larger amount of money is required to buy it.

Now actually, of course, the work that money has to do is continually undergoing some change: any change in the quantity of gold in a country is sure to coincide with changes in the supply of commodities of all kinds for purchase. It seems however clear that the mere fact that the quantity of money in a country is altered cannot have in itself—i.e. apart from any change in the proportions in which it is distributed— any tendency to alter the quantities or relative values of the commodities which are bought and sold for money, so far as the terms of exchange are settled subsequently to the alteration, by competition and not by custom. But such exchanges will not constitute the whole of the work that the altered quantity of money has to perform. Even if we leave mere custom out of account, an important part of this work will consist in the liquidation of debts and other payments fixed prior to the change and unaffected by it: hence a fall in the purchasing power of coin, consequent on an increase in its quantity, will be proportionally favourable to all borrowers of money and all persons whose income varies continually with the market value of their services. In the present state of society, therefore, such a fall must be importantly favourable to persons engaged in industry, especially to the employers of capital in wholesale trade—for such persons are habitually extensive borrowers[1]—; and must therefore tend to encourage industrial enterprise. In this way the effects of an increase in the proportion of gold to commodities may be somewhat reduced, or at least spread over a longer period, by the stimulus to industry which the transition from the smaller to the larger relative quantity gives: and a decrease may similarly act as a discouragement. Again, in other ways the actual process of change in quantity

[1] The six hundred millions of money—or thereabouts—that the bankers of the United Kingdom owe to other members of the community is mainly balanced by debts which traders or other producers have incurred to the banks; partly by discounts of bills, partly by loans and overdrafts.

of gold may alter sensibly the distribution of wealth, and thus to some extent modify the work that money has to do even in the way of mediating exchanges. For instance, when an important increase occurs in the quantity of gold in a country through the opening of new sources of supply, the new supplies do not act uniformly on the prices of things and services. They tend to raise first the wages and profits of persons engaged in gold-mining, then the prices of commodities specially consumed by them—raising these latter unequally, according to the different conditions under which they are produced—and thus to flow with varying degrees of rapidity into different channels of exchange: and it is quite possible that some of the changes in the distribution of wealth that thus tend to accompany a material increase in the proportion of gold to commodities, may also cause a material change in the need of the community for coin. E.g. they may increase the share of produce that is divided into small incomes, whose possessors chiefly use coin in making their purchases, at the expense of the share of the wealthier classes who chiefly use bankers' obligations[1]. In short, we cannot affirm more than that, in assuming the monetary work of gold to remain unchanged by a change in its quantity, and inferring that the monetary demand for gold will tend to expand or shrink in simply inverse proportion to the fall or rise in its value, we get a result which must in all cases be useful as a first approximation to the actual effect of the change considered; though it will probably always require to be corrected by taking into account minor effects, varying according to the special nature and circumstances of the change.

§ 3. In the preceding section I have considered how a change—say, for definiteness, an increase—in the amount of gold tends to affect its value, supposing the monetary work that it has to do to remain unchanged. It is obvious that if reversing the hypothesis, we suppose the quantity of gold to

---

[1] Cairnes has argued (*Essays in Political Economy*, p. 130) that the addition of 40 per cent. to our gold currency between 1851 and 1859 was prevented from affecting prices as much as it would otherwise have done, owing to the increase in the real incomes of the industrial classes in England that took place simultaneously with—and partly in consequence of—the increased production of gold.

remain unchanged, while the monetary work done by it decreases, the effect on its value would be similar: the exchange value of gold relatively to commodities in general must clearly be affected by a change in the quantity of commodities in general offered for sale,—consequent (let us say) on a change in the numbers or average wealth of the community in question—no less than by a change in the quantity of gold in monetary use[1]. And, actually, the value of gold which we have to explain is almost always a relation between a changing quantity of gold in monetary use, and changing quantities of commodities exchanged for it. But as soon as we consider this latter kind of change, we have to face the difficulties, noticed in a previous chapter[2], of measuring changes in the value of gold relatively to commodities in general, when the particular articles that make up this aggregate are undergoing changes in value relatively to each other, and also in the quantities exchanged within a given period. I pointed out that under these conditions—which are always the actual conditions—the question 'how much the general purchasing 'power of money has changed within a given period' does not admit (except by accident) of a completely definite answer. For, to answer it precisely, we have to determine the relative quantities of the particular commodities which make up the aggregate of "commodities in general"; and, as the quantities purchased at the beginning of the period have as much claim to be selected as those purchased at its close, the selection must be arbitrary. And the element of inevitable uncertainty in the very conception of a change in the standard of value is increased if the qualities of commodities have changed within the period in question; especially if the progress of industry has introduced some entirely new articles, while some old ones have fallen out of use altogether. But further, there is some difficulty in determining precisely what commodities are to be taken for comparison with gold. In

[1] It is necessary to draw attention to this obvious truth; since it seems to be often overlooked by persons who argue that though "prices"—in gold—"have fallen", the fall is not due to a change "in the value of gold";—while yet they do not definitely explain "value" to mean something different from "exchange value relatively to commodities in general."

[2] Book I. ch. ii. § 3.

Book I. ch. II., where I was considering value as a measure of the wealth of a community, I proposed to confine our attention to "consumers' commodities," in making up the price-lists for calculating changes in the purchasing power of money. My ground for this limitation was that a change in the price of "producers' commodities"—instruments or materials of production—only interests the consumer so far as it is the forerunner of a change in the price of directly consumable commodities. E.g. if the coal used by producers becomes dearer there will tend to be a material rise in the price of things in the production of which coal is extensively used, and a corresponding reduction in their supply: and when this change has taken place, the purchasing power of (consumers') money will have correspondingly fallen, so that the effect of the rise in the price of producers' coal will be thus indirectly represented. And it is, I conceive, only so that it should be represented when we are considering what a change in the value of gold is to mean, for members of the community generally.

The case is different when we ask what such a change means from a trader's point of view, or when we are considering how changes in the value of gold are caused by changes in supply or demand. For in the former case we must theoretically regard all the articles of trade as of equal importance, in proportion to the aggregate value of each: and in the latter case we must take into account the whole demand for money—the whole monetary work that gold has to do—and therefore the demand constituted by "producers'" as well as consumers' commodities. It must, however, be borne in mind that if in estimating a change in the purchasing power of gold we take into account all the commodities—including 'securities'—for which it is exchanged, we get an average result which has little practical interest for any one. No producer's interests are affected by a change in the purchasing power of gold relatively to commodities which he does not use, except so far as the change affects the aggregate price paid for such commodities;—which may or may not be the case according to the special conditions of demand for such commodities. Hence, though a change in the general purchasing power of gold may be caused by a change in the quantity of commodities in general just as much as by a change in the quantity of gold, the latter cause of change has much more general interest for producers than the former, which only interests them so far as the commodities in question are articles which they use or substitute for their own products: and in measuring the actual effect of a change, however caused, I do not conceive that there will be any *practical* advantage in deviating from the standard previously suggested[1].

§ 4. I now pass to consider an essentially different cause of changes in the value of gold; a cause, however, whose effects are often difficult to separate from those of the causes just discussed. Hitherto I have assumed the general tendency to use substitutes for gold—either bankers' promises to pay on demand or traders' promises to pay at a certain future date—to remain unchanged. Of course any important development of the banking system—or, more generally, of the use of substitutes for metallic money—in any society must by diminishing the demand for metallic money render its purchasing power less, and prices consequently higher, than would otherwise be the case: and a similar result will be produced at least temporarily by any extension of the use of credit in purchases, even if it be only the credit given by traders. Now in times of commercial hopefulness and confidence, which appear to succeed times of dullness and despondency with a certain periodicity[2], such an extension of credit in all ways,—including the use of substitutes for metallic money—tends to take place; and as prices rise in consequence, the purchasing power of gold falls, without any real change in the relation between the quantity of gold and the supply of other commodities. There has been much controversy—especially just before and after the passing of the English Bank Charter Act—as to the part taken by bankers in their transient "inflations": but it is now, I conceive, generally admitted that this is only of a secondary and subordinate kind. Where banking expedients are familiar and easily accessible, a

---

[1] Some further discussion of this question, regarded from a practical point of view, will be found in Book III. ch. iv. § 6.

[2] I do not quite think that the "decennial credit cycle" is so definite and permanent a fact as Jevons considers it (*Investigations in Currency and Finance*, vi., vii., and viii.): but his arguments are worthy of attention.

banker cannot, by the mere act of making a large loan in his own notes, induce any one to use notes who would otherwise have used coin; any more than he can induce traders to give more bank-money for goods than they believe them to be worth in gold. At the same time, banks can undoubtedly enable merchants to act on mistaken beliefs that goods are, or are about to be, worth more in gold than will prove to be the case; and in consequence to make extended purchases and raise prices. And in this way, they render possible alternations of inflated and depressed prices, which could not occur if everything were paid for in hard coin and no credit were given, and could not occur to so great an extent, even if merchants gave credit as at present, if there were no such possibility as the banking system affords of increasing the generally accepted medium of exchange[1]. How far it is desirable that Government should control the operations of banks, with the view of preventing these fluctuations in prices, is a practical question that does not now concern us; but it may be observed that at any rate the banks have no interest in producing the mistaken beliefs that tend to inflate prices. No doubt they profit by them directly through the greater demand for their commodity; but the danger of the collapse when the mistake is discovered decidedly outweighs this gain.

However this may be, it is of course true that when a buoyant state of trade causes more money to be required for the more numerous and extensive purchases of goods that are then made, the demand of traders for money supplied by bankers rises; and here as in other cases the rise in demand tends to cause at least a temporary rise in value of the commodity demanded. But it must now be observed that the rise thus caused is not primarily a rise in the "value of money," in the sense in which we have been investigating it—since the trader does not commonly purchase with goods the money he requires; —it is a rise in what for distinction's sake I have proposed to call the "value of the *use* of money," i.e. the rate of interest on

[1] It is to be observed that as all purchases in wholesale trade are customarily made on credit, any extension of purchases involves in the first instance chiefly an extension of *traders' obligations* to pay money at a future date. Hence the extended use of bankers' obligations occurs somewhat later than the rise in prices, which it sustains rather than produces.

CHAP. V.] *VALUE OF MONEY.* 245

loans of money[1]. I have already noticed that in the discussion of this latter value we are liable to find a double confusion; or rather two different confusions, made by two different sets of persons. The exchange value of the use of money, estimated in money, is more or less vaguely confounded by practical men with the exchange value of money relatively to goods; and it is more definitely and deliberately identified by Mill and other economists, with the rate of interest on capital generally. The grounds for this latter identification are obvious and plausible, and at first sight may easily appear conclusive. Since it is the essential characteristic of money that it is continually being exchanged for all other kinds of wealth, how,—it may be asked,—can competition possibly lead to the payment of a price for the use of money, different from that which is paid for the use of any portion of such capital; supposing, of course, that the capital itself is estimated at its money value? The answer to this question is somewhat complicated. In the first place, it must be remembered that interest on capital generally, as it was before defined, has to be kept carefully distinct from the other element of profit which goes to remunerate the labour of managing capital. When money is borrowed from the public for a long period or for permanence, by governments or great joint-stock companies, the price paid to the lenders for the use of it may be regarded as entirely interest in this technical sense; since such lenders do not generally obtain any remuneration for the trouble of looking after their investments. But loans made for short periods by professional lenders of money must yield the latter some "wages of management" as well as strict interest; on this ground, therefore, we might expect the rate of discount on bills of exchange to be higher than the rate of interest on capital generally. On the other hand, we have to consider that the banker to a great extent produces the money he lends, viz. his own obligations, which so long as his business flourishes

[1] The money given for a bill of exchange—that is, for an obligation to pay money at a future date—is substantially *lent* by the banker: though Mr Macleod is no doubt correct in pointing out that the transaction is formally a purchase and not a loan. The uncommercial reader should take note that as the money paid for such a bill is equal to the amount of the bill with the discount subtracted, the rate of interest obtained by the banker on this money is a little higher than the rate of discount.

he is practically never compelled to redeem[1]; and that he may easily afford to sell the use of this commodity at a price materially less than the rate of interest on capital generally. Hence so far as he increases the extent and security of his business by lending his money chiefly to traders for short periods, competition may force him to make such loans at a rate not above —or even below—that of ordinary interest on capital permanently, though not less safely, invested. And this seems to be actually the case; partly, perhaps, because traders are specially important customers of banks; but chiefly because it is convenient for bankers to lend money which the borrowers are bound to repay after definite short intervals, in order that they may at any time reduce easily the amount they have out on loan, if exceptionally large payments are required of them. Thus we have no ground for saying *a priori* that the rate of discount charged by bankers on mercantile bills will be—even on the average and after all allowance for differences of risk— the same as the rate of interest on capital generally; there is no economic reason why it should not be more than this, since the banker has to be remunerated for his trouble: and on the other hand there is no reason why it should not be materially less, if the value of the advantages above-mentioned is considerable; since a comparatively low rate of interest on the medium of exchange inexpensively produced by the banker himself would be sufficient to give him normal profit on his banking capital[2].

It should be observed that, so far as money is lent professionally by persons outside the banking system, interest on loans for

[1] That is, the amount he is continually called upon to redeem is balanced by the amount that he is able to lend afresh.

[2] The average Bank of England rate of discount on first-class short bills for the ten years 1869—1878, inclusive, was £3. 8s. 7d. which is equivalent to a rate of interest *per cent.* of £3. 10s. 6d.: and I understand that the average market-rate of discount on first-class bills was decidedly less during the same period. (See Palgrave, *Bank-rate in England, France and Germany*, c. 5.) It would seem, therefore, that the interest obtained by bankers generally on the money invested in such bills has been materially less than the interest obtainable during the same period on permanent investments of as high a degree of security—such as first-class mortgages or the bonds of the great railway companies. And so far as banks lend money for longer or more indefinite periods, as "advances on securities," they always, I believe, charge interest considerably above that charged in discounting the best mercantile bills. Hence in the argument in the text I have confined my statements to the rate of discount on bills.

short periods will generally be higher than interest on capital or 'money invested' permanently, because it must furnish the money-lender with remuneration for his trouble as well as interest on his capital. And the discredit that has often been attached to the money-lender's business must of course tend to raise the price of his loans still further; such discredit being largely due to the fact that such borrowing is often an expedient to which producers and consumers alike resort in occasional emergencies or in consequence of unthrift; the money-lender therefore is in the invidious position of making a profit out of the calamities or vices of his fellow-men.

We may conclude, then, that even the average rate of interest or discount current in the money-market will not generally tend to coincide with the average yield of invested capital. And the divergences between the fluctuations of the two rates will probably be still more marked; since the rate of discount is immediately acted on by vicissitudes of trade which only affect the other rate secondarily, and, in ordinary cases, comparatively slightly. The two rates, however, will *ceteris paribus* tend to rise and fall together; since a fall in the yield of investments generally, other things remaining the same, will induce bankers to purchase bills at a lower rate of discount, as they will gain less by investing in other securities, and will render the borrowers of their money less disposed to pay the old price for its use; and similarly a fall in the rate of discount, occurring independently of a fall in the yield of capital generally, will increase the inducement to buy and decrease the inducement to sell securities of which the interest has not risen; and therefore will cause a fall in the rate of interest on such investments actually received.

§ 5. The other confusion of which I spoke, between the rate of interest on loans of money, and the power of money to purchase goods, has never been defended by any economist: and it is easy to show that the two values in question often tend to vary in opposite directions. For an active demand for discounts on bills or advances from bankers tends, as I have said, to raise the value of the use of money; but so far as such money is mostly wanted to pay for extended purchases of goods, the increased supply and more active employment of it is generally accompanied by a rise in the price of the latter and therefore by a fall in the purchasing power of money relatively to goods. Similarly in slack times, when bankers have to make loans at very low rates, the purchasing power of money, relatively to goods, is likely to be high; for though at such times money is said to be "plentiful," what is meant is that the amount that bankers have to lend is larger than usual relatively to the demand; but since at such times there is a general lack of enterprise in trade and in the industrial investment of capital, the demand for loans is still likely to be small in comparison with the amount of production of goods.

At the same time, there are certain connexions between the purchasing power of money and the rate of discount, which go some way to explain, though hardly to justify, the common confusion between the two meanings of "value of money." It must be borne in mind that money is largely employed not in buying the consumable products and materials of production which we call 'goods,' but in purchasing land, houses, or other portions of capital with a view to interest; especially the debts of governments or joint-stock companies, or shares of the capital owned by such companies, which we call by the general name of 'securities.' Now a fall in the rate of discount will, as we have seen, tend to be accompanied by a rise in the selling price of such investments; that is, by a fall in the purchasing power of money relatively to securities generally (varying in degree, according as the securities are more or less negotiable). Thus when money is 'cheap,' in the ordinary commercial sense, i.e. when discount is low, securities will *ceteris paribus* be dear; and thus the rate of discount and the purchasing power of money will naturally be blended into one notion in the minds of persons whose attention is especially directed to the market for securities.

In the same way when the rate of discount rises the selling price of securities tends to fall correspondingly, under ordinary circumstances. This tendency, however, is likely to be much intensified if the rise in discount is occasioned by the arrival of the first stage in a commercial crisis,—that is, if it is due not merely to the keenness of the demand for loans but to a positive restriction of credit owing to a more or less wide-spread fear of bankruptcies. For under these circumstances the difficulty of borrowing money is likely to cause an extensive sale of securities, as the easiest way of obtaining what is required for the payment of debts; and consequently the selling price of securities tends to fall; and may even fall more than in proportion to the rise in the rate of discount.

But again, under the same circumstances, traders who are in pressing need of money to meet their liabilities are likely to try to obtain it by selling commodities as well as securities; consequently at such times commodities generally are likely to be cheap, so that "money" will be "dear" both in the economic and in the ordinary commercial sense.

Finally, it should be observed that those who confound the two meanings of "value of money" are not wrong in supposing that the value of the use of money tends to be lowered by an unusual influx of metallic money or bullion, and raised by an efflux; they are only wrong in overlooking the transitoriness of these effects. An increased supply of gold, not accompanied by a corresponding increase in the work that coin has to do (or a rise in the demand for gold otherwise caused), tends ultimately to lower the purchasing power of money relatively to commodities generally; but, in the first stage of the process that leads to this result, the increment of coin—or in England of notes representing the new gold in the Issue Department of the Bank—must pass through the hands of bankers, and so increase the amount of the medium of exchange that they have to lend. Hence the price paid for the use of money will tend to fall, and this fall will tend to cause increased borrowing, and consequent extended use of the medium of exchange; and then through the resulting rise in prices generally, the greater part of the new coin or bank-notes will gradually pass into ordinary circulation. Thus the fall in the purchasing power of money, consequent on an influx of gold, will normally establish itself through an antecedent and connected fall in the value of the use of money.

In the same way, when gold has to leave a country where the banking system is fully developed, in payment of commercial and other debts to foreigners, it will generally be taken chiefly from the reserves of banks; and the need of filling up the gap thus created will make it expedient for bankers to restrict their loans, and so tend to raise the rate of discount. This effect will generally be greater, the smaller the reserve of metal kept by the aggregate of banks, compared with the amount of the medium of exchange that they supply: hence it will be especially marked in such a banking system as our own, in which nearly the whole reserve of gold is kept by the Bank of England.

§ 6. Hitherto I have assumed that there is only one metal used as coin, in payments beyond a certain low limit. Let us now examine the effects of using two such metals. In the first place the purchasing power of either will obviously be less than it would otherwise be; so far as the use of the two metals actually takes place, and is not merely permitted by law. Secondly, unless either the causes of variation in the supply of both metals are the same, or one metal is decidedly more liable to such variation than the other, the chances are that the variations in annual supply when the two metals are used will be somewhat less in magnitude than when one alone is used.

These two effects are independent of the question whether (1) the two kinds of coins are both legal tender, or (2) only one is legally current, but the other is coined and commonly accepted at its market value: only in the latter case the standard of value will be entirely determined by the metal legally current.

When both metals are coined into legal tender at unlimited amounts, a rate has to be fixed at which they circulate together; since a law enacting that all debts of money may be liquidated by payment in either kind of coin, provided that there is no special contract to the contrary, would be obviously incomplete without a precise determination of the equivalence of the two metals.

So long as this legal rate does not vary materially from what would otherwise be the relative market value of the two metals, they will obviously tend to be coined and used indifferently; except so far as the choice between them is determined by the convenience of carrying or handling them. But when changes occur in the conditions of supply or demand for either metal, their effects will be importantly different from the effects that would have been produced apart from legal interference. To trace these effects in their proper order, it will be convenient to contemplate a particular case of change; which, for simplicity, we will first suppose to occur in an isolated country, entirely supplied with both metals from its own mines. Let us assume, therefore, that gold and silver are coined freely by Government and made legally current in unlimited amount at a fixed rate throughout this region; and let us assume that this rate in the first instance accurately corresponds to the relative market-values of the two metals, as they would exist apart from legal interference. Let us then suppose that the supply of silver becomes more abundant, the conditions determining the values of all other products remaining unaltered. Then, apart from legal interference, the gold price of silver would fall; but under the circumstances supposed this cannot take place, in the first instance; for no one will exchange his silver in the market for a smaller amount of gold coin than he could get by taking the silver to the mint to be coined. Hence what will happen will be that all the additional supply of silver, which the non-monetary demand will not absorb at the legal rate, will go to the mint; the purchasing power of the whole mass of coin will fall correspondingly, gold and silver being maintained at their legal relative value. As the exchange value of bullion relatively to other wares must of course fall equally an extension will tend to take place in the non-monetary demand of bullion—gold as well as silver. But as no change is supposed to occur in the conditions of supply of gold bullion, there must be a corresponding diminution in the gold sent to the mint for coinage. If the increase in the supply of silver were not very great or permanent its effects might stop at this point, so that no difference would manifest itself between the market-rate and the mint-rate of interchange of the two metals; the demand having in fact, under the pressure of governmental interference, adjusted itself to the change in supply. But if the addition to annual supply be sufficiently extensive and prolonged, the process above described may be carried on until no gold at all is sent to the mint; and then, for the first time (if the process still goes on), the market-price of gold bullion will begin to rise. When this rise has gone so far that the gold coins still in use have actually—through the continued depreciation of silver, which necessarily drags down with it the value of the coined gold as well—become less valuable than the bullion which they on the average contain, it will become profitable to melt them down; and if the same causes continue to operate, this process will continue (unless prevented by law—or even, if the difference between the two rates be great, in spite of legal interference) until the coin used in large payments is entirely composed of the metal that has fallen in value.

It thus appears that the adoption of a double standard will, up to a certain point, prevent variations in supply from affecting the relative market-value of the two metals, as it will tend to produce changes in demand sufficient to absorb their effect. But variations of a certain magnitude cannot be thus counteracted; on the contrary, such variations will nullify the formal adoption of a double standard, and render the currency practically monometallic. And it is to be observed that the change in monetary demand, by which the bimetallic system keeps the relative value of the two metals stable in spite of a change in supply, necessarily tends to affect production in the direction opposed to its own aims: i.e. it presents an enlargement in the supply of (say) silver from being checked as it otherwise would be by a corresponding fall in the value of silver.

If now we suppose the country contemplated to be in commercial relations with other countries in which the double standard is not adopted, the nullification of the double standard will be accelerated; since the single bimetallic mint will have to sustain the rated value of the two metals in the larger market constituted by all the countries concerned. Or to put it otherwise the 'non-monetary demand' for gold in the country with a double standard will be partly a demand for exportation to other countries where the value of gold is not legislatively tied to that of silver, and silver will correspondingly flow from these other countries to the bimetallic mint.

§ 7. It remains to discuss the determination of the value of 'fiat-money'; i.e. inconvertible notes issued by Government, and purporting to be equivalent to a certain amount of coin. Assuming that the government issuing such money can secure for it—as it usually can—practically complete currency as an internal medium of exchange, its value (as its cost of production is of course insignificant) depends entirely on the relation of the supply to the demand. If the amount coined in any country exceeds the amount of convertible notes of similar nominal value, which the country in question at the particular time would use, the purchasing power of the whole medium of exchange will tend to fall just as it would if there had been an equivalent addition to the amount of coin in the country—supposing that the government does not simultaneously withdraw from circulation any part of the coin in use[1]. The rise in prices, which is another aspect of this fall, will tend to increase the imports and decrease the exports of the country, and thus to cause an exportation of the standard coin—which for simplicity's sake we will suppose to be gold—to pay the balance due. If the excess in quantity of the currency still continues, the pressing need of gold to pay commercial debts abroad will cause it to be sold at a premium. When this premium has once established itself, the gold coins used in ordinary payments within the country will have a premium also: but, as the above reasoning explains, and as experience shows, some time may elapse before an excessive issue of inconvertible notes produces this result. It should be observed, too, that strictly speaking the increase of the medium of exchange through the issue of fiat-money does not tend to cause the premium to be established, until this increase has gone beyond a certain point; since, so far as such issue cuts off a portion of the ordinary demand for gold, it has a certain tendency to lower its exchange value permanently. But this tendency will be practically slight so long as the issue is confined to one country.

In the above reasoning I have supposed the region over which the fiat-money is current to be limited, and to have commercial relations with other countries outside it. But even

[1] If the amount of such coin be diminished by the action of the government, a corresponding additional amount of room will be made for the inconvertible notes. It is to be observed, moreover, that the government issuing such notes is likely to be making unusual purchases by means of them; which even if made without inconvertible notes would have occasioned a temporary rise in prices and therefore a temporarily greater room for convertible notes than would otherwise be the case.

if foreign trade were excluded—or if we suppose an issue of inconvertible notes current over the whole civilized world—the establishment of a premium on gold would still take place, if the issue of inconvertible notes were extended beyond a certain point; only it would take place more slowly and in a different way. What would happen in this case would be, first, a general rise in prices not extending to gold bullion, which would preserve its previous price in coin, and therefore in inconvertible notes. This would lead to an extension of the non-monetary demand for bullion; on the other hand, as the exchange value of bullion relatively to commodities generally would have fallen, its supply would tend to be reduced; and unless these two changes together were so slight that their effect was balanced by the simultaneous reduction of the monetary demand for bullion, a rise in the money price of bullion must ultimately take place. When this rise became so great as to make it worth while to melt down the coin, it would be checked by such melting, until the standard coin had been withdrawn from circulation; but, after this, the premium on bullion would correspond exactly to the general fall in prices resulting from the excessive issue of notes.

NOTE. It has been already noticed that Mr Jevons' theory of the relation between the 'final utility'—or final value in use—of a commodity and its value in exchange needs some modification in the case of money,—at least if we are considering its social utility. For since money is only used by being exchanged, the value in use of any portion of it is simply its value in exchange and can be nothing else. Hence, though it is true as we have seen that the value of money tends to fall when its supply is increased, just as the value of any other commodity does; this is not because the new increment of money furnishes an increment of utility or satisfaction less than that still afforded by the previously existing money; but rather because, speaking broadly, the utility of the whole aggregate remains unaffected by the addition to its quantity.

CHAPTER VI.

INTEREST.

§ 1. In the preceding discussion on the 'Value of Money' in the sense in which economists use the term—i.e. the purchasing power of money relatively to other wealth,—it has seemed desirable to include a consideration of the value of money in the ordinary commercial sense, or the Rate of Interest on loans of money; and this, again, has inevitably led us to speak of the rate of interest on capital generally. It is convenient, therefore, in passing from the theory of the value of products to the theory of the remuneration of services,—or the theory of distribution of wealth, as we at first conceived it,— to commence by examining the competitive determination of Interest.

We may conveniently begin by clearing away some controversy as to the precise nature of the service remunerated by Interest. English economists, since Senior, have generally agreed to regard Interest as the 'reward of abstinence': but the phrase has been criticised by socialists and semi-socialists, who seem to have understood it as having an ethical import, and implying that the sum paid to a capitalist for the use of his wealth was *just* compensation for the sacrifice he makes in not immediately consuming it. It does not however appear that either Senior, or his chief followers in the use of the phrase, intended any such ethical assertion. All that they meant was (1) that as any individual capitalist could, by the aid of exchange, consume in some form adapted for immediate enjoyment the wealth which he actually keeps in the form of capital, he by abstaining from such consumption renders a service to individuals, or supplies an aid to industry, for which he is paid by interest: and (2) that this remuneration is necessary, under the present social conditions, to induce the owners of wealth to postpone their enjoyment of it, to the extent required to keep in existence the actual amount of individuals' capital. Circumstances are no doubt conceivable under which the quantity of capital supplied would be practically independent of the price obtainable for the use of it: e.g. it is conceivable that the process of saving might be carried on to an adequate extent for no other 'remuneration' than the satisfaction derived from having a provision for the future needs of the person who saves, or of his family or others whom he may desire to benefit. But, actually, the price paid for the use of savings must tend to increase their total amount; though to what extent it increases it cannot, I think, be precisely known.

However, we may begin by simply regarding Interest as the share of produce that falls to the owner of Capital as such; meaning by "capital" wealth employed so that it may yield the owner a surplus of new wealth. From the individual's point of view, such capital may reasonably be considered as still existing, even when the wealth has been spent without leaving material results, whenever it has been employed so as to secure the owner a reasonable expectation of having its equivalent returned to him along with interest, or even of receiving interest only in perpetuity: but I shall not here take account of wealth spent in increasing the productive efficiency of human beings, since the economic effects of such expenditure are more conveniently considered under the head of wages. It should be observed that in the incomes of capitalists who are also employers interest can only be distinguished by abstract analysis from that other element of an employer's profit, which we have called his " wages of management "; to learn what part of the earnings of a man of business is to be called interest, we have to ascertain how much he could get for the use of his capital, supposing he withdrew it without loss from his business and lent it to other persons. Thus it is from the rate of interest actually paid on borrowed capital that we infer the theoretical interest—as distinct from employer's profit—of the capitalist who is also an employer: it is therefore convenient to begin by investigating the conditions that determine the former. The 'rate of interest' may be defined as the proportion of the price paid to the value of the capital borrowed for a certain fixed time, which we will take (according to usage) to be a year.

This definition, however, requires further explanation or qualification in two points. In the first place, we have already seen the need of distinguishing the rate of discount or interest in the money-market from the rate of interest on capital generally; since the two rates, though connected, are not identical, nor altogether determined by the same laws. Of course, when a loan is made, what is actually borrowed is, in most cases, the medium of exchange; but it is only when it is borrowed from persons who do not make a business of dealing in money, that the price paid for the loan may be regarded as substantially paid for use of the capital purchased with the money borrowed. The interest paid to professional lenders of money must, as was before observed, include remuneration for the labour of such persons; and this remuneration is obviously not Interest in the sense with which we are concerned with it in the theory of Distribution : while on the other hand so far as such lenders are also producers of the greater part of the medium of exchange at a cost considerably less than that of the coin that forms the remaining part—as we have seen to be the case with bankers—competition may force them to make loans for short periods at a rate even lower than that at which money or capital is borrowed from the public generally. It must therefore be borne in mind that our present investigation relates primarily to this latter rate; and only secondarily and with the qualifications already noticed to the former.

Secondly, we have to take into account that there is a large amount of capital not formally *lent*, of which, nevertheless, the yield is to be regarded as interest and not profit; since the capital is owned by persons who spend no labour—or at least no remunerated labour—in managing it. This is the case (e.g.) with the capital of railway companies, water companies, gas companies, and many other large masses of capital owned in joint-stock: no one who becomes a shareholder in such companies considers any trouble he may take in electing directors and criticising their report as labour requiring remuneration; hence the dividends of such companies are to be regarded as merely interest on the capital owned by the shareholders, no less than the money annually paid to the bondholders[1].

Again, it has been before observed that what we commonly speak of as the 'capital' of such companies frequently includes portions of land: and that the distinction which, in considering social production, we drew between capital—as the result of labour—and land in its original condition, has *primâ facie* no application when we are considering the question of distribution. The material capital owned by an individual is rarely to any great extent the actual results of his own labour; and its value as a source of future wealth cannot depend on whether or not it was the result of the labour of some one else. I purpose therefore, for the present, to regard the yield of land as a species of interest; reserving for the next chapter the task of examining any important characteristics peculiar to the determination of the yield[2] of land.

In considering the rate of interest on land we have to deal with a point of some subtlety as to the right mode of measuring the amount of an individual's capital. We ordinarily measure capital, as we measure wealth generally, by its exchange value; so that if any particular investment rises in value during the period investigated—as land, on the whole, has continually done—we ought (assuming that there is no cognizable change in the purchasing power of money) to consider the additional increment of value as a part of the annual yield of the investment, no less than the rent or interest nominally received. Similarly in the case of investments of which the price has

---

[1] It may be said that though ordinary shareholders in joint-stock companies obtain no remuneration for the labour of managing the business of the companies, they do obtain the remuneration of higher dividends for the labour spent in careful selection of investments. And this is no doubt true, so far as such labour results, on the average, in a more accurate estimate of the risks of different investments. But since the remark applies as much to different investments of money formally lent as it does to money employed in purchasing shares, it seems more convenient to draw attention to this remuneration of labour at a later point of the discussion. See p. 263.

[2] As will presently appear, in dealing with the (approximately) uniform rate of interest with which we are concerned in the present chapter, the chief controversies as to the determination of rent do not come before us.

fallen, we ought to subtract the difference from the interest or dividends which have been paid to the investors. But when we examine the conditions of such changes in the selling value of investments, we find that one important cause is a change in the rate of interest itself. If the rent of a piece of land were to remain the same while the current rate of interest fell from 3 to 2 per cent., the price of the land would *ceteris paribus* rise 50 per cent. From the point of view of the community, taken in the preceding book, this rise obviously does not constitute a real increase of wealth: since the command over the necessaries and conveniences of life possessed by the community is, speaking broadly, no greater because the exchange value of its instruments of production has risen in consequence of a fall in the rate of interest. But from the individual's point of view the increase of wealth is, in a certain sense, real and not merely nominal; for though the real income of the owner of the capital is not increased by the change, his power of purchasing consumable commodities has certainly increased, though he can only exercise it by spending his capital. I think, therefore, that this kind of increase of nominal wealth should be carefully noted and distinguished from other kinds; but here we may conveniently avoid any complications arising out of it by considering our problem *statically*, not dynamically; that is, by assuming that the rate of interest remains the same during the period investigated, and analysing the forces that determine it to this stable condition. Similarly, for simplicity, we may assume that there is no appreciable change in the purchasing power of money.

§ 2. Here however another question is forcibly suggested,— viz. how far, and on what grounds, we have a right to speak of "*a* rate of interest" as current at any given time. It is notorious that capital is borrowed contemporaneously at very different rates by different individuals and companies; and such differences are still more striking when we include under the notion of interest—as we have seen reason to do—the dividends paid· on the joint-stocks of companies. For such dividends actually vary from 20 per cent. or more down to zero: and when we include changes in the selling value of the investments during the year, the variations are increased manyfold, since the lower limit becomes a considerable negative quantity. In what sense, then, can we speak of a tendency to a uniform rate of interest at a given time and place?

Firstly, in so speaking we do not mean by "rate of interest" on any investment the proportion of the annual yield to the capital originally invested, but the proportion between the dividends or interest actually paid and the present selling price of the stock or bonds upon which it is paid. We can affirm no general tendency to uniformity in the former ratio. No doubt if we supposed all capital to have been originally invested with equal knowledge and foresight, we might infer that the yield of equal portions of capital would in the long run be equal, if they were invested contemporaneously or at times at which the current rate of interest was the same. But in order to draw even from this hypothesis any inference with regard to the proportion of present annual yield to capital originally invested, we should have to know in every case the amount received in previous years; since some forms of capital are more liable than others to depreciation through various causes, so that their yield in the earlier years after investment has to be proportionally greater; while other investments again take some time to rise to their full height of profitableness.

Secondly, in saying that the rate of interest even on new investments, or old investments estimated at their present value, tends to be the same, it is only meant that all differences in the rate of interest so estimated, on securities currently sold in open market, correspond to differences in the general estimate of the probabilities of fall or rise in the future yield or in the selling value of such investments[1]. So explained, the proposition follows *primâ facie* from the principle that in all pecuniary transactions each person concerned seeks the greatest pecuniary gain to himself; and there is scarcely any broad and simple deduction from this principle which approximates so closely to the actual facts of existing societies. It is generally true that men in buying debts and shares are solely influenced by the desire to get the greatest amount of interest that they can on the whole; so that if any one prefers an investment

[1] Mill's phrase "indemnity for risk" is not sufficiently general to cover all cases.

that at present yields a lower interest than another, it is because he either considers it safer or expects it to rise hereafter.

The chief exceptional cases may be classed under the following heads. (1) Some kinds of securities are purchased at a higher price than would otherwise be the case, on account of some indirect pecuniary advantage obtained by the possession of them. E.g. securities widely known and esteemed safe, for which the demand is extensive and steady, and the value in consequence comparatively stable, have a special utility for bankers and merchants, as a means of obtaining money in an emergency; again such securities (as we have noticed) are, to a certain extent, used for the payment of commercial debts in foreign countries, and have thus a special utility as an international medium of exchange. Either of these causes will have a certain tendency to raise the average price of the securities affected by it. (2) To some extent, again, the price of certain investments is raised through the operation of motives which though self-regarding, act counter to the desire of pecuniary gain. Thus the price of land in England has undoubtedly been kept up by the social consideration and power that its possession has conferred: and again, it is probable that investments reputed especially safe are purchased at a rate of interest lower, as compared with that of somewhat less trusted securities, by a difference somewhat greater than what would exactly represent compensation for the extra risk of the latter; because most persons who live chiefly on interest would suffer from a decrease of income more than they would be benefited by an increase; and again, the freedom from anxiety that safe investments give is itself a utility which has a certain price. It is to be observed, on the other hand, that the excitement of fluctuations of gain and loss is a source of keen pleasure to many minds; as is shown by the extensive existence of lotteries, gaming, betting, and speculation in stocks by private persons. It seems to be the fact that on this ground, indemnity for risk is not even sufficiently represented in the price of some very fluctuating investments[1]. (3) Again,

---

[1] If we had only to consider investments made in view of the investor's personal interests, it would perhaps be a delicate matter to balance the influence of the pleasures of excitement against that of the pains of anxiety. But in the investment of savings for posterity the former motive does not come in; here

the effect that would follow from a spontaneous willingness to pay an extra price for specially safe investments will equally tend to be produced, if a certain portion of the capital of the community is kept in such investments by legal compulsion; as is the case in England with a large part of the funds held by trustees. (4) Finally, in some cases, a diminished rate of interest is accepted out of regard for the public well-being or sympathy with private individuals. Thus considerable sums are from time to time invested in undertakings of a semi-commercial, semi-philanthropic character, which are not found by experience, and not expected, to bring in even ultimately interest at the average rate; and money is often borrowed from relatives or friends by struggling men of business, at a rate which very inadequately represents the risk of loss.

But even if we take these causes of variation fully into account, it still remains true that the differences in the rates of interest obtainable at any given time on different fresh investments of capital are mainly due to differences in the generally estimated prospects of change in the interest or selling value of the respective securities. This varying prospect is in the majority of cases a prospect of possible loss: the interest accordingly is above what would be paid for a loan of which the repayment was considered absolutely secure. In this way, for example, the interest on the ordinary stock of a prosperous railway company, taken at its selling value, comes to be generally somewhat higher at ordinary times than the interest on its 'Preference' stock or shares; this latter again being somewhat higher than the interest paid on the debentures of such a company[1]; while

therefore it seems likely that, on the whole, security will be rated somewhat above its exact pecuniary value. And the same would, I think, be true of investments made by trustees, even apart from the legal interference that actually restricts them to certain funds and stocks; since trustees are much more likely to be blamed for diminishing the funds entrusted to them by hazardous purchases than praised for increasing them by lucky hits.

[1] Joint-stock companies frequently lay by a certain part of their proceeds to form an insurance-fund against risks. In this way they diminish the hazard of their investments, and proportionally raise the ratio which the selling value of their shares bears to the annual yield; but they do not profess to make such investments "as safe as the Funds:" there still remain indefinite risks of extraordinary losses through depreciation or destruction of capital, which investors undoubtedly take into account.

the interest on the debt of the English Government would undoubtedly be less than this last, even apart from the other influences which, as we have seen, tend to raise the price of 'consols.' In such cases, evidently, the surplus receipts represent the general estimate of adequate insurance against the different risks of loss.

So far as such expectations of probable loss (and in some cases, of increased yield) are on the average well founded, it is evident that, on the whole, after a sufficient lapse of time, the differences in the original yield of different investments will have been compensated by the realization of the expected gains and losses; so that the aggregate interest on the whole capital will prove to be about as much as would have been obtained if it had all been lent on perfectly good security—allowance being made for any extra price currently paid for special advantages of safety (as before noticed). Persons of superior knowledge and foresight will of course tend to get considerably more from their investments, by estimating more accurately than others the risk of undertakings which, from their novelty or some other cause, are rightly regarded as hazardous by prudent persons without special knowledge. Such investors, in fact, obtain a certain return for the skilled labour that they perform in estimating the prospects of novel or otherwise hazardous undertakings; and if we could assume that this labour is, on the whole, undertaken by fairly competent persons, we should infer that the yield of such undertakings would on the average exceed that of safer investments by an amount sufficient to provide adequate remuneration for such labour. But this assumption would, I think, be unwarrantable as regards any actual society; since ignorant, rash and credulous persons investing in novel undertakings are commonly believed to get, on the average, considerably less interest than if they had lent their capital on the most widely esteemed security—in fact will not unfrequently be found to have lost capital as well as interest. At any rate we may say that the rate of interest on newly borrowed capital which was generally believed to be as secure as possible, would at any given time be nearly uniform, and— after allowing for the extra price of special safety—would represent approximately the common expectation of the average yield of all capital that was at that time being invested; supposing that there was no general expectation of a permanent rise or fall hereafter in the rate of interest, or in the purchasing power of money[1]. It is then with the rate of interest so understood, the expected average yield on freshly invested capital, that we are now primarily concerned. Of course in the case of any particular individual who is not an employer of capital, a fresh investment will generally be effected by purchasing some debt already contracted, or a share of some capital already in existence. But such investments are mere transfers which disappear when we are considering the aggregate of individuals' capital; from this point of view a fresh investment on which interest is paid must imply either the contraction of a new debt, or the formation by a joint-stock company of new real capital in addition to the old, the value of this latter being assumed to be kept up.

§ 3. Let us now proceed to analyse the causes which determine the rate of interest as above defined. It will be simpler to confine our consideration in the first instance to borrowed capital; and afterwards extend our view to include the case of new capital employed by its owner. Applying *mutatis mutandis*, the principles laid down in investigating the general theory of the value of products, we may assume that the use of capital is a commodity of which the amount demanded will vary inversely with the exchange value, so long as the causes of the demand remain unchanged. So far, then, as we may assume the amount of capital seeking employment at interest to be determined independently of the rate of interest, the price obtained by the owner for the use of his capital must vary with the intensity of the demand for it. So far, however, as the

---

[1] If either the rate of interest or the purchasing power of money were generally expected to rise or fall in the future, the relations of the rate of interest on loans of money with perfect security to the expected average yield of capital would become more complicated; since the price paid for the use of money would vary with the length of time for which it is borrowed; and the price of investments expected to yield a high profit at once for a short time would vary correspondingly as compared with the price of those of which the yield was likely to remain more uniform or to rise hereafter. But since it would seem that no such general expectation has ever yet influenced ordinary investors, it is hardly worth while to develop these more complicated relations in detail.

CHAP. VI.] INTEREST. 265

supply of such capital varies with the price obtainable for the use of it, the determination of the rate of interest will depend on conditions of demand and supply combined, just as the normal price of a material product does. Under these circumstances, we may conveniently begin by examining first the conditions of demand for capital.

There are two broadly different kinds of demand for loans; which we may distinguish as Industrial and Non-industrial[1]. In the former case capital is borrowed to replace itself with a profit to the user, and will therefore continue to exist in the form—chiefly—of improvements of land, buildings, machinery, raw or auxiliary materials, and unsold products, finished or half-finished. But the money of A may also be borrowed by B merely in order to increase his expenditure; in which case the commodities purchased by it will be consumed without replacement; and the interest that B subsequently pays to A will be taken out of his share of the produce otherwise obtained[2].

---

[1] A case intermediate between the two is the case of capital borrowed to prevent the ruin through temporary pressure of some individual's generally profitable industry, and the consequent destruction of some or all of his capital invested in the industry. This case resembles industrial borrowing in being favourable to the production of the community taken as a whole; but it is rather to be classed with non-industrial borrowing, when we are considering the general economic laws determining the rate of interest that such borrowers will have to pay.

[2] It is of course possible that the interest of the debt thus contracted may be from the first paid out of the yield of some kind of capital, which for some reason or other the debtor does not wish to sell. In this case the payment will for some purposes be properly regarded not as an addition to interest, but as a mere transfer of interest from the borrower to the lender. But the difference is not important for our present enquiry: since the loan when made will be a new investment of the lender's capital, while its interest will be paid from the yield of an old investment of the borrowers, so that the former will operate in determining the current rate of interest just as much as if the borrower owned no capital.

The dispute whether the debts contracted by individuals, or by the government of a community so far as it borrows from its subjects,—in excess of any capital that the borrower may own—constitute an addition to the whole aggregate of (individuals') capital in the community that includes both borrowers and lenders, turns on a merely formal—if not exactly a verbal—point. If we allow the conception of *negative quantity* to be applied to capital, we may legitimately say that a borrower without (positive) capital who is under the obligation of paying interest on a debt owns an amount of negative capital equal to the value of the debt to the lender; and therefore that the aggregate capital of the two is

Loans of this latter kind do not increase social capital; but they absorb the savings of the lenders no less than loans for productive purposes, and therefore the demand for them operates in determining the rate of interest at any particular time, just as much as the industrial demand. And it is conceivable that borrowed wealth might be chiefly used unproductively—to meet temporary deficits of income or occasions of exceptional expenditure, or by persons living habitually beyond their means,—the wealth used in production being almost exclusively employed by its owners. In such circumstances there would be no advantage in investigating the conditions of the demand and supply of capital separately: as the rate of interest would simply express the average estimate formed in the community of the comparative advantages of present and future enjoyment of wealth. But in a thrifty and progressive community, in an advanced stage of industrial development, the borrowing of producers with a view to profit—including under this term the formation of joint-stock companies in which the public invest—is much more extensive than the borrowing

not augmented by the transaction. If, however, this conception is rejected as too unfamiliar, we must certainly admit that the capital of the community—in the sense of 'aggregate capital of individual members of the community'—is increased by the kind of loans that we are considering; only we must add that such increase involves a corresponding prospect of diminished income to some other members of the same community.

It should be observed, however, that among the debts which form part of the capital of individuals, that part of the medium of exchange which consists of the obligations of bankers to pay coin on demand, occupies a peculiar position. So far as this money is used not in mediating the transfer of commodities to the consumer, but in the business of production—so far, that is, as the current account of a man of business is kept for the purposes of his business—it would ordinarily be included in an estimate of his wealth employed in production, no less than the coin that he requires for similar purposes; at the same time, so far as no interest is paid by the banker on these current accounts, he receives without deduction the interest of the investments which this acceptance of his obligations as money has enabled him to make. Thus the nominal amount of capital on which interest is paid or earned is undoubtedly increased by the creation of this medium of exchange: and this increase is not balanced,—as it is in the case (just discussed) of ordinary debts—by a correspondingly diminished prospect of income to the banker. But, as has already been said, the interest received by the banker is, from our present point of view, to be regarded as really the price paid by society for the labour of himself and his servants; except so far as it is interest on his own capital.

for expenditure: and since the amount of the latter borrowing is actually to a large extent fixed independently of the rate of interest[1], we may without material error consider this kind of demand to affect the rate of interest merely by absorbing a portion of the savings continually accumulated, and so diminishing the supply of capital available for industrial uses.

Under the general notion of 'non-industrial borrowing' we must include the hiring or renting of the durable wealth which we have previously distinguished as Consumers' Capital; of which private dwelling-houses may be taken as a principal example. The proportion of the price paid for the use of such things to their selling value will tend to vary with variations in the rate of interest—including, of course, besides interest proper, adequate compensation for gradual deterioration;—and the increased need of such articles which accompanies the growth of wealth and population in a community will absorb a certain portion of savings which would otherwise have been invested in industry. The amount thus absorbed will tend *ceteris paribus* to be somewhat greater when interest is low than when it is high; thus (e.g.) a low rate of interest will give a certain inducement to build more houses and to build them more durably. This will be true, to some extent, of the consumers' capital that is owned by the user, no less than of that which is hired: in either case such wealth is a form of investment of savings which, so far as it is managed economically, must be affected by changes in the yield of investments generally. But the economic comparison of present to future utilities, made by purchasers of such durable wealth for personal use, has not commonly the exactness of commercial calculations: and on the whole the changes in extent of demand for increased consumers' capital that would result from changes in the rate of interest are probably not great in proportion to the whole demand; so that the rate of interest on capital held in this form, in a modern industrial society, may be regarded as mainly determined by the relations of supply and demand of capital industrially invested, no less than the rate on loans of money for unproductive expenditure.

[1] The borrowing of governments for wars and other emergencies is generally thus fixed: and much of the borrowing of individuals for unproductive expenditure would be unaffected by any moderate changes in the rate of interest.

§ 4. I pass, therefore, to examine the nature and operation of the industrial demand for capital in any community. This demand, so far as it leads to the actual payment of interest, is the demand of persons wishing to employ the capital of others. But its ulterior cause lies in the existence, and recognition by such persons, of unoccupied opportunities for profitably employing capital in industry: and a portion of the aggregate of such opportunities is continually turned to account by the savings of capitalists who are themselves in business, and employ their own new capital. It will therefore be proper to include this portion in a general view of the whole industrial demand; and for similar reasons we must now include the savings employed by their owners, in our view of the whole supply offered at any time to meet the industrial demand. It should be observed, however, that the actual employment of capital in industry is likely to be somewhat different, according as the employer is or is not also the owner. Employers may sometimes invest their own savings when they would not borrow: either because they are reluctant to incur the relatively more serious loss of income that would result from borrowing if the investment failed; or because, if they can only borrow on personal security, they may be unable to obtain a loan except at a rate too high to leave them an adequate remuneration for the trouble of managing the borrowed capital. On the other hand, the field of *apparently* profitable employment tends in one way to become greater the more the capital is borrowed; since enterprising employers and promoters of companies will—without any bad faith—be often more inclined to run risks with other people's money than they would be with their own. And perhaps, in a broad view of the determination of interest we may neglect these opposite tendencies, and consider the field of employment of savings as independent of the ownership of the savings.

We must now determine somewhat more precisely the relation between the supply of capital and the field of employment. In the first place we cannot properly consider the whole addition to the stock of capital made within any given time to operate as a new investment, in determining the current rate of interest; but only that part of it with regard to which the investor's choice was perfectly free and unfettered. That is, we must exclude all the capital that is from time to time required for the completion of industrial undertakings already begun, so far as such completion is necessary to prevent the loss or diminution of the yield expected on what has already been invested. On the other hand, we must, for a similar reason, include that portion of the capital already invested in any business, which its employer could withdraw without affecting the productiveness of the remainder: since such capital is manifestly just as available for fresh investment as capital newly produced. We may perhaps designate what we have in view by speaking of the portion of capital —old as well as new—that is 'fluid' or 'floating' at any given time. The portion of what is already invested to which this term can be applied may be very different at different times in the same business; and the average proportion of floating to non-floating capital varies very much in different branches of industry; such variations depending partly on the different lengths of time for which capital is invested, partly on the extent to which it exists in a form adapted solely for the use of the particular industry in which it is actually employed, or is available for one or other of the new opportunities for investment that present themselves[1]. It should be observed that there is no clearly marked separation between "floating" and "non-floating:" that is, the loss that would be incurred by the removal of non-floating capital from a business is different for different portions; and, in fact, may vary from zero upwards to

---

[1] The distinction drawn in the text between "floating" and "non-floating" capital appears to me to require to be substituted, in this and similar discussions, for the received antithesis of "fixed" and "circulating" capital. I do not deny the importance of the difference—which these latter terms express—between instruments that aid in making many successive products of the same kind, and materials that are spent in making a single product and of which therefore the cost has to be repaid from the price of that one. But for our present purposes this is not the distinction required. Capital in this sense "fixed" may easily have, in a given case, the quality that I have expressed by "floating"; buildings, for instance, may be transferable without loss from a less to a more profitable business: whereas materials may be non-transferable, as they may be only useful for making a particular species of product—nor can it be said that when one set of materials has been exhausted another need not be purchased; since the purchase may be necessary to utilise capital fixed in machines, &c.

the whole value of the capital. Hence any rise in the rate of interest, caused by an increase of opportunities of new profitable investment would *ceteris paribus* tend to increase the amount of capital that it would be on the whole profitable to withdraw from old investments; and this increase of supply would tend somewhat to check the rise. Still it is only the supply of capital actually floating that can be regarded as directly operative in determining the rate of interest.

Let us consider, then, that at any given time there is a *quantum* of floating capital, of which—in the sense before explained—the rate of interest tends to be the same; and that the industrial demand for this is furnished by the whole aggregate of recognised opportunities for employing it profitably, that, at any given time, the existing aggregate of non-floating capital leaves open—which we may call the *effective* field of employment. The manner and degree in which this field tends to be extended or reduced, as the rate of interest falls or rises, will vary, of course, with the state of the industrial arts. But it is obvious that when interest is low, other things being the same, the cultivator has an inducement to employ more instruments in proportion to his labourers; the trader can afford to hold stocks of goods for a longer time; and there are more profitable openings for new lines of railway and other investments involving large outlay for distant returns. Similarly, if we suppose the amount of capital seeking industrial employment to increase, while the recognised modes of employing it profitably remain unchanged, we may infer that the rate of interest tends to fall, until it reaches the point at which it will seem just worth the employers' while to use the additional increment of capital. In this way the rate of interest on floating capital generally will tend to be equal to the ratio borne to the last increment of such capital by the amount of average additional wealth expected to be obtained by employing it, allowing for the varying interval that may elapse before the produce is obtained, and subtracting what we may call the employer's fee'; i.e. the portion of produce that the employers of capital will retain as their remuneration for the labour of management,—the competitive determination of which we will consider more particularly in a subsequent

CHAP. VI.] INTEREST. 271

chapter¹. The general function of capital employed in industry—as we have before seen—is to enable the ultimate net produce of labour to be increased by processes which postpone the time of obtaining it: but the opportunities for effecting this result profitably will of course vary indefinitely, with the natural resources of the country, its stage of economic development, the density of its population, and other causes:—indeed there is no one of the conditions of production analysed in a previous chapter² which may not exercise some influence on them. An obvious and striking cause of an ample field of employment is found in the natural resources of a territory, thinly colonized by an advanced industrial population, where the amount of capital already invested is proportionally small. But in considering this cause we must avoid the mistake of supposing—what the metaphor in our term 'field' perhaps suggests—that each new investment of capital tends, in proportion to its amount, to diminish the remaining field: no doubt it has this effect so far as it occupies a particular opportunity; but it may easily operate to a considerable extent the other way, by creating new opportunities. For instance, in the present state of industry, after a certain amount of capital—mainly agricultural—has been invested in a new country, it becomes profitable for the first time to invest further capital in a railway; and then, the railway being made, further investments of agricultural capital become profitable, which were not so before. Similarly, when agriculture has developed to a certain extent, extensive employment of capital in manufactures becomes profitable, then, in consequence, further developments of agriculture, and so forth.

But again, supposing that the available natural resources—as at present understood—were fully turned to account, and that population did not increase, the field of employment, as recent experience has shown, might be enlarged³ indefinitely by the progress of Invention, opening out new ways of obtaining

¹ See ch. ix. § 3.
² Book I. ch. iii.
³ It should be observed that I speak of the field of employment as "enlarged," when there is room for more capital than before at the same rate of profit; not when more is employed at a lower rate.

economic gain by expending labour for remote results. While, again, if we suppose that the arts of invention—including under this term the discovery of new lines of trade, and any other modes of improving the whole system of cooperation through exchange—remain stationary; and also that the habits and faculties of the working part of the population, so far as these are important in production, undergo no material change; the industrial demand for new capital at the existing rate of interest could only be kept up by increase of population. If this increase did not itself tend to alter the average efficiency of labour, or the share of the produce of labour that the employer of floating capital is able to secure, there would obviously be a demand of uniform intensity, so long as other conditions of production remained stationary, for an increase of capital proportioned to the increase of population. But, as I have before argued[1], in a country so thickly populated as England each increment of capital accompanying and proportioned to an increment of population would tend to be somewhat less productive to its employers than the preceding increment, and therefore to yield a somewhat lower rate of interest—apart from improvements in production due to other causes—: since the economic loss through diminished proportional return from certain kinds of labour must be taken to outweigh the economic gain from increased facilities for cooperation; which, moreover, would be partly appropriated by the owners of land and other capital so invested as to be partially exempt from the depreciative effects of fresh competition. On the other hand in the societies economically the most advanced, improvement in the arts of industry is actually progressing continuously and rapidly; and the new inventions that are continually made, including the extensions of international trade, are mostly of such a kind as to enlarge the field of employment for capital. It is not easy to ascertain the balance of these conflicting tendencies in any given country at any particular time; still less can we predict with any definiteness their probable operation in the future; especially since, as I have before said, the progress of invention may conceivably take a decided turn in the direction adverse to the employment of capital.

---

[1] Book I. ch. vi. § 3. See also the next chapter § 2.

§ 5. In investigating the factors of the demand for capital in any country, it has not been necessary to consider the different fields of employment for capital furnished by different countries. But when we pass to study the conditions of Supply, the case is different; since the attraction exercised on capital by foreign fields of employment is, in an economically advanced country like England, one of the most powerful causes of variation in the supply for home investment. In the present state of the machinery of communication and international exchange, the most enormous masses of capital can be transferred with the greatest facility from one country to another: and it is quite conceivable that this mobility of capital may before long reach a point at which the rate of interest will be approximately the same in all civilized countries, for equally safe investments; so that the whole civilized world will admit of being regarded as one community, for the purposes of the present investigation. And we may conveniently begin by supposing that this consummation has been attained; and accordingly examine the conditions of supply of capital in an isolated region, out of which issues no overflow of wealth for foreign investment, while over the whole range of it money can be borrowed at the same rate of interest on equally good security.

The investigation, thus defined, is one which we have already had occasion to make in examining the Laws of Production[1]. We then saw that the conditions of more or less rapid accumulation of capital are extremely complex. In the first place, the amount that may be saved by any community within any given period tends to be increased, *ceteris paribus*, by any cause that increases the real income of the community during that period; that is, by anything that increases the proportion of the number of effective workers to the whole population, or the average productiveness of their labour. Secondly, the proportion that is actually saved of the whole amount available for saving tends to be affected by any variation in the degree of foresight and self-control, of capacity for being influenced by remote pleasures and pains as compared with those near at hand, possessed by average members of the community; or, again, in

[1] See Book I. c. vi. § 4.

the habits and sentiments that move men to provide for posterity; and, further, so far as men save (as many in the wealthier classes would seem to do) not for any definite end but because their income is larger than is needed to defray their habitual expenditure, any material change in the various habits of luxurious consumption prevailing in different classes is likely to affect saving materially. It did not seem possible definitely to measure the combined effect of these and other causes; but we may, I think, assume, on the one hand, that *ceteris paribus* saving will increase or decrease in amount, as the rate of interest rises or falls; and, on the other hand that the amount of effect thus produced within a short period is not likely to be great in comparison with the whole amount of floating capital; so that there will be no material error in taking the rate of interest during any such short period to be determined entirely by the demand for capital. But when we consider the determination of the average rate of interest over a considerable space of time, it is clear that the effect produced on saving by changes in the rate of interest will tend to give this average rate a steadiness which it would not otherwise possess: since any rise in the rate of interest, due to a change in the conditions of demand, has a certain tendency to bring about a subsequent fall through the increase in the supply of capital which it causes; and similarly any fall in the rate has a certain tendency to cause a subsequent rise[1]. This *compensatory* or *equilibratory* action of changes in the rate of interest may be assumed to become more powerful, in either direction, as the changes themselves increase in magnitude; and it is probable that, actually, in every existing community there is a point considerably above zero below which the rate of interest could not long remain without some great change in the intellectual, moral, or economic condition of the community, as well as a higher point above which it could not permanently rise, unless we suppose a development of the arts of industry quite beyond precedent. Where, however, these points will be we have no means of determining *a priori*; and I may add that I am

---

[1] It may be observed that experience shows another way in which a fall in the rate of interest tends to bring about a subsequent rise: i.e. by leading to rash speculations, which result in a destruction of capital.

aware of no adequate empirical reason for supposing with Mill, Cairnes and others, that the rate of interest in England at the present day is very near the minimum point.

We have thus obtained a general view of the manner in which interest would be determined in an isolated region, over the whole of which the rate was (with the qualifications before given) approximately uniform. Actually, however, we find material differences in the rates of interest maintained in different regions; even where an uninterrupted trade renders it easy to transfer capital from any one of these regions to any other. The explanation of these differences is threefold. First, the general security of capital in some countries, owing to inferiority in political organization or other causes, may be materially less, even for their inhabitants, than that maintained in others. Secondly, there is a certain extra risk incurred by investing in a distant region, owing to the greater difficulty of ascertaining and estimating the dangers that from time to time may threaten the yield of any particular investment, and in taking measures to ward them off. Thirdly, there seems to be a general tendency in the members of any society to estimate the risk of investments in a foreign country more highly, *ceteris paribus*, than that of home investments; owing to their greater confidence either in the morality or in the good fortune of their own community. The extent to which each of these causes will operate, as between different countries at different times, will of course, vary indefinitely. We can only lay down as a general rule, that the yield of capital in any one country (A) does not tend to differ from the yield of capital in any other country (B) which is in permanent commercial relations with the former, by an amount more than sufficient to compensate for the extra risk of investments in B to the inhabitants of A, as estimated by the latter. Thus any new cause that operates primarily to increase the supply of capital, and consequently to lower the rate of interest, in A, tends to have its effect extended over the whole aggregate of countries with which A is in commercial relations; the intensity of the effect being, of course, diminished in proportion to the extension of its range[1].

[1] It may be said that the interest received by members of any one community on capital employed by the members of any other, ought not strictly speaking to

§ 6. So far we have considered interest as the share of produce *expected* by the capitalist as such; since it is the *expectation* of profit that determines the action of borrowers and investors; and not, except indirectly, the profit that has been earned. If now it is asked how far the actual average yield of newly invested capital is found to coincide in the long run with the expected yield, no precise answer can, I conceive, be given. Indeed, even if we could obtain accurate statistics as to the interest actually received, it would still be impossible to say exactly how much was expected; since no investment is thought to be absolutely secure; and if there were any such, its price, for reasons before given, would probably exceed that of the less secure by more than adequate compensation for risk: so that there is no means of measuring precisely the amount of risk commonly recognised in those esteemed tolerably safe. We

be included when we are discussing how the aggregate produce of the industry of the first community is distributed. But there are two reasons for not leaving it out of account in such a discussion. In the first place even if this interest were merely to be regarded as so much additional income for certain capitalists, the transmission and consumption of which did not directly affect the shares received by other members of the community, it would still tend to affect the latter indirectly: since the mere possession of this extra income, from whatever source derived, tends to give its possessors and their children certain advantages in the competition that determines the relative rewards of the higher kinds of labour—as will be hereafter explained (Ch. ix.). But, secondly, since this "tribute," if it may be so called, of interest is actually paid by transmitting the produce of the country in which the capital is invested, its payment has a direct effect on the whole foreign trade both of the country that sends and of the country that receives it. The exact nature and extent of this effect depend upon the particular conditions of supply and demand of the wares in which the trade is carried on: but, in most cases, it will be beneficial to all the inhabitants of the country receiving the tribute, so far as they are consumers of imports: since the necessity of selling the commodities in which the tribute is paid, in the markets of the receiving country, will tend to establish the equation of international demand at a rate more favourable to the latter than would otherwise be the case. This cheapening of imports may of course be detrimental to certain producers in the importing country; just as any improvement in industrial processes is liable to be detrimental to some possessors of previously invested capital and acquired skill.

These effects are of course, for the most part, indifferent to the capitalist himself, who may very likely not consume any portion of the commodities in which his interest is paid; and who, if his capital has been lent at a fixed rate of interest, only feels the effects of changes in trade so far as the fluctuations of the exchanges alter the value of the foreign money relatively to that of his own country.

can only say that we have no positive grounds for supposing that the average actual yield of capital already invested tends in the long run to differ materially from the yield expected at the time of investment. Since, however, the yield expected during the first years after investment includes, in most cases, a more or less considerable compensation for risk, it follows that the actual average yield on investments made some time ago will tend to decrease year by year, as the date of original investment recedes into the past. An important part of this decrease, in the case of capital invested in industrial instruments, is due to depreciation through the progress of invention; in consequence of which the yield of such investments—provided that they are completely exposed to competition—tends to be equal to interest at the current rate (allowing for risk) not on the sum originally invested, but on the present cost of producing instruments equally useful; which may, of course, be indefinitely less than the cost of the original investment.

There is, however, an important part of the capital of individuals previously invested at any given time, which enjoys a total or partial exemption from the depreciative effects of competition; being so invested as to give the employer who uses it, independently of his own skill and foresight, advantages in production unattainable by other employers—advantages especially marked in a community increasing in numbers and wealth. In this case there is no reason why its owner should not obtain from it a yield considerably above what interest on the original outlay would amount to. The most conspicuous case of this is that of capital invested in land. The share of produce obtained by the land owner as such—called by the special name of Rent,—has attracted the special attention of economists; it will therefore be well to devote a separate chapter to the examination of its distinctive characteristics;—especially since, so far as the value of the land is not the result of labour, it is only "capital" for the individual, and not "social capital" as we defined the term in Book I.

CHAPTER VII.

RENT.

§ 1. THE theory of value given in Chap. II. was expressly limited to material products, because in the case of these our main attention is necessarily given to analysing the combined action of Cost of Production and Demand. But even as thus limited, our investigation led us to notice cases where cost of production ceases to have any influence on the variations of value; where, accordingly, value is determined more simply by the relation of demand to quantity,—quantity being either (1) given independently of the price, or (2) tending to increase somewhat as the price rises with the demand, so as partly to counteract the changes caused by variations in the scale of demand. And it is evident that these simpler modes of determination will be generally applicable to commodities—if there be such—that are not products of labour at all. But where are we to look for such commodities? for what we call "raw" materials, in even their rawest condition, almost always require a not inconsiderable amount of labour, spent either in somehow promoting or protecting natural growth, or in extraction or detachment (of stone, wood, &c.), or in searching or hunting and capturing, or at any rate in collection and conveyance. In short we are carried back, in our search for an ultimate raw material among the important articles of current exchange, to Land: i.e. to such parts of the earth's surface as, together with the minerals below the surface, have a market value, as the indispensable primary material or instrument of the kinds of labour just mentioned. And, in fact, the share of the produce that falls to landowners as such has, by English economists generally, been treated as fundamentally distinct from Interest and Wages; as being neither remuneration of labour, nor reward of abstinence in consuming the products of labour. And it is to this share, as separated by strict analysis from interest of capital, that the term "rent"—or, as is sometimes said, "economic rent"—is now commonly applied, when used as a technical term by political economists since Ricardo. I think, however, that what is commonly known —and widely accepted—as the Ricardian theory of rent combines, in a somewhat confusing way, at least three distinct theories, resting on different kinds of evidence and relating to different, and not necessarily connected, enquiries: we may distinguish them as (1) a historical theory as to the origin of rent, (2) a statical theory of the economic forces tending to determine rent at the present time, and (3) a dynamical theory of the causes continually tending to increase rent, as wealth and population increases. It seems to me that the confusion of these three into one doctrine is partly the effect and partly the cause of the peculiar meaning given to the term Rent in Ricardo's exposition; and that in the case of agricultural land, to which Ricardo's doctrine has been especially applied, it is especially important to get rid of the confusion.

In attempting this task, it is convenient to begin by examining the ordinary use of the term Rent. As commonly used in English[1], it denotes the payment made for the use of "immoveables," i.e. either of the surface of land as used in agriculture, or of buildings erected on it, or of the minerals it contains together with the right of removing and selling them. There is, apart from any economic theory, a noteworthy difference in the nature of the obligations imposed in the lending or letting of land, houses, &c., as compared with ordinary loans for which interest is paid. In the latter case, as what is actually borrowed is money, there is no particular thing which has to be returned when the loan is repaid, but only an *equivalent* for the sum borrowed; so that here the possibility of deterioration or amelioration of the wealth borrowed does not come

---

[1] It may be worth noticing that in French "rente" is used, more widely, to denote any income that accrues without labour on the part of the person to whom it is paid.

in; whereas in the cases where rent is paid, this possibility has to be taken into account; and sometimes, as we shall see, leads to important complications. Still, rent is not the only case of payment for the use of wealth, where the same thing that was originally lent has to be restored when the contract terminates:—such payments (e. g.) are made for the use of carriages, boats, plate, pianos, and other durable articles. The amount of such payment (commonly called "hire"), as competitively determined will commonly include compensation for ordinary deterioration through wear and tear of the thing hired, interest on its value when let[1], and—in some cases at least—insurance against possible depreciation through invention or change of fashion, as well as against other risks, together with such amount of remuneration for the owner's labour of management as industrial competition may allow him.

Now an English farm, no less than a carriage or boat, is an instrument that has been adapted to its uses by human labour; it commonly contains fences, roads for economizing the labour of conveyance, and buildings for housing cattle and instruments, accumulating manure, and performing the first processes of manufacture on the produce; and further, in many cases, when it was originally made, the land had to be wholly or partially cleared of stones, trees, excess of water, or other encumbrances. It may be asked, therefore, why the price paid for the use of land thus prepared and adapted should not depend upon the cost of such adaptation no less than the price of any other durable product?

To this question Ricardo and others answer that so far as the utility of a farm is the result of labour, the price paid for the use of it should in strictness of economic language be counted profit or interest[2]; the term Rent being restricted to the price paid for the use of the "original and indestructible "powers of the soil," or the yield obtained by the owner from this source, where the owner is also the cultivator. But the

[1] The value of such an article when let will normally (as we have seen) correspond to the cost of producing something equally useful. See ch. ii. § 11.

[2] In England this price is hardly, if at all, more than ordinary interest, with a slight allowance for risk; the landlord who spends the money requires little or no remuneration for his trouble.

line thus indicated is one impossible to draw with any exactness in concrete cases, at least in a country that has long been cultivated; and, as Ricardo himself urges, it is in such a country that rent is of most importance. The *recurrent* part of the expenditure of labour in making a farm—the cost of the repairs needed from time to time to keep buildings, fences, drainage, &c. in good order—can, no doubt, be approximately ascertained; and so long as it is profitable to cultivate the farm at all, its produce must yield at least interest on this cost, as well as adequate employers' profits on the movable capital employed on the land. But this recurrent cost is, on the whole, materially less than the total expenditure that would now be required to bring the farm from its original condition up to its present degree of utility; and, as we cannot restore the original condition, we have no means of estimating definitely this non-recurrent expenditure.

This will appear more clearly when it is considered that we should have to include in such an estimate, besides the labour spent on the farm itself, a certain part of what has gone to the making of the roads, canals and railways that connect it with the markets of its produce, and with the places that supply the materials and implements of its cultivation; since the existence of these means of communication is generally necessary to the maintenance of the present value of the produce of the land, and therefore to the maintenance of the rent[1].

At the same time I think it reasonable to assume that the rent of much agricultural land in England is materially in excess of interest (at the present rate) on the expenditure that

[1] It is true, as Mill argues (II. xvi. § 5) that the rent of a farm tends primarily to be reduced by the roads, &c. that connect with its markets other more distant farms; since these are thus enabled to enter into competition with it and to lower the prices of its produce. But though this is no doubt the immediate effect of making such roads, it is not, I conceive, likely to be the ultimate effect in this case, any more than in the case of any other kind of agricultural improvement; since the increase of population and wealth in the country which these more extended means of communication render possible, tends ultimately to raise the price of the produce of the nearer farm to at least its former height. And, at any rate, the labour spent on the roads that connect a farm with its markets must be admitted to have contributed to raise its selling value and the rent payable for it.

would now be required to bring it from its original condition to its present degree of efficiency for supplying its markets with agricultural produce. I infer this from the fact that it is worth while for Englishmen to cultivate land in Manitoba in order to supply the English market with wheat: for, though I cannot compare the original condition of land in Manitoba with the original condition of land in England, I have no reason to attribute to the former so marked a superiority for wheat-growing over all English land as would even nearly compensate for the great disadvantage of its situation. Hence I infer, broadly, that a considerable portion of the rent paid for agricultural land in England—though I cannot say how much—is due not to the labour spent in fitting it for agricultural uses, but to the appropriation of the raw material to which such labour has been applied. It appears to me, however, misleading to say that even this portion is a price paid for the "original "and indestructible" qualities of the soil; since, so far as it depends on situation, it is plainly due not to the original qualities of the land but to the development of the human community inhabiting it, and the manner in which this community has disposed itself over the surface of the country.

I am unable, therefore, to accept as adequate Ricardo's account of the origin and history of rent as defined by him: viz. that it is entirely caused and its amount determined by original differences in the productive powers of the soil, which become economically operative in continually increasing degrees, as population progresses: that accordingly it is first paid on "land "of the first quality" when, in the progress of society land of the "second quality" is taken into cultivation, and rises similarly with "every step in the progress of population, which obliges "a country to have recourse to land of a worse quality[1]." This conjectural history assumes unwarrantably that the relative degrees of utility for agriculture possessed by different portions of the land of a civilized country remain always what they originally were: ignoring (1) the extent to which the labour of man has altered the original differences, and (2) the extent to which the economic value of land varies, apart from any variation in its physical conditions, in consequence of

[1] See his *Principles of Political Economy*, ch. ii.

changes (*a*) in the art of agriculture, and (*b*) in the social demand for agricultural produce.

But even if Ricardo's historical doctrine were true, and if we could generally distinguish, in any actual case, between the "original and indestructible" qualities of the soil and the qualities resulting from human labour, the distinction would still, I conceive, be irrelevant when we are considering the determination of rent, as an element of the existing distribution of produce; since the price paid for the use of land at the present time cannot be affected in any way by the extent to which its present condition is the result of labour. Hence, while I recognise that ordinary agricultural rent generally contains—besides an element that is to be regarded as interest on the present value of the results of labour previously expended,—another element due to the appropriation of a raw material scarce in quality, it does not seem to me desirable to follow Ricardo in restricting the term rent to the latter element.

It is, in fact, chiefly when we are considering what I distinguished as a "dynamical question"—the tendency of the value (and rent) of land to increase as civilization progresses—that it becomes practically important to analyse its utility into different elements, due respectively to the different causes above-mentioned; though here again what we are chiefly concerned to know with regard to any particular increase of rent is not whether it is due to labour generally, but whether it is due to labour employed by the owner or occupier. This dynamical question will be more appropriately considered in a subsequent chapter[1].

§ 2. Let us take the term 'rent' then in its ordinary sense to mean the price paid for the use of land, whatever be the source of its utility, and consider how this price is completely determined in such a country as England at the present time. So far as the demand for land is non-industrial—i.e. so far as land is used for purposes of direct enjoyment and thus belongs to the class of things before distinguished as 'durable consumers' wealth,'—there is not much use in attempting any minute analysis of the causes that affect its value or rent. We have no simple formula for determining generally how much will be paid

[1] See chap. xi. § 8, of this Book.

for the use of (e.g.) a deer-forest. We can see that it depends partly on the amount of actual and possible deer-forests, partly on the possibility of making a profit out of such land in other ways, partly on the number and wealth of the rich persons who wish to shoot deer and on the comparative utility of deer-stalking and other forms of amusement, as estimated by these persons: but it is hardly worth while to attempt to get further than this. In the case, however, of land cultivated by farmers for a profit, we can determine normal rent as the surplus which the price of its produce would be expected to afford to a farmer of ordinary ability and industry, after subtracting whatever competition allows him to claim, as remuneration for his own labour, and the sum required for replacement, with interest at the ordinary rate, of the capital employed by him upon the land;—assuming, for simplicity, that the processes by which such produce is obtained do not materially affect the utility of the land, as an instrument of future production. If the produce in question needs a special and rare kind of land, while the demand for it is strong; every part of the land so employed may yield produce that has a value above what corresponds to its cost of production (including interest on the landowner's capital that has to be from time to time reproduced). Of such produce it may be said that the price of every portion yields a certain proportion of rent to the owner:—though it tends to confuse cause and effect to say that "rent enters into its price." But with ordinary agricultural produce the case is different; since, even in a country so thickly populated as England, the supply of land capable of yielding such produce is always in excess of that actually employed for this purpose. Hence assuming that the variations in the utility of land—whether due to varying fertility or situation—are continuous[1], we may infer that even when the demand for agricultural produce is so keen that the area of cultivated land is increasing, there will always be a margin of such land of which the rent is only equivalent to interest on the outlay required to prepare and keep it fit for cultivation, *plus* whatever would be paid for the use of it if left uncultivated, for purposes

[1] This assumption is legitimate for purposes of general reasoning: since it will be true unless abrupt changes in fertility coincide with abrupt changes in situation.

of sport or rough pasture. And we may infer that the normal rent *per acre* of any other land, in the same district or supplying the same markets, can only exceed the rent *per acre* of this margin because and in proportion as it is more productive relatively to the markets which it has to supply: i.e. because and in proportion as the farmer who cultivates it can bring to market either more produce with equal expense, or an equal amount of produce with a greater expense (including the expense of conveyance).

This is the "margin of cultivation" which is said by Ricardian economists to pay "no rent": the phrase, however, is not strictly true, even according to the Ricardian definition of rent, in such a country as England; since, as I have said, something would be generally obtainable for the use of such land if left uncultivated[1]. It is further noteworthy, that when the area of arable land is diminishing—as has been the case in recent years in England—the margin of cultivation tends to be differently determined. When land has to be *brought into* cultivation it will be expected to pay interest on the expenditure required once for all—e.g. for draining or clearing—to make it fit for cultivation, as well as on any recurrent outlay required to keep it in suitable condition: but in considering whether it should be allowed to *go out* of cultivation, the non-recurrent expenditure will not be taken into account; the land will be worth cultivating, if the cultivator can afford to pay interest merely on any recurrent outlay required from the landowner *plus* what could be obtained for the use of it if uncultivated. It is owing to this essential difference in the determination of the margin of cultivation, according as the area of cultivated land is increasing or decreasing[2], that I have not thought it desirable to refer expressly to this margin in the account

---

[1] Doubtless there is always some land to be found, even when the area of cultivated land is increasing, which only yields a rent equivalent to interest on the outlay necessary to make and keep it fit for cultivation: but this is because such outlay has been partly wasted, if the land would have yielded some rent in its unlaboured condition: it does not represent the general result which economic forces tend to produce.

[2] If the area of cultivation is stationary, the normal rent of the least advantageous may vary between interest on total outlay and interest on recurrent outlay.

above given of the determination of normal agricultural rent.

There is, however, an ambiguity in this account which has to be removed. It is evident that the surplus remaining, after providing interest on the farmer's capital and remuneration for his labour, may vary with the amount of capital employed. Now in a state of thoroughly active and enlightened competition and abundant capital we may assume that the amount of capital employed on any land yielding rent would be at least sufficient to make the net produce per cent. a maximum; for if it were not so, it would be obviously profitable to leave the less productive land uncultivated, and apply the capital thus set free in increasing that employed on the more productive. But, actually, we often find the more fertile land is not cultivated up to the point at which the net produce per cent. of capital is greatest, either (1) from custom, or (2) from want of enlightenment, or (3) because the best mode of cultivation requires amounts of capital under single managements, larger than average farmers can provide themselves or procure by borrowing. So far as these causes operate, rent will actually tend to be determined not by the surplus of produce obtainable by the capital that it would be most profitable to employ, but by the surplus of produce obtainable by what an average farmer would employ.

But further, if, when the most productive land is cultivated so that its net produce per cent. of capital employed is greatest, it is still profitable to employ capital less productively on other land, it must also be profitable to cultivate the more productive land *beyond* the point at which the net produce *per cent.* is a maximum: provided we assume that, after this point is passed, the diminution in the increment of produce obtainable by an additional increment of farming capital is continuous and gradual. Indeed on this assumption, it will be obviously profitable to employ additional capital on the more productive land up to the point at which another increment would not yield ordinary interest and "wages of management:" so that we may infer that the last portion of the capital employed tends to pay no rent; meaning that the farmer does not tend to get, by employing it, any additional surplus which active competition would force him to resign to the landlord. This assumption of a "rentless" margin of agricultural capital, in the farming even of highly rented land, is, I think, legitimate for purposes of general reasoning[1]: since no one doubts that only a limited amount of capital can be profitably employed for agricultural purposes on any given piece of land: and, considering the various ways in which labour[2] may be employed directly and indirectly to increase produce, we may assume that—generally speaking—the limit of profitable employment does not coincide with the point at which net produce *per cent.* of capital is greatest, but is reached by a gradual decline in the productiveness of capital employed beyond this point. It is, however, misleading to speak—as Ricardian economists have sometimes spoken—of the "last dose of capital which pays no "rent" as if this "dose" were an element definitely ascertainable in the business-reckonings of an ordinary farmer, and could be used for calculating normal rent in any particular case. Experience certainly shows us in a broad and general way that as the demand for the produce of land rises, there is a tendency to increase the amount of capital applied to good land, as well as to extend the cultivated area: but the art of agriculture has not yet reached the degree of exactness that would be required to ascertain even approximately in any particular case the portion of capital that is to be regarded as paying no rent. Thus, while the recent fall in the value of English wheat, in consequence of the development of foreign production and trade, has led to a marked diminution in the area of wheatgrowing land in England, I cannot find that it has led to anything like an equally discernible change in the amount of capital economically applicable to the land

[1] See note at the end of the chapter.
[2] The reader will bear in mind that "employment of labour" is, from another point of view, "employment of capital": since the result of the labour is a form which a part of the employer's capital assumes. But the phrase "employment of capital" is generally more appropriate: since in calculating the cost of any application of labour we have to take into account not only the amount and quality of the labour applied, but the time intervening between its application and the realisation of the expected produce: that is, we have to regard the results of labour as constituting capital, on which interest is expected.

that still grows wheat. The most that can be said is that the fall of prices has caused a general vague tendency to diminish expense in farming wherever it can be diminished: and even this is in many cases merely due to loss of capital,—and is, in consequence, a tendency to farm more cheaply than is really economical.

§ 3. Hitherto we have assumed that the value of the land is not materially altered by the process of production. It may however happen that by using the land in the way that is economically most advantageous on the whole, the producer will either improve or deteriorate it. No difficulty is thereby introduced in the theoretical determination of rent, where the producer is also the owner; we have merely in calculating the whole amount of produce to include the increment of value added to the land, along with the value of the products taken from it; and similarly to deduct from produce any decrement due to deterioration. When, however, the producer does not own, but merely farms, the land, this possibility of improvement and deterioration renders it a matter of some difficulty to frame a rent-contract which shall give the farmer adequate inducement to treat the land in the manner most economical on the whole. To illustrate this difficulty let us suppose first that the land tends to be improved by such treatment as is, on the whole, economically desirable. Here we have to distinguish two different cases. (1) If the farmer, while using the land in the way most immediately profitable, at the same time augments its utility as an instrument of future production, the matter may be simply settled by allowing the increment of value to be appropriated by the landlord; since, in this case, such appropriation has no tendency to prevent the improvement from being made. But (2) if, as is more ordinarily the case, the outlay required for the improvement will not be profitable to the farmer, unless he secures the whole, or the main part, of the gain resulting from the increased utility of the land; it will be his interest to leave the land unimproved unless either he is bound under penalties to improve it, or this gain is somehow secured to him. The former alternative can hardly be made effectual without hampering the farmer's freedom of action to an extent disadvantageous to his industry.

Hence, in order that such improvements may be duly made, it will be needful that either (1) adequate compensation be secured to the farmer generally for whatever increment of utility may remain unexhausted when his tenure ends; or (2) a lease be given him—and continually renewed—of such length as always to allow him adequate prospect of reaping the benefit of his improvements; or (3) each improvement be made the subject of special agreement between farmer and landlord—which practically requires the latter, or his agent, to take a certain share in the management of the farm.

A somewhat similar problem is presented in the case where the land is deteriorated by the most economic use of it. This case but rarely occurs in agriculture[1]; but it is the ordinary condition of the mining industry, and of certain other branches of production which take from the land products that are not renewed[2]. In such cases the total amount of the produce in question that can be profitably taken from any particular piece of land is generally at least so far limited in prospect, that every portion brought to market tends to diminish proportionally such possibilities of future production as have a definite market value[3]. The problem, then, in letting land for the purposes of any such industry is to frame a contract which shall render it not the interest of the lessee to remove and sell an amount of such products greater than what it would be profitable for him to bring to market if he were also the owner. Now if the land in question is leased at a fixed rent, this coincidence of interests will only occur under certain special conditions. Thus, if owing to the state of competition in the industry the owner would be unable to raise the price of his product materially by limiting

---

[1] Land used for agriculture might doubtless often be deteriorated by treatment which, though uneconomic on the whole, would increase its produce for one or two years. And there would seem to be some practical difficulty in framing a contract to prevent this effectually, without interfering disadvantageously with the farmer's freedom of action; but it is hardly within the scope of the present chapter to discuss the best method of dealing with this difficulty.

[2] Such as (e.g.) Peruvian guano, timber from natural forests, &c.

[3] This is true even in the case of mines where the prospect of actual exhaustion is too remote and indefinite to be economically important; owing to the prospective increase in difficulty of extraction, at least after a certain amount has been taken.

his supply, if he has no ground for inferring a rise of any importance from the general prospects of supply and demand, and if the cost of production does not become materially greater as the amount produced within any given time increases—it would then be the owner's interest to produce as much as possible, provided that the price of the product were sufficient to pay at least the working expenses of production, including adequate remuneration for the labour of management; and under the same circumstances it would be the interest of a lessee paying a fixed rent to do the same. If, however, the owner would either have reason to expect a rise in price, or be able to produce such a rise by limiting his supply, either alone or in combination with other producers; then it would obviously be expedient for him not to produce beyond the point at which the probable rise in price, present and prospective, would more than compensate for the probable loss incurred by deferring production. But, under these circumstances, it would not generally be expedient for a lessee to adopt the same limit of production; unless the period of the lease were long enough to make it practically certain that the mine would be valueless before the end of it: since otherwise, by stopping at any given point, the lessee would lose the whole gain obtainable on the extra amount that might have been produced, whereas the owner would only lose the interest on this gain for a certain number of years. In the same way it may be shown that if there is a certain amount that can be produced within a given time by the most economic application of labour and capital, while it is still possible to produce more but at continually increasing cost, it would generally be expedient for a mere lessee to extend production beyond the limit which it would be expedient for an owner to adopt. In either of these latter cases it seems impossible, without more foresight of the conditions of the market than can be hoped for, to frame a rent-contract which will have the effect of making it always most profitable for the lessee to treat the land in question in the manner most profitable to the owner: but a rough reconciliation of the divergent interests is attained by the ordinary practice of making the lessee pay—either with or without a fixed annual payment—a certain 'royalty'; that is, a sum proportioned either to the amount of material extracted, or—

which is the more suitable arrangement—to the price obtained for it.

§ 4. When we pass from agriculture to mining, we meet with manifest and striking cases of wealth of which the value is due not to labour—at least not to labour spent on the valuable thing itself—but merely to its scarcity and its utility in its unlaboured condition; since the land containing a rich mine rises to a price far exceeding that of agricultural land, as soon as the existence of its contents is known, before the application of any part of the labour that will ultimately be needed to extract them. A still more important case in which the element of labour—applied in order to increase utility—is practically absent from the determination of value is that of land in towns; the high rent of which is entirely due to the utility attaching to such ground from its situation,—either for purposes of business, or for social communication and enjoyment. And the share of produce obtained by the owner of such land has increased in importance as towns have grown in size and density, with the development of industry and trade:—indeed, it is noteworthy that Ricardo's conception of rent as increasing independently of any outlay on the part of the landowner, as society advances in population and wealth, is much more clearly applicable to the case of building land in towns than it is to the case of agricultural land, which Ricardo has chiefly in view.

There are various other uses of land—including the permanent results of labour applied to land—by which a surplus yield is sometimes obtained, similar to that of which agricultural rent partly consists and often considerably greater in amount. Thus a railroad favourably situated or cheaply constructed is, no less than a farm, an instrument of which land in its preexisting condition may be regarded as raw material; by means of which the commodity of conveyance between certain places is produced and sold at a price that may yield its owners considerably more than ordinary interest on the cost of making the railway (including the purchase-money of the land[1]); because either it is not possible owing to legal

[1] Where—as has usually been the case—the land has been bought at a price considerably beyond its agricultural value, a corresponding share of the extra

obstacles or otherwise to construct an equally effective instrument for the same uses, or at any rate such a construction would be too costly to be profitable. A similar exemption from the ordinary effects of competition is sometimes enjoyed by certain other portions of industrial capital, such as the capital of water companies and gas companies; whose dividends are in consequence considerably higher than current interest on the original outlay.

Again, there are other results of labour, not connected with land, which yield a surplus somewhat similar in kind. This is the case, for instance, with the immaterial results of the labour of Invention, protected from imitation by patents. Even when the extra profit obtained by using the patent does not amount to more than a fair interest on the value of the labour and materials expended before the invention was perfected; still, as the intellectual result when once achieved does not require renewal, such extra yield is in any particular case determined—like the return to capital spent once for all on land—without any relation to the value of the inventor's labour. And if it is still possible for persons excluded from the advantage of the patent to use profitably inferior processes of production, the extra yield obtainable by those who use the patent will be determined in a manner exactly analogous to ordinary agricultural rent. So, again, the extra profit obtained by the Goodwill or Connexion, which gives firms of long standing an advantage in the competition for business, is often very analogous to rent; for though it may broadly be regarded as interest on the cost in labour and outlay incurred without adequate immediate return, during the earlier years of the business; still it is often mainly due to a favourable concurrence of social conditions, and when once acquired it tends to maintain itself by the mere *vis inertiæ* of habit, without any extra exertion of skill or energy on the part of those who enjoy the advantage.

In many cases, however, it is difficult to separate the extra yield obtained merely by such established connexion from that which is due to general belief in the excellence of the commodities furnished by the firm in question; and so far as this value derived from its use for purposes of conveyance has, of course, been handed over to the previous owner.

belief is really founded on the skilful conduct of the business, the additional income obtained by it—whatever may be its ultimate analysis—will be more naturally discussed under the head of Wages.

Note on the "Law of Diminishing Returns in Agriculture."

It is, I think, universally admitted by competent persons that the application of labour in agriculture is subject, in a certain sense, to the condition of "Diminishing Returns": i.e. that in a country in which population has reached a certain point of density, the agricultural produce needed is obtained partly by processes more costly than would be required if the total amount needed were less. According to the view of most economists since Ricardo, these processes are of two kinds: either (1) the application of labour and capital to land of inferior quality or situation; or (2) the application to the best land of labour and capital in excess of the amount which yields the greatest *proportional* return. A suggestive writer, however—Mr Simon W. Patten (*Premises of Political Economy*, ch. VI.) —holds that there is not really room in agriculture for the second kind of process; that the proportional return to well-applied agricultural labour increases up to the point at which no additional return at all could be obtained by any amount of additional labour; that, therefore, we ought to speak of a 'law of limited returns' instead of a 'law of diminishing returns'—so far as we have in view the returns from any given piece of land.

Now such an abrupt breach of continuity in the relation of labour to resultant utility as Mr Patten's argument assumes is contrary to our general experience of the application of human labour for the satisfaction of human wants: and nothing that I have been able to learn of the actual condition of agriculture seems to give adequate ground for assuming it to occur in this case. I think, however, that in the "intensive" cultivation of certain kinds of produce there is probably but a small interval between the point at which an additional increment of labour or capital ceases to give a *proportional* increase and the point at which it would cease to give any material increase: so that the capital earning diminished returns may sometimes be confined within limits so narrow that it is not clearly discernible, in the present state of the art of agriculture. For instance, in the case of wheat, I understand that, in the judgment of competent farmers, the outlay required on an English farm to produce wheat in the most profitable manner—even at the lowest price at which it would be remunerative to produce it at all—would, on the average, give a crop of wheat which could not be confidently expected to be much increased by any additional outlay likely to be remunerative at any price within the limits of probability. Nevertheless I do not doubt that any considerable rise in the demand for wheat would *ceteris paribus* cause some increase of outlay on land previously wheat-growing; but the change would chiefly affect what we may call the doubtful margin of expenditure: —e.g. more manure would probably be applied than was actually applied before, but not more than some competent judges would have considered economical, even at the lower price. Probably, however, any important increase in the capital applied to wheat-growing on the same land would involve an increase in the *number* of crops obtained within a given term of years: the four-crop rotation would be changed to a five-crop rotation with three corn-crops, or corn-crops might even be grown continuously for several years—on Mr Lawes' method—with only occasional changes of clover or roots. But even in this last case it would, I suppose, be difficult to say—in view of Mr Lawes' results—that the extra capital thus applied would *certainly* yield diminished returns.

CHAPTER VIII.

THE REMUNERATION OF LABOUR.

§ 1. WE now approach the part of our subject which, especially in recent years, has both excited the keenest practical interest and given rise to the most perplexing theoretical controversy—the competitive[1] determination of the wages of labour. It seems to me most convenient to follow Mill in separating the investigation into two parts; to consider first the "causes which determine or influence the wages of labour "generally, and secondly the differences that exist between the "wages of different employments[2]."

In the first chapter of this book I suggested that the term Wages might conveniently be extended so as to include the remuneration of all kinds of labour, and I shall presently urge reasons for giving this more extended scope to the first of the two inquiries above distinguished. But since Mill and other economists generally use the term 'wages' in this discussion to denote the remuneration of labour hired by employers, I have thought it best to adopt this meaning in the critical discussion which will occupy the first part of this chapter[3].

---

[1] The reader should bear in mind that throughout both parts of this investigation Competition is understood to exclude Combination, whether of employed labourers or employers. In a subsequent chapter (ch. x.) I shall consider to what extent this competitive distribution is liable to be abrogated or modified in consequence of the action of such combinations with the view of raising or lowering wages.

[2] *Political Economy*, Bk. II. ch. xi. § 1.

[3] In the chapter (Book II. chap. xi.) in which Mill treats of "the causes "which determine or influence the wages of labour generally," he expressly

We may begin this discussion by noticing one way of dealing with the question of wages which very naturally and obviously suggests itself to the mind of reflective persons, and is therefore liable to mix itself more or less unconsciously with any other theory that they may adopt, unless it is openly and clearly expressed and discussed. I mean the view in which labourers are considered as productive instruments requiring a certain quantum of food, clothing, lodging, &c., to keep them in the most efficient condition from birth to death; and this quantum, whatever it may be, including whatever is similarly required to maintain the wives and mothers of labourers, is regarded as their normal share of the social produce. It is, however, easy to show that there is no necessary tendency in a system of free competition to give them just this share and no more. For if the labourer can produce more wealth than he and his family require for necessary consumption, he may obviously, being a free agent, keep and enjoy the remainder; and we must assume that he will do this if he can. It is true

---

proceeds "as if there were no other kind of labour than common unskilled "labour, of the average degree of hardness and disagreeableness." But I am not sure that he quite realises how widely this hypothetical procedure diverges from the actual facts, in such a country as England—in 1867 Mr Dudley Baxter estimated the persons engaged in "agriculture and unskilled labour" in England as little more than a third of the whole class of manual labourers (2,843,000 out of 7,785,000), and their net annual earnings as considerably less than a third of the aggregate earnings of manual labourers (70,659,000 out of 254,729,000). At any rate I think that in the course of Mill's discussion the very hypothetical character of the assumption on which he is proceeding, rather drops out of his own mind, and is certainly liable to drop out of his reader's mind. Thus I observe that, when he passes (in chap. xiv.) to treat of the difference of wages in different employments, he speaks of his previous discussion as having been concerned with the "laws which govern the remuneration of "ordinary or average labour," without any notice of the great difference between the average remuneration of labour generally, and the average remuneration of unskilled labour. I observe too that in the corresponding chapter in Fawcett's Manual (Bk. II. ch. iv.), the doctrine of which is mainly derived from Mill, the treatment of the "average rate of wages" makes no reference to Mill's expressly hypothetical procedure, but refers apparently to the average of actual wages. And since it seems best to deviate as little as possible from actual facts in the assumptions on which our reasoning proceeds, I have taken "general wages" to mean the average remuneration of all the *hired* labour that is actually supplied in a modern civilised community; afterwards, in § 4, extending the question to include all remuneration of labour.

that in such a country as England, labourers without any capital could not produce enough to keep themselves alive; still, as capital could not any more be used without labourers, if the combination of the two produces more than is necessary to keep the labourers in efficient condition—while also furnishing what is necessary to induce the owners of wealth to keep up capital, to the extent required to make labour thus productive, —there is no general reason why the labourer should not by free contract secure a share of this extra produce.

Nor can it even be maintained that at any rate the food, clothing, &c., necessary to keep the labourer in the most efficient condition will give us a *minimum* below which the self-interest of employers, if duly enlightened, will not suffer wages to fall. This would no doubt be true if the present labourers alone were concerned and if the employer could actually feed, clothe and shelter his labourers just as he feeds, covers and shelters his horses. But when we consider the labourer as a free and independent citizen, and also as the father of a family, spending at his own discretion a considerable portion of his wages in rearing a future generation of labourers, the case is altered. Suppose that the employer knows that his labourer is under-fed and that half-a-crown a week, spent on nourishing food and warm clothing, would result in more than half-a-crown's worth of extra value in the produce of his week's labour. It does not follow that it is his interest to give him the extra half-crown: for in the first place the labourer may spend a large portion of it in alcoholic liquors, &c., which will impair rather than increase his efficiency; and secondly he may spend a large portion of it in providing better food and clothing for his family; which though it may be amply repaid to society in the additional efficiency of the future labourers whom he is rearing, will not necessarily afford any pecuniary advantage to the employer who may have no means of securing to himself any of the value of this future efficiency.

Hence it is only under special circumstances—i.e. if the employer has adequate empirical grounds for believing that the higher wages will actually be spent in increasing the efficiency of labourers whom he will himself employ[1]—that his self-

[1] It is to be hoped that many employers, in modern civilised societies, would

interest alone can be relied on to secure such provision for the labourer as would make the excess of his produce over his consumption a maximum.

§ 2. The view just discussed has not, so far as I know, ever been adopted by professed political economists. On the contrary, the doctrine which in 1869 was "presumed" by John Stuart Mill to be "found in every systematic treatise on "Political Economy,"—and which remains unretracted and unmodified in the latest edition of his own treatise—is that currently known as the Wages-Fund Theory, which appears to leave the efficiency of labour altogether out of account. The theory is stated by Mill in an essay, in which its inadequacy is admitted, as follows.

"There is supposed to be at any given instant a sum of "wealth which is unconditionally devoted to the payment "of wages. This sum is not regarded as unalterable, for it "is augmented by saving and increases with the progress of "wealth; but it is reasoned upon as at any given moment a "predetermined amount. More than that amount it is assumed "that the wages-receiving class cannot possibly divide among "them; that amount and no less they cannot but obtain. So "that the sum to be divided being fixed, the wages of each "depend solely on the divisor, the number of participants[1]." General wages being thus determined, the determination of general profits is similarly simple: profits in the aggregate are simply the excess of what the productive labourers produce over what is required to replace their wages. In this way, as was before remarked, the theory of Distribution comes to be treated by Mill and his followers as though it had but slight analogy to the theory of the Exchange Value of products.

The discussion in the preceding chapters will already have shown the reader that I do not adopt this method of treatment. But this view of wages has been so widely accepted, and by

incur the extra expenditure in the case supposed, even if the chance of securing to themselves a remunerative share of the resulting addition to the wealth of the community did not seem quite worth purchasing at the price, on strict calculations of probable gain and loss. But I do not think that we can safely reason on the assumption, that an ordinary employer will be willing to mix philanthropy with business to this extent.

[1] Mill, *Diss.* IV. p. 43, in a review of Thornton *On Labour.*

CHAP. VIII.] *THE REMUNERATION OF LABOUR.* 299

writers of so much authority[1], that it seems desirable to examine it carefully.

I may begin by observing that the language in which it is expounded by Mill in his treatise has exposed him to the charge of presenting an arithmetical truism as an economic law[2]: and, in fact, in the passage (B. II. c. XI. § 1) in which he first speaks of the wages-fund he seems rather to describe the elements of which the whole sum paid in wages is composed, than to state the law by which the total is determined. "What may be "called the wages-fund of a country," he says, is made up of "that part of the circulating capital" of the country "which is "expended in the direct purchase of labour," together with all other funds that are paid in exchange of labour. But obviously, if we knew no more of the wages-fund than that it is a total thus heterogeneously composed, the statement that "the general "rate of wages cannot rise but by an increase of the aggregate "funds employed in hiring labourers or a diminution in the "number of the competitors for hire" would be as unimportant as it is undeniable; it would be merely saying that a quotient can only be made larger by increasing the dividend or diminishing the divisor. What Mill, however, really meant was that, since the great majority of the wage-earning class are labourers hired by employers for a profit, the amount of wealth devoted to the payment of wages is mainly determined by the "law of "increase of capital," that is, by saving. It was of course always recognised, by himself and his followers, that, strictly speaking, the "capital" of which the increase is important to the labourer is "only circulating capital and not even the whole of that, but "the part which is expended in the direct purchase of labour." Notwithstanding this, it was thought a sufficient approximation to the truth to say "for shortness" that "wages depend on the "proportion between population and *capital.*" Mill certainly warns his readers that this is an "elliptical not a literal state-"ment": but it is stated without qualification in the popular

---

[1] As I have noticed, Mill himself partially renounced this theory (in the review before quoted). His leading disciples however, declined to follow him in this renunciation. See Cairnes, *Some Leading Principles of Political Economy*, Pt. II. c. I.; and compare Fawcett, *Manual of Political Economy*, Pt. II. c. IV.

[2] Cf. Cairnes, *loc. cit.*

manual of his distinguished disciple Fawcett[1], "that capital "is the fund from which labour is remunerated"...that "wages "in the aggregate depend upon the ratio between capital and "population"...and that "every law concerning wages must be "deduced from the fundamental conception of a ratio between "capital and population...if the number of the labouring "population remain stationary wages cannot rise, unless capital "is increased."

Writers who use such language as I have just quoted, can hardly, I think, have clearly recognised how small a proportion of the saved wealth in any year, in such a country as England, takes the form of wages of hired productive labourers. According to Mr Giffen[2], the "capital or property in the united kingdom" may be taken to have increased, between 1865 and 1875, at the average rate of more than £200,000,000 a year; while according to Professor Levi's estimate,—which seems to be accepted by Mr Giffen[3], who is generally regarded as taking an optimistic view of the recent progress of the working classes in wealth— the average annual increment in the aggregate earnings of the working classes during the same period can hardly have amounted to one fifteenth of this sum[4]. Hence—making all allowance for the large conjectural element that inevitably enters into these statistical calculations—it is clear that a mere knowledge of the total amount of capital saved within any period is no guide at all to the increment received by the wages-fund within the same period : everything depends on determining the proportion in which savings tend to be divided between wages and other capital. This point is discussed by Cairnes, in his development of Mill's doctrine[5]. His view is

[1] *Manual of Political Economy*, Book II. c. IV.

[2] Essay vii. in his *Essays in Finance* (First Series), p. 177. I ought to mention that Mr Giffen's estimate includes foreign investments.

[3] See *Essays in Finance*, Second Series, Essay xi. p. 433: and Prof. Levi's *Wages and Earnings of the Working Classes* (1885), p. 4.

[4] Prof. Levi estimates the increase at 103 millions for the whole period from 1867 to 1884: but as Mr Giffen remarks, there was probably little increase in money wages between 1873 and 1884.

[5] *Some Leading Principles*, Part II. c. i. § 8. Cairnes afterwards recognises (*l. c.* § 9) that the "industrial development of a progressive community follows "a well-defined course," according to which a constant growth of the national "capital is accompanied with a nearly equally constant decline in the pro-

CHAP. VIII.] *THE REMUNERATION OF LABOUR.* 301

that—assuming the condition of the arts of industry to remain unchanged—the proportion borne to labour by industrial capital that is not wages is determined by the nature of the national industries, so as not to vary with the rate of wages: from which it follows that, if the industrial capital invested in England in any year were increased by 100 millions while labour remained stationary, the whole 100 millions would be added to the wages-fund, and profits and interest—according to Cairnes' argument[1]—would be correspondingly reduced.

This consequence is, I think, sufficiently paradoxical to point us to the error in the premises from which it follows. It is unwarrantable to assume, as Cairnes implicitly does, that the industrial demand for capital other than wages will not be extended by a fall in the price paid for the commodity demanded. Both general analogy and specific experience would lead us, I think, to the contrary assumption that, given the extent of the industrial demand for capital, the amount that may be profitably employed in aid of labour will not be a fixed quantity; but will tend to be greater or less as the rate of interest falls or rises[2]. It follows that if we suppose an increase to take place in the proportion of total capital to number of labourers, other things remaining unchanged, in consequence of which the rate of wages begins to rise and the rate of interest to fall, we must also suppose, as a concomitant effect, an increase in the proportion of 'not-wages' or 'auxiliary' capital to labour. And again, from this increase in the aid rendered by capital to labour, we must further infer an increase in the average productiveness of labour, and therefore in the annual produce. Hence the increase in the wages-fund that accompanies the increase in the 'not-wages' capital

"portion of this capital which goes to support labour." But he treats this change as "the inevitable consequence of the progress of the industrial arts"; he does not anywhere recognise that the mere increase of capital through saving must have a certain tendency to produce this result, independently of any change in the arts of industry.

[1] Cairnes does not suggest that the personal efficiency of the labourers will be increased by the extra wages. Nor is there any ground for supposing that this would generally be the case to an extent sufficient to yield anything like 100 millions' worth of extra produce.

[2] This assumption was accordingly made in treating of Interest in ch. vi. p. 270.

will not be taken entirely, nor perhaps even chiefly, out of the shares of other members of the community. Nay, further, when we are considering the matter from a purely abstract point of view, and not in relation to the special circumstances of a crowded country like England, we must not exclude the possibility that new investments may tend on the average to enlarge the field of profitable employment for capital in some ways as much as they contract it in others; so that, in fact, the increase of capital may increase the efficiency of labour in as great a degree as it increases the wages-fund; and thus not cause any permanent fall in the rate of interest[1]. But, again, if any change in the arts should increase the demand for auxiliary capital, it is possible—as Mill himself elsewhere points out[2]— that the amount spent by capitalists in wages may even diminish temporarily, while the total capital of the community increases; in consequence of an extensive "conversion of circu- "lating into fixed capital."

If this reasoning be sound, it is manifest that we cannot regard the rate of wages as determined merely by taking the "ratio between capital and population;" since this alone helps us but little towards ascertaining the ratio between wages-fund and population.

§ 3. So far I have endeavoured to show the inadequacy of the "wages-fund theory," without expressly rejecting the common view, according to which a portion of the capital of employers is conceived, while remaining capital, to take the form of wages of productive labour. But this view seems to me confused and erroneous. In a certain sense, no doubt, wages are normally paid out of capital; but not in any other sense than that in which interest and rent are paid out of capital. A certain portion of capital is always—to use Bagehot's terms—"remuneratory" and not directly[3] auxiliary in its nature: that is, it does not consist of instruments

[1] In this case the limit for each employer of the amount of capital employed would be determined not by decrease in prospective profit, but by increase in disadvantages of borrowing.

[2] Book I. ch. VI. § 2.

[3] I have before explained in what sense and to what extent stocks of finished goods may be brought under the general conception of auxiliary capital. See Book I. ch. V. § 6.

CHAP. VIII.] *THE REMUNERATION OF LABOUR.* 303

that make labour more efficient, but of finished products, destined for the consumption of labourers and others. This part of capital continually *becomes* real wages (as well as real profits, interest and rent) being purchased by the labourer with the money wages he receives from time to time. But it is not therefore correct to regard the real wages as employer's capital "advanced" to the labourer. The transaction between the two is essentially a purchase by the employer of the result of a week's labour, which thereby becomes a part of the employer's capital; and he may be conceived—if we omit for simplicity's sake the medium of exchange—to give the labourer in return some of the finished product of his industry. When this transaction is complete a portion of the capital of the country has undergone one of the transformations through which capital is continually passing; and exists now in the form of the results of a week's labour, having previously existed in the form of finished but unsold products— viz. the food, fuel &c. that pass into the consumption of the labourers—; while by the same transaction the labourer has obtained a share of the produce of industry in return for his labour. This seems to be the only clear and consistent view that can be taken of the payment of wages, according to the line before drawn between "capital" and "produce": which line, again, appeared to be the only one by which we could make precise the meaning commonly attached to the two terms. Economists who have not adopted this view are liable to fluctuate confusingly between two unreconciled conceptions of wages; at one time speaking of them as "paid out of capital," whilst at another time calling them the labourers' "share of the "annual produce of labour and capital," and implying in this and other phrases that "capital" and "produce" are two distinct portions of wealth. This confusion seems to be best avoided by considering the utilities that result from hired productive labour—whether "embodied" in ploughed land, mown hay, half-finished manufactures, or any other form—as constituting the real capital of the employer who purchases them; and the commodities that continually pass into the consumption of the labourers as their share of the produce.

"Remuneratory capital," in short, does not remunerate.

while it remains capital—at least while it remains the capital of the employer[1]. We have therefore no reason to regard each addition to the total stock of capital in the country as necessarily containing an addition to the wages-fund; but only as tending to increase wages indirectly so far as it (1) increases aggregate produce by supplying industry with additional instruments, and (2) increases the labourers' share of produce, in consequence of the lower rate of interest obtained on the increased supply of capital[2].

The adoption of the other view proceeds partly—like so many other economic errors—from a one-sided attention to the more obvious and striking results of investing capital. It is of course true that when a new investment of capital is made, a large portion of the money employed is generally paid in wages to labourers; and the inference is natural, that if it were not for this investment, the labourers in question would not be receiving wages during the period in which the process of investment is going on. But the inference is mistaken; for we must assume, speaking broadly and generally, that the labourers if not employed in this way, would be earning a share of the produce—though a somewhat smaller share—in some other work. It is possible indeed that some of them would have been idle; and no doubt the sudden cessation or depression of any particular branch of industry would throw many labourers out of work; so that, under certain circumstances, the withdrawal of a given amount of capital might conceivably involve a diminution in the real wages of the employed not much less in extent. But this result is very exceptional: and, so far as it occurs, the loss thus caused to the labourers should be regarded as a transient result of the disorganisation of industry, not a permanent consequence of the diminution in the amount of capital. Speaking generally, there is no reason for supposing that a larger percentage of labourers will, on the average, be unemployed in a community with small capital than in one with large; only in the former their labour will tend to be *ceteris*

---

[1] It may of course become capital—especially "consumers' capital"—in the labourers' possession.

[2] It should be observed that these results will only follow if the increase of capital is in excess of any increased field for its employment.

paribus less productive, and their command over the necessaries and conveniences of life will generally be less in consequence[1].

The view that the amount of wages received by hired labourers is completely determined by the saving of capitalists and the number of such labourers has, however, another source: it partly arises from a hasty application of the elementary truth that the labourer must be supported on the produce of previous labour. It is incontrovertible that the ploughman in December cannot be fed on the corn to be reaped next harvest: but it does not therefore follow that the share of last year's corn which falls to ploughmen or labourers generally is strictly limited. The commodities consumed by hired labourers—or even by manual labourers—are not divided by a sharp line from those consumed by other classes: hence any cause tending to increase the reward of labour generally at the expense of interest or rent—or the remuneration of manual labourers at the expense partly of other labourers—would not be prevented from having some effect at once by the fact that the existing stocks of finished goods are adapted for a different distribution of produce: though probably a part of its effect would be temporarily absorbed in causing a rise in the market-value of the commodities which such labourers chiefly consume.

§ 4. How then is the amount of the produce that falls to labour, competitively determined? if a mere consideration of the numerical ratio between amount of capital and number of

[1] Again, it is of course true that if wages rise the capitalist employers have to spend a larger sum in purchasing the results of a given amount of labour; but then since these results have, by supposition, risen in market value, their capital (estimated at its market value) is correspondingly increased. That thus the capitalists' wealth is not decreased, while the labourers' is increased, by a simple exchange of equivalents, is certainly a paradoxical result; but I have already noticed that this paradox is an inevitable consequence of measuring Producers' and Consumers' wealth together by a common standard. In fact the capitalists' increase of nominal wealth is greater than has just been indicated; since they will obtain an equal rise in value on all similar results of labour which they have previously purchased, so far as their value depends on the cost of reproduction. No doubt, if the labour grown dearer is not really more efficient, their nominally increased capital may not bring them in any more income. But this result will not surprise us when we reflect that, if the labour grown dearer is not more productive, the rise in wages must involve a fall in interest; and it is implied in the very notion of a fall in interest that a larger amount of capital is required to bring in a given income.

labourers does not help us to determine it. In answering this question it seems to me best to include in the notion of the labour to be remunerated the exertions, intellectual and muscular, of the employer no less than those of his employees. The chief reason why this course is not commonly adopted by English economists seems to be that the remuneration of the employer's exertions, so far as he employs his own capital, is actually received by him mixed up with the returns to his capital, and can only be artificially distinguished from it by economic analysis; so that this composite employer's share is in ordinary thought obviously contrasted with the share of the employed, as tending to rise when the latter falls and *vice versâ*. And certainly it cannot be denied that the interests of employers are so far opposed to those of their employees, that an increase due to certain causes in the share of either class tends to be accompanied by a decrease in the share of the other. But this in no way places the former class in an exceptional position: since similar oppositions are continually liable to occur between the pecuniary interests of different groups of hired workers, employed in the production of competing commodities. And there is a class of hired workers—managers of joint-stock companies, or even of private industrial establishments,—who do almost exactly the same kind of work as many capitalist employers; and if, as is very likely, such a manager has capital invested somewhere else, he is practically induced to remain a manager, instead of setting up on his own account, by the consideration that he will be better remunerated for his labour in the former position than in the latter.

It may be urged, however, that the ascertainment of the amount of an aggregate, in which we lump together the earnings of employers and employed, will not really answer any question of practical interest; for what both labourers and employers are concerned to know is the amount of remuneration that the two classes respectively may look for, not the amount of produce that is somehow to be divided among them. But similarly any particular labourer is only concerned with the average wages of the whole aggregate of hired labourers in a very indirect way; so far, that is, as changes in this average rate may be expected to extend their effects to the particular branch of industry to which he belongs. And in the same way he is indirectly concerned, in only a slightly additional degree of remoteness, with the remuneration of the aggregate labour of the society of which he is a member. And there is no adequate reason for making a separate aggregate of the wages of *hired* labourers: since—if we suppose free competition excluding combination— the remuneration of labourers paid by employers, so that the results of their labour become a portion of the employer's capital, is not determined in a manner *essentially* different from the remuneration of labourers who work on their own account and are directly paid by consumers: except that in the latter case the worker is commonly paid later and therefore his remuneration must *ceteris paribus* be increased by interest proportioned to the interval that he has to wait for payment[1].

The chief advantage of considering first the reward of all labour taken in the aggregate is that it brings into prominence an element in the wages-problem which the discussion of particular wages is apt to leave in the background. When we are considering variations in the wages of this or that group of labourers we commonly assume, as it is convenient to do, that the real contribution of these labourers to the whole produce of the community is given, and that what we are concerned to investigate is merely the variation in the amount of the equivalent that society is willing to give them for this contribution. But when we are considering the reward of labour

---

[1] This will perhaps become clearer if we consider a simple hypothetical case. Let us suppose that a group of carpenters, working each on his own account and receiving payment from customers, agree to throw their private stocks of materials, instruments and half-finished goods into a common stock, under one management. Let us assume for simplicity that the manager is just worth his wages: i.e. that whatever he gets as salary is balanced by the saving he effects through better organization of labour and purchase of materials on a larger scale. Then, other things remaining the same, the other carpenters will obviously earn precisely what they earned before. Let us now further suppose that this aggregated capital becomes the property of the manager: he will of course claim to receive interest on it (including insurance against risk) and the incomes of the other carpenters will be proportionately diminished: but there is no reason why the part of their earnings which was strictly remuneration of labour should not remain the same as before. It is clear therefore that the mere transfer of a number of independent workers to the class of hired labourers will not *necessarily* produce any effect on the aggregate remuneration of manual labourers.

in the aggregate, it is obvious that it tends to be increased, *ceteris paribus*, by any cause that tends to make labour more efficient. Labour in the aggregate gets what it produces; after subtracting the price that it has to pay for the use of the results of previous labour, and whatever has to be paid for the use of land, or other portions of man's material environment, beyond ordinary interest on what it would have cost—in the present state of the arts of industry—to bring such portions of matter from their original condition to their present degree of adaptation to human uses. Consequently in the determination of Interest and Rent, as expounded in the two previous chapters, we have by implication indicated how the remuneration of labour in the aggregate is determined; so far as the quantity and quality of the labour is assumed to be given independently of its remuneration.

Accordingly, while I hold, with English economists generally that,—in such a country as England,—this remuneration tends, other things being equal, to bear a smaller proportion to the total number of labourers as that number increases, I should yet state the reasons for this conclusion quite differently from those who adopt the "wages fund" doctrine, and who determine wages simply by the arithmetical ratio between capital and population. In my view this result is due to the fact that an increase in the number of labourers will tend to raise the industrial demand for the aid of capital, and therefore to increase the portion of the total produce paid for the use of a given amount of capital; at the same time the proportion of total produce to the number of labourers will tend to be less, as the decreased utility of the additional labour, in a thickly populated country, is not likely to be compensated by the gain in efficiency from the increased advantages of cooperation[1]; while, again, the owners of land, and any other employers whose capital is partially exempted from competition, are likely to absorb a considerable share of this latter gain. On this latter ground, again, even if capital increases *pari passu* with labour, the reward of labour will tend to decrease in such a country as

[1] On account of this loss through crowding it is of course possible that interest may not actually rise even though the average remuneration of labour falls.

England, as its quantity increases; unless some improvement takes place,—through invention, education, or otherwise,—in the average productiveness of the capital-aided labour. On the other hand any such improvement is on the whole likely to increase the labourers' share of the produce; though it should be observed that different kinds of improvement operate in very different modes and degrees to bring about this result.

In the first place, improvements in the physical, moral, or intellectual qualities of labourers tend to increase the share of the produce that falls to labour, leaving the share of capital unaltered; except so far as they also increase the advantage which industry derives from the use of capital, by rendering the labourer more adapted for processes in which much capital is used. So far as this latter result accompanies the increase in the labourer's personal efficiency, a certain share of the increased produce will fall to the owner of capital as such. Similarly, labour in the aggregate tends to gain by all inventions that economize the labour necessary to produce a given utility,— whether they are discoveries of new processes in industry or new lines of trade—if they do not involve the use of an increased amount of capital; though the immediate result of such inventions is likely to be detrimental to some labourers by rendering their acquired skill less useful, and—possibly—by lowering the price of certain products more than can be made up by the consequent extension of the demand for them. Hitherto, however, the great majority of inventions have created a demand for additional capital; and in this case it is conceivable that, owing to the consequent rise in the rate of interest the owners of capital generally may obtain an addition to their share *exceeding* the whole extra produce due to the invention. In this way we reach the conclusion that the introduction of machinery, though profitable to the community taken as a whole, may conceivably, in a state of free competition, be temporarily injurious to the interests of all members of the community who are not owners of capital. This conclusion however has little practical application; most important inventions, while increasing the field of employment for capital, have at the same time effected a saving of expense to the community much greater than the addition they have caused to the capitalists' share of the produce. Still the essential difference, from the labourers' point of view, between inventions that merely economize labour without requiring extra capital, and those that enlarge the field of employment for capital, should be carefully noted.

§ 5. So far we have supposed the quantity and quality of labour to be given independently of its remuneration: but it is necessary, in order to complete our view of the causes determining the remuneration of labour generally, to take into account the extent to which the supply of labour is itself affected by its remuneration, and examine the reaction on the price of labour of this influence exercised by price on supply. For clearness we will, at first, confine our attention to the influence exercised on the number of labourers; supposing for the present that the quantity of labour supplied by each labourer, and its quality, remain unchanged. As we have before observed, the quantity of labour in a community may vary independently of any variations in the aggregate of its population, from changes in the proportion of workers to non-workers. Such changes actually occur to an extent not unimportant, and are often at least partly due to variations in wages: but I do not think that we can say generally that a rise or fall in the price of labour has a definite uniform tendency to increase or diminish the number of workers supplied by a fixed quantity of population. We will accordingly confine our consideration primarily to the influence of high or low wages on the increase or decrease of population in the aggregate; only taking note of the effect on the proportion of workers to non-workers, so far as this is inseparable from the effect on aggregate population.

We may begin by noticing an important case in which the action of price on supply may be neglected without material error, in investigating the determination of wages—the case, namely of a thinly-peopled peaceful country, cultivated, as a new colony is, by methods belonging to the most advanced stage of industry. Here no considerable number of persons are prevented from marrying by lowness of wages; and therefore, so far as native labour is concerned, supply may properly be treated as independent of price. Still even in such a country the total supply of labour will actually depend to

CHAP. VIII.] *THE REMUNERATION OF LABOUR.* 311

some extent on immigration; and this will be affected by the rate of wages—though probably not to an extent sufficient to react materially on the rate itself. But in a thickly-peopled country—according to the view of the laws of population as taken in Book I.[1]—we must regard the lowness of the real reward of labour as a continually active check to the increase of population; the force of which is no doubt diminished, but not actually removed, by emigration to other countries where the wages of labour are higher.

The check, as we have already seen, is actually applied in several very different ways; thus in England, among the upper classes of labourers, it takes almost solely the form of abstinence —prudent or vicious—from matrimony; while lower down in the social scale the "preventive" check is probably less operative than the "positive": i.e. the restriction of number results partly from the shortening of the lives of adults through unhealthy occupations or diseases caused or aggravated by an insufficient supply of necessaries, but chiefly from the mortality among young children in consequence either of insufficient provision of necessaries, or of the absence of due maternal care, in case the mother of the family has to earn wages for its support. In other countries, again, the reduction is believed to be largely effected by voluntary limitation of the number of children in a family. However, in one way or another, it may be laid down that an effective check is exercised on the great majority of labourers in all European countries by the actual lowness of the remuneration of labour: and under such circumstances it is evident that, if the earnings of labour generally rise, the force of the check will tend to be diminished, and a stimulus given to population of which the ultimate tendency will be to lower the remuneration of labour again. Similarly, any fall in this remuneration tends, by making the check more stringent and so reducing population, to cause a compensatory rise hereafter. In either case, too, the temporary variation in the reward of labour, being partly absorbed by a change in the number of non-workers requiring to be supported by the workers, is prevented from affecting proportionally the style of living of any

[1] See ch. vi. § 3.

class[1]. And if we could take as approximately constant the average standard of household expenditure in each of the higher grades of labourers,—the amount of income on which persons of average prudence would think themselves justified in marrying—then so long as population was effectively checked by want of means, this habitual standard would give us a normal rate of remuneration in each class round which the actual remuneration would slowly oscillate, just as the market-value of a material product oscillates about its cost of production. In fact we might regard this habitual standard as, so to say, a 'Quasi-cost' of Production of labour; being as closely analogous to the cost of production of a material product as is compatible with the labourer's freedom of choice.

But this supposition is only useful to facilitate our general conception of the mutual influence of Supply and Remuneration of labour: since there is, in fact, no such rigid fixity in the standards of living customary in different social grades. If in the ordinary remuneration of any class of labourers, whose real remuneration enables them to consume considerably more than the mere necessaries of life, a fall takes place from which they cannot be relieved to any material extent by industrial competition, we can hardly doubt that it will partly have the effect of lowering the standard of living; and similarly a temporary rise in the market price of such labour will have a certain tendency to raise along with it the "Quasi-cost of Production" of the labour in question. Hence we cannot say that the 'standards of comfort' of such classes tend to give us a definite normal rate of remuneration in each class; but merely that they tend to some extent to counteract the causes operating, at any given time and place, to alter the amount of produce competitively allotted to labour.

The Ricardian conception, however, of a 'natural' rate of wages, to which the actual rate tends to return after any casual fluctuations, is more plausible as applied to any class of labourers whose numbers are mainly kept down by the difficulty of procuring for their households, in sufficient quantity and quality, such

---

[1] The causes that tend to maintain different grades of labourers with different standards of comfort, even in a society where competition is unrestricted, will be discussed in the following chapter.

necessaries as food, clothing, fuel and house-room; since it would seem that any reduction in the wages of such a class must tend to cause a decline in their numbers from insufficient nutrition ; and, correspondingly that a rise in the wages of such labourers would have a stronger tendency than it would in the case of any other class to cause a subsequent increase in the supply of labourers and so *ceteris paribus* to depress wages again. And I certainly think that the Ricardian doctrine would hold good in this case, if the effect of private almsgiving and public poor-relief could be left out of account, and if we could assume that the class in question had substantially to keep up its own numbers. But I doubt its applicability to the conditions determining the lowest rate of remuneration of labour in England at the present time. For (1) the worst-paid labour of all is that of classes in large towns which are partly kept up by the economic degradation of members of other classes; and (2) the actual effect of almsgiving and public poor-relief in preventing absolute starvation renders it uncertain whether the lowest rate of wages that could be even transiently borne—without producing an irresistible demand for extraordinary aid from public funds—would have a material tendency to reduce the numbers of the class receiving it; since such a class, living from hand to mouth with little hope of material improvement of its condition and yet no sharp dread of actual starvation, is apt to be peculiarly reckless in indulging its inclinations to marriage and propagation of the species.

And further, we have to take account of an element hitherto omitted, which is here of special importance ;—viz. the effect of variations in the labourers' remuneration on their personal productiveness, whether exhibited in increase of quantity of work per head, or improvement of quality. It is evident that this kind of effect tends to react upon the remuneration of labour in the opposite way to that just discussed: since any increase in the number of labourers caused by increase in their average remuneration tends, so far as it operates, to bring down this average remuneration towards the level from which it rose; whereas so far as increased remuneration causes increased personal productiveness[1], the remuneration tends to remain

[1] So far as this increase of productiveness takes the form of increase in the

above the former level. For so far as a labourer's productiveness increases in proportion to his consumption, his share of produce may obviously be augmented, without any diminution in the incomes of other members of the community. And hence we have to note an important qualification of the general tendency of a fall in interest to be followed by a more or less compensatory rise—which from our present point of view may be described as the tendency of a rise in the aggregate remuneration of labour to be followed by a more or less compensatory fall—; for evidently, so far as increased remuneration causes increased personal efficiency, a transient fall in interest may be partly made up through the share that capital has in the advantages of the increased efficiency. And similarly any depression tends in some degree to counteract the restorative effect on average wages that a diminution in the number of labourers would *ceteris paribus* tend to cause, in such a country as England.

The extent to which changes in the remuneration of labour will produce changes—in the same direction—in its productiveness, will of course be very different in the case of different kinds of labour and different physical and moral conditions and social surroundings of the labourers. Nor can we even say that in all cases there will be some resultant effect of this kind, even if we confine our attention to the manual labourers who are recipients of "wages" in the ordinary sense; since though an increase of such wages might almost always be spent in increasing the productive power of present or future labourers, it also enables the habitual standard of living to be maintained with less energetic work, and often tempts to unsalutary indulgences[1]. But in the case of labourers scantily provided with

length of time for which each labourer works, we must of course understand by 'increase of remuneration' increase in the labourer's earnings, not in the price of labour measured in time.

[1] The diverse effects of increased remuneration on the labourers' efficiency are well illustrated by the following passages from Lord Brassey's *Work and Wages*, ch. iii.

"At the commencement of the construction of the North Devon Railway, the "wages of the labourers were 2s. a day. During the progress of the work their "wages were raised to 2s. 6d. and 3s. a day. Nevertheless, it was found that the "work was executed more cheaply when the men were earning the higher rate of

the means of maintaining physical health and vigour, and suffering from unsatisfied desire in consequence, it is reasonable to suppose that a material rise in wages would have important effects in improving the productive powers of present and future labourers; and this improvement would, so far as it went, counteract the tendency of increased population to bring down wages again. And we can still less doubt that a fall in wages which brought labourers into this condition would have a dangerous tendency to maintain itself, through the consequent fall in efficiency.

"wage than when they were paid at the lower rate. Again in London, in carrying "out a part of the Metropolitan Drainage Works in Oxford Street, the wages of "the bricklayers were gradually raised from 6s. to 10s. a day; yet it was found "that the brickwork was constructed at a cheaper rate per cubic yard, after the "wages of the workmen had been raised to 10s., than when they were paid at the "rate of 6s. a day."

"On the railways of India it has been found that the great increase of pay "which has taken place, has neither augmented the rapidity of execution, nor "added to the comfort of the labourer. The Hindoo workman knows no other "want than his daily portion of rice, and the torrid climate renders watertight "habitations and ample clothing alike unnecessary. The labourer therefore "desists from work as soon as he has provided for the necessities of the day. "Higher pay adds nothing to his comforts; it serves but to diminish his ordinary "industry."

CHAPTER IX.

PARTICULAR WAGES AND PROFITS.

§ 1. IN examining how the remuneration of labour taken in the aggregate tends to be determined, we have been inevitably led to take note of the differences which normally subsist, even where competition is legally quite open, between the wages[1] of different branches of industry. As has already been observed, it is this latter question which is most interesting to any particular labourer: the variations in an average found by dividing the aggregate of workers' remuneration among the aggregate of workers do not practically concern him, except so far as he may infer from them the variations in the wages that he may himself expect. It might be added that even the average rate of earnings in his own industry only concerns him indirectly, unless he is conscious of being an average worker. There is hardly any branch of industry in which a labourer stronger, more industrious, more skilful, or more careful than his fellows is not likely in one way or another to obtain more than the average rate of remuneration. The limits, however, within which such variations in the earnings of individuals are confined vary very much in different industries: they are naturally greater where work is paid for by the job or piece, than where the payment is customarily made for a day of

[1] In accordance with the usage of our leading economists, I extend the term wages, when used generally in this discussion, to include the remuneration of the labour of trades and professional men; but I have avoided any particular application of it which seemed odd or likely to mislead.

CHAP. IX.] PARTICULAR WAGES AND PROFITS. 317

customary length; and they tend to increase as labour becomes more skilled, except so far as this tendency is checked by custom or counteracted by combination.

When the superior labourer works on his own account, the additional remuneration that he will obtain will correspond partly to the greater quantity of work that he is enabled to do by the more urgent demand for his services, partly to the superior quality of his work so far as this is generally recognised. Similar considerations determine the extra wages that an employed labourer will receive; only that in most cases general recognition of the superiority in quality of work is more difficult to obtain: there is commonly a difference between the real value of a superior labourer to his actual employer, and his market value as estimated by employers generally, which difference is the natural remuneration of the superior insight of the employer who secures the superior employee.

In the first instance, however, we will confine our attention to the case of the worker of average ability and industry, who cannot reasonably expect more than the average rate of remuneration in his department of work. It may be thought perhaps that what such an average worker may reasonably expect, under a system of free competition, may be stated still more generally as the average net advantages[1] obtained by average labourers generally within the region over which the competition is effective:—that, in the words of Adam Smith, "the "whole of the advantages and disadvantages of the different "employments of labour and stock must in the same neighbour-"hood be either perfectly equal or continually tending to "equality...at least in a society where things were left to follow "their natural course." For "if in the same neighbourhood "there was any employment evidently either more or less "advantageous than the rest, so many people would crowd into "it in the one case, and so many would desert it in the other, "that its advantages would soon return to the level of other "employments."

[1] I use this term—taken from the *Economics of Industry*—to denote what Adam Smith calls "the whole of the advantages and disadvantages" of the different employments of labour: which is a somewhat loose phrase to express the 'balance of advantages after compensating for extra disadvantages.'

And, in fact, in Adam Smith's careful analysis of inequalities of wages "arising from the nature of the employments them-"selves," independently of "the policy of Europe," there is no express recognition of any differences inconsistent with this general statement[1]. Nor can it reasonably be doubted that industrial competition has, within certain limits, the equalizing tendency attributed to it by Adam Smith; or that in the absence of the counteracting forces of Custom and Combination, this tendency would be more strikingly manifested than it has yet been in any European community. But the further discussion which Mill and others have given to this point has brought into view important inequalities in the real reward of certain kinds of labour, which are in no respect compensatory for inequalities in the sacrifices entailed, and which yet the development of competition has no necessary tendency to remove, except in a very indirect and remote way.

The importance of this consideration we have already had occasion to notice[2]. But as the nature and conditions of these inequalities have hardly obtained sufficient recognition from the followers of Adam Smith generally, I propose to devote fuller attention to them in this chapter: confining myself for the present to the causes which would still operate, even under a system of complete "natural liberty," provided that the existing inequality in the distribution among human beings of wealth, and of marketable natural qualities, moral and intellectual, were not materially changed by some cause other than free competition.

First, however, it is to be observed that, as has already been noticed in discussing Joint Products[3], what industrial competition directly tends to equalize—with the qualifications to be presently stated—is not exactly the price of equal quantities of labour, but the whole remuneration of labourers of equal

[1] When, however, we look at the details of this analysis, we observe that Adam Smith does distinguish one case in which this tendency to equality clearly does not operate: that is, where "trust" is required. As Mill justly remarks, the superiority of reward in this case is not in any way compensatory for special sacrifices: trustworthiness has an extra value due to what I call "scarcity," and Mill "natural monopoly."
[2] See ch. II. § 8 of this book.
[3] Ch. II. § 11 of this book.

skill and energy. Hence it may fail to raise the price of a particular kind of labour, if all the labour of this kind required to satisfy the demand of society—even at a price below that of ordinary labour of the same quality—can be sufficiently supplied from the spare time of energetic persons regularly employed in some other way: as is the case with certain kinds of literary work. Secondly, we may note that, in the passage above quoted from Adam Smith, this equalizing tendency is only supposed to take effect, so far as the advantages and drawbacks of different employments are (1) "evident" and (2) "within the same neighbourhood." The first limitation requires to be emphasized, though it may seem obvious; since in practical applications of economic reasoning, based on the assumption of industrial competition, it is not always borne in mind that inequalities of remuneration only tend to be removed so far as they are "evident" to the class of persons detrimentally affected by them. Such 'evidence' is more likely to exist where the unequally remunerated employments are "in the "same neighbourhood": but a large amount of knowledge about the wages of labour in remote places is now everywhere attainable in civilized communities; and is actually attained to a considerable extent,—which, however, varies a good deal according to the different intellectual development of the classes affected. So far as this knowledge exists, industrial competition will tend to remove any appreciable differences in the real remuneration of labour of the same quantity and quality[1] in different localities, that are more than sufficient to compensate for the expense and other losses and sacrifices involved in migration from one locality to another,—supposing that the expense is not actually beyond the means of the persons affected. The obstacles presented by such expenses and sacrifices vary indefinitely at different times and between different places;

[1] In comparing qualities of labour it should be borne in mind that the processes of (nominally) the same industry are somewhat different in different places; so that labourers cannot migrate between such places without a certain loss of acquired skill. Again, if the labourers in any district have a low average standard of physical efficiency in consequence of their low wages; then, however easy migration may be to a neighbouring district where both the wages and the efficiency are greater, the difficulty an immigrant would have in earning the higher wages would be a serious obstacle to equalization.

but we may say generally that the range within which their effect is comparatively slight tends to become continually larger as civilization progresses.

Thirdly, however, it must be borne in mind that, even within such a limited range, the equalizing tendency of Industrial Competition can only take effect gradually; and, to a large extent, through the influence exercised by changes in wages on *prospective* rather than on *present* labourers. At any given time and place the competitive price of the services rendered by labourers depends on the relation of the supply to the demand just as the price of any finished product of labour does. There is thus no reason, so far as industrial competition goes, why a sudden fall in the demand for any particular kind of skilled labour should not reduce its remuneration to the level of that of altogether unskilled labour: or even below the average of this latter so far as the skilled labourer's previous habits of work have unfitted him for unskilled labour. Nor, indeed, is there any economic reason why an extensive change in processes, or local displacement, of any particular industry might not reduce the remuneration of any kind of labour in a particular district even below the point sufficient to furnish the labourers with necessaries of life; as they might be too numerous to be absorbed by such migration as their resources enabled them to effect[1].

§ 2. Let us now proceed to explain and classify the inequalities in particular wages, which industrial competition does not directly tend to remove, even within the limited range and in the gradual manner just described.

First we may place such differences as are apparent rather than real: such as the higher rate of wages in some employments, due to "inconstancy of employment" and "uncertainty "of success." In this case even the average money wages of average workmen during long periods may not be higher in such employments than they are in others with which we compare them; and it is, of course, only such an average that competition tends to equalize. In other cases an inequality in money wages merely balances some opposite inequality in advantages

[1] Some further discussion of these local and temporary variations in wages and their courses will be found in a subsequent chapter (ch. xi.).

not purchased by money, or compensates some extra sacrifice. For it must be borne in mind that the "net advantages" obtainable by labour, which industrial competition tends to equalize, have to be taken to include not merely commodities actually unpurchased—such as the free grazing and free cottage-site that an English agricultural labourer often enjoyed a century ago—but all appreciable utilities whatever, whether generally purchasable or not, which any particular kind of work affords special opportunities for obtaining. Thus, for instance,—as Adam Smith notices—the fact that any calling stands higher in social repute than another, will tend *ceteris paribus* to attach to it a lower average income. Similarly we must include on the negative side of the account not only sacrifices that indirectly involve pecuniary loss—as when a certain kind of work tends from its unhealthiness to shorten the average working period of life—but all drawbacks and sacrifices whatever. It should be observed, however, that there is no tendency to compensate special disadvantages felt by particular labourers owing to special social circumstances or physical constitution, if equally competent labourers who do not feel these disadvantages could be readily obtained in their stead. Nor, again are the extra sacrifices, which thus tend to be compensated, exactly the average extra sacrifices made by the whole body of labourers in any given employment; but rather the extra sacrifices made by that section of the body in which the strongest aversion is felt to the employment, provided that there is a demand for their services at the price required to overcome this aversion, and that such persons are equally fitted for other employments to which they are less averse, and are not compensated by any advantages similarly peculiar to them. It would be quite possible that some members of the class might have no dislike at all to their work,—or might even derive much positive pleasure from it; still, their self-interest would prompt them to demand the highest price obtainable for their services; and competition would enable them to obtain as much remuneration as was found necessary to compensate the sacrifices of their fellows. Similarly the special advantages attaching to any kind of work have no tendency to lower its remuneration, if they are only felt to be advantages by a number of persons so limited as to be unable to supply more than a fraction of the whole labour that society is willing to purchase at the higher rate which, independently of these advantages, it would tend to command.

Secondly, no exception is constituted to the general rule of equality of net advantages in different employments by any differences in wages, which merely compensate for differences in the cost of time and money, entailed by the previous training which skilled labour requires. If wealth were equally distributed and competition perfectly free, this cause would still operate to raise the net advantages earned by a given amount of skilled work above those of an equal amount of unskilled work: though the general correspondence of remuneration to sacrifice would still be maintained. Under such circumstances, supposing the rate of interest given, we could determine exactly the normal differences of wages due to this cause in any given case: it would be sufficient, if continued for the average working period of life of such a skilled worker, to replace with interest the wealth expended in teaching the worker and maintaining him during the extra years of his education—subtracting, of course, whatever was earned by the pupil before his education was completed. In short the sum so expended would tend to yield, precisely in the same way and to the same extent as any other capital, a return proportioned to the amount and the period of investment. And there can be no doubt that a considerable part of the higher wages of skilled artisans and professional men in England is actually to be referred to this cause; and to be regarded as a replacement with interest of the "personal "capital" which they possess in their expensively acquired skill.

But *thirdly*, in a society in which wealth is distributed as unequally as it is in our own, it is likely—quite apart from any influence of combination or governmental interference—that certain kinds of skilled labour will normally be purchased at an extra price considerably above that required to replace, with interest at the ordinary rate, the expense of acquiring the skill; through the scarcity of persons able and willing to spend the requisite amount of money in training their children and supporting them while they are being trained.

In explaining how precisely this scarcity is maintained, we

are met with a question to which political economists generally have given rather vague answers: viz. what general assumption may legitimately be made as to the limits of parents' willingness to sacrifice their own present comforts and satisfactions to the future well-being of their children. Probably it will correspond fairly to the facts as they exist in England at the present time if we assume that average parents in all classes are willing to make considerable sacrifices in order to give their children the training required to enable them to remain in the same grade of society as the parents themselves: but are not usually willing to make the greater sacrifices required to raise them above their own class. If so, it is easy to understand how the labour of any grade above the lowest should be maintained at a scarcity value. But even if parents generally in the lower grades of labour were desirous of doing their utmost to give their children a better education, it might easily be out of their power to do this—consistently with the maintenance of their own industrial efficiency and the health of their families—except by borrowing; from which resource they would ordinarily be cut off by their inability to give adequate security for repayment. For the parent, even if he had confidence that his child would be able and willing to repay out of his future wages the capital borrowed, is rarely likely to find a lender who will share this confidence.

In this way we are led to the conclusion that inequalities in the distribution of produce so considerable as those which exist in our own society have a certain tendency to maintain themselves which is quite independent of the mere *vis inertiæ* of custom. Such a society is likely to organize itself in grades or strata distinguished by differences of income; and so far separated that—though individuals are continually ascending and descending—the transition is yet not sufficiently easy to prevent the labour of any superior grade from being kept at what is essentially a scarcity value.

These higher rates will of course be liable to continual fluctuations from changes in the relation of the supply of the labour of each grade to the field of employment for it; and—in such a country as England—the limitation of supply necessary to maintain the higher wages of any grade requires generally speaking an effective restriction on the natural increase of population within the grade, as well as an effective barrier against intrusion from below. But such a restriction tends to result, in a general way—as we have had occasion to note—from the habitual standards of comfort prevalent in the respective grades; though, as was pointed out, the resistance offered by any such habitual standard to changes in wages is by no means rigid.

It has further to be observed that many classes of skilled workers not ordinarily regarded as capitalists use more or less expensive instruments and materials; which adds, of course, to the total amount of capital which their labour requires[1]. A further quantum of capital, in a different shape, is employed by artisans of the classes of shoemakers, tailors, the species of carpenters called cabinet-makers, and others, so far as they produce goods for sale on their own account. Such persons are in fact small traders as well as manufacturers; and their earnings, like those of other small traders, partake of the nature of profits in a varying degree, proportioned to the amount of capital that they use.

It is not improbable that the average profits made by such artisan shopkeepers, or by retail traders generally, may be sufficient after paying ordinary interest on the capital employed, to afford an extra rate[2] of remuneration for the services of these classes, as compared with the lower grade of skilled

[1] I may remind the reader that the line between outlay for production and outlay for consumption cannot always be sharply drawn; and that in some cases a portion of the expenditure ordinarily paid out of income must be partly reckoned under the former head—e.g. the expense of a physician's carriage, or a literary man's books. In other cases, again, instruments which would ordinarily be reckoned as producers' capital are partly also used unproductively—e.g. farmers' horses.

[2] I avoid speaking of this as a scarcity rate, since it might be somewhat misleading to suggest that any extra remuneration of retail traders, as compared with labourers not possessed of capital, should be referred to the 'scarcity' of such traders—although in a certain sense it would be true. For—as I shall have occasion to urge hereafter, when considering the deficiencies of *laissez faire* as a means to the most economic production,—industrial competition, in such a case as this, has no sufficient tendency to reduce the number of competitors down to the limits that economy requires; its effect is too often merely to divide the aggregate employment and earnings of the class among a larger number of individuals.

labourers who work for hire. But it is not easy to say how far this is actually the case, at any particular time and place. For, as I have before observed, the average returns to employers of capital in any branch of industry are much harder to ascertain even approximately than the average remuneration of any class of hired labourers. Numbers of small tradesmen are continually passing through the bankruptcy court; others, again, are continually extending their business and becoming large tradesmen; while the majority appear to struggle on with considerable fluctuations of income, avoiding complete failure but not adding importantly to their capital. We have no such statistics as would enable us to estimate the average earnings of this class of workers. Even if we had them it would still be doubtful whether an average obtained by dividing the total amount of profits earned by the number of persons employed in retail trade would give us approximately the remuneration which an ordinary trader might reasonably expect. For such an average would be raised by the large gains of the successful minority: and these large gains are probably in most cases due to the possession by the successful trader of special aptitudes for his business. The skill required by a retail trader is partly, no doubt, of a kind that an ordinary man can acquire by a certain definite outlay of time and instruction; so far as it consists of the arts of reading, writing, and book-keeping, together with adequate knowledge of the qualities of the articles in which he deals. But for success in trade it would seem that qualities are required which instruction cannot ordinarily give in the required degree, such as penetration, vigilance, quickness of resource in emergencies, and tact in promptly meeting the varying needs or even leading the tastes of consumers: for only thus can the trader seize the opportunities of gain great and small, and avoid the dangers of loss, which the changing conditions of supply and demand are continually bringing in the modern industrial world. Hence the earnings of traders adequately gifted with these qualities will tend to be kept high by the rarity of their talents relatively to the field of employment for them.

We are thus led to notice the only remaining important cause of inequalities in the remuneration of different kinds of labour—the scarcity of the natural gifts required for the most effective performance of their function. I have already pointed out that in almost every branch of industry to some extent—but to very different extent in different branches—wages above the average can be earned by labour of superior quality; such superiorities, speaking generally, being partly due to training and partly to the possession of natural and inherited aptitudes above the average. Where such superiority is exhibited in producing more easily and abundantly commodities of the same quality as inferior workers can supply, the extra remuneration obtainable by it is in a manner analogous to the high rent of fertile land used for ordinary agricultural purposes; since, as we have seen, the superior productiveness of land from which rent arises, is due partly to outlay and partly to natural differences independent of labour[1]. On the other hand, where the commodity produced by rare skill is valuable on account of its special qualities, real or supposed, the reward of such skill may be compared to the high rents obtained by the owners of famous vineyards and other portions of land of which the produce is peculiar and keenly desired: while again, so far as the services of any one individual have—or are believed to have—unique qualities, his remuneration is, of course, determined under the conditions of strict monopoly. Both these latter cases are exemplified by the rewards of the finer kinds of intellectual work, such as Literature, Painting, Mechanical invention: where the results which command substantial remuneration, cannot be obtained by education alone, without natural gifts so exceptional that the reward of their possessors is at most but partially affected by competition. To a less extent the same cause is operative in determining the distribution of the large incomes which constitute what are called the "prizes" of the professions of Advocate and Physician. The workers who earn these large incomes are believed by those who use their services to possess such exceptional skill as cannot

---

[1] Even in employments where the differences in skill and its remuneration are less marked, it is still to be observed that the outlay on education, &c. which constitutes Personal Capital, yields a profit varying importantly in amount in consequence of the different intellectual and moral qualities of the children educated.

be acquired by mere training and practice without rare[1] natural gifts.

Even when the skill required is not sufficiently exceptional in fact to command a scarcity value, the difficulty that people in general have in ascertaining the fact of its existence often secures a scarcity rate of remuneration to the professional men who have special means of obtaining good recommendations; such as kinship or friendship with persons who enjoy public confidence.

This leads me to notice another cause of a different kind which renders the incomes of individual traders and professional men larger than they would otherwise be; and which, like the scarcity of natural qualities just discussed, ought to be specially noted and partly discounted in estimating the average remuneration of the classes to which they belong. I mean the important economic fact that we have already more than once noted[2], under the names of Goodwill or Connexion: i.e. the widespread disposition to use the services of a particular individual rather than his competitors, not necessarily on account of any belief in their superior quality, nor even through kinship or personal acquaintance with the individual himself or his friends, but merely from the force of habit. We have already seen that this Goodwill is to a certain extent a saleable commodity; so far then as it has been purchased, the extra remuneration obtained by it is, from the point of view of the individual, interest on capital laid out. It is evident that in estimating the average return for labour in any employment in which earnings are largely increased by such Goodwill or Connexion we ought not to reckon the whole of the extra earnings due to this cause, but only the amount that an average man with ordinary training and industry may fairly expect to acquire for himself.

---

[1] It should be observed that when we speak of 'rare' skill, the term is always used relatively to the demand for the products or services of the skilled worker. It is quite possible that a given kind of skill may be confined to an extremely small minority of the members of any community, and yet may be so abundant relatively to the demand that no one possessing it is able to earn extra remuneration for his labour. This is the case (e.g.) with the faculty of writing second-rate poems.

[2] See Book I. ch. III.

§ 3. We have now come to the point at which it is desirable to concentrate our attention on that important portion of the produce of industry which is frequently but erroneously included in the "capitalists'" share: that is, the element of the profit made by the employers of capital which is in excess of the interest that they might have obtained without working, and which accordingly I have distinguished as Wages of Management. It is an important defect of English Political Economy that it has not, for the most part, conceived this element of the employers' gains with sufficient steadiness and clearness as a species of remuneration of labour—which it undoubtedly is. Even Mill's exposition—in spite of his careful analysis of profit into interest, risk, and "wages of super-"intendence,"—exhibits in important parts of the argument a want of distinction between profit and interest, and a tendency to identify "returns to capital" with the former instead of the latter, which seem to me highly confusing[1]. If we consider the large amounts of capital possessed by joint-stock companies, as well as all that is lent to private men of business, it must be evident that the greatest part of the capital of England is now really owned by persons other than those who receive the remuneration for managing it. When Ricardo and McCulloch wrote this was far less the case than it is at present; so that the identification of capitalists and employers was more naturally suggested by the facts of industry.

It is, I think, partly in consequence of this confusion that so many political economists have found no difficulty in assuming that the rate of profit[2]—allowing for difference of sacrifice and risk[3] in different employments—tends, on the average, to be simply proportioned to the amount of capital on which it is earned, just as the rate of interest does; without feeling called upon to explain how the employers' "wages of superintendence" come to vary precisely in the same ratio as the capital superin-

[1] My attention was first drawn to this point by Mr F. A. Walker's excellent book on "Wages."

[2] It may be worth while to point out, with Mr Macleod, that throughout this discussion, 'rate of profit' must be understood to mean 'rate of profit earned 'within a given period of time,' not 'rate of profit earned on each transaction.'

[3] When we are considering what average profits generally tend to amount to, the element of 'indemnity for risk' disappears.

tended. For, as I have briefly argued in a previous chapter[1], this latter result certainly does not follow as an immediate and obvious deduction from the hypothesis of unrestricted industrial competition. On the other hand, it does follow from that hypothesis, that if this proportion between employers' earnings and capital is really maintained, it must either be (1) because the trouble and anxiety of management increase in exact proportion to the amount of capital managed; or (2) because, in the competition of employers for the profits of business, the owners of large capitals enjoy some special advantages. The former of these causes can hardly be regarded as adequate to produce the effect. In trade, for instance, it seems no more trouble to order £2000 worth of sugar than to order £1000 worth; and though it is more troublesome to manage a large factory than one half the size, it can hardly be twice as troublesome. It may be said, however, that the personal sacrifice which a capitalist makes in enduring the labour and worry of business increases with the size of his capital, and the extent of the opportunities consequently open to him of enjoying life without working. And this is perhaps true, so far as we estimate sacrifice merely relatively to the individual who makes it: no doubt a certain number of large capitalists prefer to live on interest alone rather than increase their income by labour, and we may assume that a somewhat larger number would make this choice, if the additional income obtainable by labour were materially reduced. But this is not in itself a sufficient reason why free competition should provide large capitalists with the extra wages of management necessary to induce them to work; since, as we before noted, the competitive remuneration of any kind of labour does not tend to include compensation for the extra aversion felt to it by some of the labourers, except so far as such compensation is required to obtain the whole amount of the labour in question that society is willing to buy, even at the raised price. If large capitalists withdrew from business, because their average wages of management were insufficient to induce them to work, they must still leave their capital to be employed in some way, in order to get their interest; and though their withdrawal might, by increasing the supply of capital offered for loan or

[1] Ch. II. of this Book.

joint-stock investment, temporarily lower interest and therefore increase wages of management, there seems no reason why this latter rise should be permanent, supposing that an adequate supply of equally good managers is obtainable at the lower rate of remuneration which the discontented capitalists were getting. Hence if the strict proportion of employers' earnings to capital employed is, on the average, approximately realised, it must be on the second of the grounds above mentioned: the large capitalist must have special advantages in the competition of men of business which somehow enable him to sell his services to industry at a price graduated in proportion to the magnitude of his business. Let us examine how far, and in what way, this is likely to be the case.

In the first place, it is obvious that the employer's wages of management will be proportioned to his capital so far as the pecuniary cost of production to the employer, in any branch of industry, does not vary materially with the scale of production: since, under free competition, the market-price of the product must be the same—assuming that there is no difference of quality—however it may have been produced. We cannot however assume generally that cost of production is approximately the same for small and large employers alike;—e.g. we have seen[1] that in certain kinds of agriculture, where much is gained by minute and vigilant tendence, the small producer is commonly thought to have a decided advantage: so far, then, as this is the case, we may assume that the small employer will earn a higher rate of profit (per cent. of capital) than the employer who uses more capital. So, again, if retail trade is more effectively carried on in small shops, the retail trader will tend to receive a proportionally larger annual profit on his capital than the wholesale trader—independently of any additional profit on each transaction, that may be necessary to compensate for the less rapid turn-over. The question, then, is why self-interest does not in the long run prevent business from being conducted on a small scale, except when it is economically advantageous; why the small capitalist does not either (1) become a large employer by borrowing money, or (2) unite his

---

[1] Book I. ch. IV. § 7, pp. 108, 9.

capital with that of other small owners, and become a shareholder in a joint-stock company.

It is easy, however, to see that the first of these expedients can only be adopted to a limited extent. The owner of a small capital cannot ordinarily borrow beyond a small amount, except at an unremunerative rate; his whole capital being exposed to the risks of business, he cannot give adequate security to the lender. Hence the owners of large capitals are partially exempt from the competition of smaller capitalists in the management of private businesses on a large scale; from causes similar to those which, as we have just seen, partially exempt each of the different grades of labour from the competition of the grade below. It is true this exemption can only be partial, in a society with an abundant supply of capital continually available, and an active competition for customers on the part of banks and other lenders. In such societies, as Mr Walker says, if a small capitalist has a "genius for business, want of capital is not "likely to keep him under." A man who as manager for another, or as employer on a small scale, has given conspicuous evidence of skill, prudence and probity, will be able to borrow gradually increasing amounts of money; so that, by the augmentation of both his own and his borrowed capital, he may end by rivalling the largest producers. But such men are likely to be rare, no less than persons who start with large capitals; hence either class will tend, so long as industry is organized in private businesses, to obtain for its services what in a certain sense may be called a scarcity price: i.e. a rate of 'wages of management' which would be lowered if large capitals (or men with a genius for business) became more numerous, other things remaining the same.

But why then—it may be asked—do not large capitals under one management become more numerous by the association of small capitals into joint-stocks, for carrying on production on a large scale? In the first place, even supposing the rate of profit to be strictly proportioned to the capital employed, it is quite possible that the wages of management even of the comparatively small capitalist may be higher than the remuneration he would obtain for his labour in any other career; and that consequently there may not be a sufficient amount of capital owned by non-employers to offer, when aggregated into joint-stocks, a formidable competition to the large private employers. Where this is not the case, where, as in our own society at the present day the annual savings of professional men and others supply continually a large stream of capital that has to be managed by persons who do not own it, there can, I think, be no doubt that the competition of joint-stock companies does tend somewhat to reduce the rate of profit of private employers. Still, this tendency is strictly limited. For, firstly, assuming the two modes of management to be equally effective and economical, the private capitalist would still have an advantage, as he would avoid the trouble and expense generally involved in collecting the capital of a joint-stock company. And secondly—what is more important—the private employer has the economic advantage of being impelled by a stronger stimulus to exertion than the manager or directors of a company; for "no contrivance that has yet been invented can supply the "place of the feeling that the workman is labouring not for "another but for himself[1]." On these grounds, other things being the same, a man of sufficient business talents to obtain employment as the manager of a company, is likely to earn, on the average, a higher rate of remuneration if he is the owner of the capital he employs than if he is a hired manager; though his advantage varies very much with the nature of the business, being (as Adam Smith observed) less in proportion as a business is simple and can be reduced to "what is called a "routine."

Nor has it yet been shown that this advantage can be materially diminished through the adoption of the principle of "Co-operative Production" or Industrial Partnership, by which each employee in a business has a share of the profits allotted to him. It is true that by this means that part of the employer's function which consists in superintendence or overlooking, may be partly rendered superfluous through the pecuniary concern that each has in the efficiency of his own work, and still more through the concern that all have in the efficiency of the work of each. But, generally speaking, the more im-

---

[1] Hearn's *Plutology*, ch. XIII. § 9.

portant part of the work of management consists in organizing and directing the operations of a business considered as a whole: —e.g. in the case of a manufacturer, settling what is to be made and in what manner, where materials, raw and auxiliary, are to be bought, when finished products are to be sold, &c., &c.—and in distributing functions among the workers employed in the business. This work cannot be superseded or reduced by industrial partnership; and it is even liable to be made more difficult; since the secrecy necessary to the success of many operations of business is liable to arouse jealousies and suspicions among the workers who are to share the profits.

It seems, therefore, that industrial competition does not necessarily tend to prevent the services of large capitalists who engage in business from being remunerated at a rate considerably higher than that obtainable by similar labour on the part of employers who own smaller capitals. And that this result is actually produced in England and similar countries at the present time, may be inferred with a high degree of probability from the general unquestioning acceptance of the traditional economic doctrine, that employers' earnings, as well as interest, tend to be proportioned to amount of capital employed. I know, however, no adequate ground for regarding this generally accepted proposition as at all a close approximation to actual fact. It is, no doubt, a natural inference from the fact that large and small businesses exist prosperously side by side in the same industry, assuming that the respective economic advantages of the different scales of production are fairly balanced. But in many cases this assumption would be unwarranted; and even where it is legitimate, the inference that the rate of profit *per cent.* of capital is uniform overlooks, I conceive, the real nature of the source of income which I have several times spoken of as 'Business Connexion.' On the average, a large capitalist cannot obtain a large business by merely investing his money in certain kinds of real capital; he can only obtain it gradually as his connexion extends; and therefore, when obtained, a certain portion of the surplus income derived from his business, after subtracting interest on his material capital, is not properly remuneration for present work, but interest on the outlay of labour or wealth made during the earlier years of the business. I may observe further that in the important case of agriculture the received economic doctrine regards an employer as tending under competition to obtain 'ordinary profit' not on the whole amount of capital used by him, but only on a certain portion: for the farmer uses, besides his own capital, a certain amount of capital belonging to his landlord; yet he is never supposed to obtain any considerable wages of management for this latter, but only to get ordinary profit on his own or borrowed capital. And it seems on general grounds improbable that an employer tends to earn equal profit on all parts of the capital employed by him, wherever the trouble of managing different parts of the capital is materially different.

To sum up: a portion of the fund which, in the preceding chapter, we regarded as the share of labour in the aggregate, has been found on closer examination to be really interest on personal capital, by which the wages of various kinds of skilled labour tend to be increased by an amount proportioned, on the average, to the expense of time and money ordinarily needed for the acquisition of the skill. As regards the division of the remainder, industrial competition tends to equalize the shares obtained by ordinary labourers in different callings, provided they are not materially unequal either in natural qualifications or in respect of the amounts of capital possessed by themselves or their parents, except so far as differences in wages are compensatory for differences in the sacrifices entailed by different employments, or in the unpurchased advantages incident to them. But the possessors of capital, real and personal, as well as persons endowed with rare natural gifts, are likely to have— by reason of their limited numbers—important advantages in the competition that determines relative wages; in consequence of which the remuneration of such persons may—and in England often does—exceed the wages of ordinary labour by an amount considerably larger than is required to compensate them for additional outlay or other sacrifices; such excess tending to increase as the amount of capital owned by any individual increases, but in a ratio not precisely determinable by general considerations.

CHAPTER X.

MONOPOLY AND COMBINATION.

§ 1. THE effects of Combination in increasing profits and wages have attracted much attention in recent years, owing partly to the action of Trades-Unions, partly to the large gains made by successful combinations of merchants for the temporary monopoly of some indispensable or keenly demanded product. Such combinations, when manifest and manifestly profitable, have commonly excited dislike, as the gain accruing from them is *primâ facie* obtained at the expense of the rest of the community, and frequently with some loss to the community as a whole: and in the particular case of Trades-Unions, some writers have spoken of them as "interferences with the "laws of Political Economy." But if this phrase is intended to denote the laws investigated by Economic Science, the statement appears manifestly incorrect. The price of a monopolized article has its own economic laws, and can in most cases be theoretically determined on the hypothesis that every individual concerned intelligently seeks his private pecuniary interest, no less than the price of an article sold by competing dealers: and the only effect[1] of a Trade-Union or any other Combination is to bring the supply of the commodity of which the sellers combine under the conditions of a more or less perfect monopoly.

Hence—though I have followed usage in conceiving free competition to exclude combination—it seems desirable, in

[1] Provided, of course, that the combiners attain their end by purely peaceful and legal means.

working out the consequences of the general assumptions on which the theory of competitive distribution proceeds, to include an investigation of the conditions under which self-interest will prompt to combination, and of the extent of gain which the persons combining may realise. In the present chapter, then, I shall be especially concerned to trace out the economic effects of this kind of combination, regarding it merely as one mode of constituting monopoly: and I shall suppose here, as in the preceding chapters, that neither party in any exchange is restrained in the pursuit of its own interests by any regard to the interests of the other party. I do not here consider how far this supposition has been actually realised in the operations of Trades-Unions for the purpose of raising or keeping up wages, or in those of the counter-combinations of employers which have at various times and places kept down wages. Nor, again, do I consider here how far it represents a right principle of conduct, or one conducive to the economic wellbeing of the community. This latter is a question to which our attention will be drawn in the course of the next book.

In a preceding chapter I have briefly explained the general determination of the price of a monopolized commodity, in the case of material products; and the view there given has no less application to the case in which the commodity sold is labour measured by time. The monopolist, so far as he aims singly at his own pecuniary interest, will endeavour to sell the precise amount which will yield him the maximum net profit, after defraying the expenses of production. We may assume generally, that, in order that a monopoly may be a source of gain, the amount sold—within a certain time—must be somewhat less than it would be if there were no monopoly[1]; for otherwise, whatever extra profit the monopolist may make by the high price of his commodity cannot be strictly attributed to the monopoly, since the price would have tended to be the same if the supply had been in the hands of a number of sellers com-

---

[1] That is, if the price offered for the commodity is not influenced by open or tacit combination among the purchasers. As will hereafter be stated, the determination of price resulting from a struggle between a combination of sellers and a combination of purchasers, lies beyond the scope of the theory here expounded.

peting freely. The restriction in amount sold may be brought about either directly by limiting the amount brought to market, or indirectly by keeping up the price. In the latter case the restriction may not be intended by the monopolist, and he may possibly be even ignorant of its existence; but according to our general assumption as to the relation of Value to Demand, the maintenance of a high price of any commodity must *ceteris paribus* render the amount sold less than it would have been if the price had been allowed to fall; though in the case of necessaries of life, and other commodities of which the demand is inelastic, the reduction in sale may sometimes be comparatively slight, even for a considerable rise in price. The extent to which the restriction of sale has to be carried, in order to realise the maximum profit attainable, depends primarily on the precise extent to which the demand for the commodity varies with variations in its price; and, as was pointed out, it may easily happen, in the case of some articles, that several different amounts of supply would bring in about the same net profit to the monopolist. Again it has to be observed that (1) monopoly may either be permanent (so far as can be foreseen), or more or less definitely limited in time; and (2) that the supply may either be absolutely incapable of being increased—as in the case of pictures of a deceased artist—or the monopolist may control the indispensable means of increasing it. In this latter case he will have to calculate not only the variations of demand corresponding to variations of price, but also the variations of cost of production corresponding to variations in the amount supplied.

§ 2. But before we proceed to discuss this particular species of combination, it will be desirable to obtain a fuller definition of the notion of Monopoly—as we shall find it convenient to use it—and a more complete view of the different modes and degrees in which monopoly generally, and especially monopoly resulting from combination, admits of being realised[1].

[1] Throughout the discussion that follows I shall assume that the special gains of the monopolist or of the combination of sellers are realised by raising the price of the commodity monopolized. I ought however to notice the fact that—chiefly in the markets for securities—combinations of sellers are sometimes formed which are designed to have, and actually do have, the opposite effect of lowering the price of the commodity sold.

In treating of Monopoly in chap. II., I denoted by the word the control exercised by an individual seller or combination of sellers, over a commodity that no one else can bring to market. Here, however, it is convenient to use the term more widely. In the first place, it is convenient to extend it to cases in which a person or union of persons—whom, for brevity, I will call 'the 'monopolist'—cannot control more than a portion of the whole supply of the commodity; since such a partial control may render possible and profitable an artificial rise in the price of the commodity, even though the remainder is supplied by several sellers freely competing; if only the proportion controlled is so large that its withdrawal would cause a serious scarcity, and thus considerably raise the competitively determined value of the uncontrolled remainder. Such a partial monopoly confers, of course, only a limited power of raising the price of the commodity controlled; the limit of possible elevation being fixed somewhere below the price to which scarcity would raise the unmonopolized supply, if the monopolized portion were withdrawn from the market[1]. Further, if the commodity is one that can be produced in unlimited quantities, such a partial monopoly can only be effective temporarily, and

    The motive for forming such combinations is the hope of gaining ultimately, by purchasing at the lowered prices, considerably more than is lost by the sales that force the price down. There would, however, be no reasonable prospect of realising this hope, except by accident, if such sales produced no further fall in price than that which resulted directly from the increase of supply by the combining speculators: since, *ceteris paribus*, their purchases would tend to raise the price again in precisely the same proportion as their sales had depressed it. The reason why such operations are profitable lies in the imitative proceedings of other persons holding the same securities, who infer from the sales that the stock is expected to fall further, and therefore are induced to sell their own stock, in order to avoid the further fall, instead of buying. A similar explanation applies, *mutatis mutandis*, to the parallel case in which combinations of buyers are successfully made with the view of raising prices.
    Such operations are of doubtful legitimacy, even according to the ordinary standard of commercial morality: since the speculators do not merely expect to profit by the mistakes of others, but by mistakes that they have themselves intentionally caused. I have not therefore thought it necessary to give them more than this passing notice.
    [1] In the above reasoning it is assumed that the other sellers do not enter into the kind of tacit combination with the monopolist of which I shall speak presently. In practice they would, under certain circumstances, be very likely to do this to some extent.

only so far as purchasers of the commodity cannot postpone their purchases without serious loss or inconvenience. And where the monopolist *produces* as well as *sells* the commodity, he will have to take into account the future loss likely to result to him from the stimulus given by the rise in price to the production beyond his control; unless he can reckon on withdrawing his capital from the business without loss, before this stimulus has so much increased supply as to render it impossible for him to sell his own produce even at an ordinarily remunerative price.

Secondly, even where the control exercised by the monopolist extends over the whole supply of his commodity available at any particular time, we may still distinguish different degrees of completeness in the monopoly. Thus (1) the monopoly may be—so far as can be foreseen—indestructible, either permanently or for a certain determinate period: that is, it may be impossible to obtain the commodity in question at all, except from the monopolist. An artist or author of repute enjoys a monopoly of this degree; as also do the holders of certain patents and proprietors of springs or vineyards recognised as unique in quality. Or (2) the monopoly may be merely secured by the prospective unprofitableness of the outlay of wealth or labour (or both) that would be required to provide the commodity from other sources; whether such outlay were undertaken by an association of the consumers of the monopolized commodity, or as an ordinary business venture on the part of other persons. In case (2) the monopolist's calculations will be more complicated than in case (1); since he will not only have to consider the law of the demand for his commodity, but also to calculate how far any rise in his charges may seriously increase the danger of an attempt to break down the monopoly. And it will often be prudent for him to keep his price well below the point at which this danger becomes formidable, especially when he has much capital—personal or non-personal—invested in his business: since an attack on his monopoly, even when it does not turn out profitable to the undertakers, may easily have the effect of not only annihilating his extra gains, but even reducing the returns to his capital considerably below the average. This second degree of monopoly often results from the occupation of a limited department of industry, in which production on a large scale is necessary or highly expedient, by a single large firm or jointstock company, or a few such firms or companies acting in combination.

Thirdly, it will be convenient to extend the term 'mono-'poly' to include the case when it is in the power of a combination of *buyers*,—or a single wealthy buyer,—to control the price and extent of sale of a certain commodity. In speaking of this as a case of "buyers' monopoly," we are not, of course, to be understood as implying that the whole medium of exchange in any community is under a single control. All that is required, to make such a monopoly practically complete, is that a single individual or combination may furnish the only effective demand for some particular commodity: i.e. that no one else may be willing to pay anything for it. Under these circumstances, if the commodity is supplied by several persons competing freely, the buyers' monopoly may obviously exercise a control over the price substantially similar in kind and degree—though of course opposite in direction—to that exercised by a seller's monopoly. If the purchaser has not to consider future needs, and if the product cannot be kept, or if the prospect of selling it is not likely to improve, the purchaser's power of profitably reducing the price is not definitely limited except by the utility of the commodity to the seller—allowing for any disadvantage that may result to the latter in future transactions from the precedent of a low price. More ordinarily the purchaser's need will be continuous or recurrent; and in this case his reduction of price will be checked by the danger of ultimate loss through the diminution of future supply which the lowered price may be expected to cause.

It should be said that, generally speaking, a combination of buyers will be more difficult to establish and maintain than a combination of sellers, since the former are likely to be both more numerous and more dispersed. But there are important exceptions to this rule. For instance, the wholesale merchants who deal in a particular product will generally be less numerous than the producers from whom they buy. And it is probable that combinations of such dealers to keep down the prices paid by them to producers have often been successfully effected, especially in early stages of commercial development. When, however, producers as well as merchants belong to a community commercially advanced, such a monopoly of merchant buyers will be rather hard to maintain long, owing to the ease and rapidity with which capital can be turned into any branch of wholesale dealing[1].

There would generally be somewhat less difficulty in maintaining a combination of farmers or manufacturers to reduce (or keep low) the price of the labour employed by them;—supposing that the labourers did not form a counter-combination. In this case, if we assume industrial competition so perfect, that labourers can and will change their residence and employment when it is perceptibly their interest to do so, the highest limit of the employers' possible gain through combination would tend to be fixed by the point at which the corresponding loss to the labourers would outweigh the disadvantages, pecuniary and sentimental, of migrating to some district beyond the reach of the combination, or the loss of acquired skill involved in change of work: but so far as the employers are interested in the future returns of their industry, they will further avoid reducing wages so low as to drive the rising generation to other employments. In proportion, however, as the habits of the labourers, or the limitations of their intelligence or of their resources, operate as a bar to change of place or employment, the limit of the employers' possible gains through combination is obviously extended; since, supposing such change excluded, this limit would only be fixed, so far as the present supply of labour alone is concerned, by the amount of necessaries required to keep the labourers in fair working condition[2]; while so far as future supply is taken into account, it

[1] It may be observed that such a combination of dealers may exercise monopoly—in the extended sense above proposed—on two sides; i.e. in relation both to the producers from whom they purchase and to the persons to whom they sell.

[2] 'Fair working condition' is rather a vague phrase; but it is rather difficult to say how far an employer's self-interest will prompt him to add to his labourers' wages, when such additions, if properly spent, would increase the efficiency of the labourers themselves or of their children. If the employer could make sure that the extra wages would be properly spent, and that he would be able to purchase at his own price the improved labour, self-interest would obviously prompt him to give his labourers such wages as would make the

would similarly be fixed by the rate of real wages which will enable and induce the labourers to rear a sufficient supply of future labourers.

So far we have supposed that the monopoly, whether of sellers or of buyers, is not met by a counter-monopoly. But when an advantageous monopoly of either kind has been brought about by combination, it is *primâ facie* the interest of the other parties to the exchanges in question to form, if possible, a counter-combination. In this case the determination of the ratio of exchange between the two monopolies becomes an entirely different question, only partially within the range of economic science. Accordingly I defer the consideration of it till we have more completely examined the effects of onesided monopoly.

§ 3. The points that we have hitherto discussed are such as belong to monopoly generally, when considered from an abstract point of view; though in practice some of them are not likely to arise, except in the case of combinations. Let us now pass to consider some characteristics that are theoretically found only in this latter case.

In the first place, it is important to observe that a combination, however effectively it may restrict the supply of the commodity monopolized, will yet not be able to count on maintaining permanently the average earnings of the members of the combination perceptibly above the average earnings obtainable by persons of the same industrial grade in other employments imposing no greater sacrifices and requiring no scarcer qualifications, unless the number of the combining persons is also limited artificially. If entrance to the combination is left perfectly free, the ultimate effect of limiting the supply of the monopolized commodity will tend to be only a change in the mode in which competition may be expected to reduce the earnings of the combining persons; instead of bringing down prices, competition will in this case merely tend to decrease the average amount of business or employment that the combining persons are able to obtain.

excess of value of the results of their labour over what they consume (allowing for interest on the latter) as great as possible. But it will be only under special circumstances that he can feel even approximately sure on these points. See ch. viii. § 1.

Secondly, we have to take note of the various ways in which the interests of the combiners in the aggregate may be related to the private interests of individuals among them. From the point of view of general theory, Combination presents itself primarily as a consequence of the unconstrained pursuit of private pecuniary interest by each individual who combines; but even where this is the case, and where each may expect to gain if all keep their compact to restrict supply, the share of the gain of the monopoly accruing to any one member of the combination within a given period may be materially less than what he might obtain by increasing his own supply in violation of the compact; especially if such violation can be kept for some time secret. In such cases it may be necessary for the combination not only to provide against open violation of its rules by substantial pecuniary penalties, or strong social sanctions; but also to take precautions against secret evasion of rules. And such provision will, of course, have to be still more stringent, when—as is often the case in practice—the combination generally profitable to a given class of labourers has been only joined reluctantly by some individual members of the class; either (1) because they have special reason to dread the initial loss caused by the artificial restriction of supply or the sacrifices which a struggle between opposing combinations would entail; or (2) because the regulations necessary to ensure the carrying out of the combination—of which I shall speak presently—are specially disadvantageous to them.

The consideration of social sanctions for the maintenance of a combined monopoly leads me to observe that besides the express combinations which we have hitherto had in view, in which resolutions are formally taken by a whole body of combining persons or by a council representing and obeyed by the whole body, similar results may be to some extent produced by more informal communications;—or even without any communication, through the acquaintance that each member of the class has with the sentiments and habits of action of the rest. Such tacit combinations, indeed, are hardly likely to be effective for the attainment of a rise in the price of the commodity exchanged; except, perhaps, where such a general rise is obviously necessary to prevent a definite loss to the whole class, in consequence of some change of circumstances. But where the price of any product or service has acquired a certain stability through custom, the resistance which the mere *vis inertiæ* of custom would present to any economic forces operating to lower such price is likely to be considerably strengthened by the consciousness of each seller of the commodity that other sellers will recognise their common interest in maintaining the price, and that substantial social penalties are likely to be inflicted upon any one who undersells the rest. It is in this way, for instance, that the customary fees for professional services and the prices charged by retail traders, are sometimes maintained above the rate to which a perfectly open competition would reduce them[1].

In order to see more fully the effects of this necessity of imposing sanctions for the maintenance of monopoly resulting from combination, let us examine more in detail the steps which the holder of a monopoly will have to take, in order to realize the maximum of possible gain. When the monopoly is complete, it obviously confers the power of fixing exactly both the amount and the price of the commodity supplied within any given time. But from the difficulty of forecasting the demand exactly, it can rarely be most profitable to do this—except for very short periods, determined by the custom of the trade and the convenience of purchasers. And such a course will generally be still less expedient, where the monopolist has not complete control of the market. Thus an individual monopolist who wishes to approximate as nearly as is practicable to the possible maximum of gain, will in most cases find it best to leave the actual total of his receipts to be determined within certain limits by the demand; either (1) fixing the price and letting the amount sold vary with the state of the market, or (2) fixing the amount to be sold and letting the price vary—so long

---

[1] The actual extent of the operation of these unavowed, and more or less tacit, combinations is, from the nature of the case, very difficult to ascertain. Hence the mistake may easily be made of attributing to ' free competition' unfavourable effects on wages which are really due to combinations of this kind on the part of employers. And I am inclined to think that this mistake has sometimes been made by students of economic history, in dealing with states of society in which custom has ceased to determine wages, while yet manual labourers generally have not learnt to combine.

as the variations are not very great. Which of the two courses he will adopt will depend a good deal on the nature of his business; which may be such as to render either frequent changes in amount supplied, or frequent changes in price, especially inconvenient. But *ceteris paribus* he will probably prefer to effect the limitation of his supply indirectly, by keeping up the price, so that the sacrifice of his customers' interests to his own may be less palpable and offensive. When, however, the monopoly results from combination, another consideration may sometimes determine the choice between the two alternatives; viz. the respective facilities that either affords for practically holding individual members of the combination to their compact. An agreement as to price would seem to be ordinarily both the simplest and the easiest to enforce. In some cases, however, though a direct reduction of price is easy to detect and prohibit, it is more difficult to secure that none of the combining suppliers shall attract customers by indirect concessions, equivalent to a reduction of price. On these and other grounds it has sometimes been found more effective to limit the amount supplied by each seller, leaving the price to be regulated by the demand[1].

The method by which Trades' Unions, and other combinations of labourers have endeavoured to increase the earnings of their members has been mainly that of fixing a price for their labour. To a smaller extent, however, they have also adopted measures tending to restrict the amount of the labour that they control. Thus (1) they have sought to impose restrictions on the number of apprentices taken on by the employers, and (2) they have aimed at reducing the ordinary amount of hours of each week's (or day's) work of the labourers;—such reduction, however, has in some cases been not much more than a particular mode of fixing the price of labour, as there has been no regulation prohibiting work beyond the normal time, and such work has in fact been common. In any case it is evident that a union open to all properly qualified workmen in any trade

---

[1] Thus, for instance, "great coal companies......have at various times bound themselves to one another under pecuniary penalties not to exceed a certain output, which is fixed from time to time by a central committee." *Economics of Industry*, p. 182.

must in some way limit the number of those entering the trade, in order to secure permanently for its average members wages known to be higher on the whole than those earned in similar industries of the same grade. Otherwise, though the rate of wages paid to any one in actual employment might be maintained, the average wages earned from year to year would tend to be gradually reduced by an increase in the number of workmen out of employment, until the advantages of the higher price of labour were lost[1].

Hitherto we have not expressly considered the case of several products different in quality, under the control of the same monopolist. Where such differences are clearly defined, this plurality does not present any new economic problem, as the monopoly value of each separate quality of product may obviously be determined separately. But, in the case of labour, differences of quality are frequently not marked off by such definite and unmistakeable characteristics as would render it easy to frame a tariff of wages accurately corresponding to them; and especially where the processes of work performed are the same, and only the manner of performing them varies, it would be very difficult for an aggregate of workers varying in efficiency to agree upon such a tariff. One way out of this difficulty, which is that commonly taken by Trades' Unions,

---

[1] It may be observed that actually Trades' Unions are not merely associations for procuring to their members the highest possible return for their labour, but also aim at providing mutual assurance for their members by means of pecuniary assistance, against the loss caused by want of employment. The "out of "work pay" thus provided is, however, considerably less than the lowest wages earned by an ordinary worker in the trade. Hence any addition to annual wages secured by such a union, if admission to the trade were practically unrestricted, would be liable to be diminished in two ways; partly by the increased contribution that would be required from all members, to insure effectively against want of employment; and partly by the increased number of days during which each workman, on the average, would have to content himself with the out of work pay. If, as I am informed, no such effects as these have been observed in the case of Trades' Unions which do not practically restrict entrance into their trades, I should be disposed to infer that no such union has as yet raised the net advantages obtainable by its members above those obtainable in other industries that are on the same level as regards the outlay and the natural qualifications which they require—or at least that it has not done this to an extent generally perceptible for any considerable period.

is to fix a minimum rate, below which the ordinarily skilled craftsmen in the trade are not to accept employment[1].

§ 4. Let us now inquire under what conditions of Supply and Demand it will be possible for a combination of labourers to raise their average earnings by an opportune increase of the price charged for their labour. In this inquiry, however, I do not propose to take into account the loss that may be incurred through strikes, or any expense involved in carrying on the work of combination: since it can hardly be the interest of employers to run the risk of a strike, unless either they combine, or a single business is so large relatively to the particular combination of labourers as to enjoy a partial 'buyers' monopoly:'—and we have not yet come to consider the terms of exchange between two opposing monopolies.

Putting strikes, then, out of the question, we may say generally that the combining labourers will gain by raising the rate at which they consent to sell their labour, so long as this does not cause the demand for their labour to fall off so much as to reduce the total amount spent in purchasing it. Such a fall in demand may (1) be expected to occur rapidly, if an adequate substitute for the monopolized labour can be obtained from other sources, at a cheaper rate (all things considered) than that fixed by the Union: this contingency, however, it will be not difficult to exclude temporarily, if the combination comprises the majority, or even a large minority, of the labourers in the country, trained to perform the processes of the particular industry; provided the rise in wages demanded be kept within such limits that the labour controlled by the Union is still cheaper, considering its superior quality, than any other labour which the employers are able to draw from other industries, or import from other countries[2]. But (2) even if this contingency

[1] This rate is frequently different in different localities. Cf. Howell, *Capital and Labour*, c. iv. § 40.

[2] In the case of labour imported from (nominally) the same industry in other countries we have to consider not merely the actual cost of carriage, the expense incurred in procuring the labourers by advertisements, agents, &c., and the extra remuneration required to compensate for expatriation; but also the extent to which they will be inexpert in the methods and processes of the industry as practised in the country to which they are brought; and further, where the languages are different, the cost of interpreters, and the loss occasioned by inevitable misunderstandings on the part of fellow-labourers and others. Cf. Howell, c. ix. § 13.

be excluded, the fall in the demand for the monopolized labour may be expected to occur, though more gradually, through the defection of employers, if the average profits of the latter are reduced by the rise in wages perceptibly below the profits obtainable on equal amounts of capital in other industries. There are, however, several cases in which this effect is, either permanently or temporarily, unlikely to occur to any important extent: as (*a*) if the employers, being wholly or partially exempt from competition, were previously able to make profits in excess of the normal rate; or (*b*) if, apart from the rise in wages, they would be in a position to do so temporarily owing to a simultaneous rise in the price of their commodity through intensification of the demand, or to a fall in its cost of production through invention, cheapening of material, &c. It is to be observed that in the latter cases, an ultimate rise in wages might be expected to occur, even if there were no combination of labourers; since the increase in employers' profits that would then take place would tend to cause an extension of business and an intensified demand for the appropriate labour. Still, the gain that would thus accrue to the labourers might easily be less on the whole (as well as later in time) than the increase in wages obtainable by combination.

Again, if the commodity sold by the employers is of such a kind that an increase in its price tends but slightly to reduce the consumers' demand for it, so that the aggregate expenditure on the commodity is increased, the additional cost of production due to a rise in wages may be entirely thrown on the consumers, without any material reduction in the amount produced, or in the employers' demand for labour. And this is likely to be the case with any commodities which are regarded by the consumers as indispensable, except so far as the employers of the combining labourers are closely pressed in the markets which they supply by the competition of producers who are unaffected by the combination.

Further, a rise in wages may often be temporarily secured, without a corresponding reduction of business, even though the employers' profits be thereby reduced considerably below the normal rate, if their industry is one that uses a large amount of fixed capital. For in this case the employers are often unable to diminish their employment of labour materially, without proportionally reducing the yield on their fixed capital: and the loss thus incurred may be greater than that involved in paying the higher wages to their full complement of labourers. Indeed, in certain circumstances—as for instance, if an employer has contracted to do a certain amount of work under heavy penalties, or if he has a large stock of raw material that will deteriorate by being kept, or even merely if he is seriously afraid of losing his business connexion—it may be expedient for him to continue his production, even if he earns less than nothing for his labour and the use of his capital. But under such circumstances the gain to the combining labourers can obviously be only temporary, the period during which it can last being limited in proportion to the severity of the employers' loss: and it is not improbable that the ultimate loss to the combining labourers from the diminution of employment may decidedly outweigh the immediate gain.

In all the above cases it is possible for a combination of workmen to secure, either temporarily or permanently, a rise in wages; while in none of them, except the last, has such gain any manifest tendency to be counterbalanced by future loss. And it does not appear that these cases are in practice very exceptional: or that the proposition that a "trades' union cannot "in the long run succeed in raising wages" corresponds even approximately to the actual facts of industry. I am not, however, aware that any economist of repute has really maintained such a proposition—whatever may be the case with indiscreet disciples. All that Mill and his chief followers have argued is, that if one set of labourers obtain an increase of wages in this way, there must be a corresponding reduction in the wages of other labourers. Even if this were so, there hardly seems to be any reason why the labourers in any particular industry, supposing them to be "economic men" of the ordinary pattern, should be expected to sacrifice their interests to those of certain other labourers unknown. Still the conclusion, from the point of view of the philanthropist, is so important that it is worth while to examine carefully the grounds upon which it is based.

The doctrine is, in fact, a deduction from that combated in Chap. VIII., under the name of the "Wages-Fund Theory," according to which the share of hired labour in the aggregate was supposed to be "predetermined" in the aggregate bargaining between (employing) capitalists and labourers, and therefore as incapable of being altered by the successful bargaining of any one set of labourers. According to my view of the relation of capital to labour, this supposition is erroneous. We can, indeed, affirm that any increase in the wages of hired labour not accompanied by an equal increase in its productiveness, tends to be compensated to some extent by a subsequent decrease, so far as such it involves a reduction of the rate of interest in the country; since any such reduction must tend to check the supply of capital for home investment, and so ultimately to raise interest again, at the expense of wages. But there is no reason to suppose that this ulterior loss to hired labourers in the aggregate will just counterbalance their previous gain; and there are several possible cases in which the above-mentioned effect on interest will either not occur at all, or be slight in comparison to the rise in wages. Thus in the first place, when the increase in the remuneration of any class of labourers causes a corresponding increase in their efficiency, through their being more amply supplied with the necessaries of life, the gain of these labourers involves no corresponding loss to any other class. Again, so far as any rise in wages diminishes the extra profits which a particular class of employers, having certain special advantages, were previously able to make, the loss caused by it falls primarily on the wages of management of these employers; and whatever ultimate effect it may have in reducing the rate of interest is not likely to be great in proportion to its primary effect. Finally, so far as the addition to particular wages is entirely or mainly paid by an increase in the exchange value of products consumed chiefly by the rich, though there will be a consequent loss to capitalists as consumers, and thus a diminution in the real income derived from capital, there will not therefore be any diminution in interest regarded as a motive to accumulation.

In none of these cases, then, does a gain obtained through combination by one set of hired labourers tend to cause anything like an equivalent loss to some other hired labourers. There are, no doubt, many other cases in which such loss tends to be ultimately considerable, and may outweigh the immediate gain, from the point of view of labour generally, even if we leave the effect of strikes out of account. The loss in question is produced not only through reduction of the supply of capital for home employment, but also in other ways; thus (1) an increase in the cost of any particular kind of labour, so far as it causes a rise in the price of products consumed by other hired labourers, tends to diminish the real wages of the latter; (2) a rise due to combination in the price of the labour furnished by a particular class of workers will generally be accompanied by a diminution in the amount of such labour employed, and so will tend *pro tanto* to prevent some actual or possible labourers of the same class from obtaining as much remuneration as they would otherwise do; (3) the same cause tends more indirectly to reduce the demand for other kinds of labour employed either in the same industry, or in other industries cooperating directly or indirectly to produce the same consumable product.

So far I have been considering the operation of Trades' Unions, or other combinations of labourers, in restricting the supply of labour either directly or by raising its price. But, before concluding this inquiry, it should be observed that combinations of workers, avowed or tacit, have sometimes sought with more or less success to increase their earnings through an enlargement of the demand for their work; by enforcing the use of more laborious processes of production than are necessary for the result desired by the consumers of their products. Such artificial enlargement of demand is more obviously injurious to society than an artificial restriction of supply; since the extra labour of which the use is thus enforced is, from a social point of view, palpably and undeniably wasted. Hence this mode of increasing the aggregate wages of a class of workers seems to be rarely adopted in an avowed and unqualified way: that is, the more laborious process maintained by combination commonly produces, or is believed to produce, a result somewhat superior in quality to that which could be obtained by less labour, though the difference in quality by no means compensates for the additional cost.

§ 5. In the last two sections we have been engaged in

analysing the effects of monopoly resulting from combination, when it is what I have called "one-sided";—i.e. when it is not met by a counter-combination of the other parties to the exchanges in question. But—as I have said—where combination on one side gives the combiners important advantages in bargaining, at the expense of those who deal with them, self-interest will obviously suggest to the latter a counter-combination, as a means of escape from their unfavourable position. The question then arises, on what terms will exchange tend to take place when monopoly thus meets monopoly?—assuming (as we have assumed throughout) that the action of either party is governed by a single-minded but intelligent regard to its own interests. I do not think that a definite theoretical answer can be given to this question—at least according to the method adopted in the present Book—if, as will usually be the case, there is a considerable margin between the least favourable rates of exchange that it would be the interest of each side respectively to accept, if necessary, rather than not come to terms. We can say that under these conditions it is clearly the interest of both to divide this margin in any proportion, rather than not effect an exchange: but there are no general economic considerations that enable us to say what proportion would be chosen. Similarly we cannot say to what extent or for how long it is the interest of either side to suffer loss or inconvenience rather than accept the terms offered by the other party. It is a trial of endurance, of which the results are likely to vary according to the financial and other circumstances of the contending parties.

It is, therefore, only in a partial and subordinate way that Economic Science can offer assistance in dealing with the practical problem presented to Boards of Conciliation or Courts of Arbitration when they attempt to avert or close a controversy between employers and employed in any industry as to the rate of wages. Economic science cannot profess to determine the normal division of the difference remaining, when from the net produce available for wages and profits in any branch of production we subtract the minimum shares which it is the interest of employers and employed respectively to take rather than abandon the business and seek employment for their labour and capital elsewhere. All that it can do is to guard against mistakes in applying any principle of distribution of the net produce on which the two parties may agree: it can make clear what elements of gain or loss are to be taken into account in carrying out this principle under varying circumstances, and what weight is to be attached to each element. But the establishment of the principle itself lies beyond the scope of Economic Science, as conceived by the present writer. I therefore defer the detailed discussion of this practically most important problem, until, in the concluding Book, I pass from discussing Distribution as it is or tends to be to consider Distribution as it ought to be.

CHAPTER XI.

TRANSIENT AND LOCAL VARIATIONS IN DISTRIBUTION.

§ 1. THE more important conclusions reached in the five preceding chapters may be broadly summed up as follows:

The whole produce of the labour and capital employed in any country, the whole increment of its wealth in any given year, will be greater or less—other things being the same—according to the quantity and efficiency of its labour: while the supply of labour, in a thickly peopled country, will be materially influenced by the amount of produce *per head* that falls to the labourers; and again the efficiency of the labour will depend largely on the amount of aid that it receives from capital, the accumulation of which is materially influenced by the rate of interest. The earnings of labour in the aggregate (including the labour of management) may be most conveniently regarded as consisting of this total produce, after subtracting whatever payment has to be made for the use of the accumulated results of previous labour and appropriated natural agents. Industrial competition operates continually, with certain qualifications and within certain limits, to equalize the shares in which such aggregate earnings of labour are divided among the labourers; still, the wages of different classes are characterized by very striking inequalities which industrial competition has no direct tendency to remove. These inequalities are partly compensatory for inequalities of sacrifice or outlay undergone either by the workers themselves or their parents; but, in such a society as ours, they are likely to be partly due to the scarcity of persons duly qualified, through their own wealth or their parents', for the performance of certain kinds of work. The limitation of numbers necessary to this result would not, however, be maintained, generally speaking, if the standard of comfort habitual in each of the higher grades of society did not place an effective check upon increase of population within the grade. This check, moreover, may be importantly aided by the attractions which the prospects of higher remuneration abroad exercise on different classes of labourers; since the average real remuneration of any class can not remain below the real remuneration which the workers in question believe to be obtainable by them in another country, by an amount materially more than sufficient to compensate for the prospective cost and trouble of obtaining it, and the sacrifices involved in expatriation, as estimated by the persons concerned; provided that the outlay required is not actually beyond their means.

Another cause of variation in the wages of different kinds of labour is the fact that certain classes of persons possess natural qualities, physical and intellectual, which are scarce relatively to the demand for their labour; and this is, even more manifestly, a cause of differences of remuneration among individual members of the same class. Skill peculiar to a single individual renders its possessor a monopolist of the special commodity produced by his skill; and this monopoly may enable him to increase his income very considerably, if there be a keen demand for his commodity. Similar advantages, varying in extent and duration, may be gained by a combination of persons specially skilled. If the labour controlled by such a combination were strictly indispensable to the production of some strictly indispensable commodity, the combined labourers would have it in their power to exact such a price for it as would strip the rest of the community of all their superfluous wealth—that is, if we can suppose freedom of exchange to be legally maintained under these hypothetical circumstances. Practically such a case has never occurred: even where the need which the monopolized labour supplies is one which must be satisfied, some substitute can always be found either (1) for the labour or (2) for the consumable commodity which it is a means of producing; and this possibility of substitution fixes a limit to the price which the monopolized labour can obtain.

A specially remarkable instance of inequality in the remuneration of labour is furnished by the earnings or wages of management of the employer as such; since such wages tend to increase with the amount of capital employed to an extent more than proportioned to the consequent increase in the labour of management; owing to the scarcity of employers individually controlling large capitals, as compared with the field of employment for such capitals, and to the superiority, on the average, of the work done by an employer who labours for himself alone, as compared with the manager of a jointstock company.

Turning to the yield of capital itself, we observe that the returns from certain investments may be kept above the ordinary rate of interest on the original outlay—just as the remuneration of labour may—through the operation of monopoly or scarcity. A chief case of this is the rent of agricultural land in thickly populated countries, which is kept above ordinary interest on the outlay of which its utility is the result, by the limitation of land equally available for supplying the same markets with agricultural products: the excess of yield being due partly to the natural qualities of the soil, partly to the distribution of the population that purchases its produce. In some cases—such as the ground in towns or the ground containing rich minerals (supposing no outlay to have been incurred in discovering them), rent is not to any material extent paid for the use of the results of labour employed on the land: it is almost wholly to be referred to the appropriation of a natural agent scarce relatively to the demand for it. The effect of monopoly or scarcity is also exhibited by the high dividends often paid on the stocks of water-companies and gas-companies, and other investments which, either through legal interference or the force of circumstances, are wholly or partially exempt from competition. An analogous extra yield, again, is obtained by manufacturers who use processes protected from imitation by secresy or legal monopoly, and by houses of business that have an established connexion: and though such extra profit may be properly regarded as interest on the results of the labour applied in inventing and perfecting a new process or establishing a business, it is often much in excess of ordinary interest on such outlay, when the labour has been applied under specially favourable social or industrial conditions.

On the other hand the yield of capital fully exposed to competition, and not capable of being transferred without loss from the investment in which it has been placed, cannot on the average be higher than ordinary interest on the original outlay; and is liable to become indefinitely less than this, through changes in the arts of industry or in other social conditions. Nor is this liability absent, even in the case of capital partly exempt from competition.

Current interest, or the price obtained for the use of capital continually available for new investment, tends to be approximately the same for equal amounts of such capital invested for equal periods, allowance being made for differences in the security of different investments, and in the expectations of their future rise and fall. Such interest is partly paid for wealth employed in production, and partly for consumers' wealth previously lent and consumed, either by living individuals or those whose obligations they inherit, or by the community to which they belong; in this latter case the debts on which the interest is paid are to be regarded as invested capital of *individuals*, though not of the community. The ratio of this payment to the value of the principal is mainly determined, in a modern industrial community in which wealth is continually accumulated, by the relation between the supply of available capital and the field of profitable industrial employment for it; which latter tends to be enlarged as population increases— though not in proportion to such increase after a certain point of density has been reached—and which, in recent times especially, has been continually and greatly extended by the progress of invention. Since, however, the accumulation of capital in a country is influenced by the rate of interest, it may be assumed with great probability that there is, at any given time, a certain minimum rate necessary to induce saving sufficient to balance the waste of capital that is continually going on; and that as current interest sinks towards this minimum, accumulation will be more and more retarded. The supply of capital in a country, however, tends to vary from many other causes besides changes in the rate of interest there; in particular, owing to the international mobility of capital, the supply in any one country tends to be affected by any material changes in the field of employment for capital elsewhere; and also by any change—due (e.g.) to increase or decrease of mutual confidence—in the general estimate formed in any one country of the risks attending investment in another.

§ 2. The rates of remuneration for different industrial services, as they tend to be determined by the operation of the general economic causes above analysed—except Combination, which requires exceptional treatment from the difficulty of forecasting its effects, if we suppose it generally adopted—may be designated as the Normal rates. At any particular time and place, the actual shares of produce received by members of the different industrial classes are likely to vary somewhat from the normal shares, under the influence of such transient or local causes as I now propose to examine;—confining myself mainly to causes actually operative in the most advanced industrial communities, and not excluded by the general assumptions on which our theory has proceeded. We ought, however, to begin by noting that the normal shares themselves are likely to be continually fluctuating; since there is no reason to assume that any of the general causes that influence them will operate in precisely the same manner or degree for any length of time. We have already observed that both the total produce of industry, and the proportions that fall respectively to labour and to capital, tend to be continually altered by the changes that constitute the normal growth of a prosperous community—the accumulation of capital, the increase of population, improvements in the arts of industry due to invention, and the development of cooperation, especially cooperation through exchange. We have seen, too, that the growth of population within a given area tends on the one hand to increase the advantages of cooperation; but that on the other hand, after a certain pitch of density is reached, it tends[1] to diminish the efficiency of labour in agriculture, through the increased difficulty of agricultural production, and to increase correspondingly

[1] That is, the mere growth of population has in itself this tendency; though it may be counteracted by improvements in industry and trade.

the proportion of agricultural produce which falls to the landowner as such. Turning to the normal distribution of the aggregate earnings of labour among the different classes of workers, we can easily see that it will be modified in various complex ways; by changes in the distribution of wealth, altering the supply of persons capable of making a given amount of outlay; changes in the processes of industry, altering the demand both for natural qualities and for the results of training, and also altering the sacrifices required for the production of certain utilities; changes in the cost of production of certain kinds of skill, through the spread of education, &c.; changes in social habits and opinions, modifying men's estimate of commodities and of sacrifices; and other changes too numerous to mention.

Again, the continual oscillations in the market-price of commodities which we have noticed tend to be accompanied with corresponding oscillations in the profits of those who supply the commodities in question; owing to the inevitably unstable adjustment of supply to the generally varying demand. The forecast of the demand for a commodity—at any supposed price—can at best be only approximative; though with some commodities—such as a staple of food—the approximation can be made much more close than with others; in most cases, however, besides the larger alterations in demand which I shall notice later, there will be continual small tides of change from complex causes that defy calculation. And even supposing the demand for any product exactly known to all suppliers, it is still highly unlikely that at any given time supply should be so adjusted as to give the suppliers the exact remuneration that industrial competition tends to allot to them. Indeed in agriculture, hunting, and some kinds of mining the produce obtainable by a given amount of labour frequently varies very considerably on either side of the average; and it may be remarked that, supposing such variations to affect all producers about equally, it depends on the precise nature of the demand for the product whether an abundant supply will be profitable or the reverse: since if the demand is inelastic—as it is (e.g.) for corn—the producers may easily gain by dearth and lose by plenty.

Finally, even the larger fluctuations that affect different

branches of production—which we have now to examine more in detail—have already been noticed incidentally in considering the general determination of Interest; since we had to distinguish, in the returns actually received from investments of capital, that portion which is practically compensation for risk. Now it belongs to the very notion of 'risk' that we cannot predict when or how far the loss, of which we recognise a certain probability, will actually be incurred; hence even if such expectations of risk were altogether well-founded, it would be in the highest degree improbable that all owners of capital should incur the same proportion of loss in any particular year. Similarly we have taken note of 'uncertainty' as one cause of the difference in the actual remunerations of labour. Here, however, it should be observed that ordinarily a much more exact comparison of prospective remunerations is made by persons investing capital than by persons selecting a line of labour. Very slight differences in the prospective security of interest, which would have no effect on the choice of a trade or profession, find expression in the different prices of different investments of capital;—thus, for instance, the faint additional chance of the non-payment of interest on the preference shares of a first-class English railway causes such shares to be sold at a somewhat lower price than debentures of the same railway yielding the same interest. So, again, if a small capitalist is considering whether he shall go into a business, he takes into account indefinite and remote risks which can hardly enter into the view of an ordinary labourer choosing a trade for his son: for the uncertainties of which Adam Smith speaks, that tend to be compensated in the higher wages of particular trades, are dangers frequently incurred in the course of the ordinary experience of such trades. Accordingly the exceptional losses of different classes of capitalists and employers tend to be compensated by higher incomes in ordinary times to a greater extent than similar losses incurred by hired labourers. On the other hand, the fluctuations in the profits of capital employed by the owner, and even in the mere interest of capital that bears the full risks of industry, are decidedly greater on the average than the fluctuations in the remuneration of hired labour: because under the existing conditions of industry the capitalist employer mostly bears the first shock of unforeseen losses, and only passes on a part of the blow to his employees; and, in the same way, he mostly secures the lion's share of unforeseen gains.

§ 3. Let us then proceed to consider more in detail the causes and effects of the more important fluctuations in the profits of different industries. Since the danger of loss occupies a larger place in the common view of industrial capital than the chance of extra gain, we may conveniently begin by directing our attention to the former phenomenon; bearing in mind that so far as we are merely dealing with changes in distribution, loss and gain—to different sets of persons—are correlative effects of the same causes[1].

Losses in business which impair aggregate wealth as well as the wealth of individuals may be due, firstly, to dishonesty; or, without distinct dishonesty, to the pursuit of private interests by the employers of borrowed capital, with more or less culpable indifference to the interests of the persons who own the capital. Or, secondly, they may be due to mere mismanagement of the routine of business—want of care and punctuality in meeting requirements, want of vigilance in supervising subordinates, &c. These causes, however, are hardly likely to affect specially any particular branch of production; and therefore most of the damage due to them will remain with the owners or employers of the capital in question. But a third class of losses, which arise from want of the higher kind of business talent,—viz. foresight as to important changes in supply or demand, and inventiveness in adapting production to meet such changes—being liable to affect whole classes of employers simultaneously, have a much greater tendency to be passed on to the classes of labourers employed by them. It is hard to draw a line in any case defining how much of this kind of loss should be regarded as the normal penalty of unskilfulness, and similarly, how much of the corresponding gain from favourable changes is the normal reward of superior ability; since it is difficult to place definite limits to human foresight and ingenuity. But at any rate there is a

[1] It should be observed, however, that important changes in distribution are mostly accompanied by some increase or decrease in the aggregate wealth of the community.

good deal of actual loss and gain which we must place beyond the line, and consider—economically speaking—as beyond the scope of prescience and provision; and it would seem that the development of industry and trade tends to increase both the number and the magnitude of such unmerited fluctuations of income; though it also tends to mitigate their worst effects on human life and happiness.

In examining further the operation of such accidents, we may notice first those that injure the community as a whole, as well as particular classes. Such are the calamities of unusually bad seasons, plagues of noxious animals, epidemic diseases among useful animals and vegetables, extensive damage from flood or fire, &c. Losses caused in this way almost always fall with unequal weight on different portions of the community; in most cases they are borne primarily by employers engaged in the branches of industry affected; a varying portion of the loss being passed on to the consumers of their products, the labourers whom they employ, the owners of the land and borrowed capital which they use, and the other producers whose products they consume[1]. The same may be said of the destruction of property caused by war; though it is to be observed that so far as war, disease, or other calamity destroys human life, its effect on the amount of wealth *per head* possessed by the community is of a mixed kind: since the survivors, whatever they may lose by such calamities, will at any rate gain relief from the economic disadvantages of over-crowding.

Accidents of this kind favourable to production also occur, though more rarely; the most striking of these are chance discoveries of natural products suitable to human use, as in the finding of rich mines. Such discoveries, however, are more commonly made by minds that have spent time and energy in searching for them; in which case they come under the general head of Invention, the great spring of industrial progress.

More ordinarily, important changes due to invention consist in the discovery not of new sources of raw material, but new

[1] It has been observed that the producers of commodities for which the demand is of such a kind that—within certain limits—each diminution in supply tends to increase the price paid for the total amount sold, may actually gain *as a class* by any such disaster; the consumers suffering, through the rise in price, a loss greater than that which falls on the community as a whole.

modes of adapting known materials or forces to the needs of industry. Such improvements in industrial processes of course tend to make the community ultimately richer, inasmuch as they increase the amount of a given kind of commodity obtainable by a given amount of labour. But, generally speaking, they tend also to reduce the value of a certain amount of the capital already invested in instruments of production. Hence their effects on the wealth of the community at the time of their introduction are necessarily mixed; and may even be, on the whole, temporarily of a negative kind. It is even conceivable that some very important invention might reduce the value of previously existing instruments and stocks so much, that the total capital of the community would actually be diminished by an amount exceeding the value of the new commodities produced within the year; so that the community would appear to be living on its capital, in consequence of what was really a great step in the advance of material wellbeing. This paradox is the inevitable result (in the case supposed) of including in one aggregate of wealth, along with things immediately consumable, products that are only useful and valuable as a means of producing the former: but, since most of that part of real incomes which is saved exists normally in the form of such merely instrumental products, I do not see how we can conveniently adopt any other view of wealth, in discussing Distribution. We must therefore be content to note the possibility of this paradoxical result, and to guard ourselves against being misled by it.

So great a destruction of the existing value of capital as that above supposed is highly improbable; but minor effects of this kind are, as I have said, a normal incident of industrial progress; and, in considering the effects of new inventions on distribution, must be set down as losses which may temporarily more than counterbalance the economic gain of such inventions.

This gain itself will be distributed in very various ways according to circumstances. Supposing that the invention can be monopolized, through a patent or otherwise, the extra profit that its possessor can secure—which is, of course, to be regarded as the normal reward of the inventor's labour—may conceivably be equivalent to the whole of the economic gain obtained by the improvement. But, generally speaking, the monopolist will pass on a portion of this gain to others, and ultimately to the consumers; since, if (1) the improvement consists in cheapening the manufacture of some old product, it will generally be his interest to sell this at a lowered price, in order to secure possession of the market; while if (2) it leads to the production of some new consumable commodity, it will be necessary to sell this to the consumers at such a price as will give them a share of the additional utility obtained by it, in order to induce them to alter their habits of purchase. Supposing on the other hand, that the invention is not protected from imitation, competition will tend ultimately to transfer the whole gain to the consumers; but generally speaking a certain portion of it will, during an interval varying in length, be retained as extra profit by the employers who first use the invention; who may either be some or all of the persons whose fixed capital has been depreciated by the improvement, or a quite different set of persons—according as the industrial change in question is more or less sweeping in character.

The effects of such a change on the remuneration of manual labour are similarly complex and various. It is obvious that the value of what we have before called the 'personal capital' of skilled labourers—their acquired dexterities—is liable to be diminished or annihilated by improvements in industrial processes, just as the value of material instruments is. On the other hand, the fall of price caused by an improvement frequently extends the consumption of the products of the industry affected so much, as to increase considerably the total employment offered to labourers engaged in it, and to raise the price of the kind of labour required to work the new process. Sometimes however, the extension of consumption is slight in comparison to the fall in price, so that the 'labour-saving' improvement diminishes the total price obtained for the product of the industry improved. In this case it must also tend to diminish the total amount of labour employed in the industry; and since if the change takes place rapidly the labourers thus turned adrift will often find it difficult to obtain work elsewhere, it is not surprising that improvements in industrial processes should have been thought to diminish the whole field of employment for labour; and that at various times not unenlightened persons should have fancied that they were acting for the interest of the community in endeavouring to prevent this result. But, it is obvious that, if of two processes equally efficient the more laborious is chosen, the utility to the community of the extra labour thus employed is simply *nil*; and there must always be some other department of the industrial system in which it could be applied productively;—indeed it is evident that when the demand for labour in one branch of industry is diminished by a labour-saving improvement which cheapens its product, the purchasers of the cheapened product must have more to spend on other articles, so that there must be a correspondingly increased demand for labour in the branches of industry which supply these other articles.

What has been just said of the effects of newly invented improvements in the process of manufacture, applies equally to the application of inventions already published, but neglected for want of knowledge, enterprise or capital; except that the element of possible monopoly is absent in this case. Similar effects are also produced by improvements in communication and conveyance, and the opening up of new lines of trade[1]; but a full consideration of these would bring prominently into view local variations in industrial incomes, which I reserve for discussion later on.

Further, improvements in any branch of production, if they materially increase or decrease the value of its aggregate products, tend to cause secondary changes in the demand for the products of other industries, which may in some cases be important; thus if corn be materially cheapened, the demand for the luxuries of the poor may rise to such an extent as to raise temporarily the profits and wages of the producers of such luxuries above their normal amount. The new investments of capital to which invention leads are similarly a source of temporary extra gains to the producers of certain kinds of instruments and materials; thus (e.g.) the introduction of

[1] At an earlier period of our industrial history it was usual, and perhaps useful, to encourage and protect by legal monopolies, developments of trade no less than improvements in manufacture. But in the present state of commercial enterprise such artificial encouragement would seem quite superfluous; and is universally condemned by modern maxims of economic policy.

railways benefited employers and labourers engaged in the production of iron.

§ 4. Other important changes in demand continually occur, with effects similar to those just mentioned, independently of any amelioration in the processes of manufacture. To a certain extent, indeed, such changes are, in a larger sense, to be regarded as economic improvements; that is, when a general preference on the part of consumers for some commodity different from what they have previously been in the habit of purchasing is occasioned by the fact that a better or cheaper means of satisfying some need has become more generally known or appreciated. But some alterations in demand, that affect production materially, are due to the mere caprice of fashion, and thus involve no real advantage to the community. Either kind of such changes, when abrupt and extensive, may diminish the value of certain portions of real and personal capital in the way that we have seen to be an incidental effect of many industrial improvements; and may similarly affect the relative demands for certain kinds of labour.

Even if we suppose no change either in the arts of industry or the habits of expenditure corresponding to different grades of income, many important changes in the relative demands for the products of different industries must continually result from the increase of wealth and population, and from the larger changes in distribution which these tend to bring with them, through the operation of the normal conditions already investigated.

As I have already said, the highest kind of business talent is shewn in forecasting rightly all these various changes and continually adapting supply to demand; but the forecast tends to become more difficult as the range of cooperation through exchange extends. Producers are more and more led to manufacture for markets too numerous to watch carefully, too remote to understand adequately, and exposed to modifying influences of continually increasing complexity; and hence fluctuations in the adaptation of supply to demand, and consequent fluctuations in the incomes of producers, tend to become greater and to contain a larger element of mere luck. Manufacturers and traders working under these conditions have frequent and important occasions of gain through unexpected developments of demand; but they are also in continual danger of loss through oversupply of their commodities. Indeed any considerable gain is liable to tend indirectly to subsequent loss, by the exceptionally eager competition excited in the business that has suddenly become profitable. The excess of production thus caused sometimes leads to such a fall in the price of the over-abundant products that their market-value does not exceed that of the materials spent in making them—or, in the case of trade, the value of imported goods does not exceed their value in the country from which they were brought—thus allowing no return whatever to the labour and capital employed in the production. Over-production of this kind—even if it does not reach this degree—is a striking feature of the modern competitive organisation of industry, extended as it is by worldwide trade; and, owing to the intimate connexion of different branches of production, fluctuations of this kind rarely affect one branch alone, and frequently occur nearly simultaneously in a considerable number. This experience has in former times led even professed political economists to the conclusion that *general* over-production is a danger against which society has to guard; that the aggregate of labourers cooperating through exchange are liable to produce not only too much of a certain kind of commodity, but too much altogether. Now it must be admitted that this result is a possible one; an individual may obviously be led, from an over-estimate of the utilities obtainable by his labour, to work harder than he would otherwise think it worth while to do; and what is possible in the case of any one worker is possible in the case of the aggregate of workers. And I think further that this result may be expected to occur, to a certain very limited extent, when any branch of industry is abnormally stimulated by high prices; since under these circumstances the energies of employers and employed are often strained to an unusual degree, and a certain margin of extra labour is likely to be called forth, which would not have been exerted except for the high rate of remuneration which it is mistakenly supposed to be worth. But this margin—even supposing it not to be counterbalanced by an equal or greater reduction of labour elsewhere—will generally be so small a part of the whole labour thus employed that it may for practical purposes be neglected; practically the over-production of certain commodities of which we have actual experience may be regarded as merely misdirected production or temporary disorganisation of production and exchange. Indeed we may lay down, that, owing to the defects in the actual organisation of industry, which result inevitably from the limited knowledge and imperfect mutual communication of its members, society is always in a condition of *under-production*; i.e. there is always a considerable amount of available labour unemployed, for which the actual conditions of industry would, with better management, afford remuneration sufficient to bring it into employment.

Still, however they may be caused, the extensive miscalculations of supply that produce the appearance of general over-production, tend equally to depress the remunerations of employers and employed in certain branches of industry below the normal rates, and to depreciate the capital, real and personal, that has been invested in them. Indeed, when the miscalculation has been great, it may even annihilate the value of large portions of such capital, if it is of a kind that cannot be turned to other uses without great loss.

§ 5. We have now to observe that such widespread over-production will often be accompanied by important fluctuations in the rate of interest, and therefore will produce effects on distribution beyond the range of the special branches of industry in which the miscalculation has taken place. This will be especially found to be the case if the over-production has been due to a widespread over-estimate of the profit to be obtained by new investments of capital—whether in the form of additional stocks of consumable goods, destined for new openings of trade, or in railways, ships, machines and other durable instruments. We have already noticed that the demand for new capital to be productively invested depends at any particular time not upon the actual productiveness of such capital, but upon the general estimate of what it will produce. There seems, indeed, no ground for supposing that this estimate tends, on the average and in the long run, to diverge decidedly from the facts in either direction. But experience shews that the general view of the possibilities of profitable employment of capital is liable to marked ebbs and flows. Sometimes there is a general disposition to overrate it, "times of confidence," in which the over-production of which we have been speaking takes place. At such times the employers who cause the over-production avail themselves largely of the capital of others; borrowing is extended, and an unusual number of joint-stock companies are formed; in consequence of which the rate of interest rises to an unusual height. Then when the miscalculation has become manifest, numerous bankruptcies and widespread depreciation of the new investments occur; really sound investments are affected by the ruin of the unsound; the general confidence is succeeded by general distrust; and the rate of interest falls again, not merely down to, but below, the normal rate.

In these fluctuations, the rate of discount or interest charged by bankers for the use of the medium of exchange commonly fluctuates more than the rate on investments generally, as the demand for loans made by bankers increases more in proportion than the demand—made mainly by joint-stock companies—for the capital of private investors. And if the transition from confidence to distrust is sudden and sharp, it is liable to cause a very violent fluctuation in the rate of discount; bankers refuse to make loans on conditions which they would ordinarily consider acceptable, partly through fear of the bankruptcy of the applicants, partly from the necessity of protecting themselves against the consequences of a similar distrust; and thus the extreme scarcity of *trustworthy* medium of exchange forces up the price of it to an abnormal height; money being everywhere wanted, not for enlargement of purchases, but for the payment of debts already incurred. At such times there will also be a rise in the rate of interest on invested capital generally, not from an increase in the total amount of interest received, but from a fall in the selling value of securities; which are extensively sold owing to the urgent need of ready money and the high price paid for the use of it. This latter change, of course, does not affect the real income of persons who continue to hold these securities; but it involves an accidental gain to all who are at the time investing, at the expense of those who find it needful to sell their investments.

Again, other causes besides miscalculation of prospective

profits on the part of employers of capital may produce a transient rise in interest. Thus the commencement—or merely the fear—of a drain of gold from banks, for the payment of a balance of debt on the trade of the country or some other cause, may lead bankers to raise the rate of interest, in order to bring back the gold or turn the balance the other way. Such a rise in the rate tends to have the desired effect in two ways: it tends to lower prices,—because it makes holders of commodities or securities prefer selling to borrowing money, and similarly diminishes the willingness to purchase—and thus encourages exportation and discourages importation; and secondly it increases the disposition of foreign creditors to allow the debts due to them to run on, in order to obtain the higher interest.

This leads me to notice another important class of variations in Distribution, that tends to accompany critical changes in the rate of interest charged by bankers; viz. those due to variations in the purchasing power of money. I have before explained how the price paid for the use of money and its general purchasing power tend, to a certain extent, and under certain circumstances, to rise and fall together,—though under other conditions they are more likely to vary in opposite directions—; and I have shown how this similarity of variation is especially marked at financial crises. Indeed in a country where the use of bankers' obligations as a medium of exchange is general, and where the dangerous resource of inconvertible notes is eschewed, the most rapid and impressive variations in the purchasing power of money are those due to the vicissitudes of the banking system; but the more durable, though slower, variations, caused by changes in the relation of the supply of bullion to the demand for it, also produce very material effects on the distribution of incomes. These effects are of a somewhat complex kind. It has been already observed that a rise in the purchasing power of money is advantageous to all creditors, including all annuity holders and all persons whose incomes are legally fixed, and disadvantageous to all debtors; but it should be noted that it is also at least temporarily advantageous to all persons whose rates of remuneration have a partial stability through the mixture of custom[1] and informal combination of

---

[1] It should be remembered that we are contemplating a society in which

which I have before spoken; that is, to large classes of labourers. For both reasons, therefore, it is disadvantageous to employers of capital, who are generally borrowers and at the same time employers of labour; and by thus discouraging industrial enterprise, is likely to injure indirectly some of the labourers whom its primary effect benefits. Similarly a fall in the purchasing power of money causes a sensible diffusion of good fortune among employers of capital and labour; the benefit of which is likely to be ultimately shared by the labourers whom they employ, though immediately these latter tend to lose through the comparative immobility of their money incomes; while all who are legally entitled to fixed money-payments lose, of course, without compensation.

§ 6. In considering changes in the purchasing power of money, it is important to observe that such changes are only gradually transmitted, and with unequal rapidity from one part of the country to another; and also that in the same district some industries are slower in feeling their effects than others. Such inequalities are obviously due to differences in the nature and extent of the traffic carried on, directly or indirectly, between the districts in which money is produced—or the emporia of foreign trade through which it is obtained from abroad—and other parts of the country. But in order to understand these differences thoroughly, it will be convenient to take a view of the variations that tend to be found normally both in the prices of particular commodities, and in the general purchasing power of money, as we pass from district to district. These variations are due primarily to the localization of different branches of production (including exchange) in different places; which is itself traceable to a combination, sometimes rather intricate, of physical and historical causes. The most obvious of such causes are the natural economic advantages which some parts of the earth's surface offer for certain industries: thus minerals will evidently tend to be produced where they are most abundant and most easily extracted, and agricultural products where soil and climate are most favourable: large centres of trade will be formed near the mouth of navigable rivers, and manufactures

Custom pure and simple is supposed not to interfere materially with the action of Competition.

will flourish where the raw or auxiliary materials employed in them are easily obtainable. But, in any explanation of the actual distribution of industries in the complex group of communities now more or less united by trade into one industrial system, a large place must be given to the influence of differences of race, social condition, and political circumstances among the persons inhabiting different localities. It would take us too far afield to analyse these historical conditions: what we are rather concerned to observe is that when once an industry has been successfully established in any place, through whatever combination of causes, there is a certain economic *vis inertiæ* tending to maintain it there;—and to increase it in extent, if the increase of population and wealth raises the demand for its products within a given area, or if improvements in communication enlarge the area which can be profitably supplied from one centre. This *vis inertiæ* may be analysed into several elements, variously combined in different cases. Partly, a manufacturer who started elsewhere would have more difficulty in obtaining a market for his commodities, from the established reputation attaching to the locality in question: (e.g.) equally good hardware made at Halifax would not command the price of Sheffield hardware. Partly, again, he would have more difficulty in obtaining the requisite skilled labour: while further, especially in departments of industry in which the subdivision of employments has been carried to great lengths, any one branch of production tends gradually to have collected in its neighbourhood auxiliary and connected, but separately organised, industries; so that a producer by settling in this neighbourhood has superior facilities for obtaining the materials or instruments he requires.

Through this combination, then, of physical and historical conditions it comes to pass that the main part of the demand of a region often very large, for commodities of a certain quality, tends to be supplied from a district or districts, the extent of which is but small—sometimes insignificant—in comparison with the whole area[1]. And, to meet the expense of carriage,

[1] Where,—as is mostly the case in industries other than agriculture,—this development of trade leads to the close aggregation of a large number of labourers, the resulting inequality in the distribution of population is increased

the money-price paid by consumers for such commodities tends to increase, roughly speaking[1], in proportion to the distance that separates the consumer from the centre of diffusion. But it is to be observed that the real exchange-value of the commodities may vary somewhat differently from the money-price; since money itself tends to have somewhat different values in different districts. For instance, in a country which obtains its coin and bullion from abroad, the purchasing power of money will tend to be appreciably higher in districts unfavourably situated for exchanging commodities, directly or indirectly, with the emporia of foreign trade;—that is, districts between which and the places with which they trade the cost of carriage is high, while there is no such keen demand for their products outside as would enable them to throw the greater part of this cost on their customers. The theoretical maximum of possible difference between the exchange values of money in any two districts compared is constituted, as we have seen, by the cost of carrying money one way and some kind of goods the other way; but in an advanced industrial community with a fully developed banking system, the cost of carrying money itself is comparatively insignificant, at least in comparing districts not very remote, and we have mainly to consider the cost of carrying goods. This cost and the resultant differences will of course vary with the facilities, natural and artificial, for transport; hence prices may be more nearly equalised at comparatively remote places in the neighbourhood of a coast or a railway, than at places comparatively near each other, but connected only by indifferent roads.

Further, it is to be observed that local variations of prices will be more marked in the case of commodities that are either heavy in proportion to their value, or liable to injury during transport, than in the case of lighter and more durable or more safely portable articles. And since in these various ways the differences in the exchange value of money, as between any two

by the further aggregation of retail traders and artisans to supply consumable commodities to the other aggregate.

[1] The interest that manufactures and traders generally have in extending their business, induces them sometimes to take a part—or even the whole—of this cost on themselves, in transmitting their products to distant consumers.

districts compared, will tend to be different in relation to different commodities; it may easily happen that the practical purchasing power of money will have different local variations for different classes of incomes. Thus an unskilled labourer's money wages may go further in a remote rural district, owing to the cheapness of the food, fuel and house-room which they are chiefly spent in providing; while to a professional man living in the same place the gain in this way may be more than outweighed by the increased cost of certain luxuries.

All these differences have to be taken into account in considering the normal effects of industrial competition; since, as we have seen,—quite apart from any obstacles to the mobility of labour—this does not necessarily tend to equalize money-wages, but only to get rid of any considerable and generally recognized differences in the net advantages obtainable, on the average, by equally efficient and industrious labourers in the same industrial grade.

§ 7. The tendency to such equalization, however, is—as we have already noticed—still further limited by the existence of obstacles that impede the migration of labourers. These obstacles would still exist to a certain extent, even if the influence of mere inertia and easily removable ignorance, as well as the more definite hindrances to migration that have sometimes been interposed by law, and the barriers against intrusion sometimes raised by combinations of labourers[1], were altogether eliminated. There would always be a certain expense, trouble, and loss of time involved in transporting an individual—and still more a family—to a distant place; there would generally be a loss of indefinite advantages derivable from the kindly regard of neighbours, and a loss of useful knowledge of the special conditions of industrial and social life in a given locality—which would be greater if the change involved the learning of new modes of work; and there might still be a general aversion to leaving familiar scenes and breaking social relations. If, however, we suppose the distribution of industries and industrial

---

[1] It should be observed that in other ways Trades' Unions tend to aid the mobility of labour from place to place; by developing habits of concerted action among labourers, elevating the average level of their intelligence, collecting and diffusing information as to rates of wages in different localities, &c.

population to remain without material change for a considerable time, these obstacles alone could hardly hold permanently in check the forces tending to equalization, at least within a modern country; since the influences above-mentioned would not commonly affect strongly more than a part of the population of any district; and the prospect of higher wages elsewhere would continually attract the more migratory element—e.g. young unmarried or newly married persons of an enterprising turn of mind[1]. Even if the change involved expatriation and the learning of a new language, I do not think the obstacles—apart from inertia and ignorance—would be sufficient to maintain a recognized difference of wages for similar labour, between any two countries sharing the civilization of modern Europe.

Such obstacles to migration affect the more highly-paid labourers, including the employers of labour and capital, in a less degree than others; and, though the greater part of capital already invested is, at best, far less mobile than labour, still, in an industrially advanced country, where wealth grows rapidly, floating capital tends to flow rapidly and in large volume into localities specially favourable for production. Hence, supposing no material change to take place in the local distribution of industries, the net advantages generally believed to be obtainable by the employment of equal amounts of new capital in different localities would before long be roughly equalized. This equalization would not, of course, extend to rent, or to any extra profit analogous to rent accruing on capital partially exempted by circumstances from competition. Such extra yields tend rather to become more unequal, as the concentration of labour and capital in certain places becomes more intense through the growth of population and the specialisation of industries.

We may conclude, in short, that under the influence of industrial competition, the special economic advantages attached to

[1] It is assumed in this argument that the average personal efficiency of labourers in the same industry is the same in different localities. The tendency to equalization is impeded, so far as the average efficiency in different places is different, even if the difference be such as is likely to be gradually removed by migration. An important case of this kind is the low average efficiency of labour in certain places which results from the very lowness of its remuneration causing an inadequate supply of the necessaries of healthy life.

different localities, supposing them to remain substantially unaltered, would ultimately express themselves in the distribution of industrial incomes mainly in the form of rent or some extra yield similar to rent. But in fact such local advantages are continually undergoing changes so rapid and extensive, as to balance—or more than balance—during a considerable period, the equalizing forces of industrial competition. Sometimes the extension of an industry already established in a certain district is so rapid, owing to the extension of the demand through improvements either in processes of manufacture or means of communication with other districts, or perhaps to a rise in demand in consequence of a change of social habits or industrial needs, that, in spite of the continual increase in the supply of labour and capital employed in the industry, the remuneration of both labourers and employers continues for many years to remain at a scarcity height. Sometimes again, the extension of our knowledge of localized natural resources, or the discovery of new means of obtaining or using materials already known, may alter importantly the relative advantages of different districts for a certain kind of production, so that large new centres of industry may be rapidly formed in new districts, and old ones deserted. The development of the cotton manufacture in Lancashire after the inventions of Arkwright and Watt is an instance of the former kind of change; the discoveries of new valuable mines most strikingly illustrate the latter.

The effects of such changes on other inhabitants of the districts in which they occur are complex, and vary somewhat according to the precise nature of the change and the conditions of the industry primarily affected. If these latter are such that an additional amount of produce cannot be obtained except at a higher cost, a rise in demand or improvement in communication that leads to a larger sale of the produce in question outside the district must *ceteris paribus*, through the consequent rise in price, inflict loss on all consumers—as such—within the district. In the case of the products of manufactures—as distinct from those of agriculture and mining—this result is not likely to occur, except very transiently; here, as we have before seen, increased production generally leads to greater cheapness. And in all cases, the flow of labour and capital to a district where a manufacturing or mining industry is growing tends to bring gain to other industries of the same district by increasing the local market for their products :—in particular, the development of a manufacture in a town, increasing its population and demand for food, tends to benefit the agricultural producers in the surrounding country. The same process of development, however, is likely to be accompanied with a general rise in the remuneration of labour throughout the district: hence so far as the products thus locally raised in demand are easily transportable, the producers in the district are likely to be closely pressed by the competition of similar producers outside, and consequently to withdraw their capital to other departments of production in which their local advantages are less easy to dispute. In this way the successful establishment of any one great centre of industry in any district has a tendency to promote indirectly the concentration of other industries in other localities.

On the other hand, when one kind of production—say the production of hardware—develops in one district (A) through an increased sale of its products in another district (B), this development is likely to be accompanied by a decline in the production of hardware or some similar product in B or elsewhere. Such a change will, in all ordinary cases, be ultimately a gain on the whole to the larger region including the two districts; since the labour that would otherwise have produced hardware may be employed more advantageously in some other way. But it should be observed that there is no general reason for assuming that this new remunerative employment will be found within the limits of the district—say B—in which the production of hardware has been superseded: especially if the labour thus dispensed with is a considerable part of the whole labour of B. This point is not of great importance so long as A and B are within the same country; but when, in the next book, we come to consider the arguments for perfect freedom of trade between different countries, we shall have to take note of the displacements of labour that, under certain circumstances, tend to accompany the development of such trade.

§ 8. The consideration of the local and transient variations, with which this chapter is primarily concerned, naturally leads us on to inquire how far tendencies of change operating uniformly or mainly in one direction, and therefore more permanent in their effects, are discernible in the past history and present condition of industry;—how far, in short, the future economic history of our existing societies can be inferred from the experience already gained of their laws of development. This inquiry is a most fascinating one; but it does not seem to me capable of being instructively treated in any detail, according to the method adopted in the present Book;—i.e. as a problem of economic science as distinguished from general sociology. And indeed any general forecast of future economic changes, attained by any method claiming to be scientific, must, I conceive, be vague and conjectural, except so far as it is avowedly hypothetical. Hypothetical changes in production and distribution—the hypothesis being that some one of the important factors in causing the present state of things undergoes a change while the others remain stationary—are not difficult to work out: indeed I have already found it convenient to indicate such hypothetical results to some extent in previous chapters, in order to make clear my view of the economic forces whose combined operation maintains the actual distribution of produce. But any positive prophecy of the industrial future of civilized society—involving, as it must, a forecast of the probable changes, in kind or amount, of all the important factors—is indefinitely more difficult. Any such prophecy must either be in a narrow sense empirical, and therefore only useful in relation to a very limited period of the proximate future, or else, if it ventures to look further ahead, it must content itself with giving very vague and dubious answers to the questions of most interest. Still it seems desirable to attempt briefly such a vague and general forecast of economic changes as seems to me possible, without going beyond the limits that I have marked out for myself in the present treatise[1].

But in order to attain even such guarded conclusions, we must begin by making certain assumptions. We must assume that the present individualistic order of society—the *régime* of

[1] Especially since Mill has treated this part of the subject at some length in his IVth book, in a confidently dogmatic manner which I am unable to imitate.

private property and free contract—is to be maintained without any fundamental change: and we must also assume the continuance and increasing diffusion of the progressive civilization which now unites into one organic whole the inhabitants of Europe and of the countries colonized therefrom. On the basis of this latter assumption we may lay down generally that population will increase in the aggregate of countries that will share this civilization, and with it accumulated wealth, and that the arts of industry will improve: though we cannot say what will be the relative proportion of these different kinds of growth—nor can we, of course, affirm that population and wealth will increase in every part of the civilized world. Assuming improvement in the arts of industry, we may state it as probable that any given utility will be attained hereafter by a diminished expenditure of "labour and capital"—that is, labour, and delay interposed between the application of the labour and the enjoyment of the utility at which it aims—: except so far as (1) the consumption without replacement of the "unearned" gifts of nature, or (2) the diminished ratio borne by these natural bounties to the needs of the increasing population, renders it needful to use *more* labour and capital to obtain an equal *quantum* of utility. We may expect therefore that, generally speaking, commodities that are now made by complicated processes of manufacture will fall in value relatively to most products of mining and agriculture: but whether any particular class of human needs or desires is likely to be satisfied hereafter with more or less outlay of labour and capital than it is at present, cannot, I think, be clearly foreseen. *Primâ facie* the operation of the causes that tend to increase cost would seem to be most marked in the case of the products of extractive industry:—since the supply of any particular metal, from any given district where mining flourishes, is continually being consumed without replacement; and after a certain amount has been extracted, any further supply from the same district tends to be obtained at a continually increasing cost. On the other hand this tendency is counteracted by the discovery of new sources and new developments of the arts of mining: and I do not think that we have any means of deciding which of these conflicting forces is likely to be strongest—so far as the general effect on the civilized world is concerned[1]—within any period which it is worth while to consider.

An exception must perhaps be admitted in the case of gold: since, owing to the eagerness with which gold has been sought, and the comparative ease with which it has been extracted from the alluvial deposits that have furnished the largest part of the supply hitherto obtained, it is reasonable to suppose that this source of supply is by this time to a great extent exhausted over a great part of the civilized world. It seems therefore probable that before very long our supplies of gold will be chiefly obtained by the hitherto more costly and difficult process of vein-mining: and that in consequence the value of gold will rise very materially unless some great change, such as we have at present no ground for anticipating, should take place in the demand for the metal. But even this probability is, I conceive, at present too remote and uncertain to have strong claims on the attention of practical men.

The condition of agriculture in a new country is often to some extent similar to that of mining: so far as tillage is applied to naturally fertile lands whose fertility is gradually exhausted by the comparatively unlaborious methods of cultivation, which are also the most economical methods so long as land is plentiful and cheap. But this state of things passes away as the country gets filled: and at any rate after a certain density of population has been reached, the agricultural processes that are on the whole most economical are such as continually maintain the productiveness of the land cultivated: so that henceforth, apart from growth of population, there would be no important[2] reason for anticipating a future increase

---

[1] Somewhat more definite probabilities are doubtless obtainable as regards the prospects of mining in any particular country in which mines have long been worked: but even these must involve a large element of uncertainty. In the case of England special attention has been given to the prospects of coal mining with which the future of the great iron industries of the country at present seems to be bound up. The question was examined by a Royal Commission who arrived at the conclusion that the available coal in England may be expected to be exhausted in three or four hundred years, supposing the consumption of coal to increase in the future at a rate simply inferred from its past increase. But this supposition requires us to assume an increase of population which must be regarded as highly problematical.

[2] We should have, no doubt, to look forward to the exhaustion of certain

in the cost of obtaining agricultural produce. Supposing, however, that there is to be a growth of population in the world at large similar to that which has already taken place in the countries most industrially advanced, what I have called the "final" cost of obtaining the agricultural produce required for this population—i.e. the cost of the costliest portion needed to meet the demand—must some time or other be materially increased, unless an entirely novel development should take place in the art of agriculture. We may infer this by considering what would take place if England and the most advanced parts of Western Europe were now cut off from trade with the rest of the world: there can be no doubt that the price of agricultural produce would be materially raised in consequence of the more than proportional outlay of labour and capital which would be required to produce the additional amount of such produce that even the existing population would need. More land would be wanted and more expensive processes would be applied to the land now under cultivation: the price and rent of land would rise in consequence, and all members of the community except landowners would suffer proportionally as consumers. And a result similar to this must be anticipated hereafter for the civilized world, unless population is checked—or the arts of agriculture improved—in a manner which the experience of modern civilization gives us no positive reason to anticipate.

So far, I think, the Ricardian doctrine as to the tendency of agricultural rent to increase as society progresses must be admitted to be true. But this ultimate result is as yet very distant—far beyond the limits of any practical forecast. And we have no reason to expect that there will be anything like a steady rise in the price of agricultural produce, or in the price and rent of agricultural land throughout the civilized world, during the interval of time that we have to pass through before we reach this ultimate result. For a long time to come the pressure of increasing population may easily be more than counterbalanced by improvements in agriculture and trade. And, as regards increase of rent in particular, it is not impro-

supplies of manure—such as guano—but this is a kind of loss which we may fairly hope to see reduced to insignificance by improvement in the arts.

bable that agricultural improvement in the future may partly take the direction either of diminishing the natural differences in the productiveness of different kinds of land similarly cultivated, or of diminishing the differences in their economical value by a more careful utilization of their special adaptation to different kinds of cultivation[1]. If this should take place to any great extent, then, until all the land susceptible of this equalizing process has been brought under its influence, the progress of population, trade, and agriculture combined is likely to cause fluctuations incapable of being now foreseen in the rent of agricultural land; rather than the steady increase which Ricardo regards as inevitable, in the price paid "for the use "of its original and indestructible powers."

I do not, however, think that there are any corresponding reasons for doubting that the differential value of building land in towns will continue to increase steadily as civilization progresses. It is indeed possible that the growth of towns may be a less prominent feature of the development of civilization in the future than it has been in the past: but I know no positive grounds for anticipating this. And if the proportion of urban to rural population increases steadily, as a country becomes more thickly inhabited by a civilized population, it is scarcely conceivable that the proportion of the whole produce, obtained by the owners of land in or near towns, should not increase *pari passu*.

Turning from rent to interest, we again find hypothetical prediction easy, but positive forecast difficult. It is obvious in the first place that a rise in rent due to the cause just discussed,—if not compensated by improvements in other departments of industry, rendering labour and capital *on the whole* not less productive than before—must tend to be accompanied by a fall in the real returns to capital, as well as in the real remune-

---

[1] Mr Simon W. Patten (*Premises of Political Economy*, ch. vi. p. 173) argues that this is even now, to an important extent, the tendency of agricultural improvement. "The progress of civilization causes much of the poor land "to become good, not only through the increased use of capital and skill, but "also through the gradual change in the demand for food, allowing those crops "to be raised for which the land is best fitted. There are two opposing tenden-"cies, the one causing inferior land to be cultivated, the other changing the "inferior lands into good lands."

ration of labour. Putting this consideration on one side—i.e. assuming for simplicity that industrial improvement just balances the tendency of increased population to increase the "final" cost of agricultural produce—the prospect of a rise or fall in interest depends on the probable future proportion between (1) the increase of saving and (2) the increase in the industrial and other demands for capital. Neither (1) nor (2) can be predicted with any confidence: but I should conjecture that the impulses that prompt to accumulation are, on the whole, likely to grow stronger in average men, as civilization progresses: for though the development of culture may make some persons spend their time in artistic or scientific pursuits who would otherwise have been absorbed in money-making, I think that the diminution in accumulation due to this cause is likely to be more than compensated by the general increase in men's concern for the future. I think therefore that,—if the individualistic organization of society remains substantially unaltered—the proportion of capital to population is *ceteris paribus* likely to increase. Is then the increase in the demand for capital likely to balance this increase in supply? On the whole it seems to me most'probable that this will not be the case; for the non-industrial demand for the savings of individuals—chiefly for warlike purposes—which so markedly characterizes the century that has just elapsed, can hardly be regarded as likely to be a normal incident of the preponderantly industrial period of civilized history which seems to lie before us: and though hitherto, no doubt, industrial improvement has been accompanied by an increase on the whole in the industrial demand for capital, I do not see—as I have before said[1]—why this should always be the case. Some recent inventions have tended importantly to diminish the demand for capital:—e.g. the use of the telegraph by traders has tended to reduce the amount of goods that it is necessary to keep in stock, for the most economical performance of the functions of trade:—and it seems quite within the limits of probability that the inventions of the future may have this effect to a greater extent. On the whole, therefore, I should be disposed to conjecture that this demand for capital will not increase so as to balance the increase

[1] p. 152.

in supply, and that therefore the rate of interest will slowly decline. I should expect the decline to be slow, owing to the check that the fall will give to accumulation: but I see no reason for placing a definite limit to it: I do not see why it should not go on till the interest on capital not employed by its owner does not amount to more than a fair insurance against risk, so that the desire of obtaining interest ceases to be an important motive for accumulation:—though there is no reason to think that this limit will be reached until after a very long interval.

In speaking of rent and interest I have by implication said all that seems to be necessary on the prospects of increase or decrease in the average remuneration of labourers taken in the aggregate. Nor is there much that could profitably be said—even in the most conjectural way—as to the probable distribution of the aggregate remuneration of labour among different classes of labourers in the industrial community of the future, without going clearly beyond the limits of the method adopted in the present Book. For I conjecture that a very important factor in the distribution of the future will be Monopoly formed by Combination, of varying degrees of completeness: and that accordingly the case noticed at the close of the last chapter—in which Combination meets Combination and determines the division of gain and loss otherwise than competitively—is likely to be a common case. Who precisely will combine with whom, or against whom, it would be rash to predict: nor (as we have seen) does Economic Science enable us to determine the principles on which the opposing combinations will settle their disputes:—though it may give some instruction as to the application of any principle that may be accepted for this purpose[1].

[1] See ch. vii. § 7 of the next Book.

CHAPTER XII.

CUSTOM.

§ 1. IN the preceding chapters we have been chiefly endeavouring to ascertain the general way in which the exchange values of material products and the remuneration of different classes concerned in industry would be determined in a society, whose members enjoy perfect freedom of contract and freedom in the choice of domicile and calling, and further possess the characteristic of always seeking to obtain for the commodity that they exchange the largest real return that they know to be obtainable—taking all kinds of gain and loss into account. It is only in respect of the assumed universal presence of this characteristic, not in the absence of any ordinary human impulses compatible with this, that the ideal individual to whom our economic deductions directly relate—the "economic man" as he has been called—should be conceived to differ from an ordinary member of a modern civilized community. That such a difference exists, to a not unimportant extent, has been incidentally noticed several times in the preceding chapters; but it seems desirable, before concluding this part of the treatise, to analyse its causes rather more fully than has yet been done.

The main part of these causes is, by many writers on Political Economy, designated broadly under the general term Custom. Mill, indeed, goes so far as to say that "under the "rule of individual property, the division of the produce is the "result of two determining agencies, Competition and Custom."

And if we leave Combination[1] and Governmental interference out of account, and take Custom in a comprehensive sense, the assertion is approximately true: but it is important to distinguish the very different motives and economic forces whose operation is thus summed up, in order to ascertain clearly how far they can properly be said to conflict with Competition.

In the first place the word Custom is commonly used to designate two quite distinct tendencies of human nature: the tendency to do what one has done before and the tendency to do as others do. Both these tendencies equally operate to prevent that continual modification of action in order to adapt it to the continual change of men's circumstances and opportunities, which is required to realize completely the greatest possible economy in production, and the scheme of distribution that economic science contemplates. Men continually get less for their money, goods or services, because they exchange them not in the best market but in the market they have been used to frequent; and they continually produce less than they might do by a given amount of labour, because they follow not the best methods that have been invented and published but the methods followed by their neighbours. At the same time each impulse has economic effects of very different kinds and blends with and is sustained by very various motives.

To obtain a clear view of these it will be well to denominate each of these tendencies separately. For convenience' sake we will speak of the former as Habit, and reserve the term Custom to the latter (though by the usage of language it is equally applicable to the former).

I will begin by noticing the obvious fact that both Custom and Habit, though they often interfere with an alert and vigilant pursuit of amelioration, are also to a great extent economically useful in saving time and labour. By doing what he has done before, or what others do, a man avoids the necessity of deciding anew on each occasion, where the advantage that can be gained by the best decision is not worth the time and trouble spent in making it. Hence the Goodwill of a business would remain a

---

[1] As I have before observed, Combination, though opposed to Competition as the term is ordinarily used, is not excluded by the fundamental assumptions of the theory of Competitive distribution.

valuable possession, however intelligently all purchasers aimed at the maximum of economic gain in their purchases; especially if we add to the advantage of trouble saved, the further advantage which the purchaser of any commodity obtains through fixed habits of dealing, in a general disposition of the seller with whom he deals to oblige him.

Next, in explaining the obstacles which Habit continually presents to the adoption of economic improvements, we must distinguish between the mere blind adhesion to an accustomed routine, and such rational aversion to the expenditure of labour and waste of acquired dexterity involved in learning new processes as would be felt by the most perfectly 'economic' man.

Further, so far as the breach of habit involved in a change of work or residence causes actual discomfort, it is possible that, on the strictest calculations of self-interest, this drawback may outweigh the pecuniary gain that would result from the adoption of the proposed change. The ties of mere association formed by a man's previous life, no less than the ties of social or patriotic affections, constitute an economic force operating to keep a man where he is, the action of which is in no way excluded by the fundamental assumptions on which the theory of competitive distribution proceeds.

Finally, it should be observed that a man's habits of dealing are frequently sustained, even when they have become economically disadvantageous to him, through his sympathy with the expectations that they have excited in the minds of others, and the disappointment that would be produced if they were discontinued. For the tendency to do what one has hitherto done has its counterpart in the tendency to expect to be treated as one has hitherto been treated: and the breach of such expectations, if the loss caused by it is considerable, is often felt to be a hardship, if not exactly an injustice, even in cases where no legal claim could be based upon them; so that moral and sympathetic motives co-operate in preventing such a breach. Perhaps the most conspicuous effect of these mingled motives is seen in the case of domestic servants; men continually endure a moderate, and not rarely a large, amount of incompetence in an old servant rather than inflict the hardship of dismissal; and that even when they do not feel any special affection for the person thus benefited.

§ 2. In the cases just mentioned the grievance is much greater, and the motives preventing divergence much stronger, when the *habitual* conduct has been also *customary*—in the sense in which I have distinguished this term from 'habitual.' Customs thus operating vary indefinitely in usage and duration: for instance, English landlords have often allowed their farms to be let at rents below the market rate, merely because their ancestors—perhaps only their fathers—did so before them. More widely-extended customs are often regarded as morally binding even where they do not carry with them any legal obligation. It is thought to be inequitable to refuse to pay a man what persons of his class usually receive for a given service, or by taking advantage of special circumstances, to make him pay more than is ordinarily paid for any service that he receives. Indeed when a man speaks of "fair wages" for his work he often seems to mean no more than customary wages; and when he complains of being charged "extortionate" prices, he can only defend the epithet by an appeal to custom. How far such an appeal is founded on reason, we will hereafter consider: here we need only observe that even in the most economically advanced of existing communities, material divergences from purely competitive distribution are to be referred to Custom conscious or unconsciously determining notions of equity: while in other ages and countries the influence of this principle has predominated so much over that of Competition, as sometimes to reduce the operation of the latter within very narrow limits.

It is to be observed, however, that customs determining remuneration may be effective without assuming the dignity of moral rules. For instance the customary payment of fees for certain professional services—such as those of physicians and solicitors—is not, I think, supported by any general sense that the sums paid are just what the services in question are fairly worth. Rather, as I have already suggested, the effect of custom in such cases, at least in the existing condition of such a society as our own, blends with that of tacit combination, e.g. the fact that it is customary to pay a physician a guinea for his professional advice tends to produce a general acquiescence in the charge, which it is the interest of physicians generally to maintain and which it might not be quite so easy to gain for a revised tariff of fees; and therefore unless physicians as a body form a decided opinion that their average earnings would be increased by a different charge, the existing custom is not likely to be disturbed. Still if it appeared to be clearly the interest of physicians as a class to raise or lower the customary fee, it can hardly be doubted that the union of the profession is sufficiently strong to impose such a change both on the public and on any recalcitrant members of their own body. We may say therefore that the existing fee is determined by custom, but under the condition of not differing materially from what would be determined by express combination.

Again, there are certain customs of expenditure which, without being morally obligatory, are yet supported by effective social sanctions; so that the breach of them is either certain or likely to be a bar to employment, or at any rate to success, in certain callings, or otherwise to entail pecuniary loss. The obligations thence arising are in part strictly professional—such, e.g. as the necessity of wearing a certain dress; partly, again, they are attached to the social grade from which the class of labourers in question is chiefly taken; thus a clerk would incur disfavour by wearing the dress of a mechanic; a physician would not succeed who did not appear to live in a style above that of an ordinary clerk; it is even considered a part of the duty of certain highly paid officials to give costly entertainments. So far as such customary expenditure is generally felt to be burdensome, it should not be regarded as a part of the spender's consumption, economically speaking; but rather as a part of the cost of production of his services, which will therefore tend to be returned to him in the remuneration received for them. If, however, the custom corresponds to—and is, in fact sustained by—the general tastes and inclinations of persons of the social grade from which the labourers in question are chiefly drawn, it will only tend to raise the wages of such labourers so far as it constitutes an additional obstacle to the competition of aspirants from the grade below.

In some cases, again, the neglect of received customs of expenditure would hardly either prevent a man from obtaining work of a particular kind, or detract from its pecuniary emoluments; it would merely diminish his share of the social consideration that commonly attaches to these functions. This leads us to notice that the actual allotment of social rank to different callings itself depends to a great extent on the stability of custom; being often materially different from the allotment that might be expected to result from an intelligent consideration of the importance of different social functions, or of the qualities required for their efficient performance. At the same time this influence of custom, however irrational it may seem, is yet a motive force which an intelligent pursuer of private interest cannot disregard. For even if such a person were so exceptionally constituted as to derive no immediate satisfaction from social consideration, he could hardly fail to find it useful indirectly in various ways.

§ 3. It thus appears that only a part of the great and varied influence of custom can be regarded as a force opposed to competition and which the fuller development of the latter must necessarily diminish. So far as the maintenance of fixed habits of dealing, and rates of remuneration not frequently changed, leads to economy of time and labour, the development of competition has of course no tendency to modify it. So far, again, as custom determines the social consideration attaching to certain kinds of work, or imposes certain modes of outlay as a condition of obtaining such consideration, its effects should, I conceive, be treated merely as a part of the pre-existing social circumstances in which the laws of competitive distribution are supposed to operate. Customs in this latter sense may be altered, indeed are continually being altered to some extent, by the progress of civilization; but the mere development, intensive and extensive, of the intelligent pursuit of private interest has not in itself any tendency to alter them. Nor, again, can we say that such development will necessarily tend to obliterate the effect of customs that fix the money-price of services, so far as they are really supported by a veiled or tacit combination of the persons to whom they are profitable; though it will probably tend to strip off the veil and render the combination open and avowed.

There remain two important and fundamentally different

ways in which he influences of custom and habit undoubtedly counteract, to some extent, the force of competition. Firstly, so far as the mere tendency to follow use and wont operates blindly, without consideration of the consequent gain and loss, its force combines with that of simple inertia and carelessness in diminishing—or, still more often, retarding—the changes in wages or prices corresponding to changes in the conditions of industry, which competition tends to bring about[1]. Secondly, so far as men's sense of Justice or Fairness is consciously or unconsciously determined by Custom, its influence may be considered as a part of the aggregate effect of moral or quasi-moral sentiments in modifying the competitive distribution of produce. Besides the sense of Justice—which, be it observed, has sometimes acted powerfully in a direction opposed to use and wont— we may note Patriotism, Philanthropy, Pity, Friendship, Religion and other forms of devotion to an ideal, as emotional forces that come in various ways into conflict with the desire of private gain. So far, indeed, as such motives merely induce men to devote income or time and energy to other purposes than those of private enjoyment, their effects need not be included among the phenomena with which economic science is concerned:—thus almsgiving of all kinds, and other donations to individuals or public objects, may be considered as constituting a secondary redistribution of wealth, valuable as supplementing the defects and mitigating the rigours of the primary competitive distribution, but not requiring to be taken into account in economic reasonings, except in special cases in which it influences the primary distribution. And doubtless moral sentiments and ideal aims do actually exercise this kind of influence in certain cases: a certain amount of the labour from which men obtain their livelihood is performed for remuneration less than might be earned in some work no more fatiguing or disagreeable, from a deliberate postponement of the labourer's pecuniary interests to other aims. I do not, however, think that the effects of these elevated sentiments in modifying the action

[1] It is solely to this diminution and retardation of the effects of competition by the mere *vis inertiæ* of custom that I should be disposed to apply the metaphorical term "friction"; which some economists have used more vaguely and widely.

of economic forces are of fundamental importance in modern societies as they actually exist: and to investigate systematically the probability of their becoming more important hereafter, would carry us beyond the scope of the present treatise into a study of the general history of society. It appears to me, therefore, that what I have to say on the actual relations of Morality and Political Economy will be most conveniently said in connexion with the discussion, to which we are now to proceed, on the principles which *ought* to regulate the economic intervention of Government.

BOOK III.

CHAPTER I.

THE ART OF POLITICAL ECONOMY.

IN this third book of my treatise I propose to discuss briefly the principles of Political Economy considered as an Art, or department of the general Theory of Practice. It has been already observed[1], in the introductory portion of this work, that the "principles of Political Economy" are still most commonly understood, even in England, and in spite of many protests to the contrary, to be *practical* principles—rules of conduct public or private. This being so, it seems to me that confusion of thought on the subject is likely to be most effectually prevented, not by confining the Theory of Political Economy to economic *science* in the strictest sense—the study, whether by a positive or a hypothetical treatment, of the actually existing production and distribution of valuable commodities—but by marking and maintaining as clearly as possible the distinction between the points of view of the Science and the Art respectively, and the methods of reasoning appropriate to each.

How then shall we define the scope of Political Economy considered as an Art?

If we follow the indications of language, it would seem to be a branch or application of a more general art called 'Economy' without qualification. Another branch of this more comprehensive art is commonly recognised as "Domestic Economy" or "economy in household matters." Here the object with which the economist is concerned is wealth or money; but we equally speak of "economizing" time (or labour

[1] Introduction, c. II. § 1.

measured by time), economizing mechanical force, &c., &c. Comparing these different uses, we may define 'Economy' generally as the art or method of attaining the greatest possible amount of some desirable result for a given cost, or a given result for the least possible cost; 'cost' being of two kinds, either (1) the endurance of pain, discomfort, or something else undesirable, or (2) the sacrifice of something desirable, either as an end or a means[1].

The Art of Political Economy, then, would seem to be Economy applied to the attainment of some desirable result not for an individual but for a political community (or aggregate of such communities.)

So far we may hope to avoid controversy. But when we go on to ask what the desirable result is which Political Economy seeks to realise, we find the question less easy to answer. It has already been noticed[2] that Adam Smith and his earlier successors, so far as they treated Political Economy as an Art, conceived its end to be that the national *production* of wealth should be as great as possible; and hardly appear to have entertained the notion of aiming at the best possible Distribution. But this limitation of view is not in accordance with the ordinary use of the wider term 'economy.' The idea of an economic *expenditure* of wealth, of which the aim is to make a given amount of wealth as useful as possible, is even more familiar than that of economic *production* of wealth: in fact Domestic Economy, as ordinarily understood, is simply the Art or Faculty of "making wealth go as far as "possible." And it seems most in harmony with the received division of economic science, adopted in the present treatise, to recognise at least a possible Art of Distribution, of which the aim is to apportion the produce among the members of the community so that the greatest amount of utility or satisfaction may be derived from it.

---

[1] I have before urged that labour is not necessarily to be regarded as something disagreeable; all that we can ihfer from the fact that any kind of labour has to be paid for is that some out of the whole number of persons required to furnish all the labour that society is prepared to purchase, *either* dislike this labour, *or* prefer some other kind of labour either for its own sake or for its results.

[2] Introduction, c. II. § 4.

It may be said that this latter inquiry takes us beyond the limits that properly separate Political Economy from the more comprehensive and more difficult art of general Politics; since it inevitably carries us into a region of investigation in which we can no longer use the comparatively exact measurements of economic science, but only those more vague and uncertain balancings of different quantities of happiness with which the politician has to content himself. But the discussions in Book I. on the definitions of wealth and value seemed to lead to the conclusion that the real exactness of economic as compared with ordinary political estimates is generally overrated. For it there appeared that, though we could measure all wealth at the same time and place by the ordinary standard of exchange value,—i.e. money,—still in comparing amounts of wealth at different times and places neither this nor any equally exact standard was available; and we were accordingly obliged to some extent to fall back on a necessarily more indefinite comparison of utilities. Since, then, even in the reasonings of economic science, an estimate of the utility of wealth is to some extent indispensable, no fundamental change of method is introduced by adopting this estimate more systematically in the present part of our investigation.

It may however be questioned whether, so far as we regulate the distribution of produce, we should do so on the principle that I have laid down as 'economic.' Many would urge that we ought to aim at realizing Justice or Equity in our distribution. Hence it seems desirable to examine the principles of Justice or Equity that have been proposed as supreme rules of distribution: and, so far as any such principles approve themselves on examination, to consider how far their application would concide with, and how far it would diverge from, the pursuit of the 'economic' ideal.

Meanwhile we may take the subject of Political Economy considered as an Art to include, besides the Theory of provision for governmental expenditure, (1) the Art of making the proportion of produce to population a maximum, taking generally as a measure the ordinary standard of exchange value, so far as it can be applied: and (2) the Art of rightly Distributing produce among members of the community, whether on any principle of Equity or Justice, or on the economic principle of making the whole produce as useful as possible.

Here, however, it may be asked, Whose conduct the Art is supposed to direct? and some further explanation on this point seems certainly to be required. First as regards Production —the term 'Art of Production' might be fairly understood to denote a systematic exposition of the rules, by conforming to which individuals engaged in industry may produce the maximum of commodity with the minimum of cost. But Political Economy is not usually supposed to include such an exposition; and it appears to me that it would be difficult to give any general instruction of this kind, if it is to be more than a collection of common-places, without entering more fully than would be convenient into the details of particular kinds of industry. At any rate I do not propose to attempt this in the present book; I shall follow tradition in treating as the main subject of Political Economy, regarded as an Art of Production, the action of Government for the improvement of the national production: but it seems desirable, for completeness, to include in our consideration the action of private persons for the same end, so far as it is not prompted by the ordinary motives of pecuniary self-interest or regulated on commercial principles. This extension of view is still more clearly called for in dealing with the Art of Distribution; where gratuitous labour and expenditure have, especially in modern times, largely supplemented the efforts of governments to mitigate the distressing inequalities in the distribution of produce, that are incidental to the existing competitive organisation of society.

Finally, I have to observe that, in defining the scope of the Art of Production, I have implied that the mere increase of population is not an end at which it aims. This is, I think, now the generally accepted view of political economists. A statesman, however, will generally desire, *ceteris paribus*, a large population for his country: and we shall find that some important kinds of governmental interference with industry—such as the regulation of land-tenure—have been partly advocated with a view to increase of population rather than of wealth. I propose therefore in one or two cases to consider the effects of governmental interference in relation to this end.

CHAPTER II.

THE SYSTEM OF NATURAL LIBERTY CONSIDERED IN RELATION TO PRODUCTION.

§ 1. ON the very threshold of the subject of enquiry defined in the preceding chapter we find ourselves confronted by the sweeping doctrine that the sole function of an ideal Government in relation to industry is simply to leave it alone. This view in some minds seems to be partly supported by a curious confusion of thought; the absence of governmental interference being assumed for simplicity's sake in the hypothetical reasonings, by which the values of products and services are deductively determined, is at the same time vaguely regarded as a conclusion established by such reasonings. Still when modern Political Economy—according to the common view of its commencement as a special science or study[1]—was founded by the "Physiocrats" in the middle of the last century, it was an essential part of its teaching that a statesman's business was not to make laws for industry, but merely to ascertain and protect from encroachment the simple, eternal and immutable laws of nature, under which the production would regulate itself in the best possible way, if Governments would abstain from meddling. And from this time forward, under the more enduring influence of Adam Smith, the accredited expositors of Political Economy—at least until the comparatively recent movement against Individualism in Germany—have commonly been advocates of *Laisser Faire*.

[1] See note at the end of the chapter.

Hence since this doctrine, so far as it is sound, is evidently the most important conclusion of Political Economy considered as an Art, it will be convenient to begin this department of our investigation by examining carefully the grounds on which it is advocated.

Throughout this examination it is desirable, for clearness' sake, to keep distinct the two points of view which we have taken separately in the two preceding books. For the proposition that what, after Adam Smith, I shall call "natural "liberty" tends to the most economic production of wealth, by no means necessarily implies the further proposition that it also tends to the most economic or equitable distribution of the aggregate produce. It was no doubt held by the Physiocrats that natural Liberty tends to realise Natural Justice: and the same view has been commonly maintained by the more thorough-going followers of Adam Smith[1] in France and Germany,—of whom Bastiat may be taken as a type—and has been frequently expressed or implied in the utterances of subordinate members of the "Manchester "School" in England. But I am not aware that it has been expressly affirmed by any leading economic writer in England from Ricardo downwards; and since the influence of J. S. Mill has been predominant, I do not think it has been the prevailing opinion even among the rank and file of the "orthodox" school of Political Economy. Many, at any rate, of those who in England have held most strongly that it is expedient for Government to interfere as little as possible with the distribution of wealth resulting from free competition, have not maintained this on the ground that the existing inequalities are satisfactory; but rather in the belief that any such interference must tend to impair aggregate production more than it could increase the utility of the produce by a better distribution.

It will be convenient therefore to commence with an examination of the arguments by which the system of Natural Liberty is justified in its relation to production. The following is a concise statement of the reasoning to this conclusion which is more or less definitely implied, and partly expressed, in

[1] For Adam Smith's own view, see Introduction, pp. 19, 20.

numberless passages of the works of Adam Smith and his successors.

Assuming as universal a fairly intelligent and alert pursuit of the interest of self and family, it is argued that wealth and other purchaseable commodities will be produced in the most economic way, if every member of society is left free to produce and transfer to others whatever utilities he can, on any terms that may be freely arranged.

For (1) the regard for self-interest on the part of consumers, will lead always to the effectual demand of the things that are most useful to society; and (2) regard for self-interest on the part of producers will lead to their production at the least cost. That is, firstly, if any material part of the ordinary supply of any commodity A were generally estimated as less useful for the satisfaction of social needs than the quantity of another commodity B that could be produced at the same cost, the demand of consumers would be diverted from A to B, so that A would fall in market-value and B rise; and this change in values would cause a diversion of the efforts of producers from A to B to the extent required. And, secondly, the self-interest of producers will tend to the production of everything at the least cost: for the self-interest of *entrepreneurs* will lead them to purchase services most cheaply, taking account of quality: and the self-interest of labourers—including its expansion, through parental affection, into *domestic interest*—will cause them to be trained to the performance of the best-paid, and therefore most useful, services for which they are, or are capable of becoming, adapted; so far as the cost of the training does not outweigh the increment of efficiency given by it. Any excess of labourers of any kind will be rapidly corrected by a fall in the demand for their services; and, in the same way, any deficiency will be rapidly made up. And the more keenly and persistently each individual — whether as consumer or as producer—pursues his private interest, the more certain will be the natural punishment of inertia or misdirected effort anywhere, and therefore the more completely will the adaptation of social labour to the satisfaction of social wants be attained. What has been said applies primarily to ordinary buying and selling; but it may obviously be extended to borrowing and lending, hiring and letting—and, in short, to all contracts in which any exchange of utilities takes place: the only thing required of government in any such case is to secure—by the protection of person and property from force and fraud and the enforcement of freely made contracts—that every one shall be really free to purchase the utility he most wants, and to transfer what he can best furnish.

This conception of the single force of self-interest, creating and keeping in true economic order the vast and complex fabric of social industry, is very fascinating; and it is not surprising that, in the first glow of the enthusiasm excited by its revelation, it should have been unhesitatingly accepted as presenting the ideal condition of social relations, and final goal of political progress. And I believe that the conception contains a very large element of truth: the motive of self-interest does work powerfully and continually in the manner above indicated; and the difficulty of finding any adequate substitute for it, either as an impulsive or as a regulating force, is an almost invincible obstacle in the way of reconstructing society on any but its present individualistic basis. At the same time, before we accept the system of natural liberty as supplying the type to which a practical politician should seek to approximate, it is important to obtain a clear view of the general qualifications with which the argument above given has to be accepted, and of the particular cases in which its optimistic conclusion is inadmissible.

§ 2. I propose, therefore, in the present chapter, to concentrate attention on these qualifications and exceptions. And, in so doing, I think it will be most instructive to adhere, in the main, to the abstract deductive method of treatment which has been chiefly employed in the preceding book; since many persons who are willing to admit that the principle of *laisser faire* ought not to be applied unreservedly in the actual condition of human societies, yet seem to suppose it to be demonstrably right in the hypothetical community contemplated in the general reasonings of Political Economy. This supposition appears to me seriously erroneous; hence in the present chapter I am specially concerned to show that even in a society composed—solely or mainly[1]—of "economic men", the system of natural liberty would have, in certain respects and under certain conditions, no tendency to realise the beneficent results claimed for it[2].

I may begin by pointing out that the argument for *laisser faire* does not tend to show that the spontaneous combination of individuals pursuing their private interests will lead to the production of a maximum of *material* wealth, except so far as the individuals in question prefer material wealth to utilities not embodied in matter. So far as their choice falls on the latter— so far (e.g.) as the wealthier among them prefer the opera and the drama to the arts of painting and sculpture, and a greater abundance of servants, to a greater elaborateness in food, clothing, and ornaments—the result of their free action will be to render the production of material wealth less than it would otherwise be. And even taking ' produce ', as I propose to do, in the wider sense in which it has been taken in the preceding books, to include immaterial utilities as well as material, we have still to observe that men may prefer repose, leisure, reputation, &c., to any utilities whatever that they could obtain by labouring. Thus the freeing of a servile population may cause a large diminution of production (in the widest sense of the term); because the freedmen are content with what they can get by a much smaller amount of labour than their masters

---

[1] The difference between "solely" and "mainly" is important in a part of the argument that follows. See p. 410.

[2] It is from this point of view that Cairnes' interesting and persuasive essay on "Political Economy and Laissez Faire" (in his *Essays in Political Economy Theoretical and Applied*) appears to me most defective. Cairnes reaches the conclusion that *laissez faire*, though the safest "practical rule," yet "falls "to the ground as a scientific doctrine," by pointing to actual shortcomings in the production and distribution of social utility, and tracing these to the mistaken notions that men form of their interests. But this reasoning seems to me palpably inconclusive, according to the view of Political Economy as a hypothetical science, which Cairnes elsewhere expounds (*Logical Method of Political Economy*, Lect. II.). What on this view he has to prove is that there is any less reason for regarding *laissez faire* as a doctrine of this hypothetical science than there is for so regarding those deductive determinations of the values of products and services which might equally well be shown not to correspond exactly—nor, in all cases, even approximately—to the actual facts of existing societies. This, then, is the point to which I chiefly direct attention in the present chapter.

forced them to perform. In short 'natural liberty' can only tend to the production of maximum wealth, so far as this gives more satisfaction on the whole than any other employment of time.

The importance of both these qualifications becomes more clear when they are viewed in connexion with a third. In the abstract argument, by which the system of natural liberty is shown to lead to the most economic production, it has to be implicitly assumed that all the different parts of produce are to be measured, at any one time and place, by their exchange value[1]. That is, we have to assume, that utilities valued highly by the rich are useful to the community in proportion either to their market price, or to the pecuniary gain foregone in order to obtain them. And among these utilities, as we have just seen, we must include the gratification of the love of power, the love of ease, and all the whims and fancies that are wont to take possession of the minds of persons whose income is far more than sufficient to satisfy ordinary human desires. It is only by this strained extension of the idea of social utility that the production of such utility under the system of natural liberty can be said to have even a general tendency to reach the maximum production possible. Thus, for instance, there is no reason why, even in a community of most perfectly economic men, a few wealthy landowners, fond of solitude, scenery or sport, should not find their interest in keeping from cultivation large tracts of land naturally fit for the plough or for pasture; or why large capitalists generally should not prefer to live on the interest of their capital, without producing personally any utilities whatsoever.

The waste of social resources that might result in this way is likely to be greater the nearer a man approaches the close of life, so far as we suppose self-interest to be his governing principle of action. Unless he is sympathetic enough to find his greatest happiness in beneficence, it may clearly be his interest, as his end draws near, to spend larger and larger sums on smaller and smaller enjoyments. Or if we may legitimately

---

[1] A certain margin of uncertainty is introduced, so far as the interference of Government has any effect in altering Exchange-value. But this, for our present purposes, may be neglected.

assume, as political economists generally do, that a man will generally wish at least to keep his capital intact for the sake of his descendants, we still have no ground for making any similar general assumption in the case of persons unmarried or childless. Such persons, again, even if they do not spend their accumulations on themselves, may (and not unfrequently do) make an almost equally uneconomical disposal of them by whimsical or ill-judged bequests. And this leads me to another difficulty that stands in the way of the consistent realization of the system of natural liberty, if extended to include freedom of bequest. Granting that men in general will extract most satisfaction out of their wealth for themselves, if they are allowed to choose freely the manner of spending it; it does not in any way follow that they will render it most productive of utility for those who are to come after them if they are allowed to bequeath it under any conditions that they choose. On the contrary, it rather follows that any such posthumous restraint on the use of bequeathed wealth will tend to make it less useful to the living, as it will interfere with their freedom in dealing with it. How far it would therefore be generally useful to impose restrictions on bequest is a question which can only be decided by a balance of conflicting considerations; we have to weigh the gain of utility that may be expected from the greater freedom of the heirs against the loss of utility that may be feared, not so much through the diminution in the satisfactions of the testator—which perhaps need not be highly estimated—but from his diminished inducement to produce and preserve wealth. But however this question may be decided, the theoretical dilemma in which the system of natural liberty is placed is none the less clear. The free play of self-interest can only be supposed to lead to a socially advantageous employment of wealth in old age, if we assume that the old are keenly interested in the utilities that their wealth may furnish to those who succeed them: but if they have this keen interest, they will probably wish to regulate the employment of their wealth; while again in proportion as they attempt this regulation by will, they will diminish the freedom of their successors in dealing with the wealth that they bequeath; and therefore, according to the fundamental assumption of the system of natural liberty, will diminish the utility of this wealth to those successors. Of this difficulty there is, I think, no theoretical solution; it can only be settled by a rough practical compromise.

A somewhat similar difficulty arises in respect of the enforcement of contracts. If all contracts freely made are to be enforced, it is conceivable that a man may freely contract himself into slavery; it is even conceivable that a large mass of the population of a country might do this, in the poverty and distress caused by some wide-spreading calamity. In such a case Freedom of Contract would have produced a social state in which Freedom of Contract would be no longer allowed to large numbers, and therefore its effect in keeping production economic would be correspondingly restricted. It may be said that such contracts would not really be in the interest of the enslavers; and it is no doubt true, that according to the fundamental hypothesis that we are now considering, it cannot be A's interest to make a contract with B which will tend to diminish B's prospective utility to A, taking everything into account. It is, however, possible that the most valued utility which B can provide for A is the gratification of the love of power or superiority which A will obtain by a more complete control over B; so that it will be A's interest to obtain this control at the cost of rendering B's labour less productive—in any ordinary sense of the term. And, again, it may be possible for A to make a contract, which though it will tend to diminish B's productive efficiency on the whole, will tend in a greater degree to increase A's prospect of securing to himself the results of this efficiency: and, if so, A's self-interest will clearly prompt to such a contract.

§ 3. This last possibility brings us in view of another fundamental assumption of the system of natural liberty, the limited applicability of which it is both theoretically and practically important to notice. In the general argument above given it was implicitly assumed that the individual can always obtain through free exchange adequate remuneration for the services which he is capable of rendering to society. But there is no general reason for supposing that this will always be possible; and in fact there is a large and varied class of cases in which the supposition would be manifestly erroneous. In the first place there are some utilities which, from their nature are practically incapable of being appropriated by those who produce them or who would otherwise be willing to purchase them. For instance, it may easily happen that the benefits of a well-placed lighthouse must be largely enjoyed by ships on which no toll could be conveniently imposed. So again if it is economically advantageous to a nation to keep up forests, on account of their beneficial effects in moderating and equalizing rainfall[1], the advantage is one which private enterprise has no tendency to provide; since no one could appropriate and sell improvements in climate. For a somewhat different reason scientific discoveries, again, however ultimately profitable to industry, have not generally speaking a market value: the inventions in which the discovery is applied can be protected by patents; but the extent to which any given discovery will aid invention is mostly so uncertain, that even if the secret of a law of nature could be conveniently kept, it would not be worth an inventor's while to buy it, in the hope of being able to make something of it.

Here I may notice a specially important way in which the inequalities in Distribution—which natural liberty has no manifest tendency to diminish—may react unfavourably on Production. So far as the most economic production involves present outlay for remote results, it may be prevented by the fact that the persons concerned do not possess and cannot procure the requisite capital; while for others who do possess it, such outlay would not be remunerative, owing to the difficulty of appropriating an adequate share of the resulting increment of utility. In the preceding book we have been led to observe how the services of the higher grades of skilled labour, including the labour of large employers, tend to be *paid* more highly than would be the case if wealth were more equally distributed. But this result is also *primâ facie* evidence that such services are *rendered* less abundantly than would be the case if the labour and capital of the community were most productively employed: since it may be inferred that society would purchase an additional increment of such services at a price more than

[1] Cf. Rau-Wagner, *Finanzwissenschaft*, 1ter Theil, § 193.

sufficient to repay the outlay necessary to provide them,—while at the same time it would not be profitable for any capitalist to provide the money, with the view of being repaid out of the salary of the labourer educated; owing to the trouble and risk involved in the deferred payments. In this way it may be profitable for the community to provide technical and professional education at a cheap rate, even when it could not be remuneratively undertaken by private enterprise. And thus, too, the low wages of a depressed class of labourers may cause a loss of wealth to the community, from the low standard of efficiency which they tend to perpetuate in the class, even when it would not be the interest of any private employer of the labourers in question to pay higher wages.

§ 4. On the other hand, private enterprise may sometimes be socially uneconomical because the undertaker is able to appropriate not *less* but *more* than the whole net gain of his enterprise to the community; for he may be able to appropriate the main part of the gain of a change causing both gain and loss, while the concomitant loss falls entirely upon others. Thus a company A having made an expensive permanent instrument—say a railway—to the advantage both of themselves and of their fellow-citizens, it may be the interest of another company B to make a new railway somewhat more convenient for the majority of travellers—and so likely to draw the lion's share of traffic from A—even if the increment of utility to the community is outweighed by the extra cost of the new railway; since B will get paid not merely for this increment of utility, but also for a large part of the utility that A before supplied.

A still more marked divergence between private interest and public interest is liable to occur in the case of Monopoly: since, as we have seen, a monopolist may increase his maximum net profit or make an equal profit more easily, by giving a smaller supply at a higher price of the commodity in which he deals, rather than a larger supply at a lower price, and so rendering less service to the community in return for his profit. At the same time, though a monopoly in private hands is thus liable to be economically disadvantageous from a social point of view, there is in certain cases a decided economic gain to be obtained by that organization of a whole department of production under a single management, which inevitably leads to monopoly; either because the qualities required in the product are such as unity of management is peculiarly qualified to provide—as in the case of the medium of exchange—or merely from the saving of labour and capital that it renders possible. And it may be observed that cases of this kind tend to increase in number and importance, as civilization progresses and the arts of industry become more elaborate. Thus the aggregation of human beings into large towns has rendered it economically important that the provision of water for the aggregate should be under one management; and the substitution of gas for candles and oil-lamps has had a similar economic effect on the provision of light.

The practical importance of the conflict of private and social interests just mentioned is much increased by the extent to which total or partial monopoly may be affected by Combination[1]—especially when we consider that it may be the interest of the combining producers not only to limit the amount of the utilities that they produce, in order to raise their price, but also to resist any economies in production which may tend to decrease the demand for them[2]. It should be observed that wherever payment is not by results, it may easily be the interest of any individual labourer *in any particular job*, to extend uneconomically the amount of labour required, or to give as little work as he can in the time (supposing that harder work would be more irksome). But it is only where some combination of labourers exists, or custom partially sustained by combination, that it can be any one's interest *on the whole* to do this; since if the price of his services were settled by open competition, a labourer so acting would lower the market value of his services. And it is to be observed that the same

---

[1] Combination is no doubt often tacitly excluded in the reasoning by which it is argued that the most economic production tends to result from the play of individual self-interests. But I do not see how it is legitimately to be excluded.

[2] It is one of the most serious of economic objections alleged against Trades' Unions, from the point of view of the community, that the regulations of some of them are partly framed to carry out this anti-social method of increasing the remuneration of a particular class. Cp. Thornton on *Labour*, Pt. iii. ch. 5. See, however, Howell, *Capital and Labour*, ch. viii.

progress of civilization which tends to make competition more real and effective, when the circumstances of industry favour competition, also increase the facilities and tendencies to combination.

§ 5. So far we have considered combination as a possible source of economic loss to the community. But in some cases combined action or abstinence on the part of a whole class of producers is required to realise a certain utility, either at all or in the most economical way—as (e.g.) where land below the sea-level has to be protected against floods, or useful animals and plants against infectious diseases. In a perfectly ideal community of economic men all the persons concerned would doubtless voluntarily agree to take the measures required to ward off such common dangers: but in any community of human beings that we can hope to see, the most that we can reasonably expect is that the great majority of any industrial class will be adequately enlightened, vigilant, and careful in protecting their own interests; and where the efforts and sacrifices of a great majority are liable to be rendered almost useless by the neglect of one or two individuals, it will always be dangerous to trust to voluntary association. And the ground for compulsion becomes still stronger when the very fact of a combination among the great majority of any industrial class to attain a certain result materially increases the inducement for individuals to stand aloof from the combination. Take, for instance, the case of certain fisheries, where it is clearly for the general interest that the fish should not be caught at certain times, or in certain places, or with certain instruments; because the increase of actual supply obtained by such captures is much overbalanced by the detriment it causes to prospective supply. Here,—however clear the common interest might be—it would be palpably rash to trust to voluntary association for the observance of the required rules of abstinence; since the larger the number that thus voluntarily abstain, the stronger becomes the inducement offered to those who remain outside the association to pursue their fishing in the objectionable times, places, and ways, so long as they are not prevented by legal coercion.

§ 6. I have spoken above of the manner in which individuals may, through combination, avowed or tacit, make their labour less useful in order that more of it may be required. We have now to observe that, where there is no such combination, open competition may cause a similar uneconomical effect, even while fulfilling its normal function of equalizing the remuneration of producers. For suppose that the services of any particular class of labourers receive on the average a disproportionately high remuneration as compared with those of other classes; there are two ways in which this excess can be reduced, either (1) by lowering the price of a given quantum of the utilities produced by the workers in question, or (2) by increasing the number of persons competing to produce such utilities, without augmenting their aggregate produce, owing to the increased difficulty that each has in finding customers. So far as this latter result takes place, the effect of competition on production is positively disadvantageous. In actual experience this effect seems to occur most conspicuously in the case of services of which the purchasers are somewhat deficient in commercial keenness and activity; so that each producer thinks himself likely to gain more on the whole by keeping up the price of his services, rather than by lowering it to attract custom. An example of this kind is furnished by retail trade, especially the retail trade of the smaller shops to which the poorer class chiefly resorts; since the remarkable success of the cooperative stores of artisans implies a considerable waste of shopkeepers' time and labour under the system previously universal. Still even in a community of thoroughly intelligent and alert persons, the practical advantages of established goodwill or business connexion would still remain: the economic man would find it his interest under ordinary circumstances, for saving of time and trouble, to form and maintain fixed habits of dealing with certain persons. There would always be many dealers who would be trying to form, and had as yet imperfectly succeeded in forming, such connexions. Thus it appears that a considerable percentage of unemployed or half-employed labour is a necessary concomitant of that active competition for business by which industry is self-organised under the system of natural liberty: and the greater the fluctuations of demand and supply, the greater is likely to be this percentage of waste.

A somewhat similar waste, of labour and capital employed in manufactures, &c., due to the difficulty of adapting supply to an imperfectly known and varying demand, has been noticed in the last chapter but one of the preceding book, in discussing the phenomenon of (so-called) "over-production."

But again; the importance to each individual of finding purchasers for his commodity also leads to a further waste socially speaking, in the expenditure incurred for the sole purpose of attaining this result. A large part of the cost of advertisements, of agents and "travellers," of attractive shop-fronts, &c., come under this head. A similar waste, similarly incident to the individualistic organization of industry, is involved in the initial expenses of forming joint-stock companies, in the case of undertakings too large for ordinary private capitalists—expenses which could not be avoided, even in a community of economic men, though the skilled labour required for launching such companies would not be remunerated quite so largely as it is here and now.

In other cases again, the mere process of appropriating and selling a commodity, involves such a waste of time, trouble, and expense as to render it on the whole a more economical arrangement for the community to provide the commodity out of public funds. Thus (e. g.) it is an advance in industrial civilisation to get rid of tolls on roads and bridges.

§ 7. Hitherto we have not made any distinction between the interests of living men and those of remote generations. But if we are examining the merits and demerits of the purely individualistic or competitive organization of society from the point of view of universal humanity, it should be observed that it does not necessarily provide to an adequate extent for utilities distant in time. It was shown before that an outlay of capital that would be useful to the community may not be made because it would be unremunerative to individuals at the only rate at which they could (owing to poverty, &c.) borrow the money. But we may go further and urge that an outlay which would be on the whole advantageous, if the interests of future generations are considered[1] as much as those of the

---

[1] There is no abstract reason why the interest of future generations should be less considered than that of the now existing human beings; allowance being

present may not be profitable for any individual at the current rate at which wealth can be commercially borrowed.

This may be merely because the return is too distant; since an average man's interest in his heirs is not sufficient to make him buy a very long deferred annuity, even if its price be calculated strictly according to the market-rate of interest. But, speaking more generally, I do not see how it can be argued from the point of view of the community that the current interest, the current price that individuals have to be paid for postponing consumption, is the exact condition that has to be fulfilled to make such postponement desirable; though of course it is a condition inevitably exacted in a society of economic men organised on a purely individualistic basis.

§ 8. So far I have left unquestioned the assumption—fundamental in the system of natural liberty—that individuals are the best judges of the commodities that they require, and of the sources from which they should be obtained, provided that no wilful deception[1] is practised; as I have thought it important to make quite clear that, *even if this assumption be granted*, what I have called the scientific ideal' of economists —the political conditions of industry which they assume in abstract reasoning with a view to the explanation of economic phenomena—cannot legitimately be taken as the practical ideal of the Art of Political Economy; since it is shown by the same kind of abstract reasoning to be liable to fail, in various ways to realize the most economical and effective organization of industry. It may perhaps seem that these results are of merely speculative interest; since all but a few fanatics admit that the beings for whom complete *laisser faire* is adapted are at any rate not the members of any existing community. But I venture to think that the theoretical conclusion above reached has considerable, though indirect, practical importance. If it were demonstrably only from blind adhesion to custom and habit, or from want of adequate

made for the greater uncertainty that the benefits intended for the former will actually reach them and actually be benefits.

[1] The prevention of such deception is included in the functions attributed to Government by the extremest advocates of *laisser faire*; though, as we shall see in the next chapter, it is a disputed question how far Government should be allowed to interfere even for this preventive purpose.

enlightenment, that the concurrence of self-interests could not actually be relied upon to produce the best aggregate result for the community, at any rate the direction of social progress would seem to be fixed and the goal clearly in view; the pace at which we ought to try to advance towards complete *laisser faire* would still be open to dispute, but the sense that every diminution of governmental interference was a step in the right direction, would be a strong inducement to take the step, if the immediate effects of taking it appeared to be mixed, and the balance of good and evil doubtful; while optimistic persons would be continually urging society to suffer a little present loss for the sake of the progress gained towards the individualistic ideal. But if, as I have tried to show, this is not the case; if on the contrary in a community where the members generally were as enlightened and alert in the pursuit of their interests as we can ever expect human beings to become, it might still be in various cases and on various grounds desirable to supplement or correct the defects of private enterprise by the action of the community in its collective capacity,—we shall view in a somewhat different light the practical questions of the present time as to the nature and limits of governmental interference. That is, in any case where the present inadequacy of *laisser faire* is admitted or strongly maintained, we shall examine carefully whether its defects are due to want of general enlightenment, or rather to one or other of the causes discussed in this chapter; and in the latter case shall regard governmental interference as not merely a temporary resource, but not improbably a normal element of the organization of industry.

It does not of course follow that wherever *laisser faire* falls short governmental interference is expedient; since the inevitable drawbacks and disadvantages of the latter may, in any particular case, be worse than the shortcomings of private industry. These drawbacks depend in part on such political considerations as lie beyond the scope of the present discussion, and vary very much with the constitution of the government in question, and the state of political morality in the country governed. Of this kind are (1) the danger of increasing the power and influence capable of being used by government for corrupt purposes, if we add to the valuable appointments at its disposal; (2) the danger, on the other hand, that the exercise of its economic functions will be hampered and perverted by the desire to gratify influential sections of the community—certain manufacturers, certain landlords, certain classes of manual labourers, or the inhabitants of certain localities; (3) the danger, again, of wasteful expenditure under the influence of popular sentiment—since the mass of a people, however impatient of taxation, are liable to be insufficiently conscious of the importance of thrift in all the details of national expenditure. Then, further, there is the danger of overburdening the governmental machinery with work—which can hardly be altogether removed, though it may be partly obviated, by careful organization; since the central and supreme organ of government must exercise a certain supervision over all subordinate departments, and every increase in the variety and complexity of the latter must make this supervision somewhat more laborious and difficult.

Other disadvantages, in part economic, in part purely political, attach to particular modes of governmental interference. Thus when the action of government requires funds raised by taxation, we have to reckon—besides the financial cost of collection and any loss to production caused by particular taxes—the political danger of adding to a burden already impatiently borne; where, again, it requires the prohibition of private industry, we must regard as an item on the wrong side of the account not only the immediate irksomeness of restraint, but the repression of energy and self-help that tends to follow from it; where, on the other hand, the interference takes the form of regulations imposed on private businesses, in addition to any detrimental effects on industrial processes that may inevitably accompany the observance of such regulations we may often have to calculate on a certain amount of economic and political evils due to successful or unsuccessful attempts to evade them.

And, lastly, in all cases, the work of government has to be done by persons who—even with the best arrangements for effective supervision and promotion by merit—can have only a part of the stimulus to energetic industry that the independent worker feels, who may reasonably hope to gain by any well-directed extra exertion, intellectual or muscular, and must fear to lose by any indolence or neglect. The same, however, may be said of the hired labour used by private employers, to an extent which the development of industry has hitherto continually tended to increase; including even the specially important labour of management, in the case of businesses conducted by joint-stock companies. And, on the other hand, government can apply certain kinds of stimulus which private employers have either not at their command at all, or only in a less degree; it can reward conspicuous merit by honours and distinctions, and offer to faithful service a more complete security of continuous employment and provision for old age. Still the loss, in governmental service, of the enterprise and effort that is stimulated and sustained by a fuller sense of self-dependence, must be set down as very serious; and, on the whole, there seems no doubt that even where the defects of *laisser faire* are palpable and grave, they may still be outweighed by the various disadvantages incident to governmental management of industry.

But, even so, it is important to observe, first, that these disadvantages are largely such as moral and political progress may be expected to diminish; so that even where we do not regard the intervention of government as at present desirable, we may yet look forward to it, and perhaps prepare the way for it. And, secondly, even where we reject governmental interference, we may yet recognise the expediency of supplementing or limiting in some way or other the results of private enterprise: we may point out a place for philanthropic effort—as in the case of educational foundations; or for associations of consumers to supply their needs otherwise than by the competition of independent producers—as in the case of the highly successful cooperative stores managed by artisans.

§ 9. What has been said above would be true, however fully it is granted that social progress is carrying us towards a condition in which the assumption, that the consumer is a better judge than government of the commodities that he requires and of the source from which they may be best obtained, will be sufficiently true for all practical purposes. But it seems to me very doubtful whether this can be granted; since in some important respects the tendencies of social development seem to be rather in an opposite direction. As the appliances of life become more elaborate and complicated through the progress of invention, it is only according to the general law of division of labour to suppose that an average man's ability to judge of the adaptation of means to ends, even as regards the satisfaction of his everyday needs, is likely to become continually less. No doubt an ideally intelligent person would under these circumstances be always duly aware of his own ignorance, and would take the advice of experts. But it seems not unlikely that the need of such advice, and the difficulty of finding the right advisers, may increase more markedly than the average consciousness of such need and difficulty, at any rate where the benefits to be obtained or the evils to be warded off are somewhat remote and uncertain; especially when we consider that the self-interest of producers will in many cases lead them to offer commodities that *seem* rather than *are* useful, if the difference between seeming and reality is likely to escape notice.

How far Government can usefully attempt to remedy these shortcomings of self-help is a question that does not admit of a confident general answer, for the reasons discussed in the preceding section. We may, however, notice certain kinds of utility—which are or may be economically very important to individuals—which Government, in a well-organized modern community, is peculiarly adapted to provide. Complete security for savings is one of these. I do not of course claim that it is an attribute of governments, always and everywhere, that they are less likely to go bankrupt, or defraud their creditors, than private individuals or companies: but merely that this is likely to be an attribute of governments in the ideal society that orthodox political economy contemplates; of which we may find evidence in the fact that even now, though loaded with war debts and in danger of increasing the load, the English Government can borrow more cheaply than the most prosperous private company. So again—without at present entering dangerously into the burning question of currency—we may at least say that if *stability* in the value of the medium of exchange can be attained at all, without sacrifices and risks outweighing its advantages, it must be by the intervention of

Government: a voluntary combination powerful enough to produce the result is practically out of the question.

And I have already observed that where *uniformity* of action or abstinence on the part of a whole class of producers is required for the most economical production of a certain utility, the intervention of Government is at least likely to be the most effective way of attaining the result: especially if the adoption of the required rule by a majority renders it decidedly the *immediate* interest of individuals to break through it.

To sum up: the general presumption derived from abstract economic reasoning is not in favour of leaving industry altogether to private enterprise, in any community that can usefully be taken even as an ideal for the guidance of practical statesmanship; but is on the contrary in favour of supplementing and controlling such enterprise in various ways by the collective action of the community. The general principles on which the nature and extent of such collective action should be determined have been given in the present chapter; but it would hardly be possible to work out a system of detailed practical rules on the basis of these principles, by the abstract deductive method here adopted; owing to the extent to which the construction of such system ought reasonably to be influenced by the particular social and political conditions of the country and time for which it is framed. In passing therefore from abstract principles to their concrete applications—so far as the limits of my treatise allow me to discuss the latter—it seems best to adopt a more empirical treatment: the exposition of which will be more conveniently reserved for another chapter.

CHAPTER III.

THE RELATIONS OF GOVERNMENT TO INDUSTRY.

§ 1. IN the chapter that follows this I propose to discuss some of the chief cases of Governmental intervention to benefit production which forms a part of the accepted policy and practice of civilized communities at the present day: in order to examine the general principles on which they are or may be maintained, and to point out how they illustrate the general exceptions to the sufficiency of Natural Liberty which we have just been considering from an abstract point of view.

But before proceeding to this examination, it seems desirable to distinguish as clearly as we can between the strictly *economic* intervention of Government and those cases of governmental interference with industry in which the better production—or even better distribution—of purchaseable commodities is not the primary aim; and in which, therefore, economic considerations cannot be put forward as decisive, though they must always be allowed some weight. The investigation of this latter class of interventions belongs rather to the wider Art of Politics than to the special Art of Political Economy. It is, of course, fundamentally important, for the economic prosperity of the community governed, that Government should perform efficiently its main and universally admitted function of protecting private persons and their property from injury and securing the fulfilment of contracts: but the particulars and limits of this indispensable work have to be considered in relation not simply to wealth but to social well-being generally. At the same time, since—as we shall see—it is difficult to draw the line between these two classes of governmental intervention, and since even where the primary aim of the intervention carries us beyond the range of Political Economy, economic considerations are often important, I propose in the present chapter to examine briefly the chief economic questions that arise in considering the necessary action of Government in relation to private industry.

I will begin by giving a completer statement of what may be called the 'individualistic minimum' of governmental interference; which—as I briefly noticed in the preceding chapter—is generally taken for granted even by thorough-going advocates of the system of Natural Liberty. We find that, even in the view of individualists, Government has the following fundamental duties:—

1. To protect the interests of the community generally, and individual citizens so far as may be necessary, from the attacks of foreign states.

2. To guard individual citizens from physical injury, constraint, insult, or damage to reputation, caused by the intentional or culpable careless action of other individuals.

3. To guard their property from detriment similarly caused; which involves the function of determining doubtful points as to the *extent* and *content* of the Right of Property and the modes of legally acquiring it.

4. To prevent deception leading to detriment of person or property.

5. To enforce contracts made by adults in full possession of their reasoning faculties, and not obtained by coercion or misrepresentation, nor injurious to other persons.

6. To protect in a special degree persons unfit, through age or mental disorder, to take care of their own interests. Of this kind of protection the most important case is that of children; and here it should be observed that the protection may be exercised either directly, or indirectly through regulation of the relations of the sexes, so far as this may be required in order to make generally adequate provision for the care and nurture of children.

To these may be added the duty of providing for its own support and its own defence against internal as well as external foes. The enquiry into the best mode of making this provision, by taxation or otherwise, has always been regarded as an important branch of the economist's study;—indeed it constitutes a chief part of the art of Political Economy in the view of most economists since Adam Smith; and I accordingly propose to deal with it in a separate chapter[1].

§ 2. In considering the economic aspect of the action of Government, under the other heads above mentioned, it is important to note that its interference may be exerted in various modes, and various degrees of intensity. Besides (1) interference by direct prohibition or command—which may, of course, vary indefinitely in gravity—the Government may (2) indirectly prevent or discourage certain kinds of contract by refusing to enforce them; or (3) it may give to the obligations involved in certain common kinds of agreements such as Sale and Purchase, Letting and Hiring, &c., a precise definition, interpretation, or presumption, which will be held to be valid in all cases where there is no special contract to the contrary; or again (4) certain kinds of business may be undertaken by the State, though at the same time it may remain open to private individuals or joint-stock companies to enter into competition with the governmental agency if they choose. In this latter case the only element of compulsion consists in the coercive levying (by taxation) of funds required for carrying on the business in question: and where the business can be made to pay its own expenses, even this element of coercion vanishes. Which (if any) of these different modes of interference should be adopted in any particular case is a question which cannot be entirely decided by economic considerations; since even where the more intense interference by direct prohibition or command is both cheaper and more effective, a statesman may reasonably decline to employ it from fear of the displeasure and discontent which it is likely to cause; while, again, the probable amount of displeasure and discontent varies greatly with the actual state of custom and opinion in any particular community. But it should be observed that the intensity of different kinds of interference will be very differently estimated, according as we

---

[1] Chap. VIII. It should be observed, however, that fiscal considerations necessarily enter into the discussion of certain kinds of governmental interference, designed mainly for other purposes.

take a political or an economic point of view. Thus, politically speaking, interference is at its minimum, when Government, without any legal prohibition or restriction of private industry, merely prevents its development in a certain direction, by taking some new kind of business—such as the construction and management of railways—entirely into its own hands. But, economically considered, this interference is greater than when Government places private businesses under legal control and regulation; since in the latter case some of the effects—good or bad—of private enterprise are retained, whereas by the former method they are altogether excluded.

§ 3. Let us now consider separately each of the indispensable functions above enumerated. Under the first head, of Defence against Foreign enemies, the most important economic questions[1] relate chiefly to the best way of securing an adequate supply of the personal services, materials, or instruments required for war; and will therefore be more fitly discussed later, when we come to treat of the theory of the provision for national wants. Here I would only point out that the needs of war may furnish decisive considerations in favour of measures which would otherwise be inexpedient—although they are not unlikely to be advocated on other than military grounds. Thus a government may reasonably undertake for military reasons the construction of railways commercially unremunerative; or may control the arrangement of a system of railways which it would otherwise leave to unrestricted private enterprise. Again, similar reasons have often been urged for the protection of native industry in certain departments; and certainly, where there is a reasonable probability that a government would find serious difficulty in obtaining, should it be involved in war, any part of the supply of men or things required for the efficient conduct of the war, it is obvious that some kind of provision should be made in time of peace for meeting this difficulty: and we cannot say *a priori* how far it will in any particular case be better to meet it directly, by a more extensive and costly organization of the army or navy, or indirectly by the encouragement of certain branches of private industry. Thus,

[1] I pass over the abnormal and violent disturbances of production and exchange which actual war may render needful or expedient.

for instance, it may be questioned whether Adam Smith was right in commending the English Navigation Laws of his time which "endeavoured to give the sailors and shipping of Great Britain the monopoly of the trade of their own country;" but the question cannot be answered without a careful investigation of details. The restrictions thus imposed on trade must of course have increased the cost of foreign commodities to the English consumers; but they may nevertheless have been the least burdensome mode of securing a due supply of sailors and shipping for our maritime wars. On similar grounds we cannot say positively that it can never be expedient for a country situated as England is to secure itself by protection to native agriculture against the danger of having its necessary supply of food cut off by a maritime blockade.

§ 4. It is, however, of more general importance to consider the various kinds of the interference with industry which may be necessary or expedient for the due protection of the life, health, physical comfort, freedom and reputation of individuals from harm inflicted, intentionally or otherwise, by private persons. In considering the proper limits of this interference, we find much controversy on the question how far Government may legitimately go in preventing acts that are not directly or necessarily harmful, on the ground that they are likely in some indirect way to have harmful consequences to other persons besides the agent. It would be out of place here to enter fully into this controversy; but I may perhaps say that the question appears to me to be one of degree: and that I do not see how the answer to it in concrete cases can reasonably be decided by any broad general formula[1]. In some cases the burden is so trifling that no one would hesitate to impose it, if experience shows it to be at all efficacious for the attainment of either of the ends above distinguished. Of this kind are the regulations

---

[1] For instance, I do not see on what grounds it can be maintained that "it is not a merely constructive or presumptive injury to others which will justify the interference of the law with individual freedom" (Mill, *On Liberty*, c. 4). It appears to me that, on utilitarian principles, all we can say is that the presumption must be strong enough to outweigh the direct and indirect mischief of coercion.

that printers' and publishers' names should be affixed to published documents, in order to secure punishment or redress in case of libels; that poisons when sold should be manifestly designated as such; that vehicles should carry a light at night, &c. So far as more serious interference with the production or sale of certain commodities is exerted, in order to protect from disease and other physical damage either the producers or purchasers of such commodities, or other members of the community, such interference is, no doubt, liable to be attended by economic drawbacks, which have to be carefully weighed against the evils which experience shows it to be capable of preventing. But the final decision as to its expediency does not fall within the sphere of Political Economy and cannot be arrived at by strictly economic methods; since life and health are goods which it is not possible to estimate at a definite[1] pecuniary value.

The question as to the expediency of governmental interference which we may call 'indirectly individualistic'—i.e. designed for the protection of individuals other than those whose freedom of action is thereby diminished—tends in practice to be mixed with a question which, from an abstract point of view, is fundamentally distinct; viz. how far (if at all) Government ought to interfere 'paternally' to prevent injury to the life or health of an individual caused either by himself or with his own consent. In the chief cases where a man harms himself so seriously as to suggest a need of governmental interference, his conduct has also an important tendency to harm others: hence it is often difficult to say whether it is the former or the latter kind of harm that a given piece of legislation is designed to prevent. Thus the various prescriptions and prohibitions included in our own recent sanitary legislation are frequently criticized as 'paternal': but it may be fairly said that in such cases coercion is applied to individuals not primarily in their own interest, but in that of others who might suffer if their houses became a focus of disease. So again, few indi-

---

[1] I say "definite" because all reasonable persons would admit that at a certain point the machinery for saving even life and health may become too costly; and therefore the practical necessity of balancing these goods in some way against wealth cannot be evaded.

vidualists would deny that the tendency of drunkenness to cause breaches of the peace is a legitimate ground for *some* interference with the trade of selling alcohol: and the most thoroughgoing abolitionist urges his restriction more as indirectly individualistic than as paternal—i.e. more on the ground of the proved tendency of alcoholic excess to make a man beat his wife and starve his children, than on the ground of its tendency to injure the drunkard himself.

So far as any such legislation is avowedly 'paternal' it is clearly opposed to the fundamental assumption—on which (as we have seen) the economic rule of *laisser faire* partly rests—that every man is the best judge of what contributes to his own happiness; since on this principle each individual ought to set his own value on life and health, and to choose freely the means of maintaining them, just as much as in the case of other utilities. I have, however, already indicated that I do not accept this principle as universally valid: I only accept it as furnishing (as Cairnes says) a handy though rough rule of practical statesmanship, in accordance with ordinary experience of human nature, from which we ought only to deviate in special cases when there are strong empirical grounds for concluding that our general assumption is not borne out by facts. And this view is in harmony with the practice of all civilized governments. Thus (e.g.) our own government does not trust its subjects to find out for themselves and avoid unhealthy food or improperly qualified physicians, surgeons, and apothecaries: or to refrain from buying diseased meat: or to refuse to take part in industrial processes which are exposed to special dangers—as (e.g.) mining and navigation—unless due precautions are taken against these dangers. It finds that even the self-helpful Englishman cannot be trusted to take adequate care of himself in these matters: hence it endeavours in various ways to obviate the mischief liable to result from this want of care. Rarely, indeed, does it attempt by direct prohibition to prevent an individual from doing what is likely to injure himself alone; but it prescribes conditions under which certain dangerous industries are to be carried on, and does not permit them to be violated, even with the full consent of the persons who would be endangered; it directly prohibits persons not qualified in a manner which it prescribes from exercising certain trades—such as that of apothecary, and that of pilot; in other cases it indirectly hinders the employment of practitioners not properly qualified by refusing to enforce payment of fees for their services.

To meet the special arguments for these and similar measures by a simple reference to the general considerations in favour of leaving sane adults to manage their own affairs appears to me clearly irrational and unscientific. But to discuss the proper limits of this 'paternal' interference—as I have said of the 'indirectly individualistic' interference with which it is practically mixed up—would clearly carry us beyond the province of the present treatise: since all would agree that, in determining these limits, considerations of wealth cannot be taken as decisive. If we regarded a man merely as a means of producing wealth, it might clearly 'pay' to allow needle-grinders to work themselves to death in a dozen years—as they used to be willing to do in order to earn higher wages. But a civilized community cannot take this view of its members; the question whether men are to be allowed thus to shorten their lives for a few extra shillings a week has clearly to be decided on other than merely economic grounds. At the same time, it is the business of the economist to estimate the expense, trouble and loss of utility that interference of this kind tends to cause; and if he finds it in any case excessively costly, or likely to be frustrated by a tenacious and evasive pursuit of private interest on the part of the persons interfered with, he must direct attention to these drawbacks.

And the same may be said of the interference of Government for the protection of children;—whether directly, as by limiting the amount of labour that may be enacted from them, and securing to them a certain amount of education; or indirectly, by placing restrictions on the labour of married women (or women who have borne children) so far as these appear necessary in order to secure the proper performance of their maternal functions. As the system of Natural Liberty is, even by its most vehement advocates, regarded as only applicable to adults, it is not in any way opposed to the principle of such regulations; and though (1) the immediate economic loss caused by such restrictions, and (2) the ultimate economic gain to the community from the improved health and training of its children, are important considerations in determining the nature and extent of this kind of interference, they are not by themselves decisive. It is often said that parents are the best guardians of their children's interests: but this, at any rate, is quite a different proposition from that on which the general economic argument for industrial non-interference is based,—viz. that every sane adult is the best guardian of his own interests: and the limitations within which experience will lead us to restrict the practical application of the two principles respectively are not likely to coincide.

§ 5. In close analogy to the regulations above noticed that indirectly protect the person, stands another class of governmental interferences which have for their object the indirect prevention of theft. Of this kind are the regulations that hamper the easy disposition of stolen goods; such as the English law that a dealer in old metal may not at one time buy less than certain minimum quantities of lead, copper, tin, &c.; and some of the restrictions imposed on pawnbrokers. With these, again, we may class regulations that aim at the indirect prevention of fraud in exchanges; such as the prescription of standard weights and measures, and the more recent prohibition of 'truck' (that is, of the payment of wages otherwise than in money),—so far as this is designed to secure to labourers the amount of real wages that is by contract fairly due to them. If we could extend the notion of 'fraud' to include all cases in which one of the parties to an agreement 'imposes' upon the ignorance of the other, several other important interferences with industry might be brought under this head; such as the chief regulations enforced on joint-stock companies—whether framed to protect the interests of the individual members of such companies against their directors, or to protect other persons who may deal with them—the taxing of solicitors' bills, and some of the regulations of the business of carrying emigrants.

It is to be observed, however, that the element of active misrepresentation is not necessarily present in all cases of what is commonly called 'imposition.' In fact, the notion of 'imposition' affords us a transition, by which we gradually pass from exchanges in which positive deception is practised to exchanges which are merely held to be inequitable through the ignorance on one side of the quality of the article exchanged, even though there may be no active misrepresentation on the other side, and no general understanding that the other party will furnish the knowledge that is wanting. Now, in ordinary buying and selling, a purchaser is expected to protect himself against loss incurred under these latter conditions; and though experience may show that the intervention of Government to protect him is in certain cases urgently required, it must be allowed that such intervention is hardly consistent with the fundamental assumption of the system of natural liberty, that the sane adult individual is likely to be a better judge of his own interests than his government is. At any rate we may say that at this point we approach the rather delicate theoretical line that separates governmental action for the *maintenance* of real freedom of contract—which is held to be impaired by successful fraud—from action that *invades* this freedom. Various regulations tending to preve t contracts from being made under misapprehension as to material circumstances may be regarded as lying on this debatable margin: such as the rules of law obliging vendors with special opportunities of knowledge—e.g. vendors of land and promoters of joint-stock companies—to disclose any material circumstances affecting the value of what they offer for sale: or again, the compulsory registration of contracts like mortgages or bills of sale, which are liable to render the real financial position of one of the parties to the contract so materially different from his apparent position that third persons dealing with him are in danger of being seriously misled.

A somewhat similar margin presents itself when we try to define the other main condition required for the validity of contracts according to the principles of natural liberty: viz. that they should not have been procured by coercion—provided we extend the notion of coercion to include not merely physical injury or constraint, but also the moral pressure which is sometimes called 'undue influence[1].' It is, of course, in accordance

[1] The term 'undue influence' is also used to denote some kinds of what I have previously called 'imposition.'

with the strictest limitation of the sphere of Government that it should prohibit and invalidate agreements procured by the infliction or threat of any illegal harm; and further, if in any case one party to a contract is able to cause pain or alarm of a kind which the law does not generally attempt to prevent, but which is not likely to be inflicted or threatened except as an inducement to make the contract, a special interference to prevent such undue pressure may fairly be regarded as a mere defence of freedom. Thus the special protection given by our law to merchant seamen, by the invalidation of contracts alienating part of their claims to wages, may be justified by the special opportunities of undue influence which the needful discipline of a ship gives to its master. So, again, the restrictions placed on the labour of women generally, in the English factory legislation, are commonly and plausibly defended on the ground that women, owing to their normal domestic dependence, require to be protected against the undue influence of the men with whom they live. When, however, the law interferes to prevent a contract in which A merely takes advantage of the distress' of B, without being in any way responsible for it—or, otherwise, when the pressure which A puts on B is merely the threat of not rendering some service which he is in no way bound to render independently of the contract—it seems plain that such interference must be viewed not as a protection of freedom of contract, but as a limitation of it in the interests of disadvantageously placed members of the community.

I have spoken of the enforcement of contracts as a kind of protection to freedom : and there can be no doubt that a refusal to enforce such contracts is an interference with the spontaneous organization of industry which the system of natural liberty contemplates ; in which enforcement of contract is the one elementary process by the repetition and complication of which the whole fabric is bound together. At the same time there is certainly something paradoxical in calling the refusal of Government to enforce certain contracts, an 'interference' with the freedom of the individuals left alone : and it is probably for this reason that the very important restrictions, by which the enforcement of contract has actually been limited, have not commonly been treated as violations of *laisser faire*. Thus in England hardly any engagement to render personal services gives the promisee a legal claim to more than pecuniary damages;—to put it otherwise, almost all such contracts, if unfulfilled, turn into mere debts of money so far as their legal force goes. And it should be added that even the payment of debts is to a very large extent not exacted, even from persons who are now perfectly able to pay them; provided that at some previous time such persons have proved their inability to pay, given up their property for division among their creditors, and thus obtained as bankrupts protection against any future exaction of past debts. This very important limitation of the effects of contract is, I conceive, mainly to be justified as tending to promote the interests of production; being designed to restore to the bankrupt the stimulus to useful industry which an indefinite prolongation of his pecuniary liabilities would take away from all but the most energetic minds. It is thought that this can be done without any material sacrifice of the interests of creditors; since the latter, even if their claims were kept legally valid, would still have no effective means of compelling the defaulting debtor to earn the money required to satisfy them. It may be observed, however, that the same line of reasoning that thus justifies the general principle of a bankruptcy law also shows us that this kind of interference may easily be carried too far for the real interests of industry. For—even assuming that the details of such a law can be contrived and administered so as to prevent waste of the bankrupt's estate, secure its equal division among the creditors, and adequately punish not only common dishonesty on the bankrupt's part, but also such reckless and improper dealing with his borrowed resources as substantially amounts to dishonesty,—the danger still remains that the prospect of relief through bankruptcy may tempt men to run risks with borrowed property which they would not think it expedient to run with their own; and which, therefore, it is the interest of the community to prevent, although such dealing may not admit of being proved to be criminally reckless. And further, granting that a bankrupt should be exempt from legal obligation to pay his creditors in full, it still seems right that society should emphatically recognise the superior morality of the bankrupt who does exert himself to repair the losses he has caused. To attain this end, and at the same time reduce the danger before-mentioned, it seems desirable to impose on the bankrupt certain disabilities which would not seriously interfere with his earning an honest livelihood, while yet they would express the coldness that society should feel towards a man who has failed to satisfy just claims—coldness rising to disapproval if he makes no effort to satisfy them. Thus a bankrupt—so long as his debts remain unpaid—should, I think, be placed on a level with a pauper in respect of all political rights; and the protection from his creditors afforded him by bankruptcy should be made conditional on his name being kept in a register open to the inspection of all persons in the place in which he trades. This latter provision, indeed, seems expedient on a different ground, of which we have before taken note: viz. for the due information of all persons who may hereafter have dealings with the bankrupt.

I have distinguished as a special mode of governmental interference that which operates by giving a definite interpretation to customary engagements. Here again a line requires to be carefully drawn between an impartial effort to ascertain and define the probable meaning of the contracting parties,—which is obviously an indispensable function of the judicature in case of disputes—and an attempt to modify what is held to be a bad custom; especially since in the development of our own "judge-"made" law, the latter attempt has often been made in the guise of the former. Such interference by mere interpretation, which will only be operative if the persons affected do not bar it by express contract, is obviously of the very lowest degree of intensity, politically speaking, and hardly amounts to a sensible restriction on liberty; and it cannot be effective if the persons concerned are decidedly averse to the change sought to be introduced; but where there is no such aversion it may sometimes have important economic effects by overcoming the "friction" of mere carelessness and ignorance, or by forcing the tacit combination of persons who gain by the old bad custom to become open and aggressive, and so pointing it out for successful resistance.

This interpretative or quasi-interpretative intervention of law has been largely extended to the implied contracts or understandings involved in different economic relations. Thus the Law of Partnership and the Law of Agency largely consist of definitions or interpretations of this kind, designed to prevent the disappointment of normal expectations. So far as such legal definition of rights and obligations merely imposes on the persons concerned the necessity of making express contracts and announcements, if they wish to avoid the obligations that the law defines as normal, it does not materially restrict natural liberty; it is only where this avoidance is not allowed, that the restriction becomes palpable and serious. For instance, the legal obligation on common carriers to receive the goods of all applicants on similar terms is merely an interpretation of a common understanding, if it can be evaded by giving full public notice; but if it cannot be so evaded, it becomes a material interference with *laisser faire*.

§ 6. Similar delicate questions as to the line to be drawn between the intervention of Government to protect, and its interference to control, the freedom of individuals, arise when we try to determine exactly the limits of the right of property according to the system of natural liberty. Granting that the natural right of property includes the power of absolutely excluding others from the use and enjoyment of any material thing over which the right has been acquired, it still remains to be asked what kinds of things natural liberty would allow to be thus appropriated—how far, in particular, it should be allowed with regard to land, the great permanent instrument and store of material for human industry. The extremest advocates of *laisser faire* have never disputed either the justice or the expediency of keeping in common ownership certain portions of land obviously more useful when freely used in common—such as roads, rivers, and other portions required for communication and conveyance. Further, in modern European countries even such land as has been allowed to pass completely into private ownership has been held liable to special burdens to public purposes; and the right of the community to take from individuals land specially needed for important public objects, at a price corresponding to the market value that it would have had independently of such special need—which in recent times has been generally admitted and to some extent exercised in the important case of railways—may perhaps fairly be regarded not as an encroachment on private ownership, but as a reservation tacitly understood when such ownership was allowed. Again, so far as a community owns land as yet unappropriated, but likely to be more useful if allowed to pass into private ownership, it is a difficult and subtle question to determine whether the principles of natural liberty prescribe any one method of effecting this transition rather than any other: and whether any of the various complicated and elaborate regulations of the sale of public land which in English and other colonies have been adopted or proposed with a view to improve the process of colonization can properly be regarded as species of governmental interference[1].

A different kind of problem has somewhat perplexed and divided the adherents of natural liberty in respect of property in the results of intellectual labour. On the one hand it has seemed clear that the man who works with his brain has as much right to have the fruits of his labour secured to him as the man who works with his hands. On the other hand since the only effective way of protecting such fruits is to prohibit imitation on the part of others, it is not surprising that this very exceptional interference with the freedom of action of those others should have been thought by some persons to conflict with the principles of natural liberty. In the case of copyright, however, this latter view appears to me superficial; so far at least as the protection is limited to results which persons other than the author protected could not conceivably have produced by independent effort—as is mainly the case with copyright. It can hardly be an interference with A's natural liberty to exclude him, in the interest of B, from the gratuitous use of utilities which he could not possibly have enjoyed except as a result of B's labour. Hence I should be disposed to regard at least any limitation of copyright to a period falling short of the author's life[2], as an encroachment on natural liberty in the interests of the community. But I should hesitate to take a

[1] Cf. *post*, ch. iv. § 12.
[2] As I shall presently point out, the right to control any kind of property after death is a doubtful point in the system of natural liberty.

similar view in the case of patents; since here the difficulty of preventing the protection of *A* from interfering with the independent action of *B* seems practically insuperable. It is almost always within the limits of human probability that in protecting a technical invention we may be suppressing the possibility of a similar invention which might otherwise have been made by some one else; indeed such coincidence of inventions may even be said to be positively probable, whenever several ingenious minds are simultaneously pondering over the best method of meeting some definite technical need. Owing to this inevitable danger of conflicting claims, and to the undeniable hampering of industrial progress that is consequently liable to result from the protection of the first inventor, it seems hardly possible to frame the regulations of a patent law on any other principle than that of carefully balancing opposite expediencies. Indeed some able men who are not generally socialistic in their views, nor in any way opposed to the principle of copyright, have yet thought it desirable on the whole to do away with patents altogether, and to leave inventors to be rewarded by the state. And the majority of competent judges, who consider it practically impossible to give the inventor sufficient inducement to work except by securing him a legal monopoly of the results of his labour, are yet generally of opinion that the duration of this monopoly should be limited to a comparatively short term of years, in the interests of industrial progress: and many of them think it further desirable that a patentee should be compelled to allow his invention to be used by others, at a price fixed by Government, under certain circumstances; that is, either (1) when the patentee does not use the invention himself, or (2) when any other inventor has made substantial improvements in it.

Another doubtful point in the definition of the rights of private property, on the principles of *laisser faire*, relates to the right of bequest. Many even among the jurists of an earlier age, in which the hypothesis of a Law of Nature was generally accepted, preferred to treat the right of bequest as established by Positive rather than Natural law; and in fact it is difficult to maintain that we interfere with a man's natural liberty by not letting his wishes determine the relations of other men to a material world in which he is no longer living. There are, indeed, two obvious and forcible reasons for allowing free bequest in a general way, independently of the actual sentiment in its favour; first, that any law prohibiting it would be likely to be frustrated by gifts before death; and secondly, that such a law, so far as effective, would tend to diminish seriously the inducements to productive labour and care during the closing period of a man's life. But arguments of this kind can hardly be pressed to prove the inexpediency of *all* restrictions on freedom of bequest; and any such restrictions that tend to increase the utility of the wealth bequeathed by enlarging the freedom of action of those to whose management it is left, may fairly be advocated in the name of Natural Liberty, no less than in the interests of production. And in fact the tendency of modern English legislation has been to introduce, to a continually greater extent, two different kinds of limitations on the individual's right of disposing of his property after death; first in the case of bequests for public purposes, by treating the testator's dispositions as liable to an indefinite amount of revision and modification in the interests of the public, after a certain interval of time has elapsed; and secondly, in the case of private bequests, by restricting the testator's power of preventing the alienation of the property bequeathed, on the ground that such inalienable ownership is liable to lead to inferior management, especially in the case of land.

Again, since through accident, neglect or indecision a certain number of persons die without exercising the right of bequest, the government has the strictly necessary function of determining in such cases the devolution of the property left behind. *Ceteris paribus* the obvious end to be aimed at in distributing such intestate inheritances is to satisfy as far as possible any definite expectations which the general habits of bequest may have created: but the guidance of this principle is liable to be obscure and ambiguous, even on fundamental points: and even where it is not so, it cannot be regarded as an interference with natural liberty to deviate from the ordinary customs of bequest, in order to adopt an economically preferable rule of distribution—as (e.g.) by abolishing the law of primogeniture in a country where it is found to have an unfavourable effect on agriculture.

In short; neither "protection to property" nor "enforce-ment of contract" turn out to be in practice the simple matters that some theorists appear to suppose them. The determination of substantive or primary rights under either of these heads involves disputed questions of great moment, in the settlement of which the effects of different rules on the production of wealth have to be carefully considered; and further questions of hardly less importance arise in the regulation of procedure and penalties, especially in respect of enforcement of contract— e.g. as to the nature of the penalties for non-payment of debt, and the order of priority in claims to be allowed to different classes of creditors. The consideration of economic consequences should in my opinion be generally paramount in deciding important issues in these departments of law: as for instance in determining the law of Bankruptcy, the law of Patents, and the main restrictions on Bequest. Since, however, this view has not generally been taken by jurists and legislators, it has seemed to me best to treat these questions as lying on a kind of debateable border-ground where the Art of Political Economy merges in the wider Art of Politics.

CHAPTER IV.

IMPORTANT CASES OF GOVERNMENTAL INTERFERENCE TO PROMOTE PRODUCTION.

§ 1. I NOW pass to the discussion of the chief actual cases in which modern governments have distinctly encroached on the system of *laisser faire* in the interests of production, either by taking into their own management certain departments of industry, or by regulating or assisting the undertakings of private individuals or companies. I ought to premise that in speaking of 'governments' I include both "central" and "local" or "provincial" governments and do not generally take note of the division of functions between the two kinds of organs. If my limits allowed, it would be interesting to discuss the economic considerations that have to be taken into account in determining this division. We might notice in the first place the analogy between the general arguments for or against centralisation of governmental functions and the arguments for "large-scale" and "small-scale" production in private industry: in either case we have to balance the advantages of more special experience in managers and more keen concern for details of the result, against the advantages of more systematic management and generally more comprehensive views and a higher quality of skill. Again, for governmental work in which particular districts are solely or mainly interested, it is natural to select the local governments of such districts; on the other hand, care has sometimes to be taken that the local government does not exercise its functions in the interest of its locality where that is opposed to the interest of the whole country,—e.g. if a single town or district has the management of an important railroad or waterway, it may be tempted to make the greatest net profit out of its monopoly by a rate of charge inconveniently high for the rest of the community. These and other general considerations might be illustrated under more than one of the heads that we are about to discuss; but on the whole I have thought it best to avoid all questions relating to the *structure* of government, and confine myself to the determination of its economic functions.

If we put on one side (1) the promotion of Education and Culture, which it is not usual to regard simply, or even mainly, from a productional point of view, and (2) the 'burning question' of protection to native industry,—which I reserve for a separate chapter,—we find that the departments of production with which governments have actually concerned themselves are chiefly various branches of what may be called the machinery of transfer; including under this term, not only Conveyance and Communication—the establishment and management of roads and bridges, canals and railroads, harbours and lighthouses, the organization for sending letters and telegrams, &c.—but also the machinery of Exchange; i.e. the issue of metallic and paper currency, and the business of banking so far as it is connected with currency. The universality of the need of the commodities furnished by these various businesses has been sometimes put forward as the justification for governmental intervention; it has been said that the provision for such commodities, being a matter of common concern, is properly undertaken or controlled by the community through its government. But this reason is not sufficiently special; since the needs of food, fuel, clothing, and shelter—the provision for which is almost universally left to private enterprise in modern communities—are even more urgent and universal than the needs of conveyance and communication: and, further, the reason just mentioned would not explain why governments should so largely leave the provision for the moveable instruments of conveyance—carriages, ships, &c.—to private enterprise, while undertaking the establishment of the permanent and stationary instruments—roads, canals, harbours, &c. The valid arguments for governmental interference in these departments are rather, in my opinion, the following: *Firstly*, organization on a very large scale—and in some cases organization under a single control—is either necessary or obviously most expedient in important parts of the businesses concerned with transfer; so that if they were left to private enterprise, either (*a*) some important utilities would not be provided at all, or would be more expensive or inferior in quality; or (*b*) the business of providing them would become the monopoly of private persons, whose interest would not generally coincide with the interest of the public. *Secondly*, there is a special probability that the advantage to the public of improvements in the machinery of transfer may exceed very greatly the direct utilities to the persons who primarily benefit by them; which latter are generally the only utilities for which the provider is able to obtain remuneration in the way of free exchange.

There are besides certain special drawbacks or obstacles incident to the production of some of these commodities by private enterprise, which will appear when we consider some of the businesses in detail.

§ 2. *Ordinary Roads.* Both the above reasons for governmental intervention apply forcibly to the case of ordinary road-making. The indirect advantages derived from good roads, both in the improved organization of national industry which results from the development of internal trade, and in the general spread of intelligence, are universally recognised; while yet the utilities of transit, as estimated by the individuals who would purchase them, would not be sufficient to enable private undertakers to construct remuneratively the less frequented roads —at any rate if the land had to be bought—: so that to make the road system of a modern civilized community as complete as is on public grounds to be desired, the intervention of Government— central or local—would seem to be almost indispensable. On the other hand, the more frequented roads which it would undoubtedly be profitable to construct, would always be in the condition of partial monopoly; and therefore there would be no general probability that it would be most profitable for the monopolist owners of the roads to charge such a price for their use, or to keep them in such a condition, as would afford the maximum of public utility. The monopoly, no doubt, would always be partly controlled by the fear that excessive tolls or gross neglect would lead to the construction of a new road; but if the new road were less convenient to the majority of those who used it, and were therefore liable to be at any time abandoned in favour of the old road if the charges and conditions of the two were equalised, its construction would be too hazardous an undertaking to be easily entered upon.

Further, we have to observe that the use of roads managed by private enterprise must necessarily be sold; and the expense and inconvenience involved in this transaction is a serious drawback in the case of much frequented roads. In the extreme case of the streets of a town no one would propose that the expenses of construction or maintenance should be defrayed by tolls; and this arrangement is now regarded as being on the whole undesirable in the case of highways generally—in spite of its obvious equity from the point of view of distribution.

The question, however, whether ordinary roads should be generally managed by private enterprise has never been a practical one; chiefly because the portions of the earth's surface now employed for this purpose, have, to a great extent, been used in common from time immemorial, and so have remained the property of the community using them, while the rest of the land has gradually passed into private ownership.

In England, when the importance of keeping the roads themselves in good condition came, in the 18th century, to be more fully recognised, the expenses were at first defrayed by tolls, the management being what may be called *quasi-governmental*[1]: but the expense and inconvenience of collecting tolls has led to the gradual abolition of this system, and the defrayment of expenses out of the rates. The bridges that form part of roads have for the most part been similarly dealt with; in a few special cases, such as the bridges over the Thames, the construction has been undertaken by private enterprise on the security of tolls; but even these have, for the most part, been subsequently bought up by public bodies.

---

[1] I refer to the system of "turnpike trusts," by which the management of different turnpike roads was placed in the hands of different bodies of trustees, partly public and partly private, who obtained private capital on loan, paying the interest with the proceeds of the tolls, but derived no personal profit from the business.

CHAP. IV.] *INTERFERENCE TO PROMOTE PRODUCTION.* 441

§ 3. *Canals and railways.* The case is otherwise with canals and railways. Many of these more artificial and elaborate ways of communication have been constructed and managed by private enterprise. Still in some of these cases the funds for their construction have been partly obtained by the aid of Government, in the form of a guarantee of interest or otherwise; while even where the capital of railways has been raised without any assistance from the national exchequer, the companies providing it—in fully peopled countries[1]—have usually had to obtain from Government exceptional powers for the compulsory purchase of land, in return for which they have had to submit to a certain amount of governmental regulation. In many other cases railways and canals have been altogether constructed at the public expense, and managed by Government officials. The actual motive for these various kinds and degrees of governmental intervention has generally been that otherwise it did not seem likely that the improvements in question would be executed at all; the prospect of profit to private undertakers not being sufficiently brilliant and certain to overcome the difficulty of collecting capitals of the large amount required. In the case of railways in particular, the power of compulsory purchase of land has almost always been found indispensable; without it, the most enterprising companies would have shrunk from the task of bargaining with a large number of private landowners, each able by his refusal to increase the expense and diminish the utility of the line very materially. The practical issue has therefore not been between private enterprise pure and simple, and any form of governmental interference, but merely as to the kind and degree of the latter. For, on the very principles of natural liberty as ordinarily understood[2], it seems due to the owners of property on whom a forced exchange is imposed, that the power to compel such exchange should only be granted after careful investigation has shown a decided prospect of public advantage from it; while yet the necessity of making this investigation, by whatever machinery it is conducted, renders it difficult to exclude altogether the kind

[1] In the United States and the Dominion of Canada, the construction of great railways has been subvented by large grants of land as yet unoccupied.
[2] See, however, the note at the end of the chapter.

of illegitimate influences that we before noted as a danger incident to governmental management. So again, when a railway has been constructed, the more or less complete monopoly which it is sure to have of the facilities of conveyance between certain places on its line is, in part at least, due to the necessity of obtaining governmental sanction for any rival undertaking; hence Government is specially called upon to take care, if possible, that the interests of the public are not sacrificed to those of the monopolists. Further, the large amount of capital required for the construction of a railway or a canal generally excludes the independent enterprise of individual capitalists from this department: the choice, therefore, lies practically between governmental agency and the agency, under governmental control and regulation, of large joint-stock companies; and we have before observed that the latter is likely to exhibit somewhat the same defects as governmental agency, in comparison with management by private employers. The experience of different European countries, during the last fifty years has afforded considerable means of comparing the two systems: and the drawbacks that it has shown to exist in the system of management by regulated joint-stock companies may be stated as follows—taking for simplicity the case of railways, which has now the greatest practical importance.

1. In *Construction*, want of system, leading to unnecessary outlay; while yet gaps are left which it would be for the interest of the community to fill up; since local lines not likely to bring additional profit to shareholders might often pay their own expenses and greatly benefit their districts.

2. In respect of *Management*, again, so long as the separate companies are fighting each other for traffic, the public loses by the incoherent organization of its railroads—through difficulties of through-booking and imperfect correspondence—probably more than it gains in cheapness by competition. Competition, however, tends to be continually reduced by the 'Fusion' or 'Amalgamation' of companies, which it is decidedly the interest of the latter to effect;—though until it is effected the desire that each company naturally has to arrange the amalgamation on the best terms to itself tends to intensify rivalry, and prevent any effective cooperation in the meanwhile.

CHAP. IV.] *INTERFERENCE TO PROMOTE PRODUCTION.* 443

3. Amalgamation, however, increases the danger of divergence between public and private interests, that we have seen to be involved in monopoly. Nor has anything been gained, in England, by the attempt made to secure the public interest, when the construction of the line is authorized, by imposing limits on the fares charged; and attempts of this kind seem generally likely to fail, since the difficulty of forecasting the future conditions of a business like railway travelling would render it necessary to fix the limits of charges at the outset so high that it would probably not be the interest of the companies to come up to it, in case the undertaking was successful.

Again, the attempt to keep down the profits of such a monopoly, by fixing a maximum dividend, is open to the serious economic objection that when the maximum is reached, the company ceases to have any interest in preventing waste in management. This objection, however, might to a considerable extent be obviated by allowing the company to appropriate a certain share of the profits made beyond a certain limit, on condition that the remainder be applied to the reduction of charges. And in England the profits of railways have as yet not reached the point at which this particular objection would become practically important. Here the actual divergence of private from public interest lies mainly in the fact that the former excludes the possibility of such a reduction of fares as might greatly increase the utility of the railways at the risk of a *slight* loss in net revenue—a risk which it would obviously be expedient for the community to run under the circumstances, but not for private shareholders[1].

On the other hand, in a country like our own, in which large accumulations of capital are continually being made, and any opening for its profitable employment is eagerly seized, there are great counterbalancing advantages in leaving the field to joint-

---

[1] On the vexed question of "differential rates" I reserve what I have to say for a subsequent chapter (viii. § 4), in which I treat of the principles on which the governmental management of such a business as railway conveyance ought to be conducted. Here I will only say that the possible divergence on this point between the interest of the public and the real private interest of the railway company appears to me more limited in extent and importance than it is usually supposed to be by the traders who complain of differential rates.

stock companies: and there seems no reason to doubt that this agency has actually supplied us with railways both more amply and at an earlier period than governmental agency would have done, and probably with a closer adaptation of the order in time of their construction to the needs of industry.

On the whole the conclusion would seem to be, in the case of undertakings of this kind, that where the work is likely to be done by joint-stock companies if Government does not interfere, it should be left to the former during the first and more tentative stage of the undertaking, and even that private enterprise should be encouraged by concessions tolerably liberal as to charges, &c. for a limited period; but that the ultimate interests of the community should be secured by giving the Government the right of either freely revising the charges at the end of the period, or taking the business entirely into its management, on the payment of a fair price for the material capital employed, but without any extra sum in consideration of actual or expected profits[1].

In the case of railways it is not practically possible to separate the general management of the machinery of conveyance from the management of the roads over which it works[2]. But, as I have before observed, the case is different with ordinary roads and canals. Here the provision and management of the moveable instruments of conveyance has been generally left to private enterprise, without any governmental control for economic purposes, except as regards the prices charged for the use of vehicles plying in the streets of towns. The ground for this latter exception lies in the great convenience to the consumer of a uniform and stable price: otherwise the use of hackney carriages would seem to be a commodity of which the value

[1] As I shall presently point out, the same principles are applicable to other businesses besides those connected with transfer, provided they are of a kind that tend to become monopolies. It may be urged as a defect in the arrangement proposed that it would not give the company sufficient interest in the management of its business during the concluding part of the period. I think that there is some force in this objection; but that it might be obviated by a voluntary agreement between the government and the company, made a date somewhat earlier than the termination of the legal independence of the company.

[2] When railways were first introduced, it was intended that the use of them should be made available to the carriages of private individuals.

might be left to be determined by open competition, as advantageously as the value of any other article.

§ 4. *The Post-Office, &c.* The conveyance of letters is the department in which the advantages and success of governmental interference are most generally admitted—with the exception, perhaps, of coinage. The reason is that, while the business is in the main of a routine kind, adapted to governmental agency, both the gain in convenience and the saving of labour secured by unity of management is specially great: since the cost of carrying letters from office to office is but slightly increased by any increase in their number, while the reduction in the ratio of labour to utility in the work of distribution, obtained by the monopoly of it within each area of distribution, is very considerable. The saving through unity of management is less in the case of bulky or heavy parcels, since each additional parcel tends materially to increase the aggregate of carriage; but when a national machinery exists for the distribution of letters and light parcels, there seems a clear advantage in using it also for the distribution of larger parcels.

Before I pass to consider the other department of what I have called the machinery of transfer—viz. exchange—it may be convenient to notice a case of governmental interference which does not come under this head, but which in other respects has important economic affinities to the case of railways : I mean the provision of light and water. The analogy consists in the fact that these commodities have to be brought to the consumers by means of a special kind of path (pipes, wires), which can only be constructed by obtaining the partial use of long strips of land; these must either (1) be public roads (as is ordinarily the case), or (2) be obtained by compulsory sale : so that in either case some degree of governmental interference would be indispensable. Further, the expense of constructing any such special paths of conveyance, in a town or any thickly inhabited district, would be to a great extent the same whether the consumers supplied by it were all the inhabitants of the district in question or only a scattered portion of them ; hence the saving of cost obtained by keeping the whole supply of a certain area under one management is so great as to render a practical monopoly manifestly the most economic arrangement. On these grounds it is generally agreed that unrestricted competition, though it may be transiently useful, is not to be regarded as the normal condition of these branches of production: the issue is rather between governmental *regulation* and governmental *management*, and is to be decided, I conceive, in much the same way as the similar issue in the case of railways.

§ 5. *Metallic Currency.* The claims of the State to the monopoly of coining have been so generally admitted that the most uncompromising advocates of *laisser faire* have rarely thought it needful even to explain why they have not questioned it: however, the abstract economic reasons for it may be stated as follows. In the first place the ordinary advantage to the community from competition, in the way of improving processes of manufacture, is hardly to be looked for in the case of coin. It is the interest of the community that coins should be as far as possible hard to imitate, hard to tamper with, and qualified to resist wear and tear; but the person who procured the coins from the manufacturer—who would want, of course, to pass the money, and not to keep it—would not be adequately impelled by motives of self-interest to aim at securing excellence in these points.

Secondly, the admitted governmental duty of giving protection against fraud would under any circumstances have to be performed with special vigilance in the case of coin, owing to the extremely transitory interest that each individual has in the quality of the money he uses; and though this might conceivably be managed, if free coinage were allowed—by making it criminal to issue coins of the kind ordinarily used, containing less than the ordinary weight of metal—still the prevention of fraud would be far more difficult than it is at present, when all coining is illegal and all coins of the same value uniform in shape.

A supplementary argument in favour of governmental coining—in the abstract[1]—lies in the difficulty of otherwise securing a fair allotment of the loss through wear and tear of standard[2] coins. The convenience of circulation would in

---

[1] This advantage is not actually secured under our present system.

[2] 'Token' coins, would I suppose, be convertible by the issuers on demand, like bank-notes.

CHAP. IV.] *INTERFERENCE TO PROMOTE PRODUCTION.* 447

any case lead to the establishment—by common agreement if not by governmental regulation—of an allowable margin of deficiency in weight: but coins reduced through wear and tear below this margin would ultimately have to be rejected: and it is obviously unfair that the consequent loss should fall on the individual who, in the passage of a coin from hand to hand, happens to possess it at the exact point of the process of gradual attrition at which it falls below the accepted standard of weight. There seems, however, no effectual way of avoiding this result except that Government should undertake the loss and regularly call in light coin.

It is to be noted that if coinage were left to private enterprise, the expenses of producing coins would not really fall on the consumer: since, in fact, they would not fall on any one: they would merely have the effect of raising the exchange value of the coin proportionally above the value of the metal contained in it. Hence *primâ facie*, the same result ought to be brought about, where coinage is monopolized by Government: since, if Government bears the cost, the public loses collectively, without any corresponding gain to the members of the community. On the other hand the advantages of gratuitous coinage are (1) that it guards against the danger of slight fluctuations in the value of coin relatively to bullion, through temporary over-coinage and stoppage of mint; and (2) that otherwise merchants engaged in foreign trade—where coin is merely used as certified bullion—would necessarily lose the mint charge in exporting the coins, and would therefore have to raise the price of foreign goods in order to transfer the loss to consumers. But I know of no evidence from experience to show that danger (1) is considerable: and as regards (2) there does not appear to be any general reason why foreign trade should be thus specially subsidized at the public expense—in fact, as Jevons urges, the argument rather shows the desirability of establishing an international currency, if it be possible.

The general considerations, therefore, seem to be in favour of defraying the whole cost of coining by reduction in the weight of the coins; and, for the reason before given, this cost ought to include the loss through wear or tear, which should be borne by Government calling in the coins that have become too light through use—provided that fraudulent removal of the metal can be adequately prevented.

§ 6. So far we have considered (1) uniformity, and (2) protection against (a) fraud and (b) unequal incidence of loss from wear and tear, as the points at which Government should aim in managing coinage. We have now to take note of another important characteristic of a good medium of exchange: i.e. *stability* in general purchasing power. Considerable fluctuations in the value or general purchasing power of money are admitted to be an evil, from the disappointment of expectations that they cause, and the consequent uncertainty in calculating returns and remunerations, which is unfavourable to steady industry and careful trade: we may therefore assume that it is desirable to guard against such fluctuations so far as this can be done effectively without causing worse evils. There are two distinct ways in which Government may conceivably attain this end while keeping its currency on a metallic basis: either (1) by actually modifying the conditions of value of the metal used for standard coins, or (2) by measuring its changes in general purchasing power, and thus obtaining an ideal standard free from the fluctuations in value of the material medium of exchange. We might distinguish (1) and (2) as the method of *real*, and the method of *ideal* modification respectively. Let us consider the former first.

Where the medium of exchange, legally available for paying ordinary[1] debts of money, consists of coins of one metal and notes convertible into coin on demand, I know no means generally applicable for rendering its value more stable that could be recommended for the use of Government. On the one hand, a tendency to rise in value could only be resisted by promoting the use of substitutes for coin: but it is not ordinarily in the power of Government to do this, in an advanced industrial community, except so far as the use of such substitutes is actually reduced by legal restrictions. In this latter case, no doubt some effect in the desired direction may be produced by removing or modifying the restrictions:—thus in England the

[1] This is, debts that are beyond the small amount for which token coins are legal tender and that have not been contracted under the express condition of being paid in some other currency.

demand for gold coin might be to some extent lowered by allowing the use of one-pound notes; but the effect of any such measure, adopted in a single country only, is not likely to be great. On the other hand a fall in the purchasing power of gold coin might conceivably be counteracted by restricting coinage; but as this would tend to reduce the standard coins to mere tokens, the remedy would be worse than the disease.

I hold, however, that a material improvement in the prospects of stability of value of the medium of exchange may be obtained by the plan known as Bi-metallism: i.e. by coining gold and silver freely and making them legal tender in unlimited amounts at a fixed ratio. In a former part of this work I have already explained how a combination of governments may—up to a certain point—maintain the concurrent use of gold and silver as currency at a fixed ratio of exchange, even when the conditions of supply and demand are such as would—if operating unchecked—cause them to be exchanged at a different ratio. To show clearly the nature and extent of the force that such a bi-metallic union can exert, it will be convenient to distinguish (a) the monetary demand of the combining communities from (b) the rest of the demand for the precious metals—whether this be the monetary demand of countries outside the union, or the industrial or other non-monetary demand. We may call the former (a) the "rated" demand and the latter (b) the "unrated" demand, or the demand of the outside market. The force, then, by which the bi-metallic currency will tend to be maintained in effectual use,—notwithstanding changes in supply and unrated demand tending to cause a market-ratio of exchange between the metals different from the governmental ratio,—is the self-adaptation which will continually take place in the rated demand, counteracting the effect of such changes. When the outside conditions tend to make silver cheap, the rated demand will become a demand for more silver and less gold; when they tend to make gold cheap, it will become a demand for more gold and less silver; and this alternation will keep the market-ratio approximately identical with the mint-ratio, and in accordance with the ordinary law of value as dependent on supply and demand; and thus—provided that the tendency to divergence so counteracted is not too great or too prolonged—the currency will remain effectively bi-metallic, though it will be composed of the two metals in continually varying proportions.

I lay stress on the nature of the force exercised, because bi-metallists have sometimes spoken as if legal interference had some power of bringing about the concurrent use of the metals at a fixed ratio otherwise than through the operation of the ordinary law of supply and demand; while their opponents have often spoken as if the action of Governments in establishing a fixed ratio between gold and silver money was an attempt to resist natural laws, which must therefore be foredoomed to failure. Both these views seem to me misleading. On the one hand, though the fiat of Government can no doubt determine, independently of any effect on the relative market values of gold and silver, that these metals when coined shall be legal tender at a fixed ratio, it cannot secure that they shall be concurrently used, except very transiently, unless it also determines the ratio in the outside market; and the only way in which Governments can act on this outside ratio is by changes in the monetary demand as above described, which of course tend to affect market value just in the same way as any other changes in demand would affect it. On the other hand, it seems to me clear, that if the monetary demand of the bi-metallic union be large relatively to the whole demand for the precious metals, the bi-metallic character of the currency may be effectually maintained in spite of very considerable fluctuations in the outside conditions influencing the market value of the metals; and that by thus maintaining it the Governments no more attempt to override economic laws than a man attempts to override mechanical laws by erecting dams or dykes against floods.

I will illustrate the process above described by a hypothetical case; which will at the same time show how the effectiveness of the bi-metallic union will depend upon the proportion of the monetary demand that it controls to the whole demand. Let us assume that there is a bi-metallic union of countries holding three-fourths of the whole stock of gold coin in use, which we will take to be £700,000,000; that when the union begins the governmental ratio of gold to silver is that of the market,—say

CHAP. IV.] *INTERFERENCE TO PROMOTE PRODUCTION.* 451

1 : 15½—; and that three-eighths of the annual supply of gold goes to the bi-metallic mints, one-eighth being absorbed by the non-bi-metallic mints and one-half by the non-monetary demand. Let us assume further, that when the union begins, the countries are increasing in wealth, and that the annual supply of gold and silver is just sufficient to keep their values unchanged in relation to commodities generally. Now let us suppose that, other things remaining unchanged, the annual supply of gold falls from £20,000,000 to £15,000,000. Obviously the most that could be required to maintain the rated value of gold in the outside market would be that the same supply as before, £12,500,000, should go to satisfy the outside demand; but in fact slightly less than this will suffice, since the value of gold—and therefore, under the bi-metallic system, of silver also—will rise slightly in consequence of the decreased supply of gold, and this rise will cause a corresponding reduction in the unrated demand for both metals. This last effect will also involve a slight increase in the amount of silver brought to the bi-metallic mints. The bi-metallic currency will thus tend to have less gold in it than before in proportion to silver; but it will not, therefore, have positively less gold than before, since the supply that still comes to the bi-metallic mints will more than suffice to make up for the loss through wear and tear of coins. And this state of things may be conceived to go on for an indefinite time without any tendency to deprive the bi-metallic currency of its gold, or to cause a divergence between mint-ratio and market-ratio; though of course the proportion of gold coin to silver will steadily decrease under the conditions supposed.

If, however, we had inverted the supposed relation of the two monetary demands—if we had supposed a bi-metallic mint absorbing, before the fall in production, only one-eighth of the annual supply, and non-bi-metallic mints absorbing three-eighths—, the change supposed must at once have decreased the stock of gold coin held by the bi-metallic country; and each succeeding year would diminish it further until the currency became practically a mono-metallic currency of silver— with some gold coin probably circulating at a premium.

Similar results would follow, *mutatis mutandis,* if we supposed an increased supply of silver instead of a decreased supply of gold; in either case, the questions whether, and how long, the nominally bi-metallic currency can really maintain its character, must depend on the extent of the rated demand as compared with the outside demand, and on the magnitude of the changes that occur in the outside conditions determining the value of either metal.

Supposing that the bi-metallic system is effectually maintained, in the manner above explained, it will evidently have two effects: (1) it will keep the ratio of exchange between the metals approximately uniform, not only within but outside the range of the bi-metallic union; and (2) it will tend to make fluctuations in the standard of value less rapid and serious by spreading the effect of any change in the conditions of supply of either metal over the whole aggregate of the world's currency, instead of letting it operate solely on that part of the currency which is composed of the metal primarily affected[1]. The advantages of (2) are, I conceive, generally admitted: nor will the advantages of (1) be disputed, if we assume that both gold and silver are to continue to be extensively used in the whole aggregate of civilized communities effectively united by international trade: and at the present time the most eager monometallists do not appear to desire the universal adoption of a gold currency, at the risk of a great rise in the value of the medium of exchange. Indeed we may say that the trade of the world—even the internal trade of the British Empire—will in any case be carried on under what may be called, in a certain sense, "bi-metallic" conditions: and that the practical issue, so far as international trade is concerned, lies not between mono-metallism and bi-metallism, strictly speaking, but between what we might call "rated" and "unrated bi-metallism".

If, then, the advantages of effectual bi-metallism be granted, the next point in a practical consideration of the scheme would

[1] The two advantages mentioned in the text are those which appear to belong to the bi-metallic system independently of any forecast of the special conditions of production of the two metals. But in view of the unfavourable prospects of the future production of gold—mentioned in the next paragraph—some bi-metallists would lay still greater stress on the danger which a gold mono-metallic currency involves of a fall in prices so great and prolonged as to be seriously injurious to trade and industry.

be to estimate carefully the actual chance of maintaining it. But to frame such an estimate hardly comes within the scope of the present treatise: since for this purpose, as we have seen, it is fundamentally important to determine the extent and durability of the combination of Governments which can reasonably be anticipated, as well as the extent of the monetary demand that they can control, as compared with the outside demand for the precious metals. I do not profess to deal with the strictly political aspect of this question, and, in a treatise that is primarily concerned with principles, it would be out of place to discuss fully even its economic aspect :—especially as the industrial world of which England is a part seems to me to have before it a difficult choice between different kinds of risk and inconveniences, the decision of which requires a very careful estimate of the economic quantities involved. I may, however, say that at present the balance of argument appears to me to be on the side of bimetallism; provided that a stable combination can be effected —such as is now proposed—of England, the United States, Germany, and the countries forming the Latin Union. It must, indeed, be conceded to mono-metallists that if—as Soetbeer holds[1]—the present consumption of gold in arts and manufactures absorbs nearly three-fifths of the annual supply, then, considering the general reasons that we have for expecting the production of gold to grow hereafter more scanty and costly as compared with that of silver, any possible bi-metallic union has to face a serious risk of its currency coming to consist mainly of silver. On the other hand the same causes that would bring about this result would, if there were no bi-metallic union, inflict on the industry of the countries with a gold standard the serious evils of a great rise in the purchasing power of the medium of exchange :—and, though our ideal aim should be simply to keep the value of this medium stable, it must be recognised that the economic evils of a rise in value are considerably greater than those of a fall in value; since the latter change is

---

[1] See his "Materialien zur Erläuterung und Beurtheilung der wirthschaft-"lichen Edelmetallverhältnisse" (1885). He estimates the gold product in the years 1881—1884 at 589,000 kilograms, and the amount consumed in arts and manufactures—deducting old materials—during the same year, at 350,000 kilograms.

on the whole favourable to the classes that are economically most important. Further, I think that the "misery" of having to use silver instead of gold is somewhat exaggerated by English mono-metallists especially when only an easily altered law prevents an Englishman from having the one-pound notes on which his Scotch fellow-countrymen seem to thrive. Nor is the extra cost of storing silver bank-reserves, and of transmitting silver bullion in payment of international debts, an evil of such magnitude that the mere risk of it should be held to be a conclusive objection to bi-metallism. Similarly, the disturbances caused to expectation by the transition from mono-metallic to bi-metallic currency are not I conceive sufficiently important to weigh heavily in a practical consideration of the question; provided that care is taken to choose a governmental ratio not very divergent from the market ratio that would have established itself without governmental interference, if a change had taken place in the demand for gold and silver equal to that which would be caused by the action of the bi-metallic union.

§ 7. But, as I have before said, it is possible to obviate the bad effects of great changes in the purchasing power of the medium of exchange, by a method altogether different from Bi-metallism and from all other schemes that aim at actually modifying the exchange-value of standard coin. We may allow the actual standard to fluctuate, and yet maintain a stable ideal standard by measuring and allowing for these fluctuations. The adoption of such a "tabular standard" was suggested twelve years ago by Jevons in his little book on "Money¹" (ch. XXV). He suggests that a permanent government commission might be "created, and endowed with a kind of judicial power. The "officers of the department would collect the current prices of "commodities in all the principal markets of the kingdom, and, "by a well-defined system of calculations, would compute from "these data the average variations in the purchasing power of "gold. The decisions of this commission would be published "monthly, and payments would be adjusted in accordance with "them. Thus, suppose that a debt of one hundred pounds was

¹ As Jevons is careful to explain, the suggestion of such a 'tabular standard' as he advocates was first made by Joseph Lowe in 1822; and afterwards by G. Poulett Scrope in 1833.

"incurred upon the 1st of July, 1875, and was to be paid back on
"1st July, 1878; if the commission had decided in June, 1878,
"that the value of gold had fallen in the ratio of 106 to 100 in
"the intervening years, then the creditor would claim an increase
"of 6 per cent. in the nominal amount of the debt.

"At first the use of this national tabular standard might be
"permissive, so that it could be enforced only where the parties
"to the contract had inserted a clause to that effect in their con-
"tract. After the practicability and utility of the plan had be-
"come sufficiently demonstrated, it might be made compulsory, in
"the sense that every money debt of, say, more than three months'
"standing, would be varied according to the tabular standard, in
"the absence of an express provision to the contrary." It is not
intended that such a commission should take the prices of *all*
commodities into account in their computation: but merely that
they should take a considerable number of different commodities,
chosen so as to be fairly representative of the whole mass.

I concur with Jevons in regarding the scheme as theoretically
sound, though I think that a considerable time must elapse
before so unfamiliar a basis for pecuniary contracts is likely to
be voluntarily adopted to a sufficient extent to justify its formal
establishment by Government as the normal basis, any deviation
from which must be expressly announced. I think also that
the inevitable theoretical imperfections of the process by which
variations in the material standard would be measured would
render it especially necessary to proceed with great caution in
its practical application. As I have elsewhere[1] argued, it is
impossible to determine with perfect precision the extent to
which the general purchasing power of gold—or any other commodity—has changed within a given period; in consequence of
(1) the changes that take place in the relative quantities in
which different articles enter into ordinary consumption, and (2)
of the changes in quality of articles nominally the same, caused
by the development of industry. I agree with Jevons that
the inevitable element of inexactness thus introduced into the
scientific computation of a tabular standard of value would not
practically prevent us from securing by such a standard a higher

---

[1] Book I. ch. ii. § 3, pp. 61—63.

degree of stability in the value of money-debts than could otherwise be obtained. But it would have the effect of making any plan adopted by such a commission as he proposes appear somewhat arbitrary: and in carrying it out very delicate points would arise on which the decisions of the commission—when they came to involve large pecuniary interest—would be severely criticised. E.g. if any important change in consumption rendered it necessary to reduce the importance of any commodity in the selected list, or even to substitute a new commodity, or if a question arose as to the right *quality* to be chosen in the case of an article of which there were different and varying qualities,—the immense power of determining gain or loss that the scheme would place in the hands of a few persons would, I fear, arouse much jealousy and distrust. I do not urge these objections as reasons for not carrying Jevons' suggestion into effect: I should be glad to see this done: but I do not think that we can reasonably regard it as a resource for dealing with present evils or risks, arising from changes in the purchasing power of gold[1].

[1] Before leaving this subject, I ought to notice a combination of the method of Bi-metallism with the method of the Tabular standard, proposed by M. Leon Walras, which is certainly at once simple and ingenious, though I cannot regard it as practicable. M. Walras proposes that there should be a union of governments, similar to that contemplated by Bi-metallists, which should have for its object not to maintain the unlimited coinage of gold and silver at a fixed ratio, but, while coining gold freely in unlimited amounts, to circulate along with it such an amount of silver coin as should be found to be from time to time necessary to keep the purchasing power of money approximately stable. This silver coin he calls "billon regulateur", intending it to have—like ordinary token coin—a value fixed in relation to the gold coin, and higher than that of the silver contained in it. The amount of such coin should be determined from time to time by an international statistical commission, which should have the function of ascertaining at certain intervals the extent to which general prices had risen or fallen: and its coinage should be apportioned by agreement among the combining nations, according to the recommendations of this commission. Supposing such an agreement could be brought about and maintained, I think this system might prove as strong as the bi-metallic system proper to resist the disturbing force likely to be exercised on it by the expected scanty supply of gold; while, so long as this result was brought about, this regulated supplement of silver might no doubt have an important effect in preventing or reducing fluctuations in the general purchasing power of money. But the problem of determining the varying amounts of silver coin necessary to prevent these fluctuations appears to me much more difficult and complex than M. Walras

§ 8. *Paper Currency and Banking.* The governmental monopoly of metallic currency has never, so far as I know, been advocated by theorists—though in earlier ages it has been extensively used—as a source of public revenue: in fact, as we have seen, the practical question is rather whether it should be a source of expense to the nation. It is universally admitted that the alarm and disturbance to trade that would be caused, if Government tried to gain by reducing the amount of metal in coins while keeping up their value by limitation of issue, would far more than outweigh any profit that might be made by the operation. It is agreed, therefore, that Government ought to coin metal into standard coins freely for all applicants, at a price—at least—not materially greater than the cost of coining. For similar reasons, it is agreed that the tempting source of gain offered by the power of issuing inconvertible notes should be at any rate reserved for an extreme crisis of national need. But it has often been maintained that the State ought to keep in its own hands the business of issuing notes convertible into coin on demand, with the view of deriving from it a valuable contribution to the national income. And it is certainly true that by monopolizing this part of the business of banking a Government can practically borrow a considerable amount of capital, at a very low rate: i.e. at the cost of making and circulating the notes, together with ordinary interest on the metal kept as a reserve in order to secure convertibility. This, however, does not prove that it is the interest of the community that such a monopoly should be exercised: there are many highly objectionable governmental monopolies which the State could easily carry on with considerable profit to the exchequer. What has to be shown is either (1) that governmental management has some special advantages as compared with individual or associative management in this business: or, at least (2)

regards it: since the effect on prices of a given addition to the amount of metal used for monetary purposes would vary very much according to the nature and efficiency of the banking system in different countries. And, since any serious mistake in the apportionment of silver coinage among the combining countries would render the country on which an excess of silver was imposed liable to a drain of gold, I think that the difficulties of forming and maintaining such an international agreement as M. Walras' scheme requires would be quite insuperable—at least for a long time to come.

that, for some reason or other, the extra gain that bankers would make if free issue of bank-notes were allowed would not be transferred to the consumers, by a more abundant and cheap supply of the conveniences of banking. As regards (2) it is, as we have seen, theoretically possible that this transfer might not take place: the extra gains might (*a*) be retained by the banks· so far as circumstances exempt them from competition, or (*b*) might be divided among an excessive number of competing businesses, so as to reduce average profits but not charges. I do not, however, know any adequate grounds for supposing that these effects would occur; or that competition would not operate in the normal way.

As regards point (1), it certainly seems that the business of issuing notes and giving coin for them on demand is of the routine character suited to governmental management; as admitting of being conducted safely under fixed rules, by which (e.g.) the amount of reserve to be kept is once for all determined[1]: and a solvent Government seems to have an important advantage—as compared with private enterprise pure and simple—in being able to provide more complete security at a smaller expense of reserve: partly from the generally greater stability of Governments, partly because a Government, in the last resort, can suspend payment and yet keep its notes current. And this completer security is important not only because the greater confidence that a safe currency inspires is likely to increase its general use; but especially for the protection of the poor and ignorant persons who would be unable to inquire into the circumstances of the different banks whose notes they accept.

These reasons, I think, seem to me to weigh heavily against absolutely unregulated issue: it seems, however, that adequate security might be provided for the ordinary note-holder[2] by merely placing private issues under strict governmental regulation, while still leaving to private enterprise the determination

---

[1] I do not mean to affirm that this is the most economical mode of conducting the business of issuing notes. As I shall presently explain, there are strong reasons for holding that a more elastic system would be more economical.

[2] I distinguish the 'ordinary note-holder' from the man of business who is chiefly liable to suffer from a financial crisis.

CHAP. IV.] *INTERFERENCE TO PROMOTE PRODUCTION.* 459

of the amount of notes and the proportion of reserve required from time to time. Thus—to adopt a suggestion made by Mr R. H. Patterson[1]—bank-notes might be issued *by* Government, but *for* any bank requiring them, without limit, but subject to the condition that their value should be covered by a deposit of Government securities exceeding the nominal value of the notes by an amount sufficient to obviate any danger of loss from depreciation of the securities. The bank for which such notes were issued should be solely responsible for the payment of gold for the notes; but they should be legal tender until the bank stopped payment. Whenever a bank stopped payment, its deposited securities would be at the disposal of the Government for the payment of the note-holders: the notes, in fact, would become practically a kind of exchequer bills; and they would probably continue to circulate in this condition. But even if they did not circulate the ordinary note-holder would at any rate suffer no serious loss from the collapse of the bank responsible for them.

Supposing the value of any note to be secured, either in this way or by full governmental responsibility, there would seem to be no ground for prohibiting the issue of notes below a certain amount; unless such issue should be found to carry with it inevitably a material increase of forgery, which the experience of Scotland does not lead me to anticipate. Apart from this latter danger, the issue of small notes is, of course, an economic advantage to the bankers directly, and indirectly—we may assume—to their customers; no less than the issue of notes for larger amounts is.

But although it seems manifestly possible, by such regulation as that above suggested, to protect the ordinary note-holder from material loss; I hardly think that this—or any other scheme for mere *regulation* of issues, as contrasted with absolute *limitation* through State monopoly—would adequately secure the result for which the commercial world is most keenly concerned, by providing a supply of good money in a financial crisis to fill the gap caused by a general collapse of credit. It may be urged that, as things are, the agony point of such a crisis in

[1] Cf. *Science of Finance*, chap. xx.

London is reached by the Bank of England declining to lend even on Government securities, and that the dread of this point has a certain tendency to realize itself, as it intensifies the earlier stages of the crisis: and it may be thought that such a scheme as the above would remove this dread, as it would enable any bank to obtain legal tender by depositing its own Government securities. And I should admit it to be quite possible that the pressure of a crisis might in this way receive timely relaxation, so that the crisis might pass off without reaching the worst stage; but I do not see how we can be assured that this would happen; while if the worst stage were reached, if the crisis became panic, the weak side of the proposed system of legal tender notes would become manifest. Every one would fear that the particular bank responsible for his notes might stop payment, and thereby reduce his notes to the condition of mere Government debts, not immediately and certainly available for meeting liabilities; there would therefore be a serious danger of a general run for gold, and general ruin. This danger is avoided under the existing system in England; since no one is afraid of the insolvency of the Issue Department of the Bank of England, even when the limitations on issue in the Bank Charter Act of 1844 are temporarily suspended—as has been the case in the three chief crises that have occurred since 1844[1]. And it appears to me that only notes issued by Government, or by a bank which was understood to be practically secure of the support of Government in the ultimate resort, would have the unique quality required to resist the worst storms of distrust that experience shows to be possible.

§ 9. There seem to me, therefore, to be strong general reasons for keeping the function of issuing notes—and of providing a reserve of gold for their conversion—under the responsibility of Government; instead of merely regulating the issue on some such plan as that above proposed. If, however, we yield to these reasons and assume that it is desirable to have a monopolized issue of notes, sustained (in the last resort) by the credit and authority of Government, in order to guard against the extreme perils of a panic; it is manifest that a step in govern-

[1] The Issue Department is required by the act to keep gold corresponding to all the notes circulated, beyond a certain minimum.

CHAP. IV.] *INTERFERENCE TO PROMOTE PRODUCTION.* 461

mental interference, beyond what we have so far expressly considered, will become necessary. For in order that this end may be attained, in order that the abnormal issues of notes required in a panic may be properly managed, the Government must undertake—directly or indirectly—not merely the function of buying gold with notes and redeeming notes with gold, but also the function of lending notes on adequate security. Thus the department that issues notes must either (1) become a regular bank, or (2) be prepared to perform from time to time, under specially difficult circumstances, the most delicate and important part of the work of a bank; or (3) it must constitute, or enter into alliance with, some individual bank doing ordinary banking business, and entrust these duties to its management. The third of these courses seems the best; since, in the first place, the business of lending money on credit does not seem to be generally more suitable to governmental management than any other branch of commerce; rather it would seem to require the close and keen observation of the state of trade generally, and of individual traders, which it is the special advantage of private enterprise to call forth. And, secondly, a department that had no regular banking business at ordinary times, would hardly be likely to have the knowledge and trained skill required for solving correctly difficult problems of banking at special crises; it would have to depend on the advice of outsiders, liable to be biassed by urgent private interests. But even the establishment of a bank in special connexion with—though not a department of—Government tends to produce very important incidental effects on the banking system of the country. The unique security that such a governmental bank affords to depositors gives other banks an inducement to use it for the custody of their reserves; money lodged with the governmental bank is thought as safe as money in a strong box, and less troublesome; transfers of sums in its books are a very convenient mode of settling accounts among banks; and thus bankers slide naturally into the 'one-reserve system' that actually exists in England. It must be admitted, I think, that this system, increasing as it does the instability of the vast edifice of credit that is supported on this small basis of gold, renders the danger of crisis and panic proportionally greater; that is, the very need, of which the existence (as we have seen) forms the main justification for governmental interference with banking, must be partly attributed to that interference itself. On the other hand the same interference must to an equal extent be credited with the merit of the system, which lies in its economy; it enables a vast banking business to be transacted at a small expenditure in metallic reserve: and therefore those critics of our Bank Act of 1844 who complain of the large amount of gold lying idle in the vaults of the Bank of England, ought at any rate to recognise that the aggregate expense incurred by the community in keeping gold is less than it would probably be under a system of free banking, under which the leading banks (at any rate) would be likely to keep each its own reserve.

This does not of course prove that the metallic reserve actually kept under the English system might not be safely reduced; or that it might not be turned to better account, if the connexion between the Government and what we have called the 'governmental bank' were established on a different plan. Indeed it seems evident that if the Bank of England had full discretion in determining the proportion of reserve to notes issued, it would at least have the *power* of performing its functions in a manner more advantageous to the community than at present. To show this, we will suppose that the Bank is now keeping practically[1] about eleven millions of metallic reserve to meet the liabilities of the banking department, and about ten millions more to meet those of the Issue Department. Under the present strict regulation of the Issue Department this latter reserve cannot be used for banking purposes, so that its existence does not give any additional strength to the banking department; hence any given drain of gold acts on the banking reserve with much greater force than it would ordinarily exercise if the bank were left free to treat the two reserves as one. Hence it would seem that if the Bank were unfettered, the rate of discount would *ceteris paribus* be decidedly less liable to be affected by slight and transient movements of gold than is now the case; so that the rapid and large fluctuations in interest,

[1] Of course the reserve in the Banking Department actually consists mainly of notes; but the result is practically that stated in the text, since gold corresponding to these notes is kept in the Issue Department.

CHAP. IV.] *INTERFERENCE TO PROMOTE PRODUCTION.* 463

which are recognised as a bad result of our existing system, would be reduced, other things being the same. On the other hand it is bold to assume that other things would remain the same: or rather—for the present reserve may be too large—that the Bank would take all due precautions to avoid the risk of having to suspend payments. Indeed when we consider merely from an abstract point of view the proposal to give a particular joint-stock company an exclusive privilege of issuing notes the value of which will, in the last resort, be sustained by the authority of Government, without subjecting its exercise of this privilege to any governmental control whatsoever; it certainly appears a very hazardous measure. If we suppose the Bank to be governed by the vulgar desire of private gain, it will, in determining the proportion of notes to reserve, consider the risk to itself and not the risk to the community; and though the danger to itself from an inadequate reserve would be serious, it would be less than in the case of an ordinary bank—since we have supposed that Government would, in the last resort, intervene to sustain the currency of the notes.

It remains to consider briefly whether, supposing that there is a legally determined *normal* limit of the uncovered note-issue, it is desirable that the relaxation of this restriction should be only obtainable—as in England—by irregular governmental interference, or that it shall be regularly purchaseable by the Bank. If the price of the relaxation were placed sufficiently high, if (e.g.) the bank had to pay 5 per cent. for any excess over the normal amount of uncovered note-issue, the difference between the two plans would seem to be chiefly political rather than economical: neither resource would be brought into play except in an extreme emergency, but the former would have the advantage of avoiding the bad constitutional precedent set by the irregular suspension of a law. But the former measure would work very differently, if the price paid were so small that the extra issue could be counted on as an ordinary mode of relieving the pressure on the money-market; such a regulation would, I think, be an awkward combination of control and freedom: just when the Bank's relations with the commercial world became most difficult and delicate, the responsibility for yielding to the pressure for loans would be partly taken off its shoulders by what would appear to be express governmental provision for extended issue.

I have said that that part of an ordinary banker's function which consists in lending money to traders and other employers of capital is not a business in which governmental management is likely to have any special advantage. On the other hand, as a borrower of money the Government of a well-ordered and prosperous community is able to give a higher degree of security to its creditors than even a large joint-stock company can do. Hence governmental agency is specially adapted for taking charge of the savings of persons, to whom security is generally of more importance than high interest, whether such savings take the simple form of depositing money, or the more complicated form of payment for life-insurance, purchase of annuities, &c. Moreover there are particular departments of the business of lending, where the risk may be reduced to a small amount, which appear, from their routine character, to be not ill suited to governmental management. Thus there seems to be no particular reason why Government should not lend money on the security of land, as I shall presently notice; or even, for short periods, on moveable pledges, the value of which is not likely to change materially in a short time nor difficult to ascertain approximately: and in fact experience[1] renders it probable that, by establishing a governmental monopoly of pawnbroking, loans can be remuneratively made to the poor on easier terms than open competition would enable them to secure. There is the further argument for such a governmental monopoly that it considerably decreases the difficulty of preventing pawnbrokers from becoming practically receivers of stolen goods[2].

§ 10. I pass to notice certain important cases in which the interference of Government has been widely exercised and still more extensively solicited partly in the interest of production; but also largely with a view to other ends—the relief of distress, the increase of political security and stability, the amelioration of the moral or intellectual condition of large classes of citizens,

---

[1] See statistics given in an article on *Pawnbroking at Home and Abroad*, by Rev. W. Edwards, in *Nineteenth Century*, June, 1881—observing, however, that the Monts-de-Piété in France are only partially self-supporting.

[2] The distributional arguments for these measures will be noticed in ch. vii.

or the attainment of certain ideal aims of social human progress. The departments to which I refer may be briefly indicated by the names Education, Emigration and Land-tenure;—the last two being to some extent connected. I shall here consider them merely from a *productional* point of view.

Of these departments the first is undoubtedly the most important, if we take the term in an extended sense, to include all institutions or regulations for the promotion of culture, either of adults or of children. I have before observed, that— though the same machinery may partly serve the two purposes,—still the principles on which Government intervenes in the education of children are importantly different from those upon which its assistance is claimed for the intellectual improvement of adults. From the fundamental assumption of the system of natural liberty, that a man is the best guardian of his own interests, it by no means follows that he is the best guardian of his children's interests; and, in fact, in the freest of modern communities, it is found necessary to sustain by legal sanctions the parent's obligation to provide even for the material wants of his children. It is, therefore, no contravention of natural liberty —so far at least as it is maintained in the interest of production— to secure them a minimum of education by the same legal compulsion. But the expense of this education, if not artificially reduced by pecuniary aid from Government, would—in almost any civilized society—be so serious a burden on the poorest class, that it would be practically impossible to make the compulsion universal: and, as was before pointed out, the community derives an economic gain[1] from the education of its younger members—so far as they are thereby rendered more efficient labourers—which the self-interest of private employers cannot be relied upon to provide, owing to the difficulty of appropriating the advantage of the increased efficiency. Hence a national provision for education may to some extent be considered and justified as a measure for improving national production. The instruction, however, that is thus made compulsory and artificially cheap on this principle should be

---

[1] It may be observed that a certain portion of this gain to the Community will tend to appear as a definite national gain to the national exchequer, in consequence of the increased taxes paid by the more productive labourers.

strictly confined to imparting aptitudes of incontestable utility to industry; and whatever it is made universally obligatory to acquire should, of course, be universally useful.

But further; there may be the same general economic justification for cheapening by governmental aid the special training required for skilled labour, as there is for cheapening elementary general education: that is, the community may gain an adequate return for its expenditure in the greater abundance and better quality of the skilled labour so provided. This argument would hold, independently of any assumption that natural liberty is not likely to provide the right kind of training for those who can afford to pay for it. In fact, however, this assumption has been very generally made by those who have defended or solicited the intervention of modern Governments in the preparation for various trades and professions. Even in the case of the lower kinds of skilled labour, it is widely held that the traditional custom of learning a trade by apprenticeship— i.e. by mere practice and the casual intermittent instruction that persons engaged in the work can find time to give to beginners—has actually led to very unsatisfactory results: that the skill thus acquired tends to be mechanical and unprogressive, and not even so cheap as it appears, owing to the long time spent in its acquisition: and that therefore it is a socially remunerative employment of public money to organize and artificially cheapen systematic technical instruction[1]. In the case, again, of the higher kinds of skill required for what are called the learned professions, the incapacity of ordinary persons to judge of such skill has been generally recognised as a ground for governmental interference to ensure a certain degree of competence in recognised members of these professions: and most civilized Governments have not been content to secure this by requiring certain examinations to be passed by such persons; they have also given salaries to teachers appointed to impart the required knowledge at low charge, in universities or otherwise. A modern university, however, is not merely an institution for imparting special kinds of knowledge for professional purposes; it has also the function of advancing knowledge

[1] This view has gained ground considerably in England, since the publication —in 1883—of the first edition of this treatise.

generally and facilitating its acquirement by students whose aims are purely scientific. This speculative pursuit of knowledge is to a large extent—and to an extent incapable at any given time of being definitely determined—indirectly useful to industry; and since, as was before noticed, its results cannot usually be appropriated and sold, there is an obvious reason for remunerating the labour required to produce these results, and defraying the expenses incidental to the work, out of public funds,—at any rate if a provision adequate for the purpose is not available from private sources.

Besides oral instruction, in modern times, access to books is a most important means of spreading and advancing knowledge. Libraries, indeed, are among the essential instruments of academic teaching; but, as has been strikingly said, a library apart from oral instruction is itself a cheap university. The institution of free libraries and museums supported at public expense is perhaps most frequently advocated, just as a national provision for elementary or higher education is, from a *distributional* point of view, as a harmless and salutary form of communism; still the great indirect advantage that the community gains through the general spread of intelligence, and especially through facilitating the acquirement of knowledge by exceptionally gifted persons, is at any rate an important consideration from the point of view of production. And even in the case of galleries and museums of Art this consideration comes in to some extent, so far as artistic cultivation improves artistic production.

Before leaving this subject it should be observed that by far the most extensive application of public funds to the culture of adults, in most modern European communities, consists of a provision for religious worship and instruction. It would, however, be obviously incongruous to dwell on this in the present connexion: and in fact the interference of the State for this purpose, considered from a purely secular point of view, is rather to be justified on account of the value of the clergy as "spiritual police",—that is, from the indirect aid given by them to the necessary governmental function of preventing crime.

§ 11. I pass to consider the interference of Government in order to promote or regulate the migration of human beings from densely populated districts to others that are wholly or partially unoccupied. Such interference has sometimes been prompted by considerations not primarily economic; thus the colonization of a region forcibly annexed, or unable to resist the intrusion of strangers, has been fostered in order to facilitate or confirm a conquest of territory: on the other hand, in some countries the immigration of foreigners generally, or of persons of alien race or religion, has been prohibited or hampered, in order to protect the native civilization from the intrusion of subversive elements; elsewhere, again, immigration of a certain kind has been encouraged in the interests of morality and social well-being—as (e.g.) when female immigration has been promoted to prevent a great inequality of the sexes in a new colony. The grounds and limits of such kinds of interference it is beyond my province to discuss: and the same may be said of the measures now taken by our Government to secure the sea-worthiness of ships, and the sufficiency of their supply of provisions, water, medicine, &c.; since these latter regulations belong to the class of interferences for other than strictly economic ends, which were briefly surveyed in the preceding chapter. Confining ourselves to such governmental encouragement or control of emigration as has been undertaken or recommended on distinctly economic grounds, we may regard it generally as a case closely parallel to that of education, which we have just been considering: the principle of either kind of interference is that there is a possible gain to the community, —which *laisser faire* is not likely to realize,—through the increase of the efficiency of certain labourers, in the one case by developing their personal aptitudes, in the other by placing them in more favourable outward circumstances. In the case of emigration, however, the distribution of this common gain among the various classes of persons affected usually admits of being somewhat more definitely foreseen than in that of education. If the benefit consisted exclusively in an increase of income to the emigrants themselves, it would hardly, I conceive, be proposed to defray their expenses out of the general taxes. But this supposition is very unlikely to be realised in practice. In the first place, supposing the region of immigration and that of emigration to have the same government,

CHAP. IV.] *INTERFERENCE TO PROMOTE PRODUCTION.* 469

the increased taxes subsequently paid by the immigrants would generally yield the public a certain return on the cost of conveying them; against this, however, we have to set the increased expenditure required for the adequate fulfilment of the functions of Government towards the immigrants under their changed circumstances; and since it is generally reasonable to suppose that a certain portion of the assisted immigrants would have come at their own expense if they could have got no aid from Government, it would only be under very special circumstances that the increment of taxes really due to the outlay of Government in assisting them would amount to full interest on the outlay. But generally speaking, when emigration is successful, measurable advantages accrue from it, over and above this increment of taxation, to other members of the community, or to the community as a whole.

Here it is important to distinguish (1) the advantages gained by persons who employ the immigrating labourers, (2) the gain of those who exchange products with them, either as ultimate consumers or for purposes of trade and production, and (3) the relief obtained from overcrowding. In England, extensive schemes of governmental aid to emigration have often been strongly supported with a view to this last-mentioned benefit; but there is an obvious danger that the relief obtained by any one such measure would be merely temporary, and, if the aid were continually renewed, would produce comparatively little remedial effect, since it would operate mainly as a partial removal of the checks that normally keep down population in an overcrowded district. Nor can even temporary relief from overcrowding be thus secured, if free immigration is allowed into the district from which emigration is being promoted; unless the overcrowding has forced the remuneration of labour there to a level clearly below that of all other districts from which immigration thither is possible. Hence any large supply of governmental funds to emigrants, considered merely as a relief to the pressure of population in the region of emigration, is only to be recommended as an exceptional eleemosynary measure, in case of unexpected and abnormal distress. On the other hand during the long sway of the 'Colonial Policy' that Adam Smith assailed, the chief advantage derived by the mother country from colonization was generally understood to consist in the extension of trade that it brought about: and no doubt this gain, if the colony flourishes, is generally likely to be in the long run considerable[1]; but it can rarely be sufficiently certain and definite to render it anything like a profitable outlay for a community to send out colonists at the public expense, for the sake of the profit of their trade to the mother country. There remains, as the clearest economic gain resulting from emigration to others besides the emigrants, that which accrues to the owners of land and employers of capital in the region of immigration; the resources of this region being supposed to be so far undeveloped, that considerable additions to the labour and capital employed in it may be made, with an increasing rather than diminishing return to both. At first sight this would seem to be a reason for leaving the business of introducing emigrants to the private enterprise of the landowners and capitalists who might obtain a full return for it in labour; but there is a serious obstacle to private enterprise in the uncertainty of the profit on such outlay to any individual capitalist, owing to the difficulty of enforcing labour-contracts for a considerable term of years,—especially in a very thinly inhabited country—without introducing something like temporary serfdom. Hence, supposing all such serfdom—even of criminals or men of lower race—to be excluded on moral or political grounds, the intervention of the public purse is likely to be necessary for the effective introduction of the required labour.

§ 12. This intervention will be facilitated, if the unoccupied lands of the region of immigration are owned by the community, so that the sale or lease of them supplies a fund from which the expense of importing colonists may be defrayed. And in fact (as I before noticed) the question of governmental aid to immigration has had a close historical connexion with the regulation of the acquisition of land in a new country. Here the theoretical problem of determining the grounds and limits of legitimate interference is complicated by a peculiar diffi-

---

[1] The extent of this gain, as Merivale points out, will be very different in different cases; it is conceivable that large numbers of emigrants may be settled and comfortably maintained in a colony, where the net produce exported is yet comparatively insignificant. Cf. *On Colonization*, Lec. ix. and xiii.

culty of deciding what is, and what is not, interference; or, to put it otherwise, what precise action on the part of the Government would strictly conform to the principles of natural liberty. At first sight it may seem that in new countries, as Merivale[1] argues, "the 'natural' course of settlement is that "which would take place, not if land were sold at the sum which "it will fetch, but if it were granted away without any purchase "at all. Free grant is the natural system; deviations from "it...produce artificial, though perhaps very useful effects." But this view seems to me to overlook the peculiar characteristics of property in land which render it impossible or manifestly unreasonable for Government to act on the simple principle of securing it to the first occupant. In the first place, how shall we determine the extent of occupation? it cannot be said that a man is to be understood to occupy what he is able to use, because the 'use' of land by any individual may vary almost indefinitely in extent, diminishing proportionally in intensity—e.g. it would be absurd to let any individual claim possession of the whole ground over which he could hunt, as against another who wished to use it for pasturage: but if so, ought the shepherd, again, to have possession as against a would-be cultivator, or a cultivator as against a would-be miner? Even if we confine our attention to one kind of use, similar difficulties occur: there is no natural and obvious definition of the quantity of pastoral land useful for a given number of sheep or cattle, or of the quantity of tillage-land suitable for a given amount of labour—especially where the kind of tillage most immediately profitable is that which exhausts the soil—or, again, of the amount that a miner may legitimately claim. The settlement of these questions must in any case require the intervention of Government: but, apart from these difficulties of detail, the general principle of allowing complete property rights to the first occupant does not seem properly applicable to land. For the economic ground on which this jural principle is based, in the case of the produce of hunting, fishing, and other occupations by which things become property that have hitherto been unappropriated, is that the labour of search and pursuit thus receives its natural remuneration, without which there would be no adequate

[1] *On Colonization* (edition of 1861) Lec. xiv. p. 416.

inducement to perform it: but no such labour is required in the case of ordinary land in a new country: there is no advantage to the community in allowing the first comer to appropriate it gratuitously to-day, if some one else is likely to come to-morrow who will be willing to pay for it.

It seems, in short, that if land before it is occupied has a market-value, the competition of the market is the 'natural' method of determining what individual is to possess it, the price thus obtained belonging naturally to the community; and hence that—to realize Natural Liberty—Government must undertake the business of owning it, so far at least as to arrange for selling it in the most economical way. Nor can it even be laid down that this ownership should be as brief as possible, and should be transferred at once by sale to the highest bidder. Indeed, it is obvious that if more than a certain limited amount of land were offered for sale at once, at whatever price it would fetch, the value of it would fall so low that the practical effect would be nearly the same as if gratuitous occupation were allowed: and if it be said that it should only be sold to those who can really use it, the before-mentioned difficulties arising from the great variations in intensity of use recur in a different form— e.g. a wealthy shepherd could use a large province at the rate of 100 sheep per square mile, which is taken to be the carrying capacity of pastoral land in Queensland; but it would be obviously unreasonable to let him have a province for private property at a nearly nominal price, if in a few years the progress of colonization is likely to give large parts of the same land a substantial value for agricultural purposes. Rather it is clear that where land is likely to be in demand both for agricultural and pastoral use, the claims of the different uses can only be fairly adjusted by allowing the shepherd a temporary occupancy of land that is not yet required for agriculture.

I conclude, therefore, that Government is acting most in accordance with the principles of Natural Liberty if it allows the alternative of sale or lease, and the terms of either, to be decided by purely commercial considerations, merely endeavouring to make the best bargain for the community? But if so, it may be fairly argued that on strictly commercial principles, land ought only to be sold at a price that will include the present value of

CHAP. IV.] *INTERFERENCE TO PROMOTE PRODUCTION.* 473

the future increment of value which the land as a whole is likely to receive from the increased numbers and wealth of the persons residing on it. Certainly it seems that if, as seems probable, individuals are not sufficiently interested in remote and doubtful gains to rate this prospective increment at its true value, at any rate during the earlier stages of the economic life of a colony, Government ought, during this first period, not to sell the land at all, but only to let it on lease. On the other hand, we have to consider that it may be even financially more advantageous for the community to sacrifice immediate gain to the end of promoting immigration by offering absolute ownership to *bond fide* settlers: and actually, in the colonization of England, the greatest colonizer among modern communities, the financial interest of the community has been generally subordinated to this latter end.

The most obvious way of attracting settlers is by freely granting land, or selling it at low prices, in such portions and under such conditions as are thought likely to secure the actual cultivation of the land. This, in fact, is substantially the same thing as paying a part of the expenses of the transfer of emigrants out of national funds, provided the emigrants were of the class that would in any case buy and cultivate land;—since it obviously makes no difference to such an emigrant whether it is the cost of his journey or the cost of his purchase of land that is artificially cheapened at the public expense. In practice, however, this system, in the form in which it prevailed generally in the English colonies during the 18th and the first quarter of the 19th century, was not effectually guarded from being perverted to the profit of speculators[1]: and the system that has been more recently adopted of making the benefit offered to settlers to consist more in the deferring of payment than in the lowering of price, seems in every way preferable.

A different and more elaborate plan of promoting emigration through the sales of unoccupied lands, which we may call the

---

[1] e.g. in Lower Canada, the regulation restricting the amount that could be granted to a single person were so effectually evaded that 1,425,000 acres were made over to about 60 individuals, during the government of Sir A. Milne. (Merivale, Lec. xv.)

Wakefieldian system[1], was urged upon the English Government
by the Colonization Society from 1830 onwards, and partially

[1] The influence of Gibbon Wakefield on English Colonization deservedly
occupies an important place in the history of political and economic speculation,
no less than in that of English colonial policy: but it seems to be a matter of
considerable difficulty to ascertain exactly the fundamental principles or characteristics of his system. Thus Mill (*Pol. Econ.* Book v. c. xi. § 14) represents it
as an essential point in Wakefield's system that it promotes concentration of settlements; since "by diminishing the eagerness of agricultural speculators to add
"to their domain, it keeps the settlers within reach of each other for purposes of
"cooperation." But it would seem that the "uniform price" on which Wakefield insisted—as compared with the varying price that would result from sale by
auction—would tend against concentration, by increasing the settler's inducement to select land for its fertility rather than for its situation. And Wakefield
himself (*View of the Art of Colonization*, Letter LXVIII.) expressly disclaims any
wish to promote concentration of settlements, provided that combination and
constancy of labour are secured to each settler by an abundant supply of hired
labourers. "With respect to the choice of land for settlement," he writes, "the
"settlers must be the best judges...I would if possible open the whole of the
"waste land of the colony to intending purchasers...dispersion or concentration
"is a question of locality alone." Again, it was not really an essential part of
Wakefield's own scheme that the proceeds of the sale of lands should be devoted
to the support of emigration; though most writers on the subject seem to regard
this as quite fundamental to it. Mr Merivale even speaks of this (*On Colonization*, Lec. xiv.) as "the great discovery of Mr Wakefield;" and at the same
time, while emphasizing its practical value, urges as a theoretical objection
against Wakefield's system that while the "sufficient price" of which he habitually spoke had to serve two purposes,—(1) that of restraining labourers for a
sufficient, and not more than sufficient, time from the acquisition of land, and (2)
that of keeping up the supply of labourers by gratuitous importation—it was
nowhere shown that the price adequate for the one purpose might not be either
more or less than adequate for the other. But in Wakefield's own treatise this
second purpose is treated, in the most express and emphatic language, as merely
secondary and incidental. "So completely" he says (Letter LIV.) "is the
"production of revenue a mere incident of the price of land, that the price ought
"to be imposed—if it ought to be imposed under any circumstances—even
"though the purchase money were thrown away:" the decisive ground for it
being, as was explained in the preceding letter, that if only all labourers were
under the necessity of remaining labourers, it would be "possible and not difficult
"for capitalists to enforce contracts for labour made in the mother-country," as
"the temptation of the labourer to quit the employer who had brought him to
"the colony would be no longer irresistible." Under these circumstances the
plan of dealing with waste lands that was temporarily carried out in the
Australian Colonies cannot properly be called Wakefield's scheme: since,
as he reiteratedly affirmed, his "sufficient price" was never really tried, and
this was his cardinal point. But since the plan actually adopted was due to the
influence of Wakefield and his friends, and bore a certain resemblance to his
scheme, I have still ventured to speak of it as "Wakefieldian."

CHAP. IV.] *INTERFERENCE TO PROMOTE PRODUCTION.* 475

carried into effect for a limited period in some of our Australasian colonies. It will be observed that the immigration encouraged by the system of free grants or low prices is that of labourers who intend, and are expected, to become cultivators of their own land at once. Now it was believed by Wakefield and his followers that the labour of immigrants so attracted tended to lose materially in efficiency through want of cooperation; so that it would be a distinct gain to production if they were to a large extent prevented from buying land and their labour organized under the direction of capitalist employers. The characteristic principle, then, of the Wakefieldian system was that it aimed at attracting such capitalist employers by providing them with labourers willing to work for hire. With this aim it was proposed to sell land at a price so high that the mass of immigrants would not for some years afford to buy enough to become cultivators on their own account; and at the same time to devote the whole, or a fixed and substantial part, of the proceeds of such sales to the importation of immigrants, so that the immigrating capitalists might always find an adequate supply of hired labour ready to hand. The partial attempt that was made to carry out this system in our Australian colonies, for the 15 or 20 years from 1836 onward, had, in the opinion of competent judges, an important degree of success[1]. And the fact that it was afterwards abandoned is hardly evidence that it ultimately failed; since its abandonment may be probably attributed to the mere desire of obtaining land on easier terms generally felt by the labouring class, whose influence over colonial administration became preponderant when self-government with universal suffrage was granted to the colonies.

§ 13. From considering the principles of governmental interference with land in an early stage of a country's development, let us pass to examine briefly the economic reasons for continuing such interference when this stage has been passed, and the country has been fully occupied. We may conveniently divide this question into two parts; asking first under what limitations land should be allowed to pass into private ownership, and secondly why and how far, after this transition has taken place, Government should still exercise a special control

[1] Cf. Merivale, Lec. xiv., and Cairns' *Political Essays*, Essay i.

over this particular kind of property. As regards the first question, it is obvious that such portions of land as are manifestly more useful to the community when thrown freely open to common use should be retained in public ownership, and under governmental management: e. g. roads, navigable rivers and inland lakes, natural harbours, public parks, commons, &c. So, again, there are strong reasons, discussed in the earlier part of this chapter, why the land required for railroads or other similar monopolies should not be allowed to pass, except temporarily, out of public ownership: and a general right should be reserved of taking back from private owners any land that may be needed for public uses, paying for it its market-value as determined independently of such need, together with a certain 'compensation for disturbance' in consideration of the special utility that it may be fairly assumed to have for its owner. This right has been extensively exercised in recent times in the construction of railways, and is now generally recognised in the most advanced communities. Further it is quite possible to allow the surface of the soil to pass completely into private hands, while reserving to the community the rights of property in certain of the minerals contained in it: and in fact some reservations of this kind are found in the codes of some of the most advanced communities[1]. The chief argument for such reservations, from the point of view of production, is that the owner of the land, whether engaged in the business of agriculture or not, may very likely not be the person best qualified either to ascertain the presence of minerals hidden some way below the surface, or to decide whether their extraction will be remunerative; so that production will gain if the right of discovering and working them—with due compensation to the owner for the loss of the land thus rendered useless for agriculture,—be allowed to members of the community generally[2]. In special cases,

[1] Even in England, where this kind of interference is at its minimum, gold and silver mines are legally reserved to the crown.

[2] In Prussia, for instance, according to the mining law of 1865 any one wishing to bore or dig (schürfen) for any of the minerals to which this "mining-"freedom" (Berg-bau-freiheit) extends must be permitted to do so under condition of paying adequate compensation, provided that the operation is not carried on in certain specified places, as within a certain distance of buildings, in churchyards, gardens, &c. In default of agreement between the parties as to

however, governmental management of mines may be expedient either to avoid the drawbacks of monopoly in private hands— in the case of very rare minerals—or to watch over the interests of posterity, just as in the case before discussed of forests. Turning again to the surface of the land, we may say that, generally speaking, there is no reason for keeping ordinary agricultural land under governmental management,—since the general arguments in favour of private management are at least as applicable to agriculture as to any branch of production —unless, perhaps, as some small portions might advantageously be retained for purposes of scientific experiment or technical instruction. An exception, however, has to be made in the case of land on which timber is grown: where there appear to be the following special arguments in favour of Government management; first, the economic advantages of conducting this business on a very large scale, as it gains much by highly skilled and carefully trained labour which, at the same time, requires a very large area for its most economical application: secondly (what was before noticed), the interest which, in certain countries at least, a community is believed to have in preserving a due proportion of trees to the soil that it inhabits, owing to their beneficial effect on climate[1]; while, thirdly, it is thought that even the marketable utilities of trees —especially their utility, where coals are scarce, for fuel—are in danger of not being adequately or most economically provided for distant generations, if the provision is left to private enterprise, considering the slow growth of trees and the general unattractiveness of remote returns to the private undertaker.

With the exception, however, of timber, it is generally admitted that the ordinary products of agriculture, whether animal or vegetable, are likely to be most economically supplied by private undertakers. But it is a different question

the compensation, it will be determined by the "Ober-Berg-Amt." Such compensation will take the form of rent, unless the operations are continued—or may certainly be expected to last—longer than three years; in this latter case the landowner may force the miner to purchase the land. If the miner by taking portions of any given piece of land would destroy the value of the remainder, he may be forced to pay rent for, or to purchase, the whole.

[1] In England, I suppose, this consideration can scarcely have practical importance.

whether it would not be expedient to retain land in public ownership, while leasing it to private persons; so that the increase in its value which the increase of population tends to cause may be continually secured to the community. This measure, however, is more usually advocated from the point of view of Distribution, in which aspect we shall consider it in a subsequent chapter (ch. VII.). Actually the whole rent of land has never been retained by any Government; but in many cases a considerable portion of it has been reserved, either under the name of rent, or under the rather misleading name of a land-tax[1].

§ 14. Assuming that land is allowed to pass into private ownership, it remains to consider how far the conditions of its tenure and transfer should be placed under special regulation by Government. Here it should be observed that the interferences of this kind that have actually been carried out are to be classed under very different heads, even if we confine ourselves to those that have been recommended on strictly economic grounds and in the interest of production. In the first place we put aside, from our present point of view, the very important cases in which European Governments[2] have intervened not to restrict the liberty of individual owners but to render it more complete; by removing relics of feudalism which divided the rights of ownership of land generally in various complicated ways between lords and cultivators, and further impeded its transfer through the restriction of particular estates to particular classes—nobles and *roturiers*, or nobles, burghers and peasants. Akin to these are more permanent laws restricting the right of each generation to restrict the freedom of their successors, by such bequests or contracts as would hamper the alienation of land, and tend to prevent it from getting into the hands of the persons who would make the best use of it. For legislation of this kind, as was before said, can not strictly be regarded as an interference with

[1] The distinction between this reserved share of rent and an ordinary tax will be examined in a subsequent chapter (ch. viii).

[2] As in France at the Revolution of 1789; and in Prussia by the legislation of Stein and Hardenburg (1807—11), further developed and completed in 1850.

CHAP. IV.] *INTERFERENCE TO PROMOTE PRODUCTION.* 479

natural liberty; it is rather a compromise adopted in an inevitable collision of freedoms, to secure the fullest possible realization of the economic advantage of *laisser faire*. Similar to this, again, is the aim of another class of minor interferences,—such as the compulsory registration of dealings with land—which are designed to render the sale or mortgage of land more easy and less expensive, by removing the necessity of complicated and costly legal proceedings. Along with the above, again, we may class the intervention of the legislature in order to substitute, in the case of land cultivated by other persons than its owners, a certain and definite tenure for one regulated by more or less uncertain customs and understandings; so far as such legislation does not override freedom of contract, but merely interprets what is left vague in customary agreements, or defines normal conditions of letting—as regards length of tenure, compensation for improvements, &c.—in default of express contract to the contrary. When, however, the governmental determination of the conditions of letting land is compulsory, and *pro tanto* prevents freedom of contract between owners and tenants, the interference is of course of a much graver kind; and such as can only be justified by clear evidence either that it is not for the interest of the landowner to grant such terms of letting as would give the tenant the greatest possible inducement to make the land productive, or that the former, if let alone, is likely to mistake his own interest.

To illustrate the kind of evidence required, I may refer to the grounds on which the revolution in Irish land-tenure effected in 1881, and the important restriction of free contract relative to land in England in 1883, were advocated from a productional point of view. It was contended (1) that the Irish landowners, under the system of free contract, have been often found to raise the rent so high as to leave the tenants but bare subsistence, and so prevent them from having the capital[1]—or in bad times even the physical vigour—requisite to render their labour

---

[1] It may be said that it would be profitable for the tenant to borrow capital from his landlord—or some one else—if he would be more than compensated by the additional productiveness of his labour: but the additional element of risk introduced by the necessity of relying on merely personal security may render this unprofitable.

adequately efficient; and (2) that both Irish and English landowners have diminished the tenants' inducements to treat the land in the most economic way, by not securing to them the value of their improvements. How far these contentions are in fact valid, I do not now inquire[1]: but we have before seen that the first-mentioned result is quite a possible one, even on the supposition that all parties are actuated by enlightened self-interest; since even when an increase in the incomes of tenants or labourers would lead to a more than equivalent increase in the value of their labour, it is obviously not the interest of the landlord to furnish the increment of income unless he is to profit by the increased efficiency. Now in the case we are considering, the increased produce would in the first instance be appropriated by the tenant: and even where the loss to the landlord would ultimately be compensated by a rise in rent or perhaps by greater regularity in its payment, the prospect of this compensation may easily be too remote and dubious to induce a prudent landlord to make an immediate and certain sacrifice of income in order to obtain it.

So again, it may seem,—or even sometimes be—inexpedient for the landlord to give the tenant, through lease or otherwise, the fullest security of profiting adequately by his improvement of the land; because such security cannot be given without diminishing the former's control over his land more than he likes or thinks expedient. The simplest method of giving this security is by a long lease; but we have already noticed the difficulty of framing a lease that without hampering the tenant will practically make it his interest to treat the land in the best way; and, where tenants are poor, a long lease is open to the further objection, in the view of the landlord, that the benefit of an unforeseen rise in the value of the land will accrue entirely to the tenant for the period of the lease, while the landlord is likely to bear a considerable share of the loss due to an unforeseen fall, through the actual or threatened insolvency of the tenants.

[1] I ought perhaps to say that I do not myself approve of either of the legislative measures to which I have referred: though in the case of Ireland I think there were adequate grounds for extensive interference of some kind. But a sufficient discussion of either measure would be obviously irrelevant here.

Taking into account all difficulties of this kind, and not overlooking the more indefinite loss of the stimulus given to industry by the sentiment of property, we may conclude that there are inevitable disadvantages to production involved in a general separation of the ownership of land from the business of cultivating it: which would probably prevent this from being the common practice if land were held merely as an instrument of production. But in England this consideration has been outweighed by other powerful motives, in particular by the traditional social prestige and political influence attaching to the possession of land. Hence some reformers consider that an important gain to agricultural production would be secured by breaking down the tendency of large estates in England to remain in the possession of the same families from generation to generation: and that this would be attained by assimilating the law of real to that of personal property, and conferring on life-owners an inalienable right of determining the distribution of the property thus owned among their children after their death[1]. It seems doubtful, however, whether even these changes would have the desired effect in a wealthy country; since the peculiar gratification of the sense of proprietorship which the possession of land gives, and the attractions of country residence and field sports would still tend to keep great portions of it in the hands of rich persons not desirous of personally superintending its cultivation.

The question of interference on the grounds above mentioned has been practically a good deal mixed up with one which, theoretically considered, involves economic reasoning of a very different kind: the question, namely, whether agricultural production should be carried on on a large or a small scale. The ownership of land by rich persons who do not personally manage its cultivation, has a certain tendency to encourage large farms, since it is less troublesome for the owner to collect rents from a few large farmers than from many small ones; and again, the large farmer, having more capital, is not so likely, if holding under a lease, to throw the greater share of any unforeseen losses on the landlord. Hence it is *a priori* probable that this system of ownership prevents the existence

[1] This is proposed with the view of facilitating the alienation of land.

of a certain amount of small farming which might otherwise be prosperously carried on; there are, however, no adequate reasons for supposing that farming on a small scale is likely to be generally more economical, at least as regards the chief staples of agriculture.

Here, however, another consideration is often introduced, which, as was before noticed, is not directly included within the scope of the present discussion, as I have defined it. It is maintained that the system of small farming tends to give a greater gross produce, though a smaller net produce, than that of large farms; and therefore ought to be encouraged by Government, as tending to increase population—though not average wealth—within a given region. And this is certainly a possible result, if the increase in gross produce due to the small-farm system decidedly outweighs the decrease in net produce:—unless, however, the latter difference were comparatively slight, this organization of agricultural industry would be always in a state of unstable equilibrium, since the greater profitableness of the large-farm system to employers would be continually tending to introduce it.

Finally we must notice a kind of interference which has actually taken place in England, and has often been advocated in the interests of agricultural production; but which is not to be so regarded according to the definition of produce adopted in the present treatise. I refer to the law that gives the occupier of agricultural land an inalienable right to kill certain kinds of game, on account of the damage done by them to crops. For this interference with free contract can only be required for the end in view, on the ground that many landlords prefer game and sport together to what they would get by the extra produce which is expected to be obtained in consequence of the destruction of game by the occupiers. Hence —sport being a purchasable commodity—the *primâ facie* inference is that the aggregate of utilities actually obtained from the land bears a higher value than the material produce to which this legislation sacrifices it: so that the change is no more beneficial to production (as I conceive it) than the conversion of valuable vineyards into less valuable cornfields. It is, in fact, rather an interference for distribution,—as it tends to cheapen the commodities consumed by the poor, at the expense of the luxuries of the rich: though its importance from this point of view is not likely to be very great, under the existing conditions of communication and transport, provided the freedom of trade is maintained unimpaired[1].

While considering the case of game, we may note the legal prohibition of killing certain kinds of wild animals during certain parts of the year: i.e. chiefly during the breeding season, when the destruction of future supply that would result from any given amount of slaughter would be much greater than at any other time. This interference exemplifies the theoretical case discussed in § 5 of the second chapter of this book: the case, that is, of restrictions to which it would be the interest of all—or almost all—to conform, provided that each could rely on their observance by all others, but which it would be very much the interest of individuals to break if they were imposed by mere voluntary mutual agreement, without stringent penalties for non-observance.

So far we have considered Government as interfering with private management of land by way of regulation. But modern governments have also exercised an important and apparently successful influence on agriculture by carrying out certain extensive improvements of land (such as reclamation with drainage or irrigation) or by assisting private associations for this purpose with loans of capital, guarantees of interest, and sometimes powers of compulsory interference with recalcitrant landowners. This kind of interference seems to be theoretically defensible,—on the principles previously laid down in respect of railways, &c.—wherever there is a decided advantage in carrying out the improvements in question on a single system over a large area. Again, as I have before said, there seems to be no special reason why Government should not carry on the

---

[1] It may be observed that the obvious effects of such a measure are favourable to population in the region affected by it, as it tends to primarily increase that part of the gross produce of land that is consumed by the working class: but its ultimate effects are often rather hard to estimate, as we have to take into account the loss to the agricultural producers in any district that would result from materially diminishing the inducements offered to the rich to reside in the district. In an extreme case, no doubt, a general passion for sport among rich men might cause a serious and extensive depopulation of certain regions.

business of lending money to individual landowners, on certain conditions: in the chief cases, however, in which operations of this kind have been successfully undertaken by European Governments in recent times, the interference—though quite defensible from the point of view of production—has had so markedly a distributional character, that I have thought it more appropriate to reserve it for a subsequent discussion.

Before concluding this chapter I may perhaps observe that governmental interferences of which the primary intention had no relation to the production of wealth have often had important productional effects, which a statesman ought carefully to estimate in considering their expediency. Thus (e. g.) the restrictions placed in the English Factory Acts, on the labour of women and children, in order to prevent deleterious effects on their health, have practically had the effect of reducing the normal day's labour of male adults in most of the branches of industry to which they have been extended. And in the succeeding chapters in which we shall be considering measures designed to render distribution more equitable or more economical, we shall find that the chief objections to such measures are drawn from the bad effects on production which are found or believed to be inseparable from them. On the other hand it should also be observed that the interferences to promote production which we have discussed in this chapter become in effect interferences with distribution, so far as the gain resulting from them accrues to particular classes in the community, or the expense they involve is similarly specialized in its incidence. This last remark applies also to the operations of Government discussed in the preceding chapter. We shall have occasion hereafter to notice some cases in which this consideration becomes important.

Note on compulsory purchases of land.

A peculiar development of the system of natural liberty, in respect of what has always been a difficult point in this system—the appropriation of land—has been recently suggested in a vigorously written little book by Mr C. B. Clarke, called "Speculations on Political Economy." The right tenure of land, in Mr Clarke's view,

CHAP. IV.] *INTERFERENCE TO PROMOTE PRODUCTION.* 485

being a tenure "such that every piece of land shall fall into the "hands of that man who is able to make the most of it," he suggests that this might be sufficiently attained by giving any man a right to take any piece of land, provided that he was prepared to pay the price at which the land was valued by the owner himself in a "national rate-book," together with $33\frac{1}{3}$ per cent. as compensation for disturbance. The valuation being determined by the owner himself—I suppose at certain intervals—no complaint of spoliation could arise, and the necessity of "law expenses, juries, arbitrations" would be avoided: at the same time the owner would be restrained from overvaluing his land by the fear of having to pay taxes on the higher valuation, while the fear of being bought out would tend to prevent him from undervaluing it—at any rate by more than the equivalent of the compensation for disturbance. Mr Clarke, however, does not propose that any land for which an offer was made should necessarily be sold: the owner would have the alternative of raising the value of his land in the national rate-book, on payment of a fine for undervaluation. Thus a Naboth might always keep his vineyard: but with the liability of paying taxes for it in proportion to the amount that it was worth to him. There would, I think, be some difficulty as to the portions in which land held in large masses should be valued; and, unless a purchaser were always compelled to take the whole of any such portion, the scheme would hardly get rid of the necessity of arbitration so completely as Mr Clarke seems to suppose. But it is scarcely necessary to consider in detail the objections to a proposal which is certainly not within the range of practical politics: I only note it as a novel and ingenious device for harmonizing the conflicting claims of human beings to their material environment, in accordance with strictly individualistic principles.

CHAPTER V.

FREE TRADE AND PROTECTION.

§ 1. THE question of Free Trade,—in the special sense in which the term is opposed to import duties for the Protection of native industry—occupies at the present time a very peculiar and isolated position, whether we regard it from a practical or from a theoretical point of view. As a question of policy, its position is peculiar in this: that freedom of international trade is the only important part of the aims of the great 18th century movement against governmental restraint and regulation, in industrial matters, which has not been generally realized in the countries that occupy the front rank in industrial civilization. The old system under which, in its intensest form, the manufacturer could not select at will the place at which to establish himself, nor the seasons for his work, nor work for all customers, nor use the processes and materials which he found fittest for his purposes, nor give his products the form that suited his customers best,—all this has passed away so completely that we find it almost difficult to credit the historian's account of it. Within each modern civilized community, freedom of transit and residence, freedom in choice of a calling, freedom in the management of property and business—except so far as considerations of health come in—are now generally established: not indeed with absolute completeness—as we have already observed—but to an extent that constitutes a substantial victory for the system of natural liberty. But though the triumph of the new Political Economy of the 18th century has been so striking as regards the internal conditions of industry. and trade, its failure to persuade the civilized world to remove similarly barriers to international trade

CHAP. V.] *FREE TRADE AND PROTECTION.* 487

has been no less decided: not merely has universal free trade not yet arrived, but the most enthusiastic follower of Cobden can hardly persuade himself that the world is at present moving in that direction. Taking the world of West-European and American civilization as a whole, it is difficult to deny that the common sense of this civilized world has pronounced in favour of Protection.

Still, it may be said, this is not a matter in which much deference is due to common sense when opposed to the clear demonstrations of science. On a question of mathematics we do not make Common Sense the court of appeal: and, in the view of "orthodox Free-traders" the proof of the universal expediency of Free Trade is held to be as evident and cogent as a mathematical demonstration. "When I was asked," says Sir T. Farrer[1], "to write something in defence of Free Trade, it seemed to me as if I had been asked to prove Euclid": and this utterance fairly represents the sentiments of the majority of educated Englishmen who regard themselves as competent to pronounce on economic questions. But such a statement strikingly illustrates the isolated position, at the present time, of Free Trade regarded from a theoretical point of view. For only a few fanatics would now use similar language in discussing any other particular application of the general doctrine of *laisser faire*: yet surely if the universal mischievousness, to the nations imposing them, of international barriers to trade is to be demonstrated like a conclusion of Euclid, it can only be by a method equally applicable to all cases of governmental interference for production. If we still held with the Physiocrats that the self-interest of individuals would always direct them to the industrial activities most conducive to the wealth and well-being of the community of which they are members,—then, doubtless, the universal expediency of Free Trade might be simply demonstrated by mere deduction from this sweeping proposition. I conceive, however, that this old belief in the harmony of the interest of each industrial class with the interest of the whole community has lost its hold on the mind of our age: and that the need of governmental interference to promote production is admitted by economists generally in several at least of

[1] *Free Trade and Fair Trade*, p. 1.

the cases discussed in the last chapter. And, if so, it appears to me that the foundation on which the old short and simple confutations of Protection were once logically erected has now been knocked away: and that the fashion which still lingers of treating the Protectionist as a fool who cannot see—if he is not a knave who will not see—what is as plain as a proof of Euclid, is really an illogical survival of a mere fragment of what was once a coherent doctrine.

I do not mean to say that the broad general argument for industrial liberty has lost its force,—I have already expressed strongly the opposite opinion—: but I think that in the natural development of economic theory it has come to be recognised as merely a first approximation to the truth, and its necessary theoretical limitations and exceptions have come to be more clearly distinguished, classified, and systematized. And from the theoretical point of view thus attained, consistency (I think) requires us to meet the drift of the civilized world towards Protection by something more relevant than an obstinate repetition of an essentially antiquated mode of refutation. Practically I am myself decidedly opposed to this drift of popular opinion and governmental policy:—herein differing somewhat from several German writers by whom my general theoretical view of Free Trade has been anticipated, and from whom it has been largely derived. I agree, indeed, with these writers in holding, as a conclusion of abstract economic theory, that Protection, in certain cases and within certain limits, would probably be advantageous to the protecting country,—and even, perhaps, to the world—if only it could be strictly confined to these cases and kept within these limits: but I am nevertheless strongly of opinion that it is practically best for a Government to adhere to the broad rule of 'taxation for revenue only'—at any rate in a free community where habits of commercial enterprise are fully developed. My ground for this opinion is that I do not think we can reasonably expect our actual Governments to be wise and strong enough to keep their protective interference within due limits; owing to the great difficulty and delicacy of the task of constructing a system of import duties with the double aim of raising revenue equitably and protecting native industry usefully, and the pressure that is certain to be put upon the Government to extend its application of the principle of protection if it is once introduced. I think therefore that the gain that protection might bring in particular cases is always likely to be more than counterbalanced by the general bad effects of encouraging producers and traders to look to Government for aid in industrial crises and dangers, instead of relying on their own foresight, ingenuity and energy; especially since the wisest protection in any one country would tend in various ways to encourage unwise protection elsewhere.

Here, however, we are primarily called upon to consider how far abstract economic theory recognises cases in which—taken by themselves—protective duties may be expedient: and I think it clear that the sweeping answer which orthodox free-traders give to this question is not justified. I grant that the *permanent* stoppage of a channel of trade which free competition would open, could not tend to increase the wealth of the industrial society formed by the aggregate of nations whose trade is thus restricted —supposing such nations to be composed of "economic men." But I do not think that this universal negative can be established in the case of *temporary* protection, even if considered from a cosmopolitan point of view: still less if it be considered solely with reference to the interests of a particular nation.

§ 2. The most important exceptional case is that— recognised by J. S. Mill[1]—of "protecting duties imposed "temporarily in hopes of naturalizing a foreign industry, in itself "perfectly suitable to the circumstances of the country." Of course such a duty—if needed and effective—imposes a tax on the consumers of the article protected. But it is quite possible that the cost thus incurred may be compensated to the community by the ultimate economic gain accruing from the domestic production of a commodity previously imported; while yet the initial outlay, that would be required to establish the industry without protection, could not be expected to be ultimately remunerative to any private capitalists who undertook it. This would be the case if the difficulties of introducing the industry were of such a kind that, when once overcome by the original introducers, they would no longer exist for others, or would exist in a much smaller degree: since in that case,

[1] *Pol. Econ.* v. ch. x. § 1.

almost as soon as the industry began to be profitable, competition within the country would tend to bring down prices to a point at which they would be remunerative to the later comers, but not to the introducers of the industry who had borne the initial sacrifices.

It may be convenient to illustrate this by contemplating a particular hypothetical case. Suppose then that a trade is at present carried on between a mainly agricultural district (A) and a largely manufacturing district (M), in which M sends manufactures to A in exchange for corn: while yet A is in respect of natural resources not materially less adapted for the manufactures in question than M. And for simplicity, we will further suppose that there is no material difference in the average returns to labour (of the same quality) and capital in the two districts respectively[1]; and that the new manufactures can be established in A by means of floating capital which would otherwise be mainly employed in corn-growing. It is evident, then, that the employment of this capital in manufactures rather than corn-growing will be economically advantageous to the two districts taken together if the saving it causes in the cost of carriage of corn and manufactures is not outweighed by a loss of some other kind. And it seems likely that this will be the case, provided (1) that the superiority of A over M in the production of corn falls decidedly short of the degree that would render it profitable for the latter to pay the whole expense of a trade in corn from the former; and (2) that no such advantages from division of labour would be gained by the aggregation of all the manufactures in M, as would materially outweigh the gain in effectiveness of A's labour, which may be expected to result from the new opportunities of producing profitably various kinds of agricultural produce, not well adapted for transportation, and generally from the greater variety of occupations opened by the change.

Supposing then that in this way there would be a net gain to the community in the long run, from the introduction of the

---

[1] It would be easy to show that the main argument would not be substantially affected—though it would become somewhat more complicated—if the returns to labour and capital were taken to be different in the two districts.

manufacture into A, it is further apparent that the intervention of Government, by protective duties or otherwise, will be needed in order to realize this gain, if a private undertaker would have no prospect of securing a share of it sufficient to compensate him for the disadvantages against which he would have to struggle, under open competition, during the earlier years of his undertaking. Among such initial disadvantages the most important appear to be the following:

(1) the difficulty of obtaining the requisite skilled labour without paying an extra price for it:

(2) the difficulty of establishing a business connexion; likely to be aggravated by

(3) the danger of a combination of manufacturers in M, who may lower their prices temporarily to ruin their rivals in A.

(4) the difficulty of effecting simultaneously all the industrial changes required for the commercial success of any one branch of manufacture; (e.g.) the manufacturers in A may lose by having to obtain instruments or materials from M or some neighbouring region, while yet A may be no less well fitted for the production of such instruments and materials.

If on these or other grounds the manufacturer in A would have to incur a considerable temporary loss, it is easy to show that he may not be able to obtain adequate compensation by the share he could secure of the subsequent gain to society, when the manufacture is firmly established. For this gain will consist chiefly in the saving of the cost of transport of manufactures; but of this he would be only likely to secure a portion for a short time; since, after he had overcome his initial disadvantages, he would probably have to transfer a part of the saved cost to the consumer in lowered prices, in order to drive the manufacturers of M out of his home market; and he would only enjoy his remaining extra profit for a short time, before it would begin to be reduced by the competition of new men free from the burden of the initial disadvantages.

Under these circumstances, the imposition of a protective duty on manufactures in A for a certain time, sufficient to induce private capitalists to undertake the manufacture, may be a profitable outlay for the community as a whole, resembling the payment of guaranteed interest on the capital of a new railway; except that in the case of a protective duty the outlay is defrayed by the consumers of the article protected, and ought to be considered, in the adjustment of taxation, as a special tax on this class of persons.

I have never seen any serious attempt to show by general economic reasoning that the case above analysed, in which the most enlightened private enterprise would fail to turn to account an important opportunity of industrial improvement, is one that cannot occur; or to show that if it did occur, a "protecting duty continued for a reasonable time" would never be "the least inconvenient mode in which a nation could "tax itself" to defray the cost of the improvement. What Free Traders usually urge against this as a practical conclusion is that experience shows that such a duty when once imposed is not likely to be taken off,—that the protection designed to be temporary will practically become permanent. And I admit fully the force of this appeal to experience: but the consideration thus adduced does not strictly belong to economic theory: it is a political argument, the use of which tacitly concedes the economic correctness of the protectionists' reasoning.

So far we have been considering temporary protection as a means of *introducing* an advantageous change in industry. But it is theoretically possible that it may be similarly useful to *prevent* an inexpedient change. It is conceivable that under open competition a certain industry—e.g. wheat-growing—established in one district (A) may become temporarily so unprofitable as to be abandoned, in consequence of an important advantage enjoyed by the corresponding industry in another district (B); while at the same time this advantage may be so transient,—as for instance if it consists in a natural fertility that tends to be rapidly exhausted—that after a very limited period the same industry will tend to be revived again in B. In this case it is manifestly possible that the loss on the whole through the waste of capital involved in the two changes may outweigh the gain from the greater cheapness of the products of the industry during the interval between the changes: so that it would be on the whole profitable to A and B together to maintain the industry by protection. It must, however, be admitted that, actually, the difficulty of definitely forecasting future changes of industry would at best render this application of protection a highly speculative employment of social capital.

§ 3. It will be seen that the argument for temporary protection,—in both the cases above stated,—is theoretically valid from what I have called a "cosmopolitan" point of view ;—that is, if we consider the interests of the two districts taken together, and not merely that of the district whose industry is protected. But the theoretical possibility that *Laisser Faire* may not lead to the most economical local distribution of labour and capital is of practical importance at present solely from the division of the civilized world into separate nations, whose commercial policy is understood to be framed with a view to their respective sectional interests: since the arguments for protecting a nascent industry are much stronger when we consider the interests of the protecting nation alone. For not only in the case supposed would this nation receive the gain of the industrial improvement realized, while the other would bear the (smaller) loss inseparable from such gain: but it is further possible for the former in certain cases to throw a portion of the expense of protection on the foreigners whose manufactures it partially excludes[1]. This latter result would generally be possible for a time, if the protecting country supplied a considerable part of the whole demand for the foreign products against which the protective duty was directed: since the sudden and extensive reduction in the demand for these products which the duty would cause must tend to lower their price at least temporarily. Free Traders are of course right in pointing out that, so far as this is the actual effect of import duties, such duties tend to miss their primary end of protecting native industry; since to whatever extent the foreign products thus lowered in price are still purchased, to that extent the native products are not encouraged. But this in no way proves the inexpediency of the duties in question, since they may very

[1] It is also to be noted that the initial difficulties of starting a new industry are likely to be on the whole greater, when the established rival against which it would have to compete is a foreign rival: though I do not think that this would be the case necessarily.

well give adequate encouragement to native industry without completely excluding foreign products: and it cannot be an objection to them from a purely national point of view that a part of their effect is merely to levy a tribute on foreigners for the national exchequer[1]. Of course in most cases this tribute will be merely temporary; since the reduction in the foreign producers' profits which must occur in the case supposed will drive them from the industry in question, until either the price rises again or the protecting country obtains its whole supply from native sources. But, firstly, the protection that we are considering is supposed to be merely temporary: so that even a temporary sharing of the expense of it by foreign producers may reduce the burden of it to an important extent. And, secondly, if the industry happens to be one in which a large amount of capital is so firmly invested that it cannot be withdrawn from it without great loss, except very gradually, the period during which the producers will submit to lowered profits will be correspondingly prolonged. And, thirdly, the foreign producers—or some of them—may be in a varying degree exempt from the equalizing effects of competition, either generally, or in the markets of the protecting country: in consequence of which they may have been making extra profits by their transactions in these markets; so that even a considerable and permanent reduction of profits may not lead them to abandon their business. This may happen in various ways—thus (e.g.) single producers, or combinations, in a country (A) may monopolize the manufacture of certain commodities sold in another country (B); and may be thereby enabled to sell their products, if untaxed, for a price so high that even when reduced by the whole amount of a protective duty imposed in B it would still remain fairly remunerative.

[1] It may be convenient to show by a simple hypothetical case how a duty may at once protect the native manufacturer adequately and recoup the country for the expense of protecting him. Suppose that a 5 per cent. duty is imposed on foreign silks: and that in consequence, after a certain interval, half the silks consumed are the product of native industry, and that the price of the whole has risen $2\frac{1}{2}$ per cent. It is obvious that, under these circumstances, the other half which comes from abroad yields the state 5 per cent., while the tax levied from the consumers on the whole is only $2\frac{1}{2}$ per cent.; so that—apart from the cost of collecting the tax—the protecting nation in the aggregate contributes nothing to the expense of protection, which falls entirely on the foreign producers.

Under these circumstances there is no theoretical means of determining generally how far the imposition of the duty will tend, even ultimately, to raise the price of the taxed commodities in B [1]. Again, some among the producers in question may have special advantages as compared with the rest, in producing for the foreign markets. One obvious advantage of this kind is that of situation. Thus, suppose that A has been supplied with coal from two groups of coal-mines in B, one of which is situated on the side adjoining A and the other on the side remote from it: and suppose for simplicity that the mines yield coal of the same quality at the same cost of extraction. Then if a protective duty of 4s. a ton is laid by A on imported coal, raising the price of coal in A 2s. a ton, the result may be that after a time it ceases to be profitable to send coal into A from the remoter mines of B, while it still remains profitable to send it from the nearer ones, though to a diminished extent, and for a diminished profit.

In short: unless foreign products are completely excluded by import duties, such duties may partly have the effect of levying a tribute on foreign producers, the amount and duration of which may in certain special cases be considerable. Of course such tribute-levying will generally be a game that both countries can play at to a certain extent: hence the danger of suffering from retaliatory imposts may render protective duties inexpedient even when, apart from this danger, they would be economically advantageous on the whole. On the other hand, if the broad safe rule of 'taxation for revenue only' were once abandoned, it might be expedient for a country injured by the import duties of another to impose similar duties in the way of retaliation even when they are in themselves economically disadvantageous,—just as it may be expedient to incur a greater cost in actual warfare, in order to prevent or punish more violent injuries to commerce. But, in any case, to consider more particularly the conditions under which such retaliatory measures are to be recommended belongs rather to the practice of state-craft than to the Art of Political Economy.

[1] It is even possible, in the case supposed, that the price of the taxed commodities may not rise in B at all—in which case, of course, the tax would not be protective.

We have, however, in estimating the economic loss and gain of protection, to take into account certain secondary effects of protective duties, which are of a somewhat mixed kind. Supposing trade to be in equilibrium at the time that the demand in A for B's commodities is artificially restricted by import duties raising their price, and supposing that other things—including the demand in B for A's commodities—remain unchanged, one obvious result will be that B will import more than she exports; hence in order to restore the balance of trade, a certain readjustment of prices will be necessary by which B will in most cases tend to obtain a somewhat smaller aggregate of imports on somewhat less advantageous terms. This restriction on B's import trade may possibly not reduce materially the amount of her imports *from A*, if the commodities supplied by A are strongly demanded in B; since the price of such imports may be paid for indirectly by transferring to the merchants of A the debts of other countries who import from B. In this case the secondary effects of A's protection on the trade between A and B will be on the whole favourable to A. On the other hand the merchants of B will tend *ceteris paribus* to buy from a country to which they also sell: and therefore if the products of A are closely pressed in the markets of B by the competition of other countries, the protection given by A to one branch of her industry may very likely have the secondary effect of inflicting a blow upon another branch—viz. that which previously supplied the exports from A to B.

§ 4. I have now to call attention to an oversight in the ordinary exposition of the benefits of Free Trade, which is of some importance when the division of the world into separate nations is taken into account and the interests of a single nation alone are considered. It is often assumed, expressly or tacitly, that when a class in a given nation can obtain any kind of commodities cheaper through foreign trade, the nation as a whole must be benefited by their so obtaining it. What is overlooked is the possibility that the portion of the nation from which employment is withdrawn by the change cannot be employed *within their own country* without a loss of utility on the whole greater than the gain from the cheaper foreign supply of the commodities they were producing before the change. I do not think this result at all a probable one, in the case of a country as large and as industrially advanced as England. But I think it must be admitted in any theoretical treatment of the subject that in order to realise the economic advantage obtainable by free trade between two countries, a displacement of labour and capital out of one of the countries may be necessary: so that the *aggregate* wealth of the persons living *in this country* may be reduced by the change.

It may be worth while to illustrate this result by considering an extreme hypothetical case. Suppose a country (A) so thickly populated that additional agricultural produce could not be obtained from the soil except at a rapidly increasing expense; and suppose that one-third of its actual produce of this kind— say, for brevity, its corn—is now consumed by the persons engaged in its chief branches of manufacture. Suppose that the country, having been strictly protected, adopts Free Trade, and that consequently the manufactures in question are obtained at half the price from another country (B) in exchange for corn: and for simplicity let us assume that the result of the fall in price is that the same *total* price is paid for the manufactures annually consumed. What then are the manufacturing labourers thrown out of work by the change to do? The course most obviously suggested by the circumstances is that they should emigrate and supply the labour required in the extended manufactures of B, or in the newly developed trade between A and B. If they do not do this, there seems no general ground for assuming that they will all be able to find employment in A, as remunerative as that withdrawn from them. No doubt as the cost of production in agriculture may be assumed to increase continuously, a certain amount of additional labour may now be employed in agriculture which will be more productive on the whole than some of the labour employed before the trade was opened—the diminution in the amount of corn produced by each new labourer being more than balanced by the increased power of the corn to purchase manufactures. But if the additional labour is only applicable at a rapidly increasing cost, the point will very soon come at which this balance will be reversed: and it is quite conceivable that a portion of the labourers thrown out of manufacturing enployment could not, in the present condition of industry, be employed in A in agriculture so as even to provide their own consumption. And if they could not be profitably employed in agriculture it is theoretically possible that they could not be so employed at all; so that the natural result of Free Trade may be that A will only support a smaller population and that its aggregate wealth may be diminished by the change. The fear of such a result as that just described has undoubtedly been important among the motives that have operated on the side of Protection. I think that the alarm has usually been without much practical justification: but I think that it ought to be met not by a fallacious general demonstration that the result feared cannot happen, but by a careful exposition of the reasons why it is not likely to happen in any particular case to an extent that ought to influence a statesman's action.

Note. In the above discussion I have confined my attention as far as possible to such arguments as are strictly economic and naturally lend themselves to an abstract and technical treatment. There are, I need hardly say, several other considerations both for and against protection, which would have to be carefully weighed in dealing with the question from a directly practical point of view:—one of which will come to be discussed in the next chapter, in which I shall pass to consider governmental interference with a view to more equitable distribution.

CHAPTER VI.

THE PRINCIPLES OF DISTRIBUTIVE JUSTICE.

§ 1. IN the preceding chapters we have considered the grounds and limits of governmental interference so far as its end is the most economic production of purchasable utilities estimated at any given time at their market value. Many, however, of the particular kinds of interference that we have had occasion to discuss are commonly recommended not from this point of view alone, but also as conducive to a better distribution of produce; whether this better distribution is expressly judged to be such because it is more economic (in the sense above explained); or whether—as is more ordinarily the case—it is preferred and commended as more "Just" or "Equitable." On the other hand such interferences are often condemned on grounds of Justice; as involving a violation of the rights of individuals. In the following chapter I propose to discuss governmental interference with distribution—including the comprehensive schemes for such interference recommended by Socialist or semi-socialist writers—from a purely economic or utilitarian point of view; considering how far Individualism or Socialism may be expected to lead to most happiness, so far as this depends on the production and distribution of the produce of industry. In my view this is the consideration that ought to be decisive with the statesman and the philanthropist. But it seems expedient to clear the way for this discussion by a brief examination of other ethical views of the distribution of wealth and of the social order on which it mainly depends; since there are still many thoughtful persons who consider the present individualistic organization of society to be absolutely right, regarding all interference with private property as "spoliation," and all interference with free contract as "tyranny of the state over the individual." On the other hand there are Socialists who, with no less sincerity, pronounce private property generally—or private property in the instruments of production—to be "robbery," and regard the wages-contracts resulting from it as the manifestation of the "enslavement of labour by capital."

The opposition between the two views is violent and at first sight irreconcileable; I think, however, that it will be found possible to reduce it materially by careful consideration of the opposing doctrines, and so ultimately to find a common ground on which a profitable discussion may be conducted between them.

It may seem that such a discussion has not sufficient bearing on practical problems to be appropriately included in this part of my treatise. And no doubt the proposal to abolish private property—even if limited to the instruments and materials of production—cannot be said to come as yet within the range of a statesman's consideration; except as an actual or possible source of dangerous and disordering agitation among the poorer classes. But the proper application of the notions "just," "fair," "equitable," &c., to different parts of the existing distribution of wealth is undeniably a matter for practical consideration; since the demand that wages, profits, rents should be "fair" is continually made and approved by large sections of the community who would shrink from any scheme of wholesale interference with the rights of property. And we shall, I think, obtain a clearer and fuller view of the general principles of Justice or Equity which are implicitly assumed on one side or another in the discussion of such demands, if we examine the broad issue between the individualistic ideal of society, approximately realised in modern civilized communities, and the various socialistic schemes that have been constructed with the view of remedying its alleged injustices. Such an examination is not, I conceive, without interest even for those economists (chiefly English) who aim at a purely scientific treatment of the problem of distribution. For the conclusions of economic science have always been supposed to relate ultimately—however qualified and supplemented—to actual human beings; and actual human beings will not permanently acquiesce in a social order that common moral opinion condemns as unjust.

We may begin by removing a complication, by which the argument is sometimes confused, arising from the fact that the individualistic system is in possession of the field. Some persons, if the abolition of private property were proposed, would condemn the proposal as unjust, merely because the institution actually exists and has always existed from time immemorial. Reflection, however, would probably convince them that this position is untenable; since they would not deliberately maintain either that no established social order could be unjust or that if unjust it ought nevertheless to be perpetual. That any removal of legalized and long-standing social injustices should be managed with as much regard as possible to the legitimate expectations of the persons profiting by such injustices would be admitted by all reasonable persons; and more than this would hardly be demanded by any in the case of such generally approved changes as the abolition of slavery, serfdom, absolute despotism, or oppressive oligarchical privileges. Thus our question must clearly be whether the institution of private property is to be regarded, from an abstract point of view, as just or unjust. It would not even be contended, in the parallel cases just mentioned, that *full* compensation ought to be given to the persons damnified by the changes; for such compensation as would secure them advantages equal to those that they had lost would often be obviously impossible. All that can be said generally is that the compensation for the disappointment of legitimate expectations should be as nearly adequate as the circumstances of the case allow.

On the other hand we may equally neglect the argument that the existing inequalities in the division of property have had their origin in injustice; even if we grant that this is largely true in the case of the nations of modern Europe. For to disturb expectations based on ages of orderly possession, merely in order to remedy such ancient wrongs, is not defensible on any even plausible principles of jurisprudence or morality: such a measure could only be *primâ facie* justifiable if it led to the final substitution of a more equitable social order. Any plausible attack on private property must be based on objections not to its origin, but to its effects; and similarly, if the absolute justice of the institution is to be maintained, it must not be merely because it exists, but because it is based on rational principles.

§ 2. Let us ask, then, on what grounds it can be argued that individuals have an inalienable right to private property, which must avail always and everywhere against all considerations of equity or expediency that may be urged in favour of Socialistic schemes?

The most received positive answer to this question is, I think, that which treats the full right of private property—including the right of freely disposing of it by exchange or otherwise—as an indispensable element of the right to Liberty. What a Just social order (it is said) secures to individuals is Equal Freedom; whatever inequalities in the enjoyment of the material means of happiness may actually result from the exercise of this Freedom are perhaps to be deplored and voluntarily alleviated, but certainly not to be forcibly prevented by the action of Government. This Equal Freedom, then, is held to include the liberty of securing to oneself and transferring to others the sole use of any material things not hitherto appropriated.

Against this interpretation of Social Justice considerations have often been urged which may be summed up in the following dilemma. If, on the one hand, we mean by Freedom simply the antithesis of physical coercion, it does not appear that the most perfect realisation of the 'Freedom of each so far as compatible with the Freedom of all others' would include the establishment of private property at all: it would be strictly limited to protection of the individual from interference while actually using any portion of material wealth, in the same way as he would be now protected while using roads, commons, &c. If, on the other hand, we extend the notion of Equal Freedom to include equal opportunity for gratifying desires, then it does not appear how Equality of Freedom can be realised so far as any appropriation is allowed which renders things of the kind appropriated unattainable, or more difficult of attainment, by others. But, if this be granted, since land is a commodity of this kind—at least in all but very thinly peopled societies—and since most other property has come from appropriated land, the supposed basis of the right of private property can give but very little support to the institution in an advanced stage of social progress.

Similar difficulties arise if, instead of the more general "realisation of Freedom", the special principle that "every man has a right to the produce of his labour" is proposed as fundamental. Human labour is obviously not the cause of the *matter* of any material product, but only of its form; therefore if a man is to have right of property in the product he must have alread been allowed to appropriate the material; and this preliminary appropriation will require justification. To say that he has laboured in seeking it is a manifest straining of t principle that we are considering; since, as was before said, land, the grand primary material or natural instrument of that agricultural and extractive labour which is the prerequisite of all other productive work, is not something which a man would have to labour seriously in seeking, if appropriation in land had not already been allowed. And at any rate the first finder's labour cannot give him a right to diminish the opportunities of other seekers. The only mode of defending private property, on the basis of this principle, which seems to me at all tenable, is to maintain that this inevitable diminution of opportunities is adequately compensated; that the appropriation by first comers of the 'spontaneous gifts of nature' is not substantially unfair to those who come after, because though they find the land and its produce appropriated, they are placed in a better position than they would be in if there had been no appropriation. And this is, I think, true if we consider these later comers in the aggregate: it seems to me clear that existing labour, taken in the aggregate, gains more by the results of previous labour, which it finds accumulated, then it loses by the appropriation of the land; especially since a considerable portion of the utility of the land itself must be included among these accumulated results.

§ 3. But granting that the encroachment on the opportunities of existing labourers, involved in private property, is adequately compensated to such labourers in the aggregate, it does not follow that the compensation is adequate in the case of all classes of these labourers. The question still remains whether the individualistic system of private property and free contract tends to give particular labourers what their services are fairly worth. And this question is one that cannot be avoided by the advocates of this system: since the prevalent acquiescence in the results of competitive distribution is largely due to the more or less definite conviction that free competition affords the best realisation possible, in a community of human beings, of the principle that "every man should have the opportunity "of obtaining a fair return for his labour." Indeed we may say that Political Economy has importantly modified popular ethical conceptions, by defining the common moral ideal of equity in exchange, where pre-economic morality had left it vague and indeterminate. The pre-economic morality, whether of the vulgar or of philosophers, considered services and products as possessing "intrinsic worth;" and the same conception still governs the moral judgments of the vulgar, even in the present stage of economic culture—thus, one continually hears thrifty housekeepers agreeing in moral disapprobation of the present race of servants, for their persistence in demanding "more than "they are worth." But reflection soon shows that the ordinary estimate of this intrinsic worth is merely dependent on custom and habit; so that some other standard of value has to be found, unless we are prepared to condemn any deviation from custom as extortionate. And this no one in modern times is prepared to do: extended historical knowledge has shown us the wide variations of such customs from place to place, and the changes that time has continually wrought in them; and has thus irresistibly demonstrated the irrationality of setting up as a final standard the custom of a particular age and country. In this difficulty the economic ideal of free competition has been widely accepted as supplying the required standard; so that the price, which competition tends at any time to fix as the market-price of any kind of services, has been taken to represent the universal or social—and therefore morally valid—estimate of the "real worth" of such services.

But—apart from the exceptional cases noticed in a previous

chapter[1]—this view of the market-price of services is only generally true with a very important qualification. The competitive remuneration of the individual's service to society does not tend to correspond to his share of the *total* utility of the kind of services he renders: what it tends to measure is merely its *final* utility,—what the community would lose by the subtraction of a single individual's services. This distinction at once explains and is illustrated by the advantage which under certain circumstances a class of labourers may conceivably obtain by a combination which enables them to sell their services in the aggregate; for they thus force society to reckon the total utility of this aggregate, which may be indefinitely greater than the sum of the additional utilities of the portions supplied by the individual labourers, estimated separately. And when any set of scantily paid workers complain of their wages as "unfair," this discrepancy between total and final utility often seems to be vaguely present to their minds; they consider the great importance to society of the aggregate of the services of their class, rather than the comparatively trifling importance of the services of any individual worker. Often, however, the complaint expresses simply the moral dissatisfaction with the proportionment of reward to final utility, which arises when the causes that influence the latter are clearly understood and carefully considered. If a man is as industrious to-day as he was yesterday, it seems hard that he should suffer because some unforeseen decrease in the demand for his commodity, or some increase in the supply of his particular kind of labour, has reduced the final utility of his services.

But if we reject the measurement of "worth" of labour by final utility, what other standard can we take? To determine the reward of any species of labour by estimating the loss which the subtraction of the whole aggregate of such labour would inflict on society is obviously futile and impracticable. The production of necessaries and that of luxuries would from this point of view be incommensurable; all, if permitted, would

[1] See ch. ii. of this book. Some of the difficulties in determining what is a 'fair contract' in particular cases, will be again discussed in the concluding chapter.

choose the former; and no reason could be given for selecting some rather than others for this high function and remuneration.

It may perhaps be suggested that we should estimate desert not by the utility rendered to the recipient of a service, but by the effort of the worker. But though this estimate is certainly in harmony with the general notion of good and ill desert, outside the region of exchange,—since the merit of a deserving act is generally held to lie in its intention rather than its result,—the attempt to apply this principle to the distribution of social produce would involve us in insuperable difficulties. For not only should we have to abstain from rewarding physical strength and quickness, and ingenuity, so far as these qualities are independent of the agent's voluntary effort; but we should find it hard to show why even energy and perseverance are to be remunerated, unless we can prove that these qualities are not merely inherited natural gifts: so that the principle of rewarding desert would be in danger of finding no realisation, through our scrupulous anxiety to realise it exactly[1]! On the whole, therefore, we seem led to the conclusion that the demand for greater justice in distribution can only be practically interpreted as a demand that differences in remuneration, due to causes other than the voluntary exertions of the labourers remunerated, should be reduced as far as possible.

§ 4. If it be admitted that 'fair wages' may be defined, for practical purposes, as 'market wages as they would be under the condition of the least possible inequality of opportunities,' it remains to consider how such a condition is to be secured. Now it has certainly been the firm and long-cherished belief of many adherents of the traditional Political Economy, that unrestricted freedom of action and contract would tend to reduce the actually inevitable inequality of economic opportunities

[1] It may be observed that—for these or other reasons—some reconstructors of society have discarded Desert and adopted as their principle of distributive justice either simple Equality, or Equality modified by differences of Need. In the next chapter I have discussed briefly the communistic institutions in which either of these views finds its natural development; but I have not thought it fitting to introduce them here, as I do not consider these principles to be even vaguely implied in the current notions of "just" or "fair" distribution.

to the lowest attainable minimum—so soon at any rate as enlightenment should be sufficiently diffused by means of elementary education and the spread of cheap means of obtaining information by newspapers, &c. They have believed that labour thus becoming mobile would flow where the demand for it—or its final utility—was greatest, nearly as easily and rapidly as water finds its own level; so that no considerable class of persons would for any length of time obtain, as remuneration for their labour, materially more or less than the market-price of the most useful services that nature and their own or others' labour and care had qualified them to render. They have admitted that very great inequalities of income, due to inheritance, would probably continue to exist; but they have thought it not unjust that A's income should be augmented by the results of his ancestors' labour and care, whether in the form of material wealth or personal aptitudes— assuming, of course, that such augmentation did not tend to make B's income less than it would otherwise have been.

Those who hold, on the other hand, that this view of the tendencies of *laisser faire* is far too optimistic, urge chiefly the following objections. In the first place, it is impossible to prevent the effects of monopoly, especially monopoly resulting from combination, from modifying and disturbing to an indefinite extent the effects of free competition, without placing the freedom of exchange and association under restraints of a kind that the advocates of *laisser faire* could not consistently recommend. And we may add that the attempt to impose such restraints, even if made in the style of the most despotic of modern Governments, could never have more than a very imperfect and unsatisfactory kind of success. It could at most only prevent express and open combination; but, as we have before observed[1], the effects of monopoly may be largely brought about by tacit combination, which is obviously easier to the rich few than to the many poor, and which, therefore, it would be highly objectionable and invidious to favour indirectly by suppressing the only force that could effectively counteract it. On the other hand no advocate of *laisser faire* has ever supposed that a struggle among different combinations of producers, each aiming at its

[1] Book II. c. x.

own sectional interest, can have any general tendency to bring about a just distribution of produce, according to any recognised view of justice.

There is, indeed, one way in which the State may effectually prevent the disadvantageous results of monopoly without vexatious and inquisitorial legislation; viz. by taking into its own hands a business that would otherwise fall into the hands of private monopolists; since it is thus enabled both to manage the business in the interests of the community, and to secure to the public purse whatever profit it is possible and expedient to make out of it. In preceding chapters we have seen that the absence of any general coincidence between the interest of the monopolist and that of the community, as regards the extent and quality of the commodities supplied by the former, constitutes a strong argument for this kind of governmental interference from the point of view of production; we have now to note that it is also to be recommended as tending to remove an important source of unmerited inequality in distribution. On the other side we have, of course, to weigh carefully the general drawbacks of governmental as compared with private management; as these, in certain cases, might be so great as to render the loss to the community through deteriorated production more important than the gain in equity of distribution. I conceive, however that no general practical conclusion can be safely drawn from a comparison of these opposing considerations, as its results are likely to vary very much both as regards different countries and different businesses in the same country.

But further, the critics of *laisser faire* also lay stress on the growing element of fluctuation and uncertainty in the relations of demand and supply of commodities, in consequence of the more extensive organization of industry through international exchange. In this way, they maintain, the complexity of the causes affecting any worker's remuneration tends to increase in a far greater ratio than his intellectual resources for forecasting their effects; so that the element of 'desert' in his gains and losses of income tends to become continually less instead of greater. The facts at present appear to bear out this view; though we have hardly grounds for predicting the continued increase of this fluctuation and uncertainty—rather it would

CHAP. VI.] DISTRIBUTIVE JUSTICE. 509

seem reasonable to regard this increase as probably itself fluctuating and uncertain. But sudden and considerable changes in the earnings of particular classes of producers, due to unforeseen changes in the demand for (or supply of) their commodity, must be admitted to be a probably frequent incident of the world-wide extension of trade. From this point of view we must admit that there is some force in what has been urged by Protectionists as regards the tendency of Protection to keep the conditions of production more stable, and prevent the great fluctuations in local demands for labour which the changes of widely extended trade are liable to cause. On the other hand it must be admitted that the same extension of trade tends to minimize such fluctuations in supply and price of commodities as are due to unfavourable seasons or other natural causes: and if, in order to retain this advantage, Protection were limited to articles which are either but little exposed to such calamities, or are not necessaries of life or industry, the security against unmerited fluctuations in earnings would be correspondingly partial[1]: and, in any case, they would still be liable to occur from internal developments of trade and industry. And if any Government were to attempt the extensive interference that would be required to make the security against unmerited fluctuations approximately complete, it would, I conceive, find an insuperable difficulty in discriminating between losses really inevitable and those that could have been prevented or largely reduced by foresight, promptitude, and versatility in adapting action to changed circumstances; so that governmental interference, by checking this spontaneous adaptation of the industrial system to the conditions of its growth, would be liable to impair seriously its productive efficiency. Hence, though I think that a civilized community ought to be always prepared to give effective aid, through its Government, in any case of acute and widespread distress caused to any section of its members by changes in industry or trade, I hold that such intervention ought to be limited to these extreme

---

[1] It must also be borne in mind that any restrictions on trade have an indefinite but important tendency to hamper its general development, and diminish its efficiency for rendering in time of need services that may be required from it.

cases; and could never be advantageously employed as a general remedy against the divergences from equity in the competitive distribution of produce, that such changes are continually liable to cause.

§ 5. It is more plausible to hold that such a remedy is possible where the changes are mainly in one direction, and result in an "unearned increment" continually obtained by the owners of a certain kind of property, through its increasing scarcity in relation to the demand for it. The chief case of this is land in a country where population is continually growing thicker. We have seen, indeed, that the rise in the value of merely agricultural land, which the increasing demand for agricultural produce tends to bring about, may be more than counteracted by any kind of sudden and extensive improvements in production, especially by the cheapening of transport and the opening of new channels of supply through trade from abroad. But the rise of land near towns, or otherwise conveniently situated for the purpose either of building or direct enjoyment, is not on the whole affected by this cause. Hence, taking all the varied utilities of land into account, I should infer that the aggregate rental of almost all existing civilized countries will, at the close of any period sufficiently long to allow for transient oscillations, have received a considerable "unearned incre-"ment;"—provided that the existing tendencies to increase of population continue to operate without material change. And, so far as this increment can be definitely foreseen and measured, it would certainly be an important approximation to equality of opportunities if the landowners could be prevented from appropriating it by any legislation not otherwise inequitable. It should, however, be observed that if the landowner has no claim to the portion of increased rent that is not due to the labour or forethought of himself or his predecessors in ownership, no other individual member of the community can urge any more claim; hence any attempt to secure any portion of this increment for the particular persons to whom he happens to have let his land, by prescribing "fair rents" below the market-rate, cannot be justified on this score. The equitable claim must be taken to be that of the community[1].

[1] It is sometimes said that Englishmen in the aggregate have no special

I do not doubt the abstract validity of this claim: but there appear to me to be the following grave objections against any attempt to enforce it, in the case of land that has once passed completely into private ownership,—even apart from the inevitable uncertainty of any practical conclusion that assumes the continuance of the existing tendencies to increase of population. In the first place, we have every reason to suppose that at least a great part of the future unearned increment of rent is already discounted in the present market-price of land: and it would be manifestly unjust to mulct the particular persons who keep their wealth in the form of land, by taking from them a portion of the market-value of their property. It could only be unearned additions to the existing market-value of the land that could fairly be taken by the state—or rather whatever part of such additions could be shown to be due to unforeseen increase of rental[1]: and there would be much difficulty in separating this portion clearly from the *earned* increment. For in many cases the increased utility and value of the land would often be found to be only *partly* unearned, as it would be due to favourable circumstances well turned to account; and in such cases I do not know how we could pronounce what proportion of the increment was to be set down to circumstances and what to the insight and enterprise of the man who skilfully availed himself of them. And if a landowner were liable at any time to have to prove that the additional value of any part of his land was not "unearned," in order to prevent its being taken from him by an extra tax, the utilization of land by private enterprise would receive a severe check. Further, if

claims—as against the rest of the human race—to the unearned increment in the value of English land. But, firstly, this position is not tenable; since it is mainly the development of the English community and the manner in which that community has distributed itself over the country that it inhabits, which has raised the value of English land. And, secondly, whatever rights the rest of the human race may have to the land now held by Englishmen are in no degree encroached upon by an agreement of Englishmen to hold their land in common, so long as immigration into England remains as free as before. Indeed it must be obvious that the utility of English land would be more open to the enjoyment of the rest of the human race after "nationalisation" than before, so long as immigration was not restricted.

[1] As we have noticed in an earlier part of this work, a rise in the selling value of land might be merely due to a fall in the rate of interest.

the state confiscated unearned *in*crement, justice would require it to give compensation for "undeserved *de*crement:" and this, again, would involve an equal difficulty of valuation, and a dangerous withdrawal of the motive that a landowner whose land is declining in value now has to exert himself to discover some new means of turning it to account.

The only practicable way, I think, of attaining the end in view would be for the state to assume the ultimate ownership of land generally, and reward the skill and enterprise of individuals in whose hands its value increases,—according to the method before proposed in the case of railways, &c.—by allowing them to reap the whole advantage of such increase for a certain limited period. Justice would of course require that adequate compensation should be given to existing owners; and it has been urged that the financial operation that would be required, in order to buy back nearly the whole land of a fully occupied country from its private owners, would be beyond the resources even of England; or at least that the community would lose by the increased rate of interest that would have to be paid more than it could possibly gain by unearned increment. But this difficulty may I conceive be avoided, as Cliffe Leslie suggested[1], by deferring the time at which the community would enter upon the ownership of the land. The question rather is whether the diminution in production to be expected from (1) the inertness and jobbery incident to public management, (2) the inevitable divergence of interests of owner and lessee respectively, and (3) the loss of the special satisfactions, and any special stimulus to labour and care, which individuals now derive from the sense of ownership, is not likely to outweigh any gain in equity of distribution; even allowing for any advantages that may be fairly hoped from governmental administration, in spite of its drawbacks—e.g. from greater

[1] *Fortnightly Review*, October, 1880. Cliffe Leslie, indeed, held that the "requirements of justice and expediency would be satisfied" if it were simply enacted that all land should become public property in the year 2001. And certainly the value of what the landowners would lose in this case would be comparatively trifling; but I do not see why even this loss should be thrown exclusively on the particular class of persons who happen to own land, unless it can be shown to be on other grounds just that their share of the burden of taxation should be somewhat increased.

economy in the collection of rents, especially of small farms, the more uniform application of principles accepted by experts, and the power of borrowing on better terms. I should not hesitate to answer this question affirmatively in reference to most existing communities at the present time: though it is quite possible that the management of governmental business may in the future be so much improved as to render it clearly expedient to "nationalise the land."

§ 6. In any case the Nationalisation of the Land would involve so large a transfer of private capital to public ownership that its proposal must inevitably raise the further question whether other portions of the capital of individuals should not be similarly nationalised: especially since—in recent years at least—the loudest complaint against the existing individualistic system of distribution has related to the undue share of the produce of industry supposed to be obtained by "capital" in its competition with "labour." This complaint, as usually formulated, fails to discriminate between the two elements of the yield of capital which we distinguished in Book II. under the terms "interest" and "wages of management." According to the view adopted in the present treatise, the causes that determine the amount of these two elements of "profit" are so fundamentally different, that it is necessary to consider the present question with regard to each separately.

As regards "wages of management," we certainly found reason to believe that large capitalists engaged in business obtain on the average a larger proportional remuneration for their labour than any other class of workers. As we saw[1], this is implied in the assumption, commonly made both by economists and by practical men, that at least an equal percentage of profit is earned by such capitalists; since the labour of management certainly does not increase in simple direct proportion to the amount of capital managed. At the same time the question how far these extra earnings are to be regarded as unfair is not one that admits of a simple and decisive answer; since—where no combination or other monopoly comes in—they must be caused by the superior productiveness of businesses on a large scale carried on by individual capitalists; and this greater pro-

[1] Cf. *ante*, Book II. ch. ix.

ductiveness, again, must be chiefly due to the keener concern and more strenuous activity which men in general shew in the management of affairs of which they have the sole control and reap the sole profit. On the other hand, since the amount of the employers' extra gains is due not to the scarcity of possible employers personally qualified and willing to perform equally productive work, but to the scarcity of persons who being thus qualified and willing are able to obtain capital,—it can hardly be expected that other members of the community should acquiesce patiently in this large remuneration of the labour of capitalist employers, so far as it admits of being removed by associated action.

Hence I should refrain from condemning as unfair the efforts of labourers to reduce the profits of employers by combinations to raise wages: though, as has been already said, the principle on which such combinations proceed is one which could not conceivably be employed as a general basis for an equitable distribution of produce.

Hence, again, if any reduction in the extra earnings of capitalist employers can be effected by improvements in the management of associated capital, the resulting gain in aggregate produce tends to be accompanied by a greater approximation to equality of opportunities—at least as among owners of different amounts of capital. And from this point of view any successful and profitable extension of governmental management of industry—which we may regard as a peculiar species of associative management—would seem to be doubly desirable.

But further; we saw that it is not only the large capitalist whose services (as employer) tend to be at a scarcity price as compared with those of smaller capitalists; advantages similar in kind are possessed in various degrees by capitalists, or rather by the children of capitalists, of lower grades in the scale of wealth—including those who possess "personal capital" in the knowledge and skill acquired by industrial or professional training. These advantages are realized, whenever the differences in the average remuneration of different grades of labour are in excess of what would amount to ordinary interest on the additional outlay required for sustenance during an additional period of education, and for the greater cost of the education itself. Here again we may say that so far as the scarcities which cause these differences can be diminished or removed by governmental action that is socially profitable—as (e.g.) by a system of free or cheapened education, of which the cost would be repaid to the community in the increased productiveness of labour—the tendency of such action to realize greater equity in distribution may be admitted as an additional argument in its favour.

But even if such interference could be carried to the point at which there were no differences in the remuneration of different kinds of labour except such as represented ordinary interest on different outlays of capital, it might still be argued that the payment of interest at all on capital is itself a removable cause of inequality of opportunities; and that, therefore, its removal would bring about a more truly just distribution of produce. The grounds on which this has been maintained by modern Socialists are deserving of careful examination; as they have not, I think, been adequately apprehended by the individualist writers who have replied to them[1]. It may be observed, in the first place, that if the market-rate of interest is attacked at all, from the point of view of abstract justice, there is no reason for stopping short of total abolition; it would be quite arbitrary to select any particular rate of interest as ideally more just than any other. On behalf of total abolition, the contention of the Socialist is that "the full produce of labour ought to go "to the labourer." To this the Individualist sometimes thinks it sufficient to reply by urging the helpless state in which labour would be placed if deprived of the instruments of all kinds which constitute the main part of the real capital of the community. But this answer is not really to the point; as the Socialist can effectively rejoin that doubtless labour requires instruments, and the labour of making instruments should be remunerated as fully as any other kind of labour; but that interest is certainly not the remuneration for this labour; being in fact, as the economists of *laisser faire* school have been especially careful to explain, payment for what Senior and

[1] I ought to say, on the other hand, that the Socialist arguments that I have seen have been wanting in clearness of distinction between interest and that extra profit of employing capitalists that we have just been discussing.

others have called the "abstinence" of the capitalist; or, as I have preferred to say, for the delay that he allows to intervene between the application of the labour and the consumption of its product. The real question therefore is not whether instruments ought to be made but whether it is fair that this delay involved in making them should have to be paid for. On the Individualist side it is urged with truth that Labour has gained on the whole by the delay to a far greater extent than is represented by the interest paid. But the Socialist can answer that the private ownership of what I have called 'producers'' wealth is not a necessary condition of this gain. He can urge that if the community once for all took possession of the producers' capital that is now in private hands, all future accumulations of such capital might go on just as they would do on the existing system, assuming that the community would consent to devote as much labour as at present to the production of remote utilities; so that, even supposing the *present* interest to be paid to the dispossessed owners of the capital already accumulated, the labourers might still divide among themselves the increment of produce continually accruing from new accumulations of capital. In short, all the 'saving' required *could* be done without being paid for, if it were done by the community previous to the division of the produce.

It must be admitted, I think, first, that the social accumulation of instruments might conceivably be carried on by the community, and without any payment of interest; and secondly, that there is no principle of abstract equity which renders it morally obligatory to carry it on as at present, by first allowing individuals to divide up the whole produce of social industry, and then promising them future payments if they will allow a portion of their shares to take the form of fresh instruments. And if the former method of providing for the progress of industry could be trusted to work, without any counterbalancing drawbacks, the perpetuation of the inequalities of distribution that we see to be inevitably bound up with the existing system would be difficult to reconcile with our common sense of justice as I have been led to interpret it[1]. Nor do I think

[1] Even assuming, as is usually done, that it would be necessary for the complete realisation of the Socialistic scheme to refuse to enforce private con-

that the difficulties of transition from the one system to the other, or the inevitable disappointment of expectations involved in it, would necessarily be more intense—though of course they would be indefinitely greater in extent—than those which in the course of modern history have actually attended the abolition of slavery in our colonies, of serfdom in Russia, or of oppressive feudal privileges in other European States. I do not mean to imply that the transition to Socialism is to be classed with the changes just mentioned, even if it be regarded merely as a distant stage of social progress; but I conceive that in urging the reasons for not so regarding it we have to pass—as in the case of the remedies for inequality of opportunity that we have before discussed—from the point of view of distribution to that of production. I object to Socialism not because it would divide the produce of industry badly, but because it would have so much less to divide. But when this objection is urged the controversy is necessarily shifted from the tribunal of abstract Justice to one where utilitarian or, as I have called them, "economic" considerations are taken as decisive.

tracts for lending of money at interest, I cannot regard this as a fundamental objection on the ground of justice. If the interference with freedom involved in appropriation of land to individuals can—as I hold—only be justified by the gain to production that it has caused, I do not see why this other interference should not equally be justified if without impairing production it tended to bring about an adequate improvement in distribution.

CHAPTER VII.

ECONOMIC DISTRIBUTION.

§ 1. In the preceding chapter we have considered the question of governmental interference with a view to a more equitable distribution of produce. I now pass to consider how far such interference is desirable on economic grounds: that is, as was explained in the first chapter of this Book, in order that a greater aggregate of utility or satisfaction may be obtained from the produce of the labour and capital of the community. It may appear that there is no material discrepancy between the practical conclusions to which we are led by reasoning from either point of view: but the lines of reasoning themselves are widely different. So far as we aim at realizing Justice or Equity—according to the interpretation of these notions that has been chiefly discussed in the preceding chapter—the proportionment of the individual's share of produce to his Deserts is the primary end to be sought, and the removal of inequalities only as a means to this; that is, only so far as these inequalities are due to other causes than the different worth of the exertions unequally remunerated. Whereas from a purely economic point of view the relation of Desert and Equality is the reverse; a more equal distribution is—subject to certain important qualifications that will be presently stated —more economic: and though the principle of rewarding desert remains, in my view, paramount, it is rather as a stimulus indispensable to the most economic production, which thus presents itself as a condition by which all efforts to make distribution more economic ought to be confined. The distinction is perhaps rather formal than material; but it is necessary to make it clear, in order that the relation of the present to the preceding chapter may be understood.

The *primâ facie* ground, then, on which the interference of Government with the distribution of produce that results from the individualistic organization of industry appears economically desirable, lies in the very great inequalities in income to which this organization leads. The common sense of mankind, in considering these inequalities, implicitly adopts, as I conceive, two propositions laid down by Bentham as to the relation of wealth to happiness:—viz. (1) that an increase of wealth is—speaking broadly and generally—productive of an increase of happiness to its possessor; and (2) that the resulting increase of happiness is not simply proportional to the increase of wealth, but stands in a decreasing ratio to it.

The former of these propositions will be thought by many to need no support; considering the vast and varied aggregate of widely felt desires which wealth supplies the means of gratifying. Still it is notorious that it has been roundly denied by a large number of thoughtful persons. Indeed, as was before observed [1], even the Author of the *Wealth of Nations* has expressed himself with remarkable decision in the opposite sense. I think, however, that the sentimental optimism which held that happiness is equally distributed between the palace and the cottage— with a preference, if at all, in favour of the cottage—has wellnigh vanished before a more careful and impartial study of the facts of social existence. At the present day, even those who most warmly assail Political Economy on the ground of the exaggerated importance which it attaches to wealth, do not usually go so far as to maintain that increase of wealth is not important for the individual and for society so far as it can be obtained without any sacrifice of other sources of happiness. It is, indeed, probable that there are many rich individuals who would be happier on the whole if they were poorer; and, again, that the immediate effect of a sudden and considerable increase in the wealth of certain sections of the poorer classes might very likely be a diminution of happiness, on account of the increase of pernicious indulgences that it would bring with it. But, making all

[1] Introduction, c. II. § 3.

allowance for such partial or transitory exceptions, it remains true that the practical reasonings of the great mass of mankind —whether for themselves or for others in whom they are individually interested—proceed on the assumption that it is an advantage to be richer; and, further, that the judgment of the most highly cultivated, scrupulously moral and sincerely religious persons—as expressed in their conduct—does not diverge materially from that of the vulgar in the matter. The *élite* certainly disagree very much with the vulgar as to the real value of particular purchaseable commodities; but they do not practically doubt that additional control over purchaseable commodities generally is an important gain to an individual who obtains it. A man who chose poverty for himself, except for some manifest special and unpurchaseable advantage, or at the manifest call of some special duty, would be deemed eccentric: a man who chose it for his wife and children would be generally thought to deserve a harsher name.

On the other hand few, I conceive, would estimate the advantage of additional wealth so highly as even to dispute the second of Bentham's two propositions above stated, and to contend that on the average the amount of satisfaction derived from wealth tends to increase in simple proportion to the increase of the wealth itself. And from the two propositions taken together the obvious conclusion is that the more any society approximates to equality in the distribution of wealth among its members, the greater on the whole is the aggregate of satisfactions which the society in question derives from the wealth that it possesses.

Reflection, however, shews that this interference is only legitimate under certain conditions: viz. that the total amount of produce to be divided, and the number of persons among whom it is to be divided, remains unaffected by the change in distribution.; and further that the change has no tendency to diminish the happiness of the community so far as it is derived from other sources than increase of wealth. These conditions require careful examination; since it will be found that under each of these heads important, if not decisive, considerations may be urged in favour of the existing inequalities of distribution.

§ 2. In the first place it is conceivable that a greater equality in the distribution of produce would lead ultimately to a reduction in the total amount to be distributed, in consequence of a general preference of leisure to the results of labour on the part of the classes whose shares of produce had increased. It may be said that we should have no ground for supposing in this case a diminution in average happiness corresponding to the diminution in wealth; since, by supposition, the increase of leisure would be chosen as likely to give more happiness than the increase of wealth. There are, however, two considerations of some weight which may lead us to doubt the soundness of this *primâ facie* view. In the first place there is a wide-spread opinion among observant persons that human beings generally have a tendency to overvalue leisure as a source of happiness. All those who maintain that riches frequently fail to bring an increase of happiness to their possessors commonly lay great stress on this tendency; they argue that the rich miss happiness largely through an undue pursuit of passive pleasures and amusements, to the neglect of those that may be derived from strenuous activity for a serious end. I am myself disposed to take this view: and I should regard it as highly probable that a sudden and large increase of the income of the poorer classes might cause them to fall extensively into similar imprudence: while the removal of the stimulating examples which the lives of the rich now offer of the varied satisfactions to be derived from abundant wealth would probably tend still further to promote general sloth. But again, even supposing that the diminution in their labour led immediately to a real increase of happiness through increased leisure, there would still remain the objection that it might diminish the provision against social calamities causing great and sudden loss of wealth, which is now supplied by the superfluous consumption of the rich. Such calamities—whether due to natural causes, or to war,—may now be met by a restriction of the luxurious expenditure of the richer classes generally—through voluntary contributions and increased taxation combined—by which the extreme distress that they would otherwise cause to the poorer classes may be mitigated. But a community that had exchanged its superfluous wealth for greater leisure would have lost this resource; and its additional power of increasing its labour would be an inadequate substitute, owing to the difficulty of making it promptly effective. But again, even supposing that the equalization of shares did not diminish the average activity of the workers of the community, it might still diminish the efficiency of labour through its effect on the accumulation of capital. At present, the greatest part of the saving, by which the stock of instruments in the country is continually increased and the benefits of invention realized, is made from the larger incomes of the rich: and consequently there is a considerable danger that an equalization of incomes would lead to a decrease in the proportion of the aggregate income of the community thus converted into capital[1].

This argument, as just stated, assumes the continuance of the present individualistic organization of industry: since under a socialistic system the accumulation of capital would be controlled by the government and would be independent of the savings of individuals. But governments have hitherto shewn themselves timid and unenterprising in availing themselves of the results of invention; and there seems no reason to suppose that a socialistic government would be specially bold in trying expensive experiments.

Again, as we have already seen, experience would lead us to conclude that, even supposing the aggregate of accumulation not to be diminished by a more equal distribution of produce, still a quantum of capital made up of a number of small portions in different ownership is less likely to be productively administered than an equal quantum divided among a few wealthy owners. The small savings might no doubt be massed by association in amounts sufficiently large for the organization of businesses on any scale that might be found most economically expedient; but theory and experience combine to shew that

---

[1] It may be observed too that the tentative and hazardous investments, which have hitherto been necessary for the progress of industry through invention, are more appropriately made out of the savings of persons who suffer comparatively little from the partial or even total loss of their capital. I fear, however, that this possible advantage of the existing unequal distribution of wealth is but imperfectly realized at present.

the keenness of concern, and the power of prompt and unfettered action, that private ownership gives would still be wanting to the necessarily salaried and controlled managers of these businesses. Unless these advantages can be compensated, to a greater extent than they have hitherto been, either by some future development of the system of Cooperative Production or otherwise, a more equal distribution of capital must necessarily be attended with a decrease in its productive efficiency. And this conclusion holds equally whether we suppose the existing individualistic organization of society to continue as at present, or to be wholly or partially superseded by socialistic institutions; so far as we have no ground for regarding governmental management of capital as likely to be superior on the whole to average jointstock management in the points in which the latter is less efficient than management by private owners.

The objections above stated would apply with increased force, if the increase through equalization of the incomes of the poorer classes should cause the population to increase at a more rapid rate than at present; so that ultimately the increment of an average worker's share would be partly spent in supporting a larger number of children, and partly reduced through the decrease in the efficiency of the more crowded labour[1]. It would be rash, indeed, to predict confidently that this would be the effect of equalization: but it would be still more rash to ignore the risk of it.

Finally we have to consider the importance of the social functions—over and above the economic function of employing capital—which the wealthier members of a community actually fulfil, however imperfectly and with whatever waste of resources, in their customary employment of their leisure and their luxurious expenditure. I do not now refer mainly to the function of governing—including that of giving suggestions and admonitions to government—since I take it to be a disputed question of Politics whether these functions in the present stage of social

[1] Even apart from the dangers of diminishing resources against unforeseen calamity and checking the accumulation of capital, it seems at least highly doubtful whether a mere increase in the number of human beings living as an average unskilled labourer lives in England can be regarded as involving a material increase in the *quantum* of human happiness.

development may not be better fulfilled by salaried officials and professional journalists, &c. I refer rather to what may be comprehensively though vaguely designated as the function of maintaining and developing knowledge and culture. I distinguish knowledge from culture, though the latter notion would naturally include the former, because of the peculiar economic importance of the progress of science, as the source of inventions that increase the efficiency of labour. This progress in past ages has been largely due to the unremunerated intellectual activity, assisted by liberal expenditure, of rich and leisured persons. At the same time it is of course conceivable that the development of knowledge should be adequately carried on—as it is chiefly in Germany at the present time—by persons salaried and provided with instruments at the public expense. And the connexion between scientific discoveries and technical inventions is now so firmly established in the popular mind, that probably even a government controlled entirely by persons of small incomes would not refuse the funds requisite for the support of the study of physical science in universities, academies, &c. The case is different with such knowledge as has no obvious practical utility, and is therefore only likely to be valued by persons susceptible to the gratifications of disinterested curiosity. Such knowledge must be ranked, as a source of elevated and refined gratification, along with literature, art, intellectual conversation, and the contemplation of natural beauty. The capacities for deriving enjoyment from these sources constitute what we call culture; they are generally regarded by persons possessed of them as supplying a most important element in the happiness of life; while at the same time, so far as we can judge from past experience, it is only in a society of comparatively rich and leisured persons that these capacities—and, still more, the faculties of producing excellent works in literature and art—are likely to be developed and transmitted in any high degree.

There seems therefore to be a serious danger that a thoroughgoing equalization of wealth among the members of a modern civilized community would have a tendency to check the growth of culture in the community. The amount of loss to human happiness that is to be apprehended from this effect is difficult to estimate; especially since those who estimate it most highly would probably refuse to allow the question to be decided by a mere consideration of the actual amount of happiness that culture has hitherto given. They have a conviction for which they could not give an empirical justification that a diffusion of culture may be expected in the future which has no parallel in the past: and that any social changes which cripple its development, however beneficent they may be in other respects, may involve a loss to humanity in the aggregate which, if we look sufficiently far forward, seems quite immeasurable in extent.

There are, in fact, several distinct practical questions suggested by the connexion which history shews between the development of culture and the existence of a rich and leisured class in a community of human beings. We may (1) balance the additional happiness gained to the lives of the few rich by culture against the additional happiness that might be enjoyed by the poor if wealth were more equally distributed; or (2) we may consider how far whatever happiness is derived from culture by the many poor depends at any given time on the maintenance of a higher kind of culture among the few rich; or (3) we may endeavour to forecast the prospective addition to happiness when culture shall have become more diffused, which would be endangered by any injury to its present development among the limited class who now have any considerable share in it. From each of these three distinct points of view arguments of a certain force may be drawn in favour of the present inequality in distribution of wealth.

Any estimate of the force of the considerations above given must necessarily be vague; but it seems clear that they apply far more strongly against any sudden sweeping equalization, than they do against a more slow and gradual movement towards this result,—accompanied (as it naturally would be) by an improvement in the average intellectual condition of the classes who would benefit pecuniarily by the equalization.

I have not yet mentioned one important point:—the loss of the specially keen stimulus to socially useful exertion which the prospect of obtaining ample wealth by business talent, mechanical invention, or professional or artistic skill, now gives to an important minority of persons. Almost any method of introducing greater equality of incomes would involve some loss of this kind: but the extent of such loss would depend greatly on the manner in which the equalization was carried out:—which we will now proceed to consider.

§ 3. The most extreme means which have been proposed for equalizing distribution are the systems commonly designated by the terms "Communism" and "Socialism;" which involve either the almost entire abolition of private property, or its restriction to consumers' wealth. These terms, however, and especially the adjectives Communistic and Socialistic, are also used more widely to describe the general principle of any modes of governmental interference which have for their object the attainment of the same result in a more partial way. This practice appears to me convenient; but in order to prevent vagueness it will be well to give each of the terms as precise a signification as possible, without deviating materially from ordinary usage.

Of the two terms 'Socialism' is the more comprehensive: Communism being generally regarded as an extreme form of Socialism, in which the most thorough-going antagonism to the institution of private property is manifested. It would, however, be hardly convenient to restrict the term Communism to systems involving the complete abolition of this institution; since no one, I suppose, has ever seriously recommended that (e.g.) a man should not have private property in his clothes. I think therefore that the most useful way in which we can employ the terms Communism and Communistic, without deviating materially from ordinary usage[1], is to restrict them to those schemes or measures of governmental interference for equalizing distribution which discard or override the principle that a labourer's remuneration should be proportioned to the value of his labour.

The proposal to organize society on a Communistic plan, so as to distribute the annual produce of the labour and capital of the community either in equal shares, or in shares varying not according to the deserts but according to the needs of the recipient, is one of which the serious interest has now passed

[1] Cf. Mill, B. II. c. 1, where the terms are used with a denotation substantially the same as that proposed in the text.

away; though a generation ago it had not a few adherents, and was supported with earnestness and ability by more than one competent writer. And, notwithstanding what has been urged in the preceding section, the proposition that a Communistic distribution would produce more happiness than the present system, if it could be realized without materially affecting production, or removing needful checks to population, is at any rate a very plausible one. But even if it were completely true I cannot doubt that the removal of the normal stimulus to labour (bodily and intellectual) and to care, which the present individualistic system supplies, would so much reduce the whole produce to be divided, that any advantage derived from greater economy of distribution would be decidedly outweighed—even supposing that no material change took place in population. Probably few of my readers will dispute this; but I may suggest to any one who is inclined to doubt it, to compare the average energy and perseverance in labour displayed by even respectable and conscientious rich persons, even when they select their own work, with the average energy and perseverance of professional men.

If this objection be allowed to be decisive, there will be no necessity to raise the very uninviting ethical questions which would be inevitably presented by the practical problem of preventing too great increase of population in a communistic society. I do not indeed regard this problem as insoluble; but I do not see how the difficulties in which it is involved are to be overcome without such a revolution in the traditional habits and sentiments regulating the relations of the sexes as no thoughtful person could contemplate without alarm and disquiet.

The definition of Communism, as above laid down, is tolerably distinct; and it enables us to give a definite significance to the adjective 'communistic,' in its wider application to denote the tendency of minor governmental interferences. That is, we shall classify as communistic any law or institution by which a portion of the aggregate produce of a community is, by the agency of Government, distributed to individuals according to considerations of Need, without regard to their Deserts or previous services. For instance, according to this definition, the English Poor-Law is communistic in its effects—though not, perhaps, in its principle[1]. So again, public roads, parks, libraries, churches, &c., so far as they are freely used by persons who are not taxed for their maintenance, must be called communistic; though, as we shall hereafter (§ 6) notice, the bad effects of communism are thought to be avoided or outweighed in these cases.

§ 4. There is somewhat more difficulty in defining in accordance with usage the wider terms Socialism and Socialistic; since any movement for substituting governmental for private and competitive management in any department of industry is liable to be called Socialistic: while at the same time it would seem paradoxical to apply the term to such established institutions as the Post-Office, or the Mint. And even if we agree to restrict the term to those kinds of governmental intervention which not merely increase production but also equalize distribution, we still do not obtain any broad line of demarcation. For any considerable extension of the sphere of government that is really successful from the point of view of production, tends *pro tanto* to bring about the results aimed at by the advocates of more economic distribution; so far as it tends to increase the stock of capital owned by the community, and to reduce the field of employment for private capital.

This tendency may perhaps be most easily exhibited by making an extreme supposition. Suppose that, in civilized countries generally, governmental administration of all kinds of business were shewn to be economically superior, in a marked degree, to the present competitive management: it is obvious that the state might gradually buy up the land and fixed capital of different industries, paying for them out of the increased proceeds of its superior management; and the process, when once commenced, would go forward with continually increasing rapidity. The field of investment thus becoming gradually more and more limited, the return to private capital—supposing saving to continue as at present—would probably begin to fall. 'Spending' would then increase at the expense of saving, and private capital would gradually diminish from being eaten up. It would be important that the State

[1] Cf. *ante*, chap. III. § 1, and also § 5 of this chap.

CHAP. VII.]   ECONOMIC DISTRIBUTION.   529

should purchase the land of the community, and other permanent instruments of production tending to rise in value—if there be any—at an early stage of this process: not merely to gain the unearned increment, but because, as interest sinks towards zero, the selling value of land at a given rent tends to rise proportionally. The process might conceivably go on until the payment for the use of capital, as distinct from insurance against risk, became nearly evanescent; so that only such an amount of private capital would be kept up as men would be willing to keep for security of future use and enjoyment, without any view to profit. And finally when the instruments and materials of all industries had become the property of the government, the aggregate of private savings—leaving out of account the non-usurious lending and borrowing among private persons that might still go on—could only be in the form of consumers' capital,' i.e. houses, gardens, furniture, jewels, pictures, &c. Suppose further that, at the same time, by a comprehensive system of free education, elementary, technical and professional, the present scarcity values of the higher grades of labour had been deduced, so that all such skill as average persons can acquire by training was remunerated by merely a fair return for the additional outlay or sustenance during the period of education. We should thus have arrived at something very like the ideal of economic distribution which German Socialists have put forward, without any sudden shock to the expectations formed by the present system of private property. Society would voluntarily have converted its private capital into consumers' wealth; and, through the agency of its government, would have produced for itself the public capital used in its place. The income of all individual members of the community would be entirely derived from labour of some kind,—or, in the current phrase of the Socialists, labour would obtain its "full product" of consumable commodities (subtracting only whatever additional public capital had to be provided for the increase of its future produce).

I need hardly say that any such increase in social production through governmental administration as we have above imagined is beyond the limits of any rational forecast of the future development of society: it is, I suppose, even beyond the dreams of the most sanguine Socialist. My aim in imagining it has chiefly been to shew how any effective occupation by government of a portion of the present field of employment of private capital is a step toward the goal at which Socialists aim; i.e. it tends to bring with it whatever advantages attach to the reduction of existing inequalities of distribution. And it is only such mild and gentle steps towards the realization of the Socialistic ideal that I can regard as at all acceptable, in the present condition of our knowledge of man and society. I have made clear in the preceding chapter that I do not hold the proposal, that the community should prohibit interest and compulsorily purchase with terminable annuities the land and instruments of production now in private ownership, to be beyond the pale of theoretical discussion as immoral; but I think that, considering the perils of so vast a revolution, we ought to have much more conclusive evidence than has yet been offered of the advantages to be derived from it after the struggle is over, before it can be even worth while to discuss it seriously from a practical point of view. At the same time, as I have already explained, I see no reason to regard unqualified *laisser faire* as tending to realize the most economical production any more than the best possible distribution of wealth: and it seems to me quite possible that a considerable extension of the industrial functions of government might be on the whole advantageous, without any Utopian degree of moral or political improvement in human society. But at any rate to be successful such extension must, I think, be gradual; and the first experiments in this direction ought to be made in departments in which the defects of private enterprise, and the advantages of unitary administration, have been shewn to be greatest,—e.g. in departments where there is a manifest tendency to the establishment of monopolies in the hands either of single individuals or of associations. And, moreover, it ought to be an object in any such extension to maintain as far as possible in the governmental organization of industry an effective stimulus to individual exertion, and to allow scope for invention and improvement of methods.

This leads me to a point which many writers have regarded as the most fundamental objection to Socialism; the difficulty,

CHAP. VII.] ECONOMIC DISTRIBUTION. 531

namely, of distributing the produce of joint labour so as to apportion remuneration to desert. In the preceding chapter I have tried to shew that we can only hope to realize a remote approximation to this ideal of distributive justice, by getting rid of all removable differences in remuneration that are due to causes other than the voluntary exertions of the labourers. An important part of this result might, I conceive, be brought about through the assumption by government of the main industrial functions now performed by private capitalists, without any fundamental change in the principle of remuneration now adopted in respect of governmental officials, if at the same time the means of training for the higher kinds of work were effectually brought within the reach of all classes, by a well organized system of free education, liberally supported by exhibitions for the children of the poor. For as the instruments of production would be mainly the property of the nation, all the inequalities of income that now result from the payment of interest to private capitalists as such, or of profit to employing capitalists, would, speaking broadly, have ceased to exist; and though it would be impossible, without intolerable constraint on the freedom of action of individuals, to prevent the children of persons earning larger incomes or owning accumulated wealth from having a somewhat better start in life than the rest, still this advantage might be reduced to a minimum by such an educational system as I have suggested. But it is clear that in a completely Socialistic community, the remuneration of superior qualities of labour could not be determined by reference to the 'market price' of such labour, as there would be no market outside the service of government, by which its price could be fixed: the 'fair' wages of such superior labourers would have to depend entirely on a governmental estimate of the value of their work. I do not, however, see that the influence of competition need be excluded altogether; there might be competition between one locality and another for the best workers,—or even, to some extent, between different departments of a central government: and through such competition a tolerable estimate of the amount necessary to stimulate adequately to the acquisition of the required qualifications, and to compensate for any special outlay or sacrifices involved in such acquisition, might be gradually determined on the basis of experience. And for remuneration of special services—e.g. useful inventions—special rewards, pecuniary or honorific, might be added. Still, such a system, at its best, could hardly be as stimulating as the present open competition to persons with great gifts for business, or mechanical invention, or any special art or profession: our experience of governmental work affords slender ground for the belief that it would generally either give due play to the special talents of such persons, or—even if it did—would allot to the gifted individuals any adequate compensation for the additional utility which they would produce for the community.

The question remains, whether the need of organizing new checks to population—which we have seen to be incident to Communism—would also arise under such a Socialistic system as I have just sketched. There is no positive necessity that any particular department of a Socialistic government should be bound to find work for any applicant: individuals might be left to find for themselves where their services were wanted, relief being provided for the unemployed under some such deterrent conditions as those of our existing poor-law. Still, in a community in which all, or the most important branches, of production were carried on by the government, the unemployed would naturally throw on the government the whole responsibility for their situation; and if their number became at any time considerable, a strong demand would arise, very difficult to resist, that the State should provide work and adequate wages, for all applicants. It does not, however, appear to me clear that this provision, in a community successfully organized on a Socialistic basis, would necessarily give a dangerous stimulus to population. If we suppose a community in which the aggregate remuneration of labour is increased by most of the share that now forms interest on individuals' capital, while the emoluments and dignities attached to the higher kinds of labour are brought within the hopes of all classes, by a system of education which at the same time makes general such a degree of foresight and intelligence as is now possessed by the higher grade of artisans —it seems quite possible that in such a community a minimum of wages might be guaranteed to all who were unable to find employment for themselves, without drawing an ever increasing crowd of applicants to claim the guaranteed minimum, and without a serious deficit arising from the inefficient work of such as did apply.

§ 5. The question of the 'Right of Labour[1]' affords a point on which we may conveniently turn from imagining what may be in the distant future, to discuss the general economic advantages and drawbacks of such measures for the mitigation of inequalities of distribution as can be considered to be now within the pale of practical consideration: as the 'Right to ' Labour' can hardly be denied a place in this latter class, since Bismarck has declared[2] it to be one of the objects of his government to secure the German labourer work and adequate wages. I am not, however, aware that Bismarck or any influential statesman has as yet proposed any scheme for attaining this end: and I do not know any means by which it could be attained in a community like our own, without a grave danger of disastrous consequences. If the government in such a country as England guaranteed even a minimum of necessaries to all who were able and willing to give a normal day's work for them—without the deterrent conditions under which such relief is actually offered to able-bodied paupers in an English workhouse—we can hardly doubt that the labour thus purchased by the State could not, even by good organization, be made to pay the cost of its support. For a labourer employed under such a guarantee could not be dismissed for mere inertness or inefficiency, but only for such wilful and obstinate idleness as would justify his being sent to prison: hence he would have much less motive than at present either for working energetically or for seeking and qualifying himself for the employment in which he would be most useful ; and his labour would tend to be proportionally less productive. At the same time the minimum of shelter and sustenance that humanity would allow to be given him would cost more than the earnings

---

[1] This phrase is so current that it is convenient to use it: but it must be understood in the light of Whately's remark that "when a man says he wants "work, what he means is that he wants wages."

[2] In a speech delivered on the 9th of May, 1884.

of the worst-paid labourers at the present time; so that, on the whole, the measure would both materially diminish aggregate production and throw a serious burden on the public purse—both which effects would, under existing circumstances, tend continually to increase, as the security of employment would give an important stimulus to population.

Nor can I agree with those who think that—in view of the distress which the worst-paid labourers in our modern communities endure,—government might reasonably *prescribe* a minimum of wages for all labourers able and willing to give a full day's work, without incurring the dangers connected with a governmental *provision* of such a minimum. If, indeed, the commodities produced by the labourers now paid under the proposed minimum were of such a kind that if the price were raised the demand would not be materially diminished nor a competing supply obtained from elsewhere, the desired result might be attained; as the lacking *quantum* of wages could then be obtained by employers from the consumers. But I know no ground for assuming this to be generally the case: and so far as it is not the case, the legal minimum of wages would tend to throw a number of the worst-paid labourers out of work[1]: hence to prevent widespread distress it would be almost necessary to supplement the *prescription* of a minimum of wages by the governmental *provision* of employment and remuneration; so that this method of raising wages could hardly fail to land us in all the difficulties of the Right to Labour.

The dangers of the measures just mentioned may be partly illustrated by the actual experience that has been gained of the dangers incident to a kind of governmental interference with distribution which all modern communities have thought necessary, in some form or other, for the protection of their members from absolute want of the necessaries of life. I have already pointed out that, according to the received view of Communism, which I have tried to express in a precise definition, the English

---

[1] Probably an increase in the labourers' efficiency from improved physical conditions would in some cases partly compensate for the increase in the price of their services, so that the cost of these to the employer would not be increased in proportion to the rise in wages. But this effect could not be relied upon to prevent a reduction in the demand for the labour raised in price.

Poor Law must be allowed to be communistic in its effects—though it does not follow that its adoption is n any way due to a communistic design or principle. In fact if we look merely to the motive which prompts the community to grant all its members legally secu ed relief, we should rather classify this measure with the interferences to protect life and health, which I noticed in a previous chapter. But if we protect the health of a starving person by giving him necessaries at the expense of the community, our action inevitably involves to some extent the evils of communism whatever its intention may have been: that is, it tends to decrease the inducements to labour, forethought and thrift in two ways, (1) by distributing to paupers a certain *quantum* of unearned commodities, and (2) by taking from non-paupers a corresponding portion of what they have earned or saved. The former of these bad effects may be in the main averted, so far as the inducement to labour for present needs is concerned, in the case of able-bodied paupers, by exacting work from them in return for relief under somewhat disagreeable conditions; for though it is probably impossible to keep this compulsory labour up to an average degree of energy, there being no fear of dismissal for slackness, still any attractiveness that might hence attach to the position of a pauper may be more than counterbalanced by restrictions on freedom, and by the prohibition of indulgences not necessary to health, but yet so cheap that even the poorest can occasionally enjoy them: and, in fact, English experience seems to shew that the provision made for such able-bodied paupers as reside in a workhouse does not offer any serious temptation even to the worst-paid labourers to relax their energies in seeking employment elsewhere[1]. On the other hand it seems impossible to prevent even 'indoor relief' from weakening the motives that prompt the poorest class of labourers to earn and save an adequate provision against sickness and old age, or for the support of their families in case of premature death: and this is still more manifestly the case with out-door relief. And it is the expense of

---

[1] The vagrants, on the other hand, who spend single nights in the 'casual 'wards' of different workhouses, have a serious temptation to idleness in the shelter and food thus provided without adequate enforcement of labour in return.

supporting those who are wholly unable, or but very partially able, to work, which causes by far the greater part of the burden of taxation entailed by pauperism though, for the reasons already stated, the value even of the labour of the able-bodied falls seriously short of the cost of their shelter and sustenance.

The bad economic effects of this taxation on the persons taxed depend mainly on its compulsory character: since a man does not feel the reward of his labour to be lessened by the fact that he voluntarily bestows a portion of it in alms. It would seem, too, that if the destitute persons could be adequately protected from starvation by any measure that did not give them a definite legal security of obtaining relief, the discouragement to thrift which such legally secured relief entails would be partly avoided. Further, if the legally secured relief be kept inseparable from the deterrent conditions necessary to prevent its worst consequences, it cannot be regarded as a satisfactory provision for the case of deserving persons who have fallen into indigence either through inevitable and irremediable disaster, or at any rate from causes involving no serious blame to them. And, in fact the most rigid supporters of the English poor-law have generally recognised the moral necessity of supplementing it by private almsgiving. On the other hand private almsgiving, being largely impulsive, unenlightened, and unorganized, is found to give serious encouragement to unthrift, and even to imposture. These considerations suggest, first, that Government might with advantage undertake the *organization* of eleemosynary relief, in order to make its distribution as economical, effective, and judicious as possible; and, secondly, that the *provision* of funds for such relief—so far, at least, as they are used for the ordinary sustenance of adults in distress[1]—might be left mainly to voluntary gifts and bequests, with a certain amount of assistance from government, if experience shews it to be necessary, but without any legal right to relief. These two principles are maintained in the treatment of pauperism adopted in France;

[1] By this phrase I mean chiefly to exclude the sustenance of (1) destitute children, (2) the insane—whose support Government ought to undertake as a mere measure of protection to other members of the community, (3) persons incapacitated by special diseases. I also exclude medical aid generally, of which I afterwards speak.

CHAP. VII.]   ECONOMIC DISTRIBUTION.   537

and the experience of France seems to shew that voluntary provision if carefully organized may be relied on as nearly adequate for the purpose of practically securing the poor from starvation; and also that relief so provided may be distributed to the applicants in their own homes without the bad consequences that out-door relief has under our compulsory system: since the absence of legal security compensates for the absence of the deterrent conditions of the workhouse.

But again : assuming that government ought to make a legally secured provision for any sick or infirm member of the community who may be destitute of necessaries, it does not therefore follow that the expense of this provision must ordinarily be undertaken[1] by the community, so far as adults are concerned ; since it might be thrown, wholly or in part, on the individuals themselves by laying a special tax on their earnings for the purpose of compulsory insurance. There is much to be said for this method[2] of dealing with a part at least of the complex problem of pauperism, as compared with the method of the English poor-law : and though the *political* interference with natural liberty would be much more intense in the former method, the *economic* interference would be much less, so far as the measure succeeded ;—as each individual would be merely coerced into providing that he should not become a burden to others. I do not, however, see how anything like the required premiums could be exacted without great harshness from labourers who have now scarcely more than the bare necessaries of life ; and if in their case the whole or the greater part of the funds were supplied by government, the danger of weakening the normal stimulus to exertion and thrift on the part of labourers at or near this lowest level would, I fear, be decidedly greater than that which attends the English system[3].

[1] That is, in default of near relatives on whom it may properly be thrown.
[2] This method has been partially adopted by the German government in two important measures dealing respectively with insurance against sickness (1883) and insurance against accidents (1884).
[3] Mr W. L. Blackley has argued, in a series of pamphlets, that the required payments might be made by *young* labourers between the time that they become able to earn the wages of adults and the age of 21. I think he has shewn that the majority of male labourers might in this way be made to supply, without painful sacrifices, at any rate a large part of the funds required to secure them

The case of labourers thrown temporarily out of employment would also cause considerable difficulty[1].

§ 6. Besides providing the necessaries of life to persons completely destitute, modern governments have intervened in various other ways, with the view of ameliorating the economic condition of the poorer classes at the expense, more or less, of the rest of the community. But such intervention has usually —and in my opinion rightly—aimed at improving production as well as distribution, or otherwise benefiting the community as a whole, and not one part only at the expense of the rest. Accordingly the chief examples of this kind of intervention have already called for our notice in a previous chapter (ch. iv.). Thus in some cases its object has been to provide commodities specially conducive to the moral or intellectual improvement of the classes benefited, and which at the same time hardly form an element of that 'standard of comfort' which supplies the chief ordinary motive to labour and thrift; in other cases it has aimed at making such a change in the circumstances of the persons assisted as would tend to stre gthen on the whole, rather than weaken, habits of energetic industry, thrift, and self-help in the individuals assisted. Under the first head would come, for instance, the pecuniary aid, before discussed, which modern states have largely given to education—in-

against destitution in sickness and old age: nor can I see that there are serious difficulties in the way of making such saving compulsory on all persons in regular employment by laying on employers the obligation to insure their labourers. But it would be hardly possible to collect the required payments from the class of persons who pick up their livelihood by various irregular kinds of work; while if such irregulars were exempted from compulsion the increase in their number that must be expected to result from the proposed measure would be a serious economic drawback. And further it does not seem that the measure could be applied to the worst-paid class of labourers—chiefly women—without reducing their wages below the amount required to keep them in health. Even in classes above the lowest in the scale of wages there would be many exceptional cases in which such a measure as Mr Blackley proposes would cause great hardship: as (e.g) the case of young persons supporting widowed mothers, infant brothers and sisters, &c.

[1] As Brentano has pointed out, the case of insurance against accidents in dangerous industries is specially favourable for compulsion; because the workman out of employment is also out of danger. Here too the employers would properly bear a share of the cost: viz. what would be equivalent to their liability to compensate the uninsured labourer for certain kinds of accidents.

cluding the diffusion of culture by means of libraries, museums, &c.: under the second head I should place assistance to emigration, and also most interferences with the tenure of land, especially those of which the object has been to place the actual cultivators of the soil in a position more favourable to effective industry. As an example of this latter class we may notice the important assistance given in recent times by the Governments of Prussia and Hesse Darmstadt to facilitate the transition of their peasantry from feudal semi-servitude to the condition of independent proprietors. This assistance did not involve any direct pecuniary sacrifice on the part of the community; but it was nevertheless a distinctly distributional interference, since it gave the peasants the advantage of the superior credit enjoyed by the community—and also of the advantage in efficiency and cheapness which the governmental collection of rents was found to possess, compared with the collection by private individuals. From these two sources a margin was obtained enabling the cultivator to refund to the State, within a not very long period, the capital with which his landlord's rent-charge had been brought up, without any increase of his rent.

The intervention just described was for a special and temporary object. But experience has shewn that peasant cultivators are liable to become loaded with debt to money lenders who, either through the absence of effective competition—partly in consequence of a certain discredit that often attaches to their business—or perhaps sometimes through unavowed combination, are enabled to exact very onerous interest. This condition of debt tends to paralyse the productive energies as well as to cause distress: accordingly, under these circumstances governments may operate for the benefit of production no less than of distribution, by encouraging with special privileges the formation of commercial companies for the purpose of lending money on easier terms. Indeed, as was before said, the business of lending on the security of land seems to be of a kind that might even be undertaken by government itself under certain conditions, without the kind of risk that is involved in ordinary banking business. So too, where the pawnbroker is the normal resort in an emergency of poor labourers who have not saved or have exhausted their savings, governments, by undertaking the business of lending money at a moderate interest, may give sensible relief without offering any material encouragement to unthrift.

Another important case of interference primarily distributional, but which also admits of being defended as beneficial to the community, is that of measures for protecting the health of the poor, so far as the cost of these is defrayed by taxation falling on the rich. Thus the provision in certain cases of wholly or partially gratuitous medical advice and attendance both tends to benefit production by increasing the average physical vigour of the labourers, and also affords those who are taxed to pay for it a certain protection against infectious or epidemic diseases: and the same may be said of other sanitary measures primarily affecting the poorer classes, of which the cost has been, wholly or partly, borne by the community[1] on economic grounds.

How far the State *ought*, on economic grounds, to intervene in the matters above-mentioned, and others to which similar principles may be applied, is a question which involves a very difficult and complex comparison of various kinds of social utility. And I do not think that it admits of a precise general answer; as the balance of advantage in any case must depend very largely on particular circumstances and varying social conditions. One important consideration by which the answer must partly be determined is the extent to which provision has been made, or may be expected to be made, for the ends in view, either through the spontaneous association of the persons primarily concerned, or the philanthropic efforts of other individuals, or both combined. Thus experience has shewn that in important cases where mere competition among producers fails to lower sufficiently the price of certain commodities to the poorer consumers, the latter may successfully relieve themselves of the resulting disadvantages by spontaneous association—as in the case of the (artisans')

[1] An important example of such measures may be observed in the English Act of 1875 for destroying and replacing unhealthy blocks of houses in towns; since the total cost of this operation is necessarily much beyond what can be met by the rents of the new houses—due compensation being allowed to the owners of such houses as are not judged to deserve penal destruction, and to traders whose business connexion is impaired by dislodgement.

'cooperative stores' of England, and the 'cooperative banks' of Germany;—and where this remedy can be successfully applied it is doubtless preferable, both for its direct and its indirect effects, to governmental intervention. Again, the promotion of education and culture, and the cure of diseases, have been largely provided for in modern civilized communities by the voluntary contributions of individuals; partly by the donations of the living, partly by bequests. Over the gifts (or loans) of the living, the State can exercise but very slight control—except by offering to receive and administer them—without vexatious and dangerous interference with liberty; but the same danger does not attend interference with funds bequeathed for public objects: governments have always claimed the right of invalidating testamentary dispositions that are held to be contrary to public policy, and this principle might reasonably be applied to prevent bequests of which the economic consequences are clearly seen to be disadvantageous. Further, as the administration of such funds is generally removed from the influence of the ordinary economic motives prompting to the most useful employment of wealth, it is important that it should be carefully supervised by the State, in order to carry out the real wishes of the testators; and also that the schemes of the latter should be subject to thorough revision when a certain period has elapsed; since human foresight is very limited, and the fitness of any detailed regulations—even if originally well contrived—for effecting any purpose of social utility, is pretty sure to decrease as time goes on. Interference of this latter kind, however, should be controlled by a careful regard for the testators' main aims and wishes, for fear of seriously checking the disposition to make such bequests: since it is an important gain to society that such expenditure as is desirable for the purpose of ameliorating the condition of the poor should be defrayed by this means of supply so far as possible, rather than by taxation.

§ 7. If, however, the expediency of governmental interference, having a markedly distributional character, depends greatly on the extent to which provision is voluntarily made for certain social needs, we are naturally led to ask on what principles such action on the part of private persons should be determined. I shall consider this question—so far as seems suitable in such a treatise as the present—in the concluding chapter: but I may here point out that it is important to distinguish clearly between what should be morally *imposed* in the name of strict justice and what should be morally *encouraged* as wise beneficence. Any rich individual who restricts his assumption of luxuries, in order to distribute his superfluous wealth among poorer members of the community, tends *pro tanto* to bring about what I have called a more "economic" application of the material means of happiness, if only he manages his distribution so as to avoid impairing the normal motives to energy and thrift in the recipients of his beneficence. But it is much more doubtful whether "distributive justice"— so far as this diverges from the result brought about by open competition—can be effectively promoted by the voluntary action of private persons. For any such action would, from its inevitably partial and sporadic character,—since only a few moral persons could be braced up to the requisite sacrifices— tend to introduce a new kind of inequality.

There is, however, one case—of growing importance in the present organization of industry—in which there is *primâ facie* more opportunity for a private application of distributive justice. I refer to the problem of dividing the produce of industry between opposing combinations of labourers and employers. Here, as was before explained[1], economic science cannot determine a normal division, on the basis of its ordinary assumption of self-interest as the governing motive in the exchange: it can only determine roughly the limits within which it is the interest of both sides to accept any terms rather than finally break off negotiations. But if any principle of fair division could be laid down, then—provided that the division determined by it fell anywhere between these limits—the ordinary economic motive would tend powerfully to maintain it in general application, owing to the strong interest that both the opposing combinations have in avoiding strife.

At the same time, I do not think that this conflict of opposing combinations can be decided by any general principle of social justice, determining how much either party ought to receive of the value of their common product. No voluntary

[1] See p. 352.

CHAP. VII.]   *ECONOMIC DISTRIBUTION.*   543

combination of labourers could be expected to undertake the task of securing for every labourer who wants it a "fair day's wages for a fair day's work": practically actual struggles have always related to the wages of labourers in some special branch of production: there is no means of ascertaining what wages such a group of labourers would obtain if all removable inequality of opportunities were absent: and we are not even warranted in assuming that they would now be content with this, if it could be ascertained,—still less that it would be the interest of the employers to give this amount of wages rather than withdraw from the business. Hence in any rational process for determining the 'fair' wages of a group of combined labourers there must be an arbitrary point of departure: some particular ratio between their wages and the value of the net produce of their industry, under certain actual conditions, must be assumed to be 'fair,' and the definite question must be how to maintain 'fairness,' so understood, under changing conditions. This, I conceive, is the principal theoretical problem presented to Boards of Arbitration between labourers and employers: and an approximate—though necessarily rough and imperfect—solution of this problem would seem to be aimed at in the automatic sliding scales by which conflict has been partially prevented in certain industries in recent years.

So long as no material change takes place in the processes of the industry, or in the quality of the labour employed in it—including the employers' own labour—the problem offers little theoretical difficulty: net produce can be estimated with sufficient accuracy by subtracting from the price of the commodities produced the cost of the raw material and other capital consumed in producing them, and wages can be made to vary so as to maintain the same proportion to net produce. If, however, the processes of the industry change so as to alter materially the proportion of labour to capital, or of one kind of labour to another kind, a somewhat different comparison will be required. It will then be needful to ascertain the proportion borne by wages, in the division assumed to be fair, to average employers' earnings *per cent.*[1] of capital—i.e. to net

[1] There are objections, as I have before pointed out, (Book II. ch. IX. § 3) to the general assumption that a uniform rate of employers' earnings per cent.

profit with interest and allowance for risk subtracted—in order to keep the proportion approximately stable in any revision of wages. Theoretically any ascertainable change in the average quality of business management ought to affect the proportion: but in practice this point could hardly be satisfactorily investigated. On the other hand a change in the efficiency of manual labour is more easily taken into account, and ought to be so taken: the stable proportion ought to be between employers' earnings and the remuneration of labour of a given efficiency. But variations in the demand for labour ought not, I conceive, to be admitted as grounds for varying the proportional division agreed upon, though they must affect the limits within which this division will be sustained by ordinary economic motives: since the fundamental assumption in the discussion between the opposing combinations is not that the effects of free competition are to be imitated as far as possible in the settlement arrived at, but rather that they are to be resisted and modified. Again, it is obvious that changes in the purchasing power of money are not to be taken into account, unless—as may happen—they affect the prices of commodities consumed by labourers and employers respectively in appreciably different degrees.

It is probably desirable that the variations in wages, from the amount originally fixed, should be reduced by throwing on employers the larger share of loss through any fall in the price of the net produce of the industry. But if this is done it should be as a matter of express agreement, with a view to the distinct end of avoiding fluctuations in wages: and the employers should of course be compensated by a correspondingly larger share of gain from a rise in price.

of capital is normal: but I do not think that any other assumption would be practicable in the present case.

CHAPTER VIII.

PUBLIC FINANCE.

§ 1. I HAVE deferred to this chapter the discussion of the subject which, in the view of Adam Smith and many of his successors, is the main and almost the sole concern of the Art of Political Economy; viz. the "provision for the expenses of "the Sovereign or the Commonwealth:" or, as it seems convenient to call it, Public Finance. I have adopted this course, because it seemed clear that the general discussion of the principles of governmental interference, for the improvement either of production or of distribution ought, if introduced at all, to precede the discussion of the principles of Finance : since most known methods of providing for the expenses of the commonwealth involve important effects both on production and on distribution, and our judgment as to the expediency or legitimacy of these effects cannot fail to be influenced by the conclusions adopted on the questions discussed in the preceding chapters of this book. It is true that considerations of this kind cannot always be decisive : the hard necessity of obtaining supplies for the exigencies of Government may compel a financier to adopt measures whose detrimental effects on industry are generally recognised; but none the less is it desirable that he should take account of these effects, in order that, if he is unable to avoid them altogether, he may mitigate or compensate them as far as possible.

Some writers, again, have taken a somewhat narrower view of the subject of the present chapter: confining their attention to what they have designated as the "theory of taxation." And no doubt, in any modern civilized community, taxation is the chief mode by which the ordinary pecuniary wants of Government are supplied. But in no community is it the sole mode; and it appears to me that we are likely to get a clearer view of the principles on which a system of taxation ought to be constructed, if we begin by considering other methods of attaining the financier's end. Indeed my doubt is rather whether the scope of this part of our discussion should not be enlarged still further, so as to include the economic principles of governmental expenditure as well as the provision for defraying such expenditure. It is, however, difficult, in treating of the art of economically organizing governmental administration, to get beyond the general principle that we ought to aim at producing the greatest possible result with the least possible cost, without entering into the details of governmental business to an extent which seems unsuitable to the character of this treatise. I do not therefore propose to treat of the art of public expenditure, except so far as it is specially connected with the art of providing for such expenditure.

There are two ways in which this connexion becomes important. In the first place, we have to make the general observation that we cannot properly take governmental expenditure as something of which the amount is fixed prior to the consideration of the methods of supplying it and their effects. Practically, no doubt, the problem of finance is often presented to a statesman in this simplified form: but theoretically we must regard both expenditure and supply as having at least a margin within which the restriction or enlargement of either must partly depend on the effects of the corresponding restriction or enlargement of the other; within which, therefore, the gain secured to the public by an additional increment of expenditure has to be carefully weighed against the sacrifices inevitably entailed by the exaction of an additional increment of supply. This remains true even if the sphere of Government be restricted to the 'individualistic minimum' given at the outset of chap. iii. No doubt it is the worst possible economy not to make adequate provision for the necessary and acknowledged functions of Government; but adequacy in such cases cannot be defined by a sharp line. Most Englishmen are persuaded that they at present enjoy very tolerable protection of person and property against enemies within and without the country; but it would be difficult to argue that our security would not be enhanced by more and better-paid judges and policemen, or more and better-equipped soldiers and sailors. Proposals, in fact, are continually made for increased expenditure in one or other of these directions: and it is obvious that in judging of such proposals a statesman must balance—roughly no doubt, but as well as he can—the advantages of increased governmental efficiency against the difficulties and drawbacks of obtaining increased supply. And it is still more evident that any question as to the extension of what Mill distinguishes as the "optional" functions of Government must be decided by a similar balance of considerations.

But again, the theory of expenditure has another special connexion with the theory of supply, so far as particular sources of supply are specially adapted to particular kinds of expenditure.

§ 2. In order to shew the importance of this latter connexion let us consider separately each of the chief modes by which Government obtains the commodities it requires. These commodities may be divided into (1) Services, (2) Material products requiring to be continually supplied, and (3) Land, buildings and other comparatively permanent investments of capital; and both services and material products may be obtained either (*a*) without purchase, or (*b*) by purchase with money previously provided in some way. In many civilized countries an important part of the services required by Government is obtained otherwise than by free exchange. In England, for instance, the work of legislation is unpaid; and so is a considerable share of the judicial work, whether performed voluntarily, as in the case of magistrates, or compulsorily, as it is by jurymen. We are not, however, concerned to do more than notice these facts: since the desirability of imposing or accepting these unremunerated services is, I conceive, a political question in the decision of which economic considerations have but a subordinate place. This cannot be so decidedly said in the case, economically far more important, of labour obtained compulsorily for the purposes of military (including naval) service. The defenders of the compulsory system have no doubt urged other than economic reasons in its favour,—it has been said that the defence of one's country is a function which ought to be undertaken from patriotism or a sense of duty, rather than from mercenary motives and a taste for the incidents of the painful business of mutual slaughter; it ought therefore not to be made the work of a special profession recruited in the ordinary way by free contract; but rather imposed upon all citizens, whom there is not some special reason for exempting. It has been urged further that this system diminishes the constitutional dangers inseparable from the existence of a large standing army; since conscripts are less likely than professional soldiers to be seduced into fighting unjustifiably against the established political order.

But, whatever weight may be attached to these or other non-economic arguments, it seems undeniable, at any rate, that under certain circumstances there may be overwhelming economic considerations in favour of compulsory service. Where, indeed, the number of soldiers and sailors required for warlike purposes is not large in proportion to the population, and their services can be obtained at about the rate at which labour of similar quality would be hired for peaceful industry, voluntary enlistment seems clearly the most economical system; since it tends to select the persons most likely to be efficient soldiers and those to whom military functions are least distasteful; both which advantages are lost by the adoption of the compulsory system. But a nation may unfortunately require an army so large that its ranks could not be kept full by voluntary enlistment, except at a rate of remuneration much above that which would be paid in other industries for labour that requires no more outlay in training and no scarcer qualifications: and in this case the burden of the taxation requisite to provide for such an army may easily be less endurable than the burden of compulsory service.

However to present even the economical argument on this question completely we should have to consider the respective advantages of short and long service, the proper relation between the regular army and the reserve, and other details of military (and naval) organization into which my limits do not allow me to enter[1].

The material products required by the state it is ordinarily expedient to obtain by purchase, leaving the production of them to private industry; for the reasons that lead us to regard the present individualistic organization of industry as in general economically superior to a socialistic organization. But in certain cases these arguments either do not apply or are balanced by special reasons in favour of State manufacture: either where the articles required by Government are of a quite peculiar kind (such as the instruments of warfare, cannons, ironclads, &c.) so that the advantage of free competition may not be obtainable at all, or may be more likely to be obtained if Government undertakes the manufacture; or where the quality of the article is very important and at the same time difficult to test if obtained by purchase; or where systematic and costly experiments in production are required.

In the case of land, buildings, and other comparatively permanent kinds of wealth what has practically to be considered is often not how the state is to be supplied with them, but rather how far it is desirable that it should retain possession of them. Much of the land that now belongs to the public in the form of roads, commons, forests, harbours, &c. has never been private property: other portions of it, in modern European communities, have been the semi-private property of the royal families in feudal and semifeudal times, and have since gradually acquired, more or less completely, the character of public property; other portions have been taken from individuals or societies in the way of confiscation. But however such property may have been obtained, there can hardly be any valid reason for keeping it now, unless it is required for the due performance of necessary governmental functions, or unless for special reasons it is likely to be more useful socially under governmental management.

§ 3. The greater part, however, of the material provision for the needs of Government has to be obtained annually or from

[1] It should be observed that even where the services of soldiers and sailors are obtained by a compulsory system, their pay and equipment are—wholly or mainly—provided at the expense of the nation.

time to time by purchase: and we have now to consider the different sources of the funds for defraying such purchases and also paying the wages and salaries of the paid servants of Government.

The chief sources are

(1) Rent or Interest paid by individuals for the use of wealth that wholly or partially belongs to the community.

(2) Loans.

(3) Payments for commodities[1] supplied by Government.

(4) Taxes (including tributes paid by foreigners).

Such minor sources as Fines and Voluntary Gifts are too insignificant—so far, at least, as the main functions of Government are concerned—to require more than a passing notice.

Under the first of the four heads above given will come, of course, all rents paid for land or buildings that are completely public property. But besides these, wherever land has only been allowed to pass into private ownership under the condition of a periodical payment being made to the government,—or of services being rendered which have afterwards been commuted for a pecuniary payment—this payment should always be regarded, *from the point of view of distribution*, as a rent reserved by the community and not as a tax on the owner of the land; since in taking it the State does not take from the landowner wealth that has ever belonged to him, or to which he has any rightful claim. But though this is the true *distributional* view of the payment, it must be borne in mind that if it be proportioned to the total value or rent of the land, it is liable to have the *productional* bad effects of a tax in the way of checking agricultural improvement. On the other hand a payment of this kind that is guarded from such effects is a most unobjectionable mode of raising funds for public expenditure.

Interest of any other wealth besides land has hardly a place among the sources of income of modern governments, though it figures importantly among the outgoings. If they lend, it is usually borrowed money; but their borrowings have been vast. In many cases such borrowing is economically quite justifiable;

---

[1] I use this term to include services no less than material products.

but the limits of prudent indebtedness have been found practically difficult to observe.

We may say generally that the conditions under which it is prudent for a nation to borrow are, to a great extent, analogous to those under which it is prudent for a private person to do so; but there are certain important differences. In the first place, a nation can borrow without incurring any but a very trifling burden, to whatever extent its obligations can be kept permanently current, as a national medium of exchange. And secondly in the case of a nation, the matter is complicated by the difference between what we may call the strictly financial and the social points of view: i.e. between the estimates of gain and loss to the national exchequer, and the estimates of gain and loss to the community considered as an aggregate of individuals. There are two chief cases in which private borrowing is recognised as legitimate: first, where the loan is employed productively, so that the additional profit obtained by the use of it supplies a fund from which the interest may be paid, and a certain portion of the principal annually repaid; and secondly where it is employed to meet an occasional necessity for enlarged consumption, which could not be defrayed without inconvenience or even suffering out of the income of a single year, so that it is good economy to spread it over several years. Each of these cases has its counterpart in public finance. Here, however, it is not always easy to decide whether a loan has been employed productively for the nation at large. For the returns on productive outlay by government may take two quite different forms; they may either appear as increased profits on some special business carried on by a governmental department, in which the loan has been employed as capital—as when (e.g.) telegraphs or railways are bought for the State with borrowed money; or they may merely be realized in the increased produce obtained by the labour and capital of the community governed—as when a Swiss canton borrows to make a road without tolls for the use of travellers, for which it is repaid by the increased earnings of its innkeepers, tradesmen, and agricultural producers. This latter kind of outlay, however, even when socially profitable, cannot be regarded as productive from a strictly financial point of view, unless the Government secures a share of the increase of national produce, sufficient to pay something more than the interest on the loan. And it may obviously be sometimes very difficult to say how far any particular increase, either in national produce or in governmental receipts, is really due to the supposed productive outlay and not to other causes of national prosperity. Borrowing for this latter kind of expenditure therefore, though often highly advantageous, requires to be very carefully watched.

Still, on the whole, the general principle for determining productive outlay is clear, however difficult its application may be in some instances; the increased receipts accruing to the community in consequence of the outlay—whether they are obtained by the community in its corporate capacity or as an aggregate of individuals—ought to be more than sufficient to repay the loan with interest by the close of the period required to exhaust the productive effects of the outlay[1]. It should be added that when such borrowing involves loss from a strictly financial point of view, we have to take into account—as against any advantages that may be expected from it to the community at large—all the disadvantages attaching to the part of the system of taxation that might be dispensed with if the debt were not contracted.

I pass to consider the second case of legitimate borrowing; where the loan is required to meet an occasional need of extra expenditure, not positively productive. In this case the rule to be adopted appears *primâ facie* very simple; it is plain that the number of years, over which the sacrifice imposed by the emergency may prudently be extended, ought to be limited by the condition of paying off the loan before a similar emergency may be expected to occur again. Practically, no doubt, the exact application of this principle in national finance is a matter of extreme difficulty; since the chief emergencies which necessitate such loans are foreign wars (or menaces of wars) and there are no known sociological laws by which we could forecast the magnitude and frequency of a nation's future wars, in the present stage of civilization. Still, if we simply infer the

---

[1] In some cases fixed capital may be actually permanent; but in consideration of the frequent changes in industry it can never be prudent to reckon it as such.

probability of future wars from past experience, it must be admitted that the above-mentioned principle has been flagrantly transgressed by most of the leading nations of modern Europe. But the alarm which such transgression might reasonably arouse may be to some extent diminished by the consideration that we may equally infer from past experience a probable reduction in the burden of any national debt already contracted;—both an absolute reduction, from the decline of the rate of interest, and a relative reduction from the increase of the aggregate wealth of the borrowing nation. At the same time, there is so much uncertainty in all inferences of this kind that I can hardly consider a community to be justified in deliberately disregarding the rule of repayment above laid down; except, perhaps, when the taxation that would be required in order to conform to this rule would entail very serious economic or political inconveniences[1].

We have already seen that from a social point of view borrowing may be profitable, by increasing the aggregate produce of the community, even though it does not bring in an adequate return to Government, either in the form of profits on a special business in which the loan is employed, or more indirectly by an increase in the yield of certain taxes. In such a case, however, it is most probable that the increase in the total income of the community will not be equally distributed among the incomes of individual members; hence, unless the interest and repayment of the loan can be provided by imposing a rate on the persons who gain by its employment, fairly proportioned to their respective gains, it has a tendency to cause a new inequality in the distribution of wealth which

[1] I have not space to discuss adequately different modes of national borrowing: but I may briefly note the wastefulness of borrowing in such a way that the amount received is less than the debt incurred; since this method renders the borrowing nation unable to take advantage of any subsequent fall in the rate of interest, except at a serious loss. It may be said that it gives a corresponding security to the lenders, so that what the nation loses in one way will be compensated by its obtaining the loan on otherwise more favourable terms: but the security to the lenders is an indefinite and (if I may be allowed the phrase) insecure one, and therefore likely to be undervalued. If a security of this kind is to be given at all, it is more economical for the nation to guarantee its creditors against repayment for a certain period,—or for a period varying within definite limits, the variations being determined by lot.

ought to be considered in adjusting the general burden of taxation.

There is another less obvious disturbance of preexisting distribution which borrowing, whether for profitable outlay or to ward off calamities, tends to bring; viz. by raising the rate of interest, and thereby increasing the share of the aggregate produce that falls to capital. Where the outlay is of the profitable kind it is not necessary that this increase should be accompanied by a diminution in the reward of labour; as it is possible that it may be entirely supplied from the increase in the aggregate produce. But in the case of loans for wars or similar purposes, the gain to capitalists from the rise of interest inevitably involves a corresponding loss to labour, supposing that the capital is supplied by the members of the borrowing community, and that it would in any case have been saved and invested in some branch of home industry. These suppositions, however, can rarely altogether correspond to the facts; and so far as the capital borrowed is obtained from abroad, or would otherwise have been sent abroad for investment, it is quite possible that the immediate effect of the borrowing may be pecuniarily advantageous both to capitalists and labourers; both interest and wages within the community being temporarily increased by the loan. Thus the first years of a war supported by borrowing may be generally felt as years of prosperity. The day of reckoning must of course come for this expenditure; and the account must ultimately be paid in part from the share of labour,—unless the interest on the war-loan is supplied by taxes falling entirely on capitalists.

§ 4. In considering the different occasions for governmental borrowing, we have incidentally noticed that, while the major part of the ordinary income of governments is derived from taxes, a certain portion is actually in most civilized countries obtained from payments for the products of governmental industry, purchased freely by the individuals who need them, just as the commodities provided by private industry are purchased. It will be convenient to distinguish these payments as "earnings" of Government. Such "earnings" may be classed under two heads, for the purposes of the present discussion. In some cases they are obtained by selling products or services at their market-value, determined by the competition of private industries, as (e.g.) where a government possesses domain-lands and sells the agricultural products obtained by cultivating them, or similarly sells wood out of its forests, &c.[1] In other cases governments have established for themselves a monopoly in certain branches of industry, either to secure the full economic gain obtainable by organizing the industry under a single management, or for the better prevention of fraud, or sometimes with a view to taxation. In Great Britain the only business thus monopolized, besides coinage, is that of conveying letters and telegrams; in other countries various other industries are similarly conducted, as (e.g.) certain kinds of mining, the manufacture and sale of tobacco, opium, even lottery-tickets.

The financial problem is obviously very different in cases of the first and second class respectively. When the price of the commodity supplied by the government is determined by open competition with private industries, the only question is whether the government ought to carry on the business at all; whether it would not be more economically managed if handed over to private capitalists. Under ordinary circumstances, this question may be decided by a mere calculation of the financial profit of the governmental business: but, as we have seen, there are cases where it may be desirable that Government should carry on a certain branch of industry under unremunerative conditions, for the sake of some general utility which the competitive system cannot be trusted to provide.

Where, on the other hand, the industry is protected by a monopoly, there is more difficulty in determining what shall be the amount and price of the commodities supplied. A private monopolist may be assumed to aim at the greatest net gain to himself: and a governmental monopoly ought clearly to be managed on the same principle, so far as it is considered strictly from a financial point of view, as a means of obtaining money for governmental purposes. And though this ought never

[1] We may also include under this head the case of industries undertaken by Government for the sole purpose of supplying government itself with certain products: where, therefore, there are no "earnings" in the ordinary sense of the term.

to be the sole consideration for a government—since it has to regard the interests of those of its subjects who buy the monopolised commodity, and any others who are indirectly affected by its use—still there are cases in which the financial view may reasonably be allowed to prevail; as for instance where the commodity monopolised is a dangerous luxury. Even in other cases it may be on the whole expedient to keep the price of the monopolised commodity above the point that it would otherwise reach, for the sake of the profit to the treasury. But when this is done, it is clear that the purchasers of the commodity are substantially taxed for the benefit of their fellow citizens: in fact the establishment of a monopoly is a recognised mode of raising a tax on an article of consumption[1]. On the other hand if the price be reduced below a certain point, a special bounty is conferred on the purchasers at the expense of the rest of the community. It is not, however, quite clear at what point Government ought to fix the price, if it would avoid burdening one part of the community for the benefit of the other.

(1) It is thought by some that the desired impartiality will be realised, if Government sells the commodity at the lowest price which allows interest on the capital employed at the rate at which Government could borrow it, after paying all the current expenses of production, including the remuneration of all the officials employed and allowance for depreciation of capital. For—it is said—if the national exchequer gains by the business, the extra price that provides the gain is substantially a tax on those who purchase the commodity for the benefit of the rest of the community: while if it loses, the community is taxed for the benefit of these particular purchasers. There ought therefore to be neither gain nor loss.

But (2) it appears to me more strictly true that Government avoids interfering with distribution, if it sells the commodity at the price at which it would be sold if provided by private industry. This price, however, may possibly be higher than that at which Government could supply it without gain or loss; since

---

[1] This mode of taxation has obvious drawbacks, except where the production of the article is specially adapted for governmental management: but it has important advantages in some cases, especially in diminishing the cost and trouble of preventing evasions of the tax.

the article may be one which either would be less economically supplied under the conditions of free competition, on one or other of the grounds explained in chap. ii. of this book, or would be practically monopolised. In this case I should urge that the advantage which the community gains through the business being undertaken by Government is one to which the particular purchasers of the article have no claim; and that therefore if the price of the article is reduced, in the interest of production, the reduction ought to be regarded as a special benefit to them, for which allowance would have to be made in a perfectly fair adjustment of the whole system of taxation. I admit, however, that the criterion which I regard as the true one cannot easily be made exact; since under ordinary circumstances we can only conjecture roughly the price at which any commodity would be supplied by private industry.

But further: I have hitherto spoken, for simplicity, as if there were only one product to be considered: but in important cases the practical problem is to fix a scale of prices for a number of different commodities, supplied under different economic conditions as regards both cost and demand. Thus (e.g.) a railway provides conveyance suitable for different classes of persons, and for different kinds of things varying in the proportion of weight to bulk, and in the degree of care required for safe conveyance: and it conveys persons and things through a great variety of distances. On what principle, then, are the prices of these different commodities to be determined in this and similar cases? This question is often answered by saying that price should be proportioned to cost: but the simplicity of this answer ignores the normal influence of demand on price, the varying intensity of the respective demands for the different commodities, and the great difference between (*a*) the total expense of supplying the aggregate of commodities and (*b*) the sum of the additional expenses entailed by each element of the aggregate, when considered separately as an optional addition to the rest. This last consideration is conspicuously exemplified in the case of a railway: since the greater part of the annual expense of a railway—including interest on the initial outlay—does not vary materially with the amount of traffic; and even the average additional cost of each service of conveyance does not bear a fixed ratio to the amount of utility furnished, but generally a ratio that decreases as the whole amount of utility furnished increases. Now it is the interest of the community as a whole that the total amount of utility produced by the railway should be increased, so long (1) as each extra service more than pays its own extra cost and (2) the total cost is met by the aggregate of payments received; provided that this total cost is distributed among the different payments received in such a manner as to keep the aggregate demand for the commodities furnished as great as possible. If the demands for all species of such commodities were equally extensible, it would be economically advantageous—as well as obviously fair from the point of view of individual purchasers—that each payment should bear a share of the total expenses corresponding to the extra cost of the commodity paid for. But as in fact these demands are liable to be very unequal in extensibility, it may be necessary for the most economic management of the business that the unvarying element of the total expenses should be distributed unequally among the different payments: the greater share being borne by those species of commodities for which the demand is less reducible by a rise in price and the larger share by those for which the demand is more reducible. Accordingly I hold that in the governmental management of such branches of production inequalities in the charges for different commodities, based on differences of demand and not of cost, are quite legitimate; though they certainly involve inequalities in the treatment of different sets of consumers, which ought to be somehow compensated in an ideally exact adjustment of the pecuniary burdens imposed by government. But it should be observed that similar inequalities are in other ways inseparable from the most economic management of governmental monopolies:— e.g. the simplicity of our penny post is doubtless economical on the whole, but it certainly makes the internal correspondence of London pay for the correspondence between remote parts of the kingdom.

On similar grounds, the general principle of 'differential rates' must, I conceive, be admitted as legitimate, in the regulation by Government of railways under joint-stock management; so far as it can be shewn that a closer correspondence of price with cost would really render the railway less useful on the whole. The aim of government should be to prevent the supply of commodities that it regulates from being scanty and dear, but not necessarily to prevent the commodities from being unequally priced.

I do not mean to say that a private company should be left altogether unchecked in the arrangement of such differential rates, on the ground that its private interests in this matter will always coincide with the interest of the public. Such a universal coincidence cannot be affirmed: indeed a possible divergence between the two becomes manifest when we consider that one main cause, in the case of a railway, of the differences of demand above-mentioned is the partial competition of other railways and steamships—a competition which is often effective for certain long distances while leaving a multitude of shorter distances unaffected. It might be for the private interest of a railway company to make temporary reductions of price, which could not be permanently maintained without economic loss, in order to win in such a competitive struggle: but it can rarely be the interest of the community that government should do this or allow it to be done.

Sometimes, indeed, it may be on special grounds the real interest of the community, considered as an aggregate of individuals, that a commodity furnished by government should be supplied at a price *financially* unremunerative: even, it may be, at a price that will not yield ordinary interest on the capital employed. Indeed if this capital were not borrowed, and if we had not to consider the need of raising supplies for other branches of governmental expenditure, there would seem to be no reason why the condition of paying interest should be regarded at all, any more than it would be regarded in a community socialistically organized; it would be economically advantageous to extend the supply of the commodity by cheapening its price so long as it more than repaid the total cost of the labour spent in furnishing it—including the labour required for keeping in repair and duly improving the instruments used in the business. But since actually any portion of national income sacrificed in this way,—by a reduction of price below what would have to be paid apart from governmental interference—must be made up by some other tax, it will only be desirable to make such a reduction where it is important for the community generally that the commodity in question should be widely used :—as (e.g.) in the case of education.

§ 5. The discussion in the preceding section has illustrated a special difficulty of drawing the line between "earnings of "Government" and "taxes." We have now to observe that the general distinction between these two terms is not quite so clear as it appears at first sight. No one, I suppose, would apply the term "taxes" to payments for goods or services furnished by Government which the payer is left perfectly free to take or to leave—except so far as the price of the service is materially raised by the governmental monopoly—; even where, if the commodities are purchased at all, they must be purchased from the government, as in the case of payments for postal services. But, if so, it seems doubtful whether a payment of this kind acquires the character of a tax merely because it is made compulsory; as, for instance, where landowners are compelled to take a share in the cost of works of drainage or irrigation carried on by Government. On the other hand some economists hold that all taxes—i.e. all compulsory contributions of individuals to their government—ought to be regarded as payments for services received; and that the burden of taxation ought to be distributed on the principle which is ordinarily accepted in the case of such payments: viz. that every individual should pay in proportion to the cost or utility[1] of the services rendered to him. And I quite admit that this is the most consistent way of treating the problem of taxation from an individualistic point of view, so far as the services rendered by Government admit of being thus individualised. But I find it to a great extent impossible to apply this principle in the case of the most important—and actually most costly—functions of government. Take (e.g.) the case of defence against foreign foes;—modern wars are undertaken not mainly for protection of the life and property of individuals, but for the maintenance of national existence, extension of empire, &c.; and it is surely impossible to apportion the advan-

[1] I say "cost or utility" because the divergence between the two, and the difficulty of deciding to what extent and in what manner both are to be taken into account, are often overlooked.

tages thus purchased among the individual members of the community. Similarly, how are we to decide who profits by the sumptuous expenditure of the monarch and the royal family in a monarchical country? It would be going too far to affirm that all members of the nation are equally concerned in maintaining either its international position, or its monarchical constitution; still I cannot but regard as hopeless the attempt to apportion the cost of either among different classes on the principle of payment in proportion to services rendered. I hold, therefore, that at any rate for the taxation required to defray the expenses of the Court, and of the army and navy and diplomatic service, and the interest on national debts incurred for warlike purposes, some other principle of distribution must be sought.

The case is different with the expense of the administration of justice and the police. But though both judges and policemen are continually engaged in rendering special services to certain individuals, there is much force in the contention of Bentham and Mill[1], "that those who are under the necessity of going to "law are those who benefit least, not most, by the law and its "administration." It may be expedient, indeed, in order to check litigation, that the cost of administering justice should fall largely on individuals; as is actually the case so far as the services of solicitors and barristers are paid by the litigants. But it is at any rate desirable that as little as possible of this expense should fall on innocent individuals—innocent, that is, not only of violation of rights but even of undue litigiousness. It seems clear, therefore, that the support of the Judicature and police cannot, at least in the main, be defrayed by fees from the persons whom judges and policemen are more obviously occupied in protecting. At the same time, I do not think that the principle of apportioning the tax-payer's contribution to the services which he receives is so completely inapplicable here, as it is in the case of taxes for national defence: indeed we must, I think, have recourse to it to a certain extent when we come to deal with the question of determining the area of incidence of taxation.

The ordinary answer to the question, "who ought to pay "taxes to a government" is Adam Smith's,—"the subjects of

[1] Mill, *Pol. Econ.*, B. VI. ch. vi. § 3.

"the State" governed: but when the same question is raised in reference to a local tax, the ordinary answer is "the persons "residing or possessing property in the district;" and a comparison of the two answers shews the need of qualifying the first. It seems clearly just that aliens residing or possessing property in any country should pay something towards the expenses of its government; and if so, unless aliens are to be fined as such, it is clearly just that they should pay proportionally less to their own government; and the only satisfactory way of determining the ratio in which their contribution ought to be divided between the two governments is by regarding it as a price paid for services received. An Englishman residing in France is much less concerned than a Frenchman with French expenditure on armaments; but he has as much interest as a Frenchman has in the expenditure for maintaining internal order and promoting wellbeing in France; and he is also benefited by this latter outlay if without residing in France he merely holds property there. It seems therefore most proper that at least a rough division should be made of the taxes ordinarily paid by an English capitalist into three parts; one part to be paid by him to the English government wherever he may reside or hold property; another to the government of the country in which he resides; while the third should be proportioned to the property that he enjoys under the protection of his own, or any other, state.

The same principle, again, may be applied—and actually has been applied to a considerable extent—in determining the division between general and local taxation within any country. Where expenditure defrayed by taxes benefits the inhabitants in a certain locality almost exclusively, and other persons only so far as they resort to the place—thereby usually benefiting its trade—it is manifestly just, that the taxes should be correspondingly localised; as, for instance, in the case of expenditure on streets, and bridges so far as they are not maintained by tolls. Where on the other hand a more considerable share of the utilities produced tends to be diffused through the community, though residents in a certain locality benefit more than others, a division of the cost between local and general taxation is on similar principles equitable: thus (e.g.) it is reasonable that the pecuniary aid given by Government to elementary education should be furnished partly from national, partly from local, resources, so far as it is given on strictly individualistic principles —that is, with the view of benefiting persons other than the children educated. A similar division of cost would seem to be also equitable in the case of Poor-relief; but here considerations of justice appear to be overborne in England by the special need and difficulty of maintaining a very strict economy in poor-law administration.

To sum up: I do not think that any sharp line can be drawn between taxes, ordinarily so called, and any compulsory payments for services received from Government; and I accept generally the principle of fixing the amount of the individual's contribution to Government so as to correspond as closely as economic management allows to the cost of the services performed by Government to him, so far as such services can be properly regarded as rendered to individuals. At the same time I think that this principle can rarely be applied, except in a rough and partial way, to any payments that are ordinarily called taxes; and that even where it is most applicable, it must often be overborne by other considerations,—sometimes by the economic advantage of more uniform rates of payment, sometimes by the desirability of reducing the burden laid on the poorer class of contributors. Nor does it seem that there is necessarily any sacrifice of justice, even from an individualistic point of view, in throwing a part of the cost of services which men are compelled to purchase on persons other than the recipient; since from this point of view the only admissible reason for compelling any individual to purchase such services is that the interests of others will be damaged if he is allowed to dispense with them; hence it seems not unfair that these others should bear a part of their cost. And, finally, there is a large part of governmental expenditure—much the largest part in our European nations, loaded with war-debts, and armed to the teeth—the utility of which cannot be thus distributed among individuals. Let us proceed then to consider the method by which Government ought to raise the contributions required for such public expenditure as cannot reasonably or conveniently be provided for by charging individuals in proportion to services rendered; so far as there is no public income adequate to such needs derived from land or other wealth owned by the community or from the profits of governmental business. It will be convenient to call this the method of 'taxation' in the strictest sense.

§ 6. I ought, however, to premise that in the discussion which follows I do not propose to deal with the problem of constructing a system of taxation, as it presents itself practically to a statesman. It does not seem to me that this problem can be satisfactorily treated in a work on general economic theory; especially because, as I shall shew, the considerations that ought to influence a statesman in choosing, rejecting, or adjusting particular taxes are very various and complicated; and though we may usefully explain and classify them in a general theoretical discussion, we cannot pretend to estimate precisely their relative importance without careful ascertainment of the particular social and industrial conditions of the community to be taxed. Indeed there are very important political reasons for preferring some taxes to others, and for seeking to realize certain ends in taxation generally, which lie beyond the scope of a strictly economic discussion. Thus the third of Adam Smith's famous canons—that "the tax which each "individual is bound to pay" ought to be "clear and "plain to the contributor" in respect of time, manner and quantity—is a constitutional rather than an economic principle: its primary object being, as Adam Smith explains, to protect ordinary citizens against illegitimate exactions and extortions on the part of officials. So again, in a community where representative institutions are fully developed, there is an important constitutional ground for maintaining equal diffusion of the burden of taxation; viz. that the citizens generally may be equally interested in checking superfluous governmental expenditure which special classes of persons are continually prompted by strong selfish motives to extend. Indeed the force of this consideration has led some thinkers to hold seriously that the burden of taxation ought to be as much as possible *felt* by those who bear it, in order that they may have the strongest possible motives for minimizing it; and perhaps in a very orderly and law-abiding and lightly-taxed community this might be desirable: but in most actual societies the dangers arising from "ignorant impatience" of taxation are so much graver than any which "ignorant patience" could cause, that it should rather be a maxim of statesmanship to avoid if possible any species of tax that is particularly disliked by the persons on whom it falls, even if the dislike seems groundless and fanciful[1]. Further, it hardly seems within my province to deal with the very important political question, how far a statesman in constructing a scheme of taxation ought to take a cosmopolitan point of view, and not try to throw the burden of a tax on foreigners, except so far as it is fair compensation for services rendered to them, nor, in estimating injurious effects on production, consider detriment to foreign industries as indifferent —or even advantageous, if they rival industries of his own country. In a previous chapter (ch. V.), however, we have had occasion to examine the manner in which a 'tribute' may, under certain circumstances, be obtained from foreigners by means of import duties; and I shall refer to the subject again in a subsequent section: but for the most part I shall assume, for simplicity, that the burden of a tax is borne by the nation whose government imposes it.

In considering more particularly the mode of imposition of this burden, it will be desirable to keep in view our fundamental distinction between effects on Production, or on the aggregate wealth of the community, and effects on Distribution, or the incidence of the burden of taxation; though, as we shall see, it is impossible to separate the consideration of the one kind of effects from that of the other. Under the former head, the financier is chiefly concerned with effects which he would desire to avoid as far as possible[2]; namely the different extra costs of different taxes—the burden they impose on the taxpayers, over and above the net gain that they bring in to the treasury. In estimating these we have to distinguish the strictly financial cost—the expense of collection—and what may be called the extra-financial cost, i.e. chiefly the loss entailed on the

---

[1] It should be noted that there are also strictly economic grounds for this maxim, so far as dislike of a tax causes it to be *evaded*, legitimately or otherwise.

[2] Not, however, altogether: e.g. we may take into account the indirect gain that results from the restriction of the consumption of harmful luxuries.

consumers by changes in products or modes of production caused by taxes. The discussion of the former kind of cost, and of the best methods of minimizing it, belongs to the technical side of financial administration, and I shall not enter upon it further than to notice one or two considerations, so fundamentally important in constructing a system of taxation that they can hardly be omitted: what I shall chiefly consider, under the head of "effects on production" are the changes in the extra-governmental organization of industry which the financial interference of government entails.

It is, however, with the problem of distribution that we are primarily concerned, when treating of taxation in the most general way. Effects on production are properly regarded in relation to particular taxes taken by themselves; since a tax that, from the point of view of production, is bad when contemplated by itself, remains no less bad when contemplated as part of a complex system of taxation; it may be eligible as the least bad among possible alternatives, but its badness cannot be neutralized by combining it with other taxes. But the case is otherwise with effects on distribution; for when a tax is defective on account of the unequal distribution of its burden, the defect can be at least roughly compensated by the imposition of some other tax with an opposite kind of inequality— and, as we shall see, such rough compensation is all that the financier can practically aim at. Hence, in considering taxation in the aggregate, the question of distribution is the primary one: and, conversely, in considering the right distribution of the burden of taxation, we are concerned primarily with taxation in the aggregate, and only secondarily with particular taxes.

§ 7. On what principles then are we to distribute the burden of taxation in the narrower sense? that is, the burden that remains to be allotted, when the principle of payment in proportion to services received has been applied as far as is reasonable? The first point to settle is whether we should make taxation a means of redressing the inequalities of income that would exist apart from governmental interference. There is a weighty economic objection to this on account of the danger of diminishing the inducements to accumulation of capital, or driving it abroad[1],—a danger much greater here than in the case of the partially distributional interferences noticed at the close of the preceding chapter, because if the principle of redressing inequalities is applied at all, any limit to its application seems quite arbitrary; if the burden of the rich is to be twice as great as that of the poor, there seems no clear reason why it should not be three times as great, and so on. I hold therefore that the general aim of a statesman in distributing taxation should be to impose, as nearly as possible, equal sacrifices upon all. But this rule requires some very important qualifications. In the first place, I think it must be interpreted so as not to conflict with the generally accepted principle that the community ought to protect its members from starvation: from which it seems to follow that, if possible, no one's income should be reduced by taxation below what is required to furnish him with the bare necessaries of life. For if Government is to risk a serious instalment of the evils of communism in order to secure all members of the community from starvation, it hardly ought to aggravate its inroad on the motives that normally prompt the poor to energetic industry, by *taking* from those who remain independent a part of what it would actually have to *give* them if they sought its aid. And if on this ground we exempt altogether from taxation incomes below a certain low limit, it would be obviously unreasonable to exact a full quota of payment from those just *above* this minimum; for this would lead to the absurd result that persons who could only earn a very little more than the minimum would lose the *whole* of such extra earnings. I conclude therefore that we ought to treat as taxable only that portion of any individual's income which is not required to provide necessaries either for himself or for those dependent on him. Even apart from any question of poor-relief, I think that taxation proportional to what, in the widest sense, may be called superfluous consumption would tend to equalize sacrifices more nearly than the rule of proportioning taxation to total income; since deprivation of the

[1] The latter of these would be the immediate practical danger, as it is not likely that such unequal taxation of the rich would be introduced in most civilized countries simultaneously.

necessaries of life is an evil so indefinitely greater than deprivation of luxuries that the two may be fairly treated as incommensurable; and we may assume generally that if poor and rich alike are deprived of a certain proportion of their resources available for non-necessary expenditure, the loss thus incurred of purchaseable satisfaction will be at least as great to the poorest class that will be taxed at all, as it will be to any other class. The question, I think, is rather whether even this principle is not oppressive to the poor; and whether in order to equalize the real burden of taxation we ought not to lay a progressively increasing tax on the luxurious expenditure of the rich. I must admit that in my opinion, such a tax would be justifiable from the point of view of distribution alone: but it is open to the practical objection that the progression if once admitted would be very difficult to limit, owing to the impossibility of establishing any definite quantitative comparison between the pecuniary sacrifices of the rich and those of the poor; and therefore there would be a serious danger that the progression would be carried so far as to check accumulation or drive capital from the country, thus causing a loss to production which would more than outweigh the gain in equalization of sacrifice[1].

If, however, we allow the rule of equality in the distribution of financial burdens to be overborne in favour of the rich by the advantage of encouraging the accumulation of capital in the country, it seems reasonable to aim at the same result more directly by a measure that will operate generally in favour of those who derive their income mainly from labour: viz. by exempting savings from taxation. A certain minimum of savings, indeed,—enough to prevent individuals from becoming a burden to others in age or sickness—should be included in the exemption of necessaries argued in the preceding paragraph. Further than this there would be no ground for carrying the exemption, if what were saved were merely hoarded, in the form of coin or durable consumer's wealth; since the portion of

---

[1] Such a scale of taxation as I—after Mill—have proposed in the text, in which the proportion of tax to income is decreased at the lower end but not (materially) increased at the upper, is conveniently called a *de*gressive as distinct from a *pro*gressive scale.

wealth that at any given time was so hoarded would at the time be merely employed in gratifying the hoarders by giving them a sense of power or security; and there would be no reason why these personal gratifications should not bear along with others the reduction required to supply the needs of government. But, actually, since what is saved takes mainly the form of capital that aids industry, the saver,—whatever his motives may be—does in fact render an important service to production; and it seems desirable that this should at least be as little as possible discouraged by taxation.

But again; if we exempt savings on this ground, it seems reasonable to extend the exemption to what is spent by a father of a family on the education of his children, so far as it tends to make them more efficient labourers: and, similarly, to encourage by a similar exemption the devotion of funds by gift or bequest to public objects of real utility, provided that adequate security is taken that they are efficiently administered; especially if the objects are of a kind to which public money might reasonably be allotted, if private liberality were wanting. It may even be fairly urged, that a considerable part of the non-necessary expenditure of the rich is actually incurred in maintaining and transmitting culture, and that this also is a function of sufficient social importance to be properly encouraged by exemption from taxation;—though there is, of course, great difficulty of distinguishing expenditure of this kind from that which ministers to mere personal enjoyment. I should propose to recognise these various claims to exemption by throwing a large share of the burden of taxation on the consumption of commodities that are neither necessary nor promotive of culture. Such taxes on commodities, however, tend to be seriously unequal; especially since there are very strong technical reasons for concentrating such taxation on a few articles largely consumed, in order to minimize the cost—financial and extra-financial—that it involves; and it is almost inevitable that the expenditure on these particular articles should form a very variable proportion of the total expenditure of different classes of the community on things that are neither necessaries nor promotive of culture. So far as the classes thus overburdened can be distinguished as those receiving incomes of certain amounts, the inequality may be—and should be—roughly compensated by an income-tax on other classes, as is done in the English budget; but there are still liable to remain great variations in the consumption of taxed commodities among persons of similar incomes—owing to variations of taste, constitution, &c.—for which it is practically impossible to make compensation. The adoption, therefore, of this method of raising taxes must be admitted to be incompatible with any exact equalisation of the burden of taxation. But in fact any such exactness is rendered practically unattainable, on the general principle above adopted, by the vagueness of the distinction between necessaries and luxuries, and the great differences in the needs of different persons and of the same person at different times; and the method of taxing commodities has the merit of avoiding the worst inequalities which taxation proportioned to income would cause, in consequence of these differences of need; since it enables those persons whose needs are greatest to diminish their share of taxation, by abstinence from customary luxuries. For this latter reason chiefly I think it desirable that the taxation of the poor should be almost entirely thrown on commodities of the kind I have defined: as is the case in England with taxation for the purposes of the central government.

Generally speaking, it is expedient to select for taxation commodities of which the consumption is not likely to be restricted to any great extent, through the desire to avoid payment of the tax, as all such restriction increases the excess of the loss to the public caused by the tax, over and above the gain to the treasury; since the persons who are driven to consume commodities which they do not like so well suffer a manifest loss of utility. But some restriction is inevitable: hence there is a strong reason for fixing taxation on commodities which are liable to be largely consumed in excess of what is salutary: since so far as such excess is prevented by the tax, the restriction of consumption is positively beneficial to the community. And though legislative interference with the sole object of limiting the consumption of dangerous commodities is emphatically condemned by advocates of natural liberty, they have not, for the most part, pushed their antagonism so far as

CHAP. VIII.] *PUBLIC FINANCE.* 571

to maintain that the selection of taxes ought not to be partly influenced by this consideration. On the other hand, the burden of such taxes—as those on alcoholic liquors and tobacco—is liable to a special inequality; since many persons shun these dangerous commodities altogether, while among those who consume them the standard of strict moderation is vague and variable, and there are many degrees of excess possible[1]. It is desirable to prevent this inequality from being very marked:—thus, if it were necessary to increase taxation in England, there would be a positive advantage, from a distributional point of view, in reimposing the duty on sugar abolished in 1874. But imperfect equalization is a drawback inseparable from the special advantage of taxation on non-necessary commodities—viz. that the needy tax-payer can avoid it: and what is most important socially and politically in distributing taxation is to avoid marked over-taxation or under-taxation of different grades of income.

§ 8. So far we have implicitly assumed that taxes on commodities can be so imposed as to fall entirely on those who consume them; and similarly that an income or property tax will be borne by the persons on whose income or property it is laid. We have now to notice a new element of imperfection and uncertainty in the equalization of taxation, due to the fact that we can only partially succeed in making the burden either of 'direct' or 'indirect' taxes fall where we desire; the burden is liable to be transferred to other persons when it is intended to remain where it is first imposed; and, on the other hand, when it is intended to be transferred the process of transference is liable to be tardy and incomplete[2]. Indeed this process is often so complicated and obscure that it is a problem of considerable intricacy and difficulty to ascertain where the burden of a

---

[1] I agree with Mr Dudley Baxter (*Taxation of the United Kingdom*, ch. xxi.), that in estimating the burden of taxes on alcoholic liquors the extra contribution levied from the drunkard should be regarded as a fine rather than a tax: but I think fairness requires the definition of excess to be an indulgent one, since there are many other branches of luxurious consumption in which the limit of strict moderation is often exceeded.

[2] The common classification of taxes as Direct and Indirect appears to me liable to mislead the student, by ignoring the complexity and difficulty of the problem of determining the incidence of taxation.

tax actually rests: and it is not even a simple matter to state accurately the general principle for determining the incidence of a tax, supposing all the facts to be known. Thus (e.g.) Mill appears to assume as a general principle (Bk. v. ch. iii. § 3) that a tax must be "considered as paid" by "those who would be benefited if it were taken off." But it is easy to shew that, in some cases, the whole benefit of remission would be reaped by persons who have not borne any part of the burden of the tax[1]: it is not the extra income that a man would gain if the tax were taken off which gives the true measure of the burden it imposes on him, but rather the extra income that he would now be enjoying if it had never been laid on. But to get even an approximate estimate of this hypothetically determined burden may require a very careful consideration of complex consequences; and the result must often be at the best but partially satisfactory. I will illustrate by taking the most important cases; observing that whenever a tax is transferred—at once or gradually, in whole or in part—the benefit of its remission tends to be correspondingly transferred.

To begin with the simplest case.

I. A special tax on a class of persons, distinguished by characteristics either irremovable or of no economic importance tends to be wholly borne by the persons who pay it. This would be the case (e.g.) with a tax on Jews or Papists; for even if some of the Jews left the country in consequence, or some of the Papists became Protestants, the exchange value of the services of the remainder would not thereby be materially increased.

II. Taxes of the above kind are opposed to modern sentiments of equity. A nearly similar inevitability, however, attaches to a general tax on incomes, simply proportioned to their amounts, so long as it is not heavy enough to induce any particular class of the persons on whom it is imposed to diminish materially the relative supply of their labour; either voluntarily,

---

[1] This, indeed, seems to be Mill's view in another passage (Bk. v. ch. ii. § 6) in which he affirms that "there is not the smallest pretence for looking on" the existing land-tax in England "as a payment exacted from the existing race of landlords:" though it must be evident that it is the existing race of landlords who would benefit by its remission.

through emigration or abstinence from matrimony, or involuntarily in consequence of the resources of their families being reduced below the minimum required to support life. But if any considerable diminution in the relative numbers of any class takes place through these causes, it will tend to raise the market value of their labour to some extent, and to that extent to transfer the burden of the tax to other members of the community; but obviously with very different degrees of rapidity, according as the effect is produced (1) by emigration, or (2) by abstinence from matrimony or inability to rear children. Similar consequences may of course follow from any taxation that falls specially on the poorer classes of labourers; hence there is an element of truth in the old doctrine that "taxes on wages "tend to fall on profits[1]," if applied to the wages of unskilled labour, supposed to be already at the minimum required to "enable the labourers, one with another, to subsist and per- "petuate their race." And some effect of this kind might no doubt be produced even by taxes proportional (as above proposed) to non-necessary expenditure: but, unless such taxes were extremely heavy, it would generally be of so indefinite and remote a kind as not to be practically worth estimating.

III. A tax annually levied on the owners of any particular kind of durable wealth, of which the supply is absolutely limited, is in effect more intransferable than it is intended to be; since it will remain onerous to the persons on whom it was originally imposed even after they have sold the article taxed. For instance if Raphael's pictures were thus taxed, the amount of the tax capitalised would tend to be subtracted from their price, so that, after a single transfer by sale, the tax would not be really onerous to the person who actually paid it. A similar effect will be produced by a *special*[2] tax on land of fixed amount, not

---

[1] Though in fact the burden thus transferred would be divided among (1) the employers of the labour grown dearer, (2) the consumers of its ultimate products, (3) labourers in other grades, and (4) owners of capital in proportions which will vary very much according to circumstances; and which, I may add, would be very difficult to ascertain with even approximate accuracy in any concrete case, owing to the intermingled effects of other causes.

[2] The effect of a tax on land which is merely one form of a more general tax on property or income will be quite different, since in this latter case the selling

increasing with its value or rent: so far as land has changed hands by sale since its imposition, the burden of the tax will be no longer borne by the actual landowner; and therefore even if the tax was originally unjust, the actual landowner will in such case have no claim to its remission. Hence where such a tax is of old date, so that a considerable amount of land has changed hands by sale,—and all by inheritance[1],—since its original imposition, it seems best not to regard it as really a tax at all, but as a share of the rent of land reserved to the community; just as if it had been a payment imposed when the land was allowed to pass into private ownership.

IV. When, however, a special tax is imposed on land, varying in proportion to its value, the case is different, and the incidence of the tax more complicated; and it may be of some practical interest to examine it in detail, on account of the special burdens laid on land and houses—which may be regarded as a particular form of utility added to land—in our system of local taxation. At any given time there is a certain amount of outlay of various kinds for the purpose of increasing the utility of land, which would, apart from the tax, be remunerative; but a portion of which will be unprofitable, if the tax be imposed, unless the price of the produce of land rises. Hence the imposition of the tax will tend to prevent this portion of the outlay from being made, and so to restrict the supply of the utilities that it would have produced, and consequently—sooner or later—to raise their price to an extent varying according to the conditions of supply and demand for the produce in question. If (e.g.) the producers are closely pressed by foreign competition, the rise may be very slight;— thus (e.g.) an increase in local rates in England, sufficient to be a serious discouragement to the improvement of agricultural land, would still have comparatively little effect in raising the price of corn. But to whatever extent the price rises from this cause[2], the burden of the tax will ultimately rest on the price of the land will not tend to be lowered, as its purchaser will have to pay no more taxes in consequence.

[1] See § 11 for a discussion of the peculiar economic characteristics of taxes on inheritance.

[2] Here again, it will generally be very difficult to ascertain in a concrete case, how far any rise in price has actually been due to this cause.

consumer or purchaser of the utilities furnished by the land; i.e. to the occupier (who may, of course, be actually the owner) of land used for enjoyment (parks, gardens, &c.), or to the purchaser of the produce of agricultural land,—who, however, if he be a purchaser not for consumption but for sale or production, will, under ordinary conditions, hand on the whole or part of the burden still further, till it reaches what we may call the ultimate consumer.

The initial operation, however, of such a tax may be somewhat further complicated by its effects on the business of producing the increased utility of the land. To illustrate this complication, we may take the specially important case of land used for building. Suppose that a new tax proportional to value—not balanced by corresponding taxes on other sources of income—is laid on owners of land generally, including owners of land with buildings on it (the value of the buildings also being reckoned); and suppose for simplicity that the tax is annual and rent is competitively determined afresh from year to year. Then, as the imposition of the tax cannot at once affect the supply of houses or the demand for them, the whole tax will at first tend to be paid by the owner; so that the building of houses will become less remunerative, and will consequently be reduced in extent. The resulting limitation of supply—as houses cannot profitably be imported—will tend to raise their price and rent sufficiently to make building remunerative; that is, if the cost of building were unaltered the rent would tend to be increased by the amount of the proportion of the tax that falls on the rent of the building as distinct from the ground. But in fact, if the tax be a heavy one, the rise will tend to be temporarily somewhat less than this; since the cost of building will undergo some reduction in consequence of the check given to the building industry by the tax, which will tend to diminish for a time the returns to the labour and capital employed in this industry. Ultimately, however, the whole portion of the tax that is paid for the value of the house itself, will tend to fall—in the case of private dwelling houses[1]—on the consumer or occupier. The portion, how-

[1] So far as the tax falls on buildings used as producers' capital, it will have a certain tendency to be transferred through industrial competition: but the

ever, that falls on the ground-rent will continue to be borne by the owner of the ground (supposing, as above explained, that he has not sold it) unless the tax has caused a rise in agricultural produce and the land is so situated that it could be as remuneratively employed for agricultural purposes as for building. Nay further, if the tax be not uniform but higher in some districts than in others, the whole excess—and not merely the proportion of the excess that falls on the ground-rent,—will tend to remain on the owner; at least so long as the fall does not render the land more profitable for other purposes than it is for building.

So far I have supposed the tax to be formally paid by the owner. If, however, it be laid in the first instance on the occupier, the effect will be substantially the same as soon as the rent comes to be determined afresh, after the imposition of the tax.

§ 9. V. In short, a tax on land and buildings proportional to their value has partly the effect of a tax on the product of certain industries: partly, again, so far as the land or buildings taxed are 'producers' wealth,' it has the effect of a tax on the instruments of certain industries. To whatever extent it operates in either way, it comes within the large class of what we may call Taxes on Production; which occupies the most important place in modern systems of taxation. This class includes, besides (1) the important taxes before referred to on the manufacture and sale of material products, also (2) taxes on conveyance, (3) payments (fees, licenses, &c.), for leave to practise certain trades and professions, and (4) a great part of the taxes (by means of stamps) on the transfer of property—so far as these, falling with more weight on traders, may be regarded as largely taxes on trade. Such taxes on special lucrative callings are generally intended to fall, not on the persons who exercise them, but on the ultimate consumers of the commodities that the former furnish, or assist in furnishing; and it is obvious that industrial competition will tend to cause this transfer of the burden, so far as it tends to equalize remu-

incidence of the tax supposed will be so general that the extent and manner of its possible transfer is very difficult to determine—especially since producers who use land will be more heavily taxed.

nerations. Still the transfer ought not to be assumed, in estimating the incidence of taxes, without important qualifications. We may indeed take it as broadly true, in most cases, that the burden of a *long-established* tax on production does not rest on the class of persons who actually pay it;—though even here it must be borne in mind that, owing to the limited knowledge that producers have of each other's remunerations, industrial competition, however open and active, cannot tend to bring about any exact equalization of earnings; it can but operate roughly to prevent large and palpable differences. But it is only under special circumstances that a *new* tax on production can be completely and at once transferred to the consumer. For, firstly, whenever the rise in price required to effect the transfer involves a material reduction in the sale of the commodity taxed, some initial loss to producers must result; which will be greater, *ceteris paribus*, in proportion to the extent of the reduction. We have thus an additional reason for selecting, in the imposition of fresh taxes, commodities for which substitutes cannot easily be found and with which consumers will not willingly dispense, in order that the incidental loss to producers may be as small as possible. Again, the extent of loss to producers caused by a reduction in the demand for their commodities varies very much according to the degree of mobility of their capital:—thus it is usually less for traders than for manufacturers and agriculturists; which is a reason, from a strictly national point of view, for taxing imports, *ceteris paribus*, rather than the products of native industry.

But again: the tendency of industrial competition to transfer the burden of taxation from producers to consumers will not operate where the former are enjoying extra profits to an amount exceeding that of the tax; whether through monopoly, natural or artificial, or through the possession of scarce natural resources or social opportunities. Thus a moderate tax on the produce of famous vineyards would have no tendency to be transferred to the consumer; the owners of the vineyards would still produce as much as they can and get the market-price for it, as they do now, so that the whole of the tax would be substantially paid out of their incomes. Where, however, a monopoly has been constituted by means of a grant of special rights and privileges granted by government, an exceptional payment by its owners should not be regarded as, in substance, *strictly* a tax; it is rather a share in the extra profits of the monopoly reserved to the community.

It is to be noted further, that in the case of temporary and partial monopolies, protected only by the difficulties of profitable competition, it must often be very uncertain where the burden of a tax on the monopolised production really rests, after a certain interval from its original imposition. For the tax tends to operate as an additional obstacle to competition; but the force it exercises in this direction can hardly ever be known for certain. Thus the burden of a tax imposed on the receipts of a railway company, if it were practically free from the restraint of actual or prospective competition, would fall on the shareholders: for if it were profitable for them to raise their fares after the tax had been imposed, it would have been equally profitably for them to do this independently of the tax. But so far as the tax tends to remove the fear of competition, it gives a power of raising fares which *pro tanto* compensates for its burden.

Finally we must observe that taxes on commodities when laid in certain ways may actually benefit certain classes of the producers or sellers of such commodities, by giving them advantages in the competition with other producers. Thus a tax on the materials of production or on products in an early stage of manufacture, or on articles of trade some time before they are sold, has a certain tendency to increase the advantage of large capitalists, as it causes more capital to be required for a given amount of business. Hence the consumer may lose by such a tax, through a rise in price, considerably more than is gained by the exchequer; the employer being able to obtain ample wages of management, as well as interest, for the extra capital employed. Licenses again, so far as the charge for them is fixed independently of the amount of business, are similarly advantageous to large employers.

§ 10. Further, in a complete estimate of the incidence of a tax, we ought strictly to take into account not merely the burden laid on producers or consumers of the article taxed, but also the loss to the community through the non-production and non-consumption of the greater quantity and better quality of commodities which would have been produced if the tax had not been imposed. That is, we have to take into account those effects on production which we began by distinguishing from effects (merely) on distribution; so far as the former being unequally distributed, really affect distribution as well. Let us now notice briefly the chief cases of the productional effects.

Let us take first the case of taxes on the manufacture and sale of commodities. Such taxes cause an economic loss, uncompensated by any gain to the treasury, so far as the processes of production are impaired or hampered, or improvements in them precluded, by the necessity of conforming to rules imposed to guard against evasion or otherwise for the convenience of the tax-gatherer. For instance, the production of oil in Asia Minor is said to be seriously deteriorated by the fact that the olives after harvest have to be kept untouched until the tax-collector has found time to come and ascertain their amount. A further uncompensated loss results so far as such taxes admit of being evaded by the adoption of a less economical mode of producing the commodity; or by the production of substitutes for the taxed product, satisfying the same wants by inferior means. Some effect of this latter kind is almost unavoidable so far as the demand for the taxed product is decreased by its rise in price.

So far, again, as taxation of this kind reduces the normal use of materials or instruments of production, or articles whose consumption conduces to the efficiency of productive labourers, for which only imperfect substitutes can be found elsewhere, a loss results to production which may go on increasing at compound interest.

Similarly, taxes on conveyance, so far as they hinder the transfer of commodities, tend to prevent such improvements in production as result from the specialization of the labour of different places; and also, so far as they hinder the transfer of labour, they tend to prevent its most efficient employment. So again, the stamp duties on bills of exchange, receipts, drafts, &c., have a tendency to hamper the development of trade; though this effect seems inconsiderable, so long as such duties are trifling in proportion to the amount of the transactions on which they are imposed.

We have further to notice that direct taxes on expenditure, such as the taxes on carriages, horses, plate, so far as they reduce the consumption of these commodities, affect their production ultimately—though not altogether at the first imposition—to the same extent as corresponding taxes on the production of these articles[1].

On the other hand, there are certain taxes on commodities that bring in more to the national treasury than the members of the nation lose as individuals. Thus we have seen that the imposition of import duties is, under certain special conditions, an effective method of increasing a nation's income at the expense of foreigners—though on various grounds a dangerous method: and the same is true of export duties, whenever a country has a monopoly of any product keenly demanded. Again a tax imposed on things that are partly esteemed as signs of wealth, and therefore of social status, *pro tanto* increases their utility in proportion as it increases their exchange value; so that the consumers do not lose what the government gains. And, obviously taxes that reduce the consumption of commodities liable to be abused, such as alcoholic stimulants, tend to benefit consumers thus prevented from injuring themselves, and indirectly to increase production by diminishing the loss of efficiency caused by such production.

An income-tax is free from the—generally disadvantageous —effects on production of the taxes that we have been considering[2]. But it is to be observed that even an income-tax—as well as any other tax that diminishes the available resources of individuals—is liable to affect production generally, so far as it reduces the amount saved and converted into capital. And this effect cannot be altogether prevented—though it certainly tends to be reduced—by proportioning taxation (as before pro-

[1] Hence a certain share of the burden of these taxes, at least when newly imposed, will under most circumstances be borne by persons engaged in the production of the commodities taxed: no less than in the case of the 'indirect' taxes, discussed in the preceding section.

[2] The peculiar drawbacks of an income-tax, arising from the difficulty of obtaining an accurate estimate of the incomes of individuals, belong to a more technical discussion of the problem of taxation than I have here attempted.

posed) to superfluous consumption rather than to income; since the tax-payer may still prefer to let the reduction fall on his saving rather than his consumption. On the other hand, when the proceeds of a tax taken mainly from what would have been luxuriously consumed by individuals are productively employed by Government, it may be regarded as a mode of compulsory saving, by which the capital of the community—though not of individuals—may be materially increased.

It may be noticed further that, so far as saving is an affair of habit, a tax may actually cause a diminution in capital merely by the nature and circumstances of its incidence. Thus it has been plausibly maintained that the taxes on inheritance of property have a special tendency to produce this effect; because the person inheriting ordinarily considers the additional wealth thus acquired as an increase of capital, and does not spend any portion of it, but only increases his expenditure by the annual interest on it.

§ 11. This leads us to the more general question of the incidence of taxes on the acquisition of property by bequest or intestate inheritance; which I have reserved for separate consideration, because of the important peculiarities that they present, when we are considering the theoretical construction of a system of taxation. According to the criterion above laid down, it is plain that the pecuniary loss caused by any such tax falls on the person who inherits, since he would have been richer by the exact amount of the tax, if that had not been imposed; except so far as it is probable that the person from whom he inherits, being aware of the tax, may have left him a larger property in consequence—a probability which, I imagine, is not practically important in the case of most of the property obtained by inheritance.

Nevertheless, the considerations that ordinarily would lead us to limit carefully the burden of taxation falling on any individual or class do not, I conceive, apply in the case of persons taxed as inheritors. For Government, by taking a portion of what would otherwise have come to a man by inheritance, in no way diminishes the motives that prompt him to produce and accumulate wealth—if anything, it tends to increase these motives; nor does it necessarily cause even any disappointment of expectations, except when the tax is first imposed. On the other hand we ought undoubtedly to take into account the diminution in inducements to industry and care which a heavy tax on inheritances may cause, in the view of persons who look forward to leaving them. This bad effect, however, of such taxes is not likely to be at all equal in proportion to the similar effect that would be produced by extra taxes on income; in fact the limits of taxation on inheritances will be practically determined for the financier rather by the danger of evasion through *donationes inter vivos*, than by the danger of checking industry and thrift: and either danger will generally be much less where there are no children or other direct descendants to inherit. Hence it seems expedient, in the case of these taxes, to give up the ordinary aim at equality of incidence so far as to place a much heavier tax on wealth inherited by persons not in the direct line of descent from the previous owners. But if this course be adopted, it becomes theoretically almost impossible to include these taxes in an adjustment of general taxation on the principles of distribution before proposed: and it seems to me not only convenient but equitable to treat these taxes as a special burden on the class of persons owning capital in considerable amounts— inheritances below a certain value being exempted[1]. For, as was before said, the proportionment of taxation to non-necessary expenditure seems certainly to make the burden of *sacrifice* imposed on the poor heavier than that of the rich, though the excess does not admit of being definitely estimated; and it seems equitable to balance this excess roughly by the special burden that taxes on inheritance will lay on the rich.

[1] This exemption is expedient on other grounds besides that which I proceed to urge: viz. in order to encourage thrift among the poor, and on account of the greater proportional cost of collecting the tax on small inheritances.

CHAPTER IX.

POLITICAL ECONOMY AND PRIVATE MORALITY.

§ 1. We had occasion to notice in the last chapter but one, that in considering some important departments of governmental interference it is practically necessary to take account of the unconstrained action of private persons for public objects. We cannot determine what Government ought to do without considering what private persons may be expected to do; and what they may be expected to do will, to some extent at least, depend on what it is thought to be their duty to do. And, more generally, it was before observed that in the performance even of the ordinary industrial functions with which economic science is primarily concerned men are not merely influenced by the motive of self-interest, as economists have sometimes assumed, but also extensively by moral considerations. Hence it would seem that an Art of Political Economy is incomplete without some consideration of the principles that ought to govern private conduct in economic matters. But for a complete treatment of this subject, it would seem needful to begin by establishing systematically certain principles of morality, and then considering the relation of these to the principles of Political Economy as expounded in the present treatise;—a procedure which would inevitably introduce the fundamental and unsettled controversies of ethics to an extent that would be hardly suitable in the concluding chapter of a work on Political Economy. I therefore propose in this concluding chapter to confine myself to a brief reflective survey of the manner in which the morality of common sense has actually been modified by economic considerations, only trying here and there to introduce somewhat more clearness and precision than appears to be found in ordinary thought.

It is generally recognised that the current economic doctrines, and the prevalent habits of thought connected with them, have had an important effect in modifying that part of current morality which is concerned with the getting and disposing of wealth—otherwise than by merely enlightening and rationalizing the pursuit of private pecuniary interest; which, indeed, English Political Economy has for the most part rather assumed to be enlightened than sought to improve by instruction. The department of duty in which this influence has been chiefly noticed is that of liberality or charity. By many persons "hardhearted Political Economy" has been vaguely believed to dry up the sources of almsgiving; and it is undoubtedly true that almsgiving under certain conditions is shewn to be opposed to the true interests of the community by economic arguments fundamentally similar to a portion of those on which the inexpediency of legally enforced communism is usually rested. But we have also had occasion to observe that economic considerations have had an important share in defining the current conceptions of the more stringent duties of Justice and Equity: and it will be in accordance with the received order of ethical discussion to begin by considering these more comprehensively than we have yet done.

To begin with an uncontroversial definition of Justice—we may perhaps say that "just" claims to wealth or services are claims precise in their nature, for the non-fulfilment of which a man is liable to strong censure, if not to legal interference; indeed we should agree that such claims ought to be capable of legal enforcement, if the benefits of this were not in some cases outweighed by the incidental difficulties and drawbacks of judicial investigation and governmental coercion—as is (e.g.) largely the case with the mutual claims of members of a family. So far as we distinguish from strictly just claims those that we should rather call "fair" or "equitable," the latter would seem to be less definite but yet claims for the fulfilment of which gratitude is not to be expected, while their non-fulfilment is blamed.

Both kinds of claims without distinction may be conveniently classified according to their sources as follows: besides (1) claims determined by law independently of contract, with which we need not here concern ourselves, the most important class is (2) that of claims arising out of contract, express or tacit—the notion of "tacit contract" being extended to cover all normal expectations which a man knows (or ought to know) will be produced by his conduct in the minds of others. Such expectations are of course largely determined by custom: while in (3) a certain class of cases custom practically restricts freedom of contract—as in the case of fees to a physician. Further, there are (4) claims arising out of previous services rendered under circumstances under which contract would have been impossible or inexpedient; such as the claims of parents on children: and (5) claims to reparation for harm inflicted; along with which we may class claims to the prevention of harm, where A has done an act which *would* injure B if no provision were made against its harmful consequences. Under this last head would come the claims of children on parents for sustenance and nurture during infancy.

The influence of Political Economy is, I conceive, chiefly noticeable as regards the second and third of these classes. In the first place the 'orthodox' ideal of free exchange is necessarily antagonistic to the sway of custom as such—except so far as a customary determination of the price of services, modifiable from time to time by changes in supply and demand, is economically advantageous by saving time and trouble. But, as I have already observed, in a modern industrial community custom can hardly be regarded as an effective economic force, except so far as it blends with tacit combination—or, I should perhaps say, tends to turn into combination when resisted. If A pays B for certain services a customary price which he believes to be above the competition price, it is generally under the condition of both being aware that the majority of B's fellow-labourers would if necessary combine with him in refusing to accept a lower price. How far Political Economy, considered as a doctrine of what ought to be, approves of combinations to raise prices, when prompted by self-interest, I will presently consider: meanwhile there seems no doubt that the influence of economic discussion has tended to invalidate all quasi-moral obligations founded on customs pure and simple, substituting for customary terms of exchange conditions determined by definite agreements freely entered into.

The duty of observing such engagements was so clearly recognised in pre-economic morality that it can hardly be said to have been made any clearer through the teachings of economists, though no doubt these have dwelt with strong emphasis on the fundamental importance of this department of morality in a modern industrial community. It is rather in the determination of certain doubtful points that arise when we try to define exactly the conditions under which an agreement is to be regarded as really embodying the free choice of both contracting parties, that the influence of political economy appears to be traceable. It is admitted that, generally speaking, any 'really free' exchange of commodities which the exchangers have a right to dispose of is legitimate and should be held valid, and that 'real freedom' excludes (1) fraud and (2) undue influence: but how are we to define these latter terms? Is A justified in taking any advantage that the law allows him (1) of the ignorance and (2) of the distress of B—supposing that A is not himself the cause either of the ignorance or of the distress? If not, to what extent is he justified in taking such advantage? In the answers that thoughtful persons would give to these questions we may, I think, trace the influence of economic considerations, limiting the play of the natural or moral sentiments of sincerity and sympathy.

To begin with the case of ignorance: we should not blame A for having, in a negotiation with a stranger[1] B, taken advantage of B's ignorance of facts known to himself, provided that A's superior knowledge had been obtained by a legitimate use of diligence and foresight, which B might have used with equal success. We should praise A for magnanimity if he forbore such advantage: but we should not blame him for taking it, even if the bargain that B was thus led to make were positively injurious to the latter, supposing that the injury would otherwise have fallen on A, so that there is only a transfer and not an increase of damage. For instance, we should not blame

---

[1] I say "a stranger," because even a slight degree of friendship between the parties would render such a bargain a betrayal of implied confidence.

a man for selling in open market the shares of a bank that he believed was going to break, if his belief was founded, not on information privately obtained from one of the partners, but on his own observations of the bank's public acts or on the judgment of other experienced outsiders. Again if a man has discovered by a legitimate use of geological knowledge and skill, that there is probably a valuable mine on a piece of land owned by a stranger, reasonable persons would not blame him for keeping the discovery secret until he had bought the land at its market value. And what prevents us from censuring in this and similar cases is, I conceive, a more or less conscious apprehension of the indefinite loss to the wealth of the community that is likely to result from any effective social restrictions on the free pursuit and exercise of knowledge of this kind. Such use of special and concealed knowledge is only censured by thoughtful men, either (1) when it is for some particular reason against the public interest—as (e.g.) if members of a cabinet were to turn their foresight of political events to account on the Stock Exchange—; or (2) when the person using it has obtained it in some way having a taint of illegitimacy—as by betrayal of confidence, intrusion into privacy, &c.—; or (3) when the person of whom advantage is taken is thought to have some claim on the other beyond that of an ordinary stranger.

§ 2. Let us now consider the question that arises when we try to define the moral coercion or undue pressure that renders a contract unfair: viz. How far A may legitimately take advantage of the urgent need of B to raise the price of a commodity sold to the latter, supposing that he is in no way responsible for this urgent need? The question is one, I think, of considerable practical perplexity to ordinary minds; and it requires some care in distinction and analysis of cases to give even a tolerably satisfactory answer to it. In the first place, where B is under the pressure of exceptional and sudden emergency, in which A has a special opportunity of rendering assistance, while the need is so urgent that there is no room for competition to operate, it seems certain that A would be generally blamed for exacting for his service the full price which it is B's interest to pay: and this would not only be true in cases of danger to life or health, where humanity seems more obviously to dictate unbargained assistance, but even where it is a mere question of saving property. For instance we should consider it extortionate in a boatman, who happened to be the only man able to save valuable works of art from being lost in a river, to demand for his services a reward manifestly beyond their normal price: that is, beyond the price which, under ordinary circumstances, competition would determine at that time and place. Still, it is by no means clear that such extortion is "contrary to the principles "of Political Economy" as ordinarily understood. Economists assume in their scientific discussions—frequently with more or less implied approval of the conduct assumed—that every enlightened person will try to sell his commodity in the dearest market: and the dearest market is, *ceteris paribus*, wherever the need for such commodity is greatest. If therefore, the need of a single individual is specially great, why should not the price demanded from him rise proportionally? It appears to me that it is just at this point that there is a palpable divergence between the mere abstract exposition of the results of natural liberty which deductive economic science professes to give, and the general justification of natural liberty which Political Economy is traditionally held to include, and upon which its practical influence largely depends. Enlightened self-interest, under the circumstances supposed, will prompt a man to ask as much as he can get: but in the argument that shows the play of self-interests to lead to just and expedient results it is assumed that open competition will prevent any individual from raising his price materially above what is required for a due reduction of the demand. The price as thus determined competitively in an ideal market presents itself as the *fair* and—generally speaking—morally *right* price, because it is obviously an economic gain that the supply of any commodity should be transferred to the persons who value it most and *primâ facie* just that all suppliers of similar commodities should be paid the same. In exacting as much as this, the self-interest of the seller seems to be working as a necessary factor in the realization of the economic harmony of society; but any further exaction which an accidental absence of competition may render possible shows egoism anarchical and discordant, and therefore no longer under the ægis of economic morality. Such exaction could only avoid moral disapprobation if the exceptional freedom from competition, of which the seller takes advantage, were due to foresight on his part which it is for the general interest to encourage: but this case, I imagine, is rare.

The conclusion, on the whole, would seem to be that while it is generally extortionate in an individual to take advantage of the exceptional need of any other individual to drive a bargain with him on harder terms than he could obtain if competition were effectively open, it is not generally unfair for a class of persons to gain competitively by the unfavourable economic situation of any class with which they deal;—at least when this situation is not due to sudden calamity incapable of being foreseen, but to the gradual action of general causes, for the existence of which the persons who gain are not specially responsible. If such causes diminish seriously the social value of the services of any class, some change in their industrial position is undoubtedly required in the interests of the community; but the corresponding diminution of their remuneration is a natural method of bringing about this change,—a method which, though painful, is so manifestly efficacious that morality hesitates to interfere with it by censuring the persons whose self-interest prompts its application. In extreme cases, indeed, as where labour is remunerated at a rate insufficient to provide the necessaries of life without an exhausting amount of toil, strong censure is unhesitatingly passed by the common moral sentiment of the community. It seems, however, doubtful how far this censure, as it is usually applied, can be justified on reflection. For if persons who buy or sell to the poorest class are blamed as immoral for buying labour or selling house-room or other commodities at the market-price, there is a serious danger that such censure, while it will not prevent these necessary trades from being carried on, will tend to keep them in the hands of persons of low morality, and thus indirectly aggravate instead of mitigating the distress which gives rise to the censure. At any rate if we condemn "sweaters," slop-shop dealers, and other small traders who "grind the faces" of the poor by taking full advantage of competition, it should be rather for want of benevolence than for want of justice; and the condemnation should be extended to other persons of wealth and leisure who are aware of this disease of the social organism and are making no efforts to remove it. That such efforts ought to be made is undeniable: but the exact form that they will take if most wisely directed must depend upon the particular conditions of the labourers in question.

§ 3. There is another question remaining. If, on the grounds above explained, the fair price of a commodity is the price that an ideal competition would determine, it seems to follow that a monopolist who raises his prices by an artificial restriction of his commodity—not merely availing himself of the advantages of natural scarcity—is to be disapproved as deliberately sacrificing common to private interest. And I think some degree of disapproval is generally felt for this procedure; except so far as the total reward thus obtained by the monopolist is thought to be possibly not more than a normal remuneration for the total labour and outlay that he has been required to give in order to bring his commodity to market—as may easily be the case with monopolies secured by patents or copyrights. I am not sure, however, that the teaching of 'orthodox' Political Economy has actually tended to support this disapproval; because it has often produced a blind confidence in the economic harmony resulting from natural liberty, which has obscured men's perception of the opposition between the pecuniary interests of a monopolist—even when the monopoly is natural—and those of the community. This opposition, I think, has been more clearly seen in cases where the monopoly results from combination: the raising of prices by "rings" is held to be 'sharp 'practice' by many traders and by the general sense of nontraders. In recent times, indeed, a disposition has prevailed among philanthropic persons to exempt from this disapproval combinations of workmen to raise wages, even when these have been seen to involve some restriction in the supply of the commodity furnished by the combining workmen; but there are various special reasons for this exception. 1. So far as such combinations have aimed at resisting a fall in wages rather than obtaining a rise, the result sought—though no less divergent from the normal effect of competition—has not offended the moral sense of the community; partly from a general sympathy with the distress caused by loss of income, and a sense of the advantage of protecting the incomes of labourers from the fluctuations that the changes of modern industry naturally bring with them; partly too, perhaps, because the old pre-economic identification of 'customary price' and 'fair price' has not altogether lost its influence even with the disciples of economists. 2. Even when combinations of employed labourers have aimed at raising wages, the effort has usually been made when their employers have been believed to be making profits above the average; and a vague notion of implied partnership among producers lends to this attempt a certain air of resistance to unfair division of gains among partners. 3. The difficulty of preventing combinations of employers—especially tacit combinations—and the fact that large employers have frequently a partial monopoly from the very magnitude of their business confers on the counter combinations of the employed, to an indefinite extent, the character of legitimate self-defence. 4. Even independently of combination on the part of employers, their services tend to be purchased by society at high scarcity values, owing to circumstances before explained; and it seems not illegitimate that other persons dealing with them should make a systematic attempt to get some share of these larger gains, if this can be done in the mere exercise of freedom of contract[1].

We have seen in an earlier chapter that there are various other ways, not strictly involving violations of law or contract, in which individuals or combinations may promote their interests at the expense of the community. Thus they may raise or maintain the price of their services by increasing the need that others have of them—as when solicitors encourage litigation—or by resisting the introduction of more economical methods of satisfying this need—as when artisans combine against machinery; or again, within a margin allowed by the inevitable vagueness of their contract, they may reduce the quantity or quality of the services that they have engaged to render[2]; or they may make what seems, rather than what is,

---

[1] See Bk. II. c. IX. § 6, and Bk. III. c. VI. § 6.
[2] It is sometimes said that 'every workman should always do his best work:' but the principle seems ambiguous and misleading, since in fact one not uncommon mode of enlarging uneconomically the field of employment for certain

useful, and endeavour to succeed by obtrusive advertisement rather than superior workmanship. The vague condemnation passed by the moral sense of the community on these and similar anti-social practices tends to be sharpened by a keen apprehension of their economic consequences : though it would seem to have been rather blunted than otherwise by the influence of the writings of the *laissez faire* school, owing to their too optimistic reliance on the ultimate tendency of mere self-interest to eliminate the evils condemned. It may indeed be truly said that such practices are often, in the long run, contrary to the interests of the persons who have recourse to them ; but in other cases, especially when rendered respectable by custom, it seems impossible to prove that they are not really the readiest way to private gain ; and certainly they are often judged to be so by the majority of persons most keenly concerned in estimating their utility for this end.

§ 4. A consideration of facts like these leads us naturally to the widest and deepest question that the subject of the present chapter suggests ; whether, namely, the whole individualistic organization of industry, whatever its material advantages may be, is not open to condemnation as radically demoralizing. Not a few enthusiastic persons have been led to this conclusion, partly from a conviction of the difficulty of demonstrating the general harmony of private and common interest—even if we suppose a perfectly administered system of individualistic justice; —partly from an aversion to the anti-social temper and attitude of mind, produced by the continual struggle of competition, even where it is admittedly advantageous to production. Such moral aversion is certainly an important, though not the most powerful, element in the impulses that lead thoughtful persons to embrace some form of socialism. And many who are not socialists, regarding the stimulus and direction of energy given by the existing individualistic system as quite indispensable to

kinds of labour, is to make products more finished and elaborate than is required for the purpose for which they are to be used, and to charge accordingly. The right principle seems to be that every workman should do for the purchaser of his labour the kind and amount of work which seems best adapted to the purchaser's ends, provided the latter is willing to pay the price which the requisite labour would fetch if otherwise applied.

human society as at present constituted, yet feel the moral need of some means of developing in the members of a modern industrial community a fuller consciousness of their industrial work as a social function, only rightly performed when done with a cordial regard to the welfare of the whole society,—or at least of that part of it to which the work is immediately useful. From this point of view great interest attaches to the development of what is called, in a special sense, 'co-operation,' by which the conflict of interests—either between producers and consumers, or between different sets of workers engaged in the same productive industry,—has been more or less subordinated to the consciousness of associative effort for a common good. Any experiment of this kind that is economically successful is to be welcomed as a means of education in public spirit, no less than for its more material advantages.

Meanwhile it is always open to any individual who dislikes the selfish habits of feeling and action naturally engendered by the individualistic organization of society, to counteract them in his private sphere by practising and commending a voluntary redistribution of wealth for the benefit for others. This leads me to the consideration of the influence exercised by Political Economy on the moral sentiments and judgments of instructed persons in respect of this redistribution.

§ 5. Ever since Christianity has been the established religion of Europe, thoughtful and conscientious rich persons have found a serious difficulty in providing themselves with perfectly satisfactory arguments in support of the customs of luxurious private expenditure to which they have commonly conformed, in view of the obvious happiness that might be produced by devoting their superfluous wealth in some way to increase the scanty incomes of the poor; and it is a matter of some interest to consider how far modern Political Economy has diminished or increased this difficulty. I conceive that it has operated to a considerable extent in both directions; so that its resultant effect is rather hard to ascertain. On the one hand, it has exploded the comfortable belief that the luxurious expenditure of the rich is on the whole the source of wages to the poor;—it has pointed out that though labour is no doubt employed in making the luxuries, still if the money spent in them were given to the poor, labour would be no less employed in making the additional comforts of the latter; they would get, speaking broadly, the same wages and the gifts as well. Again, apart from any particular doctrines, the general habit of contemplating society in its economic aspect tends to impress powerfully on the mind the great waste of the material means of happiness that is involved in the customary expenditure even of the most respectable rich persons. On the other hand, though Political Economy has hardly had anything positively new to teach to experienced persons with regard to the dangers of almsgiving, it has certainly tended to make the common view of these dangers more clear, definite and systematic. It has impressed forcibly on instructed minds the general rule that if a man's wants are supplied by gift when he might have supplied them himself by harder work and greater thrift, his motives to industry and thrift tend to be so far diminished; and not only his motives, but the motives of all persons in like circumstances who are thereby led to expect like gifts for themselves. If, indeed, almsgiving could be confined to the relief of distress against which provision could not have been made, this danger would be eliminated; but it is obvious that any important and widespread source of distress, though perhaps incapable of being foreseen in any particular case, is—by the very fact of its frequency and importance—capable of being foreseen as a general probability, so that provision may be made against it by insurance or otherwise. If, finally, it be said that the poorest class of labourers have no superfluous wealth from which to make such provision, Political Economy answers with undeniable force that they can at any rate defer the responsibility of increasing the population until they have saved the minimum required for security against the pecuniary demands of ordinary misfortunes. It is no doubt possible for an almsgiver in particular cases to convince himself that his gift is not likely to entail any material encouragement to improvidence; but he can rarely be quite sure of this; and the general sense that care and knowledge are required even to minimize the danger has caused almsgiving to be now regarded as a difficult art, instead of the facile and applauded indulgence of the pleasurable impulses of benevolence that it once seemed to be. From such an art selfish, inert, or frivolous persons, if duly instructed, have a natural disposition to keep altogether aloof. But there is reason to hope that, in minds of nobler stamp, the full perception of the difficulties and risks attending the voluntary redistribution of wealth will only act as a spur to the sustained intellectual activity required for the successful accomplishment of this duty.

For EU product safety concerns, contact us at Calle de José Abascal, 56–1°,
28003 Madrid, Spain or eugpsr@cambridge.org.